KU-736-337

THE INTERNATIONAL ENVIRONMENT OF BUSINESS

Competition and Governance in the Global Economy

GERALD M. MEIER
STANFORD UNIVERSITY

UNIVERSITY OF WOLVERHAMPTON
LIBRARY

Acc No. 2166851 CLASS 311

CONTROL
0195116402   337

DATE   SITE   MEI
23 MAR 1999   TD

New York Oxford
OXFORD UNIVERSITY PRESS
1998

OXFORD UNIVERSITY PRESS

Oxford   New York
Athens   Auckland   Bangkok   Bogotá   Bombay
Buenos Aires   Calcutta   Cape Town   Dar es Salaam
Delhi   Florence   Hong Kong   Istanbul   Karachi
Kuala Lumpur   Madras   Madrid   Melbourne
Mexico City   Nairobi   Paris   Singapore
Taipei   Tokyo   Toronto   Warsaw

and associated companies in

Berlin   Ibadan

Copyright © 1998 by Gerald M. Meier

Published by Oxford University Press, Inc.,
198 Madison Avenue, New York, New York 10016
http://www.oup-usa.org

Oxford is a registered trademark of Oxford University Press

All rights reserved. No part of this publication may be
reproduced, stored in a retrieval system, or transmitted
in any form or by any means, electronic, mechanical,
photocopying, recording, or otherwise, without the prior
permission of Oxford University Press.

Library of Congress Cataloging-in-Publication Data
Meier, Gerald M.
The international environment of business : competition
and governance in the global economy / by Gerald Meier.
p.   cm.
Includes bibliographical references and index.
ISBN 0-19-511640-2 — ISBN 0-19-511641-0 (pbk.)
1. International economic relations.   I. Title.
HF1411.M4389   1998
337—dc21   97-29841

1 3 5 7 9 8 6 4 2

Printed in the United States of America
on acid-free paper

For those students who will
transform the
"ought"
of today into the
"is"
of tomorrow.

CONTENTS

vii

PREFACE

This is a "why" and "so what" type of book. Although we are all aware of rapid changes in the world economy, we often question "why is this particular change occurring?" And "what will be its consequences?" Seeking answers in this study, we want to acquire an understanding of the interactions between private management *in* and public management *of* a rapidly changing global economy. These interactions revolve around the forces of global competition and global governance.

Being competitive in international markets is an intensifying challenge to private management. Among nations, however, there is also competition in policy making. And the dictates of international economics frequently conflict with national politics. Public management of the global economy is therefore challenged by issues of governance and the need to establish standards of international economic conduct.

Private managers must understand the international economic context in which decision makers operate. They have to analyze the consequences of developments in the global economic environment in which their firms operate. International economic forces, national government policies, the international public sector, and strategic management are related in complex and subtle ways. This book establishes a coherent view of this mix and provides a conceptual framework for the managerial tasks of diagnosing, predicting, and responding to changes in the global trade and financial environment.

Equally, in attempting to bring order to international economic affairs, public agencies such as the International Monetary Fund, World Bank, and World Trade Organization must analyze the consequences of their policies on the private sector. Management of the international public sector requires understanding of international government-business relations. Moreover, international developments frequently determine the requisite policies for national economic management.

I therefore have in mind a range of readers—those who are concerned about the international economic environment for business, or the application of economic analysis to the functioning of the international economy, or the designation of policy prescriptions to meet current—and future—challenges in the world economy.

Over forty years of teaching have influenced this book. But eschewing the excessive formalism and heavy mathematics that deter many from the usual type of international economics textbook, I now want simply to distill the essential analytics of the major policy issues of international trade and finance. While being rigorous in analysis, I also want to seek relevance and realism in application. Accordingly, we emphasize principles of international economics, the conduct of international economic transactions, and the policies of international economic institutions.

Chapters 1 through 5 in Parts I and II establish the analytical foundations underlying the practice of "international contextual analysis" for both private and public policymakers. We shall examine how national economic and financial borders are fading, and how a new global economy is evolving. Chapter 1 sets forth the characteristics of the globalization process that will have the greatest impact on private and public management. To be able to understand and evaluate the causal forces behind economic and financial changes in the global economy, we shall then consider:

- Why changes occur in the pattern and composition of a nation's trade, and how a firm's competitive advantage is related to a nation's dynamic comparative advantage (Chapter 2).

- How trade policy (tariffs, quotas, subsidies) can affect investment opportunities and the allocation of resources, and how trade policy can deal with "unfair trade" (Chapter 3).

- What causes international flows of capital and what are their economic and financial consequences (Chapter 4).

- How balance of payments problems arise and what are the effects of the various remedial policies that governments may undertake to meet their balance-of-payments problems (Chapter 5).

We shall also apply the analytical principles from these chapters in a number of real "Policy Profiles" that relate to policy issues of contemporary and future importance in the world economy. A set of questions provides the basis for an extended discussion of a "Policy Profile."

For the reader who may want a more advanced exposition of some analytical points, there are a number of Technical Appendices.

Following these introductory analytical chapters, we shall examine in Part III international economic problems that focus on the relations between the state and market in a variety of countries and regions. A major structural change in the global economy is the new Europe—the internal market integration of the European Union and the proposed movement to an Economic and Monetary Union (EMU) (Chapter 6). Also far-reaching are the changes in Japan's global position, the question of "Japanomics," and Japan's transition to a new era (Chapter 7). The newly industrializing countries (NICs) in the less developed world are important actors in the global economy. Can the successful strategies of the Asian NICs (South Korea, Taiwan, Hong Kong, Singapore) be generalized in the future to other developing countries (Chapter 8)? Also raising crucial questions about their future development are the transition economies of Central and Eastern Europe, the former Soviet Union, and China. What is their potential and what is the likelihood of free markets taking hold there (Chapter 9)?

Finally, in Part IV, Chapters 10 and 11 synthesize the issues of competition and governance in the global economy. They do so from the perspective of recognizing the tensions that arise when the forces of international economic integration conflict with national political autonomy.

Although the argument of the book proceeds from positive analysis to the applied and the normative, the chapters are written on a stand-alone basis and may be selected according to a reader's own needs and interests. Each chapter can also be supplemented with additional analytical, empirical, or policy materials and case studies.

I owe a special debt to generations of students at the University of Oxford, Williams College, Wesleyan University, Yale University, and Stanford University. Their lively reactions have made this book stronger in style and substance.

I am also grateful for helpful comments and suggestions from Masahiko Aoki, James E. Austin, Paul Krugman, Johannes F. Linn, Sung-Hoon Park, Marcelo Selowsky, Norihiko Shimizu, John Taylor, and Peter Warr. Any number of professional colleagues will also recognize their contributions to the subject.

None of my thoughts would ever have become first drafts but for the patient efforts of Ellen Kitamura, to whom I owe special thanks. My gratitude is also extended to Marilyn Gildea. Linda Bethel kindly took responsibility for several tables and figures. And the staff of the Jackson Library saved me hours of electronic research.

Once again, as always, publishing with Oxford University Press has fulfilled my highest expectations. As editor, Kenneth MacLeod has been an author's delight—encouraging, responsive, and understanding of both the text and author.

Stanford   G. M. M.
June 1997

Website: For updated materials, comments, and answers to students' questions, contact the author at http.//www-gsb.stanford.edu/research/faculty/emeier.html.

Acronyms and Abbreviations

ASEAN	Association of Southeast Asian Nations
BOP	Balance of Payments
CEE	Central and Eastern Europe
COMECON	Council for Mutual Economic Assistance
DPR	Diagnosis, Prediction, and Response
EBRD	European Bank for Reconstruction and Development
ECU	European Currency Unit
EMS	European Monetary System
EMU	Economic and Monetary Union
ERM	Exchange Rate Mechanism
EU	European Union
FDI	Foreign Direct Investment
FX	Foreign Exchange
GATT	General Agreement on Tariffs and Trade
GDP	Gross Domestic Product
GNP	Gross National Product
G7	Group of Seven
IBRD	International Bank for Reconstruction and Development/World Bank
ICA	International Contextual Analysis
IDA	International Development Association (of the World Bank)
IFC	International Finance Corporation (of the World Bank)
IMF	International Monetary Fund
JV	Joint Venture
LDC	Less Developed Country
MFN	Most Favored Nation
MITI	Japan's Ministry of International Trade and Industry
MNC	Multinational Corporation
NAFTA	North American Free Trade Agreement
NIC	Newly Industrialized Country
NIS	Newly Independent States of the Former Soviet Union
NTB	Nontariff Trade Barrier
ODA	Official Development Assistance
OECD	Organization for Economic Cooperation and Development
PPP	Purchasing Power Parity
SDR	Special Drawing Rights
UNCTAD	United Nations Conference on Trade and Development
VER	Voluntary Export Restraint
WTO	World Trade Organization

THE INTERNATIONAL
ENVIRONMENT OF BUSINESS

PART I

THE ORGANIZING FRAMEWORK

This introductory part outlines the framework of discussion that we shall follow in this book. It sets forth the main theme of challenges to private and public management as a result of economic globilization.

For private management, the changing global economy calls for "International Contextual Analysis" (ICA) and "Diagnosis, Prediction, and Response" (DPR).

Because the globalization process creates gains or losses to different nations and to different groups within a nation, public management is also challenged to fashion governance structures that will reduce international economic conflicts and improve international economic conduct.

1 CHANGE AND CHALLENGE

D ecision makers in both the private and public sectors need greater understanding of the forces of global economic change. These multifaceted forces are commonly summarized as constituting "globalization," "interdependence," or an intensified process of "internationalization." Nothing since the Second World War has had a greater impact on private management than changes in the world economy. The practice of public management must also identify with a world of economic change. Policy makers in the international public sector—especially those in the International Monetary Fund (IMF), World Bank, and World Trade Organization (WTO)—must deal directly with global economic forces. Those responsible for national economic policy are also frequently challenged to shape domestic policy in response to changing international events.

We do not adopt the extreme view of "globalization," which maintains that national economies are completely subordinated by globalization processes and that national policy making is completely powerless before global forces.[1] Obviously, not every economic transaction is literally global in character. But the speed of global integration—the intensification of international economic linkages among nations—is accelerating.

We want to emphasize the progressive internationalization of trade and finance, the growing interdependence of nations, and the frequent conditioning of national policies by changes in the world economy. To this extent, it is now common to refer to the "global economy."

We can expect the process of globalization to be even more rapid in the future. If private and public managers are to have the capacity to manage change, they must understand the international context in which they operate. They will have to engage in what we may term *"international contextual analysis"* (ICA).

This chapter outlines features of ICA. It first focuses on the "internationalization" of the economic system and then examines the challenges to the private sector in its achievement of total efficiency and to the international public sector in its resolution of international conflicts.

"INTERNATIONALIZATION" OF THE ECONOMIC SYSTEM

It is fashionable to characterize our age in terms of interdependence. This is not a new phenomenon: for centuries the world economy has become ever more integrated. In the past quarter-century, however, the pace has accelerated. Most powerful in this process is the internationalization of markets[2]—that is, the growing flow of commodities, factors of production, management, technology, and financial capital across national borders.

Not only have the movements of these goods, services, and factors increased, but they have also become more responsive, or more elastic, to differences between domestic and foreign variables. Commodities and services flow more rapidly with respect to price differentials among nations, and financial capital moves more rapidly in response to interest rate differentials.

The internationalization process also results in a greater stock of foreign factors of production within countries—more foreign investment, foreign technology, and foreign workers.

Another feature of the internationalization process has been the internationalization of institutions. Beyond the nation state, a number of intergovernmental institutions have arisen—ranging from international organizations, such as the WTO, the World Bank, the IMF, and the United Nations Conference on Trade and Development (UNCTAD), to regional groups, such as the European Union (EU), North American Free Trade Agreement (NAFTA), Association of Southeast Asian Nations (ASEAN), or the Organization for Economic Cooperation and Development (OECD). Interest groups, such as labor unions, employer associations, and foundations, have also expanded across national borders. Above all, the population of multinational corporations has increased remarkably, and many more large firms operate an expanding number of foreign subsidiaries around the globe.

As a result of the internationalization of the economic system, we must give attention to other units of analysis than the nation state (or a variety of "actors," as the political scientist would say). We must also consider policy issues that are not delimited by national territorial boundaries. Important decision-making units are not only national governments, but also international organizations, regional organizations, transnational interest groups, and multinational corporations. These nonterritorial participants in the global economy shape decisions and events that transcend national frontiers.

Each unit has a different decision domain, characterized by different objectives, responsibilities, constituencies, time concern, and power. And yet, they all interact within a world economy that is essentially decentralized. The operational domain of world economic transactions extends beyond the jurisdictional domain of independent nations. Each decision-making unit is actually part of a larger decision process. But there is no central decision unit in the system. The relationships and interactions among different decision-making units therefore demand more analysis and evaluation.

Let us look in greater detail at the constituent elements of the internationalization process.

Internationalization of Markets for Products

Twenty years ago, only 10 percent of world production traded across national borders. Today, more than 25 percent of world production does. Table 1.1 shows the increasing

TABLE 1.1
Openness in the Postwar Period (*In percent*)

	1950–59	1960–69	1970–79	1980–89
Industrial Countries	**23.3**	**24.6**	**32.0**	**36.8**
North America	11.2	11.7	17.8	21.9
Western Europe	37.2	38.9	48.7	56.9
Japan	21.8	19.5	22.9	23.9
Developing Countries		**28.0**	**34.4**	**38.4**
Africa		48.2	55.1	54.1
Asia				
East		47.0	69.5	87.2
Other		17.2	19.6	24.0
Middle East		41.5	60.4	46.9
Western Hemisphere	26.3	23.9	24.9	27.9

Note: "Openness" is defined as nominal merchandise exports plus imports as a percent of nominal output.
Source: IMF, *World Economic Outlook* (October 1994), p. 89.

degree of openness throughout the world. The growth in world merchandise trade has been considerably faster than growth in world output—from 1950 to 1994 world merchandise output increased $5\frac{1}{2}$ times, but world merchandise trade increased over fourteen times. (Average annual rate of growth in trade has been more than 6 percent during the period since 1950, and the ratio of trade growth to output growth has averaged 1.6 a year. See Figure 1.1.) It is likely that world trade will continue to more than double in approximately a decade. Clearly, the foreign trade sector has become an ever more dynamic sector of many national economies (see Figure 1.2).

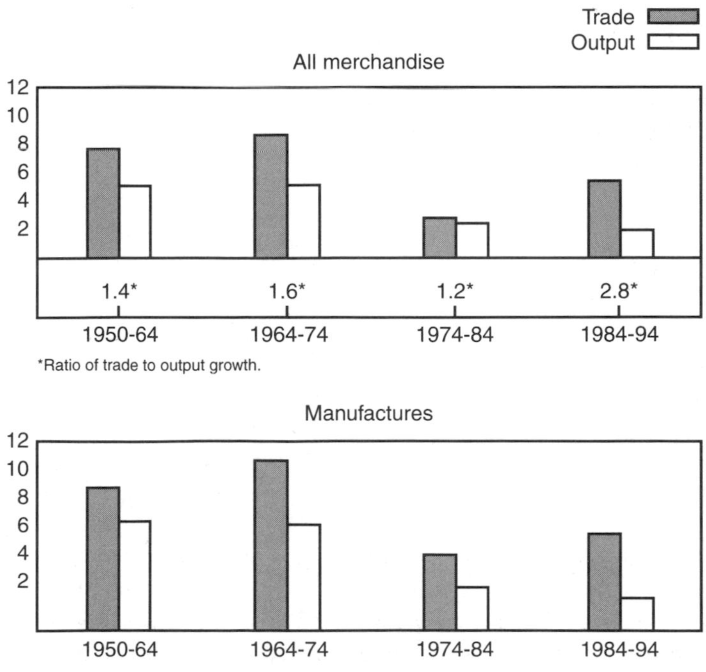
Trade
Output
All merchandise
12
10
8
6
4
2
1.4*
1.6*
1.2*
2.8*
1950-64
1964-74
1974-84
1984-94
*Ratio of trade to output growth.
Manufactures
12
10
8
6
4
2
1950-64
1964-74
1974-84
1984-94

Figure 1.1 Postwar developments in the volume of world merchandise trade and output, 1950–94 (average annual percentage in volume terms). The rising ratio of world trade to world output is striking evidence of the pace of global integration and growing interdependence among nations. *Source:* World Trade Organization, *International Trade: Trends and Statistics 1995*, (1995), p. 16.

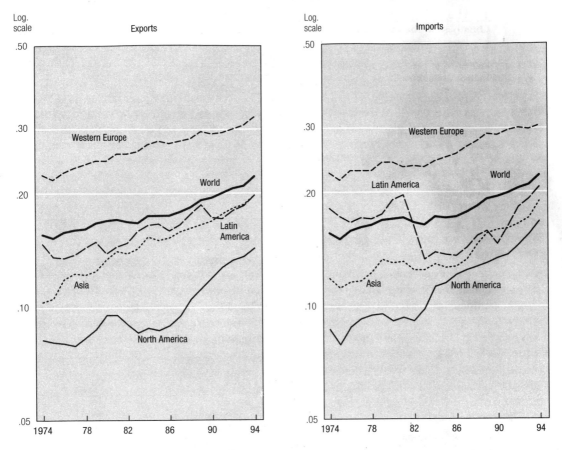

Figure 1.2 Ratio of trade in goods and services to GDP by selected region, 1974–94 (based on constant 1987 prices and exchange rates). *Source*: World Trade Organization, *International Trade: Trends and Statistics 1995*, (1995), p. 18.

Internationalization of Markets for Services

When firms are concerned about the "added cost of doing business overseas," they are referring to added service costs. But advances in communications technology have allowed these services to expand rapidly and their costs to fall, thereby quickening the pace of globalization of markets.

International trade in commercial services—which include transportation, tourism, telecommunications, banking, insurance, and other professional services—grew twice as fast as merchandise trade in the 1980s. The United States has become the world's largest merchandise exporter and also the leading exporter of commercial services. By 1995, world exports of commercial services exceeded $1.2 trillion, up 14 percent from the previous year.[3] Although still much less than world trade in goods, trade in commercial services has been the most rapidly expanding segment of world markets. Especially significant has been

---

VIRTUOUS CIRCLE OF INTERNATIONAL EXPANSION

Economies have benefited from the expansion of world trade in a number of ways. The growing access to foreign markets has allowed countries to specialize in production, engaging in activities that they do best. For example, the early postwar period saw a significant movement of employment from agriculture to manufacturing and services, particularly in Japan and some of the European countries. This promoted substantial productivity increases in agriculture and further boosted output through the high levels of productivity of these workers in the manufacturing and service sectors. New activities and products also encouraged investment, thereby contributing to faster output growth through rapid capital accumulation. In addition, the open trading system, foreign direct investment, and enhanced communications permitted technology transfers and a steady reduction in the technological gap between the leading economy—the United States—and other economies, by making high-technology investment goods available around the world and thereby encouraging convergence in economic performance across different economies. . . . Finally, faster economic growth in turn has also stimulated trade, leading to a virtuous circle of international economic expansion.

IMF, *World Economic Outlook* (October 1994), p. 89

---

trade in the "new" services—financial, communications, insurance, management, and other professional services, and royalties and license fees. In the 1970s and 1980s, the value of trade in these new services increased by an average of 15 percent a year, outperforming not only the other categories of commercial services, but also merchandise trade.

International Capital Flows

With the growth of Eurocurrency markets, international syndication of loans, government loans, and foreign direct investment, the international movement of capital has increased markedly. The international linkage of national money and capital markets has also grown rapidly with the dismantling of restrictions on financial flows across national borders, deregulation of financial institutions, and international financial innovations. There is twenty–four-hour screen-based trading around the world. A foreign exchange trader in Tokyo, dealing simultaneously in London and New York, can truly say "money knows no flag." And the competition for capital is worldwide. Long-term interest rates are increasingly determined by the integration of world capital markets.

Financial instruments such as U.S. Treasury securities have become global commodities. In the ten years to 1993, total cross-border sales and purchases of treasury bonds rose from $30 billion to $500 billion.[6]

Cross-border ownership of tradable securities in 1992 was $2.5 trillion. Gross sales and purchases of bonds and equities between domestic and foreign residents rose from only 3 percent of the U.S. GDP in 1970 to 9 percent in 1980 and 152 percent in 1996. Britain's cross-border securities transactions have grown from virtually nothing in 1970 to more than 1,000 percent of GDP.[7]

INTERNATIONAL BANKING

The managing director of Barclay's Bank states. "We know that the strategy for many international businesses is increasingly played on a global scale and we aim to be significant and winning global players."[4]

For American bankers, globalization is now an urgent challenge. U.S. domination of the global banking market has diminished. As the managing director in charge of equities at First Boston observes, "The U.S. has had a very geocentric view. Our hegemony over world capital flows was almost regarded as a birthright. As far as important capital flows are concerned, there was a real danger of the world passing us by. The U.S. was in danger of becoming irrelevant."[5]

Citicorp is trying to become the world's first global consumer bank. The chief of Citicorp's international consumer business says, "We want to be like Benetton—location indifferent." The objective of "Citibanking" consumer business is to enjoy a global brand recognition and to globalize product development and product roll-out rather than maintaining product development and design teams in every country.

Chairman John Reed looks forward to Citicorp being regarded as a microcosm of the world economy with the company's board including members from Europe, Asia, and the Americas. Managers will be as likely to hold degrees from the University of Turin or São Paulo as they will from Harvard or Stanford. Shareholders will reside in virtually every corner of the earth.

Asia has become the fastest growing region for Citibank's consumer banking, but Citibank has also moved aggressively into Latin America and has an expanding presence in Eastern Europe and the Middle East.

Equity markets in developing countries are also expanding markedly. From 1984 to 1989, the emerging equity markets in these countries quintupled in size to a capitalization of $620 billion. A recent study by the research center of the United Nations University concludes that by the year 2000 foreign investment in emerging equity markets could total $100 billion, up from an estimated $15 billion in 1989.[8] The main attraction of these emerging markets is the possibility of above-average capital appreciation over the long term.

Foreign direct investment (FDI) has also increased dramatically since the late 1970s; in 1995, FDI exceeded $275 billion, up from an average of $57 billion a year during 1981–85. Foreign direct investment has been attracted to the dynamic Asia-Pacific region, the United States, the European Union, and to a greater number of developing countries and transition economies that are now more hospitable to private foreign investment.

American companies are increasing their foreign investment at a record pace. The flow of foreign direct investment from the U.S. in 1995 was approximately $66 billion, up 27 percent from the previous record in 1993. Foreign direct investment in and out of OECD countries in 1994 was nearly $200 billion.

International investment is undertaken not only by large companies: Small American companies are also increasingly becoming global enterprises. Many of the small companies now operating abroad are niche manufacturers, making specialized products whose sales often rise more rapidly overseas than at home.

Sales by overseas affiliates of American companies now amount to three or four times the value of U.S. exports. Nearly a quarter of U.S. corporate profits now come from foreign earnings. Moreover, about 30 percent of American exports in recent years have been intracompany shipments—that is, shipment from an American company to its overseas operations. Intracompany transactions also account for about 17 percent of imports into the United States.[9]

By 1985, foreign-owned firms in the United States already had local sales that were 1½ times greater than American imports in that year. Foreign-owned firms also now account for more than half of U.S. exports and a third of its imports. In 1992, more than 20 percent of the output and 30 percent of the investment of U.K. manufacturing were by foreign-owned companies.

The increased international flow of capital is reflected on the foreign exchange market—the most liquid of markets. Foreign exchange transactions worldwide rose from a gross turnover of $200 billion a day in the mid-1980s to $1.3 trillion a day in 1995—$312 trillion in a year of 240 business days. By comparison, the annual global turnover in equity markets in 1995 was $21 trillion—equivalent to only seventeen days of trading on the foreign exchange market. The annual global trade in goods and services was $4.3 trillion—or only thirty-five days of trading on the foreign exchange market.[10] Interbank transactions and capital movements account for most of the transactions.

Increasingly, global firms are raising capital in many countries. Salomon Brothers predicts that international equity trading will expand nearly threefold to almost $3.90 trillion by the year 2000 and to $12.85 trillion by 2010. McKinsey consulting firm estimates that the total stock of financial assets traded in the global capital market increased from $5 trillion in 1980 to $35 trillion in 1992, and that it is likely to grow to $83 trillion in 2000.[11]

International Transfers of Technology

The international diffusion of technology has increased—not only through cross-border licensing agreements, but also among affiliates of multinational enterprises, and by joint ventures and cooperative R&D activities. Foreign inventors have been processing a larger share of the total number of patents issued in the United States. In 1988, they received 48 percent, a proportion that has been rising steadily for twenty-five years. Among the top 10 corporations that were awarded the most U.S. patents in 1988 were Hitachi, Toshiba, Canon, Fuji Photo Film, Philips, Siemens, Mitsubishi Denki, and Bayer, leaving General Electric and IBM as the only American companies in the top 10.

The international transfer of technology is often linked to foreign direct investment that brings to the host country a package of capital, management, know-how, and technology. Also contributing to the international diffusion of existing technologies are more international alliances that have been formed to promote cooperative R&D activities. These are especially prominent in internationally dynamic industries such as microelectronics, commercial aircraft, and pharmaceuticals.

Often, when governments liberalize their economies or undertake economic reforms, an international transfer of technology also occurs. The international transfer of technology allows innovations—in both new products and new processes of production—that decrease costs of production, improve the quality of products, and allow production of a great variety of products. Harvard's Michael Porter advises that "Today, a firm seeking competitive advantage should question its strategy if it does not have at least one foreign technology monitoring or research site."[12]

Internationalization of Industrial Organization

An ever growing number of corporations have multicountry or global operations. World business is now dominated by multinational enterprises. Distinguishing between types of multinationals, Porter refers to the "multidomestic enterprise" and the "global enterprise."[13] A multidomestic enterprise practices a stand-alone, country-centered strategy and manages its international activities like a portfolio. The enterprise is present in many countries but competition occurs on a country-by-country basis. Multidomestic enterprises characterize such industries as consumer banking, retailing, consumer packaged goods, and insurance.

The global enterprise, in contrast, engages in global scanning and worldwide sourcing, and practices a strategy that integrates the firm's activities on a worldwide basis to capture the linkages among countries. The firm's competitive position in one country significantly affects (and is affected by) its position in other countries. Global enterprises prevail in such industries as commercial aircraft, television sets, semiconductors, watches, copiers, and automobiles. A coordinated strategy gives the global firm its competitive advantage through lower cost or product differentiation. Porter foresees that many companies that are currently multidomestic companies will be moving rapidly toward fulfilling their ambitions of being global companies.

Interpreting the process of industry globalization, Porter also observes that nascent global industry leaders begin with some advantage created at home—whether it be a preferred product design, better product quality, a new marketing concept, or a cost advantage. Sustained success, however, usually requires the firm to use its home-based advantage as a lever to enter foreign markets. Once overseas, the successful global competitor complements the initial home-based advantage with the economies of scale or reputation advantages of worldwide sales. Over time, competitive advantage is supplemented by locating selected activities in foreign nations.[14]

In addition to the rise of the multinational enterprise, there is an increasing number of international coalitions or alliances among firms formed to undertake technology development, operations, and logistics, or marketing, sales, and service (Statistical Appendix, Table 1.5). These international coalitions may be in the form of joint ventures, licensing agreements, supply agreements, marketing agreements, or the pooling of R&D activities. Collaborative ventures in technologies have become frequent for automobiles, commercial aircraft, and telecommunication equipment. Licensing, however, is common in pharmaceuticals. Licensing and technological collaborations often complement one another in segments of the microelectronics and robotics industries and in biotechnology.

In response to global competition, more industries are consolidating on a worldwide basis. Motivated by the need to meet stronger competition from abroad, overcome the

---

THE EXPANDING UNIVERSE OF
TRANSNATIONAL CORPORATIONS (TNCs)

The universe of TNCs in the early 1990s was composed of at least 37,000 parent firms that controlled over 200,000 foreign affiliates worldwide, not counting numerous non-equity links. Two-thirds of these parent firms—26,000—were from 14 major home developed countries, an increase of 19,000 since the end of the 1960s. Foreign affiliates generated sales of more than $4.8 trillion in 1991, slightly more than world exports of goods and non-factor services (some one-third of which were intra-firm) and twice the sales figure at the beginning of the 1980s. The influence of the largest TNCs on output, employment, demand patterns, technology and industrial relations should not be underestimated: the world's largest 100 TNCs, ranked by foreign assets, held $3.4 trillion in global assets in 1992, of which about 40 percent were assets located outside their home countries. The top 100 control about one-third of the world FDI stock.

Transnational corporations and their activities have not only grown in quantitative terms. They also have had qualitative impact on the world economy, within the broader process of globalization.

The driving forces of technological progress and competition, combined with liberalization, have lowered barriers to international flows of goods, services and factors of production, increased the scope for international specialization and led to an unprecedented expansion in international economic transactions. Transnational corporations have played a leading role in this process—as traders, investors, disseminators of technology and movers of people—thus strengthening the links among national markets. Beyond that, the distinguishing role of TNCs is that they organize the production process internationally: by placing their affiliates worldwide under common governance systems, they interweave production activities located in different countries, create an international intra-firm division of labour and, in the process, internalize a range of international transactions that otherwise would have taken place in the market.

The strategies pursued by TNCs are of central importance to understanding the globalization process. The activities of parent firms and affiliates can be linked through stand alone strategies, in which the links are one-way, concentrating on ownership, finance and technology; simple integration strategies, in which affiliates, in addition, often provide inputs to their parent firms; or the linkages can take place through complex integration strategies, driven by the desire to exploit global economies of scale and a higher degree of functional specialization involving locating specific corporate activities in a number of locations around the world. Although all three strategies co-exist, most recently there has been a shift towards complex integration strategies, a corresponding division of the value chain into discrete functions and their location wherever they can be most effectively carried out in light of the overall needs of a firm.

Source: UN, *World Investment Report* (1994), p. XXI

---

limitations of their home markets, search for scale economies, and utilize advances in communications technology, companies are increasingly extending their operations overseas.[15] Cross-border mergers and acquisitions worldwide are growing rapidly. According to KPMG Peat Marwick, 2,707 cross-border acquisitions, joint ventures, and minority investments, with a total value over $110 billion, were announced in the first six months of 1996.[16]

THE BORDERLESS WORLD

Manufactures gradually shift their places, leaving those countries and provinces which they have already enriched, and flying to others whither they are allured by the cheapness of provisions or labour.

David Hume, *Of Money* (1752)

A merchant, it has been said very properly, is not necessarily the citizen of any particular country. It is in great measure indifferent to him from what places he carries on his trade; and a very stifling disgust will make him move his capital, and together with it the industry which it supports, from one country to another.

Adam Smith, *The Wealth of Nations* (1776), Book III, Chap. IV

A global corporation today is fundamentally different from the colonial-style multinationals of the 1960s and 1970s. It serves its customers in all key markets with equal dedication. . . . To make this organizational transition, companies must denationalize their operations and create a system of values shared by company managers around the globe to replace the glue a nation-based orientation once provided. . . . Decomposing the corporate center into several regional headquarters is becoming an essential part of almost every successful company's transition to global competitor status.

Kenichi Ohmae, *The Borderless World* (1990), p. 31

Internationalization of the Labor Market

Labor markets are being increasingly affected by international trade, foreign investment, transfer of technology, and the international mobility of labor. A World Bank report notes that as recently as the late 1970s, about one third of the world's workforce lived in countries weakly linked to international interactions because of protective barriers to trade and foreign investment. If, however, recent trends continue, by the year 2000 fewer than 10 percent of workers will be living in countries that are largely disconnected from world markets. Several developments are linking labor markets in different countries more closely together, leading to a global labor market:

- Growth of employment in industry and manufacturing in developing countries.
- Increased education in developing countries that in part underlies the growth of employment in industry and that makes an increasing share of the world's workforce able to do similar tasks.
- The growth in trade in manufacturing between developing and industrialized countries.
- Increased immigration from developing countries or transition economies to industrial countries.

- The transmission of modern technology by multinational firms around the world and the education in industrial countries of students from developing countries.[17]

Internationalization of Communication and Transportation

As a result of technological advances in communication and transportation, time has been compressed and distance has been shortened. The information revolution has made the particular geographical location of decision making less relevant, the management of international operations has been facilitated, and international transactions costs have decreased. The information explosion has also broadened the market and has increased the number of competitors, both actual and potential, in a variety of industries.

Improvements in international transportation are also accelerating, especially in aerospace technology. Although they may be at a physical distance, production centers and markets are being brought much closer together in terms of time and cost.

These advances in communication and transportation facilitate not only the movement of people and goods—even more important, they also facilitate the international transmission of ideas. They have rapid and wide educative effects—both economically and politically.

Most significantly, the speedier flow of information is accelerating change throughout the global economy, thereby intensifying competitiveness. The efficient use of time is

---

COSMOPOLITANS

The world is becoming a global shopping mall in which ideas and products are available everywhere at the same time. This puts the power of choice in the hands of customers, changing the terms of competition forever. To succeed, companies need abundant stocks of three global assets—concepts, competence, and connections—which derive from investments in innovation, education, and collaboration.

To stock the global shopping mall, international giants are increasingly developing world concepts, coordinating every aspect of their operations on a cross-border basis and empowering cosmopolitan leaders who can operate across boundaries and borders. These new business cosmopolitans push further convergence as they carry ideas from one place to another. The upper end of the cosmopolitan class forms a global elite active in cross-border networks.

No business, however locally focused, is immune from these changes, because they rattle the supply chain. Smaller businesses feel the impact of globalization through the demands of their customers, who want the world's best quality, extra services, and closer partnerships with fewer suppliers. So companies need global mind-sets whether or not they seek global markets. As they expand their horizons they must also widen their networks, for alliances and partnerships can make them seem bigger than they are and offer their customers global reach.

Rosabeth Moss Kanter, *World Class: Thriving Locally in the Global Economy* (New York: Simon & Schuster, 1995), pp. 37–38

of strategic importance. Demanding executives at aggressive companies are measuring performance in terms of the timeliness of response to changing demand, to changing technological possibilities, to changing strategies of competitors—in short, to rapidly evolving world conditions.[18]

THE NEW INTERNATIONAL INDUSTRIAL REVOLUTION

Based on developments in science, technology, and industrial organization, the forces of globalization are dramatic in constituting a new international industrial revolution. The consequences of this revolution are perhaps even more potentially far-reaching in magnitude than the introduction of the steam engine in the eighteenth century or railroads in the nineteenth century. New products and processes in microelectronics are revolutionizing patterns of industrial production; there are geometric leaps in communications technology; the development and use of new advanced synthetic materials will replace many traditional raw materials in the production of many consumer and industrial goods; and advances are being made in biogenetics and bioagriculture.

The current industrial revolution is distinctive in three important respects.[19] First, unlike industrial revolutions of the past, this one is closely linked to areas of basic science that are rapidly evolving (see Figure 1.3). Genetic engineering and the forthcoming generations of computers depend more on basic science than did the steam engine or the railroad. As economic historian Walt Rostow observes, "The fate of particular sectors and even whole national economies is likely to depend substantially in the generation ahead on success or failure in bringing into firm and steady partnership the domains of basic science, R&D engineering, and entrepreneurship."[20]

A second characteristic of the current industrial revolution is that it has repercussions beyond transformation of the older basic industries. In the advanced industrial countries, the production of automobiles, machine tools, and steel are becoming high-tech industries. But the new technologies are also transforming agriculture and a wide range of services such as communications, education, and banking.

A third characteristic is that unlike previous industrial revolutions that were national in location, this one is international in scope. Many countries are simultaneously engaged, and the ramifications of the revolution are immediately internationally diffused. The transfer of technology involves even the less developed countries of Asia, Africa, and Latin America.

Given its broad dimensions, the present industrial revolution might better be called an international *economic* revolution, for it involves more than industrial production. Global telecommunications and information services are changing the very structure of industrial organization: multinational enterprises play a prominent role in this revolution. The forces in the international economic revolution are also transforming managerial functions in production, finance, and marketing. The nature of the workplace is also undergoing change to accompany the technological advances. Closely related to technological and managerial changes, human resource development is of increasing importance. More than ever before, investment in human capital is needed to complement the technological progress that is occurring.

The real forces of science, technology, and industrial organization that underlie the international economic revolution are strong. These fundamentals should lead us to expect potentially high rates of growth in world output and international trade.

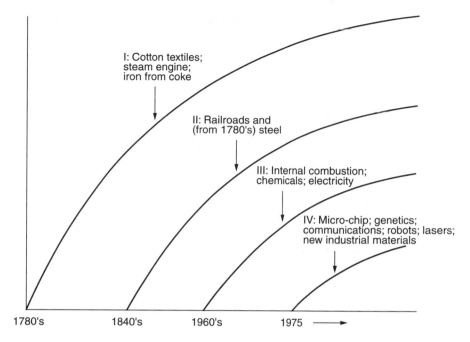

I: Cotton textiles;
steam engine;
iron from coke

II: Railroads and
(from 1780's) steel

III: Internal combustion;
chemicals; electricity

IV: Micro-chip; genetics;
communications; robots; lasers;
new industrial materials

1780's   1840's   1960's   1975 ⟶

Figure 1.3 Four industrial revolutions. *Source:* W. W. Rostow, *Rich Countries and Poor Countries* (Boulder: Westview Press, 1987), p. 139.

Tempering this optimism, however, we should recognize two counteracting forces:

- National politics may conflict with international economics, resulting in trade protectionism. Expansion of world trade depends on open markets. There must, therefore, be political support for the liberalization of trade policy.

- Although the real (nonmonetary) forces are strong in the world economy, international monetary forces may inhibit the international economic revolution. Flexible foreign exchange rates may be subject to excessive volatility and to misalignment of currencies with deleterious effects on trade patterns and international capital movements. The operation of the international monetary system is especially relevant for determining what policies a nation adopts to solve its balance-of-payments problems, and what the effects of those policies are on the nonmonetary forces of economic expansion (for instance, the effect of a tight money policy on investment).

CHALLENGE TO PRIVATE MANAGEMENT

Too often business executives fail to look beyond internal efficiency. They strive for efficient performance in the functional activities of the firm—production, finance, marketing, and organization. They hope through internal efficiency to gain a competitive advantage by lowering cost and price. But the objective of internal efficiency is too narrow a basis for achieving competitive advantage. It is limited to operations within the firm, neglecting the significance of developments in the firm's external environment. If unanticipated, these developments may hit the firm as external shocks, decreasing profitability or even threatening the firm's survival.

Internal efficiency must conform to external efficiency. There is no merit in having the captain of the *Titanic* optimize the arrangement of his deck chairs. If operations within the firm are incongruent with external realities, the manager may shortly need a lifeboat. Tomorrow's new global economy can indeed pose costly and formidable problems. But it can also offer profitable opportunities that should not be missed.

Management must be aware of the two dimensions of external efficiency: adjusting to external shocks and taking advantage of new opportunities. The appearance of a foreign competitor, policies to remedy a country's balance-of-payments deficit, rescheduling a country's external debt, the emergence of transition economies from socialism, the establishment of a regional common market, a new foreign technology, rapid development in a newly industrializing country, and the policies of the International Monetary Fund are a host of international economic and political developments that are continually changing the firm's external environment. And these changes can have even more effect on the firm's profit-and-loss statement than can its internal efficiency.

Managers therefore need to understand the international context in which their firm operates in order to achieve external efficiency. External efficiency means that the firm adapts to the ever changing international environment with appropriate response. And it does so in a timely fashion. Dynamic efficiency requires management to respond quickly and effectively to new situations.

Dynamic efficiency must complement both internal efficiency and external efficiency. The objective of seeking only internal efficiency limits management to a narrowly static and partial strategy, but the seeking of total efficiency calls for a dynamic and general strategy—a much higher understanding of what general management should do. Competitive advantage depends on achieving *total efficiency*—the proper mix of *internal efficiency plus external efficiency plus dynamic efficiency*. If a competitive edge is to be gained, business executives must have a vision and a strategy that will enable them to respond with total efficiency in the new global economy.

Many now recognize that globalization is the management credo for the future. And all the forces underlying globalization affect all firms in their need to achieve total efficiency. As a Coopers & Lybrand report to clients states:

> Sustained success—given the pace of global change and the quality of competition— requires corporations to achieve a new degree of management flexibility. They will have to become more sensitive to changes in the global business environment and be prepared to alter tactics rapidly to achieve long-term global strategic goals. The principal strategic advantage of successful global companies today—and the hallmark of corporate survivors tomorrow—will be the capacity to manage change.[21]

If managers are to develop such a capacity, they will have to understand the international context in which they operate—*international contextual analysis* (ICA)—and practice the techniques of *diagnosis, prediction, and response* (DPR).

INTERNATIONAL CONTEXTUAL ANALYSIS (ICA)

Changes in the international economy give shape to the firm's external environment. These changes occur primarily in the:

- Pattern of international trade in goods and services
- Volume and types of international capital movements
- Transfer of ideas and technology among nations

ICA focuses on these changes.[22]

Some changes in the world economy directly affect the firm through international markets (type A forces). Others operate indirectly through the impact of national governmental policies (type B forces). These are illustrated in Figure 1.4. Among the direct effects, most significant are changes in the volume of international trade, the commodity composition of foreign trade, and movements in export and import prices. The ever-changing structure of comparative advantage among nations lies behind these changes. Chapters 2 and 3 of this book point out the determinants of dynamic comparative advantage and indicate the consequences for the volume, pattern, and terms of trade (ratio of export to import prices).

Also important—and commonly linked to changes in the volume and pattern of international trade—are changes in the flow of international capital. Developments in international money and capital markets are clearly of concern for international financing activities. Private foreign investment is of increasing significance—both portfolio and foreign direct investment (equity control of the enterprise). Furthermore, attention should be given to the role of public capital movements from the World Bank, regional development

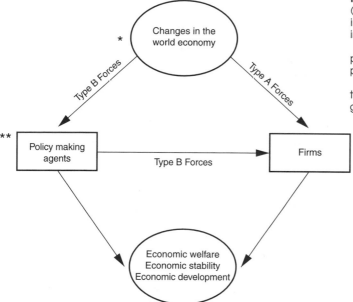

Figure 1.4 International Contextual Analysis (ICA). Type A Forces: Direct impact through international markets. Type B Forces: Indirect impact through government policies.
*Comparative advantage (Ch. 2), trade policy (Ch. 3), capital flows (Ch. 4), balance of payments (Ch. 5).
**OECD countries, less developed countries, transition economies, IMF, World Bank, Regional Development Banks, WTO, UN agencies.

banks (such as the Asian Development Bank), and the International Monetary Fund. Chapters 4 and 5 highlight the trends in international capital flows and their implications for the future.

While the changing world economy directly affects firms operating in international markets, even firms that operate only domestically feel its impact through the indirect effect of government policies. National economic management by government has an impact on private management. And national economic management is frequently determined by international events. For example, whether domestic monetary policy will be easy or tight is often dictated by a country's balance-of-payments position. A national central bank may adopt tight money policies and raise domestic interest rates to attract short-term capital from abroad in an effort to stabilize the country's foreign exchange rate. Or, to reduce the country's balance-of-payments deficit, the national government may decrease its expenditure or increase taxes in order to cut private spending. The change in the amount and composition of national expenditure will then affect domestic firms. Or a rise in the world demand for savings may cause the Federal Reserve Board to raise interest rates in the United States, thereby affecting the volume and pattern of domestic investment and consumer spending (on housing and automobiles, for instance). Dramatic political events in other parts of the world can affect the U.S. financial system.

Monetary, fiscal, and trade policies are the most important policy areas in which national governments respond to international developments. There may also be other internationally induced policies related to labor conditions, agricultural programs, or environmental controls. The chapters that concentrate on individual countries or regions (Chapters 6 to 9) will give considerable attention to the significance of such national policies.

DIAGNOSIS, PREDICTION, AND RESPONSE (DPR)

To appreciate the need for ICA, however, is only the first step. As noted in Figure 1.5, the subsequent (and more difficult) steps for management are to *Diagnose, Predict, and Respond (DPR)*. Fundamental is the *diagnosis* of current forces in the international economy (the solid arrows in Figure 1.5). What are these forces? Why do they occur? What are their consequences?

The next step requires *prediction* of future forces and their consequences (the straight, dashed arrow). This is not a matter of forecasting with a crystal ball, but of predicting in accordance with certain specified conditions. A conditional prediction states that "if x, then y." Diagnosis that establishes a causal relationship must therefore underlie such a conditional prediction. Prediction also involves expectations. The better understood are the causal relations, the more likely are these expectations to be rational. Management also learns, however, by doing. Expectations can therefore also be adaptive and thus predictions can improve.

Once future developments are diagnosed and predicted, the next step is for management to *respond* as rapidly and favorably as possible to these developments (the dashed, bent arrow). Global strategic choices must offset the negative effects of change and take advantage of positive opportunities. The manager identifies aspects of company operations that will be affected and determines what strategic response is required in various functional areas—in organization, finance, industrial relations, production, marketing, R&D, or government relations.

The basis for the analysis and prediction steps lies in ICA. Ideally, a deeper understanding of ICA may lead to the better practice of DPR, whether a firm is directly involved in international markets or is a domestic firm indirectly affected by changes in the world economy.

Our discussion, however, stops short of spelling out specific responses because that depends on each reader's knowledge and application of functional fields from other management courses and the type of firm with which he or she is concerned. Our task is the prior one of placing the firm in its international context and providing an understanding of what international forces may impinge on a firm. How the manager of each firm—or each reader—would react is ultimately a test of his or her managerial skills and vision. But we shall at least indicate some managerial implications and offer numerous suggestions that could help shape a response.

ICA focuses on three units of analysis: individual countries, international relations among countries, and the international public sector.

Diagnosis of individual countries centers on the performance of economies overseas and salient developments in these economies. Depending on the specific questions confronting management in its operations overseas, diagnosis may vary from emphasis on variables in the aggregate economy to relevant variables at the level of the firm.

In undertaking country analysis, the manager must go beyond a naive checklist and a static view of the economy. In country risk analysis, for example, a checklist of a variety of economic and political indicators tends to be simplistic and misses the interrelationships among the political and economic variables in the country. The whole may be greater than the sum of the parts. Without an understanding of the causality that lies behind the interrelationships among the indicators, there can be no basis for DPR. Indeed, a checklist may be counterproductive: A country officer may be content with simply filling in the checklist. A Gresham's law of analysis then operates in which bad analysis drives out good

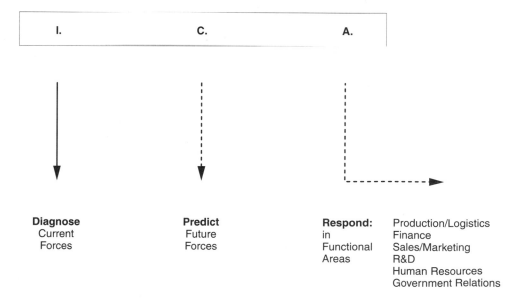

Figure 1.5 Diagnosis, prediction, response.

analysis. To make a truly meaningful country study, one must understand the macro relations determining fluctuations in national income and the micro relations determining resource allocation in the country.

A dynamic view that recognizes the crucial importance of time is also necessary. Only too often an economy is misleadingly viewed as if it were a machine, with its parts assembled and given once-for-all, and reference is made to mechanical engineering analogies (pump-priming, levers, forces). But biological analogies are more appropriate: An economy is a growing and evolving organism. It is dynamic, not stationary. Snapshots will not do. Nor will simple extrapolations. Time is highly relevant; and the evolution of macro and micro variables needs to be dated over time in dynamic analysis. Without a foundation in the appropriate dynamic analysis, the process of change cannot be interpreted, and predictions will be only guesses.

The international relations among countries call for special understanding. Attention should be given to the changing pattern of international trade in both goods and services. Management needs a basic understanding of the forces giving rise to dynamic changes in a country's comparative advantage in international trade. The connections between international capital movements and the pattern of international trade also need to be recognized.

The international public sector comprises the activities of the International Monetary Fund, the World Bank, regional development banks (such as inter-American, African, or Asian), the General Agreement on Tariffs and Trade, the new World Trade Organization, and some U.N. agencies. Rudimentary as the international public sector still is, the activities of these international institutions have considerable impact on private business. National government-business relations are important in individual country analysis, but international government-business relations will become even more significant.

CHALLENGE TO PUBLIC MANAGEMENT

Economists applaud the process of globalization because it integrates economies, promotes competition, and yields a more efficient allocation of resources on an international scale. To a national policy maker, however, internationalization is troubling: It heightens the vulnerability of a nation to external developments. Domestic autonomy in policy making is subordinated to international policy considerations. National politics is therefore likely to oppose international economics. And when the domestic economic objectives of different nations clash, international tension and conflict arise, often resulting in a zero-sum game among nations.

These conflicts then give rise to various governmental policies that, in turn, have an impact on industries and business firms. There are conflicts over markets. Each country would like free market access for its own exports. National governments, however, try to preserve domestic markets through protection for import-competing industries. They therefore resort to tariffs and quotas. To promote exports, subsidies may also be used. And access to some import markets might also be restricted, as under OPEC controls. Just as governments must watch markets, so too must markets watch governments.

There are also conflicts over the terms of trade—that is, the ratio of export prices to import prices. Each country would like to improve its own terms of trade by raising its export prices relative to import prices. Countries may therefore impose tariffs on imports to reduce the import price, or may tax exports to raise their export prices. (Chapters 2 and 3 discuss these trade conflicts in detail.)

Differences also occur over the terms of foreign direct investment. The host government would like to raise the benefit-cost ratio of foreign investment in its economy, whereas the foreign investor would like to raise the benefit-cost ratio for its own enterprise (see Chapter 4 for more detail).

Because for every country that has a deficit in its balance of payments there is a country that has a surplus, there are also conflicts over which country is to adjust to balance-of-payments problems. The deficit country may be unwilling to depreciate its exchange rate, suffer deflation in its national income, or impose direct controls over its foreign trade. The surplus country, in turn, may be reluctant to let its domestic currency appreciate in terms of foreign currencies, inflate its economy, or remove direct controls over trade. Each nation attempts to minimize the cost of adjusting to a balance-of-payments problem by avoiding remedial policies or by trying to place some of the burden of adjustment on other countries. Deficit countries call for adjustment by the surplus countries, while the surplus countries insist that the deficit countries should do the adjusting. (This problem dominates much of United States-Japan relations, as we shall see in Policy Profile 5.5 and Chapter 7.)

Conflicts also arise over domestic stabilization policies. Each nation, in trying to maintain full employment with stable prices, wishes to exercise national economic autonomy over its own fiscal and monetary policies. It does not want its domestic stabilization policies to be subject to external conditions. (See Chapter 5 for more on these balance-of-payments and economic stability conflicts.)

Finally, there are conflicts over the common resources of the world and the environment. How are nations to share common resources (for example, deep sea mining, outer space)? Environmental problems that are of a cross-border nature (such as acid rain, global warming, marine protection, pollution control) are of increasing concern.

These various conflicts arise because of economic and political changes over time as globalization occurs. The globalization process itself creates gains or losses to different nations and to different groups within a nation. As long as the forces of internationalization create dynamic change in world production and in the distribution of the world product, the distribution of benefits and detriments will be a vexing problem.

In sum, international trade and financial conflicts can be grouped in three categories:

- Those that arise because a nation seeks to acquire a larger share of the gains from trade or foreign investment

- Those that arise when a country tries to avoid being damaged by developments in another country

- Those that arise because a country wants to maintain its domestic autonomy in policy making when confronted with an international event

The driving technological, economic, and political forces behind the internationalization process will not wane, but as internationalization proceeds, we shall have to seek policy solutions for future conflicts. The challenge is to improve these policy solutions and provide more effective structures of global governance. This is difficult because the outlines of decision-making processes in the world community remain vague, supranational institutions are few, and their power to pursue international public policy making is limited. The internationalization of institutions has not kept pace with the internationalization of markets. International economics, in the sense of the internationalization of markets, will continue to be opposed by national politics, because governments desire to retain autonomy over economic policies. Nations will only too readily tend to compete among themselves in policy making, while coordination of national policies remains an ideal. Nonetheless, if progress is to be made, it will necessarily depend first on understanding the basic principles of international economic policy.

The crucial questions then are: How to resolve these conflicts and establish order in international economic affairs? How can the increasing economic and technical interdependence be managed?

Answers to these questions call for an understanding of the effects of changes in the new global economy that have an impact on both the firm and public policy.

The following chapters examine the direct impact of the forces of globalization on the firm, and also their indirect impact as a result of policies undertaken by national governments and the operation of various international decision mechanisms. An understanding of both the direct and indirect effects of international economic change is fundamental for meeting the challenge of total corporate efficiency. It is also essential for having the international public sector meet the challenges of promoting standards of international economic conduct and establishing international economic order.

To further this understanding, we shall proceed from an analysis of fundamental principles of international trade and the balance-of-payments (Part II) to an application of these principles from the perspective of state and market in various categories of countries (Part III), and finally to the more normative level with respect to global competition and global governance (Part IV).

NOTES

1. Cf. Paul Hirst and Grahame Thompson, *Stabilization in Question* (Oxford: Blackwell, 1996), Chs. 1, 9, and extensive Bibliography, pp. 212–222.
2. This process is elaborated by Assar Lindbeck, "The Changing Role of the National State," *Kyklos* 28 (1975): 23–46.
3. World Trade Organization, *International Trade, 1995*, Geneva, 1995, pp. 12–14.
4. *Barclay's Bank Briefing*, No. 83, January 1990.
5. *Financial Times*, November 20, 1989, p. 21.
6. *The Economist*, October 7, 1995, p. 11.
7. Loc. cit.
8. World Institute for Development Economics Research of the United Nations University, Study Group Series, No. 5, Helsinki, March 1990, p. 3.
9. *New York Times*, March 26, 1989.
10. Philip Gawith, "Forex Surge Masks Maturing Market," *Financial Times*, October 25, 1995.
11. McKinsey Global Institute, "The Global Capital Market," November 1994.
12. Michael E. Porter, *The Competitive Advantage of Nations* (New York: Free Press, 1990), p. 609.
13. Michael Porter, ed., *Competition in Global Industries* (Boston: Harvard Business School Press, 1986), pp. 17–20.

14. Porter, *The Competitive Advantage of Nations*, pp. 63–64. As an example, Porter refers to consumer electronics in which Matsushita, Sanyo, Sharp, and other Japanese firms initially competed on cost in selling simply designed, portable television sets. As they began penetrating foreign markets, however, they gained economies of scale and further reduced cost by moving down the learning curve. Their worldwide sales then supported aggressive investments in marketing, new production equipment, and R&D. Accordingly, the Japanese firms have long since been able to graduate from a cost focus to producing broader lines of increasingly differentiated television sets, VCRs, and other items, using world-class product and process technology.

15. International coalitions in the automobile industry indicate that the industry is rapidly losing its characteristics of being a national industry or even a multinational industry and is rapidly approaching the status of a "postnational" industry. Early in the next century, Honda and Nissan will become the first manufacturing organizations in history to perform only a minority of their design, engineering, and manufacturing work at home and the first to have payrolls with fewer than half of their employees being home-country citizens. James P. Womack, "A Post-National Auto Industry by the Year 2000," *The JAMA Forum*, vol. 8, no. 1, p. 7.

16. *New York Times*, July 30, 1996, p. C2.

17. Richard B. Freeman, Roundtable Discussion on Employment and Development, *Proceedings of the World Bank Annual Conference on Development Economics* 1994, p. 447.

18. For a detailed analysis of time as a source of competitive advantage, see George Stalk, Jr., and Thomas M. Hout, *Competition Against Time* (New York: Free Press, 1990).

19. For an insightful analysis, see W. W. Rostow, *Rich Countries and Poor Countries* (Boulder: Westview Press, 1987), pp. 136–141.

20. Rostow, op. cit., pp. 136–141. See also John W. Sewell, *U. S. Policy and the Developing Countries: Agenda 1988* (New Brunswick: Transaction Books, 1988), pp. 7–21.

21. Coopers & Lybrand, *Annual Report on the Worldwide Economic and Business Climate* (New York, 1989), p. 5.

22. For a more extensive and instructive discussion of international contextual analysis and its applications to developing countries, see James E. Austin, *Managing in Developing Countries* (New York: Free Press, 1990), Part I.

Global Trends

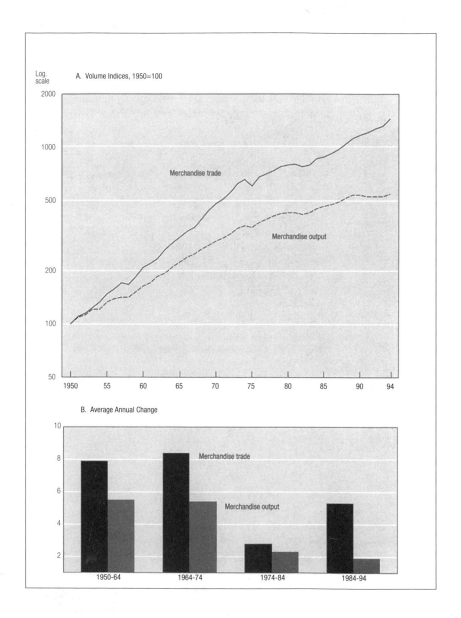

Figure 1.6 Long-term trends of world merchandise trade and output, 1950–94. *Source*: WTO, *International Trade 1995* (Geneva, 1995), p. 29.

TABLE 1.2

Growth in the Volume of World Merchandise Exports and Production by Major Product Group, 1985–95 (Annual average percentage change)

	1985–90	1990–95
I. World merchandise exports	5.8	6.0
Agricultural products	2.2	4.5
Mining products	4.8	4.5
Manufactures	7.0	6.5
II. World merchandise production	3.0	1.5
Agriculture	1.9	1.5
Mining	3.0	2.0
Manufacturing	3.2	1.0
III. World GDP	3.0	1.0

Note: World merchandise production differs from world GDP in that it excludes services and construction.

Source: World Trade Organization, *Annual Report 1996* (Geneva, 1996), p. 13.

TABLE 1.3

Growth in the Value of World Merchandise Exports by Major Product Group, 1990–94 ($ billions and percentage)

	Value	Annual Percentage Change		
	1994	1990–94	1993	1994
World merchandise exports[a]	4090	5.0	−1.0	13.0
Agricultural products	485	4.0	−4.0	13.5
Mining products	435	−2.5	−5.0	3.5
Manufactures	3040	6.0	−0.5	14.5
World exports of commercial services	1035	7.0	0.5	9.0

[a]Including unspecified products.

Source: WTO, *International Trade: Trends and Statistics 1995* (1995), p. 4.

TABLE 1.4

Leading Exporters and Importers in World Merchandise Trade, 1995 ($ billions and percentage)

Rank	Exporters	Value	Share	Annual Change	Rank	Importers	Value	Share	Annual Change
1	United States	583.9	11.6	14	1	United States	771.3	14.9	12
2	Germany	508.5	10.1	19	2	Germany	443.2	8.6	16
3	Japan	443.1	8.8	12	3	Japan	336.0	6.5	22
4	France	286.2	5.7	22	4	France	274.5	5.3	20
5	United Kingdom	242.1	4.8	18	5	United Kingdom	265.3	5.1	17
6	Italy	231.2	4.6	22	6	Italy	204.0	3.9	22
7	Netherlands	195.3	3.9	24	7	Hong Kong	196.1	3.8	18
8	Canada	192.2	3.8	16		retained imports[a]	52.1	1.0	21
9	Hong Kong	173.9	3.5	15	8	Netherlands	175.9	3.4	25
	domestic exports	29.9	0.6	4	9	Canada	168.4	3.3	9
	re-exports	143.9	2.9	17	10	Belgium-Luxembourg	154.2	3.0	21

Continued

TABLE 1.4
Continued

Rank	Exporters	Value	Share	Annual Change	Rank	Importers	Value	Share	Annual Change
10	Belgium-Luxembourg	168.3	3.3	23	11	Korea, Rep. of	135.1	2.6	32
11	China	148.8	3.0	23	12	China	132.1	2.6	14
12	Korea, Rep. of	125.1	2.5	30	13	Singapore	124.5	2.4	21
13	Singapore	118.3	2.3	22		retained imports[a]	75.8	1.5	18
	domestic exports	69.6	1.4	19	14	Spain	114.8	2.2	25
	re-exports	48.7	1.0	27	15	Chinese Taipei	103.6	2.0	21
14	Chinese Taipei	111.7	2.2	20	16	Switzerland	80.2	1.6	18
15	Spain	91.6	1.8	25	17	Malaysia	77.8	1.5	30
16	Switzerland	81.6	1.6	16	18	Mexico[b]	72.9	1.4	−10
17	Sweden	79.9	1.6	30	19	Thailand[c]	70.9	1.4	30
18	Mexico[b]	79.7	1.6	31	20	Austria[c]	67.3	1.3	22
19	Malaysia	74.0	1.5	26	21	Sweden	64.4	1.2	25
20	Russian Federation[c, d]	64.8	1.3	26	22	Australia	61.3	1.2	15
21	Austria[c]	58.1	1.2	28	23	Brazil	53.8	1.0	49
22	Thailand[c]	56.5	1.1	25	24	Denmark	43.5	0.8	21
23	Australia	53.1	1.1	12	25	Indonesia	40.9	0.8	28
24	Denmark	48.8	1.0	17		Total of above[e]	4231.8	81.9	—
25	Saudi Arabia[c]	48.2	1.0	13					
	Total of above[e]	4264.7	84.7	—					
	World[e]	**5033.0**	**100.0**	**19**		**World[e]**	**5170.0**	**100.0**	**19**

[a]Retained imports are defined as imports less re-exports.

[b]Includes shipments through processing zones (maquiladoras).

[c]Secretariat estimates.

[d]Excludes trade with the Baltic States and the CIS. Including trade with these States would lift Russian exports and imports to $82 billion and $58 billion, respectively.

[e]Includes significant re-exports or imports for re-export.

Source: WTO, *Annual Report 1996*, p. 24.

Openness in developing countries has increased sharply.

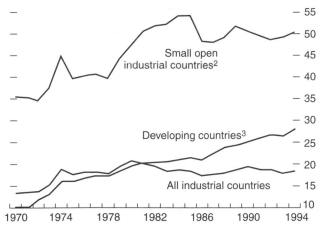

Figure 1.7 Developing and industrial countries (in percent of GDP): Openness[1] in developing countries has increased sharply. *Source*: International Monetary Fund, *World Economic Outlook*, (October 1995), p. 44.

[1] Average of exports and imports of goods and services as a percent of GDP.
[2] Belgium, Denmark, the Netherlands, and Sweden.
[3] Excludes oil exporting countries.

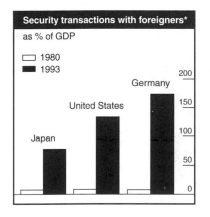

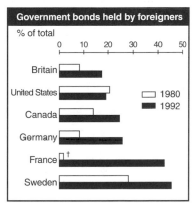

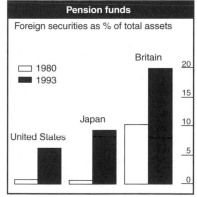

* Gross sales and purchases of bonds and equities   †1986

Figure 1.8 International financial transactions. *Source*: *The Economist* (October 1995), p. 11. ©1995 The Economist Newspaper Group, Inc. Reprinted with permission. Further reproduction prohibited.

TABLE 1.5
Growth in Strategic Alliance Formation, 1980–89

	1980–84		1985–89		
	Number	Percent	Number	Percent	% Change
Automobiles	26	100	79	100	203
USA–Europe	10	39	24	30	140
USA–Japan	10	39	39	49	290
Europe–Japan	6	23	16	20	167
Biotechnology	108	100	198	100	83
USA–Europe	58	54	124	63	114
USA–Japan	45	42	54	27	20
Europe–Japan	5	4	20	10	300
Information technology	348	100	445	100	28
USA–Europe	158	45	256	58	62
USA–Japan	133	38	132	30	−0.8
Europe–Japan	57	16	57	13	—
New material	63	100	115	100	83
USA–Europe	32	51	52	45	63
USA–Japan	16	25	40	35	150
Europe–Japan	15	24	23	20	53
Chemicals	103	100	80	100	−22
USA–Europe	54	52	31	39	−43
USA–Japan	28	27	35	44	25
Europe–Japan	21	20	14	17	−33

Source: Office of Technology Assessment (OTA), United States Congress (1993), Fig. 5.3.

TABLE 1.6
Outward and Inward Direct Investment Flows in OECD Countries ($ billions)

	Outward Flows, Cumulative Flows	
	1973–80	1981–93
United States	119.0	300.2
Japan	17.0	247.5
EU-15	117.7	813.6
Other OECD	13.9	147.0
OECD total	267.5	1,508.3

	Inward Flows, Cumulative Flows	
	1973–80	1981–93
United States	55.0	417.0
Japan	1.0	7.5
EU-15	99.4	552.9
Other OECD	23.7	166.2
OECD total	179.1	1,143.6

Source: OECD, Economics Department, Foreign Trade and Investment Division, March 1995. Reproduced by permission of the OECD.

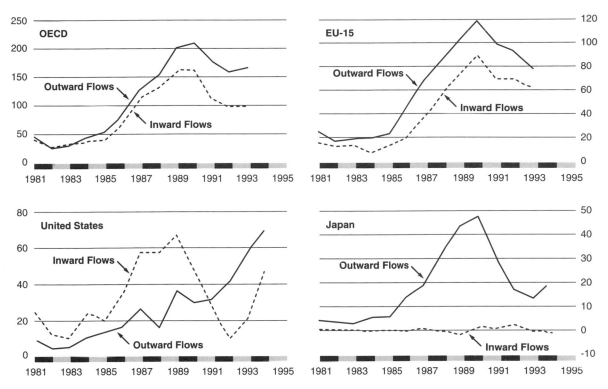

Figure 1.9   Foreign direct investment flows ($ billions). *Source:* OECD, Economics Department, Foreign Trade and Investment Division, March 1995. Reproduced by permission of the OECD.

TABLE 1.7
Growth Rates and Real Gross Domestic Product, 1977–95 (Percent change at annual rate)

Area and country	1977–86	1987	1988	1989	1990	1991	1992	1993	1994	1995
World	3.3	4.0	4.6	3.5	2.4	1.3	2.0	2.5	3.6	3.7
Industrial countries	2.7	3.2	4.4	3.3	2.4	.8	1.5	1.1	3.1	2.5
United States	2.7	3.1	3.9	2.5	1.2	−.6	2.3	3.1	4.1	2.9
Canada	3.1	4.2	5.0	2.4	−.2	−1.8	.8	2.2	4.6	2.2
Japan	4.0	4.1	6.2	4.7	4.8	4.3	1.1	−.2	.5	.5
European Union	2.1	2.9	4.2	3.5	3.0	1.1	1.0	−.6	2.8	2.9
France	2.2	2.3	4.4	4.3	2.5	.8	1.3	−1.5	2.9	2.9
Germany	1.9	1.5	3.7	3.6	5.7	2.8	2.2	−1.2	2.9	2.6
Italy	2.7	3.1	4.1	2.9	2.1	1.2	.7	−1.2	2.2	3.0
United Kingdom	2.1	4.8	5.0	2.2	.4	−2.0	−.5	2.2	3.8	2.7
Developing countries	4.5	5.7	5.2	4.2	4.0	4.9	5.9	6.1	6.2	6.0
Africa	2.1	1.6	3.6	3.4	2.1	1.7	.7	.8	2.6	3.0
Asia	6.7	8.1	9.1	6.0	5.7	6.4	8.2	8.7	8.5	8.7
Middle East and Europe	2.6	5.0	−.5	2.7	4.8	3.2	5.5	3.6	.3	2.4
Western Hemisphere	3.2	3.4	1.1	1.6	.6	3.5	2.7	3.3	4.6	1.8
Countries in transition	3.3	2.5	4.0	2.0	−3.9	−11.6	−15.2	−9.1	−9.5	−2.1
Central and eastern Europe						−11.1	−11.3	−6.1	−3.8	.2
Russia, Transcaucasus, and central Asia						−12.0	−18.7	−11.8	−15.2	−4.6

Sources: Department of Commerce (Bureau of Economic Analysis) and International Monetary Fund.

PART II

ANALYTICAL FOUNDATIONS

To be able to apply international contextual analysis (ICA), we must first understand the fundamental analytical principles of international trade and finance. The following chapters establish these principles.

Chapter 2 places the basic principle of comparative advantage in a dynamic context, thereby helping us to explain changes in the pattern and composition of a country's foreign trade. It also indicates how a firm's competitive advantage is related to a nation's comparative advantage.

Chapter 3 focuses on the effects of trade policies on investment opportunities and resource allocation. Special attention is given to policies that deal with "unfair trade."

In Chapter 4, we examine the determinants of international capital movements, as well as the economic and financial consequences of these flows of capital that have become increasingly significant in the global economy.

Chapter 5 analyzes a country's balance of payments in terms of balance of payments problems and the need for remedial policies.

At the end of some of these chapters, we shall apply the analytical principles in "Policy Profiles" that elucidate policy issues of contemporary—and future—importance in the international environment of business.

Chapter

2 DYNAMIC COMPARATIVE ADVANTAGE

P rominent among changes in the fundamentals of the world economy are changes in the volume, composition, and terms of international trade. To understand why these changes occur and their significance, we need to analyze the dynamics of comparative advantage. The theory of comparative advantage contends that when a country specializes according to its comparative cost structure, it achieves an efficient allocation of resources and hence an increase in its real national income. International specialization is simply the division of labor—and thereby greater productivity—writ large among nations. Long ago, in his *Wealth of Nations* (1776), Adam Smith observed that "the division of labor is limited by the extent of the market." For a firm, the size of its market is clearly a determinant of the variety of products that it produces and its realization of economies of scale. So too for a nation: A small economy that specializes and exports to the world market can gain higher productivity and greater real national income than if its production were limited to only the small home market—as the East Asian high performing economies have dramatically demonstrated.

If a business firm is to gain a competitive advantage, it has to locate its various activities geographically in accordance with the comparative advantage of different countries. Private management must therefore be aware of the sources of comparative advantage and anticipate how comparative advantage evolves over time. Public management also has to recognize how governments can shape a country's comparative advantage and respond to changes in comparative advantage that alter the distribution of the gains from trade among nations and the distribution of the gains within a country.

SOURCES OF COMPARATIVE ADVANTAGE

What determines the commodities and services that a country will export or import? Why did the composition of exports from Japan change from raw silk and tea in the nineteenth century to textiles in the 1890s and to metals and machinery after World War II, and then on to high-technology products? Why in the course of two decades have exports from Taiwan changed from mushrooms to electronics? How can we predict the future exports and imports of a country? The answers relate to the fundamental forces that determine a country's comparative advantage.

Labor Productivity and Wages

Adam Smith recognized that a nation should employ its resources in a way in which it has "some advantage." It was left, however, to the English economist David Ricardo to refine this insight into the logical principle of comparative advantage that has held pride of place in economic thought since Ricardo's 1817 formulation. In a simple illustration of what, under free trade, would determine trade between England and Portugal in wine and cloth, Ricardo focused on the relative differences in labor productivity (output per hour) in producing wine and cloth in England and Portugal. Ricardo wanted to "pierce the monetary veil" and concentrate instead on the nonmonetary real forces that determine trade. The focus is on the allocation of resources, not the balance of payments, which is adjusted through changes in wages or foreign exchange rates (see Chapter 5).

In the Ricardian model, even though Portugal is more productive ("better") than England in both wine and cloth, giving Portugal absolute advantage in both wine and cloth, its labor is relatively more productive ("more better") in wine than cloth. Portugal therefore has a comparative advantage in wine. England is less productive in both wine and cloth (absolute disadvantage) but has the lesser disadvantage (or comparative advantage) in cloth. In essence, technological differences in production functions between England and Portugal give relative productivity differences that allow a basis for mutually profitable trade between the countries. Ricardo did not, however, explain why technological differences exist, an important issue that is now of much concern for international competitiveness.

Given the relative productivity differentials or differences in the countries' comparative cost ratios, there is a basis for international trade. The immobility of factors across borders maintains the cost differentials and the different domestic price ratios. After opening England and Portugal to foreign trade, conditions of supply and demand will establish some international price ratio on world markets. This international exchange ratio must lie within the range of the domestic exchange ratios; otherwise, one country would not find it advantageous to trade. At home, the cost of one commodity in terms of another is greater than on world markets, and the country therefore specializes in producing the commodity that uses fewer resources than would be needed to produce domestically the commodity it imports. It exports the commodity in which it has a comparative advantage and imports the commodity in which it has a comparative disadvantage.

In a free market-price system, Portugal would then export its comparative advantage commodity wine and import cloth while England exports cloth and imports wine. As a result, both countries can consume their importable commodity at a lower cost than if each country tried to produce each commodity for itself. Specialization according to comparative advantage results in an efficient international division of labor, giving each country a higher real national income than it would have with no trade.

Significantly, the gains from trade are mutual gains in a positive-sum game. According to their relative intensities of supply and demand, one nation may gain more from trade than another, but each still gains over a no-trade situation. The gain is on the side of importables. Exports can be viewed as the intermediate goods used for the "production" of the importables. The cost of "indirectly producing" imports through direct specialization on exports is less than if the country produced the importables directly at home. Foreign trade is thus like an industry that uses exports as inputs to produce imports as output. The principle of comparative advantage becomes an efficiency rule for maximizing output (imports) per unit of input (exports).

In explaining the basis of trade, the theory of comparative costs has a remarkably high degree of generality. It can be applied widely to problems of resource allocation—whether for an individual, for a country, or for several countries or within a multiproduct enterprise. Its logic is institution-free and applicable to any decision mechanism that must exercise the logic of choice. As Lord Robbins[1] concludes,

> This analysis must surely be regarded as one of the main triumphs of abstract economic thought, far transcending in importance the problems of international trade to which it was first applied; it ultimately explains, not only the advantages arising here, but also any advantages arising from specialization anywhere where there are unequal differences in potentialities. It establishes, too, principles of action, not only for market economies, but also for any economic organization which aspires to rational allocation of resources. Other things being equal, a purely Collectivist economy should organize its resources so as to minimize the comparative opportunity costs of achieving any particular goal.

The model of comparative advantage becomes more complicated if the number of commodities and number of countries are increased, but the logic of the analysis remains the same.[2] Commodities will be ranked by their comparative factor-productivity ratios such that each of a country's exports will have a higher factor-productivity ratio than each of its imports. Any number of commodities in any number of countries can be arranged in a chain of declining comparative advantage. In this chain, the position of the dividing line between exports and imports will depend on demand conditions for each country's products and on the equilibrium conditions that world demand equals world supply and that value of exports equals value of imports for each country.[3]

Although the Ricardian analysis establishes a basis for international specialization according to comparative differences in real cost, it is, of course, necessary to translate the comparative differences in real cost into absolute differences in money prices. Obviously, any buyer of imports will only purchase imports if its absolute money price is less than the price of a domestic substitute good. This translation into absolute differences in money price will follow, provided the relative wage differentials are within the relative productivity differentials. If, for example, labor is three times more productive in country *I* than in country *II*, the absolute money price of the exports from *I* will be less than the absolute money price of the substitute commodity in *II*, provided the money wage rate is not more than three times higher in *I* than in *II*. This can be illustrated by comparing the results in Table 2.1 (a) and (b).

Under competitive conditions, the wage differences must be within the productivity differences (real cost), or else only one country would be able to export, and its wage rates

Table 2.1
Productivity, Wages, and Prices

Country	Amount of Labor Required for Producing 1 Unit of		Wage Rate per Labor Unit at Existing Foreign Currency Exchange Rate	Money Price of X	Money Price of Y
	X	Y			
(a)					
I	5	10	$2	$10	$20
II	6	30	$1	$ 6	$30
(b)					
I	5	10	$3	$15	$30
II	6	30	$1	$ 6	$30

would be bid up to compensate for this. Or the exchange rate would have to be altered to preserve the condition of balanced trade. (We shall have more to say about the balance of payments adjustment process in Chapter 5.)

We can more readily understand how comparative differences in real costs become translated into differences in absolute money prices if we appreciate the relationships between productivity, wage rates, foreign currency exchange rates, and the resultant changes in absolute prices. Suppose country *I* is more productive than country II in every commodity, and that *I* can therefore readily export to II, but II cannot export to *I*. But when the demand increases for *I*'s exports, its wage rates will also increase, thereby raising its absolute prices and reducing its competitive position. The fall in demand in *II* may also lower wage rates and absolute prices in *II*, thereby allowing *II* to acquire a comparative advantage in another commodity. Or as the demand rises for I's currency on foreign exchange markets, the price of I's currency in terms of II's currency will rise (*I*'s currency will appreciate), and this will cause the demand for I's exports to decline and will raise *I*'s demand for imports. Thus, through wage changes or foreign exchange rate movements, the goods of country *I* will rise in price and those of country *II* will fall.

Similarly, even if one industry in *I* is so competitive that it dominates the world export market, the resulting exchange rate appreciation in that country will make other export industries in *I* less competitive. Because of variations in wage rates and exchange rates the underlying differences in comparative real costs are reflected in differences in absolute market prices.

Simplified as the Ricardian analysis is, it yields the important conclusion that labor productivity and the wage rate determine unit labor cost and that this in turn is a major determinant of a country's comparative advantage. Even though in reality there are other sources of comparative advantage (examined below) and governments intervene with trade policies that affect the pattern of trade, nonetheless empirical tests validate the conclusion that a strong explanation of what goods a country will export and import can be based on relative unit labor costs.

Factor Proportions

Comparative advantage is not an antiquated nineteenth-century principle. It has been refined and generalized to modern conditions, especially by two Swedish economists, Eli

TRUE AND NON-TRIVIAL

[Economics] puts its best foot forward when it speaks out on international trade. This was brought home to me years ago when I was in the Society of Fellows at Harvard along with the mathematician Stanislaw Ulam. Ulam, who was to become an originator of the Monte Carlo method and co-discoverer of the hydrogen bomb, was already at a tender age a world famous topologist. And he was a delightful conversationalist, wandering lazily over all domains of knowledge. He used to tease me by saying, "Name me one proposition in all of the social sciences which is both true and non-trivial." This was a test that I always failed. But now, some thirty years later, on the staircase so to speak, an appropriate answer occurs to me: The Ricardian theory of comparative advantage: the demonstration that trade is mutually profitable even when one country is absolutely more—or less—productive in terms of every commodity. That it is logically true need not be argued before a mathematician; that it is not trivial is attested by the thousands of important and intelligent men who have never been able to grasp the doctrine for themselves or to believe it after it was explained to them. (Just to give one instance: "Boss" Kettering was a famous inventor of the recent epoch, having developed the self-starting auto and many other important devices. Yet this founder of General Motors and pioneer in cancer research never could understand why it might pay to send American cotton to Japan to be spun into cloth and then sent back to the United States.)

Nobel laureate Paul A. Samuelson, Presidential Address, *International Economic Relations* (1969), p. 9.

Heckscher and Nobel laureate Bertil Ohlin. Recognizing all the factors of production that may be inputs, the Heckscher-Ohlin (H-O) theory of comparative advantage focuses on factor proportions in the production of different products in different countries. The basic determinant of a country's comparative advantage is then relative factor endowment: i.e., the country's relative factor supplies of natural resources, labor, and capital (the inputs necessary for production). And this is the minimum difference among countries that is a sufficient condition for mutually profitable trade among countries, even if all the countries have the same tastes (demand conditions), same technology (production functions), and no economies of scale in production (constant returns). As long as there are relative resource differences—with some countries being relatively abundant in labor, while others are relatively abundant in capital or natural resources—there will be differences in relative costs and prices, thereby giving the foundation for trade based on comparative advantage.

The differences in relative commodity prices among countries are based on differences in relative factor rewards that are, in turn, based on differences in relative factor endowments. If a country's relatively abundant factor is labor, then wages will be relatively low, and the price of commodities that are labor-intensive in their production will also be low. The country will then have a comparative advantage in labor-intensive products. A firm that specializes in the production of such labor-intensive products will also have a competitive advantage. (Factor "abundance" is defined in terms of the relative quantities of the factors, not their absolute quantities. The production process for commodity X is labor-intensive if the ratio of labor to capital in X is greater than the ratio of labor to capital in commodity Y, at the same factor prices.)

The celebrated Heckscher-Ohlin model of trade stresses the relation between endowments and comparative advantage: countries tend to export goods whose production makes intensive use of their more abundant factors. Whereas its usual forms have emphasized relative endowments of capital, labor, and natural resources, recent variations on the model focus increasingly on the importance of skills in the trade equation, a view strongly supported by empirical evidence. A simple trade model based on the presumption that an important determinant of a country's comparative advantage is its relative endowments of skills and land illustrates this well.

In the figure below, the regression line relates the split of each country's exports between manufactures and primary products to its relative supplies of skills and land. The regional averages also are plotted. The largest contrast is between Africa and the industrial world, which lie toward opposite ends of the regression line; in between lie Latin America, South Asia, and East Asia, in that order. The ranking of Latin America and South Asia is instructive: South Asia and Africa both have low levels of schooling, and Latin America and East Asia intermediate levels. But the two Asian regions have little land compared with Africa and Latin America.

Skill accumulation increases growth by changing the nature of comparative advantage. Although the figure was estimated on the basis of cross-sectional data for 1985, it can also be used to describe the dynamics of development. Progress in the diagram consists of movement upward and to the right, reflecting a higher average skill level in a country's labor force and an increase in its comparative advantage in manufacturing over primary commodities.

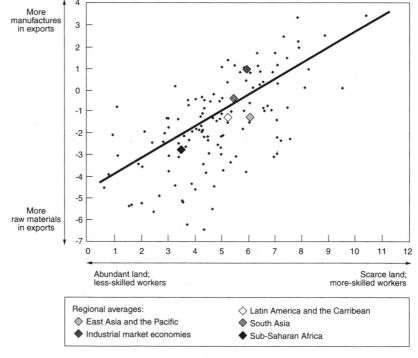

Skill intensity of exports and human capital endowment. Data are for 126 industrial and developing countries in 1985. Values along the horizontal axis are logarithms of the ratio of the countries average educational attainment to its land area; vertical axis values are logarithms of the ratio of manufactured to primary-products exports. Source: Export data from United Nations Statistical Office COMTRADE data base; education data from UNDP 1990; land data from the World Bank.

Source: World Bank, *World Development Report*, 1995 (New York: Oxford University Press, 1995), p. 59. Reprinted by permission of Oxford University Press.

Consider two countries I and II with the following relative factor endowments:

Relative Factor Endowment	I	II
Abundant	Labor	Capital
Moderate	Land	Land
Scarce	Capital	Labor

Country I would then export labor-intensive goods and import capital-intensive goods from country II.

For example, the Philippines exports labor-intensive products such as textiles, clothing, and footwear; Indonesia exports land-intensive products such as oil or timber; the United States exports capital-intensive and skilled-labor-intensive products such as chemicals, machinery, and aircraft.

It should also be noted that factors move in the guise of commodities. If labor cannot migrate from a country with low labor productivity to one with high labor productivity, the labor will in effect migrate by being embodied in labor-intensive exports. The greater are the restrictions on international movements of the factors of production, the wider are the gaps in the comparative advantages of different countries and the greater is the scope for international specialization.

Acquired Comparative Advantage

The foregoing Ricardian and H-O explanations of trade patterns are for trade at a given moment of time. But a country's comparative advantage is not static, given forever. Instead, it is dynamic—changing over time as a new comparative advantage is acquired.

In the beginning, Adam Smith actually referred to both "natural advantage" and "acquired advantage." He said, "Whether the advantages which one country has over another, be natural or acquired, is in this respect of no consequence. As long as the one country has these advantages, and the other wants them, it will always be more advantageous for the latter, rather to buy of the former than to make. It is an acquired advantage only, which one artificer has over his neighbor, who exercises another trade; and yet they both find it more advantageous to buy of one another, than to make what does not belong to their particular trades."[4]

Ricardian-type goods and H-O-type goods tend to be based on "natural advantage": i.e., historical differences in labor productivity or relative factor endowments. But, as we shall now see, comparative advantage can be acquired over time through the evolution of the product life cycle, changes in factor endowments, and the acquisition of increasing returns to scale.

PRODUCT LIFE CYCLE

Nations have a comparative advantage in industries in which their firms gain a lead in technology, thereby allowing the creation of new products or product improvement. Innovations based on new technology initially give a country a temporary monopoly position and easy access to foreign markets. American manufacturers have been technological leaders in aerospace, electrical machinery, chemicals, transportation equipment, and nonelectrical machinery. For a period of time, the innovating industry may enjoy an export monopoly as long as there is an "imitation lag" in other countries. But eventually the technological gap is narrowed, the imitation lag is overcome, and other countries may then acquire a comparative advantage in the product.

More generally, a product life cycle occurs.[5] This is based not only on technology, but also on the changing mix of other inputs in production at different stages of the product's life. As depicted in Figure 2.1, a product moves over time from being a new product to becoming eventually a mature standardized product.

In the "new product stage," production requires relatively heavy R&D expenditures and highly skilled labor. Product design is still being adapted, costs are high, and sales are low. The suppliers therefore concentrate on the home market, where any technical difficulties in production can be most readily solved and where demand is less elastic.

In the second "growth" stage, marketing and capital costs dominate, and mass production and distribution become possible. Costs and price fall, and the product becomes exportable (in the amount given by the difference between the solid production curve and dotted home consumption line in Figure 2.1). In this stage of the product life cycle, suppliers may deem it a strategic competitive advantage to establish foreign subsidiaries to produce overseas.

In the third "mature" stage, the product and manufacturing operations have become standardized and routine, and can be absorbed in other countries. Sales then level off, price-elasticity of demand is high, and exports diminish. Whereas in the first two stages, the innovating country had advantages from introducing and producing the new product, these advantages are lost by the third stage. The technology may now be licensed to foreign producers, or the technology may have become publicly available. The trading partner, which formerly imported the product, may now be able to duplicate its routine type of production.

The determinants of the trade structure may change so much over time that a country that initially imported a product begins to substitute home-competing production for the import, becomes more efficient in its import-substitution production, and eventually acquires a comparative advantage for the mature product based on its lower costs of production. This is the other side of the product cycle—what Japanese economists call the "catching-up product cycle."[6] Overseas producers may then actually begin to export the "old" product to third countries and to the first country, which has lost its initial comparative advantage. A global product life cycle can thus occur over several country markets. For example, the production and export of TV sets from the United States gave way to imports from Japan and then from South Korea and Taiwan. Finally, in 1995, a Korean firm acquired control of Zenith, the last American manufacturer.

As the technological gap narrows and imitation lag shortens, so too does the product gap. As the comparative advantage in the mix of input requirements alters over the product's life cycle, so does the comparative advantage of producing the product in one country rather than another. Through technological change, there is a continually changing international division of labor. Modifications in comparative advantage can be expected to be even more rapid in the future as technological progress accelerates, imitation lags shorten, and product life cycles speed up.

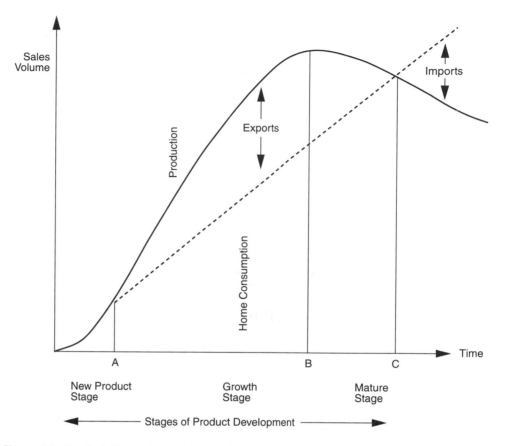

Figure 2.1 Product life cycle and trade. A country may initially innovate and then, after time A, become an exporter of a new product. After time B, the innovating country loses its comparative advantage when the product becomes standardized and foreign countries compete with the innovating country's exports. Finally, after time C, the innovating country becomes an importer of the product.

   The product cycle explains from the viewpoint of a more developed industrial country how comparative advantage of a new product is first acquired in the advanced economy and then transmitted to less developed economies through trade and investment. The catching-up process in the less developed countries describes the sequence from imports to eventual exportation of the standardized product as domestic costs reach the international competitive cost threshold. For the history of Japan's development, this has been called the "wild geese-flying pattern of industrial development,"[7] as depicted in Figure 2.2.
   Kazushi Ohkawa outlines a framework of phases and their shifts as follows: (1) traditional product export; (2) primary import substitution of nondurable consumer goods; (3) primary export substitution of light manufactured goods for agricultural products; (4) secondary import substitution of durable goods for producers and consumers by further development of domestic manufacturing; and (5) secondary export substitution in which export of nondurables is replaced by durable goods export. The series of shifts from one phase to another, (1) → (2) → (3) → (4) → (5), has been empirically observed through the

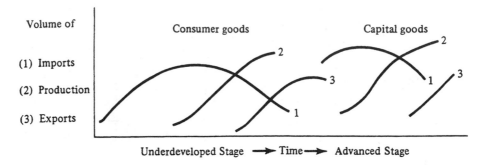

Figure 2.2 The catching-up product cycle. The developing country proceeds over time from imports of a particular product to its import-substitution production and eventual export of the commodity. The catching-up process may begin with simple consumer goods; at a more advanced stage of development, the pattern may be repeated for capital goods.

entire process of industrialization in East Asia, first in Japan, and then in the postwar period in Taiwan and South Korea.[8]

FACTOR ENDOWMENTS OVER TIME

The product life cycle model explains some changes in comparative advantage as the mix of factors required to produce a product varies over the life of the product. More generally, comparative advantage changes as a country's factor endowment evolves over time. A country that is initially labor abundant may become relatively labor scarce over time; a country that is capital scarce may become more plentifully endowed with capital (see Table 2.2). South Korea and Taiwan, for example, have now reached a situation in which labor is relatively scarce, and inexpensive labor has disappeared. At the same time, capital accumulation has been rapid, and more of their exports reflect capital intensity.

In the more developed countries, the evolution of factor endowments increasingly favors capital-intensive and research-intensive products. Over time, labor skills are upgraded, R&D efforts become more extensive, and technological progress occurs. In essence, factors are created. And as Harvard's Michael Porter emphasizes, "Nations succeed in industries where they are particularly good at factor creation."[9] But knowledge of the processes by which factors are created is still limited.[10]

Table 2.2
Rates of Resource Growth, 1963–80 Relative to Total Labor Force

	Capital	Skilled Labor	R&D Scientists
United States	1.4	1.0	−1.1
Japan	8.3	2.7	5.1
Germany	3.0	2.5	5.6
United Kingdom	3.3	1.5	5.6
Canada	2.0	1.3	1.1
Newly industrialized countries	6.2	2.6	

Source: Harry P. Bowen, "Changes in the International Distribution of Resources and Their Impact on U.S. Comparative Advantage," *Review of Economics and Statistics* (August 1983): 405.

The factor proportions model can be extended and more broadly applied to incorporate human capital and R&D as "research endowments." These endowments may differ among countries, but even if they were the same, it would be most unlikely that each country's endowment would be used to develop and produce the same "research-intensive" products at the same time. The extensive range of product differentiation within industry provides a strong source of international trade, and country's export industries may well show higher rates of technical progress through "research effort" (either in product innovations or process innovations) than the same industries in its trading partners.[11] In an industrial export industry of an advanced economy, the characteristics of high skill-intensity, high research-intensity, technical change, innovations, and economies of scale are all likely to be strongly interrelated.

A number of empirical studies demonstrate how the evolution of relative resource endowments have affected comparative advantage. An extensive study for the Washington-based Institute for International Economics traces changes in the comparative advantages of Japan and the United States.[12] The study calculates indices of "revealed" comparative advantage that can be used to gauge changes in international specialization. The export index of "revealed" comparative advantage is defined as the ratio of a country's share in the exports of a particular commodity category to the country's share in total merchandise exports. A value greater than (less than) one for a particular industry is interpreted as reflecting comparative advantage (disadvantage) in that industry.

In 1967, Japan had a comparative advantage in unskilled labor-intensive commodities, such as textiles, apparel, rubber and plastic products, leather and leather products, stone, clay, and glass products, and miscellaneous manufactured products. This is shown in Table 2.3.

The study also shows that as a consequence of its poor natural resource endowment, Japan had a comparative disadvantage in 1967 in food, beverages, and tobacco, agricultural raw materials, and nonoil mineral products.

From 1967–80, however, Japan's pattern of international specialization changed considerably. It shifted from a position of comparative advantage to one of comparative disadvantage in apparel and leather and leather products, the most unskilled labor-intensive categories. Japan's initial comparative disadvantage increased further in natural resource-intensive commodities, whether in a primary form or in a processed state (lumber and wood products, furniture). Furthermore, Japan reduced somewhat its specialization in physical capital-intensive products. At the same time, it greatly strengthened its comparative advantage in skill-intensive products, with the largest change occurring in nonelectrical machinery.

By 1985, Japanese industries enjoyed a greater than 60 percent share of total world exports in motorcycles, TV image and sound recorders, dictating machines, calculating machines, mounted optical elements, photo and thermocopy apparatus, still cameras and flash apparatus, cash registers and accounting machines, outboard marine piston engines, and electric gramophones.

The data for Japan may be contrasted with those for the United States, as shown in Table 2.4. In 1967, the United States had a comparative advantage in primary products, physical capital-intensive products, and human capital-intensive products. It had a comparative disadvantage in most unskilled labor-intensive commodities. Processed natural resource-intensive products were an intermediate category. Between 1967 and 1983, the United States generally increased its comparative advantage in natural resource-intensive

Table 2.3
Revealed Comparative Advantages for Exports, Japan, 1967–83

Industry	0	1.0	2.0	3.0	4.0	5.0
Food, beverages, and tobacco	←					
Agricultural raw materials	◄					
Non-oil mineral products	►					
Textile mill products			←—————————————			
Apparel and other finished textile products		◄—————————				
Lumber and wood products	←					
Furniture and fixtures	←					
Paper and allied products	◄					
Printing and publishing	►					
Chemical and allied products		◄—				
Rubber and plastic products				←		
Leather and leather products		◄———				
Stone, clay, and glass products			◄——			
Primary metal and allied products				◄		
Fabricated metal products			◄—			
Nonelectrical machinery		————→				
Electrical machinery						—→
Transportation equipment				———→		
Instruments and related products				————————→		
Misc. manufacturing products		◄———				

Note: Values greater than (less than) one reflect the comparative advantage (disadvantage) in a given industry. The direction and length of each arrow indicate the direction and size of the shift in comparative advantage during the 1967–1983 period.
Source: Bela Balassa and Marcus Noland, *Japan in the World Economy* (Washington, DC: Institute for International Economics, 1988), p. 30. Copyright 1998 by the Institute for International Economics. All rights reserved.

products, at the expense of manufactured goods. But it increased its comparative advantage in research-intensive products and maintained the strength of its comparative advantage in human capital-intensive products. The U.S. comparative advantage in physical capital-intensive products, and its comparative disadvantage in unskilled labor-intensive products, underwent little change during this period.

The pattern of comparative advantage in high-technology products (defined as those for which R&D expenditures accounted for at least 3.5 percent of the value of a given product's output in the United States in the mid-1970s) is of particular interest. The relative importance of these products is indicated by their average ranking on the comparative advantage scale of each nation. On this scale, high-technology products are a more important component of American than of Japanese exports. In fact, the average ranking of these

Table 2.4
Revealed Comparative Advantage for Exports, United States, 1967–83

Industry	0	1.0	2.0	3.0	4.0
Food, beverages, and tobacco			→		
Agricultural raw materials			———→		
Non-oil mineral products			——→		
Textile mill products	→				
Apparel and other finished textile products	←				
Lumber and wood products		→			
Furniture and fixtures	←				
Paper and allied proudcts		→			
Chemical and allied products			◄		
Rubber and plastic products		←			
Leather and leather products (no change)					
Stone, clay, and glass products		←			
Primary metal and allied products	←				
Fabricated metal products			→		
Nonelectrical machinery			→		
Electrical machinery (no change)					
Transportation equipment			←		
Instruments and related products			←		
Misc. manufacturing products	→				

Note: Values greater than (less than) one reflect the comparative advantage (disadvantage) in a given industry. The direction and length of each arrow indicate the direction and size of the shift in comparative advantage during the 1967–1983 period.
Source: Bela Balassa and Marcus Noland, *Japan in the World Economy* (Washington, DC: Institute for International Economics, 1988), p. 32. Copyright 1998 by the Institute for International Economics. All rights reserved.

products was higher in the United States at the beginning of the period than it was in Japan at the end.

It further appears that, with a few exceptions, the United States increased its comparative advantage in high-technology products over time (Table 2.5). By 1983, such products occupied the first four places on the revealed comparative advantage scale of the United States (aircraft, aircraft engines, office machinery, steam engines and turbines); this had been the case for only one product group (aircraft) in 1967.

Japan extended its comparative advantage in twelve out of nineteen high-tech nology product categories (Table 2.6). The exceptions were aircraft, optical instrume agricultural chemicals, synthetic fibers, cellulose fibers, steam engines, and turbine declines in these product categories were the mirror image of the increases obser United States.

Table 2.5
Revealed Comparative Advantages for High-technology Exports, United States, 1967–83

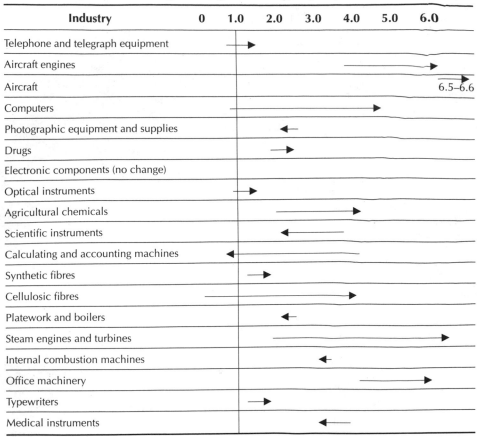

Industry	0	1.0	2.0	3.0	4.0	5.0	6.0
Telephone and telegraph equipment	→→						
Aircraft engines					→	→	
Aircraft							→ 6.5–6.6
Computers		←——————→					
Photographic equipment and supplies			←				
Drugs			→				
Electronic components (no change)							
Optical instruments		→→					
Agricultural chemicals				———→			
Scientific instruments			←				
Calculating and accounting machines		←————————					
Synthetic fibres		→→					
Cellulosic fibres		————————→					
Platework and boilers			←				
Steam engines and turbines				——————————→			
Internal combustion machines				←			
Office machinery					———→		
Typewriters		→→					
Medical instruments				←——			

Note: Values greater than (less than) one reflect the comparative advantage (disadvantage) in a given industry. The direction and length of each arrow indicate the direction and size of the shift in comparative advantage during the 1967–1983 period.
Source: Bela Balassa and Marcus Noland, *Japan in the World Economy* (Washington, DC: Institute for International Economics, 1988), p. 34. Copyright 1988 by the Institute for International Economics. All rights reserved.

It is significant that the data show a complementary pattern of specialization in the high-technology area, with Japan having a comparative advantage in products in which the United States has a disadvantage and vice versa.[13]

ECONOMIES OF SCALE

When monopolistic competition exists, other sources of specialization and trade are frequently created through the differentiation of products and also the realization of economies of scale in production.[14] (Increasing returns to scale exist when output increases in greater proportion than inputs—for example, a doubling of expenditure on inputs results in a more than double expansion of output.) Even if relative factor endowments were identical in all countries, there would still be a basis for trade when imperfect competition results in

Table 2.6
Revealed Comparative Advantage for High-technology Exports, Japan, 1967–83

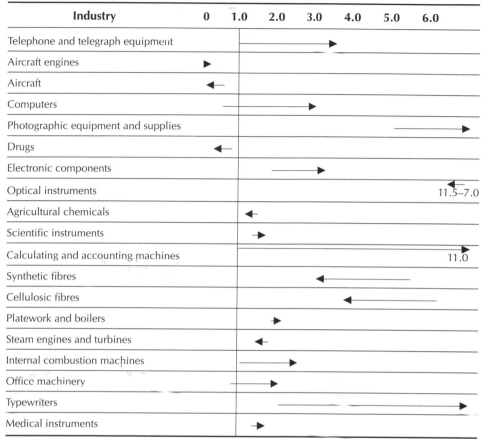

Industry	0	1.0	2.0	3.0	4.0	5.0	6.0
Telephone and telegraph equipment							
Aircraft engines							
Aircraft							
Computers							
Photographic equipment and supplies							
Drugs							
Electronic components							
Optical instruments							11.5–7.0
Agricultural chemicals							
Scientific instruments							
Calculating and accounting machines							11.0
Synthetic fibres							
Cellulosic fibres							
Platework and boilers							
Steam engines and turbines							
Internal combustion machines							
Office machinery							
Typewriters							
Medical instruments							

Note: Values greater than (less than) one reflect the comparative advantage (disadvantage) in a given industry. The direction and length of each arrow indicate the direction and size of the shift in comparative advantage during the 1967–1983 period.
Source: Bela Balassa and Marcus Noland, *Japan in the World Economy* (Washington, DC: Institute for International Economics, 1988), p. 35. Copyright 1988 by the Institute for International Economics. All rights reserved.

differentiated products or increasing returns to scale. These conditions explain *intraindustry* trade (for example, the exchange of automobiles for automobiles or office machines for office machines) unlike the *interindustry* trade that is explained by the Ricardian or H-O theories (wine for cloth or labor-intensive for capital-intensive products).

A study of U.S. trade in 1990 concluded that in trade with developing countries, the United States tends to be a net exporter of skill-intensive goods, and a large net importer of nonskill-intensive goods, in conformity with the H-O theory of interindustry trade. The composition of trade with other advanced industrial nations, however, was based much more on intraindustry trade in differentiated products than on differences in factor proportions.[15]

A sizable and growing proportion of international trade is intraindustry trade, about one fourth of world trade. This type of two-way trade in similar, but not identical, products is determined by R&D expenditures and innovations that differentiate products. The trade of manufactures against manufactures (accounting for some 60 percent of world trade) is closely related to differences in technology among countries and their economies of scale in production. The dynamic quality of intraindustry trade and trade in manufactures underlies many of the changes in the composition of trade over time, especially in trade among the advanced industrial nations. The developed industrial countries that trade among themselves tend to have more similar factor endowments and hence more intraindustry trade, while the less developed countries trading with the more industrialized countries tend to have different factor proportions and conduct mainly interindustry trade.

LADDER AND QUEUE

Over time, an industrializing country tends to proceed up a ladder of comparative advantage—from initially exporting commodities that are natural resource-intensive (sugar or rice) to commodities that are unskilled labor-intensive (textiles) to semiskilled and skilled labor-intensive (electronics) to capital-intensive (machinery) and finally to the export of knowledge-intensive commodities (computers, control equipment). As depicted in Figure 2.3, the upward movement is from exports that embody basic factors such as natural resources and unskilled or semiskilled labor to exports that embody more advanced and specialized factors such as highly educated and skilled personnel and R&D activities. The basic factors are passively inherited, representing natural or historical comparative advantage based on differences in labor productivity (Ricardo-type goods) or in factor endowments (H-O-type goods). They give a cost-based advantage in the production of some products. But the basic factors dominate only the lower rungs of the ladder. As a country develops, the advanced factors that dominate the top rungs are upgraded over time through considerable investment in human and physical capital to allow the country to acquire comparative advantage in differentiated products and proprietary production technology (Porter- and Krugman-type goods).[16] This gives a product-based advantage derived from differentiated products or increasing returns to scale.

At the same time as the early-comers climb the ladder of comparative advantage, late-comers in the queue can occupy the vacant rungs. For example, as Japan has proceeded up the ladder, South Korea has come behind it—first exporting primary products in the late 1950s, subsequently moving upscale to textiles and plywood in the 1960s, and then iron and steel products and electrical machinery in the 1970s. By 1995, Korea's top three semiconductor makers were expanding to take away most of the global memory chip market from Japan.

Taiwan has also moved rapidly up the ladder. The government now encourages the substitution of machines for labor and is letting labor-intensive and low-tech factories close or move offshore. Firms are moving toward high technology and higher value products. For example, Microelectronics Technology Inc. was making components for microwave receiving equipment; now it makes complete systems for ships. Inventa Electronics Co., which made almost-disposable calculators, now builds personal computers. Kennex International Corp. is designing high-end sporting goods. And Vidar-Sun Moon Star Co., which formerly produced electronic parts, now makes mobile phones and digital microwave radios.

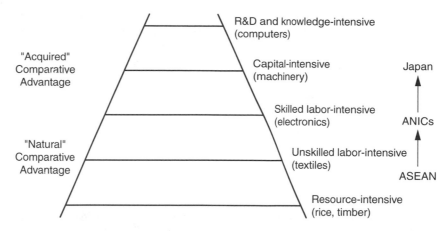

Figure 2.3 Ladder of comparative advantage. The sources of comparative advantage evolve over time, thereby changing a country's composition of trade and its position on the ladder of comparative advantage. At the lower rungs, "natural" comparative advantage is related to Ricardian and H-O-type of goods that have a cost-based type of advantage. The higher rungs of "acquired" comparative advantage relate to Porter- and Krugman-type of goods that have a product-based type of advantage.

Numerous examples of this character cause the *Wall Street Journal* to speak of "the new Taiwanese economy—moving from imitation to innovation."[17]

While Japan proceeds up the ladder of comparative advantage, it is now being followed by the Asian NICs (Taiwan, South Korea, Hong Kong and Singapore). Accordingly, Japan now imports more of the labor-intensive, low price manufactures (footwear, watches, radios, and TVs) from the late-comers to development. As the upper tier country moves on to specialization in the more sophisticated products, the lower tier countries also expand their exports of the lower technology products to the markets of third countries. Japan's labor cost advantage in textiles and consumer electronics has long since been lost to South Korea and Hong Kong. The Asian NICs export textiles and the simpler consumer electronics products to North America and Europe as Japan specializes on even higher technology exports. Indeed, competition between Japan and the Asian NICs has been occurring more often in third country markets than in their own.

As the Asian NICs, in turn, move up the ladder of comparative advantage, their former positions on the lower rungs of the ladder are being taken by those behind them in the queue: Thailand, Malaysia, Indonesia, the Philippines. Thailand and Malaysia, in particular, have in recent years gained impressive footholds in export markets for manufactures. The dynamics of "the ladder and the queue" have certainly been pronounced within the Asia Pacific region. Figures 2.4 through 2.6 show the changes in revealed comparative advantage for East and Southeast Asian countries from 1970 to 1986.

The changing pattern of Asia Pacific trade has also carried over to changes in trade patterns between the OECD countries (North America, Japan, European Union) and Asia Pacific. The more industrialized OECD countries engage in complementary trade with Asia in manufactures, exchanging capital goods for final consumer goods. Capital-intensive and technology-intensive goods are exchanged for labor-intensive and lower-technology consumer goods. To a lesser extent, the same is true for the OECD area and

Latin America. Europe's trade with Africa, however, has remained of the more traditional type of manufactures for primary commodities, because sub-Saharan African countries have not yet become exporters of manufactures. While the major source in the developing world of U.S. consumer goods imports is Asia Pacific, the major destination of American exports is Latin America. Japan's trade is the most complementary and integrated with the Asian countries.

DYNAMIC GAINS FROM TRADE

We have so far emphasized the static gains from trade—the increase in each country's real income based on efficient international resource allocation. But the dynamic aspects of trade are of equal importance. The gains from trade do not result merely from a once-over change toward efficient resource allocation among industries, but are being continually augmented by the dynamic gains. Whereas the static gains from trade, as a result of reallocating resources in accordance with comparative advantage, explain a once-over change to a higher level of real income, the dynamic gains from trade explain the higher rate of growth in income over time.

Although dynamic elements were not central in classical and neoclassical thought, they were not ignored. John Stuart Mill, for one, was particularly clear on the dynamic gains. Trade, according to comparative advantage, results in a "more efficient employment of the productive forces of the world," and this Mill considered to be the "direct economical advantage of foreign trade." But, emphasized Mill, "there are, besides, indirect effects, which must be counted as benefits of a high order." One of the most significant "indirect" dynamic benefits, according to Mill,[18] is

> the tendency of every extension of the market to improve the processes of production. A country which produces for a larger market than its own can introduce a more extended division of labour, can make greater use of machinery, and is more likely to make inventions and improvements in the processes of production.

More generally, Hla Myint has emphasized the dynamic "productivity" theory of international trade that was part of classical thought. The "productivity" theory links growth of the domestic economy to a country's foreign trade by interpreting trade as a dynamic force: Trade widens the extent of the market and the scope of the division of labor, permits a greater use of machinery, stimulates innovations, overcomes technical indivisibilities, raises the productivity of labor, and generally enables the trading country to enjoy increasing returns and further growth.[19] Many of the dynamic gains stem from trade in ideas and the educative effect of trade.

In modern terminology, free trade may promote "X-efficiency,"[20] which means the presence of some forces cause the firm to purchase and utilize all its inputs "efficiently," so as to reduce real costs per unit of output. Motivational elements contribute to an increase in productivity and make the firm produce closer to its minimal cost equilibrium. X-efficiency improves allocation within the firm, as distinct from the orthodox allocative efficiency among firms or industries.

Trade, with the exposure that it brings to the competition of world markets, can stimulate greater managerial effort and hence improve X-efficiency. Free trade makes it

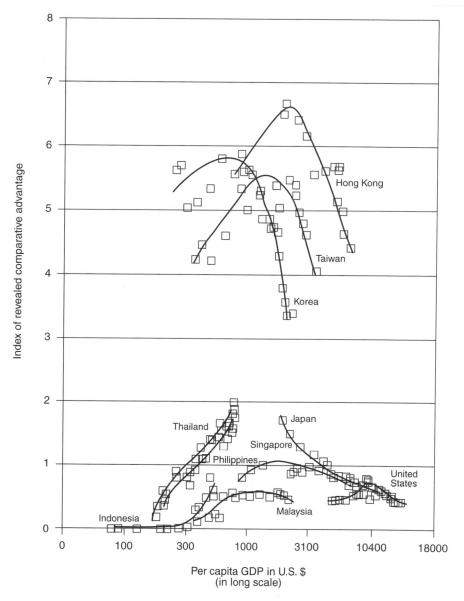

Figure 2.4 Revealed comparative advantage: unskilled labor-intensive goods. The index of revealed comparative advantage compares the shares of a commodity group within a single country's exports to the same share in world markets. If the ratio for a commodity group exceeds one, then the country has a comparative advantage in that type of commodity group. *Source*: Seiji Naya, William E. James, and Michael Plummer, *Pacific Economic Cooperation in the Global Context: Macroeconomic Structural Issues of Trade, Finance and the Adjustment Process* (Honolulu: East-West Center, 1989).

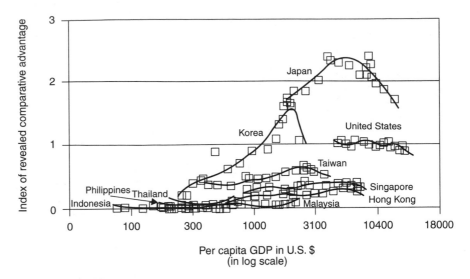

Figure 2.5 Revealed comparative advantage: human capital-intensive goods. *Source:* Seiji Naya, William E. James, and Michael Plummer, *Pacific Economic Cooperation in the Global Context: Macroeconomic Structural Issues of Trade, Finance and the Adjustment Process* (Honolulu: East-West Center, 1989).

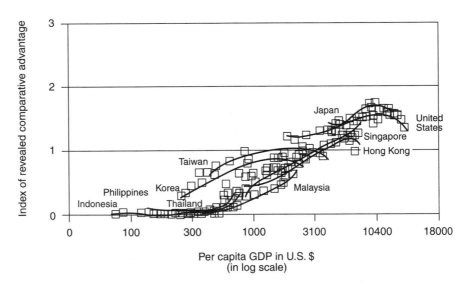

Figure 2.6 Revealed comparative advantage: technology-intensive goods. *Source:* Seiji Naya, William E. James, and Michael Plummer, *Pacific Economic Cooperation in the Global Context: Macroeconomic Structural Issues of Trade, Finance and the Adjustment Process* (Honolulu: East-West Center, 1989).

impossible for management to enjoy the quiet life of a monopolist in a sheltered industry. In defensive response to the greater competitive pressures from overseas, import competing firms will have to reduce their managerial slack and pursue cost-reducing methods of production through greater effort, more intensive search for best methods of production, or the utilization of new information.

This view of the impact of trade emphasizes the supply side of a country's growth—the opportunity trade provides a country for removing its domestic shortages and overcoming the diseconomies of the small size of its domestic market. This advantage is especially crucial for small developing countries. Also important is the opportunity trade offers for the exchange of goods with less growth potential for goods with more growth potential, thereby quickening the progress that results from a given effort on the savings side. An obvious example is the opportunity to import capital goods and materials required for development projects. (We shall discuss more thoroughly the particular problems of "development through trade" as related to poor countries in Chapter 8.)

Classical economists also noted the effects of trade on the domestic factor supply, especially on capital accumulation. Real income rises through the more efficient resource allocation associated with international trade, and the capacity to save, in turn, increases. The stimulus to investment is also strengthened by the realization of increasing returns in the wider markets overseas trade provides. There are also some benefits from foreign investment attracted to the export sector.

Of increasing significance in a rapidly changing technological world is technological diffusion and adoption, the transfer of skills, and know-how—all the elements that might contribute to accelerating the county's "learning rate." Theories of the determinants of a country's "learning rate" are not yet formalized.[21] But foreign trade has to be allotted a substantial role in these theories via the competitive stimuli it creates, its "cost reduction" effects through the realization of economies of scale, and its contribution to increasing productivity and developing new skills. Dynamic learning scale economies are important consequences of international specialization.

COMPARATIVE ADVANTAGE AND COMPETITIVE ADVANTAGE

Having examined the sources of and changes in a country's comparative advantage, we should now ask how this is related to the competitive advantage of a firm. At least 70 percent of U.S. manufacturing output faces international competition in the form of imports or competition in export markets. Under free trade, a country would import those commodities in which it has a comparative disadvantage. A domestic firm that then competes with these imports is unlikely to have a competitive advantage: Costs will be too high or there will be greater demand for the imports because of nonprice attributes such as style, quality, or service. Lacking a competitive edge against imports, the domestic firm may seek protection through government restrictions on the imports. (In the next chapter, we examine the case for and against such protection.)

The competitive advantage of a firm with a global strategy, however, depends on where the firm locates its various activities. If the global competitor locates its different activities in different countries according to each country's comparative advantage, it will then at the same time achieve competitive advantage.

Although the classic reason for locating an activity in a particular nation is factor costs, competitive advantages also arise from dispersing activities to several or many nations to perform R&D, gain access to specialized local skills, or develop relationships with private customers.[22] As Porter observes, "One of the potent advantages of the global firm is that it can spread activities to reflect different preferred locations, something a domestic or country-centered competitor does not do. Thus, components can be made in Taiwan, software written in India, and basic R&D performed in Silicon Valley, for example."[23] Intrafirm trade (i.e., imports from a firm's own subsidiaries abroad) characterizes many multinational firms. Beyond horizontal international specialization among different final products, multinationals are important in promoting vertical international specialization among different intermediate stages of production. By decomposing the production process into different activities that are located in various countries according to factor endowments, and by undertaking worldwide sourcing for inputs and commodities, the multinational is seeking corporate advantage in conformity with the comparative advantages of the countries in which it operates.

The multinational thus acts as a unit of integration in the world economy. By investing overseas and transmitting technology, together with its realization of economies of scale in R&D and marketing, the multinational is a unit of real international integration.

By its multinational operations and intrafirm transactions, the multinational corporation (MNC) transcends the national barriers to commodity trade and impediments to international factor movements. As such, the MNC becomes the mechanism for making effective the LDC's potential comparative advantage. The MNC provides the complementary resources of capital, technology, management, and market outlets that may be necessary to bestow an "effective" comparative advantage to the labor-surplus factor endowment in the host country.

This can be appraised as efficient international production. The MNC views production as a set of activities or processes, and the global strategy of the MNC is tantamount to the solution of activity models of production, with production processes in many countries. A competitive equilibrium solution to the programming problem is imposed within the MNC when it operates efficiently as a planning unit.

This interpretation of the MNC as an efficient technical and allocational unit of integration means that whereas intrafirm trade conforms to corporate advantage, it is also identical with the realization of comparative advantage. If the nation–state fragments the world economy through restrictions on commodity and factor movements and thwarts international economic integration, the MNC may serve a complementary—rather than competitive—function to the nation–state: The MNC may be the vehicle for evoking, in practice, the principle of comparative advantage in world trade, for trade in both outputs and inputs. The internal resource allocation in the MNC is a substitute mechanism for the market; when it realizes comparative advantage in processes and activities, the resource allocation decisions of the MNC will be more efficient than those in unintegrated markets that are characterized by imperfections and uncertainty. For global technical efficiency, the world economy is the territorial unit of international production, not the nation–state, which is a unit of international politics.

Dynamic comparative advantage is what matters in allowing enterprises to proceed up the nation's comparative advantage ladder. The stock of factors at any particular time is less important than the rate at which they are created, upgraded, and made more specialized to particular industries providing management and innovation.[24] Over time, to maintain its competitive advantage or to achieve higher-order competitive advantages, a firm must invest and innovate. As Porter maintains, "Sustaining advantage requires still further improvement and innovation to broaden and upgrade the sources of competitive advantage through advancing the product, the production process, marketing methods, and service."[25]

To retain the competitive advantage of a firm, management must continually anticipate changes in the comparative advantage of nations and be prepared to respond to these changes. Over time, a country's comparative advantage in the production of different products may widen or narrow, according to changes in factor supplies, factor quality and factor prices, the opening and closing of technological gaps, the dynamics of innovations, and variations in learning curves. A firm's competitive advantage in those products will thereby also change, and strategic responses then become necessary to achieve total efficiency. Without the efficient practice of international contextual analysis, firms in the more developed countries will not be able to reach the top rungs of the ladder of comparative advantage. And firms in the less developed countries will not be able to move in the queue to a higher rung on the ladder.[26]

NOTES

1. Lionel Robbins, *Political Economy: Past and Present* (1976), p. 154. Fritz Machlup also concludes that "the invention of the law of comparative advantage may be regarded as one of the greatest achievements of economic theory." Machlup, *A History of Thought on Economic Integration* (1977), p. 42.
2. Ricardian trade theory has been refined continually and generalized down to the present day. For an advanced discussion, see R. Dornbusch, S. Fischer, and P. A. Samuelson, "Comparative Advantage, Trade, and Payments in a Ricardian Model with a Continuum of Goods," *American Economic Review* 67 (December 1977): 823–839.
3. See J. Bhagwati, "The Pure Theory of International Trade: A Survey," *Economic Journal* 74 (March 1964): 5–6; and Ronald Findlay, *Trade and Specialization* (1970): 62–69.
4. Adam Smith, *Wealth of Nations* (1776), Book IV, Chap. II.
5. Raymond Vernon, "The Product Cycle Hypothesis in a New International Environment," *Oxford Bulletin of Economics and Statistics* (1980): 255–268.
6. Kiyoshi Kojima, *Japan and a New World Economic Order* (London: Croom Helm, 1977), pp. 150–152.
7. Kaname Akamatsu, "A Historical Pattern of Economic Growth in Developing Countries," *The Developing Economies* (March–August 1962): 3–25.
8. Kazushi Ohkawa and Hirohisa Kohama, *Lectures on Developing Economies* (Tokyo: University of Tokyo Press, 1989), p. 5.
9. Michael Porter, "The Competitive Advantage of Nations," *Harvard Business Review* (March–April 1990): 78.
10. Porter's concern is with the types of factor creation that lead to innovations and private investments of companies. In contrast, the "new growth theory" seeks greater understanding at the macro level. See Paul Romer, "Endogenous Technological Change," *Journal of Political Economy* (October 1990).
11. W. Gruber, D. Mehta, and R. Vernon, "The R&D Factor in International Trade and International Investment of United States Industries," *Journal of Political Economy* 75 (Feb. 1967): 20–37.
12. Bela Balassa and Marcus Noland, *Japan in the World Economy* (Washington, DC: Institute for International Economics, 1988), pp. 27–35. The following pages in this section summarize pp. 27–35 of this study.

13. For a more detailed explanation of these results, see Ibid., pp. 33–34 and Appendix A.

14. For a detailed analysis, see Elhanan Helpman and Paul R. Krugman, *Market Structure and Foreign Trade* (Cambridge, Mass.: MIT Press, 1985), Chs. 2, 6–9; Krugman, ed., *Strategic Trade Policy and the New International Economics* (Cambridge, Mass.: MIT Press, 1986), Chs. 1, 12.

15. Jeffrey D. Sachs and Howard J. Shatz, "Trade and Jobs in U. S. Manufacturing," *Brookings Papers on Economic Activity* 1 (1994): 13–21.

16. Porter, op cit., p. 77; Krugman, op cit., pp. 8–14.

17. "Unlikely Leader," *The Wall Street Journal,* June 1, 1990, p. 1.

18. See John Stuart Mill, *Principles of Political Economy* (1848), Vol. II, Book III, Chap. XVII, Sec. 5. See also Smith's earlier statement on the benefits of trade by widening the extent of the market: Smith, *Wealth of Nations* (1776), Book IV, Ch. 1, par. 31.

19. Hla Myint, "The 'Classical Theory' of International Trade and the Underdeveloped Countries," *Economic Journal* 68 (June 1958): 318–319; and Myint, "Adam Smith's Theory of International Trade in the Perspective of Economic Development," *Economica* 44 (Aug. 1977): 231–248.

20. H. Leibenstein, "Allocative Efficiency versus 'X-Efficiency,'" *American Economic Review* 56 (June 1966): 392–415; and Leibenstein, *General X-Efficiency Theory and Economic Development* (1978). Also, cf. W. M. Corden, *Trade Policy and Economic Welfare* (1974): 224–231.

21. Elements of such a theory might be found in the writings on "learning by doing" and "X-efficiency." Cf. Kenneth Arrow, "The Economic Implications of Learning by Doing," *Review of Economic Studies* 29 (June 1962): 155–173; Leibenstein, op cit.; and Allyn Young, "Increasing Returns and Economic Progress," *Economic Journal* 38 (Dec. 1928): 527–542.

22. Michael E. Porter, *The Competitive Advantage of Nations* (New York: Free Press, 1990), pp. 56–57.

23. Michael E. Porter, *Competition in Global Industries* (Boston: Harvard Business School Press, 1986), Ch. 1.

24. Porter, *The Competitive Advantage of Nations*, p. 74.

25. Ibid., p. 173.

26. For a clarification of the distinction between comparative advantage that applies to a country and competitive advantage that applies to a firm, see Peter G. Warr, "Comparative and Competitive Advantage," *Asian-Pacific Economic Literature* (November 1994): 1–14; Warr, *Comparative Advantages and Competitive Advantage in Manufactured Exports*, EDI Working Paper, World Bank, 1992; John H. Dunning, "The Competitive Advantage of Countries and the Activities of Transnational Corporations, Review Article," *U. N. Transnational Corporations* (February 1992): 135–168.

Factor Proportions Model of Trade

The Heckscher-Ohlin (H-O) analysis can be summarized in a series of diagrams, as follows:

Consider two countries, *I* and *II*;

two commodities, *w* and *c*;

two factors, *L* and *K*.

Let the production of *w* be *L*-intensive, and the production of *c* be *K*-intensive.

Let the factor endowment in *I* be relatively *L*-abundant,

and in *II* relatively-*K*-abundant.

With this $2 \times 2 \times 2$ model (2 countries, 2 commodities, 2 factors) we can illustrate diagrammatically the basis for international trade and the equilibrium conditions of trade. The logic of the analysis would be the same for a multi-country, multi-commodity, multi-factor model; but for simplicity we draw only two-dimensional diagrams.

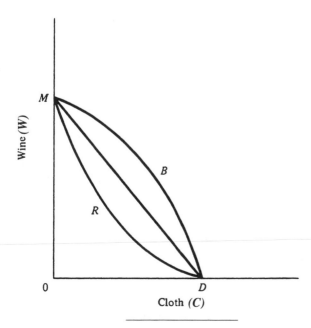

Figure 2.7 Production-possibility frontiers.
The slope of the production-possibility frontier, or product transformation curve, represents the opportunity cost of producing *c* in terms of *w*. This is equivalent to the marginal rate of domestic transformation (MRT_d) of *w* for *c*. *MBD* represents increasing opportunity costs or diminishing marginal rate of transformation of *w* for *c* (as more *c* is produced, greater amounts of *w* must be sacrificed to produce one additional unit of *c*). *MD* represents constant opportunity costs, or constant marginal rate of transformation of *w* for *c*. *MRD* represents decreasing opportunity costs, or increasing marginal rate of transformation of *w* for *c*.

Reprinted from Gerald M. Meier, *International Economics* (New York: Oxford University Press, 1980).

We can first recognize the generality of production conditions, as in Figure 2.7. For country *I*, three alternative production-possibility frontiers are represented: *MBD, MD,* and *MRD. MD* represents the Ricardian case of constant costs, previously considered. *MBD* denotes increasing costs (the production frontier is concave to the origin). There are diminishing returns to the variable input in the production of each product. As *I* produces more *c*, it must sacrifice production of more *w* (the slope of *MBD* becomes steeper as production moves from *M* toward *D*). Cost is a sacrificed benefit, and thus, this is a case of increasing opportunity costs. As more *c* is produced, the marginal opportunity cost of producing *c* rises, and the price of *c* in terms of *w* rises (the absolute slope of *MBD* becomes greater).

In contrast, *MRD* represents decreasing opportunity costs (the production frontier is convex to the origin). As *I* produces more *c*, it need sacrifice less *w* because of increasing returns to scale.

We may next establish the pre-trade equilibrium position. In Figure 2.8, the area *OMBD* represents *I*'s production-possibility set, and the curve *MBD* its production-possibility frontier. In order for production to be in equilibrium in perfectly competitive markets, the price of $w(P_w)$ must equal the marginal cost of $w(MC_w)$, .and price of $c(P_c)$ must equal the marginal cost of $c(MC_c)$. Let the line P_1, tangent to *MD* at *B*, represent the domestic price line. The slope of this line is the commodity exchange ratio of *w* for *c* before international trade. This slope shows the relative price of *c*, that is, the amount of *w* that must be sacrificed for 1 unit of *c*. The relative price of *c*, or the commodity exchange ratio of *w* for *c*, is equal to the inverse of the ratio of the absolute money prices. For example, if P_w is \$20 and P_c is \$10, the ratio of the absolute prices of *w* to *c* is 2/1. The relative price of *c* is the inverse of this ratio, or 1/2, indicating 1 unit of *w* has to be sacrificed for 2 units of *c*. The domestic price line P_1 has a slope of 1 unit *w* downward and 2 units of *c* to the right.

At *B*, the commodity exchange ratio (slope of the domestic price line) equals the marginal cost ratio (slope of the production frontier), which is the MRT_d (marginal rate of transformation in domestic production). At this production point, the marginal cost of each commodity equals its price. Producers would therefore be in equilibrium producing the combination of *w* and *c* represented at *B*.

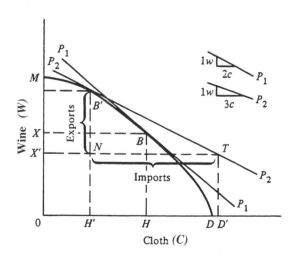

Figure 2.8 Country *I*: Pre-trade Position. P_1: domestic price line (slope is commodity exchange ratio). *B*: home production and consumption point: $P_c/P_w = MRT_d = MRS$. *OH*: home production and consumption of *c*. *OX*: home production and consumption of *w*.

Post-trade Position:
P_2: international price line (common to P'_2 for Country *II*). *B'*: equilibrium production point. *B'N*: exports of *w* in exchange for NT = imports of *c*. *T*: equilibrium consumption point (OX' of *w* and OD' of *c*): $MRT_d = MRT_f = MRS$.

If *B* is the pre-trade equilibrium position, then consumers must also be in equilibrium at this production point. This means that consumers are willing to substitute *w* for *c* in their consumption pattern—call this the marginal rate of substitution of *w* for *c* in consumption, or MRS—at the same rate as the domestic commodity exchange ratio of 1*w* for 2*c*. Each consumer would be at a consumption point where the individual's $MRS = P_c/P_w$, and this would be the same for all consumers consuming both goods.[1]

Therefore, at *B,* we arrive at the following set of pre-trade equilibrium conditions:

$$\frac{P_c}{P_w} = MRT_d = MRS, \tag{1.1}$$

where P_c/P_w is the slope of the domestic ~~price line~~; MRT_d, the slope of the domestic production frontier; and *MRS,* the ratio of substitution in consumption. This means that the rate at which commodities exchange on domestic markets, the rate of their transformation in domestic production, and the rate of their substitution in consumption are all equivalent. Producers are maximizing profits while consumers maximize their "satisfaction" ("utility," or reach their maximum indifference curves). Production is on the frontier (full employment and efficient resource allocation), the relative valuation of products by consumers (*MRS*) is equal to the relative costs of production (*MRT_d*), and the *MRS* and *MRT_d* are equal to the relative prices of the commodities.

Now consider country *II*. A similar analysis can be applied, but the production possibility set for *II* is now given as the area *ORES* in Figure 2.9. The production-possibility frontier *RES* is biased toward the production of *c,* and *w* is more expensive to produce in *II*.

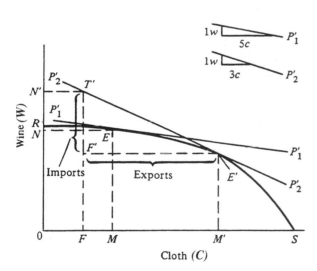

Figure 2.9 Country *II*: Pre-trade Position: P_1': domestic price line. E: equilibrium production and consumption point: $P_c/P_w = MRT_d = MRS$. *OM*: home production and consumption of *c*. *ON*: home production and consumption of *w*.

Post-trade Position:
P_2': international price line (common to P_2 for country *I*). *E'*: equilibrium production point. $E'F'$: exports of *c* in exchange for $F'T'$ = imports of *w*. *T'*: equilibrium consumption point: (*ON'* of *w* and *OF* of *c*): $MRT_d = MRT_f = MRS$.

---

[1] Each consumer's *MRS* (the absolute slope $-\Delta w/\Delta c$ along the individual consumer's indifference curve between *w* and *c*) must equal the price ratio P_c/P_w (the absolute slope of the consumer's budget line). These equilibrium conditions are developed fully in any of a number of elementary texts. See, for example, Robert Dorfman, *The Price System* (1964), 105–25; and Jack Hirshleifer, *Price Theory and Application* (1976), 443–46. A "community indifference curve" could be drawn at *B,* tangent to the production frontier and price line. But such a curve indicating *community* preferences is only the product of the economist's geometrical skill, not an empirical construct. Instead of retreating to this facile geometrical escape, it is better to understand the meaning of consumer equilibrium and recognize that its conditions must hold for each consumer.

In contrast, the production frontier in country I is biased toward the production of w, and c is more expensive to produce in I. The different shapes of the production frontiers reflect different relative factor endowments. The slope of a country's production-possibility frontier (MC ratio) is its comparative cost ratio. Therefore, as long as the slopes of the production-possibility frontiers differ at the points of pre-trade equilibrium (B and E), there is a basis for trade between I and II.

Suppose in II, before trade, the domestic commodity exchange ratio was $1w{:}5c$. At this ratio, the equilibrium pre-trade production and consumption point would be at E. In each country, $P_c/P_w = MRT_d = MRS$. But the MRT_d in I at B differs from that in II at E. If the countries are opened to trade, some commodity price ratio could be established on world markets between $(MRT_d)_I$ and $(MRT_d)_{II}$. Assume that equilibrium conditions of demand and supply set this international commodity exchange ratio at $1w{:}3c$. The international exchange ratio can be termed the marginal rate of transformation through foreign trade (MRT_f); this shows the rate at which one commodity can be transformed (exchanged) into another on world markets. This trade in effect introduces another "technological" process of transforming domestic resources (exports) into foreign resources (imports). This foreign rate of transformation is the slope of the international price line P_2 (Figure 2.8) or P_2' (Figure 2.9). In response to the additional possibilities for transforming w into c on world markets, country I will reallocate resources away from c into w, the labor-intensive commodity that has a relatively low cost of production because I's factor endowment is relatively labor-abundant. Resources will be reallocated toward w, which has a relatively higher price on world markets, until finally the equilibrium allocation is reached at production point B' (Figure 2.8), where the MC ratio or MRT_d is now equal to the international exchange ratio or the marginal rate of transformation through foreign trade (MRT_f). Then I will consume OH' of c and $H'N$ of w at home and will export $B'N$ of w in exchange for NT of c, consuming the bundle of w and c at T after trade ($D'T$ of w and OD' of c).

We know that the post-trade consumption position must lie on the international price line (consumption frontier), but its exact position at T is determined by the equilibrium condition that the international exchange ratio equals the MRS in consumption. Therefore, in equilibrium after trade (at T), the following equilibrium marginal conditions hold:

$$MRT_d = MRT_f = MRS, \tag{1.2}$$

where MRT_d is the slope of the production-possibility frontier; MRT_f, the slope of the international price line; and MRS, the ratio of substitution in consumption.

A similar analysis applies to country II (Figure 2.9), which will also trade along the international price line P_2' (P_2' has the same slope as P_2 for I). Resources will therefore be reallocated from E to E', into the capital-intensive commodity c because this is the relatively inexpensive commodity in II. Total home production will be OM' of c and $M'E'$ of w. Out of this home production, OF of c and FF' of w will be consumed domestically. The difference of $M'F = E'F'$ of c will be exported in exchange for $F'T'$ imports of w. Country II's exports equal country I's imports, and II's imports equal I's exports. The final equilibrium consumption point after trade will be T' at which point the same type of marginal conditions as expressed in equation (1.2) will also hold for II.

We can note that, after trade, each country continues to produce some w and some c: specialization is incomplete in this model, unlike the complete specialization of the

Ricardian model. There is incomplete specialization because the model allows for increasing costs, as reflected by the concave production frontiers. Each country has a comparative advantage in the product intensive in its abundant factor over a certain range of production. At a certain output (B' and E'), the relative costs of producing c and w are equal in I and $II,$ and the specialization does not proceed beyond this output.

If, however, each country had decreasing costs, as indicated by a production frontier convex from the origin (as MRD in Figure 2.7), then a country would never lose its comparative advantage as it produced more of its comparative advantage commodity. Indeed, the range of comparative advantage would widen, and the country would continue producing the commodity until specialization became complete.

The factor proportions model also illustrates the important principle that when factors are not freely mobile between countries, the factors in effect move in the guise of the commodities traded if trade is unrestricted. Although labor does not physically move from I and II, it does so indirectly by being embodied in the labor-intensive commodity from I. Commodity trade therefore tends to be a substitute for international factor movements. If the exchange of commodites is restricted, there will be larger discrepancies in factor prices, which will increase factor movements or create differences in factor returns if factors are not mobile internationally.

If there were free trade in commodities, there would be a tendency toward partial factor price equalization. When the demand for the abundant factor increases in the exportable commodity, and the demand for the scarce factor falls, there will be a rise in the price of the abundant factor relative to the price of the scarce factor.

THE SCOPE FOR INTERNATIONAL SPECIALIZATION

When we recognize the dynamic quality of comparative advantage and the continually changing character of the international division of labor, we may naturally wonder about the prospects for international trade. As national economies grow, it is to be expected that the volume of trade will increase from forces on the demand side. But at a given level of income, the volume of trade will also depend on the structure of comparative costs. The scope for international specialization will be wider, and the trade potential greater, the wider the gaps in the comparative advantages of different countries. Further, as national output grows, the composition of that output might be pro-trade biased, in the sense that exports increase in greater proportion than import-competing commodities. Or national growth might be anti-trade biased, in the sense that import substitutes increase in greater proportion than exports.

Since World War II, the volume of international trade has grown not only absolutely but also as a percentage of world output. Can we expect that international trade will continue to acquire greater relative importance? The answer will depend on changes in the pattern of demand, the differences in production conditions among countries, and the course of technical change. (We ignore government imposed restrictions on the free flow of goods and capital.)

It could be inferred from the factor proportions theory that the gap of comparative advantage will narrow as national relative demand patterns become more similar, as technology is more rapidly diffused internationally, and as technological change provides synthetics that can replace natural resources. But even if a larger number of countries become technically capable of producing a wider range of commodities, it does not follow, of course, that they could all produce at anything near the level of comparable real costs. The issue remains whether differences of "efficiency" between countries will narrow or widen.

There are strong forces that tend to widen the gap of comparative advantage and expand the scope for international specialization and trade. Technological change, both rapid in pace and extensive in range, keeps production functions different in various countries. Technical advances in transportation and communication also promote specialization. Economies of scale in the production of exportables widen comparative advantage. As income rises, the income-elasticity of demand also tends to increase, and this creates a greater demand for more differentiated products—and hence more specialization. Finally, two other developments in recent years have had a significant effect on widening comparative advantage. One is the increased skewness in the geographical location of consumption and production of raw materials. The second is the growth of the multinational corporation. This intensifies international specialization by allowing a potential comparative advantage in an overseas country to become effective through the receipt of capital and technology. For example, natural resources or labor, which had not been utilized for lack of capital or technology, may now become economically productive. By bringing into existence these resources that earlier were essentially non-existent economically, the migration of capital and technology actually increases differences in factor endowments. The multinational corporation is also often an agent that introduces the production of a new product in another country, thereby "short circuiting" some of the stages of the product cycle.

It is therefore not surprising that the forces that have accelerated the process of internationalization of markets should also be the forces that will increase the scope for international specialization. The international transmission of real forces affecting productivity over the longer run deserves as much attention as the shorter period transmission of monetary forces (to be examined in Chapters 4 and 5).

Evolution of South Korea's Exports

Illustrative of dynamic changes in comparative advantage is the evolutionary pattern of South Korea's exports, as summarized in the following tables.

It is clear that foreign trade grew in importance and changed in composition as Korea underwent the process of structural transformation, with a substantial decline in agriculture and a rise in manufacturing. Exports grew as a share of GNP, and as the tables indicate, in the course of two decades, Korea moved from being a primary commodity exporter to being a net importer of primary commodities and an exporter of manufactures. Within the manufacturing category, exports have become ever more capital- and skill-intensive, and added domestic value has increased in the export sector.

In only a decade, the semiconductor industry grew to account for 13 percent of the country's exports in 1994. Overseas sales of computer chips exceeded cars, ships, and consumer electronics, amounting to at least $17 billion in 1995. South Korea's top three semiconductor makers are cutting heavily into Japan's global memory chip market. There has also been a rapid increase in Korean chip production overseas: In 1995, Hyundai announced it would build a $1.3 billion semiconductor plant (the world's largest) in Oregon by 1997, and Samsung announced it will invest $1 billion in a new chip plant in Europe, and also in the United States and Southeast Asia. Unlike the 1970s, when Korea's overseas investments were mainly in trading and construction, most of the recent investments are in manufacturing.

Table 2.7
Composition of Exports and Imports, Korea, 1962, 1970, 1985 (Percent of Total)

	1962		1970		1985	
Industry	Exports	Imports	Exports	Imports	Exports	Imports
Commodities and processed foods[a]	75.6	33.7	21.5	37.3	5.1	17.5
Mineral fuels[b]	5.0	7.3	1.0	6.9	3.1	23.6
Chemicals[c]	1.8	22.4	1.4	8.3	3.1	9.0
Manufactured goods[d]	17.6	36.6	76.1	47.6	88.7	49.9
Machinery and transport equipment	2.6	16.5	7.4	29.7	37.6	34.2

[a] Standard industrial trade classification (SITC) 0–2 and 4.
[b] SITC 3.
[c] SITC 5.
[d] SITC 6–9.
Source: Bank of Korea, Economic Planning Board (EPB), *Major Statistics of Korean Economy*, various issues. Numbers may not add to totals because of rounding.

Table 2.8
Korea's Major Exports in 1961 ($ millions, %)

	Commodity	Amount (%)
	1961	
1	Iron ore	5.3 (13.0)
2	Tungsten	5.1 (12.6)
3	Raw silk	2.7 (6.7)
4	Anthracite	2.4 (5.8)
5	Squid	2.3 (5.5)
6	Fish	1.9 (4.5)
7	Graphite	1.7 (4.2)
8	Veneer board	1.4 (3.3)
9	Grains	1.4 (3.3)
10	Pig's hair	1.2 (3.0)
	Total	25.3 (62.0)
	Others	15.6 (38.0)
	Grand total	40.9 (100.0)

Source: Korea Institute for International Economic Policy, 1995.

Table 2.9
Korea's Major Exports in 1970 ($ millions, %)

	Commodity	Amount (%)
	1970	
1	Textiles products	341.1 (40.8)
2	Veneer board	91.9 (11.0)
3	Wig	90.1 (10.8)
4	Iron ore	49.3 (5.9)
5	Electronic products	29.2 (3.5)
6	Candy	19.5 (2.3)
7	Footwear	17.3 (2.1)
8	Tobacco and relative products	13.5 (1.6)
9	Iron and steel products	13.4 (1.5)
10	Metal goods	12.2 (1.5)
	Total	660.6 (77.1)
	Others	174.6 (22.9)
	Grand total	835.2 (100.0)

Source: Korea Institute for International Economic Policy, 1995.

Table 2.10
(Korea's Major Exports in 1980 ($ millions, %)

	Commodity	Amount (%)
	1980	
1	Textiles products	5,014 (28.6)
2	Electronic products	2,004 (11.4)
3	Iron and steel products	1,854 (10.6)
4	Footwear	904 (5.2)
5	Vessels and floating structo	618 (3.5)
6	Plastics	571 (3.3)
7	Metal goods	433 (2.5)
8	Veneer board	352 (2.0)
9	Fish (deep sea)	352 (2.0)
10	Electrical machinery	324 (1.9)
	Total	12,426 (71.0)
	Others	5,079 (29.0)
	Grand total	17,505 (100.0)

Source: Korea Institute for International Economic Policy, 1995.

Table 2.11
(Korea's Major Exports in 1989 ($ millions, %)

	Commodity	Amount (%)
	1989	
1	Electronics and electrical products	17,087 (27.4)
2	Textiles products	15,140 (24.3)
3	Iron and steel products	4,298 (6.9)
4	Footwear	3,587 (5.8)
5	Motor vehicles	2,370 (3.8)
6	Chemicals and chemical products	1,815 (2.9)
7	Vessels and floating structo	1,786 (2.9)
8	Marine products	1,690 (2.7)
9	Machine tools and engines	1,408 (2.3)
10	Plastics	1,277 (2.0)
	Total	50,458 (80.9)
	Others	11,919 (19.1)
	Grand total	62,377 (100.0)

Source: Korea Institute for International Economic Policy, 1995.

Table 2.12
Korean Exports

	1989	1990	1991	1992	1993	1994	1995
Exports ($ millions)	62,377	65,016	71,870	76,632	82,236	96,013	125,058
Volume of exports	94.2	100.0	109.9	119.1	127.2	146.1	181.1
Market exchange rate (won per $)	679.60	716.40	760.80	788.40	808.10	788.70	774.70

Source: IMF, *International Financial Statistics* (October 1996): 368.

3 TRADE POLICY

Free trade versus protection has been the longest standing policy debate in economics. Remarkably, it is more alive today than ever. Economists extol the virtues of free trade, but governments still intervene with mercantilistic policies to protect particular industries. As *The Economist* laments, "trade protection is probably the biggest avoidable cause of economic harm in the world." The controversy persists, however, because national politics contradict international economics.

In the beginning was Adam Smith, who in his *Wealth of Nations* (1776) advised, "never to attempt to make at home what it will cost more to make than to buy." Successive generations of economists have supported and refined Smith's argument that "If a foreign country can supply us with a commodity cheaper than we ourselves can make it, better buy it of them with some part of the produce of our own industry, employed in a way in which we have some advantage."[1]

Indeed, it is disheartening that—more than two centuries after Adam Smith—there should still be so much disagreement over free trade. The disagreement is not because economists are unclear on its merits. By words, diagrams, mathematics, and the computer, economists have proved the logical validity of the principle of comparative advantage on which rests the case for free trade. Empirical evidence also supports it. The disagreement persists because of special interests with political influence.

If economists were listened to, free trade would be the rule. National borders would not be allowed to interfere with the best global allocation of resources. Exceptions would be few and confined to strictly limited conditions.

Free trade, however, needs enforcement. Otherwise, for national political objectives, governments will frequently intervene in international markets. Absent an international mechanism for the enforcement of free trade, national trade policies frequently contradict the economist's prescription.

FREE TRADE AND ITS EXCEPTIONS

The traditional case for free trade rests on the basic—but often ignored—principle of comparative advantage. A decentralized market system that allows producers and consumers the freedom to choose according to market prices will provide the most efficient allocation of scarce resources, resulting in a gain in real national income. This is as true for international markets as it is for domestic markets.

Through free international trade a country can export a commodity that is relatively cheap to produce in that country for the importation of a commodity that is relatively expensive to produce at home. By specializing its production on the export commodity—the country's comparative advantage commodity—the country indirectly produces its importable commodity. It thereby gains more of the importable through free trade than if it had tried to produce it directly at home. Under free trade, comparative advantage dictates that a country exchange what it can produce most efficiently for what others can produce most efficiently. Even if a country could produce every commodity better (absolute advantage), it would still gain by specializing in its "more better" products (comparative advantage). National real income would then increase (recall Chapter 2).

To the economist, the exceptions to free trade are extremely limited. They arise only when the domestic market or international market fails to allocate resources efficiently. Or a noneconomic objective receives priority. The age-old argument of national defense is a case in point. As Smith recognized, "Defense before opulence." The empirical problem, however, is to determine which industries truly deserve protection for national security reasons. Presently there is much discussion of this argument with respect to segments of the electronics industry.

Infant Industry

Another age-old exception has been protection for an "infant industry." When properly stated, the case for protecting an infant industry arises when there is a domestic market failure in which prices do not equal the future social benefit from the industry. The industry may confer a social benefit outside its own production but is not paid for this external benefit. By training labor, for example, an industry provides experienced labor to other industries at no cost. Or by introducing technology that can be used by other firms, it confers an external benefit for which it is not paid. The essence of the case for government support is that the infant industry yields an external economy, but cannot appropriate payment for it through the market price system. There is then justification for government intervention to promote a greater output from the industry that confers external benefits: The social gain is greater than the private profit, and more output should be encouraged.

The argument, however, must be carefully circumscribed. When expressed in its precise modern form, its applicability is narrowly limited. Infant industry protection is not justified simply because a firm may initially make losses until it becomes competitive. Why cannot a new firm go to the capital market and borrow the necessary funds or obtain credit lines to underwrite early losses? Why should not the firm capitalize early losses as part of its initial investment, and go ahead as long as the eventual return will cover this investment at a satisfactory profit?

The validity of the protectionist argument rests on "dynamic learning effects," such that after a period of learning-by-experience, an industry that is not currently competitive may achieve comparative advantage through a temporary period of protection. Learning by doing may give rise to external economies; without protection there would then be underproduction from the social point of view. If the learning experience results in dynamic internal economies in which the learning benefits remain wholly in the firm, the market failure may be in the imperfection of capital markets that makes the financing of such investment difficult or too expensive because capital markets are biased against this type of "invisible" investment in human capital, or because the rate of interest for such a long-term investment is too high owing to private myopia. If capital markets are imperfect, the firm may not be able to borrow, so that even if a firm were to acquire a long run comparative advantage in some product, it would not be privately feasible to produce.[2] The first best policy would be to remove imperfections in capital markets. But if this cannot be implemented, a second best case can be made for a protective trade policy.

It is necessary, however, to stress that the protection be limited in time and that it allow a sufficient decrease in economic costs such that the initial excess costs of the industry will be repaid with an economic rate of return equal to that earned on other investments. In the more developed countries, protection should not persist from infancy to the geriatric or even senile stages of an industry that has long lost its comparative advantage. In the less developed countries, a costly import-substituting industrialization policy that protects infant industries beyond the first easy stage of import substitution is only too likely to result in excessive costs to the economy and adverse spillover effects on agricultural development and export promotion. The direct costs of import-substitution industrialization are discussed in Chapter 8. The subsidization of an import-competing industry implicitly taxes agriculture and exports. The neglect of agricultural development is harmful to the economy's growth. An overvalued exchange rate and the cost of home inputs above world prices reduce the competitiveness of exports.

When the narrow conditions for government intervention are met, a subsidy on the activity that gives rise to the external benefit would be the best feasible policy. This is because it induces more output, but does not raise the price to consumers. A next best policy would be a tariff. Third best would be a quota on imports. The quota is inferior to a tariff because it physically limits the amount of imports and completely paralyzes the price system, unlike the tariff. (For diagrammatic analysis of this hierarchy of trade policy, see the Technical Appendix, pp. 99–105). We must recognize, however, that whether the industry is subsidized directly or indirectly through a tariff or quota, infant industry protection will redistribute income from taxpayers and consumers to the owners, and probably also to the employees, of the industries protected. If given the opportunity to vote, would taxpayers and consumers endorse such a redistribution?

Terms of Trade

Another exception to free trade because of international market failure is based on the argument that a country may have sufficient market power to improve its terms of trade (raise its export prices relative to import prices). If, for example, the country is a monopoly exporter of a product, it may tax its exports and increase their prices to foreign buyers. If, on the other hand, the country is the major importer and the supplier has to reduce its price f.o.b. in order to get under a tariff imposed by the country that is its largest market, the tariff-imposing country may again make the foreigner in effect pay the duty by lowering the price of its export. The tariff-imposing country's terms of trade would then improve.

This terms of trade argument can be traced back as early as J. S. Mill in the nineteenth century. But neither Mill nor successive generations of economists have seen much empirical validity in the argument. In general, these instances of market failure, whether domestic or international, are extremely limited.

Even if the industry had a monopoly position, a government must be careful not to reduce the gains from the volume of trade so much that it offsets the marginal gain from improvement in its terms of trade. A monopolist maximizes total profit, not the unit price. (Consider the optimum tariff argument in Technical Appendix 3.2, pp. 101–3.)

Moreover, governments are rarely able to apply protective measures in a technically correct fashion. They lack the necessary information and the capacity to fine tune. Long ago, when he appraised the terms of trade argument, the distinguished British economist Edgeworth stated, "The direct use of the theory is likely to be small. But it is to be feared that its abuse will be considerable. Let us admire the skill of the analyst, but label the subject of his investigation *Poison*."[3] Instead of fine tuning, government is more likely to overdo the protectionist intervention to the detriment of the economy. And there is always the possibility of retaliation by the other countries, with a resultant trade war that makes everyone worse off. The free trade case is based on a cosmopolitan viewpoint, with all trading nations benefiting in a positive sum game; in contrast, protectionist arguments are based on national advantage: What one country gains another loses in a zero sum game.

Strategic Trade Policy

Some new arguments for protection are now stirring considerable discussion among economists and policy makers. At the theoretical level, these arguments are stimulated by game theory—by the notion of strategic behavior by competitors in a zero sum game. The techniques of game theory establish the conditions under which trade policy targeted to particular industries facing foreign competition might result in more profits for "us" in world markets. The theory indicates that export subsidies can affect the structure of the game among a small number of firms (oligopoly) that are domestic and foreign competitors so as to allow "our" domestic firms to achieve extra profits from exports at the expense of foreign competitors.

With today's discussion of whether American industry is losing its international competitive position, this is not a theoretical issue, especially when foreign governments give strategic support to their firms. The popular belief is that if Japan, France, Korea, or other countries are "targeting" profitable industries, why shouldn't the United States also use trade policy as an instrument of industrial policy? Should not the American government promote its export industries? Is it not especially important for the government to ensure that American firms gain the profits to be realized in high-tech sunrise industries of the future? Why can't trade policy be used to shift profits from foreign firms to domestic firms?

MIT's Professor Paul Krugman has been a leading expositor of the strategic trade policy argument.[4] In the simplest case, the argument maintains that a subsidy to domestic firms, by deterring investment and production by foreign competitors, can increase the profits of domestic firms by more than the subsidy, thereby raising national income. Suppose, for example, there is a product that could be developed and sold either by a U.S. or a European firm to a third country, but is not sold at home. (Krugman refers to Airbus and Boeing.) If either firm developed the product alone, it could earn large profits; however, the development costs are large enough that if both firms tried to enter the market, both would lose money. If the European government offers an export subsidy to its firm, that firm will expand sales abroad. As the American firm responds by reducing its own output, profits are shifted to the European firm. If the firm's profits increase by more than the amount of the subsidy, the national interest of the European country is served by export promotion at the expense of the American firm.

A favorable outcome to strategic trade policy, however, rests on some narrow assumptions. Krugman's example allowed room for only one profitable firm. But if additional firms can enter the industry, monopoly profits cannot be retained by the protected firm, and the protection does not secure excess returns for domestic producers. Or, if in contrast to the assumption that the competing European and American firms sell only in a third market, the firms also sell in their home markets, then prices in the European country may rise to consumers and offset the national gain. Or if the increased output of the European firm draws resources away from other industries in the home country, then costs will rise, in turn, for these adversely affected industries. The gain is also overstated if it is not recognized that in reality there are substantial costs to raising the revenue to finance subsidy schemes. Moreover, if the United States retaliates, as is especially likely if applied to high-tech industries, the gain will also be offset. Or if the American firm does not reduce output for its own strategic reasons, the favorable result will not be realized.

The force of the argument for a strategic trade policy depends crucially on what assumptions are made about the second firm's reaction to the first firm's move in expanding its output. If the firms follow the strategy of each firm selecting its optimal level of output, taking the output of the rival as given, then the case for an export subsidy holds. But if the firms instead engage in a strategy of setting prices and letting outputs adjust to the demands at those prices, the policy should not be an export subsidy, but rather an export tax. The correct policy is thus very sensitive to assumptions about the nature of the game that will be played by the firms. But this information is difficult to come by and is unlikely to be known by government policy makers. Most analysts therefore reject the practical significance of strategic trade policy.

Indeed, despite his exposition of strategic trade theory, Krugman's own judgment is that "new trade theory offers some subtle arguments for sophisticated government policy, but it could all too easily be used for a cloak for crude protectionism. . . . There is still a case for free trade as a good policy, and as a useful target in the practical world of politics."[5] Strategic trade policy, for Krugman, is not, at base, an argument for protectionism per se. It is instead an argument for a limited government industrial policy consisting of carefully targeted subsidies, not for tariffs and import quotas. But Krugman worries that it may provide "a new intellectual gloss" for old-school protectionists and for those, like Clyde

Prestowitz and Robert Kuttner, who advocate "managed trade."[6] According to Krugman, however, none of the international economists responsible for the new strategic trade theory has come out as an advocate of Kuttnerian trade policy. "This is not because they are afraid to break the free-trade ranks. It is because the actual prospects for a successful strategic trade policy are not very good."[7]

Krugman concludes that there are four overriding questions: Can we identify strategic sectors? Can we successfully pursue a strategic policy? Can we trust ourselves to use the new ideas wisely? How will other governments respond? Given negative answers to the first three questions and the high probability of retaliation by other governments, the scope for applying strategic trade policy is extremely limited. Strategic trade theory notwithstanding, free trade is not passé.

Trade and Wages

A new argument for protection has been propounded as a result of the growing importation of unskilled labor-intensive goods from the less developed countries into the United States, where since the late 1970s the real wages of less-skilled labor have declined relative to skilled labor. Some argue that, in accordance with the Heckscher-Ohlin factor endowment theory of comparative advantage, trade with the less developed countries should make skilled labor scarcer in the more developed countries, raising their wage, while it makes unskilled labor effectively more abundant, reducing its wage. It is also claimed that because of the movement of capital and the transmission of technology to the less developed countries, their productivity has increased. It is then contended that higher productivity combined with low wages have led to imports from the developing countries that push down the relative real wages of low skilled labor in the industrialized countries.[8] Moreover, because of wage inflexibility in European labor markets, it is claimed that the importation leads to the pressures being felt in high unemployment in Europe.

Empirical studies confirm the trends in earnings inequality during the 1980s and 1990s. For instance, the percentage by which the average annual earnings of those with a college education exceeded the average earnings of those with only a high school education rose steadily from 27 percent in 1979 to 65 percent in 1993 (see Figure 3.1). The drop in the relative position of the less skilled also appears in other ways: greater earnings differentials between older and younger workers; greater differentials between high-skilled and low-skilled occupations; in a wider earnings distribution overall and within demographic and skill groups; and in less time worked by low-skill and low-paid workers.[9] The essential question, however, is whether trade is responsible.

Many analysts interpret the growth in earned income inequality as equivalent to a rise in skill premiums and an increase in economic returns to skills.[10] Bigger wage differentials are especially evident for extra education, occupational skill, and work experience.

Although growth in imports of unskilled labor-intensive goods has been rapid, the amount is still too small to have a significant effect on wages. Since the industrialized nations spend only a little more than 1 percent of their combined GDPs on imports of manufactures from the developing countries, the net flows of labor embodied in that trade are small compared with the overall size of the labor force.[11]

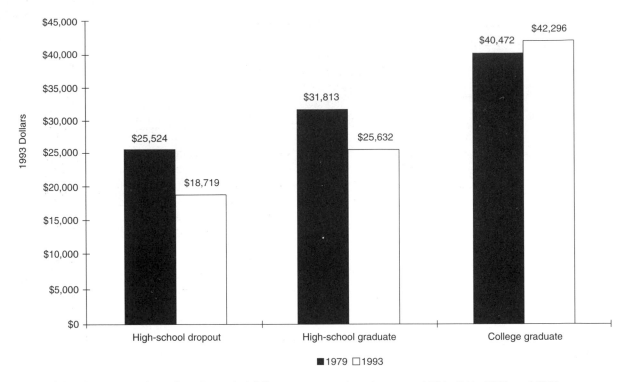

Figure 3.1   Mean annual earnings for male full-time, year-round workers, aged 25 to 34 in 1979 and 1993. *Source:* Council of Economic Advisers, *The Outlook for Economic Growth* (November 14, 1995), processed.

Although the relative wage decline for the unskilled is economy-wide, only a small proportion of workers—some 17 percent in the United States—are employed in manufacturing. Most of the unskilled are in service sectors where their wages can scarcely be determined by traded goods.[12]

Furthermore, if trade lowered the relative wages of unskilled workers, we would expect to see a decline in the relative price of unskilled labor-intensive goods. Companies should then also substitute unskilled workers for more expensive skilled workers. But the evidence does not show these effects.

Moreover, the popular notion that the manufacturing affiliates of U.S. multinationals are established abroad primarily in low-wage countries to produce for the American markets is unfounded: In 1992, for instance, only 12 percent of sales by manufacturing majority-owned foreign affiliates were to U.S. customers.[13] And only one-quarter of that came from developing countries. Further, if the transfer of technology by multinationals leads to increasing productivity, this should also in turn raise wages in the developing countries. On the consumption side, low-income groups tend to be the major consumers of the cheaper imported goods embodying unskilled labor and gain from the lower prices; protection would have the opposite effect.

The evidence suggests that the rise in demand for skilled workers was overwhelmingly caused by changes in demand within each industrial sector, not by a shift of the United States's industrial mix in response to trade. The declining demand for less-skilled U.S.

TRADE AND WAGES

The new debate focuses on one issue: whether in a global economy the wages or employment of low-skill workers in advanced countries have been (or will be) determined by the global supply of less-skilled labor, rather than by domestic labor market conditions. Put crudely, to what extent has, or will, the pay of low-skilled Americans or French or Germans be set in Beijing, Delhi and Djakarta rather than in New York, Paris or Frankfurt?

On one side of the new debate are those who believe in factor price equalization—that in a global economy the wages of workers in advanced countries cannot remain above those of comparable workers in less-developed countries. They fear that the wages or employment of the less skilled in advanced countries will be driven down due to competition from low-wage workers overseas. On the other side of the debate are those who reject the notion that the traded goods sector can determine labor outcomes in an entire economy or who stress that the deleterious effects of trade on demand for the less skilled are sufficiently modest to be offset readily through redistributive social policies funded by the gains from trade. They fear that neoprotectionists will use arguments about the effect of trade on labor demand to raise trade barriers and reduce global productivity.

Richard B. Freeman, "Are Your Wages Set in Beijing?" *Journal of Economic Perspectives* (summer 1995): 16.

workers has been across a whole range of industries, not simply those that produce tradable goods. Indeed the evidence is that between 1969 and 1993 industries unaffected by trade cut their use of low-skilled workers even faster than trade-affected industries.[14] The reduction in the relative demand for less-skilled workers throughout the economy is primarily the result of technology and biased technological change. The substitution of capital and skilled labor for unskilled labor has been much more important than the effect of trade.[15] Technological progress has made it profitable to use relatively more of better educated labor despite the fact that the less educated labor has become relatively cheaper. Besides biased changes in technology, the unskilled and less skilled have also been adversely affected by forms of business organization, economic deregulation, new patterns of immigration, and the diminishing influence of trade unions. It is also apparent that the wage gap between high- and low-skilled workers has been accompanied by the growing segregation of workers by skill. It has become less common for high- and low-skilled workers to work in the same firm. An increase in the mean skill level in a firm raises wages of highly skilled workers but causes those of poorly skilled workers to decline.[16]

From these empirical studies, we can conclude that trade is not a major cause of the inequality in relative wages in the United States. For OECD countries, a study also found no major impact of trade on OECD employment or wage differentials either in total or by type of labor.[17]

Finally, to the extent that imports may cause a problem of dislocation for labor, the superior policy reaction should be education and skill training and job relocation assistance rather than the nth best policy of protection. Although particular groups within a nation may be adversely affected by imports, the total real national income still rises, thereby allowing some form of compensation, and the long-term gain outweighs any short-term loss.

Reciprocity

The desire to react to another country's trade policies gives rise to other arguments for protection. Ever since Adam Smith, the liberal free trade view has recognized less costly imports as the "gain from trade" and has maintained that if other countries drop rocks in their harbors, that is no reason for the free trade country to do the same. The traditional view has been that unilateral free trade is still better than protection. Now, however, popular arguments question whether the United States should unilaterally liberalize its trade if other countries protect theirs. Should not the United States reduce its tariffs only if other countries reduce theirs? Should not the United States demand equal market access in other countries or else retaliate with tariffs and quotas against them? Moreover, economists now recognize that another country's comparative advantage might be artificially or arbitrarily created through government policies in that country. Foreign governments might subsidize their exports. Should not such "unfair trade" be countervailed with duties equal to the subsidies? Foreign firms may also engage in dumping their exports; that is, selling abroad at a lower price than at home, or selling exports at a price below cost. Should not there also be antidumping duties on this type of "unfair trade"?

These questions raise the issue of how one country should react to the trade policies of another. On the matter of tariff reductions, the General Agreement on Tariffs and Trade (GATT) does not adopt the pure free trader's position of unilateral free trade but instead bases negotiations to reduce tariffs on the principle of reciprocity—a country negotiates to reduce its tariffs only on the condition that other countries reciprocate (see Policy Profile 3.3). Reciprocity is politically necessary to induce nations to liberalize their trade because the public sees the "gain from trade" on the side of exports; the benefits of obtaining importables at lower cost impresses them less than they do the economist. Even a free trader should go beyond the static resource allocation gains to recognize the dynamic gains from trade that result from an increase in exports. These dynamic gains consist of increases in productivity, more competitive market structures, higher investment, realization of economies of scale, greater capacity utilization, and technological progress. It is commonly believed that "we" should not allow another country to export freely to "us," if we cannot do the same to them. Economists support this belief by saying that all countries should be able to enjoy the dynamic benefits from exports. Open markets benefit all trading nations.

The basic principle of GATT is reciprocity. This is applied to multilateral negotiations with all members of GATT, and reciprocity is sought in terms of a broad balance of concessions on all products considered together. In contrast, some critics of free trade propose that the U.S. government should achieve reciprocity through bilateral negotiations and should seek reciprocity by and within specific industries. The proposals include threats of retaliation if the reciprocity is not achieved.

In recent years, such an aggressive stance has been directed primarily against Japan. The focus on Japan stems from the stubborn U.S. trade deficit with Japan. As will be discussed in Chapter 5, however, the policies of the U.S. Treasury and the Federal Reserve—not the bilateral trade negotiations—are what will solve the deficit problem. Bilateral negotiations are likely to create a nationalistic backlash in Japan while doing little to reduce the trade deficit. William Cline of the Institute for International Economics points out, "Surely bilateral trade balances cannot be the criterion for trade equity. It must be recalled that the United States runs a large surplus with Europe, but U.S. policy makers would be incensed if Europeans cited this fact as evidence that the U.S. market is more closed than the European market."[18]

The demand for reciprocity frequently degenerates into a form of export protectionism. Recognizing this, Columbia's Jagdish Bhagwati emphasizes three essential objections to bilateral approaches aimed at specific industries in specific countries:

- It is essentially the United States that decides if the foreign markets are unfairly closed. Where the weak are confronted, they will concede but will be resentful. Where the strong are confronted, retaliation and trade skirmishes are a distinct possibility.
- Faced with demands they cannot refuse, the weaker trading partners are likely to satisfy bilateral U.S. demands by simply diverting their imports away from other countries in favor of the United States. This is not an opening of markets, but rather a way of increasing U.S. exports by diverting them from more efficient suppliers who have less political clout.
- As for seeking reciprocity by and within each industrial sector, this has the disadvantage of creating demands that are hard to accept politically and hence may readily lead to the risk of confrontation degenerating into punitive tariffs that would in turn invite retaliatory tariffs.

For these reasons Bhagwati states that he remains "profoundly opposed to this turn to the bilateral 'open foreign markets aggressively' policies, based on exaggerated 'I am more open than thou' presumptions, that afflicts current U.S. policy makers. It would be wise to pull back from these policies at the first opportunity, and to display statesmanship and commitment to the goals of a liberal trading regime."[19] Most economists agree with Bhagwati that instead of stressing trade policy by results with one, there should be an emphasis on trade policy by rules with all.

UNFAIR TRADE: SUBSIDIES

Charges of "unfair trade" multiply as globalization intensifies international competition. In the interest of "fair trade," many now argue not only for reciprocity of market access for exports, but also for protection against imports that are subsidized or dumped. Almost daily a business executive complains that it is unfair to have to compete with foreign governments that promote their exports. To compete with a foreign firm is one thing, but to compete against the deep pockets of a foreign government is quite another matter. A "level playing field" is wanted. But care must be taken not to equalize costs among nations, as some executives wish. For to do so would mean no trade. A plea for "fair trade" becomes only too easily a plea for protection.

Considering the issue of "fairness," economists maintain that it is wrong for foreign governments to pursue policies that violate a country's natural comparative advantage and competitive markets. The free competitive market is the standard that is normally adopted as fair trade: Market economic principles should apply equally to all trading firms. Insofar as an export subsidy makes private costs less than social costs, and exporters acquire an artificially larger share of world markets, economists would deem such trade unfair.

Other economic and legal considerations, however, call for a complex exercise in line drawing between fair and unfair trade. This is apparent in an assessment of the major policies aimed at unfair trade—namely, countervailing duties on export subsidies and antidumping measures. These measures are good politics, but again, care must be taken that their misuse or overuse does not result in bad economics. What action should "we" take if a foreign government provides low-interest funds for targeted industries, special amortization provisions for capital investment, or R&D support for technology? What if that government gives general subsidies to all industries through education, fire and police protection, and roads? What action should be taken if Korea exempts export industries from tariffs on imported inputs? If the European Union (EU) remits the value-added tax on exports? If Mexico allows a lower income tax on income earned from exports? If the EU subsidizes wheat and then exports pasta made out of the subsidized wheat? If Brazil has no environmental laws? If Japan's government supports the growth of knowledge and capital-intensive industries, semiconductors, electronics, robotics, aerospace, biotechnology, and telecommunications? In all these cases, how should other governments respond?

Answers to these questions are now provided by the Subsidies Code of GATT and national legislation. The answers, however, do not attempt a substantive resolution of what is unfair trade, but designate certain technical procedures as defined by legislation. For example, the U.S. Trade Agreements Act provides for a countervailing duty on imports when a foreign nation extends a "bounty or grant" on its exports, and this inflicts "material injury" as claimed by a competing domestic firm. The finding is to be made by the Commerce Department, and the president cannot change the finding.

The meaning of a subsidy through a bounty or grant is, however, ambiguous, and what type of subsidy is acceptable or unacceptable is controversial. Cases decided by the Commerce Department recognize three types of subsidy: (1) a direct subsidy on exports; (2) a domestic subsidy that is provided to a specific enterprise or industry; and (3) upstream subsidies (subsidized component used in a final export good). General government benefits such as police, education, and public works are not considered subsidies. Although the U.S. legislation equates all forms of government intervention with subsidies, the EU interprets only the expenditure of government funds as an indispensable requirement of any subsidy. Under EU practice, for example, an export credit is a subsidy to the extent that the rates charged are below those that the government has to pay for the funds. American authorities, however, compute the subsidy by comparing what a company would pay a normal commercial lender with what it actually pays on the preferential-rate loan.

Agricultural subsidies are widespread in the United States, Japan, and the EU. For political reasons, these have not been subjected to countervailing action. The GATT Subsidies Code permits subsidies for agricultural products as long as the subsidies do not result in the exporter obtaining "more than an equitable share of the world market." This has had little bite in practice. In the Uruguay round of trade negotiations, the United States sought multilateral agreement to eliminate farm subsidies over a ten-year period. But this met opposition by the EU.

When there is a finding of subsidization and injury, the remedial action is scaled to offset the subsidy, not the injury. A countervailing duty is calculated equivalent to the amount of the subsidy. This is a complex calculation that depends on the time profile of the subsidy, its duration, and discount rate.

Regardless of what definition of subsidy is used, no consideration is given to the possibility that the subsidy might improve resource allocation in the subsidizing country by correcting a market failure (an external economy such as in R&D activity) in that country. Such a subsidy might also improve resource allocation in the world and increase the value of world output. An infant export industry might justify promotion by subsidization when the social return is greater than the private return.

Moreover, in imposing countervailing duties, governments do not consider the costs imposed on consumers through higher prices, costs to the government of administering the law, and the lobbying expenditures of domestic producer groups that seek a rent from the protection. These may not be offset by benefits to producers or by duty revenues, and the cases in which countervailing duties can generate a net benefit to the economy are difficult to identify in practice. Foreign governments are also likely to retaliate.

Given these costs, many economists and lawyers take a much less favorable view of U.S. policy against subsidized exports than do business executives. In a critical analysis of U.S. trade policy, University of Chicago's Law Professor Alan Sykes concludes:

"The imposition of countervailing duties on 'subsidized' imports does not systematically promote national economic welfare, and existing law is poorly tailored to identify the cases in which countervailing duties are arguably beneficial. Indeed, the duties are imposed mechanistically under conditions that may often produce a considerable new welfare loss to the U.S. economy. As a consequence, duties under existing law will enhance national economic welfare only by chance."[20]

Some also believe that because the buyer in the importing country benefits by imports of subsidized products, the export country should simply receive a "thank you note" instead of a countervailing duty on its exports. In answer to this, Bhagwati counters:

"An economist is right to claim that, if foreign governments subsidize their exports, this is simply marvelous for his own country, which then gets cheaper goods and thus should unilaterally maintain a policy of free trade. He must, however, recognize that the acceptance of this position will fuel demands for protection and imperil the possibility of maintaining the legitimacy, and hence the continuation, of free trade. A free trade regime that does not rein in or seek to regulate artificial subventions will likely help trigger its own demise. An analogy that I used to illustrate this 'systemic' implication of the unilateralist position in conversing with Milton Friedman on his celebrated *Free to Choose* television series is perhaps apt: Would one be wise to receive stolen property simply because it is cheaper, or would one rather vote to prohibit such transactions because of their systemic consequences?"[21]

Notwithstanding criticisms of existing trade law, and regardless of theoretical analyses of ideal trade policy, countervailing action against subsidized exports will undoubtedly become even more important in the future. U.S. law has provided for countervailing duties ever since the tariff act of 1897; but until 1974, only fifty-eight countervailing duties were imposed. Changes in the law since 1974 have facilitated petitions for countervailing duties. Moreover, as international competitiveness has intensified with globalization, the number of countervailing duty cases has risen rapidly—to over 300 petitions from 1980 to 1989 (see Statistical Appendix, Table 3.7). In addition, there have also been any number of "settlements" in which the American petitioners withdrew their petitions following the negotiation of alternative trade restrictions (as with Canada Softwood Lumber Products after Canada agreed to impose a 15 percent tax on its exports to the United States; later the Canadian government agreed to raise the price charged for the right to harvest timber on government lands). Dozens of countervailing duty petitions on steel products were withdrawn after the Reagan administration negotiated voluntary restraint agreements with major foreign steel suppliers.

As long as firms do not like to surrender markets for any reason, action against foreign subsidies will remain a major trade issue in the competitive future.

UNFAIR TRADE: DUMPING

Antidumping duties are another major weapon against unfair trade. The threat of dumping was a rationale for the adoption of the first U.S. protective tariff in 1816, and since 1916 there has been an antidumping law. While the countervailing duty on subsidized exports reacts against action of a foreign government, the antidumping duty responds to the action of a foreign firm. The number of antidumping investigations initiated between 1980 and 1988 in the United States was 409, in the EU 357, Canada 319, Australia 465, but only 1 in Norway, and 2 in Sweden. A total of 160 were initiated in 1994–95, of which 37 were by the EU and 30 by the United States.

The traditional definition of dumping is selling at a lower price in one national market than in another—that is, price discrimination between national markets. ("Reverse dumping" is selling goods at a lower price in the home market than abroad, but this does not create international tensions.) One test of dumping is simply foreign price less than home price for the goods. Another test is selling to country two at an export price f.o.b. lower than in country three. Still another is foreign price less than cost of production.

These tests call for complex calculations. In comparing the U.S. price and foreign market value, American legislation specifies adjustment for "differences in circumstances of sale." If sales are held to be below cost, the statute calls for a "constructed value of the exported product." "Less than fair value" is constructed by comparing the price in the importing country with (*a*) cost of materials and fabrication plus (*b*) general expenses that must be calculated as not less than 10 percent of (*a*) plus profits equivalent to not less than 8 percent of (*a* plus *b* plus interest). It can be argued that this gives a high dumping margin. Further, if firms are highly leveraged, as in Japan, the "profit" calculation can be unusually high.

After the Commerce Department determines whether goods are being sold, or are likely to be sold, in the United States at less than fair value, the International Trade Commission must find "material injury," or the threat thereof, in the U.S. industry. The statute defines "material injury" as "harm which is not inconsequential, immaterial, or unimportant." Instances are a decline in output, sales, market share, profits, productivity, or return on investments, or negative effects on cash flow, inventories, employment, wages, growth, or ability to raise capital. Considering the gain to buyers from low import prices, one might again think the importing country should simply send a thank you note. Reference to material injury forecloses this option. There is not, however, any weighing of the injury against gains. In 1989, for example, U.S. dumping duties were placed on a wide range of ball bearings, but the protests from firms that used the imported ball bearings in production—such as Caterpillar, Hewlett-Packard and General Electric—were ignored.

The practice of dumping represents price discrimination, which can be a common practice for maximizing profits when a firm faces a more elastic demand in foreign markets than at home, and realizes economies of scale. During periods of slack demand, a firm that has high fixed costs and low variable costs will rationally produce in the short run if it can sell at any price above variable costs. It may then export to a country where firms have higher variable costs. But persistent sales at a loss tend to indicate a lack of comparative advantage, and if they continue over the longer run then it must be because of some assistance provided by government. The rationale of the antidumping law then merges with that of the countervailing duty law.

An antidumping duty is also rationalized by claiming that it prevents predatory dumping—that is, a temporary period of selling below marginal costs to either forestall the development of competition or eliminate competition in the importing country, followed by an increase in price above marginal cost. Even during the period of dumping there can be injury to import competing producers who lose market share and to other domestic producers from whom demand has been diverted on to the dumped goods.

Proponents of countervailing and antidumping duties maintain that "free trade" is a mirage and that what matters is "fair trade." But when protectionist sentiment is strong, care must be taken not to overextend and overuse these restrictive policies. When duties are imposed, fairness to the producer means higher cost to the buyer. When the U.S. Special Trade Representative uses Super 301 of the U.S. Trade Act to gain market access for American exports, the action is trade enhancing.[22] But when the United States imposes countervailing and antidumping duties, the action is trade restricting. These measures should therefore not be used in trivial cases, nor as harassment of successful foreign competitors. Such action is likely in periods of intense international competition and as long as the petitioner has nothing to lose. Discipline and transparency are therefore required if the truly unfair cases are to be resolved without being protectionist for high-cost firms competing against imports.

More generally, fair trade should not mean that all countries play by U.S. rules. This would lose all the gains from trade that arise because of different environments. The case for free trade rests on gains to all countries because of different environments (resources, political systems, laws, and so forth).

Nor should fair trade mean that costs of production should be equalized in all trading nations. This would violate the basic logic of comparative advantage and eliminate any gains from trade.

Finally, fair trade should not mean equal market shares. This too would result in less gain from trade.

DEMAND FOR PROTECTION

Although some arguments for protection are based on sound economic logic, rarely does protection in practice conform to these arguments. Instead, protection is determined in political markets where the demand for protection by interest groups gives rise to a supply of protection by lawmakers who seek their support. The demand for protection is expressed by special interests through lobbying, contributions to candidates who support their position, and filing at administrative and regulatory hearings. Normally, those demanding protection are special interest groups who face losses because of imports. Their losses are concentrated within a small group and come immediately with the market disruption from imports. In contrast, buyers who benefit from the imports are numerous, dispersed, and unorganized; individually, their gains are small and accrue over a longer period. Collective action can be well organized by the few who claim to be injured, not by the many who benefit. The special interests thereby win out over the general interest. For instance, the Federal Trade Commission estimated that the U.S. sugar quota costs consumers over 60 percent more than the gains to sugar producers. The consumer loss, however, is less than $5 per capita, and the individual consumers have neither the interest nor the organization to oppose the protectionist quota.[23]

Protectionist efforts are all the more successful in periods of slow economic growth, unemployment, balance of payments problems, or intense international competition. Protection for special interests can then be masked by advocating interventions to protect employment, remove a trade deficit, or counter unfair trade. Moreover, to diminish opposition, it is politically astute to adopt policy measures that are indirect and opaque—for example, tariffs or quotas rather than subsidies, and voluntary export restraints (VERs) rather than tariffs.

Associated with the desire to increase competitiveness in world markets, possibly in association with industrial policy, there is now also a demand for targeting exports and in effect giving them government protection. More voices urge the United States to pursue a "tit for tat" strategy with governments that promote their exports. This, however, can be excessively costly. As Princeton's economist Gene Grossman observes:

"The risk that any scheme of targeted export promotion would fall prey to much the same sort of special interest pressures is cause for grave concern. If an apparatus for discretionary industrial policy of this type were to be erected, each and every export sector would have ample incentive to argue the (alleged) merits of its own case for subsidization. And even if the policy analyst could somehow solve the difficult technical problems of identifying industries worthy of promotion, there could be little guarantee that these would be the ones to emerge from a politically influenced process of selection. In all likelihood established industries would win out over emerging ones, those in politically contested regions of the country over those in areas clearly in the camp of one party or the other, and those that could most easily overcome the free-rider problems associated with industry wide lobbying campaigns over those that could not. In short, the market failures in the political realm might easily outweigh those in the economic realm, leaving us with a set of strategic trade policies that would serve only the interests of those fortunate enough to gain favor."[24]

The continuing process of globalization creates both protectionist and pro-trade interests. A lack of consensus among business managers around the world is revealed in Figure 3.2. Managers in more domestically focused companies and those in countries that lag in international competitiveness are less supportive of free trade. High cost, inefficient firms seek protection as international competition intensifies. Other firms, however, that maintain a competitive advantage in world markets are antiprotectionist. These firms are likely to be borderless companies, multinationals that are engaged in direct foreign investment to export into home and world markets, or are participating in joint ventures and international alliances. For such firms, their global network of interrelationships and multiple loyalties makes them want to avoid protectionism in other countries and to promote trade liberalization on a worldwide basis. When their home country becomes protectionist, they lose in their operations elsewhere in the world.

In 1990, Donald V. Fites, who was then president of Caterpillar, said the following at MIT's Sloan School of Management:

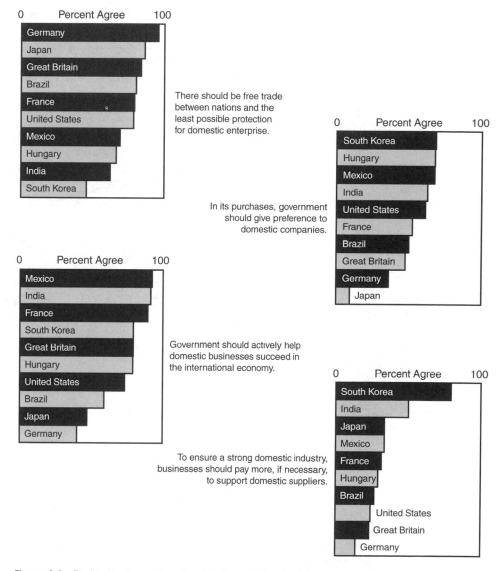

Figure 3.2 Protectionism or free trade? A world leadership survey conducted by the *Harvard Business Review* gave these responses from managers in following countries. *Source*: Reprinted by permission of Harvard Business School Press. From Rosabeth Moss Kanter, "Transcending Business Boundaries: 12,000 World Managers View Change," *Harvard Business Review*, Boston, MA (May–June 1991): 156. Copyright © 1991 by the President and Fellows of Harvard College; all rights reserved.

"Some of you might think that Caterpillar would support [a protectionist] solution because our most formidable competitor is Japanese. Komatsu, a $5.6 billion company, is a major force in the U.S., Japanese and European construction equipment markets. . . . Komatsu is a global competitor in every sense of the word. They're aggressive and tenacious . . . and they'd like nothing more than to replace us as industry leader. So why don't we want the U.S. government to step in and help us manage the situation? Quite simply, because in the long run, managed trade weakens our own competitiveness and threatens the strength and vitality of the entire world trading system. We, Caterpillar—and we, the nation's business community—have little to gain and much to lose if the managed trade concept is allowed to drive U.S. trade policy.

"What's at stake for Caterpillar? Three things: sales, profit, and jobs. We traditionally do more than half our business outside the United States, so any policy that affects world trade affects Caterpillar.

"I should emphasize that Caterpillar is more than just a U.S. exporter. We're a global competitor. . . .

"When you put it all together, we have a global presence our competitors are trying to match. Protectionist trade policies weaken that presence and can do irreparable damage to our worldwide competitive position."[25]

A recent study of the politics of antiprotection also concludes that those who matter most in the political process opposing protectionism are not household consumers, but the special interest groups that benefit most from the specific trade that would be restricted: industrial users of imports, retailers of traded consumer goods, U.S. exporters who sell to the countries whose goods would be restricted, and the companies and governments of those countries. For example, in opposition to a bill that was introduced in Congress in 1985 that would cut textile and apparel imports, heavy political activity was undertaken by the Retail Industry Trade Action Coalition, American Free Trade Council, private or government groups in Hong Kong and China, and the American Association of Exporters and Importers. Moderate activity included retailers such as J. C. Penney, K-Mart, and The Limited, Inc., and importers such as Levi Strauss, Liz Claiborne, Nike Inc., Samsonite, and others.[26]

COSTS OF PROTECTION

The narcotic of protection is only too tempting. But as a former director of the U.S. Treasury's Office of Trade Research says:

"The first task for the leadership of the trade policy community is to recognize the instinct of policy makers to see foreign scapegoats for the effects of domestic indecision or wrong decisions. Efforts should be made to publicize the simple truth of classical economics, namely that trade restrictions by one country, no matter what any other country does, has for that country larger costs than benefits."[27]

The costs of protection can indeed be substantial. When a tariff is imposed, producers in the tariff-imposing country are in essence subsidized, and consumers are in essence taxed. The marginal high-cost, inefficient firm can now meet foreign competition, and the inframarginal firms make more profit. Consumers pay a higher price and buy a smaller quantity. Tariff revenue goes to the government. In the case of a quota, however, there would be no government revenue unless the government chose to auction off import licenses. Otherwise, market power would determine whether the exporter or the importer gains the scarcity premium from the quota. In addition to the loss to consumers, there is also a deadweight loss of economic efficiency resulting from the distortion of producer decisions and consumer decisions. There is too much domestic production: High-cost resources are allocated to the production of goods that can be imported at lower cost. Consumer choice is restricted, and there is too little consumption of the good.

Beyond these costs, there is also the cost of rent seeking: Those who lobby for protection expend real resources to capture excess profits in a protected market. There is also another cost involved in expenditure-seeking—that is, lobbying to be a beneficiary of the government's expenditure of the tariff revenue.

These static costs are potentially high. Equally important are dynamic costs that mount up over time through a reduced rate of economic growth. The sheltering of home firms from competition, the distortion in resource allocation, and the handicap that protection places on export industries all combine to lower the country's growth rate. Protection limits the gains from trade in both imports and exports.

Table 3.1
Some Estimates of the Costs to Consumers of Protection in Selected Sectors ($ Millions)

Sector and Country	Year and Source	Cost
Clothing		
United States	1984 (Hickok 1985)	8,500–12,000
United States	1984 (Hufbauer, Berliner, and Elliott 1986)	18,000
Textiles		
United States	1980 (Munger 1984)	3,160
United States	1981 (Wolf 1982)	2,000–4,000
Textiles and clothing		
United States	1980 (Consumers for World Trade 1984)	18,400
Steel		
United States	1980 (Consumers for World Trade 1984)	7,250
United States	1984 (Hickok 1985)	2,000
Specialty steel		
United States	1984 (Hufbauer, Berliner, and Elliott 1986)	520
Automobiles		
United States	1983 (Tarr and Morkre 1984)	1,109
United Kingdom	1983 (Greenaway and Hindley 1985)	265
Videocassette recorders		
United Kingdom	1983 (Greenaway and Hindley 1985)	121
EC	1984 (Kalantzopoulos 1986)	459

Source: World Bank, *World Development Report 1987* (New York: Oxford University Press, 1987), p. 150.

Numerous studies have calculated these costs of protection. The amounts have been sizable even when the calculations are limited to the direct static effects within the protected industry and do not allow for adverse repercussions elsewhere in the economy or the dynamic costs. Table 3.1 presents estimates of only the costs to consumers of protection in various industries in the United States, the United Kingdom, and the European Community (EC). The striking fact about protection to preserve jobs is that each job costs the consumers much more than the worker's salary.

Table 3.2 shows the net cost of protection after deducting the gain to local producers and the gain in government revenue from the cost to consumers. There is still a sizable extra cost to the economy as a whole in producing more of the goods domestically rather than importing them. The net cost would be greater if allowance were made for the cost of rent seeking and expenditure seeking.

The costs of import quotas are even greater than tariffs. The current system of import quotas and price supports for American sugar producers gives them about 90 percent of the U.S. sugar market. Foreign imports amounted to about 4.4 million tons per year during 1975–1981 when there were no quotas. The 1989 quota, however, allowed only 1.2 million tons to be imported, restricting imports to about 12 percent of the U.S. sugar market. As a result, sugar prices are artificially high: In 1990, the average world price was 12 cents per pound wholesale, but the average U.S. price was 23 cents per pound wholesale. A commerce department study estimated that sugar quotas and subsidies add an average of

Table 3.2
Some Estimates of the Welfare Costs of Protection in Selected Sectors ($ Millions)

Sector and Country	Year and Source	Cost
Clothing		
Canada	1979 (Jenkins 1980)	92
EC	1980 (Kalantzopoulos 1986)	1,409
United States	1980 (Kalantzopoulos 1986)	1,509
Textiles and clothing		
United States	1984 (Hufbauer, Berliner, and Elliott 1986)	6,650
Steel		
United States	1985 (Kalantzopoulos 1986)	1,992
Specialty steel		
United States	1984 (Hufbauer, Berliner, and Elliott 1986)	80
Automobiles		
United States	1981 (Feenstra 1984)	327
United States	1983 (Kalantzopoulos 1986)	2,192
United States	1983 (Tarr and Morkre 1984)	994
Videocassette recorders		
EC	1984 (Kalantzopoulos 1986)	442

Source: World Bank, *World Development Report 1987* (New York: Oxford University Press, 1987), p. 151.

$3 billion annually to American consumers' grocery bills.[28] Moreover, some 8,900 U.S. food manufacturing jobs have been lost because sugar-containing imports are cheaper than U.S. food products. Ten U.S. sugar refineries have closed and 7,000 U.S. sugar refinery jobs have been lost since 1981 because of the import restrictions.[29]

Although small in number, the 12,000 domestic sugar growers have become one of the most powerful lobbying groups in Washington. They are joined by the corn growers (producers of corn syrup), who benefit from the higher prices for all sweeteners that result from inflated sugar prices.

The peanut quota system can also be criticized for distorting the market. Only 1.7 million pounds of imports—a tiny fraction of U.S. consumption—are allowed in each year. "That might keep Skippy running for one afternoon," says James Mack, lobbyist for the Peanut Butter and Nut Processors Association. "It's a virtual embargo."

At the same time, the government limits the number of farmers who can sell peanuts in the United States. And it sees to it that the minimum selling price for their so-called quota peanuts is about 50 percent higher than the world price. The program costs the Federal Treasury about $4 million a year. But, as *The Wall Street Journal* asks: "Who else pays? Every mother feeding her children peanut butter sandwiches, say peanut processors, and every baseball fan munching on ballpark peanuts. One processor estimate has consumers paying an extra $369 million a year—a hidden subsidy to quota holders. . . . Take away the subsidy, processors assert, and consumers could save as much as 40 cents on an 18 ounce jar of peanut butter priced at $1.79."[30]

Studies consistently demonstrate that—through tariffs or quotas—the cost of preserving a job through protection is considerably more than the worker's salary. For example, each job preserved in the car industry in the United States is estimated to have cost consumers between $40,000 and $108,500 a year. This cost to American consumers of preserving one worker in car production was equivalent to six workers earning the average industrial wage in other industries. Voluntary export restraints in the U.S. steel industry cost consumers $114,000 per protected job each year. For every dollar paid to steel workers who would have lost their jobs, American consumers lost $35, and the net loss to the entire U.S. economy was $25.[31] In sunset industries or industries left behind by changing comparative advantage, the injury to workers who lose their jobs could be compensated more cheaply by a combination of financial payments, retraining, and new job creation than by protection.

Another careful study of the costs of protection in twenty-one sectors in the United States in 1990 concluded that the cost to the economy and to consumers of preserving jobs in these industries is high. "In a fourth of the 21 sectors, the consumer cost per job saved is $500,000 or more. There is only one sector (costume jewelry) in which the estimated cost of saving a job through trade protection is less than $100,000. On average, the consumer surplus loss per job saved is an astounding $170,000 per year. In other words, consumers pay over six times the average annual compensation of manufacturing workers to preserve jobs through import restraints. But in two thirds of the cases, production workers' hourly wages (excluding compensation) are at or *below* the average hourly manufacturing wage in 1990 of $10.80. In terms of net national welfare, the cost per protected job is about $54,000. This figure far exceeds the cost per worker of even a 'gold-plated' adjustment program entailing income maintenance, retraining, and relocation."[32]

For Japan, the costs to the economy and to consumers of preserving jobs through import protection are even higher. A study of highly protected sectors concludes that on average in 1989, the Japanese consumer cost per job saved amounted to ¥83 million ($600,000). In some sectors, the costs were much higher. In chemical products, the cost was nearly ¥330 million ($2.4 million), followed by a figure of ¥133 ($1 million) for metal products.[33]

All these studies underestimate the cost of protection insofar as they do not include the cost of rent seeking and expenditure seeking, the adverse repercussions elsewhere in the economy, or the dynamic costs. As an example of adverse spillover, the president of Caterpillar argued in 1989 against extending quotas on steel imports, pointing out that the voluntary restraint agreements in steel "had created artificial shortages which increased our steel costs by about 10 percent, caused inefficiency in our manufacturing operations, compromised our $1.5 billion factory modernization, and frustrated our efforts to increase production in U.S. facilities."[34]

The dynamic costs of inward-looking import-substitution policies have been especially high in the developing countries. Comparative studies consistently demonstrate that countries that looked inward had lower rates of economic growth than those that promoted exports. As we shall see in some detail in Chapter 8, trade liberalization in the newly industrializing countries did much to stimulate their growth.

In sum, when it is recognized that the costs of protection outweigh the gains, there is much to the saying that protection is like practicing acupuncture with a two-pronged fork: Even if one of the prongs finds the right spot, the other prong can only do harm.[35]

REGIONALISM AND TRADE POLICY

In recent decades, the formation of regional blocs has spread (see Tables 3.3 and 3.4). Most prominent are the European Union (EU) and the North American Free Trade Agreement (NAFTA), but there is also movement toward regional trade arrangements for the Association of South East Asian Nations (ASEAN) and some discussion of a Trans-Atlantic Free Trade Area. Of increasing concern are the implications that regionalism and preferential trade arrangements (PTAs) might have for the normative economics of trade policy.

Under specified conditions, Article XXIV of GATT allows a preferential trading arrangement as an exception to GATT's basic principles of nondiscrimination and most favored nation treatment. A trade bloc in the form of a customs union or free trade agreement is permitted provided that the member countries that discriminate in favor of one another must eliminate all restrictions on a substantial part of all their trade, and that the formation of the bloc must not result in an increase of barriers for states outside the bloc. In a customs union, trade barriers among the member countries are reduced to zero, but a common external tariff—no higher than the previous average of the members—exists on imports to the union. In a free trade area, members also remove trade barriers against one another, but can retain individual country tariffs instead of a common tariff against outside countries.

The rationale behind Article XXIV is that "half-a-step" toward free trade (within the customs union or free trade area) is better than none. But the basic issue is whether such a trade bloc is actually a step toward multilateral free trade—a building block—or is rather a stumbling block that fragments the world economy.

Table 3.3
Regional Integration Agreements Notified to GATT and in Force as of January 1995
Reciprocal Regional Integration Agreements

EUROPE
European Union (EU)

Austria	Germany	Netherlands
Belgium	Greece	Portugal
Denmark	Ireland	Spain
Finland	Italy	Sweden
France	Luxembourg	United Kingdom

EU free trade agreements with

Estonia	Latvia	Norway
Iceland	Liechtenstein	Switzerland
Israel	Lithuania	

EU association agreements with

Bulgaria	Hungary	Romania
Cyprus	Malta	Slovak Rep.
Czech Rep.	Poland	Turkey

European Free Trade Association (EFTA)

Iceland	Norway	Switzerland
Liechtenstein		

EFTA free trade agreements with

Bulgaria	Israel	Slovak Rep.
Czech Rep.	Poland	Turkey
Hungary	Romania	

Norway free trade agreements with

Estonia	Latvia	Lithuania

Switzerland free trade agreements with

Estonia	Latvia	Lithuania

Czech Rep. and Slovak Rep. Customs Union
Central European free trade area

Czech Rep.	Poland	Slovak Rep.
Hungary		

Czech Rep. and Slovenia Free Trade Agreement
Slovak Rep. and Slovenia Free Trade Agreement

NORTH AMERICA
Canada-United States Free Trade Agreement (CUFTA)
North American Free Trade Agreement (NAFTA)

LATIN AMERICA AND THE CARIBBEAN
Caribbean Community and Common Market (CARICOM)
Central American Common Market (CACM)
Latin America Integration Association (LAIA)
Andean Pact
Southern Common Market (MERCOSUR)

MIDDLE EAST
Economic Cooperation Organization (ECO)
Gulf Cooperation Council (GCC)

ASIA
Australia-New Zealand Closer Economic Relations Trade Agreement (CER)
Bangkok Agreement
Common Effective Preferential Scheme for the ASEAN free trade area
Lao People's Dem. Rep. and Thailand Trade Agreement

OTHER
Israel-United States Free Trade Agreement

Table 3.4
Share of Regional Trading Schemes in Intraregional Exports and World Exports, Selected Years, 1960–90

Scheme (year founded)	1960	1970	1975	1980	1985	1990
Australia–New Zealand Closer Economic Relations Trade Agreement (1983)						
Share in intraregional exports[a]	5.7	6.1	6.2	6.4	7.0	7.6
Share in total world exports[b]	2.4	2.1	1.7	1.4	1.6	1.5
European Community (1957)						
Share in intraregional exports	34.5	51.0	50.0	54.0	54.5	60.4
Share in total world exports	24.9	39.0	35.9	34.9	35.6	41.4
European Free Trade Area (1960)						
Share in intraregional exports	21.1	28.0	35.2	32.6	31.2	28.2
Share in total world exports	14.9	14.9	6.3	6.1	6.3	6.8
Canada–U.S. Free Trade Area (1989)						
Share in intraregional exports	26.5	32.8	30.6	26.5	38.0	34.0
Share in total world exports	21.9	20.5	16.8	15.1	16.7	15.8
Association of South East Asian Nations (1967)						
Share in intraregional exports	4.4	20.7	15.9	16.9	18.4	18.6
Share in total world exports	2.6	2.1	2.6	3.7	3.9	4.3
Andean Pact (1969)						
Share in intraregional exports	0.7	2.0	3.7	3.8	3.4	4.6
Share in total world exports	2.9	1.6	1.6	1.6	1.2	0.9
Central American Common Market (1961)						
Share in intraregional exports	7.0	25.7	23.3	24.1	14.7	14.8
Share in total world exports	0.4	0.4	0.3	0.2	0.2	0.1
Latin American Free Trade Area/Latin American Integration Association (1960, 1980)						
Share in intraregional exports	7.9	9.9	13.6	13.7	8.3	10.6
Share in total world exports	6.0	4.4	3.5	4.2	4.7	3.4
Economic Community of West African States (1975)						
Share in intraregional exports	—	3.0	4.2	3.5	5.3	6.0
Share in total world exports	—	1.0	1.4	1.7	1.1	0.6
Preferential Trade Area for Eastern and Southern Africa (1987)						
Share in intraregional exports	—	8.4	9.4	8.9	7.0	8.5
Share in total world exports	—	1.1	0.5	0.4	0.3	0.2

—Not available.
[a]Intraregional exports as percentage of the region's total world exports.
[b]Region's exports as percentage of total world exports.
Source: International Monetary Fund, *Direction of Trade Statistics* (Washington, DC).

In a trade bloc, the conditions of market access for member countries differ from the conditions outside the bloc. The movement to free trade within the bloc may or may not be desirable when there are still trade restrictions for nonmembers. The theory of second best becomes relevant: To optimize in a subpart of a system may not necessarily be desirable if there are distortions elsewhere in the system.[36] A regional trade bloc may therefore lead to "trade diversion," which worsens the international allocation of resources, instead of to "trade creation," which improves international resource allocation. Trade creation occurs when a member country in a trade bloc imports from another member country that is a low-cost producer. Previously the former country did not import at all because of a duty on the foreign product. When the duty is removed, and the other country is a lower-cost source, the international division of labor is improved as resources shift into more efficient production. If, however, a member country now imports from another member that is a higher-cost producer than an outside country from which it formerly imported because imports from the outside now face a discriminatory tariff, the bloc is trade diverting. In this case, there is an uneconomic diversion of production from the low-cost outside source to the high-cost supplier within the bloc, and the gains from trade are diminished.[37]

In considering whether trade creation or trade diversion is likely to dominate in a particular union, we have to take into account the preunion level of tariff rates among the members, the level of the postunion external tariff compared with the preunion tariff levels of each member country, the elasticities of demand for the imports on which duties are reduced, and the elasticities of supply of exports from the members and foreign sources. Conditions are more propitious for trade creation when each member's preunion duties are high on the others' products, the members are initially similar in the products they produce but different in the pattern of relative prices at which they produce them, the external tariff of the union is low compared with the preunion tariff levels of the members, and the production within the union of commodities that are substitutes for outside imports can be undertaken at a lower cost.[38]

The formation of a free trade union might also result in an improvement—or at least the forestalling of a deterioration—in the region's commodity terms of trade. This is possible if there is a reduction in the supply of exports from the union, the demand by members of the union is reduced for imports from outside, or the bargaining power of the members in trade negotiations is strengthened. But unless the members of the union are the chief suppliers of their exports or major buyers on the world market for their imports, they are unlikely to be able to exercise sufficient monopolistic or monopsonistic power to influence their terms of trade by raising duties on their trade with the outside world or by inducing outsiders to supply their goods more cheaply. Moreover, when free trade is confined only to the region, there is the risk of retaliation through the formation of other economic blocs. A union may thereby inhibit the realization of the more extensive gains from the "universal" approach to free trade.

Regional integration might also be beneficial in encouraging competition among the member countries. Technical efficiency in existing industries might then be improved as marginal firms are forced to reduce their costs, resources are reallocated from less efficient to more efficient firms, and monopolies that had previously been established behind tariff walls are no longer in a sheltered position. Further, the stimulation of competition within each country may yield not only a better utilization of given resources, but may also raise the rate of growth of productive resources. This may result from stronger incentives to adopt new methods of production, to replace obsolete equipment more quickly, and to innovate more rapidly with more and better investments.

The effects of a regional trade organization may differ according to whether it is a North–South type of integration as in NAFTA, or is a South–South type of integration involving only a developing country integrating with another developing country. Gains from South–South integration tend to be considerably less than for North–South integration, and in many cases have been harmful because the regionalism has become an instrument of protection.[39]

There are several economic objections to a union among developing countries. To begin with, it may be argued that the case for an economic union is in reality weak when the constituent countries have not yet established many industries. Limitations on the supply side may be more of a deterrent to the creation of an industry than is the narrow market on the side of demand. If production conditions do not also improve, the mere extension of the consumer market will not be sufficient to create industries. Moreover, when manufacturing industry is only at a rudimentary stage in the member countries, there is not much scope for eliminating high-cost manufacturers within the region. Nor is there much scope for realizing the benefits of increased competition when there are not yet similar ranges of rival products, produced under different cost conditions, in the several member nations. A union will not cause substantial improvement in the utilization of resources unless industries that have already been established need wider markets than the national economy can provide for the realization of economies of scale and unless the member countries have been protecting the same kind of industry, but have markedly different ratios of factor-efficiency in these industries to factor-efficiency in nonprotected branches of production.

The case for a union is strongest among countries that have little foreign trade in proportion to their domestic production, but conduct a high proportion of the foreign trade with one another. When these conditions prevail, there is less possibility for introducing, within each member country, a distortion of the price relation between goods from other member countries and goods from outside the union, and more of a possibility for eliminating any distortion by tariffs of the price-relations between domestic goods and imports from other member countries. There is therefore greater likelihood that the union will improve the use of resources and raise real income.

A union among underdeveloped countries, however, is unlikely to conform to these conditions. The ratio of foreign trade to domestic production is generally high for these countries, and the actual volume of intraregional trade is normally only a small proportion of the region's total foreign trade. The gain from regional integration would therefore be small. The basic difficulty is that, with existing trade patterns, the formation of a union is likely to cause a considerable amount of wasteful "trade diversion." Over the longer run, comparative costs and trade patterns may change, and economies of scale may give rise to competitive advantages as development proceeds, so that the scope for "trade creation" will become greater within the union. But the immediate gain is small, and the longer-run prospects for the creation of new trade are not likely to influence current decisions to join a union.

Besides the possibility of "trade diversion," other undesirable consequences may result from a union. The member countries are unlikely to benefit equally, and some members may believe the others are gaining at their expense. A country may have a strong comparative advantage in only primary products and will sell to other members only goods that it could as readily export to outside countries. At the same time, the location of manufacturing industry and ancillary activities may become localized within one member country, and "polarization" results. Other members may then contend that if they too had been able to adopt tariff protection against their partners, they would have also been able to attract industry. A nonindustrialized member country may further complain that in buying from an industrialized partner, instead of importing from the outside, it is losing revenue equal to the duty on outside manufacturers. And, with a common external tariff, member countries no longer have the discretionary power to use variations in the tariff for the purpose of adjusting their national revenues to their own requirements. The internal strains that arise from uneven development among the member counties may thus make it extremely difficult to preserve a regional grouping.

It may, however, be possible for the union to redistribute benefits among members through a system of public finance transfers, a regional development bank, balance of payments support, regional policies for the location of industry, the pooling of overhead costs of public services, or coordination of development policies. But unless the union is strong enough to adopt these other measures and distribute the gains more evenly, its dissident members will threaten its stability.

The issue of trade creation versus trade diversion denotes the immediate static impact of the formation of a regional trade arrangement. Equally important is whether the dynamic time path of the arrangement leads toward outward-looking multilateralism and the eventual benefits of the goal of nondiscriminatory, multilateral free trade.[40] Over time, will regional blocs merge into a single world bloc, or will they fragment the world economy?

The answer depends on whether new members are readily admitted to the bloc and whether market access is granted for outside countries. Governments and producer interest groups must have the incentives to keep the blocs open and moving toward multilateral free trade.

Can the rules of the game be reformed in such a way that regionalism will complement rather than substitute for the multilateral approach? If regionalism is not to pose a threat to international economic peacekeeping, regional blocs must be supplementary to GATT and the WTO, promoting external liberalization along with internal liberalization in order to support nondiscriminatory multilateral trade. To this end, it is suggested that Article XXIV of GATT be reformed to rule out free trade areas and allow only customs unions with low common external tariffs. Second, recourse to antidumping measures and voluntary export restraints also need to be curtailed through the strengthening of GATT's articles that pertain to these practices. Third, countries should be encouraged to adopt liberal rules of entry when designing regional arrangements.

NOTES

1. Adam Smith, *An Inquiry into the Nature and Causes of the Wealth of Nations* (1776; Glasgow edition, Oxford University Press, 1976), Book IV, Ch. III.
2. For the problem of technical change and imperfect capital markets, see Joseph E. Stiglitz, "Financial Markets and Development," *Oxford Review of Economic Policy* (winter 1989): 62–63.
3. F. Y. Edgeworth, "Appreciation of Mathematical Theories," *Economic Journal* (1908): 556.
4. Paul R. Krugman, ed., *Strategic Policy and the New International Economics* (Cambridge, Mass.: MIT Press, 1986).
5. Paul R. Krugman, "Is Free Trade Passé?" *Journal of Economic Perspectives*, vol. I, no. 2, p. 132.
6. Clyde Prestowitz is author of *Changing Places* (New York: Basic Books, 1988). Robert Kuttner is an economics columnist.
7. Paul Krugman, "Protectionism: Try It, You'll Like It," *The International Economy* (June/July 1990): 38.
8. For analysis of this argument, see Paul Krugman, "Does Third World Growth Hurt First World Prosperity?" *Harvard Business Review* (July–August 1994): 120–121; Gary Burtless, "International Trade and the Rise in Earnings Inequality," *Journal of Economic Literature* (June 1995): 800–816, with bibliography; Adrian Wood, *North-South Trade, Employment, and Inequality:*

Changing Fortunes in a Skill-Driven World (New York: Oxford University Press, 1994); J. David Richardson, "Income Inequality and Trade: How to Think, What to Conclude," *Journal of Economic Perspectives* (summer 1995): 33–55.

9. For an illuminating evaluation of many of the empirical patterns that have been observed in the labor market, see Jagdish Bhagwati and Marvin H. Kosters, eds., *Trade and Wages: Leveling Wages Down?* (Washington, DC: AEI Press, 1994), Ch. 2; Freeman, op. cit., pp. 18–32.

10. Burtless, op. cit., pp. 802–803.

11. Krugman, op. cit., p. 120.

12. Robert Z. Lawrence, "Trade, Multinationals and Labor," NBER Working Paper No. 4836 (1994): 15–17.

13. Raymond J. Mataloni, Jr., "A Guide to BEA Statistics on U. S. Multinational Companies," *Survey of Current Business* (March 1995): 46.

14. Gary Burtless, "Worsening American Income Inequality," *The Brookings Review* (spring 1996): 30.

15. Paul R. Krugman and Robert Z. Lawrence, "Trade, Jobs and Wages," *Scientific American* (April 1994): 49; Jagdish Bhagwati, "Free Trade: Old and New Challenges," *Economic Journal* (March 1994): 243–244; Jeffrey Sachs and Howard Shatz, "Trade and Jobs in U. S. Manufacturing," *Brookings Papers on Economic Activity* (1994): 1–84; Burtless, op. cit., p. 815; John Bound and George Johnson, "Changes in the Structure of Wages in the 1980s: An Evaluation of Alternative Explanations," *American Economic Review* 82 (1992): 371–392; Bhagwati and Kosters, op. cit., Ch. 2.

    But see Robert C. Feenstra and Gordon H. Hanson, "Foreign Investment, Outsourcing, and Relative Wages," *NBER Working Paper* #5121, May 1995, for a contrary analysis that maintains that rising imports can explain a significant part of the decline in relative employment and wages of unskilled workers in the United States during the 1980s.

16. Michael Kremer and Eric Maskin, "Wage Inequality and Segregation by Skill," National Bureau of Economic Research Working Paper 5718, August 1996.

17. *The OECD Jobs Study: Evidence and Explorations* (Paris: OECD Publications, 1994).

18. William Cline, *Reciprocity: A New Approach to World Trade Policy* (Washington, DC: Institute for International Economics, September 1982), p. 12.

19. Jagdish Bhagwati, *Protectionism* (Cambridge, Mass.: MIT Press, 1989), p. 126.

20. Alan O. Sykes, "Countervailing Duty Law: An Economic Perspective," *Columbia Law Review* (March 1989): 213–215. This article originally appeared at 89 Colum. L. Rev. 199 (1989). Reprinted by permission.

21. Bhagwati, *Protectionism*, p. 35.

22. Super 301 is the provision of the U. S. Trade Act that specifies retaliation against countries designated as unfair traders. Notable applications have been against Japan, Brazil, and India.

23. Paul R. Krugman and Maurice Obstfeld, *International Economics* (Glenview, IL: Scott, Foresman, 1988), pp. 189, 215; David G. Tarr, *Aggregate Costs to U.S. Tariffs* (Washington, DC: Federal Trade Commission, 1984).

24. G. M. Grossman, "Strategic Export Promotion: A Critique," in Paul R. Krugman, ed., *Strategic Trade Policy and the New International Economics* (Cambridge, Mass.: MIT Press, 1986): 65. © Massachusetts Institute of Technology, 1986.

25. Donald V. Fites, *Managed Trade: Beyond the Rhetoric* (Caterpillar 1990).

26. M. Destler and John S. Odell, *Anti-Protection: Changing Forces in United States Trade Politics* (Washington, DC: Institute for International Economics Policy Analysis, no. 21, September 1987).

27. J. M. Finger, "Incorporating the Gains from Trade into Policy," *The World Economy* (December 1982): 375.

28. *The Wall Street Journal*, July 29, 1991, p. A6.

29. U. S. Department of Commerce estimates, as reported in Jasper Womach, "Sugar Policy Issues," (Washington, DC: Congressional Research Service, CRS Issue Brief, March 20, 1989), p. 4.

30. Reprinted by permission of *The Wall Street Journal*, May 1, 1990, p. 1. Dow Jones & Company, Inc. All Rights Reserved Worldwide.

31. World Bank, *World Development Report* 1987 (Washington, DC: Oxford University Press, 1987), p. 152.

32. Gary Clyde Hufbauer and Kimberly Ann Elliott, *Measuring the Costs of Protection in the United States* (Washington, DC, Institute for International Economics, 1994), p. 11. Copyright 1994 by the Institute for International Economics. All rights reserved.

33. Yoko Sazanami et al., *Measuring the Costs of Protection in Japan* (Washington, DC, Institute for International Economics, 1995), p. 43.

34. Fites, *Managed Trade: Beyond the Rhetoric.*

35. Bernard M. Hoekman and Michael Pleidy, "Policy Responses to Shifting Comparative Advantage," *Kyklos* (1990): 25–51.

36. R. G. Lipsey and K. J. Lancaster, "The General Theory of Second Best," *Review of Economic Studies* (1956–57): 33–49.

37. Jacob Viner, *The Customs Union Issue* (New York: Carnegie Endowment for International Peace, 1950).

38. For a formal model of a basic trading bloc, see Paul Krugman, "Is Bilateralism Bad?" in E. Helpman and A. Razin, *International Trade and Trade Policy* (Cambridge: MIT Press, 1991). Krugman concludes that world welfare reaches a minimum when there are a few large blocs, and would be higher if there were more blocs, each with less market power.

    For an extension of the welfare implications of Krugman's model, see Jeffrey Frankel et al., "Trading Blocs and the Americas: The Natural, the Unnatural, and the Super-natural," *Journal of Development Economics* 47 (1995): 61–95.

39. Jaime de Melo and Arvind Panagariya, *The New Regionalism in Trade Policy* (World Bank and Centre for Economic Policy), pp. 14–21. A World Bank study by Alexander Yeats claims that Mercosur (the regional grouping of Argentina, Brazil, Paraguay, and Uruguay) has artificially diverted trade flows by maintaining much higher tariffs and nontariff barriers on imports from third countries than they impose on members within Mercosur. The preferential arrangements cause producers in Mercosur to concentrate on selling in each other's markets products that are not internationally competitive. Motor vehicles, sheltered by tariffs as much as 70 percent, exemplify the problem. *Financial Times*, October 24, 1996, p. 5.

40. This issue is raised by Jagdish Bhagwati, "Regionalism and Multilateralism: An Overview," in Jaime de Melo and Arvind Panagariya, eds., *New Dimensions in Regional Integration* (Cambridge University Press, 1993), pp. 31–45.

Optimality of Free Trade

OPTIMALITY OF FREE TRADE

We shall first note how the case for free trade can be argued in terms of partial welfare economics analysis. Partial welfare analysis does not consider all hypothetical welfare distributions, but merely those that exist before and after the contemplated policy change in one industry. A convenient approach to this type of analysis is to consider what happens to consumers' surplus and producers' surplus after there is a policy change that affects an industry.

Marshall (1890) defined consumer's surplus or rent as "the excess of the price which he [a consumer] would be willing to pay rather than go without the thing, over that which he actually does pay." The economic measure of this "surplus satisfaction" is the area between the demand curve and price line (such as DP_hE in Figure 3.3, when the market price is P_h).

On the side of supply, "the price required to call forth the exertion necessary for producing any given amount of a commodity may be called the supply price for that amount during the same time." But producers will have "differential advantages," resulting

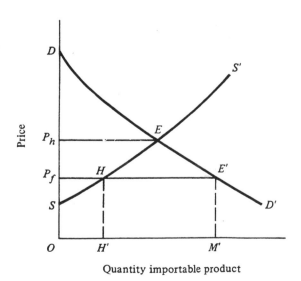

Figure 3.3 Free trade is superior to no trade. SS' is the domestic supply curve. The home price with no trade is P_h. A prohibitive tariff would be at the specific rate P_fP_h, or at the *ad valorem* rate P_fP_h/OP_f. When trade policy changes from prohibitive protection at P_h to free trade at P_f, the excess of the gain in consumers' surplus over loss in producers' surplus is $EE'H$, OH' is produced at home, and $H'M'$ is imported at P_f.

Quantity importable product

Reprinted from Gerald M. Meier, *International Economics* (New York: Oxford University Press, 1980).

in different levels of their cost curves. Thus, the supply curve SS' slopes upwards to the right, with a higher price being needed to bring forth a supply from the higher-cost firms. The difference between the price line and the supply curve is producer's surplus or rent—a surplus remuneration that is greater than the amount necessary to call forth the supply from the lower cost firms. Producers' surplus under prohibitive protection with the domestic price at P_h, would amount to $P_h ES$ in Figure 3.3.

Consider now a change from no trade to free trade. In Figure 3.3, let P_h represent the domestic price before trade, and assume that there is a prohibitive tariff—say, at the specific rate of $P_f P_h$ per unit of import, or the *ad valorem* rate $P_f P_h / O P_f$—sufficiently high to prevent any imports, so that all the demand is filled from home supply. Under free trade the price would be P_f, the border price that includes transportation costs to the importing country. The country would then produce $O H'$ at home and import $H' M'$. For simplicity we assume that the import supply curve is infinitely elastic at P_f (the importing country can demand all the commodity desired at a constant price). When the country moves from no trade to free trade, consumers' surplus increases from DEP_h to $DE'P_f$, a gain to consumers of $P_h EE'P_f$. Producers' surplus decreases from $P_h ES$ to $P_f HS$, a loss to producers of $P_h EHP_f$. But the gain to consumers is greater than the loss to producers by the amount of $EE'H$. It would therefore be possible for the gainers (the consumers) to compensate the losers (producers) and still be better off in the free-trade situation than in the no-trade situation. Conversely, it would be impossible for the future losers (producers) to bribe the future gainers (consumers) not to "vote" for free trade. If it were politically desired, the government could tax consumers an amount equivalent to $P_h EHP_f$, and taxes could be remitted by this amount for producers. Since potential economic welfare (real income) has increased, the producers could be brought back to their initial income level, while consumers could be left better off after the policy change.

Consider next a change from protection to free trade. In Figure 3.4, the price with tariff (P_t) falls to the free-trade price P_f. Home production would then decline from $O H'$ to $O H''$, while imports would increase from $H' M'$ to $H'' M''$. The effects would be

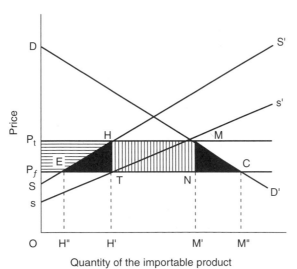

Figure 3.4 Free trade is superior to restricted trade. If the tariff $P_f P_t$ or $P_f P_t / O P_f$ is eliminated, the effects are: increase in consumers' surplus: $P_t MCP_f$; decrease in producers' surplus: $P_t HEP_f$; loss in government tariff revenue: $HMNT$; net gain: HTE (production gain) and MNC (consumption gain). An increase in price from the free trade P_f to price with tariff P_t would result in the production and consumption "deadweight losses," HTE and MNC, respectively.

Price

Quantity of the importable product

an increase in consumers' surplus: $P_t M C P_f$

a decrease in producers' surplus: $P_t H E P_f$

a loss in government tariff revenue: $HMNT$.

Gains to consumers exceed losses to producers and the government by the amount of the two shaded triangles HTE and MNC.

Alternatively, we can note that the value of output produced elsewhere in the economy after the tariff is reduced is $H''EHH'$ (the area under the supply curve represents the opportunity cost of factors that can be used elsewhere in the economy). But the imports equivalent to the domestic goods that these resources produced under the tariff now cost only $H''ETH'$. The net production gain to the economy is therefore HTE. And the net consumption gain to the economy is MNC. Potential welfare has increased. It would be possible, if politically desired, to tax consumers an amount equivalent to the loss in producers' surplus and government revenue, remit taxes to producers so that they are no worse off than before the policy change to free trade, and still leave consumers better off under free trade by the amount of the shaded triangles.

This gain from free trade will, however, be overstated if the resources displaced from domestic production are not absorbed in alternative employment. The value of the released resources that were previously involved in the sheltered domestic production are represented by $H''EHH'$ in Figure 3.4. If these resources are not immediately absorbed elsewhere at earnings rates equal to their marginal productivity, then the relevant part of the area $H''EHH'$ that remains idle should be deducted from the two triangles HTE and MNC. To be precise, the net direct gain or loss of welfare from reducing the tariff is the present value of the two shaded triangles—determined by discounting the sum over the appropriate time period and at some appropriate interest rate—minus the present value of the loss of productive output during the transitional period when displaced resources are idle.

Finally, consider the reverse movement from free trade (P_f) to protection (P_t). We assume that the tariff does not cause the foreign suppliers to lower their export price—that is, the tariff-imposing country is a small country that cannot affect its terms of trade. Home production would then expand from OH'' to OH', while imports would fall from $H''M''$ to $H'M'$. The effects would be

a decrease in consumers' surplus: $P_t M C P_f$

an increase in producers' surplus: $P_t H E P_f$

an increase in government tariff revenue: $HMNT$.

The decrease in consumers' surplus is offset in part by the gains to the producers and government. But consumers still lose more than the producers and the government gain. There remain the two shaded triangles HTE and MNC, representing the production and consumption "deadweight losses," respectively.

The production deadweight loss is transferred from consumers to inefficient domestic producers. The consumption deadweight loss means less is consumed at a higher price. It would be impossible for the gainers under protection (producers and government) to compensate the losers (consumers) sufficiently to leave consumers as well off as they were under free trade. If, however, there were a "vote" for protection or free trade, it would "pay" the consumers to bribe producers not to vote for protection (a tariff). Or under free trade, taxes could be imposed on consumers in an amount sufficient to compensate producers and government for lost tariff revenue, while still leaving consumers better off under free trade than protection.

The cost of protection therefore consists of a production cost and a consumption cost. The production cost is the excess real cost of securing $H''H'$ from inefficient home producers instead of from imports. This can be calculated as the "cash cost" or "subsidy-equivalent"—the cash cost to the Treasury of a production subsidy to the protected industry that would have the same protective effect as the tariff. The subsidy-equivalent of the tariff in Figure 3.4 is $P_f P_t HT$. If there were a production subsidy (a negative tariff), designed to obtain the same amount of protection for home industry, the *ad valorem* subsidy would shift the domestic supply curve down to the new position ss'. This subsidy would raise home output to OH', with a protection effect identical with that of the tariff-equivalent. But there would be no consumption effect because P_f does not rise. And, although there will be a redistribution to producers, the increased revenue to home suppliers comes not from consumers, as in the case of a tariff, but from the Treasury.

The consumption cost under a tariff can be calculated by a compensating variation in income—that is, by the amount consumers' money income would have to increase to leave them as well off after protection as they were in the free-trade situation before prices rose.

From a consideration of the gains and losses in this type of partial analysis, we can conclude that

free trade is superior to no trade, and

free trade is superior to a tariff.

In each case, the gains from trade are composed of a consumption gain and a production gain. Whether expressed as an increase in the "mass of commodities and sum of enjoyments," an increase in consumers' surplus, or an increase in real income, the consumption gain amounts to the substitution of lower-cost imports for higher-cost domestic goods. The production gain arises from the allocation of resources away from the direct production of importables in higher-cost home production to the specialization in the lower-cost production of exportables. The export sector indirectly "produces" the importables on the world market, and this conversion of domestic resources into foreign resources will raise the trading country's real income if the alternative domestic employment of resources used in the export sector would have lower productivity. Moreover, the gains from trade are mutual gains: every trading nation enjoys a consumption gain and a production gain.

A UBIQUITOUS AND TIMELESS PRINCIPLE

Whether a country is rich or poor, big or little, new or old, with or without high standards of living, agricultural, industrial, or mixed, makes no difference. It is a matter of mathematics, quite independent of environment, that there is an inherent gain in the specialization along the lines of comparative competence which unshackled trade tends to develop.

There is no possible refutation of this analysis. Advocates of a restrictive commercial policy must, in logic, accept it as a fact and attempt to show that the gain may be outweighed by economic or other considerations of superior importance. . . . The presumption is always in favor of free trade, since the gain therefrom is certain, and the loss, if any, dependent upon incidental circumstance. This presumption is rebutable but it is ever present; and, in this sense, the classical economists were right in insisting that free trade is a ubiquitous and timeless principle. Other things being equal, it will enable people to have more goods of every kind than would otherwise be possible.

Frank Graham, *Protective Tariffs* (1934), 58–59

Technical Appendix 3.2

Optimal Trade Interventions

It is now time to temper some of our conclusions from the preceding chapters. Are there any exceptions to the conclusions that free trade is Pareto-superior to no trade, and free trade is Pareto-superior to restricted trade? If the logic of our previous analysis is correct, then exceptions can arise only if we make one or more of the following modifications to our earlier analysis: (i) we no longer adopt the cosmopolitan viewpoint, but instead consider only that of national advantage; (ii) some of the postulated conditions of a perfectly competitive economy do not exist; and (iii) we change the goal from that of Pareto efficiency to some other social objective with non-economic elements.

Any of these changes expands the context of the free-trade versus protection debate. And in this wider context, some of our prior conclusions have to be modified.

THE WELFARE ECONOMIST'S CONCLUSIONS

We know that in practice governments resort to a number of policy instruments to restrict trade for various objectives. Tariffs, quotas, voluntary export restraints, taxes, subsidies, exchange rate restrictions—all these, and more, appear in a country's foreign trade regime. In most cases, these trade restrictions are imposed to stimulate exports or restrict imports in order to protect particular interests,[1] promote employment, ease a balance of payments problem, foster industrialization, or to retaliate against a foreign country.

But which of the various policy instruments is optimal or "first best" to achieve the desired objective? The actual practice of protection is likely to deviate enormously from what the welfare economist would specify as optimal policy interventions. In practice, the policy measures undertaken are likely to be second best, third best, or nth best. Moreover, the arguments on behalf of the policy interventions are likely to be non-economic. And frequently what purports to be an "argument" for protection is really a "non-argument" for protection, but rather an argument for some other type of policy.

What, then, would be the optimal trade interventions? To answer this, we shall now adopt the perspective of the welfare economist. After summarizing the welfare economist's conclusions, we shall explain how these conclusions were reached.[2]

Reprinted from Gerald M. Meier, *International Economics* (New York: Oxford University Press, 1980).

[1] These interests can be to protect the status of specific industries confronting foreign competition, the income distribution for a certain group, or to protect against "low-wage" foreign labor.

[2] In elaborating these conclusions, the following sections draw on H. G. Johnson, "Optimal Trade Intervention in the Presence of Domestic Distortions," in R. E. Caves et al. (eds.), *Trade, Growth and the Balance of Payments: Essays in Honor of Gottfried Haberler* (1965), 3–4; Jagdish Bhagwati and V. K. Ramaswami, "Domestic

Summary of the welfare economist's analysis:

Free trade is Pareto-superior to no trade.

Restricted trade is Pareto-superior to no trade.

Free trade is Pareto-superior to restricted trade.

Except: An "Optimum tariff" is Pareto-superior to free trade when there are international market distortions and the criterion is only "welfare" of nationals.

And: An "Optimum subsidy" is Pareto-superior to a tariff when there are domestic market distortions.

Stated succinctly, the welfare economist would argue that "the only first-best economic argument for protection is the optimum tariff. All other arguments for protection should really be arguments for some form of government intervention in the domestic economy, and the use of tariffs in these cases would be sub-optimal policy."[3]

RANKING OF ALTERNATIVE POLICIES

If trade intervention is to be justified economically, it must be because conditions depart from the marginal equivalencies established earlier for the optimality of free trade. Free trade fulfills the following (first-order) marginal conditions of Pareto efficiency:

(i) Marginal rates of substitution of factors are equal among all producers (absence of factor market distortions).

(ii) Marginal rates of transformation of goods in domestic production (MRT_d) are equal among all producers (absence of differential producer taxation, or absence of distortion in producer prices).

(iii) Marginal rates of substitution of goods in consumption (MRS) are equal among all consumers (absence of differential consumer taxation, or absence of distortion in consumer prices).

(iv) Marginal rates of transformation in production are equal to marginal rates of substitution in consumption (absence of commodity taxation).

(v) Marginal rates of transformation are equal in domestic production and in foreign trade (MRT_f) (non-intervention in foreign trade).

Either externalities or absence of perfect competition in any of the commodity or factor markets can lead to violations of these conditions. The equivalence is then destroyed

Distortions, Tariffs and the Theory of Optimum Subsidy," *Journal of Political Economy,* 71 (Feb. 1963), 44–50; Bhagwati, "The Generalized Theory of Distortions and Welfare," in Bhagwati et al. (ed.), *Trade, Balance of Payments and Growth: Essays in Honor of C. P. Kindleberger,* (1971), 69–90; and Bhagwati, *The Theory and Practice of Commercial Policy: Departures from Unified Exchange Rates.* Princeton Special Papers in International Economics No. 8 (Jan. 1968).

[3] J. Bhagwati and T. N. Srinivasan, "Optimal Intervention to Achieve Non-economic Objectives," *Review of Economic Studies,* 36 (Jan. 1969), 27.

between MRS, MRT_d, and MRT_f. If there is a divergence between marginal social costs and marginal private costs or between private and social benefits or between revenue or marginal cost and price in the country's international trade, then trade interventions may be called for to correct the divergences. If divergences cannot be removed directly, as they usually cannot, then they must be offset or neutralized by some trade intervention. But which of the alternative trade interventions should be adopted?

To determine the optimal type of trade intervention, we shall obviously have to be able to rank alternative policies that correct the divergences. The prevalent policy choices of an international character are trade tariffs, subsidies, and quantitative restrictions.[4] The most common domestic policies that affect a country's pattern of foreign trade are taxes and subsidies on production and consumption and taxes and subsidies on factor use.

Ranking alternative policies involves the "theory of the second best."[5] In a world in which the first-best conditions of Pareto optimality do not actually exist throughout the entire system, we have to use the second-best criterion. We have to ask: Given a policy constraint that does not allow the removal of some other distortion in the general system, what is the optimum policy for the remaining part of the system? The optimum policy will be second best in comparison with the standard first-best conditions of the entire system. For example, if free trade cannot be achieved throughout the world, will free trade within a customs union or a free-trade area for a limited number of countries still be desirable? It does not follow that the removal of tariffs in part of the world necessarily leads to an increase in economic welfare as long as another part of the world maintains tariffs.[6] But the economist might show what policy leads toward or away from the second-best welfare maximum. In this sense, the economist recognizes that the actual economy is inferior to the ideal, first-best optimum conditions, but the economist as policy advisor then seeks to establish policies that are second best instead of third best or fourth best or nth best. The degrees of inferiority away from the ideal are minimized, so that the result is quasi-optimal (a constrained optimum). If the economy must have distortions, the best set of distortions is established (the second-best solution is found instead of the third-best).

More directly, economists evaluate the optimal way of offsetting the distortions that cannot be removed. "Optimal" in this context means that the policy intervention should be directed specifically to the point at which the divergence occurs and should correct the source of the divergence itself without creating any other by-product distortion elsewhere in the system. For any given marginal divergence, or set of divergences, there is then a first-best optimal policy or set of policies.[7] This is, in simplest language, the "first-best partial policy in a second-best world"—the best policy in a suboptimal world where general first-best conditions cannot be established uniformly.[8] Inferior to the first-best policy will be other policies that create by-product distortions as they attempt to correct the initial distortion.

---

[4] Voluntary Export Restraints and Orderly Marketing Agreements are variants of quantitative restrictions. Foreign exchange restrictions can also be used for trade intervention purposes.

[5] J. E. Meade, *Trade and Welfare* (1955), Chap. VII, and R. G. Lipsey and K. Lancaster, "The General Theory of Second Best," *Review of Economic Studies,* 24 (1956), 11–32.

[6] The reduction in tariffs to zero within the customs union may cause trade diversion, and a superior policy might be to reduce tariffs within the customs union to a level below the external tariff maintained by the union, but greater than zero. See Lipsey and Lancaster, *op. cit.*

[7] W. M. Corden, *Trade Policy and Economic Welfare* (1974), 28–31; also, references in note 2, above.

[8] For a more elegant (but more complex) statement that clarifies the different meanings of "second best,' see J. Bhagwati, "The Pure Theory of International Trade: A Survey," *Economic Journal,* 74 (March 1964), 56–57, n. 1.

These policies can then be ranked as second best, third best, fourth best, etc., according to the number of additional by-product distortions the successive policies impose. We shall adopt this practice of establishing a hierarchy of policies that correct a given distortion, ranging from the first-best downward.

The number of alternative policies considered will, of course, depend on the policy adviser's interpretation of what is technically feasible and politically conceivable.

Because they are secondary issues that do not affect the central logic of the analysis, we normally make the following assumptions: (i) Subsidies can be financed by "non-distortionary" taxes, such as lump sum taxes that do not affect incentives. Financing can also be realized not by raising taxes, but by forgoing other governmental expenditure. The equivalence of a subsidy on one product can also be achieved by taxing other products or by remitting taxes on the product that is to be subsidized. (ii) Taxation involves no collection costs. (iii) There are no costs of disbursement of subsidies. (iv) The income distribution effects of various policies can be neglected.

If, in contrast to these assumptions, there actually are costs to financing a subsidy, then we should seek the minimum-cost package of taxes, that is, a policy that minimizes the by-product distortion costs of financing and disbursing the subsidy.

It is an empirical question whether departure from these assumptions will change the ranking of policies in any particular situation. For example, if the collection costs of financing a subsidy through taxes were so much larger than those of a tariff, it is conceivable that the tariff would then become superior to the subsidy, even though on other grounds we had originally established that a subsidy was a first-best way and a tariff a second-best way of correcting the distortion. The subsidy would then have to be just high enough for the marginal gain from partially correcting the distortion to be equal to the marginal by-product costs.

It is reasonable, however, to argue that in practice the ranking of policies is unlikely to be affected by the existence of collection and distortion costs because the first-best policy is initially selected by the criterion that it be directed precisely to the point of the divergence.

OPTIMUM TARIFF

A long-standing argument for protection has been the "terms of trade" argument. From the viewpoint of national advantage, a country with monopoly power or monopsony power in its foreign trade can improve its terms of trade by taxing its exports (if it has monopoly power) or taxing its imports (if it has monopsony power). A tax on exports can be passed on to the foreign buyer, whereas a tariff on imports can result in a lowering of the price of the imports—calculated before the duty—in order to retain the market of the tariff-imposing country. In either case, the commodity terms of trade would improve.

The "terms of trade argument" was well known to classical economists, who recognized it as an exception to free trade. But they noted that the gain to one country was a loss to another: the cosmopolitan viewpoint of mutual gains had changed to the national viewpoint in a zero-sum game. Moreover, they were cautious about the application of this argument: they thought that a government could readily overdo its application to the detriment of even the tariff-imposing country. As Edgeworth warned, "the direct use of the theory is likely to be small. But it is to be feared that its abuse will be considerable. Let us admire the skill of the analyst, but label the subject of his investigation *Poison*."

The essence of the terms of trade argument is that "the foreigner pays the duty." By taxing its exports, the monopolist country raises its export price. By taxing its imports, the monopsonist country causes the foreign country to reduce its export price. The tax is thereby absorbed by the foreigner. To the extent that the export price declines, the production loss and the consumption loss of the tariff will be less, at the limit zero, if the exporter lowers the foreign price by the full amount of the tariff. The more elastic the import demand of the tariff-imposing country and the less elastic the export supply of the exporting country, the more will the export price be reduced and the terms of trade improve for the tariff-imposing country.

While the terms of trade improve, however, the volume of trade decreases. Gains at the margin in the terms of trade are being offset by losses "on the average" in the gains from trade through the reduced volume of trade. An optimal degree of taxation should therefore be sought. The optimum tariff will be one that improves the country's terms of trade just up to the point where the marginal gain from the improved terms of trade is equal to the marginal loss from a reduced volume of trade.

The conditions for an optimum have been spelled out with considerable refinement. The case for a tariff arises initially because of the existence of a distortion in international markets—there is a divergence between marginal revenue or marginal cost and market price in international trade. Just as a monopolistic firm equates marginal revenue and marginal cost instead of price and marginal cost, so too should a country with national monopoly power. This market imperfection means that world market prices diverge from the MRT_f. There is an international distortion so that $MRT_f \neq MRT_d = MRS$. Free trade makes the price ratio or average terms of trade equal to the marginal cost ratio (MRT_d). But the average terms of trade equal the marginal terms of trade only if national monopoly power does not exist. The existence of national monopoly power means that the exporting country can gain more by equating its marginal terms of trade MRT_f (i.e., its marginal revenue or marginal receipts from exports) to its MRT_d (i.e., its marginal opportunity cost in domestic production). This can be done through a tariff that corrects the divergence in international markets. Because the distortion relates to foreign transactions, the intervention in trade will be the first-best remedial policy: it will achieve equality between MRT_d and MRT_f without destroying the domestic equality between MRS and MRT_d. (A second-best policy would be either a tax-cum-subsidy on production or on factor use.)

But what is the optimum degree of trade restriction? The objective is not to maximize, but to optimize, the terms of trade. The optimum degree of trade restriction equates the marginal gain from improved terms of trade to the marginal loss from the contraction of the international division of labor. Just as a monopolist does not charge the highest possible unit price, but instead maximizes total profit by equating marginal revenue and marginal cost, so too a country with monopoly power should not try to maximize the terms of trade, but should make the marginal receipts from exports equal to its marginal cost ratio (MRT_d). As long as the foreigner's demand is not perfectly elastic, the terms of trade can be improved by the exercise of monopoly power. If the foreigner has a very inelastic demand for imports from the exporting country, a tax on exports may even allow the country to obtain more imports for fewer exports. In the normal case, the terms of trade would improve, but the volume of trade would also decrease. The optimum tariff rate would then be a rate that would improve the terms of trade just up to the point where the gain from improved terms of trade begins to be offset by a loss from the smaller volume of trade: the marginal value of exports would equal the marginal value of imports. The lower the elasticity of foreign supply to the tariff-imposing country, or the more inelastic the demand for the country's exports, the higher is the optimal tariff rate.

Although there is a symmetry between export taxes and import duties, more countries tend to have monopoly power than monopsony power and to seek an improvement in their terms of trade through export taxes. The effectiveness of this policy, however, will depend on the inelasticity of the foreigner's demand for imports, the bargaining power of the respective countries, and the capacity for retaliation by the importing country. It also depends on whether the government spends the revenue on imports or on the country's exportables or whether it increases the government's surplus or reduces other taxes. It must also be remembered that the optimum tariff situation represents only a potential optimum: the distribution of income issue still has to be settled by some welfare criterion.

OPTIMUM SUBSIDY

If an international distortion calls for an optimum tariff, a domestic distortion requires an optimum subsidy as the first-best remedial policy. Just as there exists an optimum tariff policy for a divergence between foreign prices and the MRT_f, so too does there exist an optimum subsidy policy for a divergence between domestic prices and MRT_d. Domestic distortions commonly take the form of a divergence between private cost and social cost within the country because of externalities in production or imperfections in a factor market. Domestic prices will then not measure social opportunity costs as indicated by the MRT_d. The domestic distortion will mean that $MRT_d \neq MRS = MRT_f$. The first-best policy to bring the MRT_d into equality with the MRS will involve a domestic tax-cum-subsidy policy, aimed specifically at the source of the divergence between market prices and social opportunity costs.

External economies in product markets can occur when expansion in industry *1* confers a side-effect benefit on industry *2,* but industry *1* cannot appropriate the whole of the social return. If fewer units of inputs are required to produce a unit of output in industry *2* as a result of the expansion of industry *1,* there is an external economy from *1*'s expansion; but the price system does not register this benefit, and industry is not paid for this external benefit. This may occur when industry *1* trains labor that becomes freely available to industry *2* or when the expansion of industry *1* creates and diffuses knowledge that becomes freely available to industry *2.* The output of industry *1* will therefore be less than it should be if its private costs were lowered to the true social cost or if the value of its output were raised to its true social benefit. When domestic prices do not reflect the true social marginal cost or social benefit, the true $MRT_d < MRT_f$.

If in Figure 2.9, p. 59, there was an externality in the production of *c,* such that the market does not remunerate *c*-firms for the increment that *c* creates in *w*-output, the production externality would result in non-tangency between the MRT_f and the production-possibility frontier. A production subsidy on *c,* equal to the degree of external economies, would then bring about the tangency of MRT_f and MRT_d at a greater output of *c.*

If the external economies arise in an import-competing industry, then the first-best policy would be a subsidy on production in that industry. If the external economies stem from expansion of an export industry, the first-best policy is subsidization of that industry.

A tariff would correct the distortion of domestic prices from opportunity costs, but it would achieve this production gain at the expense of introducing a consumption-distortion cost through the rise in prices. In other words, a tariff could equalize MRT_d and MRT_f, but at the same time it would cause a by-product distortion of destroying the equality between MRS and MRT_f. A tariff would therefore be a second-best policy in comparison with the subsidy. A quota on imports would create even more by-product distortions, and would therefore be a third-best policy.

A diagrammatic analysis of the optimum subsidy argument is presented in Figure 3.5.[9] Let there be external economies created in the import-competing industry. There is then a marginal divergence between private and social cost. This is represented in Figure 3.5 by noting that SS', the private money cost, exceeds ss', the social cost, by the proportion d of SS'. Under free trade, P_1 is the price, OQ_1 is home output, and Q_1Q_4 are imports. When $ss' < SS'$, this import-competing industry ideally should produce OQ_2, because at this output the marginal social cost of production would equal the marginal cost of imports. Therefore, there should be a subsidy on production at the rate d per unit, where d is the proportional excess of private over social cost. This raises P_1 to $P_2 = (1 + d)P_1$ for producers, and stimulates home output to OQ_2. The subsidy increases domestic output by Q_1Q_2, but consumers still pay P_1.

The social gain brought about by the subsidy can be calculated as follows. The social cost of the protected output is the area under the social marginal cost curve Q_1KLQ_2. The

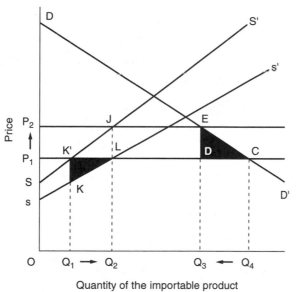

Quantity of the importable product

Figure 3.5. Optimum subsidy.
Pre-subsidy:
P_1 = free trade price; OQ_1 = home output; Q_1Q_4 = imports.

Post-subsidy:
Subsidy = P_1P_2 per unit, or *ad valorem* rate (d) of P_1P_2/OP_1; $P_2 = (1 + d)P_1$ = price for producers; P_1 = price for consumers; OQ_2 = optimum home output because at OQ_2 the marginal social cost of home output = marginal cost of imports (P_1); Q_1Q_2 = increase in home output; Q_1KLQ_2 = social cost of Q_1Q_2; $Q_1K'LQ_2$ = cost of imports replaced; $KK'L$ = social gain from subsidy. If the country had imposed a tariff at rate d, instead of an equivalent subsidy, the price would have risen from P_1 to P_2; imports would have decreased from Q_2Q_4 to Q_2Q_3; and the consumption loss would have been EDC as the result of the tariff.

[9] See Corden, *op. cit.,* 9–12.

value of the imports that are replaced is $Q_1 Q_2 \cdot P_1$ or $Q_1 K' L Q_2$. The import replacement cost is therefore less than the value of the imports by the shaded triangle $K K' L$.

The subsidy at the rate of $P_1 P_2$ per unit, or alternatively, the *ad valorem* rate $P_1 P_2 / O P_1$, is the optimal rate because a higher subsidy would reduce this total gain by stimulating home output to a point where the marginal social cost of production exceeds the marginal cost of imports (to the right of $O Q_2$), whereas a lower subsidy would cause home output to be at a point where the marginal social cost of import replacement is still less than the marginal cost of imports (to the left of $O Q_2$).

If the subsidy is financed by taxation, the redistributive effects of the subsidy are as follows: the taxpayers lose $P_2 J L P_1$; home producers gain $P_2 J K' P_1$; and the beneficiaries of the external economies created by the extra output gain $K' J L K$. There is a net gain to the country of the amount $K K' L$.

If the trade intervention had taken the form of a tariff, instead of a subsidy, the same production effect could have been realized, but a by-product distortion would be created in the form of a consumption loss. Thus, if the government had intervened with a tariff at the rate $d(P_1 P_2 / O P_1)$, the consumption loss would have been an increase in price to consumers from P_1 to P_2, a reduction in quantity demanded by $Q_4 Q_3$, and a loss in consumers' surplus by the shaded triangle *CED*.

The infant industry argument for intervention can be expressed best in terms of external economies, and hence, as a case of a domestic divergence justifying an optimum subsidy. The essential argument is that when an infant industry expands, it yields external economies over time by creating and diffusing knowledge or training labor that becomes freely available to other firms. The infant industry creates an asset from which other firms freely benefit. The social returns on the creation of long-term learning capital are then greater than the private returns, and the market would not provide enough of the activity that creates the external economy.

Sometimes the argument is mistakenly based on the premise that an industry suffers losses on an investment for a certain period and then realizes profits, at a later date, after the industry grows and overcomes the initial production difficulties. But this delay in the realization of profit does not in itself justify government protection. The initial investment will have private profitability if the future output allows the interest to be earned on the inital investment. The costs of growth, which are later recovered, can form part of normal market calculations and require no special subsidization. If, however, the capital market is imperfect and the social rate of discount is less than the current market rate of interest, then we have a situation that may justify a subsidy on the creation of long-term learning capital.

If, for example, a pioneer firm incurs expenses on acquiring knowledge, which is then available free to later entrants, there is a case for an optimal subsidy to the learning process. Similarly, one firm's investment can give rise to an externality if, in accordance with "learning by doing," productivity in the capital goods industry is a function of cumulative gross investment, so that if a firm invests more today, the return on any given level of investment undertaken by any firm tomorrow will be higher. An optimal subsidy on investment would then be justified. These cases indicate that the private market may underestimate the future benefits of an investment in the acquisition of knowledge. It is also possible that the private capital market overestimates the time preference for returns, with private firms desiring returns within a shorter period of time than would society, which may have greater concern for the future than has the firm. The social rate of discount is then less than the current market rate of interest, and the investment may be socially profitable even though privately unprofitable. Again, subsidization of investment would be appropriate.

In factor markets there is also a case for an optimum subsidy policy whenever there is a divergence between social and private marginal costs in factor use. A factor market imperfection will again cause $MRT_d \neq MRS = MRT_f$. A distortionary wage differential between activities for the same factor is a common instance of this, especially in less developed countries. The market wage in the advanced manufacturing sector of the economy tends to be greater than the alternative opportunity cost of labor in agriculture. When labor migrates from the rural to the urban sector, the sacrifice in agricultural output is less than the value of the manufacturing wage. The market price of the factor does not reflect the social cost of the input: a true accounting or shadow wage would be less than the actual wage facing the manufacturing sector. The result is that the price ratio understates the profitability of transforming agriculture into manufactures. The manufacturing sector, which is an import-competing sector, employs less labor than would be socially desirable. To offset the distortionary wage differential, the first-best policy would be a factor subsidy geared directly to the amount of labor employment provided by the import-competing firms. Second-best policy would be a subsidy on manufacturing production, and third-best a tariff to protect import-competing manufacturing firms. The production subsidy and tariff would shift production toward more manufacturing output, but it would not remove the wage differential, and therefore the economy would still operate on an inefficient production-possibility frontier. Moreover, the tariff would create an added consumption cost. A quota to protect the import-competing manufacturing firms would be fourth-best policy because of its additional consumption cost and physical limitation on imports.

In each of these cases, it is most desirable that the subsidy be directed as specifically as possible to the exact source of the externality. The optimal subsidy is geared to labor training or to investment in creation of knowledge or to labor employment—not simply

---

PROTECTING DUTIES

The only case in which, on mere principles of political economy, protecting duties can be defensible, is when they are imposed temporarily (especially in a young and rising nation) in hopes of naturalizing a foreign industry, in itself perfectly suitable to the circumstances of the country. The superiority of one country over another in a branch of production often arises only from having begun it sooner. . . . But it cannot be expected that individuals should, at their own risk, or rather to their certain loss, introduce a new manufacture, and bear the burden of carrying it on until the producers have been educated up to the level of those with whom the processes are traditional. A protecting duty, continued, for a reasonable time, might sometimes be the least inconvenient mode in which the nation can tax itself for the support of such an experiment.

John Stuart Mill, *Principles of Political Economy* (1848), Book V., Chap. 10.

a general subsidy to the firm. A general subsidy would not distinguish among production activities or type of factor inputs and hence would lead to some by-product distortion.

THE OPTIMAL AND THE ACTUAL

The welfare economist's canons may be honored more in the breach than in the observance. But if the quality of policy-making is to be improved, it is first necessary to identify the deviation between the ideal "first-best" policy and the actual practice.

In practice, the optimum tariff argument is only too likely to degenerate into retaliatory rounds of tariff increases. The process is harmful to all concerned. But as long as it remains in the individual interest of each country separately to raise tariffs, a collective attempt to arrest the process is ineffectual if not backed by international sanctions. Free trade is not a natural state for the world economy; it must be enforced by some international code of conduct.

There are also practical limits to the optimum subsidy argument. The calculation of external economies is obviously difficult. Furthermore, it is unlikely that in practice the subsidy can be financed by non-distortive, lump sum taxes and disbursed in a costless manner. If the act of financing the subsidy is likely to impose inevitable distortion and collection costs, then in practice it is not optimal to correct the original distortion completely or to use only a subsidy and not a tariff. A first-best policy must in practice also entail a first-best financing package. These costs in financing may weaken the case for a subsidy over a tariff. So too will subsidy-disbursement costs. But the size of these costs is really an empirical issue, requiring comparison of the collection and distortion costs for alternative financing packages. The subsidy can be provided directly from general tax revenue or by a decrease in government expenditure elsewhere or by a tax exemption, or a rebate of another tax for the industry to be subsidized, or by an increased tax on a competitive industry.

Without the empirical studies, there is, however, an initial popular bias in favor of a tariff over a subsidy. For a tariff taxes consumers and refunds part or all of the revenue to subsidize producers—thereby bringing about the collection and simultaneous disbursement in a less costly way than the financing of a subsidy. Moreover, the tariff subsidizes producers in a covert fashion. The protected industry tends to prefer this to a subsidy, which is explicit and therefore subject to continual budgetary review. For these reasons, the tariff, rather than the subsidy, is the prevalent form of trade intervention in practice.

GOVERNMENT FAILURE

(P)rotection might procure economic advantage in certain cases, if there was a government wise enough to discriminate those cases, and strong enough to confine itself to them; but this condition is very unlikely to be fulfilled.

F. Y. Edgeworth, "Theory of International Values," *Economic Journal*, 4 (March 1894): 48.

THEORY AND PRACTICE

Finally, something should be said about the bearing of theoretical analysis of the arguments for protection on practical policy-making and the assessment of actual tariff systems. The demonstration that in certain carefully defined circumstances a tariff levied at a theoretically specified rate would make a country better off than it would be under free trade is not—contrary to the implication of many economic writings on protection—equivalent to a demonstration that past or present tariffs have in fact made the nations imposing them better off than they would have been under free trade, or a justification of whatever tariffs legislators might choose to adopt. Modern economic analysis of the cases in which a tariff or other governmental intervention in the price system would improve economic welfare, in other words, does not constitute a defense of indiscriminate protectionism and a rejection of the market mechanism; rather, it points to a number of respects in which the market mechanism fails to work as it should, and indicates remedies designed to make the market function properly. The usefulness of the exercise depends precisely on the assumption that legislators do not normally know what makes for improvement of economic welfare, and would be prepared to act on better information if it could be provided. If economists did not customarily accept this assumption, their work on economic policy would have to be oriented entirely differently; in particular, research on commercial policy would—depending on the theory of government adopted—be concerned with inferring from actual tariff structures either the divergences between social and private costs and benefits discovered by the collective wisdom of the legislators to exist in the economy, or the political power of various economic groups in the community, as measured by their capacity to extort transfers of income from their fellow-citizens.

H. G. Johnson, "Optimal Trade Intervention in the Presence of Domestic Distortions," in R. E. Caves et al. (eds.), *Trade, Growth and the Balance of Payments* (1965), 8.

The infant industry argument is most likely to be misdirected in practice. Again the problem of estimating the magnitude of external economies and forecasting changes in cost conditions is formidable. And what is termed an infant industry in practice is not retricted to the demonstration of external economies, as it should be. Nor is the temporary condition of the protection respected: instead, the industry is likely to acquire a vested interest to be sheltered far into adulthood. Indeed, protection of senescent industries becomes even more widespread than protection of infant industries.

Finally, the welfare economist's canons are completely ignored when trade interventions are used for balance of payments purposes, employment creation, or non-economic objectives.

Not surprisingly, the gap between the ideal "first-best" policy and actual practice is indeed wide. But we must first understand the ideal and recognize the gap before there can be improvement.

GATT and the World Trade Organization

Introduction

For the past half-century, the major international institutional structure shaping trade policy has been the General Agreement on Tariffs and Trade (GATT), now incorporated in the World Trade Organization (WTO).

GATT attempted to establish a common code of national conduct in commercial policy, and it tried to facilitate the negotiation of multilateral trade agreements by indicating the rights and obligations of each trading nation and by providing a forum for the discussion and settlement of trade problems. The basic principles are those of reciprocity and nondiscrimination through most-favored nation treatment by which a member country agrees to levy the same tariff rates on imports from any other GATT member.

It is, however, a striking puzzle of the GATT legal system that the substantive obligations of the agreement form a long, complex, and carefully drafted instrument that is fairly rigorous in its demands, but at the same time, GATT's enforcement procedures are highly ambiguous and uncertain. The jurisprudence of GATT has been termed a "diplomat's jurisprudence," insofar as the GATT diplomats attempted to develop an approach toward law that tries to reconcile, on their own terms, the regulatory objectives of a conventional legal system with the turbulent realities of international trade affairs.[1]

The text of GATT is highly technical, consisting of many articles, supplemented by agreements. The major articles cover general most-favored nation treatment (Article I), antidumping and countervailing duties (Article VI), quantitative restrictions (Article XI), restrictions to safeguard the balance of payments (Article XII), subsidies (Article XVI), market safeguards (Article XIX), customs union and free trade areas (Articled XXIV), tariff negotiations (Article XXVIII), and trade and development (Article XXXVI).

Three broad principles underlie the various articles: (i) trade should be conducted on the basis of nondiscrimination with all contracting parties of GATT bound by the most-favored nation (MFN) clause in the application of import and export duties; (ii) protection of domestic industries should be exclusively through the customs tariff and not through other commercial measures, such as import quotas; (iii) there should be consultation among the parties to avoid damage to the trading interest of all contracting parties.

GATT has been most successful in negotiating tariff reductions. There have been eight rounds of multilateral trade negotiations, the last being the Uruguay round from 1986 to 1994. The negotiation process is as follows: The basic feature of the trade negotiations is a "concession"—that is, a promise either to lower the duty on a commodity and keep it at or

---

[1] R. E. Hudec, "The GATT Legal System: A Diplomat's Jurisprudence," *Journal of World Trade Law* (Sept.–Oct. 1970): 615–665.

[2] When Part IV on trade and development was added to GATT, an exception was made to this rule of reciprocity for less-developed countries.

110

below that level, or a promise not to raise the duty on that item. Concessions are negotiated usually with the principal supplier and then, in accordance with the most-favored nation principle, they are generalized to all suppliers. Before each negotiating session, countries prepare lists of their export products on which they seek tariff reductions. After receiving the lists of requests for concessions, each country prepares a list of responses or offers and submits it to GATT. The contracting parties then meet in a negotiating session in which multilateral bargaining ensues. The multilateral negotiating session concludes with the submission by each country of its revised tariff schedules including all those items on which concessions have been granted. When a concession on a product is granted it is referred to as "binding," and the duty on that product is said to be "bound." An important principle of the negotiating process has been that of reciprocity. Governments agree to reduce tariffs only in exchange for equally valuable tariff reductions by others, and any subsequent action that upsets the exchange is deemed an injury deserving some compensation equivalent to the value of the concession that is unbound.[2] Such compensation may take the form of either a concession by the offending party on another item of import or withdrawal by the injured party of the concession granted to the offending party. There is no explicit provision in the general agreement regarding the value of a concession, but the assumption has been that the value of a concession, or the breach of the concession, on a product is measured roughly by the amount of trade in that product moving to the importing country in a base period multiplied by the change in the rate of duty.

This approach to trade negotiations is not what a pure free trader would advocate. Instead of insisting on reciprocity, the free trade economist sees the gain from trade as being able to gain the importable at lower cost than if produced at home. Hence, unilateral liberalization of trade is to the country's benefit. For pragmatic political reasons, however, GATT introduced the condition of reciprocity: A country is more willing to reduce its trade barriers if other countries reduced theirs. Market access into a country will be granted if the country also gains market access for its exports into other countries.

Paul Krugman has interpreted this negotiating process in terms of "the principles of GATT-think":

> To make sense of international trade negotiations, one needs to remember three simple rules about the objectives of the negotiating countries:
>
> **(1)** *Exports are good.*
>
> **(2)** *Imports are bad.*
>
> **(3)** *Other things equal, an equal increase in imports and exports is good.*
>
> In other words, GATT-think is enlightened mercantilism. It is mercantilist in that it presumes that each country, acting on its own, would like to subsidize exports and restrict imports. But it is enlightened in that it recognizes that it is destructive if everyone does this, and it is a good thing if everyone agrees to expand trade by accepting each others' exports.
>
> GATT-think is also, to an economist, nonsense. In the first place, general equilibrium theory tells us that the trade balance has very little to do with trade policy. A country that restricts imports will indirectly be restricting its exports as well. So even if

one agreed with principles 1 and 2, one would argue that countries gain nothing from import restriction.

Nor do economists agree that exports are good and imports bad. The point of trade is to get useful things from other countries, that is, imports, which are a benefit, not a cost; the unfortunate necessity of sending other countries useful things in return, that is, exports, is a cost rather than a benefit.

Moreover, standard trade theory does not see export subsidies and import restrictions as similar policies. On the contrary, in general equilibrium an import tariff is equivalent to an export *tax*. Furthermore, in standard trade theory an export subsidy is a stupid policy but not a malicious one, since it generally worsens a country's terms of trade, and thus benefits the rest of the world. . . .

Finally, standard trade theory generally argues that free trade is the best *unilateral* policy, regardless of whether other countries do the same. That is, in standard theory one does not need to justify free trade in the context of international agreements. (The qualification is the optimal tariff argument, which generally plays no part at all in real-world trade discussion.)

In effect, GATT-think sees the trade policy problem as a Prisoners' Dilemma: Individually, countries have an incentive to be protectionist, yet collectively, they benefit from free trade. Standard trade theory does not agree. It asserts that it is in countries' unilateral interest to be free traders—as Bastiat put it, to be protectionist because other countries are, is to block up one's own harbors because other countries have rocky coasts.

Yet although GATT-think is economic nonsense, it is a very good model of what happens. Indeed, it is embedded in the very language of the negotiations. Suppose that the United States succeeds in pressuring the European Community to stop exporting wheat that costs it three times the world market price to produce, or Japan to take a little rice at one-tenth the cost of domestic production. In GATT parlance these would represent European and Japanese "concessions"—things that they would do unwillingly (and at present appear unwilling to do at all). That is, as GATT-think predicts, countries seem to treat exports—almost any exports, at almost any price—as desirable, and imports—no matter how much better or cheaper than the domestic substitute—as undesirable.

Moreover, over the years a trading system based on the principles of GATT-think has, on the whole, done very well. No amount of lecturing by economists on the virtues of free trade could have achieved the extraordinary dismantling of trade barriers accomplished by lawyers in the thirty years following World War II. If there are problems with the system now, they have more to do with perceptions that some countries are not playing by the rules than with a dissatisfaction of the political process with the rules themselves. . . .

The result of applying the principles of GATT-think has up to now been pretty good. The reason is the process of multilateral negotiation, which, in effect, sets each country's exporting interests as a counterweight to import-competing interests; as trade negotiators bargain for access to each others' markets, they move toward free trade despite their disregard for the gains from trade as economists understand them. . . . [3]

To encourage countries to offer trade concessions, GATT allowed some forms of contingent protection under specified conditions. Article XIX of GATT provides for market safeguards if as a result of a reduction in tariffs "any product is being imported . . . in such

---

[3] Paul Krugman, "The Move Toward Free Trade Zones," in *Policy Implications of Trade and Currency Zones: A Symposium* (Jackson Hole, Federal Reserve Bank of Kansas City), 1991.

increased quantities . . . as to cause or threaten serious injury to domestic producers of like or directly competitive products." Tariff concessions can then be withdrawn. Contingent protection can also be imposed through antidumping action and duties to countervail the effects in the domestic market of foreign subsidies, again provided that a domestic industry is injured.

Many countries, however, have circumvented Article XIX and imposed unilateral safeguards in the form of voluntary export restraints (VERs) or orderly marketing agreements (OMAs) to restrain imports. Most notable has been the United States's restrictions on semiconductors and automobiles from Japan. Instead of invoking Article XIX, countries have resorted to unilateral action because Article XIX requires the precedent condition of a tariff reduction, most-favored nation treatment in the withdrawal of a concession, and the withdrawal of substantially equivalent concessions by the other country. Since the 1970s, new protectionism in the form of unilateral administrative action imposing quantitative controls has spread.

The Uruguay round promoted more trade liberalization, extended the reach of GATT into new areas, refined some articles, established new agreements, and strengthened dispute settlement provisions. Developed countries agreed to reduce their tariffs on industrial goods by 40 percent, with the proportion of industrial products entering developed country markets under MFN zero duties more than doubling from 20 percent to 44 percent. In the four largest developed country markets in terms of imports from MFN sources, the average post-Uruguay round tariff on industrial products ranges from 1.7 percent (Japan) to 4.8 percent (Canada). Among the developing countries, India, Korea, and Singapore agreed to reduce their average tariffs on industrial products by more than half.

Greater market access was also achieved through increased bindings of tariffs—that is, agreement not to increase the tariff after it has been lowered. The percentage of industrial tariff lines bound rose from 78 percent to 99 percent for developed countries, from 21 percent to 73 percent for developing economies, and from 73 percent to 98 percent for transition economies.

The GATT secretariat estimates that this liberalization of trade in goods will increase world income by $510 billion per year by the time the market access commitments are fully implemented in 2005.[4]

Some liberalization of nontariff measures was also achieved. The most important quantitative measures scheduled for elimination are the restraints on textiles and clothing applied in the context of the Multifibre Arrangement (MFA). MFA restraints are to be phased out in a series of steps until 2005. Consumers in developed countries and exporters in developing countries should benefit from this trade liberalization.

The Uruguay round also made some revisions in Article XIX on market safeguards. The Agreement on Safeguards bans VERs, but enforcement will be difficult because the many forms of VERs are difficult to identify and because arrangements between industries can be made without the transparent involvement of governments. The agreement also restrains the use of Article XIX to imports "in such increased quantities, *absolute or relative to domestic production*." The italicized words have been added. The exporting country's right to compensation is restricted insofar as it cannot be exercised for the first three years that a safeguard measure is in effect, provided that the safeguard measure has been taken

---

[4] GATT Secretariat, *The Results of the Uruguay Round*, 10 November 1994.

as a result of an absolute increase in imports. The application of Article XIX is, however, tightened insofar as measures taken pursuant to it must be terminated within eight years of its first application. The agreement also calls for progressive liberalization at regular intervals during the period of application.

Antidumping legislation has been a gray area that GATT has not successfully defined or controlled. National action has varied and has frequently been contrary to GATT's vision of an open international trading system. This is because an opposite view of GATT's antidumping rules is that they should reflect the right of a national government to take action to protect its industries from certain forms of import competition. The Uruguay round's Antidumping Agreement remains equivocal on these two views. To limit antidumping actions, some procedural changes are made, a sunset clause is added, the requirement of injury is strengthened, and "domestic industry" is normally to refer to all domestic producers, not just one company. But governments still have a wide scope for antidumping actions to defend "legitimate interests."

As a leading trade analyst observes, "What is missing in this is not the scope for any government to take action, either anti-dumping action, or anti-anti-dumping action. What is missing is an objective standard of 'legitimate interest.' Anti-dumping will remain the instrument of choice for interests seeking relief from import competition. It would seem, however, that further negotiation to perfect an objective standard, or even an agreed standard, of 'legitimate interest' is a pipe dream. Anti-dumping is not a matter of 'legitimate interests,' it is a matter of practical politics. The 'objective'—to sensible people—is not 'better' antidumping actions, it is 'fewer.'

"One route to fewer follows the strategy of Asian martial arts: to use the enemy's strength against him. It will be very difficult to discipline anti-dumping because it has become an entitlement for protection-seeking interests, particularly in the United States. The Asian martial arts defense against this entitlement is not to attempt to throw it back, but to broaden it. The entitlement should be extended beyond import-competing interests, to consumers of goods that are imported as well as produced at home. An import-restricting action should not be taken unless its benefits to domestic interests exceed its costs to other domestic interests. These other domestic interests should have the same standing in law (GATT law as well as national law) and regulation as import-competing interests, including the entitlement to petition for removal of an import restriction."[5]

The Uruguay round also recognized new commercial realities by extending GATT rules within the WTO to these new areas: services, trade-related investment measures (TRIMs), and trade-related intellectual property rights (TRIPs). The promotion of liberalization of trade in services is of value to exporters of financial services, advertising, insurance, managerial and technical services, telecommunications, and transportation in rapidly expanding sectors of world trade that need to be subject to multilateral rules. So too is the agreement on TRIPS needed "to promote effective and adequate protection of intellectual property rights" while ensuring "that the measures and procedures do not themselves become barriers to legitimate trade." The agreement adopts the multilateral discipline of nondiscrimination and a commitment to transparency for minimum standards of protection

---

[5] "Subsidies and Countervailing Measures and Antidumping Agreements" by J. Michael Finger, in OECD Documents.

and guidelines to foster greater harmonization of rules and practices for protection of such intellectual property as copyrights, trademarks, industrial designs, and patents.

Negotiation on import barriers to agricultural products led to a 36 percent reduction in export subsidies and a decline of 18 percent in domestic support to agricultural producers. On several agricultural products, commitments were made for minimum market access, as nontariff barriers are to be converted into tariffs that will subsequently be reduced. And virtually 100 percent of agricultural product tariff lines will be bound. Most notable was the attempt to introduce market mechanisms into agricultural production and trade, but this met with limited success: Liberalization will come only slowly. Even by 2002, trade in temperate agricultural commodities will be significantly less liberal than is trade in manufactures now.

If the rule-oriented system of GATT is to be enforced, there obviously must be an effective mechanism for dispute settlement among the trading nations. The Uruguay round sought an improved mechanism that would be more transparent, predictable, and consistent. Agreement was reached on the establishment of a Dispute Settlement Body as part of the new WTO. The dispute settlement process now has these features:

1. It establishes a unified dispute settlement system for all parts of the GATT/WTO system, including the new subjects of services and intellectual property. Thus, controversies over which procedure to use will occur less frequently, if at all.

2. It reaffirms the right of a complaining government to have a panel process initiated, preventing blocking at that stage.

3. It more carefully outlines the steps of the procedure as follows:

   - First consultation must occur.
   - The parties can utilize "good offices" to help them achieve a settlement.
   - If there is a failure to agree then a panel can be requested.
   - The panel is usually three persons, and if agreement on its composition fails, the director general can impose a panel.
   - The panel proceeds as before, to receive oral and written advocacy.
   - Express provision is made for third-country advocacy (by nondisputants that have a legitimate interest).
   - The panel drafts its report and the rules call for certain consultation about it with the disputing parties.
   - The first panel examination normally is supposed to take no more than six months.

The WTO rules establish a new appellate procedure that will substitute for some of the council approval process of a panel report, and overcome blocking. A panel report will automatically be deemed adopted by the council unless it is appealed by one of the parties to the dispute. If appealed, the dispute will go to an appellate panel. After the appellate body has ruled, its report will go to the council, but in this case it will be deemed adopted unless there is a consensus *against* adoption, and presumably that negative consensus can be defeated by any major objector. Thus the presumption is reversed, compared with the previous procedures. The ultimate result of the new procedure is that the appellate report will in virtually every case come into force as a matter of international law.[6]

Members are required to use the dispute settlement mechanism when they seek redress for a violation of one of the agreements or nullification or impairment of the benefits of the agreements. The automatic nature of the new procedures should improve the enforcement of the substantive provisions in the agreements.[7]

The institutional arrangement and procedural structure for implementing the substantive rules of the Uruguay round have been embedded in the WTO. How the WTO implements the various agreements, deals with disputes, and relates to regional arrangements will be decisive for the future of the multilateral trading system.

THE WTO: WHAT IT IS, WHAT IT DOES

Introduction

THE WORLD TRADE ORGANIZATION (WTO) was established on 1 January 1995. It will take charge of administering the new global trade rules, agreed in the Uruguay Round, which took effect on the same day. These rules—achieved after seven years of negotiations among more than 120 countries—establish the rule of law in international trade, which for goods and services together are estimated to have approached some $5 trillion this year. Through the WTO agreements and market access commitments, world income is expected to rise by over $500 billion annually by the year 2005—and annual global trade growth will be as much as a quarter higher by the same year than it would otherwise have been.

HOW DIFFERENT IS IT FROM GATT?

- The WTO is more global in its membership than the GATT. Its prospective membership is already around 150 countries and territories, with many others considering accession.
- It has a far wider scope than its predecessor, bringing into the multilateral trading system, for the first time, trade in services, intellectual property protection, and investment.
- It is a full-fledged international organization in its own right while GATT was basically a provisional treaty serviced by an *ad hoc* Secretariat.
- It administers a unified package of agreements to which *all* members are committed. In contrast, the GATT framework includes many important side agreements (for example anti-dumping measures and subsidies) whose membership is limited to a few countries.

---

[6] OECD Documents, *The New World Trading System*, 1994, pp. 118–119.
[7] For an appraisal of the potential benefits for U.S. business as a result of the Uruguay round, see symposium in *Business America*, January 1994, pp. 4–27.

- It contains a much improved version of the original GATT rules plus a lot more. The new version, called GATT 1994, clarifies and strengthens the original GATT rules for trade in goods.
- It reverses policies of protection in certain "sensitive" areas which were more or less tolerated in the old GATT. Under various agreements, export restraints on textiles and clothing will be dismantled, trade in agriculture reformed and "grey-area" trade measures—so-called voluntary export restraints—phased out.

WHAT DOES IT DO?

The WTO administers, through various councils and committees, the many agreements contained in the Final Act of the Uruguay Round, plus a number of plurilateral agreements, notably on government procurement and civil aircraft. It also oversees the implementation of the significant tariff cuts (averaging 40 per cent) and reduction of non-tariff measures agreed to in the negotiations.

It is a watchdog of international trade, regularly examining the trade regimes of individual members. In its various bodies, members flag proposed or draft measures by others that can cause trade conflicts. Members are also required to notify various trade measures and statistics, which are maintained by the WTO in a large data base.

As in any partnership, conflicts can arise among members. The WTO, from the very start of these conflicts, provides several conciliation mechanisms for finding an amicable solution. Trade disputes that cannot be solved through bilateral talks are adjudicated under the WTO dispute settlement "court". Panels of independent experts are established to examine disputes in the light of WTO rules and provide rulings. This tougher, streamlined procedure ensures equal treatment for all trading partners and encourages members to live up to their obligations.

The WTO is also a management consultant for world trade. Its economists keep a close watch on the pulse of the global economy, and provide studies on the main trade issues of the day.

Finally, the WTO will be a forum where countries continuously negotiate exchanges of trade concessions to further lower trade barriers all over the world.

WHO IS IN IT?

ALL THE 128 MEMBERS of the old GATT automatically become WTO members upon acceptance of the Uruguay Round Agreements and submission of commitments on trade in goods and services. On the assumption that negotiations on the current membership applications of over 20 countries are ultimately concluded successfully, then the WTO will cover virtually the whole of world trade.

Participating and presiding over WTO meetings are representatives from members' diplomatic missions in Geneva and specialists from capitals.

The WTO Secretariat—numbering 420 of many nationalities—services all meetings of WTO bodies at its headquarters in Geneva. The Secretariat works witith developing countries and countries undertaking economic reform to help them negotiate accession and draw maximum benefit from the WTO.

WTO, *Focus*, no. 1, Jan.–Feb., 1995.

FREE TRADE TARGET DATE ESSENTIAL TO REMOVE "SPAGHETTI BOWL" OF BARRIERS

From Prof Jagdish Bhagwati, Prof Arvind Panagariya, and others.

Sir, Recently the idea that the World Trade Organisation should have a target, such as 2015, to achieve worldwide free trade has been proposed independently by many, among them principally by Martin Wolf in your newspaper. It has been endorsed by Mr Donald Johnston, OECD's secretary general, and by the UK's trade secretary, Ian Lang. There have also been indications of interest in the proposal by Mr Renato Ruggiero, director general, WTO.

As economists deeply interested in the future of the world trading system, and keeping in view the first WTO ministerial in December in Singapore and the opportunity it presents for undertaking a significant initiative on trade, we and a group of economists worldwide would like to lend our support to the idea and to urge the member states of the WTO to make the endorsement of such a WTO target their first priority. Among its advantages, a few are significant.

While consistent with Article 24 of the General Agreement on Tariffs and Trade, there are now so many preferential trade arrangements (PTAs) such as North American Free Trade Agreement and the European Union's numerous free trade areas with other countries, that a virtual "spaghetti bowl" of criss-crossing preferential trade barriers has arisen, with different duties applying depending on which country the product being imported is assigned to.

We are therefore in danger of reproducing the chaos created by the absence of most favoured nation status during the 1930s, produced then by protectionism but now, ironically, by free-trade intentions. Given the politics that often drives these PTAs, any attempts at reducing their spread do not seem to be likely to succeed. While some of us have indeed suggested reforms in Article 24, and in disciplines such as the use of anti-dumping duties on non-members, as ways of minimising the adverse effects of the preferences that the PTAs inherently imply, the worldwide achievement of free trade appears to be the most effective remedy. The reason is that preferences relative to zero duties are zero: preference would be effectively killed at source.

Then again a principal advantage of PTAs, which seems to attract trades-oriented businesses in particular, is that they offer target dates that will lead on schedule to ultimate free trade, albeit within a limited area. By contrast, the Gatt/WTO lurches from one round of multilateral trade negotiation to another, the end of a round never linked for sure to the start of another, as is in fact the case again with the end of the Uruguay Round.

A WTO target would thus cut through this fundamental weakness and simultaneously eliminate multilateralism's chief disadvantage vis-a-vis the inherently discriminatory PTAs, contributing to the current efforts at restoring the primacy of the WTO in the world trading system.

It would also set the WTO firmly on to the task of completing the agenda of worldwide free trade, an objective which Gatt pursued diligently through successive rounds of multilateral trade negotiations and whose advantages have been demonstrated by nearly half a century of experience.

Jagdish Bhagwati, Department of Economics, Columbia University, Arvind Panagariya, Centre for International Economics, University of Maryland. Letters to the Editor, *Financial Times*, June 25, 1996.

Antidumping and Countervailing Duty Cases

Table 3.5
Countervailing Cases Initiated, 1985–92

A	B		C		D		E		F		G	
			Against Exports From									
	Total Number of Cases[a]		**Industrialized Countries**[b]		**Eastern Europe (including former Soviet Union)**[b]		**Latin America Developing Countries**[b]		**Africa and Middle East Developing Countries**[b]		**Asian Developing Countries**[b]	
Initiating Country	No.	(%)	No.	(%)	No.	(%)	No.	(%)	No.	(%)	No.	(%)
Australia	278	(27)	144	(52)	15	(5)	22	(8)	10	(4)	87	(31)
Austria	4	(0)	0	(0)	4	(100)	0	(0)	0	(0)	0	(0)
Brazil	14	(1)	3	(21)	3	(21)	3	(21)	0	(0)	5	(36)
Canada	128	(12)	73	(57)	13	(10)	10	(8)	1	(1)	31	(24)
European Union	159	(15)	42	(26)	46	(29)	14	(9)	6	(4)	51	(32)
Finland	13	(1)	2	(15)	11	(85)	0	(0)	0	(0)	0	(0)
India	5	(0)	1	(20)	0	(0)	3	(60)	0	(0)	1	(20)
Japan	3	(0)	0	(0)	1	(33)	0	(0)	1	(33)	1	(33)
Korea	9	(1)	8	(89)	0	(0)	0	(0)	0	(0)	1	(11)
Mexico	63	(6)	37	(59)	0	(0)	10	(16)	0	(0)	16	(25)
New Zealand	31	(3)	7	(23)	0	(0)	0	(0)	0	(0)	24	(77)
Poland	24	(2)	24	(100)	0	(0)	0	(0)	0	(0)	0	(0)
Sweden	11	(1)	2	(18)	9	(82)	0	(0)	0	(0)	0	(0)
United States	298	(29)	131	(44)	30	(10)	45	(15)	12	(4)	80	(27)
Total All countries	1,040	(100)	474	(46)	132	(13)	107	(10)	30	(3)	297	(29)
Of which: Total developing countries[c]	91	(9)	49	(54)	3	(3)	16	(18)	0	(0)	23	(25)
Of which: Total industrialized countries[d]	949	(91)	425	(45)	129	(14)	91	(10)	30	(3)	274	(29)

Notes: [a]The total number of cases initiated (column B) by each country is the sum of the number of cases of all the exporting groups (i.e. columns C to G). Percentages in column b are percentages of the total number of cases for the initiating countries (i.e. of 1,040).

[b]Percentages in columns C to G are percentages of the total for the initiating country (given column B) and therefore do not add up to the 'total number of cases' percentages in column B.

[c]Includes Brazil, India, Korea and Mexico.

[d]Includes Australia, Austria, Canada, European Union, Finland, Japan, New Zealand, Poland, Sweden and the United States.

Source: GATT, *Basic Instruments and Selected Documents*, various issues.

Table 3.6
Numbers of Antidumping and Countervailing Duty Investigations in the United States, 1980–89

Year	Antidumping	CVD	Year	Antidumping	CVD
1980	37	69	1985	63	31
1981	15	17	1986	71	20
1982	65	116	1987	15	3
1983	46	8	1988	42	8
1984	74	26	1989	23	3
Total 1980–89	451	301			

Source: Richard Boltuck and Robert Litan (eds.), *Down in the Dumps* (Brookings Institution, Washington, DC, 1991).

Table 3.7
Target Industries of U.S. Antidumping and CVD Investigations, 1980–89

Industry	Antidumping	CVD
Chemicals	58	37
Food	16	45
Iron and steel	201	149
Leather	—	6
Machinery	8	6
Nonferrous metals	16	5
Oil country tubular goods	12	8
Textiles and apparel	15	6
Lumber	—	4
Other	125	35
All products	451	301

Source: Richard Boltuck and Robert Litan (eds.), *Down in the Dumps* (Brookings Institution, Washington, DC, 1991).

Table 3.8
Target Countries of United States Antidumping and Countervailing Duty Investigations, 1980–89

Country	Antidumping	CVD	Country	Antidumping	CVD
Belgium	10	17	India	3	3
Canada	25	18	Indonesia		1
Denmark		7	Malaysia	1	1
France	22	28	Pakistan		3
Greece	2	1	Philippines	1	1
Ireland	1	6	Thailand	3	
Italy	26	24	Argentina	6	
Luxembourg	6	13	Brazil	24	36
Netherlands	9	13	Chile	2	1
Portugal	3	1	Columbia	4	
Spain	15	21	Costa Rica	1	
United Kingdom	18	18	Ecuador	1	
West Germany	29	18	El Salvador	1	1
Economic community		3	Mexico	8	2
Austria	5	5	Peru	1	
Finland	4		Trinidad & Tobago	1	
Norway	1	1	Uruguay		1
Sweden	6	4	Venezuela	13	10
Switzerland	4		Iran	1	
Turkey	2	4	Israel	5	4
Australia	3	1	Kenya	1	
New Zealand	2	3	Czechoslovakia	2	
South Africa	7		East Germany	7	
Hong Kong	3		Hungary	4	
Japan	58	6	Poland	6	
Korea	27	17	Romania	9	
Singapore	6	1	Soviet Union	2	
Taiwan	28	7	Yugoslavia	5	
China	17				

Source: Richard Boltuck and Robert Litan (eds.), *Down in the Dumps* (Brookings Institution, Washington, DC, 1991).

Number of cases filed

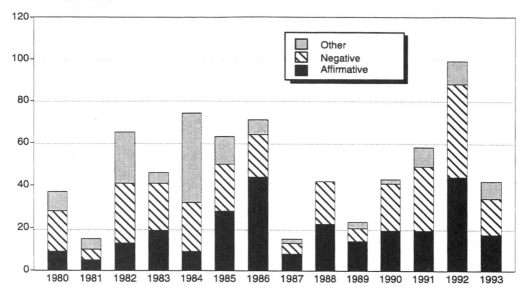

Figure 3.6 Antidumping case summary, United States, 1980–93. *Source*: U.S. International Trade Commission.

Number of cases filed

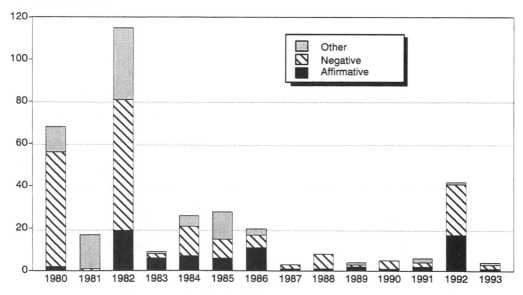

Source: U.S. International Trade Commission.
Figure 3.7 Countervailing duty case summary, United States, 1980–93. *Source*: U.S. International Trade Commission.

DISCUSSION QUESTIONS

1. The Uruguay round did not consider the relationships between trade and labor standards, or trade and the environment. What action, if any, would you advocate that the WTO take in these areas to induce countries to adopt social policy standards?

2. Would you expect the dispute settlement mechanism of the WTO to intensify or diminish the incidence of trade disputes? Intensify or diminish unilateral adoption of trade restrictions?

3. Will the outlawing of voluntary export restraints lead to an increase in the imposition of antidumping tariffs and countervailing duties on subsidized exports?

4. U.S. trade law provides four significant ways by which a domestic firm or industry may petition the U.S. government for protection against import competition:

   a. Escape clause or market safeguards (Section 201 cases)

   b. Antidumping

   c. Antisubsidy or countervailing duty

   d. Unfair import practices (Section 337 cases)

   In addition, Section 301 of U.S. trade law allows complaints by U.S. exporters against unfair treatment in foreign markets. It attacks foreign restrictions with the threat of more U.S. restrictions.

   Do you support these policies? How do these remedial policies relate to the provisions of GATT?

5. Although the Uruguay round continued the concept of special and differential treatment for developing countries, it limited such treatment and made it more time-bound than previously. After the end of a transitional period, LDCs are expected to adopt most of the same disciplines as the more developed countries. Do you believe that special and differential treatment should be accorded LDCs? If so, in what ways?

6. GATT is based on the principles of nondiscrimination and reciprocity in tariff bargaining; the notion that when protection is allowed in exceptional circumstances, it should be practiced by tariffs and not by nontariff barriers; the provision for compensatory action if the benefits from tariff reduction are subsequently modified; and regular arrangements for consultation among member countries as parties to the agreement.

   a. Do you think the unconditional most-favored nation principle has the effect of increasing or diminishing a country's willingness to reduce its tariffs? Is most-favored nation treatment the closest international parallel to "equal protection of the laws?" Should most-favored nation treatment be the universal principle for international trade negotiations?

   b. Do you think that the principle of reciprocity agrees with the free-trader's notion that the "gains from trade" are to be calculated on the side of less costly imports? Or is it actually reflective of a protectionist attitude that other countries should "pay for" the tariff-reducing country's "sacrifice" in having to import more?

   c. Consider the degree of strictness with which GATT treats quantitative restrictions, tariffs, and subsidies to domestic producers. Are all three devices contrary to free trade? Why are the devices treated differently?

    d. What are the enforcement powers of the WTO? Can there be freer trade without the provision of more international sanctions?

7.   a. The strategy of trade negotiations might be likened unto those in a "game." Do you think game theory illuminates any of the key decisions in trade negotiations? Or might the negotiations be better explained in the old-fashioned terms of "national power" and "personality" of the negotiators and political leaders?

    b. Another view would be to liken trade negotiations to a process of dispute settlement. The critical questions then are who shall decide the issues? By what standards? And under what procedures? Consider how these questions were answered in the Uruguay round negotiations.

    c. Were the crucial questions of the Uruguay round negotiations empirical in the sense that they could be answered by numerical data, or were they political insofar as they involved decisions about competing values?

    d. Does the prolonged and complex process of negotiations in the Uruguay round suggest that a more expeditious method of trade negotiations be instituted? What would you propose? The former director-general of GATT has suggested that future tariff negotiations could usefully take the form of attempts to reach global free trade in particular industries. But would the elimination of all tariffs in a particular industry generally by itself satisfy the principle of reciprocity?

Do you think that members of the world trading community are ready to de-emphasize the principle of reciprocity? If not, do you think it is possible to work out other procedures of negotiations that will allow the principle of reciprocity to be used in the direction of trade liberalization?

8. If a domestic industry suffers dislocation because the government lowers tariffs and imports rise, do you think it is legitimate to argue that the industry should receive adjustment assistance because the injured had invested and operated in reliance upon a certain governmental commercial policy?

    a. Would a similar argument apply to injury as the result of a change in monetary policy or fiscal policy? If you take a different view for commercial policy, why?

    b. If imports should rise—not because of a reduction in governmental protection, but simply because the imports become competitive—should relief in the form of governmental assistance still be given?

    c. Should adjustment be broadened to provide assistance to workers and firms engaged in production for export when there is a decline in the market for particular exports?

    d. If adjustment assistance does not take the form of an increase in tariffs or the imposition of quotas, does a foreign nation have any basis for objecting to the adjustment assistance?

Chapter

4 INTERNATIONAL CAPITAL FLOWS

T rade in assets on international financial markets has become increasingly important—and challenging—to private management and public management alike. This
chapter considers the remarkable growth in international money and capital markets,
the determinants of various types of international capital movements, the special significance of capital flows to developing countries, and the important policy issue of whether
world savings are adequate.

As with trade in goods and services, there are also gains from international trade
in financial assets. The international integration of national financial markets allows the
transferring of savings from one country to another where returns are higher. The lending
country gains. Clearly, a borrowing country that is short of domestic savings also gains if
it has access to the international capital market, thereby allowing it to increase its domestic
investment and enjoy a higher future income. Alternatively, a capital inflow may allow the
borrowing country to gain by consuming more currently than it can produce. An efficient
international capital market would be characterized by highly mobile capital that flows to
the most productive uses worldwide. The result would be another set of gains from trade
that result from intertemporal trade: Goods and services are presently being exchanged for
future goods and services, that is, for assets.[1]

For the individual investor, international trade in assets allows portfolio diversification
and hence reduces the riskiness of the return on the investor's wealth. And for the financial
manager of a firm, the integration and deepening of international money and capital markets
allow the manager to pursue more alternatives for raising capital and for protecting the value
of the firm's financial assets. Financial managers can also find profitable opportunities by
shopping the international markets.[2]

Moreover, as the IMF observes, "In addition to their traditional functions of chan-
neling resources from units that are net savers to those that are net dissavers, of providing
liquidity, and of allocating, pricing, and diversifying risk, international capital markets
have acquired increased clout as an indicator of the credibility of the government's actual

or prospective policies, as a disciplining mechanism for errant or inconsistent government policies, and as an impetus for reform of financial markets and practices in industrial and developing countries alike. But if international capital markets are to perform all these functions well—and to avoid the potential systemic risks that go along with increased size and integration—it is important that the supervisory and regulatory framework itself be sensitive and responsive to the changing structure of those markets, including their increasingly 'international' dimension."[3]

The growth of international trading in securities, bonds, and other debt instruments is closely related to the growth of international trade in goods and services. In part, this is because multinational enterprises in the global marketplace gain a competitive advantage not only through exports, but also through foreign investment. In many industries, as a manifestation of the need for a global strategy, trade and foreign investment are complementary. Since the 1970s, however, the rate of growth in lending and investing across national borders has been even more rapid than the growth in world trade.

INTERNATIONALIZATION OF FINANCIAL MARKETS

A rapidly changing world economy has stimulated the integration of financial markets and an increasing amount of international capital flows. The variety and amount of international capital movements have grown at a fast pace for a number of reasons: New types of financial markets have arisen, beginning with the inception of the Euromarkets in the 1960s. Fundamental reorganizations have occurred in the financial systems of the world centers of finance (New York, Tokyo, and London).[4] The barriers among national financial markets have been continually reduced as countries have liberalized their national financial markets by eliminating capital controls. There is increased mobility of capital across national borders as transaction costs fall with advances in telecommunication and computers. Securities-market facilities are also expanding rapidly, allowing ever-increasing sales of stocks and bonds directly to foreign buyers without the participation of banks.

As a result of these changes, national money and capital markets are increasingly influenced by international financial intermediaries, foreign assets, foreign investors, and conditions in other national financial markets. Especially significant now are short-term capital movements (foreign bank deposits and securities with less than a year's maturity), international portfolio investment (purchase of stocks and bonds without control of the issuing enterprise), cross-border sovereign lending to foreign governments by commercial banks, more private foreign debt and equity financing in developing countries, and more private foreign direct investment (FDI, exercising control of the enterprise).

By 1991, estimates of some of the amounts of international capital flows were $7.5 trillion a year for international bank lending, and approximately $2½ trillion a year for cross-border ownership of debt and equity holdings.[5] In 1995, receipts of investment income on U.S. assets held abroad were nearly $183 billion, while payments of income on foreign-owned assets in the United States were over $190 billion.

The growth of international financial markets is reflected in the rapid increase in transactions on international currency markets. Cross-border financial transactions in most industrial countries expanded from less than 10 percent of GDP in 1980 to in excess of 100 percent of GDP by the early 1990s (see Table 4.1). Since the late 1980s, the foreign exchange (forex) business has attracted investment institutions with huge portfolios of assets and capital, as well as the large numbers of commercial banks and large corporations that trade currencies for their own books. Overall, the flows generated by investment institutions are far greater than those of banks. Now trading activity often exceeds $1 trillion a day in the global forex spot market, a twenty-five-fold increase since 1980.[6] This huge increase in turnover makes it increasingly difficult for a central bank to control its foreign exchange rate by intervening on the exchange markets with its only limited amount of foreign reserves.

TYPES OF CAPITAL FLOWS

The major categories of capital flow transactions are official or private and short term or long term. Consider transactions in financial assets between U.S. residents and residents of foreign countries.[7] U.S. official capital flows include changes in the reserves of U.S. monetary authorities in monetary gold, foreign exchange, special drawing rights (SDRs) at the IMF, and loans and credits to foreigners by U.S. government agencies. Changes in foreign official assets in the United States occur through transactions in U.S. Treasury securities, other U.S. government obligations, and bank deposits, as well as U.S. corporate bonds and stocks.

Private capital flows encompass foreign direct investment and portfolio investment undertaken by both American residents abroad and foreigners in the United States. The U.S. government defines a direct investment as "the ownership or control, directly or indirectly, by one person of 10 per centum or more of the voting securities of an incorporated business enterprise or an equivalent interest in an unincorporated business enterprise." Portfolio investment is defined to include "any international investment which is not direct investment." All investment transactions between parent organizations and their foreign affiliates are direct investment flows. Portfolio investment primarily refers to ownership of financial securities, broadly defined to include sales and purchases of securities and amounts of outstanding claims and liabilities reported by banks and nonbanking concerns.

In the next chapter we shall consider the balance of payments accounts. In these accounts incomes on direct and portfolio investment are reported in the current account; exchanges in financial assets between U.S. and foreign residents are measured in the capital account. The value of accumulated stocks of U.S. assets abroad and of foreign assets in the United States—resulting from capital flows in and out of the United States over time—is compiled in the statement of U.S. international investment position (see Tables 4.2 and 4.3).

TABLE 4.1
Cross-Border Securities Transactions (as a percent of GDP)

	1980	1992
United States	9.3	109.4
Japan	7.0	69.9
Germany	7.5	91.2
France	8.0	122.0
Italy	1.1	118.4
United Kingdom	266.0	1015.8
Canada	9.6	113.1

Source: IMF, *World Economic Outlook*, May 1995, p. 80.

TABLE 4.2
U.S. Net International Investment Position

End of Year	$ Billions		Percent of GDP	
	At Current Cost	At Market Value	At Current Cost	At Market Value
1982	379	265	11.9	8.3
1987	−23	58	−.5	1.2
1990	−251	−224	−4.5	−4.0
1993	−556	−508	−8.6	−7.8

Source: Department of Commerce, *Survey of Current Business*, annual.

TABLE 4.3
Summary Components of the U.S. Net International Investment Position ($ Billions)

	1994	1995
Net position		
At current cost	−580.1	−814.0
At current stock-market value	−492.5	−773.7
U.S. government and foreign official assets	−301.3	−420.3
Direct investment		
At current cost	199.5	241.6
At market value	287.0	281.9
U.S. and foreign securities	−463.2	−665.8
Bank- and nonbank-reported claims and liabilities	−15.0	30.5

Source: Department of Commerce, *Survey of Current Business*, January 1997, D-61.

The value of foreign-held assets in the United States continues to exceed the value of U.S. assets abroad. Foreign private and official holdings of U.S. bonds are especially large. For direct investment, however, U.S. assets abroad continue to exceed foreign assets in the United States.

A significant episode in the evolution of international capital markets was the formation of the Eurodollar market in the 1960s. To escape the regulations of national monetary authorities, holders of dollars—and later holders of other strong currencies—deposited them in Eurocurrency markets—i.e., money markets outside the borders of the national currencies. The Eurocurrency market has become the major international money market.

Transactions in Eurocurrency markets involve mainly short-term capital movements, the dominant instruments being certificates of deposit, time deposits, and bank loans. When banks intermediate Eurodollar deposits between depositors and borrowers who are citizens of different nationalities, there is a short-term capital outflow from the depositor's country to the borrower's country.

In the 1970s, after OPEC countries invested their petrodollars in Euromarket bank deposits, international banks had considerable amounts of liquidity to recycle through syndicated bank loans from the Euromarkets to developing countries. The rate of interest on bank credits is normally some margin over LIBOR—the London Interbank Offer Rate—depending on the credit rating of the borrower. These flows peaked with the debt crisis in the early 1980s. Official bank lending to developing countries then rose to partially offset the decline in private lending. In the 1990s, private flows to developing countries increased, and foreign direct investment and portfolio investment in developing countries now constitute a growing share of global capital movements.

As the long-term counterpart of the Eurocurrency market, the Eurobond market is a long-term (normally ten- or twenty-year maturities) market for bonds denominated in a currency other than that of the country where the market is located. For the growth in foreign bond markets and Eurobond markets, see Table 4.8 in the Statistical Appendix.

The foreign exchange market is the major international money market. An extended analysis of the determinants of foreign exchange rates and their relation to balance-of-payments policy will be presented in the next chapter. Here we should note that the bulk of foreign exchange trading involves international flows of short-term capital as commercial banks facilitate the exchange of interest-bearing bank deposits.

With international economic integration and the removal of restrictions in financial markets, short-term capital movements have increased markedly. Foreign exchange can be viewed as an asset, and the demand for a foreign currency bank deposit or a foreign short-term security is determined by the same considerations as for any other asset—namely, its expected real rate of return, the risk involved, and the asset's degree of liquidity. Holders change their desired asset holdings according to changes in the levels of interest rates, exchange rates, and size of portfolio. Individuals and institutional investors balance their portfolio holdings according to their estimates of expected rates of return on various assets, and their degree of aversion to risk. The changes in portfolio balance will lead to financial capital movements.

The foreign demand for assets denominated in the currency of a given country will be determined by the expected yield on that country's assets relative to the expected yield on assets denominated in other currencies. This expected relative yield reflects the interest rate differential between the home country and the foreign country, and the expected movement in the exchange rate. Exchange rate risks and the risk preferences of speculators will determine the degree of substitutability between assets denominated in domestic currency and assets denominated in foreign currencies. The degree of substitutability will determine, in turn, the elasticity of demand for domestic currency assets with respect to their expected relative yield. The change in the demand for foreign assets during a given time period will depend on changes in the interest rate differential and in the expected exchange rate depreciation or appreciation. A rise in a foreign currency's interest rate tends to attract an inflow of short-term capital, provided that the investor does not expect the foreign currency to depreciate in the future and reduce the real rate of return in terms of the investor's currency.

In determining one's portfolio balance, a prospective lender of financial capital (purchaser of a foreign security) will estimate the range of possible yields on a foreign security after converting the payments of interest into domestic currency, allowing for the possibility of depreciation in the foreign currency during the period until maturity of the security. To hedge against the risk of depreciation, the lender can buy forward "cover" on the forward exchange market against the risk that a future change in the exchange rate might affect the capital value of the investor's holdings of foreign assets. The forward market provides contracts of varying maturities for the future delivery of a currency. By selling expected foreign exchange rate forward, the lender can be assured of the amount of domestic currency that will be received thirty or ninety or 180 days hence. Short-term capital flows quickly in response to interest rate differentials among countries in order to hedge against or speculate on foreign exchange rate movements.[8] Considering the relative returns from a domestic security and a foreign security, an investor would find covered interest arbitrage profitable if the proportionately higher interest yield on a foreign security exceeds the proportional discount on the foreign currency in the forward exchange market.

If the foreign currency on the forward exchange market is trading at a sufficiently high forward premium, it may still be profitable to invest in foreign securities even though the foreign rate of interest is below the domestic rate. Interest arbitrageurs and currency arbitrageurs operate on the differentials, engaging in transactions from a cheap market to a dear one. Besides arbitrageurs, there may be speculators on the forward markets, and these may drive the forward rate to a margin that is considerably different from what would have been determined by only the arbitrageurs.

Based on the foregoing considerations, economists have propounded an asset-market theory of exchange-rate determination. This approach views the exchange rate as an asset price—the relative price at which the stock of money, bonds, and other financial and real assets of a country will be willingly held by domestic and foreign asset holders. Variability in the factors that influence expected rates of return or relative risk will therefore tend to result in variability of exchange rates in a regime of floating rates. Only when the actual stocks of domestic and foreign assets that are held are equal to the desired stocks will the current demand for and current supply of a currency establish a flow equilibrium. In a short period of time, the potential demand for a currency resulting from changes in desired stocks of financial assets can be large relative to the flow demand that arises from current account transactions. This is because prices in goods markets normally change more gradually, there are longer lags in the adjustment of commodity trade to price changes, and the expectational factors are not as prominent as they are for financial transactions.

The asset-market theory is primarily directed to the short-run determinants of the exchange rate. Other forces operate to determine the longer-run equilibrium rate. Shifts in interest differentials and changes in risk preferences of participants in the foreign exchange markets can therefore lead to sizable movements in short-run exchange rates that are inconsistent with effective adjustments in the longer run. Perhaps the major value of recognizing the influence of financial capital flows and portfolio changes is in devising policies of exchange-rate management to reduce the instability arising from the short-run asset-market disturbances and to indicate policy action that can reduce the short-run variability from the appropriate level for longer-run equilibrium.

The asset-market approach is also mainly relevant for countries that have financially deep capital and money markets and an absence of exchange controls so as to permit substantial arbitrage between domestic and foreign assets. In countries with thin financial markets, or limited possibilities for arbitrage, the exchange rate will be determined slightly by financial capital flows, but mainly by supply and demand in good markets (under freely floating rates) and the amount of official intervention in currency markets (under managed floating). See the next chapter regarding balance-of-payments policy.

INTERNATIONAL PORTFOLIO EQUITY INVESTMENT

Portfolio equity investment across borders has also grown as investors have sought international diversification for maximum risk-adjusted returns. Table 4.4 shows the dramatic expansion of net international equity trading. In 1993, U.S. investors provided most of the

TABLE 4.4
Net Cross-Border Equity Flows ($ Billions)

	1986	1987	1988	1989	1990	1991	1992	1993[1]
Investor from								
North America	3.68	−2.18	4.03	21.04	12.03	48.25	46.39	70.90
United States	2.61	−2.68	1.95	19.00	10.26	43.31	41.99	66.40
Canada	1.07	0.50	2.08	2.04	1.77	4.94	4.40	4.50
Japan	8.15	16.87	2.99	·17.89	6.26	3.63	−2.73	15.30
Europe	21.32	9.42	14.29	38.40	4.58	39.55	7.56	45.20
Of which:								
United Kingdom	8.85	3.77	9.66	24.16	−0.88	25.84	−2.96	24.20
Emerging markets	1.48	−5.73	1.47	0.79	−5.47	6.58	2.57	21.50
Pacific rim	0.79	−5.39	1.31	−0.61	−5.79	5.49	−3.78	12.50
Latin America	0.47	−0.42	0.09	1.49	0.30	0.53	6.33	7.50
Other[2]	0.22	0.08	0.07	−0.09	0.02	0.56	0.02	1.50
Rest of world	7.35	−1.95	10.07	8.48	−14.22	2.62	−0.62	6.30
Australia	0.60	0.92	1.44	2.08	−1.31	2.71	−0.59	1.50
Other	6.75	−2.87	8.63	6.40	−12.91	−0.09	−0.03	4.80
Equity from								
North America	19.82	20.26	−3.69	13.80	−15.89	9.60	−3.95	28.60
United States	19.11	16.47	−1.39	11.42	−14.61	11.02	−4.20	21.10
Canada	0.71	3.79	−2.30	2.38	−1.28	−1.42	0.25	7.50
Japan	−15.76	−42.84	6.81	7.00	−13.28	46.83	8.96	20.00
Europe	33.38	29.67	22.75	47.11	15.29	23.35	24.83	56.10
Of which:								
United Kingdom	7.83	19.50	9.72	11.24	5.35	5.84	10.08	19.60
Emerging markets	3.34	5.88	3.47	10.07	13.16	15.78	22.45	52.00
Pacific rim	3.43	6.03	2.45	3.36	3.89	4.73	10.95	30.00
Latin America	0.20	0.43	0.72	6.98	9.89	11.15	9.64	20.00
Other[2]	−0.29	−0.58	0.30	−0.27	−0.62	−0.10	1.86	2.00
Rest of world	1.20	3.46	3.51	8.63	3.90	5.06	0.87	2.50
Australia	0.76	2.16	3.76	0.96	1.48	1.86	0.15	2.00
Other	0.44	1.30	−0.25	7.67	2.42	3.20	0.72	0.50
Total	41.98	16.43	32.85	86.60	3.18	100.63	53.17	159.20

[1]Data for 1993 are estimates.
[2]Africa, Middle East, and Eastern Europe.
Source: IMF, *International Capital Markets*, 1994, p. 71.

demand, investing an unprecedented $66 billion in foreign equity while receiving an inflow from sales to foreign investors of $21 billion. European markets benefited the most from international portfolio flows with sales to foreign investors of $56 billion in 1993. As large and recurring government fiscal deficits in the industrial countries have raised the ratios of government debt to GDP, there has been a strong trend toward increasing the nonresident ownership of government debt. For the major industrial countries as a group, the ratio of general government debt to GDP was about 43 percent in 1980, but had risen to 68 percent in 1994. Given the size of their debt, governments cannot rely on only domestic investors but have had to turn to institutional investors overseas.

Most recently, the emerging stock markets in developing countries have become an attractive feature of global integration. See Figure 4.1. In 1990, there were 232 emerging market funds worldwide, with total net assets of $14 billion. By mid-1995, their number had increased almost sixfold, with estimated net assets of about $123 billion. Most attractive have been the emerging markets in East Asia and Argentina, Brazil, and Mexico in Latin

America. The combined capitalization of emerging equity markets—the market value of the equity of quoted firms—increased from less than $100 billion at the end of 1983 to nearly $1 trillion in 1993. Expressed as a ratio to GDP, market capitalization in Chile, Hong Kong, Malaysia, and Singapore exceeds that in the United Kingdom or the United States.[9]

To the foreign investor, the attraction of emerging markets is the prospect of higher returns. The opportunity of cross-country diversification also reduces overall portfolio risk. As the developing countries continue to grow and their money and capital markets deepen, investors will be increasingly attracted to the emerging markets. Considerable potential exists for an increase in supply of funds into emerging markets. This is because of the very low percentage of institutional money (mutual funds, pension funds and insurance companies' investable surplus) that is already in developing markets: less than 1 percent for U.S. institutional investors, and perhaps 5 percent for U.K. investors (see Figure 4.2). Even small absolute increases in these numbers would yield very large percentage increases in investable resources.[10]

Emerging markets contribute to the mobilization of domestic and foreign savings in the developing economies by deepening financial markets and broadening the financial instruments for investors who wish to diversify their portfolios. The inflow of external equity finance reduces reliance on external debt, thereby making the developing country less vulnerable to increases in international interest rates and to problems of debt servicing. Growth of the private sector and the accumulation of capital leading to increases in productivity in the private sector can be promoted by higher capitalization, liquidity, or turnover on the nation's stock exchange.

Large portfolio inflows may, however, be volatile and potentially destabilizing in financial markets and the economy.[11] We discuss (pp. 144–46) the problem of managing volatile capital inflows. The case study of the Mexican devaluation (pp. 208–24) also relates to this policy problem.

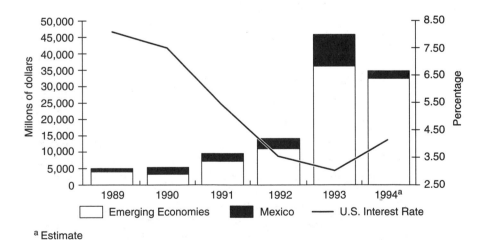

a Estimate

Figure 4.1 Resources attracted by emerging economies and the U.S. interest rate. *Source*: Economic Research Department of BANAMEX. Based on data provided by the International Monetary Fund, and from the *International Financing Review*.

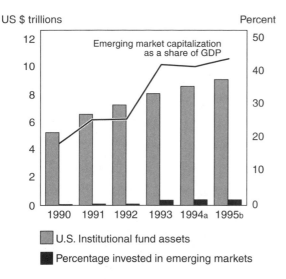

US $ trillions   Percent

Figure 4.2 Growing emerging markets set to attract greater foreign institutional investment. *Source*: IMF, *International Capital Markets*, 1995, p. 20.

■ U.S. Institutional fund assets

■ Percentage invested in emerging markets

Note: U.S. institutional funds include pension funds, life insurance companies, non-life insurance companies, and mutual funds. The market capitalization ratio includes the countries covered in the IFC's 1994 emerging market index, excluding Portugal and Taiwan (China). It is a weighted average of the total stock market capitalization of emerging markets over their total GDP.

a. Estimated.

b. Preliminary.

To realize further gains from the integration of their emerging stock markets, developing countries still have to lower barriers to equity flows in their countries. A study has shown that poor credit ratings, high and variable inflation, and exchange rate controls are barriers that have a high rank-correlation with measures of lack of market integration. So too are the lack of a high-quality regulatory and accounting framework and the limited size of some stock markets.[12]

FOREIGN DIRECT INVESTMENT AND MULTINATIONAL CORPORATIONS

The flow of foreign direct investment has intensified in recent years as more companies have expanded across borders by making foreign acquisitions and mergers and investing in greenfield sites. See Figure 4.3. Between 1983 and 1988, FDI worldwide rose by more than 20 percent annually, four times faster than world trade. By the early 1990s, annual flows of FDI amounted to around $230 billion, with the stock of this investment having reached some $1.7 trillion. Table 4.5 indicates the global pattern of FDI. For the OECD countries, inflows of FDI exceeded $200 billion in 1995 (50 percent higher than 1994), and outflows rose by 40 percent to over $250 billion, an all-time high. The United States invested $97 billion abroad in 1995, and received inflows of $74 billion.

The increase in FDI is being undertaken mainly by multinational corporations (MNCs)—not only for activities in industrial countries, but also in developing countries

TABLE 4.5
Global Pattern of Direct Investment

	1976–80	1981–85	1986–90	1991	1992	1993	1994[1]
			($ billions, annual averages)				
Total outflows	39.7	43.2	167.7	187.1	179.4	199.0	233.5
Industrial countries	39.0	41.4	158.6	177.7	161.4	168.4	197.8
of which: United States	16.9	7.6	25.3	31.3	41.0	57.9	58.4
Japan	2.3	5.1	32.1	30.7	17.2	13.7	17.9
United Kingdom	7.8	9.2	28.1	16.4	19.4	25.7	30.0
Other Europe	10.0	15.1	63.9	91.3	80.2	63.2	80.1
Developing countries[2]	0.8	1.8	9.1	9.5	18.0	30.5	35.7
of which: Asia	0.1	1.1	7.8	7.2	15.3	26.4	30.2
Latin America	0.2	0.2	0.6	1.3	0.8	2.2	2.9
Total inflows	31.8	55.3	152.4	152.0	153.2	177.4	239.7
Industrial countries	25.3	36.2	126.8	108.7	94.8	96.8	135.1
of which: United States	9.0	18.6	53.4	26.1	9.9	21.4	60.1
Japan	0.1	0.3	0.3	1.4	2.7	0.1	0.9
United Kingdom	5.6	4.3	21.7	16.1	16.5	14.6	10.9
Other Europe	8.7	9.9	38.8	57.5	55.7	52.4	51.5
Developing countries[2]	6.4	19.1	25.6	43.3	58.4	80.6	104.6
of which: China	—	1.0[3]	3.1	4.4	11.2	25.8	33.8
Other Asia	2.1	4.6	12.1	20.5	26.2	25.5	33.3
Latin America	3.6	5.6	6.6	11.2	12.6	16.1	25.9

[1]Preliminary.
[2]Including Eastern Europe.
[3]1982–85.
Source: Bank for International Settlements, 65th Annual Report (Basle, 1995), p. 66.

and transition economies. More than 30,000 firms own or control assets in more than one country through equity arrangements, and those firms own or control more than 150,000 foreign affiliates.[13]

Why does a firm make a decision to engage in direct investment overseas? The firm has various modes of entry into a foreign country: exporting, licensing, a sales branch, production subcontracting, and finally, direct production investment.[14] Why would a firm then decide on direct investment overseas to produce output or secure inputs, instead of using markets to export its final product, import inputs, or license its technology?

The motives for FDI are varied, relating to both considerations at a microeconomic or firm level and to the macroeconomic and political environment in which the investment is to be implemented.

Foreign investment may readily become a part of competitive strategy in oligopolistic industries (a few large competitors) where a firm reacts to the moves of another firm in the industry. In such an industry, foreign investment may be undertaken to gain control over an input and thereby to create a barrier to entry of new competitors. The foreign investment may also be undertaken as a reaction to a competitor's move in a foreign country: The investment is an attempt to match the leader and maintain market share.

More generally, analysts identify four main motives for foreign direct investment:

- To acquire natural resources, the price of which is lower and/or the quality is higher than in the investing country.

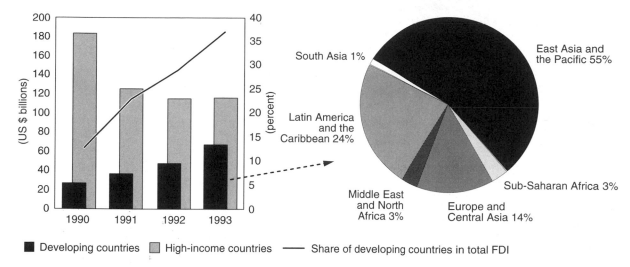

Figure 4.3 Global foreign direct investment, 1990–93. *Source:* World Bank staff estimates based on balance-of-payments data reported by the International Monetary Fund and data on net foreign investment reported by the Organization for Economic Co-operation and Development.

- To service foreign markets, particularly in the country in which the investment is being made.

- To restructure existing foreign value-added activities, so as to improve overall efficiency and change the range of products produced.

- To acquire assets that might be complementary to existing assets, or competitive to them, so as to reduce risk, capture the economies of scale or synergy, or generally strengthen the acquiring firms' competitive position in national or world markets.[15]

A so-called "eclectic theory" of FDI offers a fuller explanation of these motives. This theory—abbreviated as OLI—is based on ownership-specific advantages (O) and location-specific advantages (L) of the MNC. These advantages allow the MNC to realize additional profits overseas by internalizing (I) various activities through FDI. The combined elements of the theory of OLI advantages explain why an MNC chooses the route of FDI over alternative modes of entry into a foreign country, and why the MNC can gain a competitive advantage over domestic firms in the foreign country.[16]

Ownership (O) advantages stem from specific endowments internal to the multinational that gives the firm three kinds of advantages. The first comprises those that any firm may have over another producing in the same location—advantages that stem from size, monopoly power, and better resource capability and usage. The second and third kinds of O advantage arise from the ability of enterprises to coordinate the interaction among separate but complementary activities better than the market can. The second advantage is that which a branch plant of a national enterprise may enjoy over a domestic enterprise when the branch plant can benefit from many of the endowments of the parent company at zero or low marginal costs—for example, access to cheaper inputs, knowledge of markets, centralized accounting procedures, administrative experience. The third type of advantage arises specifically from the multinationality of a company, and is an extension of the other two. The larger the number of, and the greater the differences between, the economic environments in which an enterprise operates, the better placed it is to take advantage of different country-specific characteristics and risk profiles.[17]

The O advantages stem mainly from intangible assets, such as superior technology, innovative capacity, and product differentiation. As competition is a function of innovation and product differentiation, this leads to more foreign direct investment. The capital investment allows the transfer of other resources than capital—namely, technology, management, organizational and marketing skills (and it is the expected return on these owner-specific advantages, rather than simply on the capital, that prompts enterprises to become multinational enterprises investing overseas). The capital investment becomes a conduit for the transfer of other resources, and it is on these other resources associated with proprietary knowledge that the multinational enjoys additional rents.

Given the ownership advantages, it is more beneficial for the multinational possessing these advantages to use them itself rather than to sell or lease them to foreign firms. It realizes the internalization (I) advantages by placing these transactions within the organization instead of relying on transactions at arm's length in markets. If markets were perfectly competitive, transactions through the market mechanism could not be improved upon; but once there are imperfections in the market mechanism, internalization becomes a better form of organizing the transactions. Internalization of transactions become more profitable when there are barriers to competition and economic rents can be earned, when transaction costs are high, or when the economies of interdependent activities cannot be fully captured. Internalization advantages are frequently a matter of the international economics of information. There is often an inherent informational asymmetry when the multinational owns proprietary knowledge. The multinational may benefit from retaining its knowledge by internalizing transactions instead of transacting at arm's length on markets by selling the knowledge to another firm and thereby losing its monopoly advantage.[18]

Given O advantages and I advantages, it is in the global interest of the enterprise to utilize these advantages outside its home country by investing overseas rather than by serving foreign markets entirely by exports and domestic markets by domestic production. These are the locational (L) advantages of countries. Location advantages are related to decision making at the macroeconomic level. The international economic and political environment—the international context in its widest sense—is equally important in shaping the MNC's decision to invest abroad. Locational advantages are a part of this international contextual analysis. But also important are the macroeconomic levels and rates of growth of national income in the host country and the source country. Econometric studies conclude that the GNP growth is especially significant.[19]

Policies undertaken by the host country's government may also affect the MNC's operations. Especially important for locating its investment in a developing country is the firm's reaction to public policies that restrict or welcome FDI.

Based on internalization advantages, location advantages, and ownership advantages, FDI allows the investor to profit from a competitive advantage in creating, exporting, and capturing private returns on information and new technologies. While this analysis describes generally the determinants of FDI, it does not indicate why a specific country will receive the investment over another country. Recent research on the determinants of foreign direct investment from the United States is informative on this issue. Relative costs influence location decisions, but low direct labor costs are not of as much importance as is commonly

THE ECLECTIC PARADIGM OF INTERNATIONAL PRODUCTION

1. Ownership-Specific Advantages (of enterprise of one nationality (or affiliates of same) over those of another)

Hierarchical-Related Advantages	Alliance or Network-Related Advantages
a. Property right and/or intangible asset advantages (Oa). Product innovations, production management, organizational and marketing systems, innovatory capacity, non-codifiable knowledge: "bank" of human capital experience; marketing, finance, know-how, etc. b. Advantages of common governance, i.e., of organizing Oa with complementary assets (Ot). (i) Those that branch plants of established enterprises may enjoy over de novo firms. Those due mainly to size, product diversity and learning experiences of enterprise, e.g., economies of scope and specialization. Exclusive or favored access to inputs, e.g., labor, natural resources, finance, information. Ability to obtain inputs on favored terms (due, e.g., to size or monopsonistic influence). Ability of parent company to conclude productive and cooperative inter-firm relationships e.g., as between Japanese auto assemblers and their suppliers. Exclusive or favored access to product markets. Access to resources of parent company at marginal cost. Synergistic economies (not only in production, but in purchasing, marketing, finance, etc., arrangements). (ii) Which specifically arise because of multinationality. Multinationality enhances operational flexibility by offering wider opportunities for arbitraging, production shifting and global sourcing of inputs. More favored access to and/or better knowledge about international markets, e.g., for information, finance, labor etc. Ability to take advantage of geographic differences in factor endowments, government intervention, markets, etc. Ability to diversify or reduce risks, e.g., in different currency areas, and creation of options and/or political and cultural scenarios. Ability to learn from societal differences in organizational and managerial processes and systems. Balancing economies of integration with ability to respond to differences in country-specific needs and advantages.	a. *Vertical Alliances* (i) Backward access to R&D, design engineering and training facilities of suppliers. Regular input by them on problem solving and product innovation on the consequences of projected new production processes for component design and manufacturing. New insights into, and monitoring of, developments in materials, and how they might impact on existing products and production processes. (ii) Forward access to industrial customers, new markets, marketing techniques and distribution channels, particularly in unfamiliar locations or where products need to be adapted to meet local supply capabilities and markets. Advice by customers on product design and performance. Help in strategic market positioning. b. *Horizontal Alliances* Access to complementary technologies and innovatory capacity. Access to additional capabilities to capture benefits of technology fusion, and to identify new uses for related technologies. Encapsulation of learning and development times. Such inter-firm interaction often generates its own knowledge feedback mechanisms and path dependencies. c. *Networks* (i) of similar firms Reduced transaction and coordination costs arising from better dissemination and interpretation of knowledge and information, and from mutual support and cooperation between members of network. Improved knowledge about process and product development and markets. Multiple, yet complementary, inputs into innovatory developments and exploitation of new markets. Access to embedded knowledge of members of networks. Opportunities to develop 'niche' R&D strategies; shared learning and training experiences, e.g., as in the case of cooperative research associations. Networks may also help promote uniform product standards and other collective advantages. (ii) business districts As per (i) plus spatial agglomerative economies, e.g., labor market pooling. Access to clusters of specialized intermediate inputs, and linkages with knowledge-based institutions, e.g., universities, technological spill-overs.

2. Internalization Incentive Advantages (i.e., to circumvent or exploit market failure)

Hierarchical-Related Advantages	Alliance or Network-Related Advantages
Avoidance of search and negotiating costs.	While, in some cases, time limited inter-firm cooperative relationships may be a substitute for FDI; in others, they may add to the I incentive advantages of the participating hierarchies, R&D alliances and networking which may help strengthen the overall competitiveness of the participating firms. Moreover, the growing structural integration of the world economy is requiring firms to go outside their immediate boundaries to capture the complex realities of know-how trading and knowledge exchange in innovation, particularly where intangible assets are tacit and need to speedily adapt competitive enhancing strategies to structural change.
To avoid costs of moral hazard, information asymmetries and adverse selection; and to protect reputation of internalizing firm.	
To avoid cost of broken contracts and ensuing litigation.	
Buyer uncertainty (about nature and value of inputs (e.g., technology) being sold).	
When market does not permit price discrimination.	
Need of seller to protect quality of intermediate or final products.	
To capture economies of interdependent activities (see b. above).	Alliances or network related advantages are those which prompt a 'voice' rather than an 'exit' response to market failure; they also allow many of the advantages of internalization without the inflexibility, bureaucratic or risk-related costs associated with it. Such quasi-internalization is likely to be most successful in cultures in which trust, forbearances, reciprocity and consensus politics are at a premium. It suggests that firms are more appropriately likened to archipelagos linked by causeways rather than self-contained 'islands' of conscious power. At the same time, flagship or lead MNCs, by orchestrating the use of mobile O advantages and immobile advantages, enhance their role as arbitragers of complementary cross-border value-added activities.
To compensate for absence of future markets.	
To avoid or exploit government intervention (e.g., quotas, tariffs, price controls, tax differences, etc.)	
To control supplies and conditions of sale of inputs (including technology).	
To control market outlets (including those which might be used by competitors).	
To be able to engage in practices, e.g., cross-subsidization, predatory pricing, leads and lags, transfer pricing, etc. as a competitive (or anti-competitive) strategy.	

3. Location-Specific Variables (these may favor home or host countries)

Hierarchical-Related Advantages	Alliance or Network-Related Advantages
Spatial distribution of natural and created resource endowments and markets.	The L-specific advantages of alliances arise essentially from the presence of a portfolio of immobile local complementary assets, which, when organized within a framework of alliances and networks, produce a stimulating and productive industrial atmosphere. The extent and type of business districts, industrial or science parks and the external economies they offer participating firms are examples of these advantages which over time may allow foreign affiliates and cross-border alliances and network relationships to better tap into, and exploit, the comparative technological and organizational advantages of host countries. Networks may also help reduce the information asymmetries and likelihood of opportunism in imperfect markets. They may also create local institutional thickness, intelligent regions and social embeddedness [Amin and Thrift 1994].
Input prices, quality and productivity, e.g. labor, energy, materials, components, semi-finished goods.	
International transport and communication costs.	
Investment incentives and disincentives (including performance requirements, etc.).	
Artificial barriers (e.g. import controls) to trade in goods.	
Societal and infrastructure provisions (commercial, legal, educational, transport, and communication).	
Cross-country ideological, language, cultural, business, political, etc. differences.	
Economies of centralization of R&D production and marketing.	
Economic system and policies of government: the institutional framework for resource allocation.	

Source: John Dunning, "Reappraising the Eclectic Paradigm in an Age of Alliance Capitalism," *Journal of International Business Studies* (1995), pp. 475–76.

believed. In many industries, direct labor costs now account for only 10 percent to 15 percent of manufacturing costs, and the share is even smaller in some industries. In contrast, because white-collar and supervisory labor costs have been rising in the more developed countries, it has become increasingly attractive to invest in countries that offer a well-educated pool of labor. (The software industry in India is one example.) As multinationals transfer ever more sophisticated production lines to developing countries, the availability and cost of skilled labor becomes of growing importance.

Market size is also significant in affecting location decisions. Larger economies have attracted the bulk of FDI. This is because of the potential for local sales and also the existence of more diverse resources that make local sourcing more feasible. In the smaller economies, FDI usually concentrates on production for export. In relation to their size, the smaller developing countries have actually attracted more foreign investment than have the larger ones.

There is also somewhat of a herd effect with would-be investors following where others are already operating successfully. Further, as more firms invest in a country, synergies and linkages develop among them. Regional concentration, as in South China, may result.

For understandable reasons, the quality of a country's physical infrastructure will also influence location, as will the general degree of industrialization, especially for investment in the more technical industries.

The research on FDI from the United States therefore concludes that foreign investors are strongly influenced by structural factors such as market size, the quality of infrastructure, the level of industrialization, and the size of the existing stock of FDI.

The growth of MNCs tends to promote more foreign investment because, as we have seen (pp. 53–55), the MNC is also a unit of integration in the world economy. As long as goods are freely traded, the profit-maximizing MNC has an incentive to locate where opportunity costs are lowest—that is, according to a country's comparative advantage. Empirical studies conclude that comparative advantage of the factor proportions type (H-O theory in Chapter 2) is a statistically significant determinant of the location of inward FDI.[20]

POLITICAL RISK

Once entry is secured, and conditions of performance specified, the foreign investor still runs the risk of renegotiation, abrogation of some concessions, or changes in governmental policies. To assess the noncommercial risks, it is necessary to practice political risk analysis. A "political assessment function" has to be incorporated in an international firm to establish managerial contingencies generated by the political environment. Political events and political forces may cause a loss to the firm's cash flow or returns. Managers worry in a vague and general way about "the investment climate or the business environment," but these are empty boxes that must be filled with content by more rigorous political risk analysis.

The political risk is not so much that of a dramatic revolution type or macro changes affecting ownership, but rather more of a micro character affecting operations. Revolutionary changes involving social and political upheaval that lead to nationalization or confiscation are relatively rare occurrences. If on entry, the negotiation process between host government and foreign investor has resulted in a development contract with a payoff to each party, this can be the best guarantee against nationalization or expropriation as long as the government gains the benefits that it expected from the foreign investment. Political risk analysis can anticipate the coup or revolutionary type of widespread change by focusing on trends in the distribution of income, unemployment, asset distribution, ethnic and racial tensions, political participation, and political legitimacy. The major task of political risk analysis, however, is not to identify the relatively rare upheavals such as those that follow an election as in Chile in 1971 or a revolution as in Cuba in 1959 that may lead to the expropriation of most, if not all, foreign-owned firms. Instead, the major task of political risk analysis is to identify the politically generated managerial contingencies in routine policy making by the government.

Empirical studies show that the number of major discontinuities that significantly affected the operations of foreign firms in the past three decades is limited. In the vast majority of instances, the impact of politics on firms varies widely, even given the same environmental scenario; it is a function of industry- , firm- , and even project-specific characteristics. The relationship between environment and firm varies in accordance with strategy, organizational structure, and managerial style.[21]

In most countries the impact of political events varies from firm to firm and from project to project. It is of a micro character and normally affects operations rather than termination of ownership.[22] The most frequent political risk is a change in public policy that might entail partial divestment, price controls, changes in taxation, foreign exchange remittance restrictions, local content rules, labor law revisions, or changes in tariffs and quotas. These policies do not relate to a general "investment climate" but are industry specific, firm specific, or even project specific. They are far short of nationalization or confiscation, but they do affect cash flows and returns.

The object of political risk analysis should be to mitigate these noncommercial risks caused by political change. How can this be done? To meet the risk of changes in public policies that would have adverse impact on the firm, the investor should try to reduce exposure, share the risk with others, or create deterrent structures. At the outset, the forestalling of political vulnerability is closely related to the bargaining power of the foreign investor. The degree of bargaining power is, in turn, dependent on certain characteristics of the investment project. These characteristics lead to certain likely outcomes independent of the ideology or political regime in the host country. The greater is the firm's bargaining power, the less likely is the investment to be vulnerable to political factors. A number of studies have determined those characteristics of an investment that will give the investor greater bargaining power and ensure less political vulnerability. These are:

- The bargaining power tends to be greater, the larger the size of the required fixed investment.
- The higher is the technical intensity of production.
- The higher is the marketing intensity of production (marketing companies whose sales are determined to a large degree by brand identification and consumer loyalty occupy a strong position vis-à-vis host governments).
- The higher is the managerial intensity of production.
- The less is the extent of competition among investors (more investors mean more

alternatives for host authorities to choose from and more rivals to play off against one another, thereby increasing the strength of the host government).[23]

These characteristics of the foreign firm and its investment projects may allow the foreign investor to gain more generous terms at the outset. Over time, however, to avoid increasing vulnerability during a long payback period, it is necessary to continue to demonstrate a high benefit cost ratio to the host government. As long as the host country remains serious about accelerating its development, the continual beneficial economic performance of foreign investment will be the decisive determinant of the investment security. The ultimate source of security resides in the underlying community of interests between investor and host government. The protection of private foreign investment rests less in legal doctrines than in a benefit–cost analysis of the economic realities of the development process.[24] (For more on this analysis see Chapter 8.)

CAPITAL FLOWS TO DEVELOPING COUNTRIES

Although the preponderance of international capital flows is among the major industrial countries, the flows to developing countries have increased markedly in recent years. And in so doing, they raise significant policy issues for private investors, recipient governments, the World Bank, and the IMF. As our later discussion of developing countries will explain in more detail (Chapter 8), a less-developed country normally experiences a shortage of savings to cover planned investment. In macro economic terms, when government expenditure plus private investment exceeds government revenue and private savings, there is a "savings gap" that constitutes a "resource gap." This internal balance will spill over into an external imbalance of imports greater than exports, and hence constitute a foreign exchange gap. International financial intermediation is then required to fill the foreign exchange gap with an inflow of foreign capital. This can be accomplished by loans from a multilending agency such as the World Bank and commercial banks, or by private foreign investment.

This two-gap analysis of savings and foreign exchange is based on the relationship between national income analysis and the balance of payments, as we shall see in detail in the next chapter. For now, suffice to recognize that a net capital inflow contributes to the filling of the savings gap and the foreign exchange gap. The inflow increases the amount of resources available for capital formation above what can be provided by domestic saving. As long as a development program emphasizes investment, and home savings are deficient, there will be a need for an increased supply of long-term capital from overseas. To finance the foreign exchange gap and allow imports to be greater than exports, the country must rely on foreign savings that enter the country through the international capital flows. This is as true for Mexico as for Brazil—and just as true for the United States when it has a net governmental fiscal deficit and domestic private savings fall short of domestic private investment. Foreign savings must make up the deficiency of domestic savings.

International capital flows to developing countries are both public and private, composed of foreign aid (official development assistance), commercial bank loans, foreign direct investment, and international portfolio investment. A major change in the 1990s was the increase in the volume of private capital flows to developing countries, far surpassing official flows from governments and multilateral institutions. See Table 4.6 and Figure 4.4.

In 1995, private capital flows accounted for three-quarters of the total net resource flows to developing countries, up from 43 percent in 1990. Official development finance (comprising grants and bilateral and multilateral loans) amounted to $55 billion in 1994, while private flows were $173 billion. Most of the official development assistance has been going to the lowest income countries, such as those in Africa. Developing countries with higher per capita income have been expanding their access to international capital markets.[25]

Commercial bank lending to governments in less-developed countries raises important policy issues. Beginning in the 1970s, with the large increase in petrodollar deposits, commercial banks undertook Eurocurrency syndicated loans to the governments of developing countries. Their external debt doubled between 1973 and 1977, and then doubled again by 1981. The total debt burden of developing countries continued to rise from $836 billion in 1982 to nearly $1.3 trillion in 1990. More than two thirds of that increase was due to a rise in official debt to governments and to international financial institutions. By the

TABLE 4.6
Aggregate Net Long-term Resource Flows to Developing Countries, 1990–96 ($ billions)

Type of flow	1990	1991	1992	1993	1994	1995	1996[a]
Aggregate net resource flows	100.6	122.5	146.0	212.0	207.0	237.2	284.6
Official development finance	56.3	65.6	55.4	55.0	45.7	53.0	40.8
Grants	29.2	37.3	31.6	29.3	32.4	32.6	31.3
Loans	27.1	28.3	23.9	25.7	13.2	20.4	9.5
Bilateral	11.6	13.3	11.3	10.3	2.9	9.4	−5.6
Multilateral	15.5	15.0	12.5	15.4	10.3	11.1	15.0
Total private flows	44.4	56.9	90.6	157.1	161.3	184.2	243.8
Debt flows	16.6	16.2	35.9	44.9	44.9	56.6	88.6
Commercial banks	3.0	2.8	12.5	−0.3	11.0	26.5	34.2
Bonds	2.3	10.1	9.9	35.9	29.3	28.5	46.1
Others	11.3	3.3	13.5	9.2	4.6	1.7	8.3
Foreign direct investment	24.5	33.5	43.6	67.2	83.7	95.5	109.5
Portfolio equity flows	3.2	7.2	11.0	45.0	32.7	32.1	45.7

Note: Developing countries are defined as low- and middle-income countries with 1995 per capita incomes of less than $765 (low) and $9,385 (middle).
[a]Preliminary.
Source: World Bank Debtor Reporting System. World Bank, *Global Development Finance* 1997, (Washington, DC, 1997), p. 3.

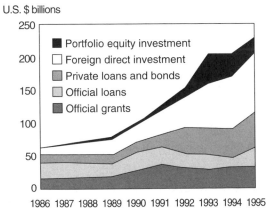

U.S. $ billions

■ Portfolio equity investment
□ Foreign direct investment
▓ Private loans and bonds
░ Official loans
▒ Official grants

Figure 4.4 Aggregate net resource flows to developing countries reached a record $231 billion in 1995. *Source:* World Bank, *World Debt Tables* 1996, p. 3.

end of 1982, however, U.S. banks had lent 176 percent of bank capital to Latin America alone, and 287 percent of bank capital to all developing countries. In 1990, Africa's debt to commercial banks was $35 billion, Latin America's bank debt was $242 billion (rising from $18 billion in 1982), and Asia's bank debt was $124 billion (up from $82 billion in 1982).

The legacy of the commercial bank loans to Latin American countries in the 1970s and 1980s now constitutes the "MBA problem"—the problem of managing the external debts of Mexico, Brazil, and Argentina. Other countries have similar problems, but the magnitude of debt servicing from Latin American countries is especially large.

In the 1970s and 1980s, the capital markets of Latin American economies were not attractive for foreign savings in the form of a short-term capital inflow. Nor was private foreign investment in real property or business enterprises sufficient to cover the shortfall in domestic savings. And the amounts of foreign aid plus loans from the World Bank and regional development banks were inadequate to support growth targets. The developing countries therefore turned to the commercial banks for Eurocurrency loans.

If only their growth rates had been sufficiently high in the 1970s and 1980s, and if a rise in domestic private saving and government revenue had progressively closed the savings gap, the debtor countries would have been able to manage their debt servicing without default. But in the most heavily indebted countries, inappropriate governmental policies limited national economic growth rates, and the rise in government expenditure continued to outstrip government revenue. Added to the inappropriateness of domestic policies were adverse external shocks in the early 1980s—an international recession, falling primary commodity prices, deterioration of the developing countries' terms of trade, and increasing real interest rates on external debts. Moreover, the growth of private lending declined sharply in 1982, as net commercial bank lending to the developing countries (that is, new lending minus repayment of principal) fell from $43 billion in 1981 to $22 billion in 1982. Net lending in 1982 was not enough to cover interest payments. In the second half of 1982, for the first time net lending was negative. A debt crisis occurred in the early 1980s. With a sharp fall in commercial bank lending, developing countries then had to cut their imports, reduce investment, lower real wages, create unemployment, and limit their growth—resulting in Latin America's lost decade of the 1980s.

It can be argued that if initially the commercial banks had correctly assessed the country risk of these cross-border sovereign loans, they would not have had to deal with rescheduling problems as they have since the early 1980s. But only slowly have the techniques of country risk analysis been refined and appreciated. Meanwhile, too many loans went to projects that appeared financially profitable in local currency, but turned out to be operating in an economy that could not raise sufficient foreign exchange to service the loans internationally. The risk that had to be analyzed was not corporate risk, but *country* risk. And this called for lenders to undertake a less familiar type of macroeconomic analysis beyond the usual microanalysis of project feasibility and the project's financial return on investment. Now it is recognized that a debt service problem is a balance-of-payments problem and that this in turn stems from inappropriate development policies in the debtor country.

Table 4.6 shows international capital flows to all the developing countries, 1990–96. Along with the trends already noted, it is evident that new lending from commercial creditors (commercial banks and suppliers) is low. Unlike the 1970s and early 1980s, the developing countries are not now relying on commercial banks for sovereign loans. Many countries, however, have a legacy of an external debt problem from earlier loans. After some necessary background analysis of the balance of payments in the next chapter, we shall return in Chapter 8 to this problem of managing external debt.

While commercial banks are now less willing to engage in cross-border sovereign lending to developing countries, the countries are more receptive to foreign direct investment (FDI). It is understandable why developing countries now desire to increase the equity/debt ratio on foreign capital: There are some relative advantages of FDI over foreign loans from the standpoint of balance-of-payments adjustment. Equity investment requires payments only when it earns a profit, but debt requires payments irrespective of the state of the economy. The host government can also control payments on FDI, whereas the terms for the servicing of external debt are set in international markets. In contrast to the need to service debt (amortization as well as interest), earnings from private foreign investment are frequently reinvested and only a part repatriated. Moreover, the maturity structures of the earnings from a direct investment and payments on its financing tend to be more closely matched, thereby avoiding the liquidity problem that arises when countries borrow short term to finance long-term investment. With private FDI, both the commercial risk and the exchange rate risk are passed on to the investor, rather than having to be borne by the host government.

In Chapter 8, we shall undertake a social benefit-cost analysis of FDI in developing countries. From that perspective, we shall also analyze the negotiating process between foreign investor and host government.

For more empirical evidence of the capital flows to LDCs, see the Statistical Appendix of this chapter.

MANAGING CAPITAL INFLOWS

Emerging markets—the domestically expanding stock markets in developing countries—have recently attracted large capital inflows. Foreign investors increased their annual net investment in emerging markets from less than $4 billion in 1990 to approximately $40 billion in 1994. Private portfolio investment in developing countries has increased as a share of the capital inflow into these countries. The capital movement has been attracted by the prospect of higher returns and as a means to reduce overall portfolio risk. Governments have also encouraged more investment by liberalizing or eliminating capital restrictions in both source and recipient countries and by emphasizing international private equity investment as an alternative to more debt in developing countries. Given the relatively small percent of equity securities from developing countries in the typical portfolio of large and institutional investors in the more-developed countries, the potential for large capital inflows in the developing countries is high.

A large inflow of private equity capital can, however, create adjustment problems for the recipient country. Unlike FDI, the portfolio type of capital is short term, highly volatile, and possibly reversible. The inflow may be only to take advantage of one-time gains as the host country undertakes policy reforms, and an outflow can occur abruptly and rapidly in response to rising interest rates in other countries or as a result of sensitivity to political instability and to any loss in policy credibility.

Beyond its volatility, the capital inflow may feed inflation and cause a real exchange rate appreciation. The foreign exchange rate is the price of one currency in terms of another and should reflect the purchasing power of the two currencies. The nominal exchange rate should then adjust to offset a differential in the rates of inflation in the two countries. When a government, however, chooses to fix its exchange rate and when inflation is higher in that country than in its trading partners, the fixing of the exchange rate may lead to an overvaluation of the currency in real (or purchasing power) terms. The value in local purchasing power of a country's foreign currency cash flows will then be decreased by an appreciation in the real exchange rate. The firm's ability to compete in international markets will also be diminished. Valuation of the country's exchange rate may result in a current account deficit in the balance of payments as exports decrease and imports increase. Although the capital inflow may be offsetting a current account deficit, the loss of credibility in the country's national economic management and increasing uncertainty by investors can force a devaluation crisis as the country overexpands its money supply, begins to lose foreign exchange reserves, experiences capital flight, and the inflow of foreign capital falls. Once a market attack on the domestic currency occurs, the central bank may not have sufficient reserves to fight the market. If the assets held by foreigners are indexed to hard foreign currency (dollars), there will be a loss of official reserves. When the foreigners convert the local currency (pesos) into the foreign currency (dollars), the government will have to increase interest rates in an attempt to induce the foreigners to hold their assets, or reduce the domestic money supply to reduce the demand for imports, or devalue the local currency (peso). Policy issues are illustrated in Policy Profile 5.1 on the Mexican devaluation at the end of the next chapter.

In many developing countries, experience has demonstrated the difficulty of maintaining a fixed exchange rate, or an exchange rate within a narrow band in the face of open capital markets. Countries confront an adjustment problem when they incur inflation and appreciation in the real exchange rate. Efforts at trade liberalization are also jeopardized. And economic growth is stalled.

Policies are needed to manage the repercussions of the capital flows. National policy measures in the recipient countries may attempt to avoid monetizing the inflow and to follow a tight fiscal policy. To prevent a rapid expansion of the money supply and to protect the exchange rate from appreciation, the government may sell domestic bonds to absorb the liquidity when it buys foreign exchange. This policy of sterilization of short-term inflows tends, however, to keep interest rates high. Under a fixed exchange rate regime, capital inflows are then likely to persist, and countries eventually have to seek other measures to accommodate the sustained inflows. Many Asian countries have therefore attempted to control their fiscal deficits to avoid the upward pressure on domestic interest rates that may induce shorter-term inflows. Fiscal policy, however, is generally not sufficiently flexible to deal with the volatility of short-term fluctuations in international capital flows.

As late as the mid-1990s, South Korea chose not to liberalize its financial markets and open the bond market fully until the differential between the Korean and international interest rates had narrowed sufficiently to make a destabilizing inflow unlikely. Chile has widened the band within which its currency can fluctuate, and has discouraged capital inflows with a special stamp tax and high minimum reserve requirements on foreign credits. The government has also instituted a minimum requirement of holding assets at least one year within the country. Several Asian countries have also restricted foreign borrowing by domestic companies and instituted higher reserve requirements on foreign capital inflows. Because they can be imposed quickly and easily, many countries resort to restrictions on the capital inflow, such as ceilings on foreign borrowing, minimum reserve requirements on foreign loans, and interest rate equalization taxes.[26]

A unique proposal by Nobel laureate James Tobin advocates an international tax on foreign exchange transactions.[27] The so-called Tobin tax has two main objectives to reduce volatility in exchange rates caused by short-run speculation and to defend the autonomy of national macroeconomic and monetary policies against the growing internationalization of money markets. The tax, say 1 percent, on spot conversions of one currency into another, would drive a wedge between short-term interest rates in different national markets and thereby reduce the international mobility of short-term capital that is not based on fundamentals. The revenue that is raised could be devoted to international purposes.

Objections to the Tobin tax center on whether the objectives would be achieved, on practical feasibility issues, on asset substitution to avoid the tax, and on the possible superiority of alternative measures to control speculative pressure on exchange rates.

Controls on capital mobility, however, go against the most efficient use of capital in the world economy. These national measures should be only temporary and the international financial community should seek better ways to meet the problem of volatility and reversibility through policies other than simply stopping the inflow to prevent a future outflow. Longer-term solutions are needed. The box on p. 147 summarizes some policies to manage capital flows. The fundamental question remains whether there should be new institutional international arrangements such as an IMF stabilization fund that might operate as a safety net and exercise more effective surveillance of exchange rates and national policies in order to manage international financial crises in today's world. In contrast, some, such as MIT's Rudiger Dornbusch, worry about "moral hazard" if there is so much collective defense against a currency crisis that it weakens individual defenses. As Dornbusch maintains, it may be better that capital importing countries and private investors "have to be made to understand they are on their own."[28]

ARE WORLD SAVINGS ADEQUATE?

In macroeconomic terms, the significance of international capital flows is that the savings of the capital-exporting country are being channeled into real capital accumulation (FDI) or financial investment (portfolio investment) in the capital-receiving country. International financial intermediaries are transferring the resources—i.e., savings—from one country to another. The net real capital transfer—the net resource transfer—comes to the recipient country through imports being greater than exports in its current account balance of payments. (For more on this see the next chapter on the balance of payments.) If, then, there is to be a "sufficient" flow of international capital, there must first be a "sufficient" amount of savings.

The question of the adequacy of world savings is therefore of major concern in the changing global economy. If productivity is to increase, and the real rate of world economic growth is to be satisfactory, there must be sufficient investment financed by a sufficient supply of saving. Demands on the supply of savings have increased not only in industrial countries because of the deficit in the public sector that absorbs private savings, but also

TOOLS FOR MANAGING CAPITAL FLOWS

Sound macroeconomic policy keeps inflation under control, encourages productive investment, and minimizes distortions in both internal and external transactions. Within such a framework, authorities have a wide variety of tools for managing capital flows. Indirect instruments are consistent with overall liberalization programs and are generally more effective than direct interventions.

LONG-TERM POLICIES

- Macroeconomic policy balance that favors relatively tighter fiscal policy and somewhat more relaxed monetary policy
- Liberalization of external and domestic trade
- Positive investment climate, with minimal restrictions on foreign ownership of assets
- Promotion of high domestic saving
- Relatively wide intervention bands on the exchange rate, with periodic revisions if needed
- Support for a strong financial sector, with foreign participation
- Sound prudential regulation and enforcement in financial and capital markets
- Free capital movement in both directions
- Collection and dissemination of information by rating agencies and other means
- Reduction or elimination of government financial guarantees
- Encouragement of private hedging markets, with adequate prudential regulation

SHORT-TERM POLICIES FOR DEALING WITH PRECIPITOUS FLOWS

- Sterilization of "excess" inflows
- Higher reserve requirements for banks (on all transactions or on foreign transactions)
- Limitations on open foreign exchange positions of financial institutions
- Informal pressure by authorities on the financial markets
- Foreign borrowing limits on classes of liabilities or public borrowers
- Taxes on short-term foreign borrowing
- Restrictions on foreign ownership of certain short-term assets
- Restrictions on certain speculative transactions

The short-term policies tend to impose costs on the financial system; if maintained for too long, they may lead to distortions as bad as the ills they are supposed to cure. They are primarily designed to help governments react to sharp changes in capital flows and buy time to assess more fundamental causes and cures. The farther down the list, the less desirable the policy, and the sooner it should be reversed. If such policies cannot be reversed in a reasonable time, more fundamental changes are needed in other policies. As countries develop, maintain high rates of growth, and continue to attract capital, gradual appreciation of the exchange rate should be expected.

Source: John D. Schilling and Yan Wang, *Managing Capital Flows in East Asia*, (Washington, DC: The World Bank, 1996), p. 120.

from the investment requirements in developing countries and the transition economies where investment demand has outstripped net capital inflows.

Figure 4.5 indicates that the average world saving rate was considerably lower in 1981–96 than in 1973–80 or even 1960–72. During 1992–96, the world saving rate averaged nearly 22 percent of GDP—down over two percentage points from the late 1960s and 1970s. Private saving in industrial countries has remained roughly steady at about 20 percent over the past three decades. But for industrial countries, which account for roughly half of world saving, virtually all of the decline in the saving rate took place in public sector saving. The public saving rate of major industrial countries averaged 4 percent during 1960–72, but only one half of 1 percent during 1981–95.[29] As a result of the low saving rate, there has been a high real interest rate as indicated in Figure 4.6.

World capital flows are determined mainly by savings in the major industrial countries. Do changes in domestic saving in the industrial countries translate into international capital flows to the LDCs and transition economies, or does an increase in saving simply translate into more domestic investment? This depends on the relative demands for savings in the industrial countries, developing countries, and transition economies relative to their own domestic supplies of savings. It also depends on the efficiency of international capital markets in providing sufficient international financial intermediation from countries with excess savings to countries requiring a net resource inflow. As for the future supply of saving, a study by the IMF concludes that "overall the prospects for world saving over the next 15 or 20 years are not necessarily grim, especially if rapid growth in high-saving countries can be sustained. The key will be what happens to public saving. Even a modest swing in the world's public saving position over the next couple of decades will probably dominate other movements.

(In percent of GDP; PPP basis)

Figure 4.5 World saving rate. *Source:* IMF, *World Economic Outlook*, May 1997, p. 200.

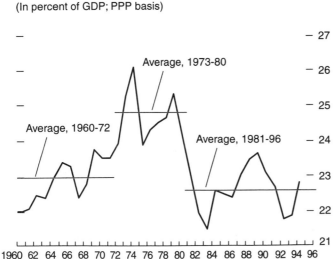

[1]Data before 1970 represents less-than-complete country coverage.

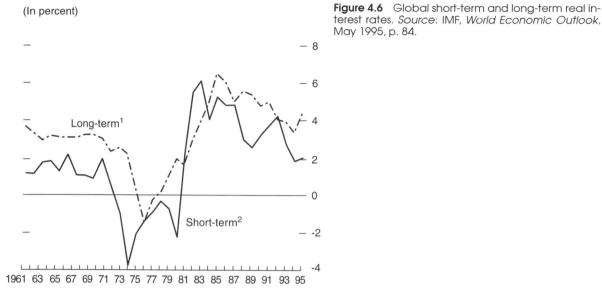

(In percent)

Figure 4.6 Global short-term and long-term real interest rates. *Source:* IMF, *World Economic Outlook,* May 1995, p. 84.

[1]GDP-weighted average of ten-year (or nearest maturity) government bond rates for the United States, Japan, Germany, the United Kingdom, Canada, Belgium, the Netherlands, and Switzerland minus long memory inflation estimate.
[2]GDP-weighted average of three-month treasury bill note for same countries minus actual inflation.

"On balance, the future supply of world saving depends upon two critical variables: the pace of economic growth among developing countries, and the amount of public dissaving among industrial countries. If some large developing countries grow rapidly and experience high saving rates, and if the industrial countries return to their public saving rates of the 1960–72 era, the world saving rate could easily increase by two to four percentage points—despite steady declines in private saving rates in Japan and other industrial countries. This might be called the optimistic saving scenario. On the other hand, a pessimistic saving scenario might develop: In the face of stagnant economic growth in key developing countries and even larger budget deficits in industrial countries, the world saving rate could decline by an additional two to three percentage points over the next 15 to 20 years."[30]

Even with the optimistic saving scenario, however, there is still a need for further integration of international capital markets and for the more efficient operation of international financial intermediation. Both the source country and recipient country benefit if international capital can flow to where it earns a risk-adjusted premium and to countries that provide international portfolio diversification. This calls for ever more integrated capital markets through a reduction in capital restrictions and a deepening of money and capital markets within developing countries and the transition economies.

The optimistic scenario should also be supplemented with the requirement of further liberalization of international capital markets. Despite the integration that has occurred, the integration process is still limited. This is indicated in a variety of ways. One might simply identify barriers to capital flows, including regulatory barriers such as capital controls and limits on foreign ownership, and also less tangible barriers, such as language, information, and relevant cultural differences. Another approach is to examine the extent to which returns on similar assets that are traded in different markets have been equalized, presumably by capital flows. Most of these "law of one price" tests study the equality of nominal or real interest rates on short-term government bonds across countries. A third approach is to compare actual investment portfolios with the highly international diversified portfolios that standard finance theory predicts in an integrated global capital market. Although cross-border transactions and holdings of foreign securities have increased, there is still the question of how far portfolios have moved toward an "optimally diversified portfolio." The answer is not very far. Empirical studies also indicate that investors in major industrial countries still have a strong "home-asset preference," implying limited international diversification. From these studies we can conclude that despite the clearly impressive trends in the capital market integration process, the world economy still has a long way to go before a fully efficient world capital market is established. Except for the wholesale markets for heavily traded, highly liquid, largely default-free financial assets, international integration of asset markets for the broader categories of world saving appears to be limited.[31]

Beyond the policy issues that we have examined in this chapter, we have to discuss in subsequent chapters other policy problems associated with international capital. The next chapter relates capital movements to balance-of-payments policy. It also considers management of the exchange rate. Chapter 8 on developing countries will examine country risk analysis and the negotiation process between foreign investor and host government. As in other policy problems, we shall see that those associated with international capital markets raise issues of both market failure and government failure.

NOTES

1. Paul R. Krugman and Maurice Obstfeld, *International Economics,* 4th ed. (New York: Harper Collins, 1997), Ch. 4.
2. Raymond Vernon and Louis T. Wells, Jr., *The Manager in the International Economy,* 6th ed. (Englewood Cliffs, Prentice-Hall International, Inc., 1991), pp. 62–65.
3. International Monetary Fund, *International Capital Markets* (Washington, D.C., September 1994), p. 33.
4. For details on the evolution of the financial systems of the United States, Japan, and the United Kingdom, see David M. Meerschwan, *Breaking Financial Barriers* (Harvard Business School Press, 1991), Part II.
5. *The Economist*, September 19, 1992, p. 9.
6. Most of the foreign exchange transactions involve trading among banks. The U.S. dollar acts as a vehicle currency with most of the transactions in the foreign exchange market being exchanges of U.S. dollars for another currency.
7. For a more detailed discussion of data systems for U.S. capital flows, see Robert E. Baldwin, *Behind the Numbers*, pp. 158 ff.
8. The forward foreign exchange market is used by traders and investors to hedge against exchange-rate risk. The forward rate can be at a premium or discount, compared with the spot rate, depending on demand and supply conditions in the forward market. The premium is used to compute the "covered interest differential" that adjusts the ordinary interest-rate difference for the cost of hedging in the forward market. When the covered interest differential is positive, investors buy foreign bonds and sell the foreign-currency proceeds forward. This is

covered interest arbitrage, which tends to maintain "covered interest parity." When, however, speculators expect a currency to appreciate by an amount larger than the forward premium, they buy it forward. For details of expectations, exchange rates, and capital movements, see Peter B. Kenen, *The International Economy*, 3rd ed. (1994), Ch. 16.

9. IMF, *World Economic Outlook* (May 1994), p. 26.

10. Pedro-Pablo Kuczyynski, "Why Emerging Markets?" *Columbia Journal of World Business* (summer 1994): 12.

11. This issue is examined fully in several articles in *The World Bank Economic Review* (January 1995). An article by Claessens, Dooley, and Warner takes issue with the conventional view that short-term flows are inherently more unstable than other types of capital flows and require some policy action.

12. Geert Bekaert, "Market Integration and Investment Barriers in Emerging Equity Markets," *World Bank Economic Review* (January 1995): 12.

13. John H. Dunning, ed., *The Theory of Transnational Corporations* (London: Routledge, 1993), p. vii.

14. S. Hirsch, "An International Trade and Investment Theory of the Firm," *Oxford Economic Papers* 28 (July 1976): 258–270.

15. John H. Dunning, ed., *The Theory of Transnational Corporations* (London: Routledge, 1993), p. 8.

16. For an exposition of OLI, see John Dunning, *Explaining International Production* (London: Unwin Hyman, 1988), pp. 13–40; Dunning, "Reappraising the Eclectic Paradigm in an Age of Alliance Capitalism," *Journal of International Business Studies*, vol. 26 (3), 1995: 461–493.

17. These advantages are listed and examined in more detail by Dunning, *The Theory of Transnational Corporations*, op cit., pp. 191–199.

18. This interpretation of internalization is developed by Wilfred J. Ethier, "The Multinational Firm," *Quarterly Journal of Economics* 101 (1986): 805–830.

19. DeAnne Julius, *Global Companies and Public Policy* (New York: Council on Foreign Relations Press, 1990), pp. 36–37.

20. Keith E. Maskus and Allan Webster, "Comparative Advantage and the Location of Inward FDI: Evidence from the United Kingdom and South Korea," *The World Economy* (March 1995): 315–328.

21. See Stephen J. Korbin, *Managing Political Risk Assessment* (Berkeley: University of California Press, 1982).

22. Ibid., p. 40.

23. Donald J. LeCraw, "Bargaining Power, Ownership, and Profitability of Transnational Corporations in Developing Countries," *Journal of International Business Studies* (spring/summer 1984): 27–43.

24. For empirical studies see Bryan Levy, "The Determinants of Policy in LDCs," *Journal of Development Economics* 28 (1988): 217–231; Donald J. LeCraw, ibid.; Dennis J. Encarnation and Louis T. Wells, Jr., "Sovereignty on Guard: Negotiation with Foreign Investors," *International Organization* 39-1 (winter 1985): 47–78.

25. The World Bank labels countries as "middle income economies" if their GNP per capita was more than $725 but less than $8,956 in 1994. Low income economies are those with a GNP per capita of $725 or less in 1994.

26. See IMF, *World Economic Outlook* (October 1994): 57–61.

27. Mahbub ul Haq, et al. eds., *The Tobin Tax* (New York: Oxford University Press, 1996).

28. Peter Passell, "Economic Scene," *New York Times*, February 9, 1995.

29. IMF, *World Economic Outlook* (May 1995): 67 ff.

30. IMF, *World Economic Outlook* (May 1995): 77, 79.

31. IMF, *World Economic Outlook* (May 1995): 81.

Capital Flows

TABLE 4.7
Sources of International Capital Markets Financing

	1987	1988	1989	1990	1991	1992	1993	1994
	(Gross issues in $ billions)							
Syndicated loans	91.7	125.5	121.1	124.5	116.0	117.9	136.7	202.8
Euronotes	102.2	93.2	81.6	73.2	87.9	134.6	160.2	279.8
Euro-commercial paper	55.8	57.1	54.1	48.3	35.9	28.9	38.4	31.8
Euro-medium-term notes	8.0	12.6	15.5	16.0	43.2	97.9	113.2	243.0
Bonds	180.8	227.1	255.7	229.9	308.7	333.7	481.0	426.9
Straight bonds	121.3	160.2	154.6	158.9	242.7	265.4	369.1	288.8
Floating rate bonds	13.0	22.3	17.8	37.1	18.3	43.6	69.8	96.3
Convertible bonds	18.2	11.3	14.1	10.6	10.1	5.2	18.1	21.7
Bonds with warrants attached	24.8	29.7	66.2	21.2	31.6	15.7	20.6	9.9
Other bonds	3.5	3.6	3.0	2.1	6.0	3.8	3.4	10.3
International equity offerings	20.4	9.1	14.0	14.2	23.8	25.3	36.6	58.1
Depository receipts								
(ADRs/GDRs/Rule 144A)	4.6	1.3	2.6	1.7	4.6	5.3	9.5	11.0
Total	395.1	454.9	472.4	441.8	536.4	611.5	814.5	967.6
Memorandum items								
Global bonds	—	—	1.5	9.7	15.4	25.1	34.4	49.0
Cross-border equity trading[1]								
Gross equity flows	1,377.8	1,166.7	1,562.6	1,390.9	1,322.5	1,404.9	2,266.1	2,550.0
Cross-exchange trading	508.6	342.6	582.9	873.9	779.1	968.7	1,547.5	2,000.0
Net equity flows	16.4	32.9	86.6	3.2	100.6	53.7	196.3	119.6
Cross-border mergers and acquisitions	70.9	109.6	117.5	128.4	83.7	91.0	95.1	156.2
	(In percent of total)							
Syndicated loans	23.21	27.59	25.64	28.18	21.63	19.28	16.78	20.96
Euronotes	25.87	20.49	17.27	16.57	16.39	22.01	19.67	28.92
Euro-commercial paper	14.12	12.55	11.45	10.93	6.69	4.73	4.71	3.29
Euro-medium-term notes	2.02	2.77	3.28	3.62	8.05	16.01	13.90	25.11
Bonds	45.76	49.92	54.13	52.04	57.55	54.57	59.05	44.12
Straight bonds	30.70	35.22	32.73	35.97	45.25	43.40	45.32	29.85
Floating rate bonds	3.29	4.90	3.77	8.40	3.41	7.13	8.57	9.95
Convertible bonds	4.61	2.48	2.98	2.40	1.88	0.85	2.22	2.24
Bonds with warrants attached	6.28	6.53	14.01	4.80	5.89	2.57	2.53	1.02
Other bonds	0.89	0.79	0.64	0.48	1.12	0.62	0.42	1.06
International equity offerings	5.16	2.00	2.96	3.21	4.44	4.14	4.49	6.00
Depository receipts								
(ADRs/GDRs/Rule 144A)	1.16	0.28	0.55	0.39	0.86	0.86	1.17	1.14
Total	100.00	100.00	100.00	100.00	100.00	100.00	100.00	100.00

[1]The data for 1994 are estimates.
Source: IMF, *International Capital Markets*, August 1995, p. 189.

TABLE 4.8
Foreign Bond and Eurobond Market Characteristics ($ millions)

	1981	1984	1985	1987	1990	1993
Eurobonds						
Total euro	31,616	79,458	136,731	140,535	199,584	406,694
US dollar	26,830	63,593	97,782	58,070	70,070	146,935
German mark	1,277	4,604	9,491	15,023	21,150	57,904
British pound	501	3,997	5,766	15,051	18,030	43,868
Japanese yen	368	1,212	6,539	22,563	33,065	46,805
European currency units	309	3,032	7,038	7,397	17,526	7,161
Other	1,697	3,020	10,114	22,431	12,561	104,021
Foreign Bonds						
Total foreign	21,369	27,953	31,025	40,253	30,385	76,806
US dollar	7,552	5,487	4,655	7,416	5,940	24,795
German mark	1,310	2,243	1,741	n.a.	n.a.	n.a.
British pound	746	1,292	958	n.a.	n.a.	n.a.
Swiss franc	8,285	12,626	14,954	24,301	13,741	27,394
Japanese yen	2,457	4,628	6,379	4,071	n.a.	14,770
Other	538	1,677	2,339	4,465	n.a.	9,847
Grand total	52,985	107,411	167,756	180,788	228,904	483,500

n.a. = not available.

Source: Morgan Guaranty Trust Company, *World Financial Markets,* various issues; Salomon Brothers, *Bond Market Research,* (various issues).

TABLE 4.9
Flows of FDI into and out of Developed Countries, 1967–92 ($ millions)

Country and Country Group	1967–72	1973–78	1979–84	1985–88	1989–92
Outflows of Domestic Capital (annual average)					
United States	6,412	11,641	7,510	22,160	31,402
Canada	269	967	3,113	3,852	5,515
Western Europe†	4,792	10,495	12,974	46,433	120,570
Austria	18	49	117	—	1,452
Belgium-Luxembourg	100	308	309	1,667	7,604
Denmark	42	68	98	—	1,909
Finland	35	36	205	785	2,115
France	376	1,051	2,342	6,137	27,293
Germany	836	2,137	3,023	7,070	21,255
Italy	251	262	1,170	2,489	5,780
Netherlands	463	877	543	4,095	13,707
Norway	12	123	253	889	1,254
Spain	25	81	251	516	2,324
Sweden	175	452	659	2,568	8,014
Switzerland	1,145	3,243	—	3,040	6,415
United Kingdom	1,314	3,438	5,422	17,177	21,098
Japan	331	1,809	3,587	14,760	35,048
Southern Hemisphere‡	118	303	1,091	3,206	2,173
Australia	95	193	751	3,095	1,492
Total†	11,923	25,209	29,774	90,411	316,420
Inflows of Foreign Capital (annual average)					
United States	925	4,309	14,903	31,815	34,838
Canada	712	704	231	1,407	6,103
Western Europe†	4,419	8,241	9,690	25,309	89,933
Austria	62	114	212	—	476
Belgium-Luxembourg	319	959	1,032	1,817	8,891
Denmark	101	110	73	—	1,198
Finland	21	35	19	141	311
France	444	1,411	2,006	3,886	15,122
Germany	927	1,741	884	1,213	8,475
Italy	657	555	771	2,281	3,527
Netherlands	454	509	26	2,542	7,945
Norway	78	365	246	435	755
Spain	206	456	1,426	3,402	10,208
Sweden	103	59	131	473	2,385
Switzerland	252	517	—	1,284	3,000
United Kingdom	798	1,670	2,906	7,835	24,368
Japan	111	89	138	348	11,975
Southern Hemisphere‡	1,052	1,112	1,683	2,362	7,063
Australia	813	860	1,589	2,677	6,097
Total†	7,218	14,455	26,694	61,241	242,670

*Includes reinvested earnings.
†Including countries not listed separately.
‡Includes Australia, New Zealand, and South Africa.
Source: International Monetary Fund, *Balance of Payments Yearbook* (Washington, DC: IMF, 1993).

TABLE 4.10
Major Capital Flows in Selected Industrial Countries[1]

	1976–80	1981–85	1986–90	1991	1992	1993	1994
			($ billions, annual averages)				
			Total Capital Flows				
Outflows[2]	153.7	231.1	678.9	510.8	543.6	975.7	725.8
As a percentage of GDP	*3.0*	*2.9*	*5.4*	*3.3*	*3.2*	*5.3*	*3.6*
United States	43.3	44.1	77.4	96.9	82.5	125.4	164.3
Japan[3]	15.4	53.5	242.2	117.2	25.4	65.0	162.0
Western Europe[4]	95.0	133.5	359.2	296.7	435.7	785.3	399.5
Inflows	168.2	270.7	745.6	510.4	557.6	941.8	635.7
As a percentage of GDP	*3.3*	*3.4*	*5.9*	*3.3*	*3.3*	*5.1*	*3.2*
United States	33.6	100.0	177.7	82.1	108.2	160.7	278.2
Japan	15.2	30.3	178.3	27.2	−93.5	−43.0	30.8
Western Europe[4]	119.4	140.4	389.6	401.1	542.9	824.1	326.6
			of which: Portfolio Investment				
Outflows	21.3	63.6	182.7	267.3	244.1	424.6	232.6
United States	5.3	6.5	13.6	44.7	45.1	120.0	60.6
Japan	3.4	25.0	85.9	74.3	34.4	51.7	83.6
Western Europe[4]	12.6	32.0	83.1	148.3	164.6	253.0	88.4
Inflows	26.3	68.3	172.3	354.0	305.8	520.4	175.4
United States	5.2	29.4	44.7	54.0	66.7	104.9	91.5
Japan	5.1	12.6	26.9	115.3	8.2	−11.1	34.7
Western Europe[4]	16.1	26.4	100.7	184.8	230.9	426.5	49.3
			Direct Investment				
Outflows	36.9	37.0	149.4	169.8	157.8	160.5	186.4
United States	16.9	7.6	25.3	31.3	41.0	57.9	58.4
Japan	2.3	5.1	32.1	30.7	17.2	13.7	17.9
Western Europe[4]	17.8	24.3	92.0	107.8	99.6	88.9	110.0
Inflows	23.3	33.2	114.2	101.0	84.8	88.5	123.5
United States	9.0	18.6	53.4	26.1	9.9	21.4	60.1
Japan	0.1	0.3	0.3	1.4	2.7	0.1	0.9
Western Europe[4]	14.2	14.3	60.6	73.6	72.2	67.0	62.5

[1]Excluding official monetary movements.
[2]Including errors and omissions.
[3]Including *net* short-term capital of the non-bank sector.
[4]Including intra-regional flows. Data for 1994 are partly estimated.
Source: IMF, OECD, national data and BIS estimates.

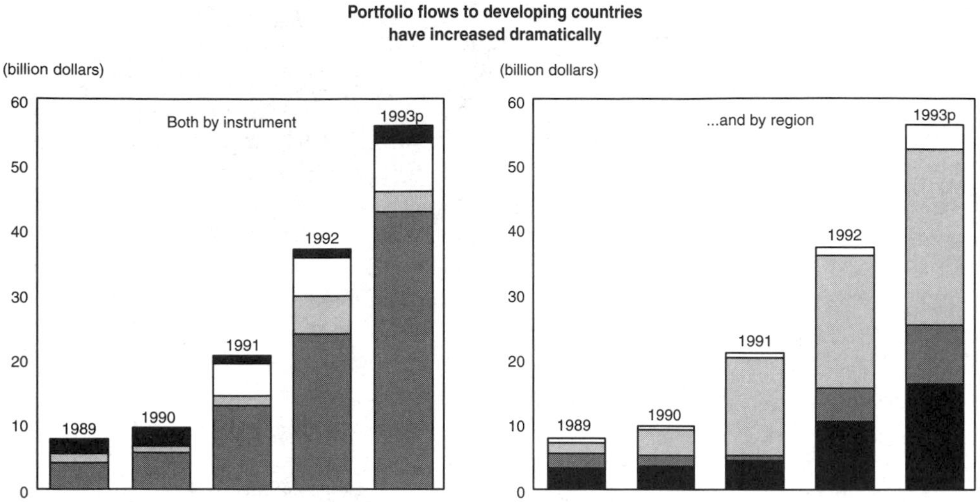

**Portfolio flows to developing countries
have increased dramatically**

(billion dollars)

	1989	1990	1991	1992	1993p
Bonds, CPs & CDs	4.0	5.5	12.7	23.7	42.6
Direct equity investment	1.3	0.8	1.5	5.8	3.2
Depository receipts	0.0	0.1	4.9	5.9	7.3
Country funds	2.2	2.9	1.2	1.3	2.7
Total	**7.5**	**9.3**	**20.3**	**36.7**	**55.8**

p = Projected

(billion dollars)

	1989	1990	1991	1992	1993p
East Asia & Pacific	2.88	3.14	4.04	10.00	15.92
Europe and Central Asia	2.3	1.91	0.80	5.17	9.22
Latin America & the Caribbean	1.39	3.77	14.96	20.47	27.20
Global investment funds	0.08	0.04	0.25	0.14	2.64
Other regions	0.86	0.47	0.22	0.93	0.82
All developing countries	**7.52**	**9.33**	**20.27**	**36.71**	**55.79**

Figure 4.7 Portfolio flows to developing countries. *Source:* World Bank, *World Debt Tables, 1993–94.*

TABLE 4.11
Emerging Stock Markets (first quarter 1995)

Market	Market Capitalization ($ millions)	Number of Listed Companies	Average Daily Value Trade for Quarter ($ millions)
Latin America			
Argentina	32,374	156	22.60
Brazil	132,139	545	329.17
Chile	65,937	317	28.70
Colombia	16,826	190	5.47
Mexico	75,069	204	145.49
Peru	7,472	223	8.69
Venezuela	3,668	90	1.29
East Asia			
China	43,832	298	94.40
Korea	178,339	702	664.62
Philippines	45,747	192	44.63
Taiwan, China	234,386	323	1,733.00
South Asia			
India	105,735	4,702	49.82
Indonesia	44,164	221	48.72
Malaysia	205,520	494	315.78
Pakistan	10,274	738	13.41
Sri Lanka	2,612	222	1.17
Thailand	128,355	403	203.42
Europe/Mideast/Africa (EMEA)			
Greece	15,397	219	12.72
Hungary	1,263	40	1.00
Jordan	4,616	95	1.62
Nigeria	881	179	0.10
Poland	2,853	47	7.06
Portugal	17,414	180	16.60
South Africa	232,741	636	54.39
Turkey	27,887	184	190.15
Zimbabwe	1,640	64	0.49
IFC Indexes			
Composite	894,038	1,389	
Latin America	212,057	331	
Asia	633,480	787	
EMEA	48,501	271	
Regional Totals			
Total	1,637,141	11,664	
Latin America	333,485	1,725	
Asia	998,964	8,295	
EMEA	304,692	1,644	

Source: International Finance Corporation, *Quarterly Review*, First Quarter 1995, p. 2.

Foreign Direct Investment in the United States

Foreign investment in the United States raises a number of policy issues—economic and political. As Figure 4.8 shows, the flow of foreign direct investment (FDI) in the United States rose rapidly in the 1980s, reaching a peak of $73 billion in 1988, falling to a low in 1992, and then increasing again by 70 percent in 1993, by 80 percent in 1994, and 19 percent in 1995. The United States received more investment from foreign firms than any other country in the mid-1990s, supplanting China as the leading investment destination. In 1995, the inflow of FDI was nearly $59 billion. By the end of 1995, foreign companies had invested more than $560 billion in the United States, up from $80 billion in 1980 (at historical cost).

Table 4.12 shows the FDI position in the United States by major area, and Table 4.13 shows FDI by industry.

The British continue to be the largest direct investor with the Japanese in second place. British investment accounts for nearly 25 percent of total FDI in the United States while Japanese investment accounts for some 19 percent. Japan's direct investment has been concentrated in manufacturing and real estate. After 1990, the flow of investment from Japan declined for several reasons: a termination of the initial starting-up phase of the FDI movement that had begun in the early 1980s; the generally low profitability of Japanese subsidiaries abroad, aggravated by a slowdown in the United States; and the collapse of the Japanese "bubble economy" and subsequent sluggish domestic economy, which further contributed to a relatively cautious investment strategy. Related to the latter condition, the Japan Centre for Economic Research notes that although the ratio of production abroad by Japanese affiliates to domestic production by parent companies in Japan rose from 3 percent to 6 percent during 1985–92, the ratio remains low compared to those of U.S. and German companies, at 28 percent and 20 percent, respectively.[1]

Interestingly, as Japanese investments declined in the early 1990s, those from Korean companies increased. In 1995, L G Electronics purchased a controlling share in Zenith Electronics, the last American manufacturer of TVs. Other Korean investments in American electronics firms have been made by Samsung Electronics and Hyundai Electronics who are also building semiconductor factories in the United States.

Foreign multinationals have acquired equity holdings in Wall Street firms, real estate, and foreign ownership of such familiar household names as Firestone, General Tire, Doubleday and Company, Viking Press, A&P, Grand Union, Carnation and a host of other formerly U.S. companies. The buying of such American trophies as Columbia Pictures by Sony and Rockefeller Center by Mitsubishi aroused considerable public concern. So, too, has the foreign holding of bank assets.

---

[1] GATT, *Trade Policy Review: Japan*, vol. I (Geneva, May 1995), p. 28.

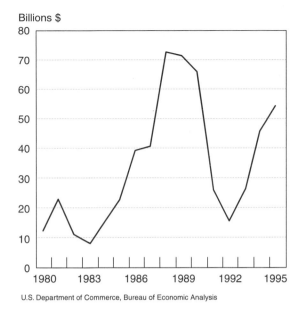

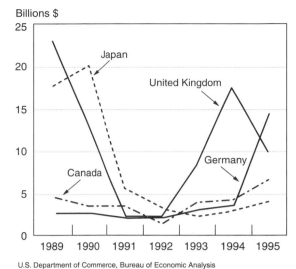

U.S. Department of Commerce, Bureau of Economic Analysis

U.S. Department of Commerce, Bureau of Economic Analysis

Figure 4.8 Outlays for new investment in the United States. (A) By foreign direct investors, 1980–95. (B) By foreign direct investors from selected countries, 1989–95. *Source: Survey of Current Business,* July 1996, p. 102.

TABLE 4.12
Foreign Direct Investment Position in the United States on a Historical Cost Basis, by Major Area, 1982–95

Year	All Areas	Canada	Europe	Latin America and Other Western Hemisphere	Africa	Middle East	Asia and Pacific
				($ millions)			
1982	124,677	11,708	83,193	14,229	105	4,401	11,041
1983	137,061	11,434	92,936	15,035	95	4,446	13,115
1984	164,583	15,286	108,211	16,201	194	5,336	19,355
1985	184,615	17,131	121,413	16,826	461	4,954	23,830
1986	220,414	20,318	144,181	16,763	250	4,870	34,032
1987	263,394	24,684	181,006	10,103	521	4,973	42,108
1988	314,754	26,566	208,942	11,243	441	6,570	60,992
1989	368,924	30,370	239,190	16,218	505	7,588	75,053
1990	394,911	29,544	247,320	20,168	505	4,425	92,948
1991	419,108	36,834	256,053	14,546	937	4,864	105,873
1992	427,566	37,843	255,570	17,473	896	4,797	110,987
1993	466,666	40,487	287,940	19,716	1,003	5,220	112,299
1994	502,410	42,133	309,415	25,042	925	5,565	119,331
1995	560,088	46,005	360,762	22,716	936	5,053	124,615
Average annual growth rate (percent)	12.3	11.1	11.9	3.7	18.3	1.1	20.5

Source: Department of Commerce, *Survey of Current Business,* July 1996, p. 54.

TABLE 4.13
Investment Outlays by Industry of U.S. Business Enterprise, 1989–95
($ millions)

	1989	1990	1991	1992	1993	1994[r]	1995[p]
Total	**71,163**	**65,932**	**25,538**	**15,333**	**26,229**	**45,626**	**54,368**
By industry:							
Petroleum	1,189	1,141	702	463	882	469	1,731
Manufacturing	35,958	23,898	11,461	6,014	11,090	21,218	28,493
Food and kindred products	6,515	997	1,247	404	1,294	4,567	4,233
Chemicals and allied products	11,584	7,518	2,897	1,644	5,035	6,905	13,716
Primary and fabricated metals	3,545	2,447	797	1,187	1,297	1,485	578
Machinery	4,346	3,795	4,929	1,002	1,778	1,867	5,350
Other manufacturing	9,969	9,141	1,591	1,778	1,686	6,393	4,616
Wholesale trade	2,634	1,676	623	698	837	2,156	(D)
Retail trade	1,861	1,250	1,605	256	1,495	1,542	2,957
Depository institutions	349	897	482	529	958	2,026	2,592
Finance, except depository institutions	4,186	2,121	2,199	797	1,599	2,195	5,751
Insurance	1,901	2,093	2,102	291	1,105	450	(D)
Real estate	6,438	7,771	3,823	2,161	1,883	2,647	2,679
Services	10,058	19,369	2,256	2,023	4,162	7,163	4,142
Other industries	6,587	5,716	284	2,101	2,218	5,760	3,983

[r]Revised.
[p]Preliminary.
[D]Suppressed to avoid disclosure of data of individual companies.
Source: *Survey of Current Business*, July 1996, p. 120.

Responding to the wave of foreign investment, the best-selling book *Buying into America* has raised the fear of "giving away America's future," and has argued that policy makers must shield citizens from the negative impact of foreign investment and assert some control over its future direction. The authors conclude: "The United States is sinking deeper and deeper into the condition of a developing country: importing capital when a few short years before it was the world's largest creditor nation. Advanced countries export, and that's the company this country should keep.

"The forces of the international market place have begun to overwhelm America's capacity to deal with them. The surge of foreign investment is only one glaring example. The manner in which the nation's leaders respond will determine how we meet the most difficult economic challenge of our times: to retain U.S. sovereignty in the global economy."[2]

Most economists, however, do not take such a negative view of foreign investment in the United States. They do not even see the inflow as simply a result of the U.S. trade deficit. The growth began back in the 1970s when the United States still had a trade surplus. Nor do they attribute the buying of American enterprises to "bargains." True, depreciation of the dollar does make the purchase of assets cheaper in terms of foreign currency. But so too does the depreciation of the dollar make profit streams less valuable in foreign currency.

---

[2] Martin and Susan Tolchin, *Buying into America: How Foreign Money Is Changing the Face of Our Nation* (New York: Times Books, 1988), p. 274.

Rather than following these popular views, economists look to more fundamental causes. These are to be found in the corporate strategy of multinationals and the determinants of direct foreign investment as part of the firm's global strategy. These determinants are similar to those already discussed on pp. 134–39. Moreover, the inflow of foreign capital into the American economy is testament to the strength of the economy, not its weakness. An additional influence on foreign investment is the threat of protection against imports. This has been especially significant for some Japanese investment. Jagdish Bhagwati has called this quid pro quo investment—foreign investment in the United States to deter tariffs or quotas against Japanese imports.[3] For example, Komatsu Limited has said that the company's fear of rising protectionism was one of the major reasons for its decision to invest in an American plant in Tennessee.

What are the economic implications of the growth in foreign investment in the United States? Unlike the critics, proponents of foreign direct investment argue that it creates new and desirable jobs for Americans and that it brings with it new technology that can help maintain U.S. competitiveness in world industries. Proponents also say that as long as the United States maintains a large balance-of-payments deficit on current account, foreign direct investment is a more satisfactory source of necessary financing than other alternatives. These arguments are spelled out by Edward M. Graham and Paul Krugman in their careful and thoroughgoing study of foreign direct investment in the United States.[4] Contrary to the critics' view that foreign investment costs jobs for American labor, Graham and Krugman demonstrate that the foreign firms actually create new and desirable jobs. They conclude that value added and compensation per worker employed in U.S. subsidiaries of foreign firms are comparable to those in U.S. firms; indeed, overall the foreign subsidiaries do a little better than all U.S. firms. They also refute the myth that foreign controlled firms in the United States do all their R&D activities in their home countries, as R&D layouts per worker for foreign manufacturing affiliates are slightly higher than the U.S. figure. The foreign firms are actually bringing new technology to the United States. Critics point to differences in import behavior, claiming that foreign subsidiaries, particularly those of Japanese firms, import considerably more per employee than do U.S.-domiciled firms. Given that the subsidiaries are relatively new in the United States, however, their reliance on their parent organizations is understandable. Over time, imports per employee by foreign subsidiaries should come down to levels similar to those of American firms.

More generally, the foreign direct investment helps solve the U.S. balance-of-payments deficit. To finance the current account deficit, the United States must rely on foreign savings—either through portfolio investment or foreign direct investment. The case made by proponents of foreign direct investment is that this type of investment is typically held for a much longer term than are other forms of U.S. assets that can be sold to foreigners to finance the current account deficit. Therefore, foreign direct investors are less likely to liquidate precipitously and en masse their holdings of U.S. assets than would foreign holders of U.S. assets such as treasury bills or portfolio equities. A large and sudden liquidation by foreign investors would trigger a precipitous fall of the dollar and an ensuing

[3] Jagdish Bhagwati, "The Political Economy of Foreign Direct Investment," in Anne O. Krueger and Ronald Jones, eds., *The Political Economy of Trade Policy* (Oxford: Basil Blackwell, 1989), pp. 222–227.

[4] Edward M. Graham and Paul R. Krugman, *Foreign Direct Investment in the United States*, 3rd ed. (Washington, DC: Institute for International Economics, 1995).

UNANSWERED QUESTIONS

To the Editor:

A small army of former high Government officials, whose law firms and brokerage houses represent foreign investors in the United States, resort to epithets to stifle discussion of the [impact of foreign investment in the United States] . . .

They paint with a very broad brush. Having concluded that foreign investment is beneficial, as indeed much of it is, they ignore numerous policy issues. These include:

- The wisdom of having states compete for foreign capital, providing millions of dollars in tax abatements and other incentives, thus letting United States taxpayers subsidize foreign acquisitions and investments.

- The wisdom of United States laws that discriminate against United States companies and in favor of foreign investors. Thus, Citicorp was precluded from buying a California bank, which was ultimately sold to a Tokyo bank that was subject to no such restrictions.

- The question of whether some industries are so vital to our national security or industrial strength that the United States should maintain a controlling interest in them. These include banking, transportation, communications, machine tools, semiconductors and biotechnology.

- The question of whether it is protectionist to demand that our trading partners end restrictive practices on United States investments abroad.

- The need for basic information. At least 50 percent of all foreign investment goes unreported, because of loopholes in United States laws.

- The fear that we have become so profligate that we have become addicted to foreign capital to subsidize a life style we cannot afford. The wisdom of becoming the world's largest debtor nation and its impact on our national sovereignty.

- The question of whether it is good to become a nation of tenants. Prime commercial property in our nation's largest cities—Houston, Los Angeles, New York, Honolulu and Washington—is increasingly being acquired by foreign interests.

These are among the dozens of questions that are raised by the surge of foreign investment in the United States. They cannot be shunted aside by accusations of xenophobia, protectionism or racism. They deserve rather to be the subjects of a national debate.

Susan J. Tolchin
Professor of Public Administration
George Washington University
Washington, June 9, 1988
The writer is co-author, with Martin Tolchin, of *"Buying Into America: How Foreign Money Is Changing the Face of Our Nation."*

New York Times, June 22, 1988

economic crisis.[5] If the United States continues to have to finance its debt internationally, then FDI is preferable to other forms of foreign investment in the United States. To the extent that foreign direct investment helps to settle the balance-of-payments accounts, the Federal Reserve need not increase interest rates to attract an inflow of short-term capital; nor need monetary and fiscal authorities undertake a deflation of the American economy or a further depreciation of the dollar.

As the *Wall Street Journal* observes, the "Buying of America" is a half-truth at best. Foreign investment is flowing into the United States, but capital is also flowing out rapidly. In 1995, U.S. direct investment abroad increased by over $90 billion. Western Europe and the Newly Industrializing Countries of Asia are the big investment targets. Since 1992, FDI from the United States has surpassed Japan's direct investment overseas. The *Wall Street Journal* concludes, "The large issue is whether U.S. companies are likely to be leaders or laggards in the trend toward the globalization of markets and industries. Companies operating in the major markets of North America, Europe and Asia are far more likely to prosper in the 1990s than those that don't, experts say. So, U.S. companies' stepped up activity abroad is an encouraging sign."[6]

DISCUSSION QUESTIONS

1. Although European firms have invested considerably more than Japanese firms in the United States, Japanese investment has received the most attention. Why?

2. Do you think that the eclectic OLI theory of the determinants of FDI (pp. 135–38) explains why Japanese firms have invested in the United States? Does it also explain the fluctuations in the flow of investment funds?

3. How would you respond to the questions raised by Professor Susan B. Tolchin in her *New York Times* letter (p. 162)?

4. Do you believe that FDI in the United States results in net benefits or net costs to the American economy?

5. Does it matter whether foreign companies set up new plants in the United States, or buy into existing companies?

6. Do you believe that the outflow of FDI from the United States results in net benefits or net costs to the American economy?

7. Should FDI into the United States be screened and evaluated on "national interest" grounds with respect to the firm's operations in the United States?

8. After 1990, the flow of FDI from Japan into the United States fell sharply. Why? Do you believe that this is a permanent break in trend and that the large inflow in the 1980s was a one-time event?

---

[5] Edward M. Graham, "FDI in the USA: Threat or Opportunity?" *JAMA Forum*, vol. 8, no. 3, p. 3.
[6] The *Wall Street Journal*, April 9, 1990, p. 1.

External Debt Management

Despite years of negotiations between the commercial banks and debtor governments, the problems of managing an external debt still remain. Especially vulnerable are some Latin American, African, and Eastern European countries. For developing countries, Tables 4.14 and 4.15 and Figure 4.9 provide some data on the stock of external debt and debt servicing. Although the banks have improved their exposure, the highly indebted countries have not been able to raise their growth rates and reduce the burden of their debts. There is still a challenge to the international financial community to find a way out of the debt problem. To resolve the debt problem, the international financial community has to answer some central questions:

- Who should bear the risk of default—the private commercial banks, the IMF, or the creditor governments?
- How can the social costs of default be decreased?
- How can sufficient growth in the debtor countries be insured and their cash flow strains reduced?
- Can there be a general solution for all debtor countries or only case-by-case negotiations?

Agreement on the answers to these questions is not readily forthcoming because of the different interests of the commercial banks, debtor governments, creditor governments, World Bank, and IMF. The answers lie in the future. But the way in which these questions are answered will have considerable consequences for business enterprises. At the worst, there may be repudiation of obligations, thereby amounting to a "tax" on creditors and a risk to the world financial system. Or creditor governments will have to bail out the banks and debtor countries. At least, if the process of growth with debt cannot be reinvigorated, the exports from the more-developed countries will continue to suffer.

To meet the debt problem, any number of proposals have been promulgated by economists, businesspeople, and government policy makers. These proposals can be categorized as (1) financing the debt; (2) forgiving a debt overhang; or (3) emphasizing internal adjustment. These can be examined in turn.

Rescheduling of loans on a case-by-case basis has been the main way for dealing with the debt problem. This involves financing the debt by stretching it out over time, setting interest at the market level (LIBOR) plus some risk premium on the rescheduled portion of debt, and providing new lending to refinance part of the interest due. The problem is viewed as one of illiquidity not insolvency, and such a rescheduling does not reduce the present value of the debt that is due. Between 1980 and 1989, commercial banks restructured about $320 billion of maturities.

TABLE 4.14
Developing Countries External Debt, by Maturity and Type of Creditor, 1989–98

	1989	1990	1991	1992	1993	1994	1995	1996	1997	1998
Total debt	1,125.4	1,227.9	1,298.1	1,373.6	1,488.0	1,609.7	1,732.2	1,783.3	1,853.4	1,949.2
By maturity										
Short-term	163.2	185.3	219.9	259.6	294.2	294.4	304.9	335.1	337.9	362.6
Long-term	962.1	1,042.7	1,078.2	1,113.9	1,193.8	1,315.3	1,427.3	1,448.2	1,515.5	1,586.5
By type of creditor										
Official	547.0	579.3	627.0	639.7	681.0	744.6	791.4	757.7	745.4	745.9
Banks	391.9	386.7	399.0	410.1	424.3	404.6	422.1	425.0	434.9	453.8
Other private	186.4	262.0	272.2	323.8	382.7	460.5	518.6	600.6	673.1	749.5

Source: IMF, *World Economic Outlook*, May 1997, p. 192.

TABLE 4.15
Debt Indicators, 1990–95 (percent)

Country Group	Share of 1995 Total Debt	Debt to Export Ratio						Debt Service to Export Ratio					
		1990	1991	1992	1993	1994	1995[a]	1990	1991	1992	1993	1994	1995[a]
All developing countries	100	161.6	175.3	166.7	168.6	162.8	150.0	18.3	18.6	17.1	17.6	16.6	16.3
Severely indebted	33	327.3	365.6	346.6	347.3	332.2	323.2	25.8	28.0	29.2	28.9	26.5	29.2
Low-income	10	457.1	498.5	494.8	530.0	529.4	492.8	23.2	23.2	22.2	17.4	20.0	21.2
Middle-income	23	294.5	331.5	310.9	307.2	290.9	288.0	26.5	29.3	30.9	31.4	27.9	30.8
Moderately indebted	45	192.7	214.0	221.7	219.8	209.3	199.1	24.7	26.8	26.2	26.2	24.4	24.4
Other countries	22	58.3	63.4	59.4	65.3	68.3	64.0	10.0	9.1	8.4	9.4	8.9	7.8
By region													
Sub-Saharan Africa	11	225.7	239.4	235.6	251.9	265.7	269.8	17.8	16.4	15.7	14.9	14.0	14.7
East Asia and the Pacific	23	106.6	106.0	101.6	101.3	93.3	83.3	15.3	13.4	13.1	14.7	12.0	10.7
South Asia	8	315.9	311.7	319.4	287.9	271.6	245.7	27.6	25.0	24.7	23.7	25.6	24.9
Europe and Central Asia	18	120.2	157.8	143.6	151.5	153.7	144.6	16.8	20.5	12.8	12.4	14.6	15.4
Latin America and the Caribbean	29	277.4	282.0	276.2	274.6	258.6	254.2	26.3	26.2	28.9	30.0	27.5	30.3
Middle East and North Africa	11	109.8	129.2	126.1	134.5	148.5	136.9	14.7	16.8	16.2	15.5	15.4	13.7
Highly indebted poor countries	11	489.2	529.9	531.8	561.3	526.3	565.4	20.8	21.3	17.2	17.2	18.2	23.8

Note: Based on (nominal) debt stock at year-end.
[a]Preliminary.
Source: World Bank, *World Debt Tables*, vol. 1, 1996, p. 27.

The rationale for financing the debt is the belief that the debtor country can grow out of debt, and the new money makes it possible to reduce the debt servicing burden. As growth occurs, the ratio of debt to GNP or to exports can decline, thereby improving creditworthiness. If, for example, world prices are rising 3 percent annually, and real growth in national income of the debtor country is 4 percent annually, then as long as its debt grows less than 7 percent annually, the country's ratio of debt to national income will fall.

Similarly, the debt-to-export ratio will decline if the growth rate of exports exceeds the real rate of interest. If the growth rate of export earnings is high and interest rates are

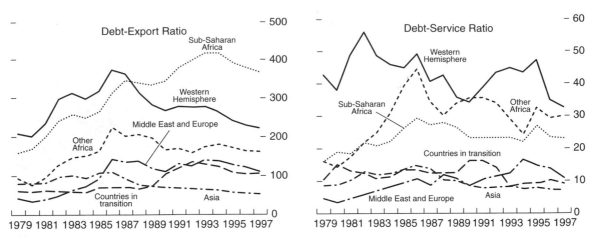

Figure 4.9 Debt ratios. Debt service refers to actual payments of interest on total debt plus actual amortization payments on long-term debt. *Source:* IMF, *World Economic Outlook*, May 1996, p. 39.

low, then the debt crisis can be only temporary. The debtor country can then grow out of its debt by instituting an adjustment program of restraint that will allow it to avoid further debt buildup by paying most of the interest out of a trade surplus generated through devaluation of its foreign exchange rate and domestic demand restriction, while export growth reduces the debt-to-exports ratio.

Creditor banks may have an incentive to provide new money for part of their interest due if they believe that this is a way of protecting the value of the loans they have already made. The financing of the debt is in the nature of defensive lending that allows the existing creditors to buy an option to collect on their claims in the future if economic conditions improve. Under conditions of uncertainty, this is preferable to a fairly likely default if the new money is less than payments of interest and principal that would be stopped in the event of a default. The defensive lending improves the expected value of the initial debt.

Those who support a strategy that relies on new financing of debt believe that the incentive for defensive lending is sufficiently strong, and that combined with adjustment efforts by the debtors and an improving external environment, problem debtors could become creditworthy and be able to return to normal capital markets in a few years.

Critics of this strategy, however, are pessimistic and assert that banks would simply be throwing good money after bad, the costs of their increased exposure are not justified, and what is really needed is policy reform in the debtor countries. In recent years, a number of analysts have maintained that the necessary way to solve the debt problem is by eliminating the "debt overhang" through debt reduction. The "debt overhang" can be defined as the portion of debt which, if forgiven, would allow the remaining debt to trade near par on secondary markets. The rationale is that the debt overhang in itself restricts the country's economic growth. It is argued that a heavy debt burden reduces the incentive to invest. For if exports increase as a result of more investment, most of the benefits accrue to creditors in bigger debt service payments rather than to the country itself. This depresses the returns to the country from investment and thereby weakens the incentive to invest.

Debt fatigue has set in, and debt reduction would therefore now be of greater benefit than new lending. A lower present value of payments is required through rescheduling below market interest and through cancellation of principal. Debt forgiveness, it is claimed, would then actually result in a higher value of expected payments. Less becomes more.

In 1989, the Bush administration called on U.S. commercial banks to accept an orderly process of debt reduction. In contrast with earlier Treasury policies, Treasury Secretary Brady urged creditor banks to agree voluntarily to reduce the value of their claims through a cut in principal or interest in return for guarantees on the remaining portion of the debt. The Brady Plan offered the banks a "menu of options" of debt reduction mechanisms: buybacks, conversion of debt into bonds with lower principal or interest, and exchanging debt for equity in the debtor countries.

In a buyback, the debtor country uses cash reserves to repurchase some of its debt from its creditor banks but at the deeply discounted price on the secondary market. In 1987, Bolivia and commercial banks negotiated a program of debt buybacks in which Bolivia could use money from third governments to repurchase its debt on the secondary market. In this way, Bolivia bought back almost half of its commercial debt in mid-1988 at an average discount of 89 percent (at a price of 11 cents on the dollar). Now the World Bank and IMF also allow debtor governments to use a portion of their financial support from the Bank and Fund to repurchase their debt directly for cash.

Debt reduction can also be achieved by converting some of the existing debt into a new asset that has a lower contractual debt service burden. For example, the banks and debtor government might agree to convert some of the existing debt, which might carry a floating market interest rate, into a new debt that carries a fixed, below market interest rate, with some or all of the future interest payments guaranteed. The new asset could be made safer than the original debt by backing it with guarantees or collateral.

A debt-equity swap involves the debtor government repurchasing existing bank debt using local currency, which must then be used by the seller to make a foreign direct investment in the debtor country. The seller can be a creditor bank, or a private company that purchases the debt from a bank and then sells the debt to the debtor country's central bank at a higher price in local currency. Multinational companies with operations in the country in effect obtain cheap local currency to meet their local costs when the debt matures.

Debt-equity swaps, however, have decreased since 1988. Brazil and Mexico suspended their debt to equity programs on the grounds that repurchasing debt for local currency causes an increase in the money supply and is thereby inflationary. If the government then offsets the monetary effects of the transaction by selling a bond in the domestic financial market, the bank debt is reduced, but not the overall debt. Because the local debts carry much higher interest rates, the overall interest payments will tend to rise, not fall, after the debt-equity swap.

In practice, given the persistence of the debt problem, the amounts of new financing and debt reduction through voluntary measures have proved inadequate. To go beyond the conventional and inadequate strategy of debt management, the architect of Bolivia's adjustment program and Poland's shock treatment, Harvard economist Jeffrey Sachs, now advocates a much stronger program of debt forgiveness.[1] Sachs maintains that the U.S. Treasury must emphasize the need for "concerted participation"—less euphemistically, "imposed" participation of the banks in debt reduction, with no free riders. All banks should accept an equivalent reduction of their debt, although they may choose among methods of participation, for example, buybacks or debt conversions. Perhaps the simplest mechanism would be to cut the interest charge on the debt to a fixed level below market rates, combined with official guarantees on part or all of the payments. Negotiations would be carried out in a case-by-case manner, conditioned on prior economic reforms in the participating country. The general goal would be sufficient debt reduction to enable the debtor to pay the remaining debt service routinely and to resume growth.

Sachs emphasizes the importance of involving creditor governments, the World Bank, and the IMF in a program of debt reduction. The U.S. Treasury, he maintains, will have to choose between the easy path of overseeing a small amount of debt reduction and the much harder path of active engagement to achieve debt reduction needed to solve a debt crisis. According to Sachs, the market alone will not achieve the necessary extent of debt reduction. He further argues that, unlike the situation in the early 1980s, the commercial banks are now in a position to accept a reduction in debt without serious risk to banking institutions. American commercial banks have rebuilt their capital base at the same time that they stopped increasing their debt exposure. Sachs also believes that debt relief can be structured with a guaranteed interest stream that does not damage the book value of the capital base of the banks.

Critics of debt relief, however, claim that banks would not voluntarily participate in a debt relief program that would reduce their profits and their capital, and there is no legal way to force their participation. Future credit standing of the debtor country would also be weakened and it would make it more difficult for debtors to return to financial markets in the future as creditworthy borrowers. Moreover, debt relief would reduce the pressure to carry out necessary domestic policy reforms in the debtor countries. The question of equity is also raised since there is a moral hazard problem in rewarding through debt forgiveness the debtor countries that misuse their borrowed funds and in punishing the debtor countries that manage their economies efficiently. Although concessional relief may be necessary for sub-Saharan African countries, this is questionable for such middle income debtors as Argentina, Colombia, or Venezuela. Yet, debt forgiveness would spread through political considerations to countries where the economic case is not strong. Finally, would less really mean more? Does the debt actually act as a tax on economic reform? Would the debt relief really provide the incentive for higher investment and greater growth?

Contrary to the Sachs program, the chairman of the restructuring committee at CitiCorp/CitiBank, William Rhodes, has stated "We hear proposals to abandon the current case-by-case, country-by-country evolutionary process, including voluntary debt reduction, in favor of an 'imposed' solution.

"I believe that mandated solutions are simply not the answer. . . . Imposed debt forgiveness would seriously retard the countries' return to the marketplace. Commercial banks, once losses were imposed on them rather than contracted on a voluntary basis, would probably stop or severely curtail lending to the countries in question—including vital short term lines to support trade. Many developing countries would have to rely exclusively on capital flows from official sources. This would severely limit their growth. . . .

---

[1] For details, see Jeffrey Sachs, "Making the Brady Plan Work," *Foreign Affairs* (summer 1989): 87–104. Also, Sachs, "New Approaches to the Latin American Debt Crisis," Princeton University, *Essays in International Finance* 174 (July 1989).

"As we move ahead, creditor governments, the multilaterals and the commercial banks must find additional ways to help developing countries which are making efforts to restructure their economies. I believe that the combination of new money, where needed, and accelerated debt reduction on a voluntary basis, is the most promising way to bring some of the countries back to the private capital markets. That is our major challenge."[2]

So far, however, neither the Brady plan nor the Sachs program has come to rule debt negotiations. All would agree that it is a perverse capital movement when the net interest payments from poor countries to rich exceed net new loans. All would like the development process to be reinvigorated in debtor countries. All parties may be suffering from debt fatigue, but no one proposal has gained general acceptance. The debt problem remains to be solved.

DISCUSSION QUESTIONS

1. You are on the staff that practices country risk analysis for a private commercial bank. The bank is considering a cross-border loan to the government of a Latin American country. What variables would you analyze to determine the creditworthiness of the borrowing country?

2. Debtors have the option to default. In weighing whether to default on its inherited debt, the debtor country will balance the cost of continued debt servicing against the cost of defaulting. What are these costs?

3. The central issue that creditors have to confront is whether to refinance or forgive a debt to avoid the debtor's repudiation of its existing debt. What is the case for refinancing? The case for debt forgiveness?

4. What determines the capacity of debtor countries to grow out of their debts?

5. Would you recommend any general solution to the external debt problem of the Highly Indebted Countries, such as the creation of a new International Debt Facility? Or must it remain a matter of only country-by-country negotiations, with the outcome dependent on the bargaining power of the respective participants?

---

[2] William Rhodes, "Voluntary Measures Are Already Working," *Financial Times* (April 12, 1989).

5 BALANCE-OF-PAYMENTS POLICY

R apid changes in international monetary conditions make balance-of-payments problems a major concern for national economic management and private management
alike. Operating exposures to exchange rate volatility clearly affect global competition and create challenges for financial management. Policies that a government adopts to
remedy a balance-of-payments problem will also condition a firm's activities. The practice
of International Contextual Analysis (ICA) and Diagnosis Prediction and Response (DPR)
therefore call for an understanding of the transactions in the balance of payments and the
policies that a government can undertake to meet a balance-of-payments problem. The
practice of ICA requires management to analyze not only the nonmonetary (real) forces
that shape the pattern of trade, but also the monetary forces that determine foreign exchange
rates and a country's balance-of-payments position.

Whether multinational or purely domestic, the firm will have to practice DPR when a
government's central bank or monetary authority intervenes on foreign exchange markets
with its own foreign exchange reserves to hold or alter the foreign exchange rate. Firms
will also be affected when, because of its balance-of-payments deficit, a government uses
monetary policy (a rise in interest rates, or a decrease in the money supply) to attract
foreign capital or to slow down domestic expansion and, hence, lower the demand for
imports. Similarly, there will be an impact from fiscal policy (a decrease in government
expenditure and/or an increase in taxes) again to slow down domestic expansion and the
demand for imports. Or, if the government attempts to lower the demand for imports by
imposing foreign exchange controls and trade restrictions, there will also be repercussions
on the firm.

To facilitate ICA and DPR, we shall have to understand some balance-of-payments
accounting, how to recognize a balance-of-payments deficit or surplus, operation of the
foreign exchange markets, various policies for the correction of a deficit, and the role of
the International Monetary Fund.

MULTIPLE POLICY OBJECTIVES

From the perspective of ICA, we should first recognize that a country operates within an uneasy triangle of multiple objectives: freer trade, internal balance, and external balance. The reduction of trade barriers is a frequently avowed policy target for most countries. Even more vigorously, national governments seek economic expansion—a satisfactory rate of growth in rich countries and the acceleration of development in poor countries. Internal balance requires this domestic expansion to maintain full employment and stable prices. External balance—the avoidance of balance-of-payments problems—is sought not as an end in itself but to achieve the other policy objectives of internal economic stability and freer trade. If a country were autarkic, it would not need to worry about its balance of payments. Or if a country were content to have a stationary economy, without full employment and growth, again it need not worry about its balance of payments. But, given the policy objectives of internal balance and freer trade, a country has to have external balance to achieve its policy objectives.

The state of its balance of payments is fundamental in determining whether a country can pursue monetary and fiscal policies to achieve economic stability and also trade negotiations to liberalize trade. A balance-of-payments deficit can prevent the other objectives from being achieved. And, it is those other objectives—not the balance of payments in itself—that contributes to a country's economic welfare.

The pursuit of full employment is paramount, and countries are often willing to forgo external balance to pursue economic expansion. But, as a country raises aggregate demand to achieve full employment, its imports will increase or its exports may fall so much that a deficit arises in the country's international payments balance. Some trade-off must then occur between internal balance and external balance, or between internal balance and free trade. The central challenge for an international monetary system is how to allow nations to pursue their domestic economic objectives without having to forgo the gains from trade, or to suffer external imbalance.

Before analyzing these uneasy policy trade-offs, we must first ask what constitutes a balance-of-payments problem? And, what is the process of adjustment when there is such a problem? Having outlined the fundamental analytics of balance-of-payments policy, we may then examine the significance for ICA and DPR. As with most statistics, those of a country's balance of payments do not in themselves provide answers to the analytical questions we ask. Instead of limiting our diagnosis to the numbers, we must realize that the balance of payments always balances, but this is no sign that the country does not have a balance-of-payments problem that requires remedial policy action. A government has to analyze how its balance of payments is brought into balance and whether this requires a remedial policy. Because the ensuing policy action may have profound effects on business, firms must understand how to identify a balance-of-payments problem and then to anticipate the policies that a government might undertake to remedy the problem.

BALANCE-OF-PAYMENTS ACCOUNTING

To begin with the accounting: The balance of payments is simply a systematic summary record of all the economic transactions in goods, services, and financial assets during a given period between a country's residents and residents of the rest of the world. As such, it records the sources (receipts) and uses (payments) of funds for a country's external transactions. The balance of payments is neither a balance sheet nor an income statement, but a form of flow-of-funds statement that shows changes in assets, liabilities, and net worth over time. The sources of funds are exports, investment income, transfer payments received, and long-term and short-term borrowing. The uses of funds are imports, investment income paid abroad, transfer payments abroad, long-term and short-term lending and investing abroad, and increases in official reserve assets.

The balance-of-payments accounts are constructed according to the principles of double-entry bookkeeping; every transaction has two equal sides, a debit and a credit. (Any transaction giving rise to a receipt from the rest of world or increasing net claims on foreigners is recorded as a credit. Whatever its form, the receipt is recorded as a debit. Conversely, any transaction giving rise to a payment to the rest of the world or increasing net liabilities to foreigners is recorded as a debit; the payment is recorded as a credit.)[1] If all the international transactions in the balance of payments are divided into vertical debit and credit columns, the sum of the debits will be identically equal to the sum of the credits.[2] There is always an identical equality between credits and debits insofar as credit items that result in receipts from sales of goods, claims, or official reserves must be matched by debit items that result in payments for purchases of goods, claims, or official reserves.

Horizontally, the balance of payments can be divided into three broader subaccounts: the "current account," which records transactions in goods and services and transfer payments[3]; the "capital account," which represents a change in a country's financial assets and liabilities; and the "official international reserve account," which records transactions in monetary gold and other reserve assets such as convertible currencies, the country's "reserve tranche" at the International Monetary Fund (IMF), and its holding of special drawing rights (SDRs) at the IMF.[4] Table 5.1 illustrates a consolidated balance-of-payments table.

The table is constructed from illustrative transactions. The sum of the debits is identically equal to the sum of the credits, and the algebraic summation of the net balances of the current account, capital account, and official reserves equals zero. The balance on the current account must always equal the balance on the capital account plus official reserves (with sign reversed), because the balance of payments is constructed as an accounting identity. In terms of the economic transactions that are occurring, this means that if increases in claims on foreigners are to exceed increases in liabilities to foreigners by any amount— that is, if the country is to be able to invest abroad—exports must exceed imports. If, however, the country is running a deficit on current account, this must be offset by investment from abroad and/or a loss of reserves. In Table 5.1, the net balance on current account shows exports greater than imports by 25. This is offset by a capital inflow of 20 and a reserve outflow of 5.

Table 5.2 presents a synopsis of the U.S. balance of payments over a number of years. The dramatic change to a deep deficit in the U.S. current account during the 1980s is illustrated in Table 5.3. Since 1988, the deficit as a percentage of GNP has diminished moderately, but is still of policy concern, especially in relation to Japan's trade surplus (consider Policy Profile 5.5).

The other side of the trade deficit has been the United States's change from being the world's largest creditor to becoming the world's largest debtor. Figure 5.1 illustrates this change in the difference between the value of U.S. assets abroad and foreign assets

TABLE 5.1
Consolidated Balance of Payments

	Debits	Credits	Net Balance	Cumulative Balance
Current Account	(−) 100	(+) 75	−25	
A. Goods and Services				
Merchandise exports		+		
Merchandise imports	−			
				Balance of Trade
Shipping payments	−			
Tourist expenditures	−			
Interest and dividends received		+		
				Current Account Balance
B. Unilateral Transfers				
Private remittances received		+		
Government transfers abroad	−			
Capital Account			+20	
Long-term capital inflow		+		
Repayment on long-term loans	−			
				Basic Balance
Short-term capital outflow (net)	−			
Official Reserves			+5	
Monetary gold inflow	−			
Official purchases of foreign currencies	−			
Allocation of SDRs received		+		
Reserve position in IMF		+		
			$\Sigma = 0$	

TABLE 5.2
U.S. Balance of Payments, Selected Years, 1960–95
($ billions)

	1960	1974	1985	1987	1989	1991	1993	1995
Exports of goods, services, and income	30.6	148.5	382.7	449.3	641.7	717.7	762.9	969.2
Imports of goods, services, and income	−23.7	−137.3	−484.0	−592.7	−719.5	−731.8	−825.1	−1,082.3
Unilateral transfers, net	−4.1	−9.2	−23.0	−23.9	−27.7	4.5	−37.6	−35.1
U.S. assets abroad, net[a]	−4.1	−34.7	−39.9	−72.6	−168.7	−57.9	−194.6	−307.9
Foreign assets in the United States, net[b]	2.3	34.2	141.2	243.0	218.5	94.2	−194.6	424.5
Memoranda								
Balance on goods, services, and income	6.9	11.2	−101.3	−143.5	−77.9	−14.0	−62.3	−113.1
Unilateral transfers, net	−4.1	−9.2	−23.0	−23.9	−27.7	4.5	−37.6	−35.1
Balance on current account	2.8	2.0	−124.2	−167.4	−105.6	−9.5	−99.9	−148.2

[a]Increase/capital outflow (−).

[b]Increase/capital inflow (+).

Source: U.S. Department of Commerce, Bureau of Economic Analysis. *Survey of Current Business* (July 1996), pp. 68–69.

in the United States. As long as its current account deficit persists, the United States will remain a net debtor and will depend on an inflow of foreign capital to balance its balance of payments.

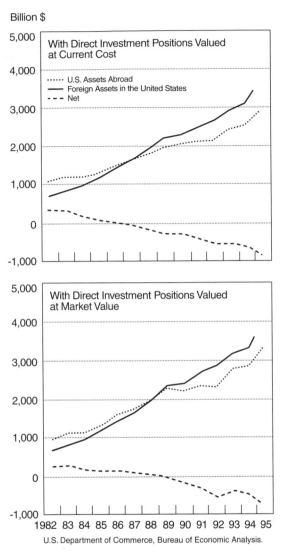

Billion $

Figure 5.1 New international investment position of the United States, 1982–95. The value of foreign assets in the United States exceeds the value of U.S. assets abroad. The net international investment position of the United States became negative after 1989. Except for direct investment, foreign holdings of assets in the United States exceed U.S. holdings abroad, mostly reflecting large private and official holdings of U.S. bonds. *Source*: U.S. Department of Commerce, *Survey of Current Business* 76, 7 (July 1996): 36.

U.S. Department of Commerce, Bureau of Economic Analysis.

CONCEPT OF "DEFICIT"

No matter when we look at a country's balance of payments, it will always balance, but this does not mean that the country is not experiencing international payments difficulties. On the contrary, even though the balance of payments balances, there can be a "deficit" or "surplus" in the balance of payments. The determination of a balance-of-payments disequilibrium is a matter of analytical judgment, requiring interpretation and economic analysis of the international transactions. If we exclude from consideration some transactions—namely, those that act as "settlement" transactions—then the balance of the remaining "ordinary"

TABLE 5.3
U.S. International Transactions as Percent of Nominal GNP, Selected Years, 1960–89

Year	Merchandise Trade	Net Investment Income	Other Items[a]	Current Account Balance
1960	1.0	0.7	−1.1	0.5
1965	0.7	0.8	−0.7	0.8
1970	0.3	0.6	−0.6	0.2
1975	0.6	0.8	−0.2	1.1
1980	−0.9	1.1	−0.1	0.1
1981	−0.9	1.1	0.1	1.3
1982	−1.1	0.9	0.0	−0.2
1983	−2.0	0.7	−0.1	−1.3
1984	−3.0	0.4	−0.2	−2.8
1985	−3.0	0.4	−0.2	−2.8
1986	−3.4	0.5	−0.2	−3.1
1987	−3.5	0.5	−0.1	−3.2
1988	−2.6	0.0	−0.0	−2.6
1989[b]	−2.2	−0.2	−0.1	−2.2

[a]"Other Items" include net military transactions, net travel and transportation receipts, other net services, remittances, pensions, and other unilateral transfers.
[b]International transactions for 1989 are for the first three quarters expressed as an annual rate.
Source: *Economic Report of the President* (February 1990), Table C-102

transactions can be in deficit or surplus. The items that we include as ordinary transactions are placed "above the line" that separates ordinary from settlement transactions. The items we exclude as settlement items are placed "below the line," in the sense that they are induced to accomplish the financing of any deficit in the ordinary items above the line. Ordinary transactions, or autonomous transactions, are undertaken for their own commercial sake, arising from the fundamental differences between countries in prices, incomes, interest rates, and conditions of demand. Settlement or induced transactions are the residual money flows that occur to fill any gaps left by autonomous transactions. They arise because of an imbalance above the line and reflect increases or decreases of the net foreign liquidity of a country. The transactions below the line are the best measure of surplus or deficit in the balance of payments.

The analysis of the balance of payments becomes therefore an exercise in line drawing. Where should we draw the line through the accounts and place below the line the settlement (or balancing, or residual) items that finance the ordinary (or autonomous) items above the line? In determining whether a country has a deficit in its balance of payments, we are in effect determining whether it needs to take some remedial policy action. If gold acts as an official international monetary reserve (not as a simple commodity), the changes in gold reserves act to balance the international payments. Monetary gold would therefore be placed below the line, and a gold outflow (a credit item) would indicate the size of the deficit, or the negative balance above the line. Official international reserves are now composed of foreign assets (convertible foreign exchange) held by a country's central bank, the country's reserve position in the IMF, and its holding of Special Drawing Rights at the IMF. (Countries may include the holdings of gold by their monetary authorities as reserves, valued by some at market price and by others at a fixed price [$42.22 an ounce for the United States] or an average price. But the gold is not considered a liquid asset because the market is thin and if a monetary authority were to sell the gold, the price would fall markedly.)

When we consider capital items, however, judgment differences vary over which capital transactions should be placed above the line and which should be regarded as settlement items to be placed below the line. Borrowings from commercial banks, foreign governments, the World Bank, or the International Monetary Fund should be placed below the line. Long-term capital inflows in the form of direct or portfolio investment, however, should be placed above the line, insofar as they are ordinary market-type transactions. They are not induced in an accommodating or compensatory fashion to finance a deficit above the line. Similarly, an inflow of foreign short-term private capital—for example, the increase in holdings of U.S. bank deposits by foreign individuals, foreign firms, or foreign commercial banks—is to be treated as an autonomous transaction primarily in response to market forces and placed above the line. This assumes that the short-term private capital inflow has been motivated by an increased foreign demand for dollars for investment purposes and for working balances. If, however, the inflow is purely speculative, it might be placed below the line because there is always the possibility that the foreign private holder of short-term dollars can sell his dollars to his own central bank, and the changes in liquid liabilities to private foreigners can thus be transferred to foreign central banks and result in a claim on foreign exchange reserves.

References are frequently made to the "basic balance," which places only current account transactions and long-term capital movements above the line (see Table 5.1). References are also made to the "official settlements balance," which places everything above the line except official reserve transactions.

NATIONAL INCOME ACCOUNTS AND BALANCE OF PAYMENTS

We can recognize the relationships between the balance-of-payments accounts and national income accounts in the following accounting equalities. Consider first a closed economy. The value of the economy's national income (Y) will be identically equal to the value of its domestic output (O) and to the value of its national expenditure (E); or

$$Y = O = E = C + I + G \tag{5.1}$$

where C is consumption expenditure; I, investment expenditure; and G, governmental expenditure on goods and services.

Now open the economy to foreign trade. The value of domestic output (O) is then

$$O = C + I + G + X - M \tag{5.2}$$

where C, I, G, and X (exports) are now gross of any import content, and M represents imports that are subtracted from (C + I + G + X) to obtain the value of domestic output, or the income produced by resources within the country.

National income is now, however,

$$Y = O \pm (D \pm U) \tag{5.3}$$

where $\pm$D represents receipts (+) or payments (−) of dividends and interest on foreign investment, and $\pm$U represents unilateral transfers (gifts and grants) received (+) or given abroad $(-)$. Unlike a closed economy, the national income of an open economy can exceed the value of domestic output if net income payments are being received from abroad.

In an open economy, national expenditure (E), or the rate of total absorption of goods and services, can also exceed the value of domestic output by having imports exceed the country's exports. National expenditure is now

$$E = C + I + G = O - (X - M) \tag{5.4}$$

or

$$X - M = O - E \tag{5.5}$$

If $(D + U)$ are assumed to be zero, then $Y = O$, and

$$X - M = Y - E \tag{5.6}$$

It follows that a current account surplus $(X > M)$ in the balance of payments is equivalent to:

- National income (Y) > national expenditure (E)
- Household and business saving (S) > (I_d) and/or taxation revenue (T) > government expenditure (G) [follows from the accounting relationship, $(S+T) - (I_d+G) = (X-M)$].[5]
- Net foreign investment: A current account surplus is a measure of how many new claims the nation is acquiring on foreigners—i.e., a measure of net foreign investment. If the country is engaged in net foreign investment, it will be investing a part of its national savings abroad instead of in domestic investment. The net foreign investment also means that the value of output produced in the country exceeds what the country is spending for all purposes including domestic investment.

Conversely, a current account deficit $(M > X)$ is equivalent to:

- National expenditure (E) > national income (Y)
- National investment (I_d) > household and business saving (S), and/or government expenditure (G) > tax revenue (T)
- Net foreign borrowing

If a country is experiencing a current account deficit, it means that national expenditure is greater than the value of national output produced. The internal imbalance between expenditure and output spills over into the external imbalance of imports greater than exports on current account. To finance this excess spending, the nation must be disinvesting abroad or becoming more of a net debtor to pay for the extra net imports on current account.

A central proposition that can be deduced from this analysis is that a "domestic imbalance" between investment and saving and an "international imbalance" between exports and imports are not two different kinds of disequilibria, but are the mirror images of each other: The external imbalance reflects internal imbalance.

From equation (5.6), it is clear that if at full employment real E is greater than the country's real Y, then the excess absorption by consumption, investment, and government expenditures can only be made possible by an excess of imports over exports. The external deficit reflects an excess of spending over income at home. And this deficit in the balance of trade must be financed by an induced capital inflow or loss of foreign reserve assets.

We may note that at an equilibrium level of Y, it must be true (*ex post*) that $I_d + X + G = S + M + T$. We may say that "full equilibrium" would mean the simultaneous achievement of "internal balance," in the sense that $I_d + G = S + T$, and "external balance" in the sense that $X = M$.

But is it possible that Y is at an equilibrium level, although there is not both "internal balance" and external balance"? Indeed, the absence of "external balance" is a reflection of the absence of "internal balance"; without the external disequilibrium, the equilibrium level of Y could not be supported. If, for example, at a full employment equilibrium level of national income, $I_d + X + G = S + M + T$, but $I_d > S$, and $G > T$, then it must be true that $M > X$. This is equivalent to $E > Y$. In this situation, the trade imbalance is a direct manifestation of internal disequilibrium, and we may as readily speak of excess spending as of a balance-of-payments deficit, or as easily of "overabsorption" as of "overimporting." Under fixed rates, the excess absorption must be supported by an induced capital inflow or loss of foreign reserve assets. A country borrows from abroad—that is, utilizes foreign saving—to the extent that its current account is in deficit. Under flexible rates, the home currency will depreciate when $E > Y$.

If, in contrast, $S > I_d$ and $T > G$, then it must be true that $X > M$. This is equivalent to $Y > E$. In this case, with fixed rates, the excess savings will flow overseas in the form of foreign investment (a capital outflow) or there will be an inflow of foreign reserves. A country saves and invests abroad to the extent that it has a surplus on current account (equal to a deficit on capital account). With flexible rates, the home currency would appreciate when $Y > E$.

It should be emphasized that a country that is engaged in net foreign borrowing will have an import surplus on current account, and a country engaged in foreign investment will have an export surplus on current account. The real transfer of capital is effected through the export surplus.

From these accounting relationships, it is clear that to reduce a current account deficit, it is necessary to raise national output relative to national expenditure and to reduce the excess of domestic investment plus government expenditure over savings plus taxation. This has been the challenge to the American economy since the early 1980s as it has experienced the double deficits in the trade balance $(M > X)$ and the federal budget $(G > T)$.

Referring back to Table 5.2, we can now give more meaning to how the balance of payments of the United States has evolved. Before the 1970s, the United States had a positive balance of trade in goods and services and a positive but falling balance on current account. After 1971, the balance of goods and services turned negative and became especially large after the early 1980s. From 1964 through 1975, America was a net lender, and its rising receipts of interest and dividends from abroad allowed the trade balance to become negative without requiring the United States to engage in net borrowing between 1973 and 1976. But from 1977 on, the United States had not only rising trade deficits, but also a current account deficit, and consequently became a net borrower. By 1985, the United States had become even a net debtor: The accumulated net foreign assets had become negative, for the first time since World War I.

FOREIGN EXCHANGE MARKETS

Balance-of-payments problems are, of course, reflected in the foreign exchange markets. Ordinary supply and demand analysis applies to foreign exchange markets. The only peculiarity is that we express the price of one money in terms of another money. In Figure 5.2, the price of foreign exchange is on the vertical, expressed as the number of units of domestic currency (d) per unit of foreign currency (f). On the horizontal is represented the quantity of foreign exchange (f) demanded and supplied. The view is from the d country. Going up the vertical scale, the d currency depreciates—more units of d are offered per unit of f. Correspondingly, there is an appreciation of the f currency as we go up the vertical axis. When the d currency depreciates, the prices of imports from f country increase in terms of d. We would, therefore, expect the quantity demanded of f currency to decrease as the d currency depreciates. As the d currency appreciates (going down the vertical scale), the prices of imports from f country become lower in terms of d. We would, therefore, expect a greater quantity of f currency to be demanded. The demand curve for foreign currency DD_f therefore slopes down to the right, as in Figure 5.2. What lies behind DD_f are all the transactions that give rise to payments from d country to f country for the import of goods, services, and financial assets (ordinary payments above the line).

The supply of f currency is derived from transactions for goods, services, and financial assets above the line that give rise to receipts in the d currency. The supply of f is the flip side of the demand for imports that must be paid for in d currency. If the f currency appreciates and the d currency depreciates, the price of imports from d country will fall in terms of f currency. We would then expect a greater quantity of f to be supplied. Conversely, a lower quantity of f will be supplied when the f currency depreciates (d appreciates). The supply curve for f currency, therefore, slopes up to the right as represented by SS_f in Figure 5.2.

If there is a free market in foreign exchange, the market would establish a market clearing exchange rate where the quantity demanded of f equals the quantity supplied of f. In Figure 5.2, this would give a market clearing exchange rate of 1.80d : 1f.

If now domestic investment rises, or domestic saving falls, or there is an increase in government expenditure, or a fall in tax revenue, then the national income of the d country would increase and there would be a greater demand for imports from f country. This would mean that at each and every exchange rate, the d country would demand a greater quantity of f currency. This is represented in Figure 5.2 by a shift of the demand curve from DD_f to $D'D_f'$.

If the exchange rate is then held by central bank intervention, there will be excess demand for foreign exchange represented by the amount GP in Figure 5.2. To hold the rate, the central bank will have to fill the foreign exchange gap of GP with the sale of reserves of f, in effect, increasing the supply of f from SS_f to $S'S_f'$. Even though there is now a regime of flexible exchange rates, intervention is common by central monetary authorities in order to defend the existing rate by selling or purchasing reserves. The present international monetary regime can be characterized as one of "managed floating."

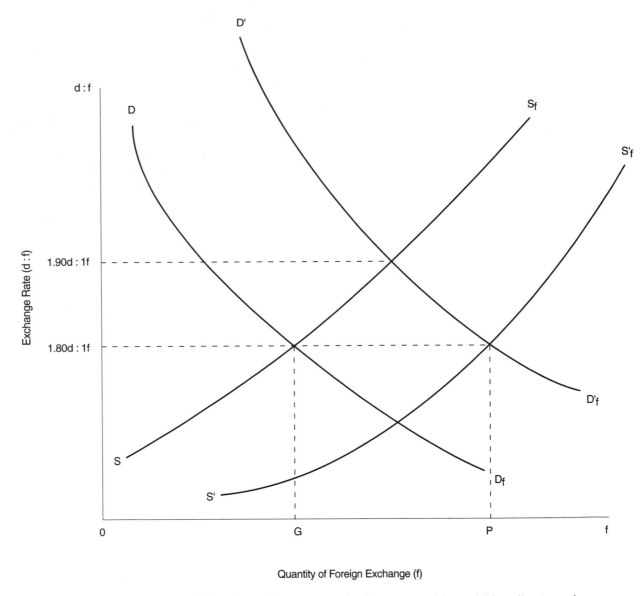

Figure 5.2   Foreign exchange market. d, domestic currency; f, foreign currency. Viewpoint from the d country.

If the monetary authority intervenes to hold the rate, as in Figure 5.2, then the rate remains overvalued. If demand and supply were allowed to operate freely in this foreign exchange market, the rate would go to 1.90d to 1f. If, however, the rate is held, how can we tell that the rate is overvalued? Some economists would want to calculate "purchasing power parity" to determine this—that is, compare the domestic cost relative to foreign cost for a given basket of goods. The calculation of purchasing power parity is complex, and is subject to a number of qualifications and criticisms. More directly, it is possible to judge an exchange rate as being overvalued if the central bank continues to lose reserves in an attempt to hold the rate, or if the country has to borrow capital from overseas to fill the gap GP (these are induced compensatory capital flows below the line), or if the country has to license foreign exchange, or impose tariffs and quantitative restrictions to restrict the demand for foreign exchange. All these actions would indicate that the exchange rate is inappropriate compared with a market clearing rate.

More generally, how would one forecast the foreign exchange rate? The analytics of DPR would suggest that the price of foreign currency depends on home and foreign interest rates, expected inflation rates at home and abroad, and the home country's current account balance. According to this analysis, the home country's currency will depreciate—the price of a foreign currency will be raised—by the following changes in "fundamentals":

- A rise in the home country's money supply relative to the foreign country's money supply.

- A rise in the foreign country's real income relative to the home country's real income.

- A rise in the foreign country's real interest rate relative to the home country's real interest rate.

- A rise in the home country's expected inflation rate relative to the foreign country's expected inflation rate.

- A deficit in the home country's current account balance.[6]

PURCHASING POWER PARITY

Our willingness to pay a certain price for foreign money must ultimately and essentially be due to the fact that this money possesses a purchasing power as against commodities and services in the foreign country. On the other hand, when we offer so and so much of our money, we are actually offering a purchasing power as against commodities and services in our own country. Our valuation of a foreign currency in terms of our own, therefore, mainly depends on the relative purchasing power of the two currencies in their respective countries. . . .

Given . . . normal free trade between two countries A and B, a certain exchange rate will establish itself between them, and, apart from slight fluctuations, this rate will remain unaltered so long as no variations take place in either of the currencies' purchasing power, and no obstacles are placed in the way of trade. . . .

Thus the following rule: When two currencies have undergone inflation, the nromal rate of exchange will be equal to the old rate multiplied by the quotient of the degree of inflation in the one country and in the other. There will naturally always be found deviations from this new normal rate, and during the transition period these deviations may be epxected to be fairly wide. But the rate that has been calculated by the above method must be regarded as the new parity between the currencies, the point of balance toward which, in spite of all temporary fluctuations, the exchange rates will always tend. This parity I call *purchasing power parity*.

Gustav Cassel, *Money and Foreign Exchange After 1914* (1922): 138–140

Although a prediction of the foreign exchange rate rests on such fundamental economic changes, there is, of course, always the possibility of the random event or shock that will upset the economist's prediction. In the long term and in a structural sense, however, the economic determinants are central.

CORRECTING A DEFICIT

If there is a deficit in its balance of payments, what policies can a country undertake to remedy the problem? What policies will institute a process of balance-of-payments adjustment so as to remove the deficit? Various possibilities are illustrated in Figure 5.3 that represents the $:£ foreign exchange market from the standpoint of the United States. On the vertical is the foreign exchange rate expressed as number of dollars per unit pound sterling. On the horizontal is the volume of sterling traded for dollars. Let the initial demand curve be represented by DD and the initial supply curve by SS. The equilibrium exchange rate is then initially $2.00:£1:00. Suppose national income then rises in the United States, or consumer tastes change toward imports. The demand for dollars will then rise from DD to D'D', and a foreign exchange gap of GP will appear.

What remedial policies are then possible? First, the gap can be "filled" by an outflow of foreign reserves, illustrated by (1) in Figure 5.3. Alternatively, the gap GP can be suppressed by imposing direct controls on imports through tariffs or quantitative restrictions that will suppress D'D' back to a level of DD, illustrated by (2) in Figure 5.3. Or, the foreign exchange gap GP can be removed by reducing demand from D'D' back to DD through deflation of national income via a tight monetary policy and/or a tight fiscal policy. This is illustrated as (3) in Figure 5.3. Finally, the exchange rate may be allowed to fluctuate freely, and the dollar will then depreciate and the pound will appreciate to a new equilibrium exchange rate of $2.50:£1:00. The quantity of foreign exchange supplied will then increase (4a), and the quantity of foreign exchange demanded will decrease (4b) as the prices of exports and imports change. The foreign exchange gap is then removed.

In summary, the policy options are (1) fill GP; (2) suppress GP; (3) remove GP with deflation; and (4) remove GP by depreciation. Although many countries undertake policy option (1) as long as they have sufficient foreign exchange reserves, or then proceed to (2), only the policies involved in (3) and (4) really remove the foreign exchange gap by correcting the underlying causes that gave rise to GP.

When is the policy option of currency depreciation needed? The "real exchange rate" is frequently used as an indicator of the need for depreciation. The real exchange rate can be calculated by comparing the relative costs of manufactures in two countries, or an alternative measure is to compare wage levels within the country with those abroad, adjusted for productivity. When the real exchange rate appreciates, current account difficulties may lie ahead. The larger the increase in domestic cost relative to foreign cost, the more likely it is that a currency depreciation will be necessary. Falling reserves are another indicator of depreciation to follow. The reserves can fall because of a current account deficit, or because there is capital flight from the domestic currency toward foreign currencies that are expected to appreciate.

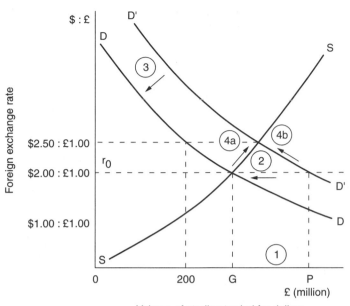

Figure 5.3 Policy options to correct a deficit. Equilibrium exchange rate (r_o) is initially $2.00:£1.00.

Demand for £ then rises from DD to D'D', and a foreign exchange gap of GP appears. This gap can be "filled" by an outflow of foreign reserves (1); or "suppressed" by imposing direct controls on imports (2); or "removed" by reducing demand through deflation (3).

With freely fluctuating exchange rates, the $ depreciates and the £ appreciates to the new equilibrium exchange rate of $2.50:£1.00. The quantity of foreign exchange supplied will then increase (4a), and the quantity of foreign exchange demanded will decrease (4b).

No mechanism of adjustment is without its burden. The central policy problem is to determine which of the alternative adjustment processes is least burdensome and how the burden of international adjustment is to be shared among deficit and surplus countries.

In assessing the burden or costs of adjustment through depreciation, we should note the following consequences. Depreciation will have a general effect on all prices in the foreign trade sector, acting as an *ad valorem* subsidy on all exports and as an *ad valorem* tax on all imports. A 10 percent depreciation of a country's currency is equivalent to a 10 percent uniform import duty and a 10 percent uniform export subsidy. Instead, however, a government may want to be selective and alter only some prices of selective exports (such as nontraditional new exports) and selective imports (such as luxuries, but not necessities). Depreciation may then be costly in not being selective and in being overly general in its impact.

Depreciation will also require a shift in resources as the demand for exports increases, the demand for imports falls, and the demand for import-substitutes rises. Resources must then be transferred into the export and the import-competing sectors unless excess capacity already exists in these sectors. These readjustments in resource allocation are not frictionless or timeless: They involve costs of transfer. If the country's capacity to transform is low, the costs can be substantial.

Further, depreciation entails a change in the distribution of income. Those who consume importables suffer a rise in their cost of living and a fall in their real incomes. Exporters, on the other hand, reap a windfall because a unit of foreign currency is now worth more in terms of home currency. Factors employed in export and import-competing sectors are also likely to benefit as demand shifts toward these sectors.

From the viewpoint of a debtor country, debt-servicing payments fixed in terms of the creditor's currency are equivalent to an import that rises in value in proportion to the country's exchange depreciation. If debt servicing is considerable, depreciation will make it all the more burdensome.

Unless other countervailing policies are taken, depreciation will also generate inflationary forces that exacerbate the resource allocation and distribution of income effects. The increase in exports and decrease in imports will have an inflationary impact through the rise in aggregate demand. In addition, there may be a cost-push type of inflation to the extent that imports rise in price, they are inputs, and firms have sufficient market power to raise commodity prices when their costs rise. Wages will also rise as the cost of living increases, and labor seeks to maintain real wages. If such price increases in the products and labor markets are allowed, the depreciation may become abortive as prices rise to offset the depreciation. If this is to be prevented, the country may have to impose contractionary monetary and fiscal policies, and possibly wage-price controls or some type of "social contract" to restrain increases in factor payments.

Another consequence of depreciation can be a deterioration in the country's commodity terms of trade. This depends on how export prices change relative to import prices when expressed in the same currency. Export prices decline in terms of the foreign currency, and import prices rise in terms of the home currency. But when export and import prices are both expressed in terms of one currency, the terms of trade might improve or deteriorate. Whether the terms of trade turn against the depreciating country depends on the relative size of the demand elasticities of the trading countries and their supply elasticities. The terms of trade are more likely to deteriorate under the following conditions: the less the demand shifts away from importables to exportables; the more elastic the supply of exports, so that export prices do not rise; and the more elastic the supply of imports, so that import prices do not fall. In general, depreciation tends to worsen a country's terms of trade, the less elastic are demands relative to supplies. If the terms of trade do deteriorate, then even though the country's balance of payments improves, each unit of the country's exports would buy fewer imports. The rise in import prices relative to export prices would thus reduce real income per unit of output in the depreciating country.

Finally, if depreciation is effective in correcting the balance-of-payments deficit through price changes, it will ipso facto do so by increasing the volume of exports or reducing the volume of imports, thereby reducing the total amount of resources available for home consumption and investment. The "rest of the world" gains greater command over the depreciating country's resources, or the depreciating country has less command over foreign resources. The ultimate consequence of depreciation is that the deficit country's real expenditure must decline. Even though the mechanism of adjustment operates through price changes, its ultimate impact is on real income. When the value of a country's imports is initially greater than the value of its exports, then the removal of this deficit—by increasing exports or decreasing imports—must result in fewer resources being available to fulfill aggregate home demand.

Although depreciation has these undesirable side effects, the deficit country still is spared the alternative burden of a more general and deeper deflation in employment and income or the costs of direct controls on trade and capital movements. The prices of exportables and importables rise as compared with prices of domestic goods, and this shifts the demand from internationally traded to domestic goods, while stimulating foreign demand for and domestic production of exports. By operating directly on the value of exports and the value of imports through the effects of price changes, depreciation still allows the price mechanism to guide the allocation of resources. Finally, depreciation does not restrict the volume of trade to the extent that the deficit country's exports increase even if its imports decline. In this way, the international division of labor and mutual gains from trade are maintained.

The various policy options of financing the deficit and internal and external adjustment can be illustrated in Figures 5.4 and 5.5. Figure 5.4, the so-called "Cooper triangle," is depicted with the vertices of the triangle indicating the following:

At L: exclusive use of international liquidity to fill the foreign exchange gap with official reserved assets. This corresponds to policy option (1) from Figure 5.3: It allows national expenditure to be sustained. As long as the country has enough reserves, or there is a lender of last resort in the system that will provide official liquidity, the country need not reduce its national expenditures to correct the balance-of-payments deficit. Conversely, the more the international monetary system dictates that an international imbalance should exercise discipline over a country's domestic policies, the less access the country should have to official international liquidity. The less the country's access to liquidity, the more it would then have to resort either to internal measures to remove its balance-of-payments problem or to external measures.

At I: exclusive use of "internal measures" of adjustment to a country's balance-of-payments deficit through reduction of aggregate demand by deflating the domestic economy through an increase in interest rates, a decrease in the money supply, and increase in taxes,

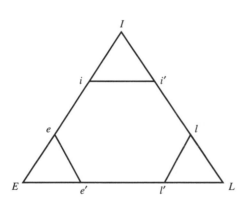

Figure 5.4 Policy options. L, international official liquidity; I, internal policy measures; E, external policy measures. *Source:* Adopted from R. N. Cooper, "The Relevance of International Liquidity to Developed Countries," *American Economic Review*, Papers and Proceedings, LVIII (May 1968): 620–629; and Cooper, *The Economics of Interdependence* (New York: McGraw-Hill, 1968), pp. 17–22.

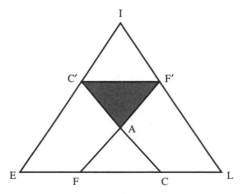

Figure 5.5 The feasible policy-space for coping with international imbalance. L, international official liquidity (expenditure-sustaining policies). Policy option (1). E, External measures (expenditure-switching policies). Policy options (2) and (4). I, Internal measures (expenditure-reducing policies). Policy option (3). EL, Size of *ex ante* deficit. Shaded triangle represents boundaries of the feasible policy-space. At A, EF of the deficit is financed by international liquidity, LC of the deficit is removed by external measures, FC of the deficit is removed by internal measures. *Source:* Adopted from R. N. Cooper, "The Relevance of International Liquidity to Developed Countries," *American Economic Review*, Papers and Proceedings, LVIII (May 1968): 620–629.

or a decrease in government spending. These policies are "expenditure-reducing." They correspond to policy option (3) from Figure 5.3.

At E: exclusive use of external measures such as tariffs, quotas, and exchange controls—policy option (2). These measures are "expenditure-switching": They switch national expenditure away from imports on to import-competing goods at home or domestic goods.

Depreciation of the country's exchange rate—policy option (4)—is also expenditure-switching by changing the prices of importables and exportables, so that demand switches on to exports and import-competing goods as the exchange rate changes.

Within the triangle, governments operate in a "feasible policy space," according to the degree of international liquidity that is available in the international monetary regime, and according to national preferences with respect to adjustment policies.

In Figure 5.4, for example, the country is only able or willing to deflate to the boundary of ii': any point south of ii' can be chosen. With respect to expenditure-switching policies, the country may be constrained to the boundary ee'. Any point to the northeast of ee' can be realized. Finally, the access to international liquidity is limited to ll': Freedom of choice of this "expenditure-sustaining" policy exists anywhere to the northwest of ll'.

What policies will a government actually undertake when it has a balance-of-payments deficit? This depends on what the country can do in the context of the particular type of international monetary regime that exists—for example, fixed exchange rates or flexible exchange rates.[7] It will also depend on what the government wants to do in accordance with the state of its domestic economy—whether there is already domestic deflation or inflation—and the expected reaction of foreign governments to any policy that the deficit country undertakes.

There are, therefore, bounds on what may be called a "feasible policy space" in which the government is able and willing to operate. This is represented by the shaded area in Figure 5.5. Let the triangle be an equilateral triangle (equal sides), with the length of a side representing the size of the deficit in the balance of payments before adjustment (a large triangle, a large deficit; a small triangle, a small deficit). If the government chose only the policy option of deflation, it would be at the vertex I in Figure 5.5, indicated as internal measures that are expenditure–reducing. Each of the other vertices represents exclusive use of a sole policy option. At E, the country undertakes external measures of direct controls on imports or depreciation. At L, the country has unlimited access to official international liquidity. In reality, however, the political process will lead to a mix of the policy options. For instance, for political reasons the government may be unwilling to deflate the economy beyond the line represented as C′F′ in Figure 5.5. It may also be unwilling to go in the direction of depreciation or direct controls as represented by the boundary C′C. And it may be unable to use official liquidity beyond the boundary F′F.

A feasible policy space is then represented by C′F′A. Some combination of policies will be adopted within this feasible policy space. Suppose the position adopted is at A. This means that EF of the total deficit would be financed by the use of international liquidity. LC of the deficit would be removed by the external measures of controls on imports and depreciation of the domestic currency. This would leave FC of the deficit to be removed by the internal measures that reduce national expenditure through monetary and fiscal policies.

It can also be noted that the more a government can make use of one type of measure—for example, internal expenditure-reducing measures—the less it needs the other two of expenditure-switching measures or expenditure-sustaining measures of international liquidity. There is a three-way trade-off among L and I and E-measures.

In the mix of policy measures, those that reduce national expenditure or switch national expenditure will have an impact on the business firm. Only if the deficit country has sufficient official international liquidity and chooses to sell these reserves will there be no need to undertake policies that either reduce national expenditure or switch the composition of national expenditure. In contrast, the usual case will have the government undertaking policies that have income effects and price effects to which the business firm must respond.

Although the focus has been on the deficit country, a surplus country also has a balance-of-payments disequilibrium, but the surplus country need not take remedial action to the extent that a deficit country sooner or later must. A deficit country, however, will urge the surplus country to undertake policies of adjustment just as the surplus country believes that the deficit country should undertake the adjustment.

INTERNATIONAL MONETARY FUND

What role in all this for the International Monetary Fund (IMF)? Designed at the Bretton Woods conference after the Second World War, the IMF was to be a supranational authority that would establish international monetary order and was to provide an international code of conduct that would avoid currency crises. The accomplishments of the Bretton Woods conference can be interpreted in terms of the uneasy triangle of policy objectives as an attempt to allow nations to pursue their domestic economic goals without being required to forgo the gains from trade liberalization, or to suffer the costs of correcting balance-of-payments disequilibrium. In the interests of their pledge to full employment, nations would no longer tolerate—as under the historical pure gold standard—deflation in national income as a means of removing a balance of payments. Nor did nations want to endure again successive rounds of competitive currency depreciations as had occurred in the interwar period. To allow domestic autonomy for the pursuit of full employment, countries at Bretton Woods established the IMF with a pool of currencies as a source of additional official liquidity for its member countries. To avoid the extremes of a freely fluctuating exchange rate or a fixed exchange rate, there was to be initially some fixity of exchange rates as determined by the IMF, but subsequently some provision for periodic adjustments in the value of a country's currency.

To achieve these objectives, the fund's code of international monetary conduct was initially based on four fundamental principles. First, a country's foreign exchange rate is a matter of international concern; a par value system should be the subject of international scrutiny and endorsement. All member countries of the fund must establish par values for their currencies, expressed initially in terms of gold or of the U.S. dollar of specified gold content, and may not change them without consultation with the fund. Exchange rates should be fixed with fluctuations only within 1 percent of either side of the fixed parities. The exchange rate, however, may be subject to periodic change—the adjustable peg feature. But this variation in the exchange rate was to be allowed by the fund only to correct a "fundamental disequilibrium" in the member's balance of payments.

The second basic principle of the IMF was that exchange controls on current international payments should be prohibited except temporarily under certain extraordinary conditions. A country's currency should be convertible, and multiple exchange rates should be reduced to a unitary exchange rate.

Third, national gold and currency reserves were to be augmented so that countries need not be forced to meet short-run balance-of-payments deficits by suffering domestic deflation and unemployment. This should be in the form of prescribed "drawing rights" by a member country on its "quota" at the fund. The amount of a member's subscription to the fund is equal to its quota. The financial resources subscribed to the fund by all of its members constitute an international reserve pool of currencies against which a member can draw for short-term financial assistance.

A member's right to purchase other currencies from the fund with its own currency is subjected to complex rules. A member has "drawing rights" up to a certain percentage of its quota, divided into five equal tranches. Only the first tranche of 25 percent of the member's quota can be drawn on automatically and unconditionally to achieve international liquidity. Beyond the first tranche, discretionary factors—"conditionality"—enter into the fund's decision on whether the member country can exercise its drawing rights and under what conditions of national economic management. A drawing country must repurchase its own currency from the fund within a certain number of years by payment to the fund in the foreign currency previously acquired, or in any other currency acceptable to the fund. This temporary access to the fund's financial resources offers only short-term financing to help ease the adjustment process for short-term balance-of-payments problems. For "fundamental disequilibrium," the adjustable peg was to come into force.

Finally, the IMF adopted the principle that a balance-of-payments disequilibrium is necessarily two-sided between deficit and surplus countries. The adjustment obligations are therefore the joint responsibility of both surplus and deficit countries, although the fund had no powers to enforce action by the surplus country. This system was not designed to grant a member country immunity from the "discipline of the balance of payments." A member's access to the fund's resources is contingent on the member's undertaking some process of adjustment when it has a deficit. Balance-of-payments discipline will ultimately be exercised, though a country may gain some breathing time by using its drawing rights at the fund.

The most important features of the IMF turned out to be its system of pegged—but adjustable—rates and provisions for liquidity. If gold was not completely demonetized at Bretton Woods, it was at least dethroned from its old position under the pure gold standard. Gold was initially left as an official reserve asset, and the value of local currencies could be expressed in terms of gold or the dollar; the dollar was expressed in terms of gold, so that par values connected with gold or the U.S. gold price. Throughout the 1950s and 1960s, the IMF was successful in increasing international liquidity through periodic increases in the quotas of its members. In 1969, countries also agreed to create new reserve certificates—Special Drawing Rights (SDRs)—in the fund. These were allocated to members in proportion to their IMF quotas in return for their payment of a convertible currency.

Pressure on exchange rates, however, became more extensive and severe in the 1960s, and large devaluations became necessary, especially for the pound sterling and the French franc. Strains were also placed on the system by having it become increasingly dollar centered, but the dollar still had to coexist with other reserve assets, especially gold. America's basic balance went into deficit between 1950 and 1970 as the outflow of private long-term capital and government grants and capital transactions exceeded the U.S. surplus in the balance on current account. The persistent basic balance deficit was financed by an increase in foreign holdings of dollar assets and a fall in the U.S. gold stock. While the deficit in the U.S. balance of payments served to provide additional liquidity to the international monetary system, the very creation of the deficit also undermined confidence in the future exchange rate stability of the dollar.

Yale Professor Robert Triffin repeatedly warned that the persistent deficit and piling up of short-term indebtedness of the United States, as a reserve center, were bound to undermine, in the end, the confidence of other countries in the ability of the United States to honor its commitment to redeem dollar holdings in gold. By 1971, the monetary reserve assets of the United States were down to their lowest level in the post-World War II period. The balance on current account had also gone into deficit, thereby increasing all the more the deficit in the basic balance. The United States was in the precarious position of being an investment banker that was lending long (through the outflow of capital) and, at the same time, a deposit banker that was borrowing short (through the buildup of external liabilities to foreigners holding dollar assets). Finally, in 1971, with the "Nixon shock," the U.S. Treasury closed the gold window and made the dollar inconvertible into gold.

Following the suspension of gold convertibility by the United States, the Bretton Wood system gave way to a hybrid exchange rate regime of nationally managed floating, joint floats, and pegged exchange rates. By 1978, the IMF's Articles of Agreement were amended to allow governments wide latitude in choosing exchange rate arrangements. Since the 1970s, exchange rates have been flexible. Revealing that they desire the flexibility to be less than full flexibility, however, governments commonly intervene in foreign exchange markets, buying or selling foreign exchange to manage the range of floating—hence, the term "managed" or "dirty" float. In mid 1996, 65 members of the IMF pegged their currencies—either to another currency, to the SDR, or to some composite of currencies.

While the IMF has abandoned its code of conduct with respect to exchange rates, except for a weak gesture of "surveillance," it continues to exercise the significant functions of providing members with official liquidity through periodic increases in quotas and drawing rights and in imposing conditionality on the use of the fund's resources. Various facilities of the IMF now allow member countries to accumulate over 400 percent of their quota in drawings.[8]

The principal way the fund makes its resources available to members is to sell to them currencies of other members or SDRs in exchange for their own currencies. Such transactions change the composition, but not the overall size, of the fund's resources. A member to whom the fund sells currencies or SDRs is said to make "purchases" (also referred to as "drawings") from the fund.

The purpose of making the fund's resources available to members is to meet their balance-of-payments needs. The fund's resources are provided through permanent policies for general balance-of-payments purposes (the tranche policies), permanent facilities for specific purposes (the extended fund facility, the compensatory and contingency financing facility, and the buffer stock financing facility), and temporary facilities (i.e., the supplementary financing facility or the policy on enlarged access to the fund's resources).

Since the fund's resources are of a revolving character to finance temporary balance-of-payments deficits, members that purchase from the fund must subsequently repurchase their currencies with the currencies of other members or SDRs.

ACCESS LIMITS AT THE IMF ARE GUIDED BY QUOTAS

The rules governing access to the IMF's general resources apply uniformly to all members. Access is determined primarily by a member's balance of payments need, the strength of its adjustment policies, and its capacity to repay the IMF. Access is permitted up to limits defined in relation to the member's quota.

The Executive Board reviews the access limits in the credit tranches and under the extended Fund facility (EFF) annually in light of many elements, including the magnitude of members' payments problems and developments in the IMF's liquidity. Guided by the principle that strong adjustment programs deserve strong support and by the need to safeguard the monetary character and catalytic role of the IMF, the Executive Board decided that, for a three-year period beginning October 24, 1994, the *annual* limit for access to the IMF's general resources in the credit tranches and under extended arrangements would rise to 100 percent of quota from 68 percent of quota. The *cumulative* access limit was left unchanged at 300 percent of quota, net of scheduled repayments.

These limits may be exceeded in exceptional cases. The limits exclude drawings under the compensatory and contingency financing facility (CCFF), the buffer stock financing facility (BSFF), the enhanced structural adjustment facility (ESAF), and the systemic transformation facility (STF). The current overall access limit under the CCFF is set at 95 percent of a member's quota. For the BSFF, the access limit is 35 percent of quota.

Access Limits
(percent of member's quota)

Under stand-by and extended arrangements[1]	
Annual	100
Cumulative	300
Under special facilities	
Compensatory and contingency financing facility (CCFF)	
Export earnings shortfall[2]	30
Excess cereal import costs[2]	15
Contingency financing[3]	30
Optional tranche[4]	20
Combined	95
Buffer stock financing facility (BSFF)	35
Under ESAF arrangements[1]	
Three-year access[5]	190

[1]Under exceptional circumstances, these limits may be exceeded.
[2]When a member has a satisfactory balance of payments position—except for the effect of an export earnings shortfall or an excess in cereal import costs—a limit of 65 percent of quota applies to either the export earnings shortfall or the excess cereal import costs, with a joint limit of 80 percent.
[3]A sublimit of 25 percent of quota applies on account of deviations in interest rates.
[4]May be applied to supplement the amounts for export earnings shortfalls, excesses in cereal import costs, or contingency financing.
[5]Average access expected at 110 percent of quota for first-time ESAF users.

Access under ESAF arrangements also differs according to members' balance of payments needs, the strength of their adjustment efforts, and their capacity to repay. An eligible member country may borrow a maximum of 190 percent of its quota under a three-year ESAF arrangement, although this limit may be increased, under exceptional circumstances, up to a maximum of 255 percent of quota. ESAF access is expected to average about 110 percent of quota for first-time users.

IMF Survey, September 1996, p. 14

The policy objectives represented by the uneasy triangle still continue to be of major concern, just as they were at the original Bretton Woods conference. There is still a need to resolve the three major problem areas of an international monetary system—provision of liquidity, an adjustment mechanism, and confidence in the system. Ever since the 1970s breakdown of the original Bretton Woods regime, there have been numerous proposals for international monetary reform. Any future reform will have to focus on the exchange rate regime, control of international monetary reserves, balance-of-payments adjustment, and the role of the IMF as an international monetary authority. Different policies are advocated in these areas, not only because of differences in technical interpretation, but even more because of the political and distributional implications of various proposals.

If not international monetary reform, there must be better coordination among national macroeconomic policies. Speedier balance-of-payments adjustment at lower cost depends on better coordination of policy, especially among the United States, Japan, and the European Union. To facilitate international financial diplomacy and peacekeeping in the international monetary arena, a revitalized IMF with stronger financial and consultative functions is necessary. This would dampen the volatility of exchange rates, reduce business uncertainty, and diminish the disruption from adjustment policies. (In the last chapter, we shall return to the problem of international monetary reform.)

ONCE AGAIN, ICA

Balance-of-payments policies have a wide range of implications for ICA. Most significant are how the foreign exchange rates may change, the nature of the policies undertaken to correct a balance-of-payments deficit, and the influence of the IMF.

The price of foreign currency is a very special price, and the variation in the foreign exchange rate has significant effects on business firms. A change in the exchange rate recalibrates the prices of all exports and imports. If the domestic currency depreciates, it is equivalent to imposing an *ad valorem* tax on all imports and an *ad valorem* subsidy on all exports. The price changes in the tradable goods also spread to the prices of domestic goods. How managers respond to the ups and downs of movements in foreign exchange rates can determine whether their firms earn profit or suffer loss.

The remedial policies taken by a deficit country to adjust its balance of payments also affect business. If the deficit country undertakes a tight money policy, the increase in interest rates will affect the cost of capital, and a decrease in the money supply will reduce demand in the economy. If the government resorts to controls on imports, there will be a switch in the composition of demand on to domestic goods that compete with imports.

The role played by the IMF can also be significant. For the IMF can be instrumental in determining the amount of official liquidity—the ultimate means of settling international payments. When the fund imposes "conditionality" on a country—that is, a set of required policy measures to justify drawing from the fund—it also affects the country's creditworthiness for lenders and modifies the country risk analysis undertaken by lenders. Finally, the IMF may facilitate policy coordination among deficit and surplus countries, thereby easing the process of adjustment and reducing currency fluctuations.

While managers in undertaking ICA should give considerable attention to the features of balance-of-payments policy that we have discussed in this chapter, their next step is to proceed from diagnosis to prediction and response (DPR). This must be related to strategic considerations of the specific conditions in particular countries. In the following chapters, we shall relate DPR to developments in the Triad (U.S., Europe, and Japan), the newly industrializing countries, and the transition economies of formerly planned economies.

NOTES

1. A capital inflow is a credit item (think of the sale or export of the corresponding security). A capital outflow is a debit item (purchase or import of the corresponding security). A reserve outflow is a credit item (think of the sale or export of the reserve asset). A reserve inflow is a debit item (purchase or import of the reserve asset).
2. For accounting details, see IMF, *International Financial Statistics*, annual.
3. Within the current account, the "balance of trade" account refers to the balance of "visible" current transactions—the sales and purchases of merchandise. Other items in the current account are "invisibles," such as freight, insurance, travel, investment income, and unilateral transfers.
4. When a country initially joined the IMF, it deposited with the IMF its subscription, of which 25 percent was paid in gold and 75 percent in its own currency. The former "gold tranche" of 25 percent is now the "reserve tranche," and countries may pay this with convertible currencies or SDRs. On the basis of its subscription, the country has "drawing rights" with the Fund by which it can draw other convertible currencies. A country's drawings from the IMF enter as a credit item in its balance of payments.
5. This relationship is explained more fully on pp. 201 and 227.
6. For a more detailed analysis, see Peter H. Lindert, *International Economics* (Homewood, IL: Irwin, 1991), Ch. 16.
7. At various times, the world economy has been on a gold-bullion standard, an inconvertible paper standard, and a gold-exchange and reserve-currency system. Under the gold-bullion standard, as it existed in the pre-1914 period and from 1925 to the early 1930s, the exchange rates were fixed and the international reserve asset was gold. Under a paper standard, as it existed in the interwar period, the exchange rates were freely floating and the need for reserves was removed, unless the monetary authorities wanted to intervene to hold the exchange rate fluctuations within limits. Under the gold-exchange and reserve-currency standard, as established in the post-war period with the institution of the IMF, exchange rates were fixed, but subject to adjustment under conditions of "fundamental disequilibrium," and reserves consisted of a substitute for gold in the form of drawing rights at the IMF. (Details of this will be examined below.)
8. For details of IMF's operations, see the IMF *News Survey* and the IMF *Annual Report*.

International Transactions

TABLE 5.4
U.S. International Transactions (selected years, $ millions)

(Credits +; debits −)	1975	1985	1995
Exports of goods, services, and income	157,936	382,747	969,189
Goods, adjusted, excluding military	107,088	215,915	575,940
Services	25,497	73,155	210,590
Income receipts on U.S. assets abroad	25,351	93,677	182,659
Imports of goods, services, and income	−132,745	−484,037	−1,082,268
Goods, adjusted, excluding military	−98,185	−338,088	−749,364
Services	−21,996	−72,862	−142,230
Income payments on foreign assets in the United States	−12,564	−73,087	−190,674
Unilateral transfers, net	−7,075	−22,954	−35,075
U.S. assets abroad, net (increase/capital outflow [−])	−39,703	−39,889	−307,856
Foreign assets in the United States, net (increase/capital inflow [+])	15,670	141,183	424,462
Balance on goods	8,903	−122,173	−173,424
Balance on services	3,501	294	68,360
Balance on goods and services	12,404	−121,880	−105,064
Balance on investment income	12,787	20,590	−8,016
Balance on goods, services, and income	25,191	−113,079	−101,290
Unilateral transfers, net	−7,075	−22,954	−35,075
Balance on current account	18,116	−124,243	−148,154

Source: Department of Commerce, *Survey Current Business*, July 1996.

TABLE 5.5
Balance of Payments, Selected Developing Countries
Current Transfers ($ millions)

	Exports of Goods and Services		Imports of Goods and Services		Net Workers' Remittances		Other Net Private Transfers		Current Account Balance before Offical Transfers		Gross International Reserves	
	1980	1994	1980	1994	1980	1994	1980	1994	1980	1994	1980	1994
Low-income Economies												
Ethiopia	590	563	797	1,189	22	247	58	61	−126	−317	262	588
Malawi	315	390	638	639	0	0	13	18	−310	−230	76	48
Uganda	331	333	450	901	−2	0		304	−121	−264		
Vietnam		4,918		6,218				170		−1130		
Bangladesh	976	3,220	2,622	4,830	197	1,090	13	154	−1,436	−366	331	3,175
Kenya	2,061	2,666	3,095	2,844	0	−3	27	151	−1,006	−30	539	588
Nigeria	27,749	9,879	22,044	12,504	−410	546	0	0	5,295	−2,079	10,640	1,649
India	12,348	35,020	18,105	43,692	2,786	4,976	74	1,224	−2,897	−2,473	12,010	24,221
Nicaragua	514	459	1,049	1,429	0	30	2	0	−534	−940	75	146
Zambia	1,625	1,185	1,987	1,593	−61		−122	−19	−545	−427	206	
Ghana	1,213	1,386	1,264	2,123	−4	12	0	259	−54	−466	330	689
Pakistan	3,010	8,401	6,042	12,812	1,748	1,446	147	945	−1,137	−2,020	1,568	3,716
Zimbabwe	1,719	2,016	1,900	2,338	8	0	−129	26	−302	−295	419	585
China	20,901	124,665	24,752	118,334	640	395	0	441	−3,211	7,157	10,091	57,781
Côte d'Ivoire	3,640	3,177	4,761	3,590	−716	−312	0	0	−1,836	−726	46	221
Sri Lanka	1,340	4,087	2,269	5,646	152	698	−16	−72	−793	−933	283	1,686
Egypt	6,516	10,511	9,745	16,121	2,696	5,073	95	0	−438	−536	2,480	14,413
Myanmar	556	1,125	869	1,776	0	0	7	312	−307	−339	409	518
Lower-middle-income Economies												
Peru	4,832	5,996	5,080	9,197	0	280	0	−14	−248	−2,935	2,804	7,420
Costa Rica	1,219	3,399	1,897	4,004	0	0	20	89	−659	−516	197	906
Poland	16,200	22,189	20,338	25,898	0	0	593	991	−3,545	−2,718	574	6,023
Thailand	8,575	59,161	10,861	68,429	0	0	75	986	−2,212	−8,282	3,026	30,280
Venezuela	22,232	19,170	17,065	15,993	−418	−746	0	436	4,749	2,450	13,360	12,459
Upper-middle-income Economies												
Brazil	23,275	50,674	36,250	54,474	1	0	126	2,597	−12,848	−1,203	6,875	38,492
South Africa	29,258	29,580	25,989	30,215	0	0	94	−19	3,363	−654	7,888	3,295
Czech Rep.	—	19,602		19,744		0		126		−16		6,949
Malaysia	14,836	65,795	15,100	70,106	0	0	−43	48	−307	−4,262	5,755	26,339
Chile	6,276	14,881	8,360	15,987	0	0	64	52	−2,020	−1,045	4,128	13,802
Hungary	9,780	11,441	10,374	16,404	0	0	63	896	−531	−4,067		6,853
Mexico	22,240	53,607	33,496	86,406	687	3,705	106	216	−10,463	−28,878	4,175	6,441
Uraguay	1,594	3,442	2,312	3,892	0	0	2	33	−716	−416	2,401	1,622
Saudi Arabia	114,208	54,598	62,710	52,159	−4,094	−15,717	0	0	47,404	−13,278	26,129	9,139
Greece	8,374	15,650	11,670	22,732	1,066	2,576	21	53	−2,209	−4,453	3,607	15,809
Argentina	11,202	21,029	15,999	31,421	0	0	23	318	−4,774	−10,074	9,297	16,003
Korea, Rep.	22,577	116,228	28,347	121,364	0	0	399	832	−5,371	−4,304	3,101	25,764

Note: Low-income economies: GNP per capita of $725 or less in 1994.

  Lower-middle-income economies: $725 to $2,800.

  Upper-middle-income economies: $2,800 to $8,955.

Source: World Bank, *World Development Report*, 1996, pp. 218–219.

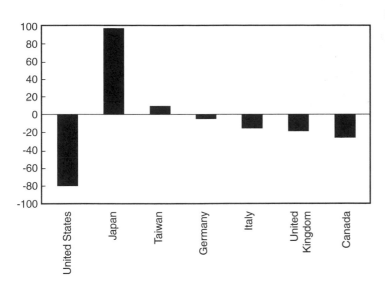

Figure 5.6 Current account balances, 1990–95 average, in $ billions. *Source*: IMF, *International Financial Statistics*.

TABLE 5.6a
Foreign Exchange Rates, 1969–95

Period	Belgium (franc)	Canada (dollar)	France (franc)	Germany (mark)	Italy (lira)	Japan (yen)
March 1973	39.408	0.9967	4.5156	2.8132	568.17	261.90
1969	50.142	1.0769	5.1999	3.9251	627.32	358.36
1970	49.656	1.0444	5.5288	3.6465	627.12	358.16
1971	48.598	1.0099	5.5100	3.4830	618.34	347.79
1972	44.020	.9907	5.0444	3.1886	583.70	303.13
1973	38.955	1.0002	4.4535	2.6715	582.41	271.31
1974	38.959	.9780	4.8107	2.5868	650.81	291.84
1975	36.800	1.0175	4.2877	2.4614	653.10	296.78
1976	38.609	.9863	4.7825	2.5185	833.58	296.45
1977	35.849	1.0633	4.9161	2.3236	882.78	268.62
1978	31.495	1.1405	4.5091	2.0097	849.13	210.39
1979	29.342	1.1713	4.2567	1.8343	831.11	219.02
1980	29.238	1.1693	4.2251	1.8175	856.21	226.63
1981	37.195	1.1990	5.4397	2.2632	1138.58	220.63
1982	45.781	1.2344	6.5794	2.4281	1354.00	249.06
1983	51.123	1.2325	7.6204	2.5539	1519.32	237.55
1984	57.752	1.2952	8.7356	2.8455	1756.11	237.46
1985	59.337	1.3659	8.9800	2.9420	1908.88	238.47
1986	44.664	1.3896	6.9257	2.1705	1491.16	168.35
1987	37.358	1.3259	6.0122	1.7981	1297.03	144.60
1988	36.785	1.2306	5.9595	1.7570	1302.39	128.17
1989	39.409	1.1842	6.3802	1.8808	1372.28	138.07
1990	33.424	1.1668	5.4467	1.6166	1198.27	145.00
1991	34.195	1.1460	5.6468	1.6610	1241.28	134.59
1992	32.148	1.2085	5.2935	1.5618	1232.17	126.78
1993	34.581	1.2902	5.6669	1.6545	1573.41	111.08
1994	33.426	1.3664	5.5459	1.6216	1611.49	102.18
1995	29.472	1.3725	4.9864	1.4321	1629.45	93.96

TABLE 5.6b
Foreign Exchange Rates, 1969–95

	Netherlands (guilder)	Sweden (krona)	Switzerland (franc)	United Kingdom (pound)[1]	Multilateral Trade-weighted Value of the U.S. Dollar (March 1973 = 100)	
					Nominal	*Real*[2]
March 1973	2.8714	4.4294	3.2171	2.4724	100.00	100.0
1969	3.6240	5.1701	4.3131	2.3901	122.4	
1970	3.6166	5.1862	4.3106	2.3959	121.1	
1971	3.4953	5.1051	4.1171	2.4442	117.8	
1972	3.2098	4.7571	3.8186	2.5034	109.1	
1973	2.7946	4.3619	3.1688	2.4525	99.1	98.8
1974	2.6879	4.4387	2.9805	2.3403	101.4	99.3
1975	2.5293	4.1531	2.5839	2.2217	98.5	94.0
1976	2.6449	4.3580	2.5002	1.8048	105.7	97.5
1977	2.4548	4.4802	2.4065	1.7449	103.4	93.3
1978	2.1643	4.5207	1.7907	1.9184	92.4	84.3
1979	2.0073	4.2893	1.6644	2.1224	88.1	83.2
1980	1.9875	4.2310	1.6772	2.3246	87.4	84.9
1981	2.4999	5.0660	1.9675	2.0243	103.4	100.9
1982	2.6719	6.2839	2.0327	1.7480	116.6	111.7
1983	2.8544	7.6718	2.1007	1.5159	125.3	117.3
1984	3.2085	8.2708	2.3500	1.3368	138.2	128.8
1985	3.3185	8.6032	2.4552	1.2974	143.0	132.4
1986	2.4485	7.1273	1.7979	1.4677	112.2	103.6
1987	2.0264	6.3469	1.4918	1.6398	96.9	90.8
1988	1.9778	6.1370	1.4643	1.7813	92.7	88.2
1989	2.1219	6.4559	1.6369	1.6382	98.6	94.4
1990	1.8215	5.9231	1.3901	1.7841	89.1	86.0
1991	1.8720	6.0521	1.4356	1.7674	89.8	86.5
1992	1.7587	5.8258	1.4064	1.7663	86.6	83.4
1993	1.8585	7.7956	1.4781	1.5016	93.2	90.0
1994	1.8190	7.7161	1.3667	1.5319	91.3	88.7
1995	1.6044	7.1406	1.1812	1.5785	84.2	82.5

Note: Certified noon buying rates in New York.
[1]Value U.S. dollars per pound.
[2]Adjusted by changes in consumer prices.
Source: Board of Governors of the Federal Reserve System.

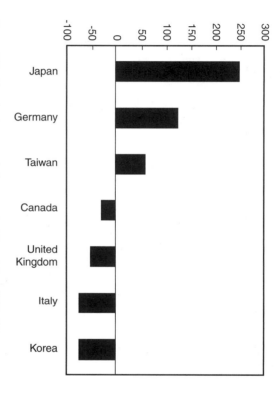

Figure 5.7 Nominal appreciation against the dollar: 1970–94, cumulative change, in percent. *Source:* IMF, *International Financial Statistics,* and the Bank of Japan, *Economic Statistics Monthly,* various issues.

TABLE 5.7
International Reserves, Selected Years

Area and Country	1952	1962	1972	1982	1992	1993	1994	1995 Oct.
All countries	49,388	62,851	146,658	361,209	725,550	789,096	844,242	936,928
Industrial countries[1]	39,280	53,502	113,362	214,025	424,229	440,423	460,716	509,312
United States	24,714	17,220	12,112	29,918	52,995	54,558	52,510	59,458
Canada	1,944	2,561	5,572	3,439	8,662	9,299	8,552	10,520
Australia	920	1,168	5,656	6,053	8,429	8,359	8,007	7,694
Japan	1,101	2,021	16,916	22,001	52,937	72,577	87,062	122,454
New Zealand	183	251	767	577	2,239	2,430	2,540	2,761
Austria	116	1,081	2,505	5,544	9,703	11,288	12,165	13,908
Belgium	1,133	1,753	3,564	4,757	10,914	9,187	10,382	11,293
Denmark	150	256	787	2,111	8,090	7,557	6,260	7,108
Finland	132	237	664	1,420	3,862	4,009	7,374	6,762
France	686	4,049	9,224	17,850	22,522	19,354	20,851	21,063
Germany	960	6,958	21,908	43,909	69,489	59,856	56,325	59,324
Greece	94	287	950	916	3,606	5,792	10,222	10,193
Iceland	8	32	78	133	364	312	202	227
Ireland	318	359	1,038	2,390	2,514	4,326	4,201	5,659
Italy	722	4,068	5,605	15,108	22,438	22,387	24,435	24,655
Netherlands	953	1,943	4,407	10,723	17,492	24,046	24,872	25,239
Norway	164	304	1,220	6,273	8,725	14,327	13,074	15,700
Portugal	603	680	2,129	1,179	14,474	12,094	11,189	
Spain	134	1,045	4,618	7,450	33,640	30,429	29,021	23,447
Sweden	504	802	1,453	3,397	16,667	14,081	16,141	15,725
Switzerland	1,667	2,919	6,961	16,930	27,100	26,674	26,704	25,251
United Kingdom	1,956	3,308	5,201	11,904	27,300	27,420	28,739	
Developing countries:								
Total[2]	9,648	9,349	33,295	147,184	301,321	348,673	383,526	427,616
By area:								
Africa	1,786	2,110	3,962	7,737	12,826	13,778	16,367	16,504
Asia[2]	3,793	2,772	8,129	44,490	164,403	190,810	229,296	249,709
Europe	269	381	2,680	5,359	15,171	17,176	19,374	31,130
Middle East	1,183	1,805	9,436	64,039	44,151	47,319	46,341	50,309
Western Hemisphere	2,616	2,282	9,089	25,563	64,770	79,589	72,148	79,964
Memo:								
Oil-exporting countries	1,699	2,030	9,956	67,108	46,144	46,532	44,445	44,369
Non-oil developing countries[2]	7,949	7,319	23,339	80,076	255,177	302,141	339,081	383,247

Note: International reserves are comprised of monetary authorities' holdings of gold (at SDR 35 per ounce), special drawing rights (SDRs), reserve positions in the International Monetary Fund, and foreign exchange. Data exclude U.S.S.R., other Eastern European countries, and Cuba (after 1960).

U.S. dollars per SDR (end of period) are: 1952 and 1962—1.00000; 1972—1.08571; 1982—1.10311; 1992—1.37500; 1993—1.37356; 1994—1,45985; October 1995—1.49455; and November 1995—1.48615.

[1]Includes data for Luxembourg.

[2]Includes data for Taiwan Province of China.

Source: International Monetary Fund, *International Financial Statistics*.

Money and Income in an Open Economy

Earlier parts of our analysis have established some relationships between saving, investment, interest, money, and national income, and also the balance of payments. As a summary device, we can incorporate all these relationships in a single diagram, commonly referred to as the *IS-LM-BP* diagram.[1] In Figure 5.8 the IS curve shows the various combinations of the interest rate and income levels that will make investment equal to saving. Investment will be greater with a lower rate of interest, and saving will increase with a higher level of income. The IS curve therefore slopes down to the right. The IS curve is drawn for a given level of exports and imports. "Investment" is therefore to be considered more generally as injections into the income stream—that is, domestic investment, exports, and government expenditure. "Savings" are to be considered more generally as leakages from income—that is, savings, imports, and taxes. The IS curve is also drawn initially under the assumption of a given exchange rate.

The *LM* curve shows combinations of the interest rate and income levels that will make the demand for money or liquidity preference (*L*) equal to the supply of money (*M*). The real money supply is constant along a given *LM* curve, and it is assumed that the money supply is completely controlled by the central bank's monetary policy. (A net international flow of money can be "sterilized" and not allowed to affect the domestic money through open market operations and changes in reserve requirements.) The *LM* curve is also drawn initially under the assumption that the exchange rate is given. The real demand for money to hold as cash balances depends on the transactions motive and the speculative motive. Transactions balances are related to the level of income, rising as income rises. Speculative balances are a function of the interest rate, falling when the rate of interest rises (the higher the interest rate, the more willing are investors to forgo a position of liquidity in favor of holding securities with higher yields). The *LM* curve slopes up to the right, indicating that financial markets are in equilibrium at lower levels of interest and income and at higher levels of interest and income. At lower levels of income, transactions demand is lower, leaving more of the given money supply available to satisfy the higher speculative demand at low interest rates. At higher income levels, transactions demand is higher, leaving less of the given money supply available to satisfy a smaller speculative demand at the higher interest rate. The more responsive the demand for money to a change in the interest rate, the flatter the *LM* curve. The *LM* curve would be vertical if the demand for money did not depend at all on the interest rate, but only on the level of income. And an increase in the

---

Reprinted from Gerald M. Meier, *International Economics* (New York: Oxford University Press, 1980).

[1] For a more detailed exposition of the IS-LM-BP model, see Paul R. Krugman and Maurice Obstfeld, *International Economics* (4th ed., 1997), pp. 476–80. Dennis R. Appleyard and Alfred J. Field, Jr., *International Economics* (1995), pp. 498–515.

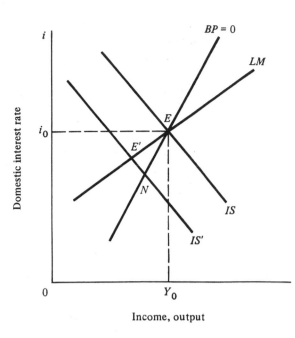

Figure 5.8 Income Determination in the Open Economy. Given the schedules that equate injections and leakages in the income stream at different levels of interest rates and income levels (IS), and the demand for and stock of money (LM) and the demand and supply of foreign exchange (BP), the equilibrium position of the economy is determined at E. At E, the interest rate is i_0 and the level of income is Y_0. There is equilibrium in all three markets—domestic goods, assets, and foreign exchange.

If I then falls to the level IS', a new equilibrium is established at E'. But E' is now to the left of $BP = 0$, indicating that there is a balance of payments surplus.

real money supply will shift the LM schedule down and to the right, whereas a monetary contraction has the opposite effect of shifting LM up and to the left.

Now consider the balance of payments. The trade balance is a function of income, and the capital account is a function of the domestic interest rate. An increase in income will cause imports to rise, thereby worsening the balance of payments. But an increase in the interest rate will induce more short-term capital inflows, which could offset the trade deficit and leave the balance of payments in equilibrium. In Figure 5.8, the schedule $BP = 0$ represents combinations of interest rate and income that provide balance of payments equilibrium. The schedule is drawn for given exports (a country's exports are not a function of its own income level) and a given foreign interest rate. The BP curve will be flatter, the higher the degree of capital mobility with respect to the differential between domestic and foreign interest rates. The lower the marginal propensity to import, the flatter also the BP schedule. (A low marginal propensity to import means that the trade deficit does not increase so much when income rises, and therefore the interest rate need not rise so much to offset the rise in imports by a capital inflow.) The schedule is upward sloping, indicating that when income expands, interest rates must also be higher to attract the capital flows that finance the trade deficit. Thus, BP schedules above and to the left of $BP = 0$ would indicate a balance of payments surplus, whereas BP schedules below and to the right of $BP = 0$ would indicate a deficit.

The full equilibrium level in the economy can now be represented by E in Figure 5.8. Injections into the income stream equal leakages (IS); international receipts equal international payments ($BP = 0$); the money supply is therefore unchanging, and the demand for money equals the actual stock of it (LM). There is equilibrium in the domestic goods market, the assets market, and the foreign exchange market.

Departures from full equilibrium can be introduced by considering changes in any of the variables. Suppose, for instance, that I falls. The IS curve then shifts down to the left to

IS' in Figure 5.8. The equilibrium level changes from E to E', where $IS' = LM$. But E' is now off the BP schedule, indicating by its position to the left of BP that there is a balance of payments surplus. The equality $I + X + G = S + M + T$ holds, but $(S + T) - (I + G)$ is positive and equals the balance of payments surplus $(X - M)$. International receipts exceed international payments, and the central bank purchases foreign exchange (with unchanged exchange rate), thereby increasing the money supply. The given interest rate i is then consistent with a higher level of income, meaning that the LM curve now shifts down to the right until it passes through N where a new full equilibrium is established.

As expected from our earlier analysis, a decline in investment reduces income (via the multiplier effect); a surplus appears in the balance of payments as imports decline; the interest rate falls as the money supply expands; and investment and income then rise until the balance-of-payments surplus is removed.

In contrast, an increase in domestic investment will shift the IS curve to the right. Income will then rise. And so will imports. At the new equilibrium income level, the central bank will have to finance the trade deficit by selling foreign exchange if the exchange rate is to be maintained.

Depreciation of the domestic currency will shift the LM curve upward and to the left. This is because the depreciation will cause a rise in the domestic price level through higher prices of tradable goods, and at the higher price level, the public will demand more money for transactions purposes. The higher demand for money can be fulfilled from the speculative money balances only if the interest rate rises. After the depreciation, the demand for money and supply of money become equal only if at any given income level the interest rate is higher than it was before the depreciation.

In the case of a depreciation, the BP schedule also shifts downward and to the right. This is because imports fall and exports increase, thereby improving the trade balance. Equilibrium in the balance of payments would then require a lower interest rate to induce a greater outflow of capital if the balance of trade is in surplus.

Monetary policy can also shift the LM curve, and fiscal policy shifts the IS curve.

If we now allow for capital movements, less of the adjustment process will depend upon changes in the exchange rate. To illustrate the role of capital movements and changes in interest rates, we may consider an *IS-LM-BP* diagram, as in Figure 5.9. Positions of balance of payments equilibrium at a given exchange rate $(BP = 0)$ are now determined by both the trade balance (as a function of aggregate demand and the exchange rate) and capital movements (as a function of the interest rate and the exchange rate).

Consider first the effects of monetary policy under floating rates. Suppose the country undertakes an expansionary monetary policy. The LM curve then shifts outward and to the right to LM'. The interest rate falls. As a result, short-term capital flows out of the country, and the exchange rate depreciates as the demand for foreign currency rises. The exchange-rate depreciation will cause, in turn, a shift in the IS curve upward and to the right, because the depreciation increases exports (injections) and decreases imports (leakages). The balance of payments also improves, and the BP curve shifts to the right to BP'. (BP' represents balance of payments equilibrium at the new exchange rate.) At T', a new equilibrium is established at a higher level of income with the intersection of IS' and LM' on the BP' schedule. A key element in this process of income expansion is the mobility of capital: the more mobile the capital, the greater the increase in income as a result of an increase in the money supply.

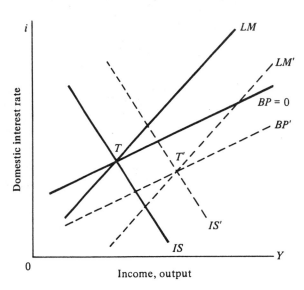

Figure 5.9 Monetary Policy with Flexible Exchange Rates. The LM curve first shifts to the right with monetary expansion, and interest rates fall. Capital flows out, and the exchange rate depreciates. This causes IS to shift to IS'. The balance of payments improves and BP shifts to BP'. Along BP', the balance of payments is in equilibrium at the new exchange rate. At the new equilibrium position T', $IS' = LM' = BP'$, and income is higher.

Now consider the effects of fiscal policy. If the country increases government expenditure, the IS curve shifts upward to IS'. This causes interest rates to rise and capital to flow in, and the greater supply of foreign currency causes the domestic currency to appreciate. The currency appreciation causes imports to rise and exports to fall. This has a deflationary effect and shifts the IS curve back until it is at its original position. The more mobile is capital, the less effective is fiscal policy under floating rates. (In the limiting case of perfect capital mobility, fiscal policy has no effect under flexible exchange rates. This is because there is only one income level that can make the demand for money equal to the supply when the interest rate is fixed and the money supply is constant. An increase in government expenditure, therefore, cannot change this equilibrium income, but can only lead to a trade deficit that offsets the fiscal expansion, which is financed by the capital inflow.)

Price and Income Effects in the Adjustment Process

The international economy is clearly not composed of countries with constant real income, and to the extent that a country's income is variable, its balance of payments will also change. It is also obvious that prices are not constant, and exports and imports are responsive to price variations. In reality, the adjustment process operates through both "price effects" and "income effects." We must now attempt to synthesize the two approaches.

We have already seen that when a country's exports fall, imports are not likely to decline by the same amount—and the country is left with a deficit if only "automatic" income adjustments are considered. To complete fully the adjustment process, we must then remove the assumption of neutral government policy and allow the government to pursue active policies that will deflate national income further. As noted, a tight money policy, for example, may then be necessary to raise interest rates and thereby to cause a reduction in domestic investment in order to depress national income further.

In reality, however, some prices are also likely to change to support the adjustment process. The reduction in the home demand for exportables will result in a fall in export prices unless supply is perfectly elastic. If the demand for exports is relatively elastic, then the initial price reduction will result in an increase in exports, so that the initial reduction in exports is offset, and the deficit is not so large. With the decline in domestic expenditure, the domestic price level may also fall. If the prices of inputs used in import-competing goods decline, and the prices of import-competing goods also fall, then there may be a "switching" in demand from imports to import-competing goods. And this increased demand for import-competing goods need not again raise import-competing prices if the elasticity of supply of import substitutes is sufficiently high. The result of this type of price change would also ease the adjustment process by supporting the income change with a price change that reduced imports.

Although it is a longer-run phenomenon, labor productivity might also increase in the export sector and in the import-competing sector. If wage rates can be held constant, or do not rise so much as to offset the entire increase in labor productivity, then "efficiency wages" and prices may decline in the deficit country and lessen the need for income changes to re-equilibrate the deficit country's balance of payments.

The interactions of income and price changes can also be recognized in the case of the depreciation of a country's currency. The depreciation will change not only price relationships; it will also have an impact, via the multiplier, on domestic income, output, and employment. Instead of considering only the partial-equilibrium analysis of the elasticities approach, we should recognize that changes in production and expenditure in one sector

Reprinted from Gerald M. Meier, *International Economics* (New York: Oxford University Press, 1980).

will have repercussions on the equilibrium of the rest of the economy. Ideally we would want to know the value of the "total" elasticities—that is, the value of the elasticities after allowing for all the changes involved in a depreciation.

In the first place, assuming that the partial elasticities are sufficiently high so that the country's exports increase or its imports decrease, there will then also be a stimulating effect on the country's national income via the foreign trade multiplier. As its income increases, its demand for foreign exchange shifts upward, and this has to be "automatically" offset or the country has to restrain deliberately this increase by appropriate "expenditure-changing" policies that limit the level of expenditure or income. The effect on prices may be interpreted as the "impact effect," the stimulus to exports and check to imports caused by the rise in the price of foreign exchange. The induced changes in income accompanying the rise in exports and decline of imports may then be interpreted as the "reversal effect," since they tend to counteract the initial impact effect of the depreciation.

The essence of the absorption approach then becomes relevant: only if the depreciation leads, directly or indirectly, to a smaller increase in national expenditure (E) than in national income (Y) can there be an improvement in the balance of trade (B). The balance of trade will improve only if the multiplier effect of higher output on total absorption is less than the increase in output itself. How far a country will have to allow depreciation of its currency in order to re-equilibrate its balance of payments will therefore depend not merely on the potential price-elasticities of demand for its imports and exports, but also on the income effects and the country's general policies directed to restraining inflation. If, prior to the depreciation, the economy is less than fully employed, then the income effect will not be so strong and will not be so significant in offsetting the initial impact effect of price changes. Expenditure-switching policies can succeed without any expenditure reduction only if the domestic economy has the capacity to increase output. If, however, the economy is already fully employed, then as exports increase and imports decrease with the impact effect, money income, but not real income, will increase; domestic prices will rise; and expenditure will be diverted to importables and exportables, thereby having a strong "reversal effect" that may swamp the initial price effects.

When a country is initially in an inflationary situation, and it then allows its currency to depreciate, the depreciation will be abortive unless the country also undertakes policies to deflate and offset the inflationary forces of the depreciation itself. Depreciation is inflationary insofar as domestic prices for imports rise, domestic resources are transferred from the production of nontradable goods to tradables, and an increase in exports, or a decrease in imports, results in positive income effects via the multiplier. For this reason, depreciation is considered an inappropriate policy as long as inflation is allowed to persist. If a country allows its exchange rate to fluctuate freely, and it continues to tolerate domestic inflationary forces, its currency will continue to depreciate in terms of foreign currencies until the initial inflationary forces and the inflationary impact of the depreciation are offset.

This is merely to reiterate the fundamental principle that if depreciation is effective through the elasticity approach, it will then increase home income in the deficit country and have an income effect that makes the absorption approach relevant. To correct the balance of payments through depreciation, there must be an increase in the country's real output relative to its national expenditure. At less than full employment, the balance of payments improvement can be realized by increasing national output more than "absorption." After full employment, however, as inelastic supplies are encountered and prices increase, the level of money income, but not real income rises, and correction of the balance of payments then depends on whether absorption can be reduced. If there is to be "disabsorption" in the private sector, this will have to be equivalent to an increase in savings. This might happen even under inflationary conditions if individual savers are subject to money illusion (that is, savings increase with rising money rather than real income), if there is income redistribution from lower to higher marginal savings rate groups, or if there is income redistribution from the private to the government sector through progressive income taxation.

According to the absorption approach, it can also happen if the "real balance effect" is strong (the real value of cash holdings declines when prices rise, and the holders of cash want to restore their real holdings) so that a depreciation leads to a reduction in real expenditure if the money supply is kept constant. This agrees with the monetary approach. The crux of the monetarists' analysis is the real balance effect and the associated stock-adjustment behavior by which actual real balances are adjusted to desired levels by international reserve flows in an open economy.

According to the monetarists, depreciation operates on the volume of real balances, and a depreciation is therefore equivalent to domestic credit contraction and works by deflating domestic real balances through a rise in the domestic price level. As the depreciation gives rise to an overall payments surplus, it will cause a net inflow (or slow down a net outflow) of money. To a monetarist, the depreciation improves the balance of payments by raising the money supply to meet demand. Or savings may respond to a rise in interest rates, or may increase in the foreign trade sector as profits rise in the export and import-competing industries at the expense of the real wages of those who import at a higher price. If monetary authorities would resist expansion of the money supply, deflation would balance trade following depreciation. These results, however, are unlikely to occur automatically in sufficient magnitude in many cases. Disabsorption will then have to be sought by active governmental policies that reduce $C + I + G$. Monetary policy becomes necessary to sterilize (that is, to offset through open market sales and credit contraction) the growth of domestic credit.

Nonetheless, it may be simplistic to contend that real income will not increase after full employment and, hence, that the balance of payments remedial measures can operate only on the side of cutting absorption instead of increasing real income. Even at full employment, depreciation may still effect an increase in real income through changes in resource allocation that will result from the change in the exchange rate. As the overvaluation of the domestic currency is reduced, resources will now be reallocated from domestic uses to the export and import-competing sectors where their contribution to real income is greater.

If the elasticities and absorption approaches emphasize that the adjustment mechanism must operate through both price effects and income effects, the monetary approach stresses that all balance-of-payments disequilibria could be handled by the use of domestic monetary policy. Thus, depreciation is only a substitute for domestic credit contraction, operating by reducing the world value of a country's money supply. According to the monetary approach, the preference for depreciation as a means of avoiding the equivalent domestic monetary contraction must be because of price and wage rigidity and money illusion. Further, the depreciation will be ineffective if an expansion of domestic credit offsets the exchange-rate change. And the depreciation will have to continue unless the initial exchange-rate change is supported by slower domestic credit expansion.

We can now offer a summary comparison of the different approaches to the adjustment mechanism. The elasticities approach has been the traditional theory in which the demand for foreign exchange is determined by the demand for imports, measured as a flow of foreign money, and the supply of foreign exchange is determined by the amount foreigners spend on domestic exports, measured as a flow of foreign money. The elasticities are therefore significant in determining whether a devaluation or depreciation will re-equilibrate the balance of payments.

In contrast, the monetary approach views the exchange rate as the relative price of national monies instead of as the relative price of national outputs. The monetary approach also interprets the exchange rate as being determined by the conditions for equilibrium in the market for stocks of assets instead of by the conditions for equilibrium in the markets for flows of funds, as in the absorption approach. Although the monetary approach does not deny that changes in the exchange rate can have significant effects on relative commodity prices and that these price changes affect the balance of payments, it is contended that these effects must come through the impact of the relative price changes on the demand for money. A depreciation therefore operates through a rise in the demand for domestic money and a fall in the demand for foreign money, associated with the expansion of domestic output and the contraction of foreign output. To be in harmony with the elasticities approach, the monetarist approach would contend that price changes are merely the indirect means by which the national money demand and supply are equated.

The monetary approach also emphasizes the markets for stocks of assets instead of the markets for flows of funds. The effects of asset flows on asset stocks are usually not considered in the elasticities, absorption, or income-multiplier approaches. The monetary approach recognizes that although flows of funds occur to correct monetary disequilibrium, the demands and supplies of flows of funds are themselves a reflection of the requirement for asset-market equilibrium.

Because the monetary approach maintains that a balance-of-payments deficit reflects excess supply of money as a stock, the deficit represents only a phase of stock adjustment and is thus temporary and self-correcting. Provided that the monetary authorities do not create new domestic credit, the excess supply of money will be removed by an increase in purchases of foreign goods and foreign assets. When stock equilibrium is restored in the goods and assets markets, the deficit will have been removed. Being concerned with long-run equilibrium, the monetary approach views the effect of depreciation (or appreciation) as only transitory and maintains that in the long run, depreciation (or appreciation) will have raised (or lowered) only the domestic price level and not affected real variables. Being concerned with the long run, the monetarist model assumes that output and employment tend to full employment levels, with reactions to changes taking the form of price and wage adjustments. In contrast, the Keynesian income-multiplier model assumes that employment and output are variable at constant prices and wages. But in agreement with the absorption approach, the monetary approach recognizes that depreciation can reduce real money balances and thereby reduce absorption (E) out of a given real income (Y).

The emphasis on both price effects and income effects implies that the correction of the balance of payments will depend on decisions taken throughout the economy (as emphasized by the absorption approach) and not merely in the foreign trade sector (though this sector will ultimately be affected by decisions taken elsewhere). This double emphasis on both price and income effects is reflected in policy measures that may be "expenditure-switching" or "expenditure-reducing." Expenditure-switching policies divert spending on foreign-produced goods to home-produced goods. Among such policies are depreciation and the various forms of direct controls on imports. Expenditure-reducing policies reduce $C + I + G$ directly and through multiplier effects indirectly—policies such as higher taxes or tight monetary policies.

Some of these price and income effects may be automatically instituted, but some need to be realized through adjustment policies that are deliberately pursued. The nature of the existing international monetary system and the initial state of a country's domestic economy will determine which effects are automatically brought about—and the degree of their automaticity. Whether price effects or income effects play the dominant role in the adjustment process, the way in which price and income effects are interrelated, and the policy choices open to a country, will depend on whether the international monetary system is based on fixed exchange rates, freely floating rates, or "managed floating." The sources of international liquidity will also matter. So too will the state of the domestic economy—whether the economy is in recession or in an inflationary situation.

Devaluation of the Mexican Peso

In December 1994, the new government of President Zedillo took office in Mexico. Within three weeks, the government devalued the peso. Turmoil then ensued on the currency, capital, and stock markets.

The new finance minister was Jaime Serra Puche who, as the previous commerce minister, had been Mexico's chief negotiator for the North American Free Trade Agreement (NAFTA). During the six years of the previous administration, the international financial community had hailed Serra (Yale PhD) and his other cabinet colleagues (several MIT and Stanford PhDs) as brilliant technocrats who achieved remarkable policy reforms in the Mexican economy.

Since the mid-1980s Mexico had adopted an outward-oriented and private–sector-led reform strategy. Key structural reforms included budget deficit reduction, privatization, and trade liberalization. The government's budget changed from a primary (noninterest) deficit of 8 percent of GDP in 1981 to a surplus of 8 percent by 1988–90. The public enterprise privatization program emphasized greater efficiency and also made Mexico more attractive to foreign investors. The switch from import substitution to export promotion brought an elimination of import quotas, a reduction in tariffs, and finally the implementation of NAFTA at the start of 1994. The anti-inflation stabilization program succeeded in reducing inflation from an annual rate of 159 percent in 1987 to 8 percent in 1993.

Another feature of the stabilization and reform program was the adoption by government, labor unions, and business of a series of *pactos* aimed at controlling wages and prices. To gain the restraint of labor and business, the government undertook to control the nominal peso-dollar exchange rate. A fixed trading band for the peso was established in 1987, and by central bank intervention as needed, the peso was allowed to depreciate only occasionally by a very small daily amount. The minute daily nominal devaluations were, however, insufficient to offset the rate of Mexican inflation, and the real exchange rate appreciated by some 10 percent in 1991, 8 percent in 1992, and 5 percent in 1993.

The structural reforms dramatically improved the fundamentals of the Mexican economy and enabled the country to regain international creditworthiness. There was a dramatic reversal of capital flows, from an outflow of $0.1 billion in 1988 to a net inflow of $20 billion in 1991, $26 billion in 1992, and a record $30 billion in 1993. The capital inflows allowed Mexico to increase its foreign reserves from $9.8 billion at the end of 1990 to $25.1 billion at the end of 1993, and to a peak at $29.3 billion by the end of February 1994.

Mexico's stock market became a leading emerging market. While interest rates were falling abroad, values on the Mexican stock exchange rose rapidly—from an index of 500 at the beginning of 1991 to over 2,500 at the beginning of 1994. In mid-May 1994, the Bolsa stock market stood 225 percent above its 1988 level in real terms. Foreign investment—both portfolio in the emerging market and direct investment induced by Mexico's policy reforms and the prospect of ratification of NAFTA—increased markedly in the early 1990s, especially at the end of 1993 and the beginning of 1994.

An inflow of capital, however, was needed to cover an ever-increasing current account deficit in Mexico's balance of payments. The current account deficit rose from $7.4 billion in 1990, to $14.8 billion in 1991, $24.8 billion in 1992, and $23.3 billion in 1993. Large capital inflows had to be attracted via large increases in domestic interest rates. In 1994, the net total of capital flowing into Mexico rose to $30 billion, more than 8 percent of Mexico's GDP. Before 1990, the inflow of foreign capital had come mainly from commercial banks, foreign direct investment, and foreign aid. From 1990 to 1994, however, Mexico financed nearly three-quarters of its external deficit by selling stock and bonds to foreign financial institutions. Portfolio investment from overseas amounted to $12 billion in 1991, $19 billion in 1992, nearly $28 billion in 1993. But while the inflow of foreign capital did help to offset a rising current account deficit, the repercussions from the inflow also put more pressure on the current account.

A relaxation of credit constraints on domestic borrowing allowed a rise in consumption and a fall in savings—the rate of personal saving fell from about 15 percent in 1988 to about 7.5 percent in 1994. Domestic prices also rose. And the peso continued to appreciate as a result of the large portfolio reallocation of foreign and Mexican investors into domestic assets, the tight anti-inflation monetary policies, and the government's use of the exchange rate as a nominal anchor to reduce inflation.

The real peso appreciation together with trade liberalization encouraged an increase in imports. Between 1985 and 1994, the current account moved from balance to the large deficit of $30 billion, equivalent to 8 percent of GDP.

Moreover, during 1994, political difficulties stemming from a peasant revolt in the southern state of Chiapas, two political assassinations, and the election campaign caused some capital flight. In addition, the inflow of portfolio investment fell sharply in March 1994 as U.S. interest rates rose. In April 1994, there was a net outflow of capital and again between September and November. Accordingly, with the rising current account deficit, foreign exchange reserves fell as the government used them to fill the financing gap rather than opting for a policy of devaluing the peso. At the end of February 1994, international reserves of Banco de Mexico (the central bank) were about $29 billion. Attacks on the currency then began, and by mid-November the reserves were down to $16.2 billion. Interest rates were raised to counter speculative attacks on the peso. But foreign investors were increasingly uncertain about the peso's parity against the dollar and moved out of *Cetes* (peso-denominated treasury bills) to *Tesobonos*, bonds that are denominated in pesos but indexed to equal the U.S. dollar. Outstanding Tesobonos rose from about $1.8 billion in February 1994 to $28 billion by November 1994—an increase from 6 percent to 50 percent of the value of all Mexican government securities outstanding. Of this total, $11 billion were held by Mexican investors (mainly banks), $1 billion by Japanese investors, and the bulk of the remaining by U.S. institutional investors (mutual funds and pension funds).

When the new administration assumed office on December 1, 1994, Mexican officials estimated that no less than $4.8 billion of foreign reserves had flowed out in the previous month, and the reserves were down to $12.9 billion by the end of November. Further, the government was to confront within a month the maturity of some $3 billion of Tesobonos.

To meet its balance-of-payments problem, the government could have undertaken any one or a combination of the remedial policies discussed in this chapter (pp. 181–87). Deflation through tight money and fiscal policies could reduce the demand for imports, but the deflation would slow the economy's growth. An increase in interest rates might give foreign investors a necessary risk premium, but would the rise actually be high enough to prevent an outflow without also slowing the economy's growth? Direct controls on imports would go against the prior achievements of trade liberalization. Devaluation of the peso could avoid the costs of deflation or import controls, albeit with the risks of inflation, further speculation against the peso, and an adverse effect on foreign investment.

Foreign reserves were down to $11.1 billion on December 16, 1994. On December 19th, the exchange rate was 3.47 pesos to the U.S. dollar. Although he followed the usual practice of first denying any possibility of devaluation, Finance Minister Serra announced on December 20 that the government would no longer support the peso within a narrow band. The government devalued the peso by 15 percent before reimposing the former limits on the peso's daily movement. But investors did not consider this action sufficient. During the two days of December 20 and 21, foreign exchange reserves declined by $4 billion.

Market pressure on the peso immediately forced the government to abandon its efforts to defend the peso's new value within the exchange-rate band. Given its loss of credibility and the uncertainty of investors, the government on December 22 had to leave the market free to correct the overvaluation of the peso. The hope was that this free float of the peso would overcome the current account deficit and promote the economy's growth through exports. By the close of the foreign exchange market on December 22, the peso had declined by an additional 20 percent to 4.80 to the dollar. Foreign reserves still continued to fall to the level of $6.4 billion on December 31.

In a move to restore confidence and credibility for future policies, Serra had been forced to resign on December 29, and was replaced by Guillermo Ortiz (Stanford PhD). In his PhD thesis, Ortiz had concluded—from a mathematical model of adjustment that allowed for devaluation expectations—that "a development strategy which relies on foreign borrowing does not seem viable in the long run." Now the December attack on the peso had vividly demonstrated the problem of trying to maintain a fixed exchange rate with open capital markets.

In view of the increasing current account deficit, why didn't the government shift to a contractionary monetary policy earlier or devalue earlier? Several reasons can be suggested. If the central bank had refused to buy assets from foreign investors and had not extended credit to the banking system, sales of foreign-owned assets to Mexicans would have caused markets to fall and interest rates to rise. But this would have led to a recession. As for the alternative action of devaluation, although the peso was appreciating, was it overvalued? Guillermo Ortiz had earlier argued that:

"It is true that the Mexican currency has appreciated, but such a fact is far from implying a strong devaluation of the currency. That depends on the equilibrium of the real exchange rate, which is difficult to calculate, adding to the fact that the peso had undergone a strong devaluation before the current stabilization effort started, which probably made it undervalued . . . the appreciation process is a natural, and not necessarily negative, consequence of the reform process in Mexico."[1]

---

[1] Guillermo Ortiz. "Comment on Rudiger Dornbusch: Stabilization and Monetary Reform in Latin America," in *A Framework for Monetary Stability*, edited by J. Beaufort Wijnholds. (Boston: Kluwer Academic, 1994), p. 306.

The governor of the Bank of Mexico, Miguel Mancera, also questioned whether the peso was overvalued. He believed that "the losses of international reserves during 1994 were clearly associated with unfortunate political or criminal events . . . and did not result from an expansionary monetary policy . . . it was entirely reasonable to believe that the adverse political shocks would cease once a convincingly legitimate presidential election had been held." Moreover, Mancura maintained that "manufacturing exports [had] been growing at an increasingly fast rate, which reached 22% in January–November 1994 (compared with the same period in 1993), the highest increase since 1989. In this light, could the peso be viewed as overvalued?"[2]

Insofar as imports were composed of investment goods, it could also be argued that these imports would increase productivity and lead to greater output and exports. If pressure on the balance of payments was coming from the private sector—not from a fiscal deficit by the government—many thought that the balance of payments could be treated with benign neglect. With NAFTA, there was also the belief that exports would continue to increase.

Given additional time, it was argued that the fundamental reforms would become more effective, but a devaluation would cause the government to lose credit for its reform program. And for political reasons, an election year was not a time for a devaluation.

The new finance minister attempted to calm the volatile markets. He announced a comprehensive program aimed at stabilizing the economy and restoring financial market confidence. The major objectives were to be the containment of inflation and the reduction of the current account deficit by about four percentage points of GDP to a deficit level of less than $14 billion that was believed sustainable. To accomplish these objectives, a fiscal surplus of 0.5 percent of GDP was to be achieved through cuts in government expenditure equal to 1.3 percent of GDP. Monetary policy was to be tight. A 7 percent cap was to be placed on wage increases. Privatization of more state-owned assets was expected to yield $12 to $14 billion. A hoped-for retention of government bonds was to be sought through an increase in interest rates on the Tesobonos to 20 percent and by the issue of new longer-term higher-yield bonds that would encourage foreign investors not to withdraw dollars when their bonds matured.

It was essential to calm the currency and stock markets and to restore confidence for foreign investors. The finance minister went to New York to give a two-hour presentation of his program to a standing room only crowd of banking and brokerage officials in the ballroom of the Pierre Hotel. After the meeting, Ortiz held a smaller lunch with representatives of ten major U.S. banks. William R. Rhodes of Citicorp, who organized the lunch, said Ortiz gave "a forceful presentation, which impressed everyone with his realism as to what has to be done."

To give credibility to the proposed stabilization program, the Mexican government announced the arrangement of a key Exchange Stabilization Fund of $18 billion, composed of a $9 billion line of credit from the United States, $1.07 billion from Canada, $5 billion from the Bank for International Settlements, and $3 billion from international commercial banks. Mexico also requested four commercial banks in Japan to provide credits of $1.2 billion, and the Bank of Japan began considering the provision of $1 to $5 billion of loans through the Bank for International Settlements. In addition, the IMF was expected to provide a secondary line of reserves from a standby agreement in 1995. This would subject the Mexican government to the IMF's monitoring of its conditions for

---

[2] *Wall Street Journal,* January 31, 1995, p. A22.

drawing on the standby agreement—a possible confidence-building signal to international investors.

In mid-January 1995, Mexico's central bank began to make modest drawings from its international credit line to buy pesos. In addition, overnight interest rates paid by banks on peso deposits doubled to 55 percent. But many analysts feared that in allowing interest rates to rise, the central bank was causing stock prices to fall further and was increasing the amount of nonperforming loans in Mexican bank portfolios.

With a pledge to "do what is necessary to restore confidence," the U.S. administration announced that it would ask Congress to approve a package of loan guarantees as high as $40 billion, to come—if needed in the event of Mexican defaults—from Federal Reserve Bank currency dealings and the Treasury's Exchange Stabilization Fund. New loans guaranteed by the United States could last as long as ten years, allowing Mexico to reschedule its external debt to a longer maturity profile. Acting in essence as a co-signer for Mexico's longer-term debt, the United States was to receive "insurance" fees for its guarantees.

Although investment banks and Wall Street traders applauded the guarantee plan, Congress showed considerably less enthusiasm. Indeed, many in Congress complained that the arrangement would be simply a "bailout" for wealthy investors, that the risk should not be borne by the American taxpayer, that more stringent economic and even political commitments should be asked of Mexico—such as border control of migrants, environmental protection, increase in minimum wages, privatization of Pemex (the state-owned oil monopoly), and cessation of Mexican relationships with Cuba.

As Congress continued to debate, the currency markets and stock market continued to be apprehensive. The second weekly auction of Tesobonos was poorly subscribed: The government was left with $125 million of its $400 million offering, and the government had to offer a rate of 24.98 percent on ninety-one-day Tesobonos—among the highest auction rates on record.

Although many in Congress remained hostile, the IMF—in a period of two weeks—concluded with Mexico a standby agreement of $7.58 billion. Mexico could add these funds to the reserves of its central bank over the next eighteen months, and repay the fund in three to five years. The managing director of the IMF said that Mexico's recovery plan was "strong, coherent and credible."

Meanwhile, Congress had still not acted. On January 30, uncertainty drove the peso to its lowest level—falling by another 10 percent to 6.35 pesos to the dollar, a loss in value of 45 percent since the devaluation of December 20, 1994. And the Mexican stock market fell to 1898.9—its lowest level since October 1993. Foreign reserves were only $3.4 billion on January 31, enough to cover only three weeks of imports. More than $2 billion of the special $9 billion credit line from the U.S. Federal Reserve had already been used. And some $29 billion in the dollar-indexed Tesobonos and $20 billion in Mexican bank obligations were to come due during the year.

Fearing that the international economy could not afford any further Congressional delay on the proposed $40 billion guarantee agreement, President Clinton then announced on January 30 that by executive authority he was granting Mexico $20 billion in loans and guarantees from the U.S. Treasury's Exchange Equalization Fund (normally used to stabilize the dollar in international markets).

In addition, the rescue package would raise the IMF's support to Mexico to $17.8 billion in an eighteen-month standby credit—3½ times more than the fund had ever approved for any country. Of the IMF total, $7.8 billion would be available immediately. The Bank of

International Settlements, supported by the central banks of the major industrial countries, would contribute another $10 billion in short-term loans. Canada would swap $1 billion of its currency for pesos, and a group of Latin American countries would also arrange a similar $1 billion package. This new $50 billion package would replace the $21.8 billion in earlier pledges.

After the late morning announcement of this new rescue plan, the peso immediately regained more than 10 percent of its value against the dollar, strengthening from an intraday record low of 6.55 pesos to the dollar to 5.75 pesos to the dollar. And the Mexican stock market saw its biggest one day gain of 10 percent to close at 2093.98. Other emerging markets around the globe also gained.

Of the financial support package, Ariel Buira, vice governor of Banco de Mexico, said: "Our problems are over. This is real money. It gives us more flexibility, it will allow us to meet our short term obligations and restore confidence in the Mexican peso."

And Michel Camdessus, managing director of the IMF, stated that the fund's action had averted "the first major crisis of our new world of globalized financial markets."

The United States and Mexico signed their $20 billion loan agreement on February 22, 1995. Like the IMF's conditionality for its standby agreement, the United States also imposed some conditions. Mexico should:

- Limit its credit expansion to 10 billion pesos for all of 1995
- Maintain "substantially positive" real interest rates
- Raise $12 billion to $14 billion through privatizations over the next three years

To ease any concern over a possible default, Mexico also agreed to collateral terms requiring importers of Mexican crude oil, oil products, and petrochemicals to remit their payments to a special Mexican account at the Federal Reserve Bank of New York. The United States could exercise first claim in the event of a default.

The United States made $3 billion immediately available. Another $7 billion will be provided during the next four months, and the remaining $10 billion would be disbursed beginning in July 1995, subject to the economic policy conditions being met. Initially, the rescue package was to help Mexico retire the short-term Tesobonos, and was also to provide guarantees for medium-term bonds that Mexico plans to issue. Mexico's central bank was also permitted to use American funds to support holders of dollar-denominated certificates of deposit in Mexico's banking system.

The day after the agreement, interest rates on benchmark twenty-eight-day treasury bills (Cetes) were allowed to rise to 59 percent—the highest level in seven years. Mexican stocks gained 1.73 percent and ended the day at 1708.28. And the peso closed at 5.845 to the dollar—a loss of 40.7 percent since the peso was first devalued on December 20.

Many analysts believed the immediate liquidity crisis was over. But the unprecedented $50 billion financial support package was only the beginning of the resolution of Mexico's problems. Troublesome questions for the future remained. The success of the programs formulated by the Mexican government and supported by the financial rescue package depended on future answers to a number of questions. Would Mexico be able to lengthen its debt profile? Would new foreign capital flow in? Could Mexico avoid a deep and long recession? Would savings increase? Would exports increase and imports decrease? Could inflation be avoided? Would Mexico succeed in regaining a credible rate of economic growth?

Aggregate domestic and private savings declined...

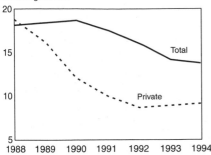

Source: World Bank staff estimates.

...the real exchange rate appreciated...

Source: World Bank and International Monetary Fund.

...and the current account balance deteriorated

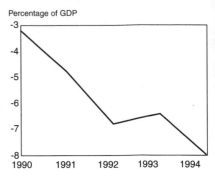

Source: Bank of Mexico.

In the face of loss of investor confidence, some policy mistakes were made...

The nominal exchange rate band was not adjusted...

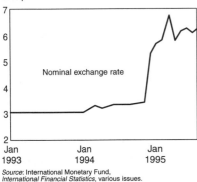

Source: International Monetary Fund,
International Financial Statistics, various issues.

...the increase in domestic interest rates was moderated by sterilization...

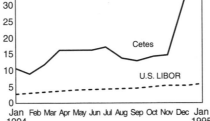

Source: Bank of Mexico and U.S. Department of Commerce,
Survey of Current Business, various issues.

...and public debt was shifted to short-term dollar-linked instruments

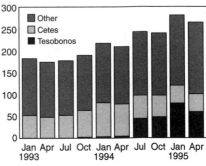

Source: Bank of Mexico.

With the result that...

The current account balance deteriorated further...

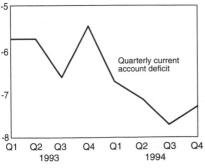

...and there was a sustained loss of reserves...

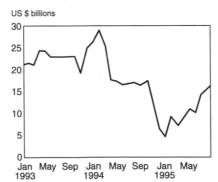

...and a sharp decline in reserve cover

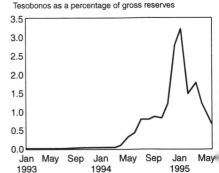

Figure 5.10 Mexico: what happened and why? The surge in private capital flows to Mexico during 1990–93 was associated with increased vulnerability to shocks. Source: IMF, International Capital Markets 1995, p. 13.

TABLE 5.8
Mexico

Population mid-1992 (*millions*)	85.0				Income group: Upper-middle	
GNP per capita 1992 (*US$*)	3,450				Indebtedness level: Severe	

Key Ratios	*1980*	*1985*	*1991*	*1992*	*1993*
Gross domestic investment/GDP	27.2	21.2	22.4	23.3	21.7
Exports of goods and nfs/GDP	10.7	15.4	13.9	12.6	12.8
Gross domestic savings/GDP	24.9	26.3	19.3	17.7	15.9
Gross national savings/GDP	21.6	22.4	17.9	15.7	13.5
Current account balance/GDP	−5.5	0.2	−5.2	−7.5	−6.8
Interest payments/GDP	2.4	5.1	2.2	1.8	1.6
Total debt/GDP	29.5	52.5	40.2	34.4	34.6
Total debt/exports	258.1	286.5	203.0	187.9	185.9

Investment to GDP ratio (%)

Sharesof GDP by sector (%)

GDP: Production (*% of GDP*)	*1980*	*1985*	*1991*	*1992*	*1993*
Agriculture	8.2	9.1	7.7	8.4	8.5
Industry	32.8	33.3	30.0	28.3	28.4
Manufacturing	22.1	23.4	22.3	20.4	20.4
Services	59.0	57.6	62.2	63.2	63.2
(*average annual growth*)	*1980*	*1985*	*1991*	*1992*	*1993*
Agriculture	2.1	0.2	1.0	−0.2	1.7
Industry	0.1	3.0	3.4	2.7	0.1
Manufacturing	0.1	3.4	4.0	1.7	−0.9
Services	1.8	2.2	4.1	3.7	0.5
GDP	1.2	2.3	3.6	3.0	0.4

Growth rates of GDI and GDP (%)

GDP: Expenditure (*% of GDP*)	*1980*	*1985*	*1991*	*1992*	*1993*
Private consumption	65.1	64.5	71.7	72.2	74.8
General government consumption	10.0	9.2	9.0	10.1	9.3
Gross domestic investment	27.2	21.2	22.4	23.3	21.7
Exports of goods and nfs	10.7	15.4	13.9	12.6	12.8
Imports of goods and nfs	13.0	10.3	17.0	18.1	18.7
(*average annual growth*)	*1980–85*	*1985–93*	*1991*	*1992*	*1993*
Private consumption	−0.7	4.8	6.2	6.7	0.0
General government consumption	4.2	1.3	3.9	2.3	3.0
Gross domestic investment	−9.3	6.1	7.2	14.6	−3.3
Exports of goods and nfs	10.5	4.5	5.4	0.8	3.5
Imports of goods and nfs	−13.0	17.0	16.4	21.2	−1.2
Gross national product	0.8	2.7	4.4	2.3	0.2
Gross national income	−0.1	2.9	3.7	2.6	−0.9

GDI — GDP

Change of GDP deflator and CPI (%)

Prices and Goverment Finance (*Domestic prices*) (*% change*)	*1980*	*1985*	*1991*	*1992*	*1993*
Consumer prices	26.4	57.7	22.7	15.5	9.8
Wholesale prices	24.5	53.6	20.5	13.4	8.9
Implicit GDP deflator	26.7	56.5	21.7	14.4	4.6
Government finance (*% of GDP*)					
Current budget balance	2.9	−2.0	4.2	5.9	5.0
Overall surplus/deficit	...	...	...	...	...

GDP def. — CPI

Table 5.8 (*continued*)

Poverty and Social	1980–85	1985–93
(annual growth rates)		
Population	2.2	1.8
Labor force	3.2	3.1

	most recent estimate (mre)
Poverty level: headcount index (*% of population*)	10.1
Life expectancy at birth	70.3
Infant mortality (*per thousand live births*)	35.0
Child malnutrition (*% of children under 5*)	13.9
Access to safe water (*% of population*)	78.0
Energy consumption per capita (*kg oil equivalent*)	1,524.8
Illiteracy (*% of population age 15+*)	12.7
Gross primary enrollment (*% of school-age population*)	114.0

Development diamond*

Trade	1980	1985	1991	1992	1993
(millions US$)					
Total exports (fob)	18,031	26,757	42,688	46,196	51,886
Fuel	10,441	14,767	8,166	8,307	7,418
n.a.	...	...	...	...	
Manufactures	5,549	10,072	31,602	35,421	41,685
Total imports (cif)	20,644	17,039	49,968	62,130	65,467
Food	2,448	1,082	5,640	7,744	7,842
Fuel and energy	...	...	...	...	...
Capital goods	5,174	3,165	8,471	11,556	11,156
Export price index (*1987=100*)	126	114	122	126	...
Import price index (*1987=100*)	62	87	102	101	...
Terms of trade (*1987=100*)	202	131	119	128	...
Openness of economy (*trade/GPD,%*)	24	26	31	31	31

Export and import levels (mill. US$)

Balance of Payments	1980	1985	1991	1992	1993
(millions US$)					
Export of goods and nfs	20,844	31,503	51,402	55,388	61,239
Import of goods and nfs	25,189	23,741	60,508	73,617	76,395
Resource balance	−4,345	7,762	−9,106	−18,229	−15,156
Net factor income	−6,669	−9,157	−8,679	−9,595	−10,924
Net current transfers	275	1,799	2,745	3,020	2,687
Current account balance					
Before official transfers	−10,739	404	−15,039	−24,804	−23,393
After official transfers	−10,700	1,077	−14,853	−24,804	−23,393
Long-term capital inflow	10,535	861	20,509	20,586	30,416
Total other items (net)	−573	−5,581	2,051	7,113	−6,178
Changes in net reserves	738	3,643	−7,707	−2,895	−846
Memo:					
Reserves excluding gold (*mill. US$*)	2,960	4,906	17,726	18,942	...
Reserves including gold (*mill. US$*)	4,175	5,679	18,052	19,171	...
Official exchange rate (*local/US$*)	2.3E-02	0.3	3.0	3.1	3.1

Current account balance to GDP ratio (%)

External Debt	1980	1985	1991	1992	1993
Export ratios					
Long-term debt/exports	185.4	261.6	152.6	137.4	137.1
IMF credit/exports	0.0	8.8	11.9	9.9	7.5
Short-term debt/exports	72.7	16.1	38.5	40.7	41.3
Total debt service/exports	49.3	45.2	24.1	34.3	26.6
GDP ratios					
Long-term debt/GDP	21.2	47.9	30.2	25.2	25.5
IMF credit/GDP	0.0	1.6	2.4	1.8	1.4
Short-term debt/GDP	8.3	3.0	7.6	7.5	7.7
Long-term debt ratios					
Private nonguaranteed/long-term	17.7	17.8	8.8	12.9	15.3
Public and publicly guaranteed					
Private creditors/long-term	71.4	72.2	62.2	56.6	54.9
Official creditors/long-term	10.9	10.0	29.0	30.5	29.8

Structure of external debt (%)

*The development diamond shows a level of development in the country compared with its income group average.

TABLE 5.9
Real Exchange Rate, Terms of Trade, and Real Wages in Mexico, 1980–93

Index, 1980=100

Year	Real Exchange Rate[a,b]	Real Exchange Rate[a,c]	Real Exchange Rate[a,d]	Terms of Trade	Terms of Trade Adjusted[c]	Minimum Wage	Real Wages, Manufactures	Real Wages, Maquiladora Operations
1980	100.00	100.00	100.00	100.00	100.00	100.00	100.00	100.00
1981	118.72	124.43	106.71	97.47	112.41	101.40	104.68	100.91
1982	86.80	91.87	75.84	84.98	76.33	110.91	103.21	110.65
1983	79.73	52.23	67.98	77.63	61.52	79.30	79.48	87.29
1984	97.20	54.47	81.08	76.13	62.77	75.07	74.72	85.88
1985	100.94	54.42	83.56	72.02	64.18	73.34	76.66	85.55
1986	69.15	35.66	67.68	51.86	46.90	79.76	65.74	83.52
1987	63.64	33.33	67.17	57.31	59.40	89.95	66.00	85.03
1988	77.44	41.32	82.39	51.78	53.63	51.92	64.65	81.21
1989	84.09	47.79	84.24	54.47	57.18	54.52	70.41	86.98
1990	84.22	50.10	87.68	55.57	60.99	50.81	72.92	87.55
1991	92.61	54.52	98.34	51.94	57.71	46.40	77.23	86.24
1992	98.90	59.09	108.14	51.62	56.74	40.17	83.34	87.49
1993	102.80	59.79	114.82	49.40	55.10	39.56	81.89	83.87

[a]An increase in the real exchange rate index indicates appreciation.

[b]The real effective exchange rate estimated on the basis of consumer prices for 133 countries.

[c]The real effective exchange rate estimated on the basis of unit labor costs for Mexico's six largest trading partners: United States, Germany, Japan, Canada, United Kingdom, and France. These countries account for 85 percent of Mexico's trade in manufactures.

[d]The Mexico-U.S. wholesale relative price levels.

[e]Takes into account the effect of international interest rates on the cost of debt service.

Sources: Authors' calculations based on real exchange rate and terms of trade data from Banco de México (1993) and from *International Financial Statistics*: wage, exchange rate, and terms of trade data from Salinas de Gortari (1993); and the relative price measure of the real exchange rate from Morgan Guaranty Trust Company (various issues). Dornbusch and Werner, *Brookings Papers on Economic Activity*, 1 (1994): 294.

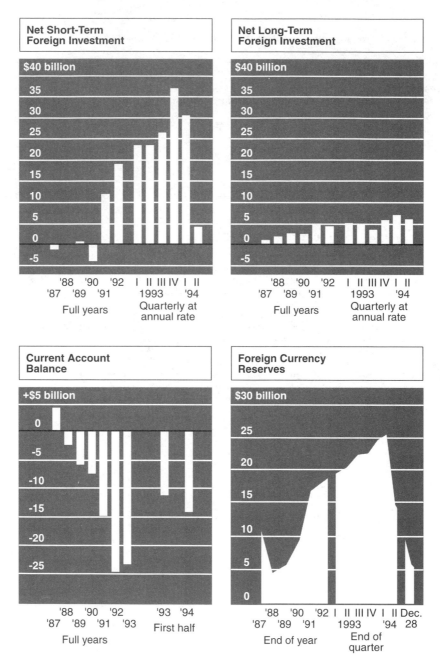

Figure 5.11 Mexico: International Transactions, 1987–1994. *Source: International Monetary Fund.*

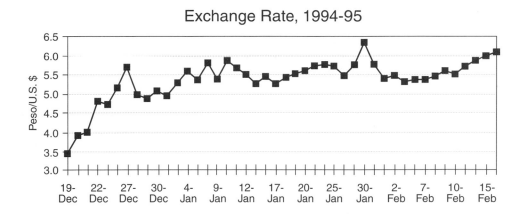

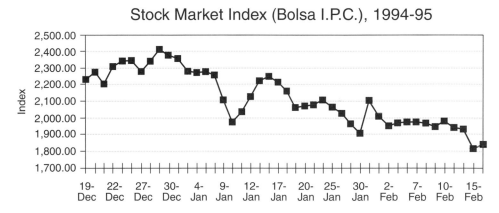

Figure 5.12   Mexico: Exchange Rate and Stock Market Index

THE 1995–96 PROGRAM

The program formulated by the Mexican authorities, and supported by the stand-by credit, must be seen against the background of Mexico's favorable economic fundamentals and its past record of macroeconomic and structural reforms. The program involves a two-pronged approach aimed at consolidating the progress made in the past several years and addressing the current liquidity problem of dealing with substantial short-term obligations falling due. The availability of external financing to support the conversion of short-term government debt into medium- and long-term debt and to help domestic commercial banks to meet their short-term external obligations is expected to ease investors' immediate concerns about the situation in Mexico, and reverse the overshoooting of the depreciation of the currency that has occurred.

The program's specific objectives for 1995 are the reduction in the external current account deficit from 8 percent of GDP in 1994 to 4 percent of GDP in 1995, and to 3–3½ percent of GDP in 1996; and a lowering of the annualized rate of inflation to around 9 percent in the fourth quarter of 1995, from more than 30 percent in the first quarter of the year. Economic activity is expected to decline in the first half of the year, as the effects of the change in relative prices and the financial adjustment work through the economy. However, it is expected to recover in the second half of the year as financial conditions stabilize. Real GDP should grow by around 1.5 percent for 1995 as a whole.

To achieve these goals, the program is centered on a policy of wage, price, and credit restraint supported by an improvement in the fiscal position. The revised 1995 budget for the nonfinancial public sector provides for a fiscal surplus of 0.5 percent of GDP (compared with a balanced position in 1994), and a primary surplus (the overall balance excluding interest obligations) of 3.4 percent for the year as a whole, compared with a primary surplus of 2.6 percent of GDP in 1994. The contribution of the public sector to the adjustment process is to be particularly large in the first half of 1995. Moreover, the authorities stand ready to strengthen the public finances through additional measures if necessary.

The fiscal tightening should help to achieve an early stabilization of financial and exchange markets, and the measures can be expected to boost savings and result in a substantial reduction in imports. In addition, an acceleration in export growth should result from the real depreciation of the currency.

The policy on wages and prices that has been formulated within the context of the Agreement of Unity to Overcome the Economic Emergency signed between the Government, the Bank of Mexico, and the labor and business sectors, will set the path for the evolution of wages and public sector price rises during 1995. This agreement implies a significant reduction in real wages on average and represents a major contribution on the part of labor to set the basis for a resumption of growth. Wage policy under the agreement provides for an increase of 7 percent in minimum and public sector wages, and an additional 3 percent through an income tax credit for workers with incomes of up to twice the minimum wage. Contractual wage negotiations will adhere to these guidelines and, in addition, will include productivity bonuses freely negotiated between labor and business. The pact also limits the increase in public sector tariffs during 1995 to about 10 percent, or about two thirds of the expected average rate of inflation. The price strategy will result in a revenue loss for the public sector (of about 0.6 percent of GDP) that will be compensated by other fiscal measures. The authorities recognize the need to address price distortions that may result from these measures in due course.

Credit policy will play a critical role in achieving the objectives of the program. The monetary program establishes a limit on the growth of net domestic assets of the Bank of Mexico of MexN $10 billion in 1995, compared with MexN $60 billion in 1994. Under this limit, credit expansion by the Bank of Mexico would be 17 percent of the monetary base at the end of 1994, a rate which is less than that of projected nominal GDP and is consistent with the inflation target of 19 percent for 1995 as a whole. The Bank of Mexico stands ready to tighten credit conditions further to counter unforeseen pressures in the exchange market.

The program provides for a reduction in the rate of credit expansion by the development banks of more than one half (to 2.1 percent of GDP) in 1995. However, the development banks and trust funds will continue to provide net financing to priority sectors, including exports and agriculture.

The substantial depreciation of the exchange rate that has taken place is expected to contribute to a significant improvement in the current account of the balance of payments. Merchandise exports are projected to grow by close to 25 percent in 1995 helped by the devaluation, the increase in investment in export industries in recent years, and the contraction in internal demand. In addition, the effect of the peso depreciation, the policy of credit restraint, and the expected fall in real incomes should lead to a decline in imports of 7 percent in U.S. dollar terms.

The Bank of Mexico will support the floating exchange rate regime through limited intervention in the foreign exchange market. The authorities envisage that the strength of their economic program, together with external financial support, will help to stabilize financial markets and result in a significant correction of the recent overshooting of the exchange rate.

For 1996, the authorities have indicated they will follow policies to lower inflation to single digits and further reduce the external current account deficit to 3–3½ percent of GDP. With the return of financial and exchange market stability, investment could be expected to recover which, together with continued export expansion, would contribute to a rebound in real GDP growth to around 4 percent.

While specific proposals for 1996 will not be developed until the 1996 budget is prepared in the second half of 1995, the authorities are committed to review tax policies to at least maintain the surplus position of the public sector and improve the equity of the tax system.

STRUCTURAL REFORM POLICIES

Over the past several years, Mexico has made substantial progress in the area of structural reform. The program consolidates and extends this progress in important ways. It provides a reinforcement of the Government's strategy for privatization and the granting of concessions to the private sector in areas previously reserved for the public sector. In the past, the privatization efforts had focused mainly on commercial enterprises (although some concessions have been granted for the operation of highways). Beginning in 1995, privatization also will involve basic infrastructure (rail, ports, airports, electricity generation, and radio and telecommunications). The implementation of the new strategy will require some constitutional changes as well as reforms in the regulatory environment which are already under way.

The authorities expect revenues from privatization and concession operations to be about $6 billion in 1995 and an additional $6–8 billion in 1996–97. The privatization proceeds will be used largely for the cancellation of the public external debt.

INTERNATIONAL FINANCIAL SUPPORT

In addition to the IMF's $17.8 billion stand-by credit, the United States is expected to provide $20 billion; the G-10 central banks through the Bank for International Settlements, $10 billion; and the commercial banks, $3 billion.

ADDRESSING SOCIAL ISSUES

During the late 1980s and early 1990s, there was a significant reduction in the number of families living in extreme poverty, reflecting the strong economic growth and increases in real wages in this period, complemented by a program of targeted social expenditures. The authorities recognize, however, that the peso crisis and the adjustment measures that it entails could complicate efforts to sustain the steady improvement in the well-being of the poorest sectors in the short term. A number of policy measures are being implemented to protect the poor from the adverse effects of the adjustment process. While overall lending by the development banks is being scaled back sharply, it will be focused more heavily on financing of agriculture through specialized agencies that lend to small farmers. To limit the real wage adjustment for the lowest wage earners, employers will be allowed to supplement wages of those earning up to twice the minimum wage and to claim a corresponding tax credit.

THE CHALLENGE AHEAD

The Mexican authorities have embarked on a strong adjustment program to help deal with the current crisis in financial and foreign exchange markets. The domestic adjustment package, combining prudent fiscal and strong monetary and credit policies, a disciplined incomes policy, and further structural reforms, provides an appropriate policy response to current circumstances. Furthermore, the authorities stand ready to strengthen the program as needed to achieve the program's objectives. The support of the international financial community is crucial to the success of the program.

Mexico is an original member of the IMF; its quota is SDR 1,753.3 million (about $2.6 billion); and its outstanding use of IMF financing currently totals SDR 2,594.7 million (about $3.8 billion).

IMF *Survey*, February 6, 1995

DISCUSSION QUESTIONS

1. Of the Mexican problem, Treasury Secretary Robert Rubin argued at a White House briefing in mid-January 1995, that "This is a liquidity crisis. It's a crisis of confidence."

   "This is not a liquidity crisis," said Texas Senator Phil Gramm, speaking at virtually the same moment on Capitol Hill. "Mexico is broke for some very good reasons."

   Fred Smith, president of the Competitive Enterprise Institute, observed that "Giving Mexico a new loan is like giving an alcoholic one last drink. Mexico must be forced to deal with the consequences of economic management."

And Michael Bruno, the chief economist at the World Bank, said, "The fundamentals of the Mexican economy remain sound, and the measures announced over the past few weeks should strengthen the balance of payments and lay the foundations for renewed economic growth" (*Washington Times*, Jan. 23, 1995).

Do you agree with any of these statements? What are the policy implications of the different statements?

2. By December 1994, the peso had clearly appreciated. But was it overvalued? By what measure?

3. (a) Do you believe that Finance Minister Serra was inept in denying the possibility and then devaluing? In allowing the market to determine the value of the peso, without government intervention?

(b) Would it have been better for the Mexican government to act earlier with small devaluations (a crawling peg) instead of the maxi devaluation and uncontrolled float? Or would the best timing for a devaluation have been when NAFTA was ratified in 1993?

4. (a) What arguments could have been made against a devaluation?

(b) Do you agree with the director for international economics at Bear, Stearns & Co. in New York who wrote in the *Wall Street Journal*, Jan. 11, 1995, that:

"Some root-canal experts will say that Mexico was right to devalue in order to make Mexican labor cheaper and boost competitiveness. However, it should be clear now to President Zedillo and his advisers that neither the Chiapas problem nor worries about too many imports justified the devaluation.

"The devaluation occurred when the Mexican central bank allowed dollar-indexed interest rates to fall to record low levels in the weeks leading up to the devaluation. This looked like an inflationary monetary policy. The peso hit new lows each day as the central bank expanded its balance sheet. The proper solution, instead of devaluation, was to shrink the balance sheet, pushing dollar-indexed interest rates temporarily higher to re-establish credibility.

"Mexico's international reserves were stable from April through October, indicating that the private sector was easily financing strong imports and the current account deficit without government support. In devaluing, the Mexican government made a massive miscalculation both as to the nature of the problem and as to the results of the devaluation."

5. Who were the gainers from the sequence of events after December 20, 1994? The losers?

6. In his *New York Times* foreign affairs column (Jan. 25, 1995), Thomas L. Friedman wrote:

"There was a telling story in the *Washington Post* last week quoting 'Congressional sources' as saying they saw 'little political gain in approving . . . a plan to bail out Mexico's economy when members, particularly Republicans, believe they were elected to deal with problems closer to home.'

"I've got news for those Congressional sources: In today's intertwined global market, Mexico *is* 'home.' There is far more American industrial investment and mutual-fund investment in Mexico today than there is in our own state of New Mexico. And the economic collapse of Mexico would damage the U.S., Latin America and Canada far more than the bankruptcy of New Mexico. To some extent, 'home' is where the wallet is, and right now, if you check your pension fund or mutual fund, you will find that your wallet is spread from Toronto to Tierra del Fuego.

"The Mexico crisis also demonstrates how we have gone from a world dominated by superpowers to a world dominated by supermarkets. It is the Tokyo, New York, London and Frankfurt bond markets that will have as much say as governments in determining Mexico's fate."

Do you agree with this view?

7. Do you support the actions taken by the IMF? The U.S. Treasury? The U.S. Congress?

8. After President Clinton's announcement of financial aid to Mexico on January 31, 1995, some media commentators said the president's action was a "bailout" at the expense of the American taxpayer, was undemocratic in bypassing Congress, and was an action contrary to the wishes of the American public as expressed in recent public opinion polls.

Are these criticisms valid?

9. At the end of February 1995, would you have believed that the program announced by the Mexican government and President Clinton would be sufficient to achieve external balance and internal balance? Sufficient economic growth?

10. It was reported (*New York Times*, Jan. 9, 1995) that the drop in the peso's value has Nike Inc. considering expanding in Mexico to make shoes that the company now produces exclusively in Asia. A company official said that Mexican production could begin within a year, but added that "nothing's final yet."

What do you think Nike should consider in making its final decision?

11. The head of Henry Kaufman & Co. (an international money management and financial consulting firm) wrote in the *Wall Street Journal* (Jan. 26, 1995) that the alarms did not ring earlier over Mexico in part because of "the decision of many financial institutions to emphasize near-term over longer-term profit opportunities and to utilize their researchers in this pursuit. . . . Financial institutions were enchanted by the hope of high profit margins, revved up by new institutional arrangements to funnel money into Mexico and other developing countries. . . . In this milieu, the objectivity of many analysts and economists has been compromised. They've become part of a broader marketing, underwriting and distribution effort."

Barton Biggs, chairman of Morgan Stanley Asset Management Inc., also observed that "A lot of smart young guys who took Spanish in prep school got hired for $400,000 as Latin American analysts" (*Wall Street Journal*, Feb. 1, 1995). Biggs suggests that Wall Street firms should do an agonizing reappraisal about whether they want to continue their commitment to emerging markets.

What is your reaction to these statements?

12. Are there any general lessons to be learned from the Mexican experience?

United States Deficit with Japan

A perplexing and persistent policy problem has been the payments imbalance between the United States and Japan.[1] What have been the trends in the balance of trade and balance on current account? Why the U.S. deficit? And what policies can provide an effective adjustment mechanism?

WHAT HAS HAPPENED?

The United States confronted a deficit in its balance of trade every year from 1980–95. A large proportion of that deficit—in several years over 50 percent—was with Japan. From a surplus of $5 billion in 1981, the U.S. current account went into a deficit of over $11 billion in 1982, and was at a peak of $167 billion in 1987 and was still as high as $148 billion in 1995 (see Table 5.10).

While the United States has had a current account deficit, Japan's current account, negative in 1980, has been in surplus since 1981, albeit by a smaller amount than Japan's balance of trade surplus because of a net negative imbalance on services. The surplus in Japan's current account, 1989–95, is shown in Table 5.11. The surplus supported a capital outflow in various ways: portfolio investment, direct foreign investment in plants in the United States and Europe, purchase of real estate and financial institutions, and the purchase of U.S. Treasury securities. In 1995, private investors alone bought a record $99 billion worth of treasury securities. The result was that Japan's net external assets, negative in 1980, were in surplus by more than $650 billion in 1995. During Japan's economic downturn of the 1990s, there was some retrenchment in long-term capital exports, as Japanese creditors sold long-term assets to repay short-term foreign liabilities.

At the same time as Japan acquired overseas assets, the United States, which was the world's largest creditor in 1981, went into debt in 1986, and became the world's biggest debtor. The net investment position of the United States in the world economy has gone from a sizable surplus at the beginning of the 1980s to a deficit of more than $500 billion in 1995.

The foreign exchange rate between the dollar and yen also showed dramatic trends. Under the Bretton Woods standard, the dollar:yen rate was $1:¥360 from 1949 to 1970. After the floating rate regime came into being, the dollar:yen rate reflected a depreciation of the dollar and an appreciation of the yen, especially in the 1980's. From an annual average rate of $1:¥238 in 1985, the yen appreciated to $1:¥94 in 1995. In 1996, the rate averaged $1:¥108.

---

[1] Some readers may prefer to consider this Policy Profile in conjunction with Ch.7, especially pp. 264–71.

TABLE 5.10
U.S. Current Account Deficit with Japan

Year	Current Account Deficit ($ billions)	Current Account Deficit with Japan ($ billions)	The Share of Current Account Deficit with Japan in Current Account Deficit (%)
1982	11.4	15.4	134.8
1983	44.5	18.4	41.8
1984	99.7	34.8	35.1
1985	125.4	45.3	36.4
1986	151.1	56.3	37.0
1987	167.1	57.2	34.2
1988	128.3	50.6	39.4
1989	102.9	43.9	41.5
1990	91.7	38.2	40.3
1991	9.5	28.0	294.5
1992	67.9	43.5	69.6
1993	99.9	53.5	53.5
1994	148.4	64.6	43.6
1995	148.2	60.3	40.7

Source: Survey of Current Business, various issues

TABLE 5.11
Japan's Balance on Current Account, 1989–95 ($ billions)

Year	Balance on Current Account*
1989	57
1990	36
1991	68
1992	112
1993	132
1994	131
1995	111

* Balance on goods, services, income from overseas, and unilateral transfers
Source: IMF, *International Financial Statistics*, September 1996, p. 348.

WHY THE DEFICIT?

A facile, but questionable, popular explanation is to blame American trade deficits on Japan's barriers to imports—highly questionable, because the U.S. deficit began in the 1980s during a period when Japan did not increase barriers to imports, but actually liberalized its trade policies. Overt Japanese protection in the form of tariffs and quantitative restrictions is arguably lower than protection in most industrialized countries, except in agriculture. It can, however, be maintained that "invisible protection" restrains imports through customs procedure, standards testing requirements, public procurement policies, and government guidance to business. The complicated distribution system may also make imports uncompetitive as do "in house" buying habits and the behavior of *keiretsu* (networks of affiliated firms). These invisible barriers allegedly account for Japan's low volume of manufactured imports.

Studies differ on whether Japan's level and pattern of trade are abnormal. Some claim that Japan's import of manufactures are unusually small—less than one half of other major industrial countries; others conclude that Japan's total trade is normal and that its trading pattern is consistent with what would be predicted from its factor endowments of capital-abundance and few natural resources.[2] Japan's intra-industry trade in manufactures is also unusually low.

Nonetheless, given the magnitude of the American trade deficit with Japan, it is not reasonable to maintain that greater market access would alone eliminate the deficit. Rather than focusing on trade policy or microeconomic forces, most analysts believe that macroeconomic forces have determined the trade and current account imbalances. This follows from the differences in macro performance between the United States and Japan. As stated again by the President's Council of Economic Advisors, there is a fundamental relationship between national income analysis and balance-of-payments analysis:

> The net borrowing of the Nation can be expressed as the sum of the net borrowing by each of the principal sectors of the economy: government (Federal, State, and local), firms, and households. In other words, the current account deficit (CAD) is equal to the government's budget deficit ($G - T$, or net borrowing by the public sector) plus the difference between private sector investment and private sector saving ($I - S$, or net borrowing by the private sector):

$$
\underset{\substack{\text{Government} \\ \text{deficit}}}{(G - T)} \quad + \quad \underset{\substack{\text{Private} \\ \text{investment}}}{(I} \quad - \quad \underset{\substack{\text{Private} \\ \text{saving}}}{S)} \quad = \quad \underset{\substack{\text{Current account} \\ \text{deficit}}}{CAD}
$$

> The crucial insight of this identity is that the current account deficit is a macro-economic phenomenon: it reflects an imbalance between national saving and national investment. The fact that the relationship is an identity and always holds true also means that any effective policy to reduce the current account deficit must, in the end, narrow the gap between U.S. saving and U.S. investment.[3]

In 1994, Japan's household saving rate of nearly 15 percent contrasted markedly with personal saving in the United States of only 3.5 percent during the early 1990s. The national net saving rate that had averaged 8 percent of national income in the 1960s fell in the 1980s, reaching a low of 2 percent between 1990 and 1993.

With low private saving, a large federal budget deficit, and a relatively tight monetary policy, real interest rates in the United States rose from minus 1.1 percent from 1970–80 to 3.6 percent in 1980–86.[4] The higher real interest rates attracted an inflow of foreign capital, thereby allowing the United States to finance its current consumption by incurring a large foreign debt. In the early 1980s the tight monetary policy and a portfolio shift toward dollar assets also contributed to the real exchange rate appreciation of the dollar and current account deficits. These trends were reversed somewhat in the late 1980s.

---

[2] In many econometric studies, conclusions differ about what quantitative effect the elimination of formal and informal barriers to trade in Japan would have on American exports. See Marcus Noland, "U.S.-Japan Trade Friction," *The World Economy* (March 1995): 238–267, with extensive references; P. R. Krugman, ed. *Trade with Japan*, 3rd ed. (1995).

[3] *Economic Report of the President 1995*, p. 251.

[4] Treasury bill rate adjusted for the realized rate of consumer price index inflation.

In the early 1990s, however, recessions in Japan and Europe, combined with recovery in the United States, resulted in a worsening of the U.S. current account deficit. There is evidence that the United States's income elasticity of demand for imports from Japan is considerably higher than Japan's income elasticity demand for imports from the United States. The growth rate in the United States has not, however, been so high as to blame the trade deficit on an especially strong demand for imports. Moreover, the inflation rate in the United States fell to low levels during the 1980s and 1990s.

The basic problem of low saving has entailed a high cost of capital, and the result in low investment has led, in turn, to low productivity. From a prior trend of 3 percent per year from 1960–73, labor productivity fell to a trend of 1.1 percent per year after 1973. The low labor productivity means that relative wages have to fall to keep American industry competitive internationally.

WHAT ADJUSTMENT POLICY?

Of particular concern is the issue of whether the adjustment mechanism has been—or will be—effective in reducing the United States's payments imbalances in trade and on current account. A prior question, however, is whether the United States's economic policy should simply be that of "benign neglect," refusing to adjust and continuing to borrow overseas (not only from Japan, but also European and East Asian countries) to sustain current levels of consumption through its current account deficit.

Alternatively, because of the risks involved in benign neglect, the United States has undertaken some adjustment policies. Foremost has been a restrictive budget policy in an effort to reduce domestic consumption, raise domestic savings, and thereby eliminate the need to borrow overseas. After increasing for most of the period since 1980, the real dollar value of the budget deficit and the budget deficit as a percentage of GDP have declined since 1992. A continued decrease in the budget deficit would increase national saving and thereby tend to lower the interest rate, increase investment, and hence raise productivity. If, because of a declining interest rate differential between the United States and other countries, the dollar should depreciate on foreign exchange markets, the fall in the exchange rate would still be of benefit to tradable-goods firms through their price competitiveness in world markets and expenditure switching. In contrast, if foreigners expect less inflation in the United States, and greater confidence in the American economy attracts more foreign investment, the dollar might strengthen as the budget deficit is reduced. Any prediction about whether elimination of the budget deficit would weaken or strengthen the dollar must be conditional with respect to the macro state of the American economy, world interest rates, foreigners' expectations, and the reaction of foreign governments.

While the United States reduces its budget deficit and lowers consumption, many advocate that Japan should undertake monetary expansion to stimulate consumption and investment and thereby reduce its current account surplus. Between 1985 and 1990, Japan grew at an average rate of 4.4 percent per year; from 1990 to 1993, Japan's growth rate actually declined, and GDP grew by less than 1 percent in 1994–95. Easier fiscal and monetary polices, involving increased spending and a larger budget deficit in Japan, are therefore advocated to stimulate growth and imports.

The major adjustment policy has come through exchange rate movements. The dollar depreciated markedly from 1971–95, falling in April 1995 to a postwar low of 80¥. The yen appreciated to new highs. At times, interventions by central banks attempted to halt the exchange rate movements. But the Federal Reserve's buying of more dollars and the Bank of Japan's selling of yen generally failed to carry conviction in the market; at best, interventions merely slowed the dollar's fall. By early 1995, the yen was 32 percent above where it was at the end of 1992. In terms of purchasing power parity, the yen was increasingly overvalued from 1986. This is evident in Table 5.12, where the real exchange rate—i.e., the ratio of the nominal exchange rate (e) to purchasing power parity (e^p) in yen–dollar terms—was on a downward trend since the mid-1970s. This reflected lower inflation in Japan relative to the United States. From 1979–85, the yen was exceptionally cheap. But since 1986, the real value of the yen increased sharply. From an index number of 100 in 1990, Japan's real effective exchange rate increased to 155 in 1995.[5]

By acting as an ad valorem tax on imports and an ad valorem subsidy on exports, the depreciation of the dollar was expected to improve the United States's balance of trade. The appreciation of yen was expected to reduce exports to the United States and to induce a surge in imports from the United States.

Other policies were also expected to reduce the deficit. In the Reagan administration, voluntary export restraints were sought to limit imports of Japanese automobiles, steel, and machine tools. In the Clinton administration, U.S. trade negotiations sought new

TABLE 5.12
Japan's Real Exchange Rate, ¥:$, 1970–92

	e	*e^p*	*e/e^p*
1970	360.00	241	149
1971	349.33	242	144
1972	303.17	245	124
1973	271.70	260	105
1974	292.08	286	102
1975	296.79	280	106
1976	294.35	284	104
1977	268.51	283	95
1978	210.44	277	76
1979	219.14	261	84
1980	226.74	250	91
1981	220.54	237	93
1982	249.08	226	110
1983	237.51	222	107
1984	237.52	219	108
1985	238.54	217	110
1986	168.52	216	78
1987	144.64	210	69
1988	128.15	204	63
1989	137.96	200	69
1990	144.79	196	74
1991	134.71	192	70
1992	126.65	190	67

Note: e = annual average of the exchange rate; e^p = purchasing power parity (¥: $).
Source: Kazuo Sato, "Economic Growth in Japan," *World Economy* (March 1995): 207.

---

[5] IMF, *International Financial Statistics* (September 1996), p. 346.

agreements to open Japanese markets to American imports of semiconductors, automobiles, and automobile parts. At the macro level, since the early 1980s, policies have sought to limit inflation in the United States and thereby reduce the demand for imports and maintain the competitiveness of exports. And the federal deficit as a percentage of GDP has fallen from a high of nearly 5 percent in 1992 to about 2 percent in 1995.

Taken together, these policies did provide some adjustment. Japan's current account surplus as a percentage of GDP fell from a peak of 3.2 percent in 1992 to about 2.2 percent in 1995. Japan's trade surplus, however, continued to rise in dollar terms, mainly because when the yen-based trade accounts are translated into dollars, the dollar value of the surplus is inflated. But in volume terms, the surplus diminished. In 1994, Japan's imports increased 14 percent while exports increased only 2 percent. Nonetheless, even with the volume improvement, the trade surplus in dollars did not decline because of the yen's appreciation. And it is the imbalance expressed in dollars—not in yen or volume—that matters for financial markets and for the adjustment problem.

A major—and perplexing—question is: Why has the exchange rate not had greater effect? One explanation is that Japanese firms have undertaken strategic adjustments by squeezing their profit margins, increasing productivity, and cutting costs. They have practiced "pricing to market" to hold market shares, thereby reducing the prices of exports to hold down their dollar prices. Accordingly, there has been a low pass-through from the higher yen to higher export prices from Japan. A study by the Fuji Bank, for instance, concluded that from 1985–88, the pass-through to Japanese export prices varied from 10 percent for videocassette recorders to 92 percent for integrated circuits, with an average of 56 percent for total exports.[6] The higher yen also had a deflationary impact as Japanese companies cut prices to remain competitive with imports and as they constrained corporate profits and capital spending. The corporate restructuring to cut costs also increased the unemployment rate and thereby limited consumption.

Another explanation is offered by Stanford's Ronald McKinnon who suggests that because exchange rates are determined in forward-looking asset markets, spot exchange rates reflect current and expected future monetary policies. If the yen rises above its purchasing power parity with the dollar, it therefore implies that Japan is following (or is expected to follow) a deflationary monetary policy relative to the United States. The appreciation of the yen dampens domestic investment and causes recession—what is known in Japan as *endaka fukyo* (high yen-induced recession). Thus a high yen fails to reduce Japan's current account surplus or the United States's deficit. While it slows growth in exports, it depresses the domestic economy and Japan buys less from the rest of the world. Any effect on its current account surplus is ambiguous.

Finally, while most economists believe that adjustments in exchange rates do affect trade flows, they recognize that there is a considerable time lag. From econometric analyses, William Cline of the Institute for International Economics has found that the trade ratios of the United States and Japan respond to the real exchange rate with approximately a two-year lag.[7] The numerator of the trade ratio is the value of nonoil imports of goods and nonfactor

---

6 See also Kenichi Ohno, "Exchange Rate Fluctuations, Pass-through and Market Shares," *International Monetary Fund, Staff Papers*, No. 37 (1990): 294–310.

7 William R. Cline, *Predicting External Imbalances for the United States and Japan*, Institute for International Economics (September 1995), pp. 1–5.

services; the denominator is the value of exports of goods and nonfactor services. The lag is due to the time taken for recognizing the change in the exchange rates and for switching orders and delivering. Higher growth rates of income in the United States and lower growth rates in Japan have also diminished the effect of the exchange rates. Even with the same proportional growth rates, Japan's surplus with the United States would tend to increase because the United States has a higher propensity to import from Japan out of income than does Japan to import from the United States.

As of 1997, the U.S. administration eschewed deflation or direct controls on imports as means of adjustment. Instead, reliance was on an adjustment mechanism that worked through a further decline in the federal budget deficit, the exchange rate, and future growth in Japan. Many analysts maintain that the foremost policy measure for dealing with the external deficit should be further reduction of the fiscal deficit.[8] Lower interest rates resulting from fiscal correction can directly reduce the deficit on capital services and can indirectly induce easing of the dollar and make American exports more competitive.

DISCUSSION QUESTIONS

1. Do you think the diagnosis of "Why the Deficit" (pp. 226–28) is adequate and valid?

2. Professor Paul Krugman has said that, "If one asks how a higher saving rate translates into a smaller trade deficit, it is not enough to insist that the accounting ensures that it must. A consumer deciding between a Ford and a Honda cares nothing about the U.S.'s national income accounts. How does a lower U.S. budget deficit persuade Americans to buy fewer foreign goods and foreigners to buy more U.S. products?" Krugman answers that changes in the government's financial balance translate into changes in physical trade flows through the exchange rate mechanism. "Higher savings will normally reduce the trade deficit because they result in a weaker dollar."

   Do you agree? If not, how else could higher U.S. savings reduce the trade deficit?

   If you were associated with a tradable goods industry (import substitution or export), what prediction would you make about how the elimination of the federal budget deficit would affect the demand for your product?

3. Do you believe that because balance-of-payments adjustment has costs, and the dollar enjoys a unique position as a reserve currency, the U.S. Treasury and Federal Reserve should simply follow benign neglect with respect to the United States's current account deficit and let the dollar's weakness be Japan's problem of declining exports to the United States?

4. Would you advocate trade sanctions against Japan to lower the United States's trade deficit? Would you consider such actions to be superior to depreciation of the dollar?

5. What measures could the Japanese government undertake to drive down the yen relative to the dollar?

6. If Japan removed all its barriers to imports and to an inflow of foreign capital, do you believe that Japan's current account surplus with the United States would fall to zero?

---

[8] See, for instance, Cline, op cit., pp. 65–70, 73–74.

7. Professor Martin Feldstein has said that, "If the U.S. doesn't free up the resources to shrink its trade deficit by higher savings or smaller budget deficits, the falling dollar and shrinking inflow of funds from abroad will cause domestic interest rates to rise and investment in equipment and construction to fall. The resulting decline in economic growth should of course be blamed on the low rate of domestic saving and not on the falling dollar." Do you agree?

8. The fiftieth anniversary of the Bretton Woods agreement was in 1995. Does the instability in the dollar:yen rate during the 1980s and 1990s indicate a need to bring more stability back into the international monetary system?

PART III

STATES AND MARKETS

Utilizing insights from the previous analytical chapters, we now want to identify forces of economic change in various categories of countries and to analyze their significance in the global trade and investment environment. We shall focus particularly on the international consequences of new economic and political directions in the European Union, Japan, developing countries, and countries in transition from state planning to a market-price system.

Throughout the following chapters run the issues of the state's relationship to the market, international competitiveness, international markets versus national politics, and the question of maintaining international economic order.

How these issues will be resolved is important for international private management and international public management. We are ultimately concerned with how firms will react to these changes, how a national government will manage the increasing proportion of its economy that is subject to external influence, and how the international public sector will manage a changing world economy.

The discussion in each chapter brings the reader up to the point of considering an individual response to the managerial challenge. Although the chapters indicate in a general way the nature of some possible responses, a specific response by a specific firm in a specific country will have to depend on the particular conditions of that firm and its own managerial judgment.

Chapter

6   THE NEW EUROPE

T he New Europe, with its two major objectives—market integration and monetary integration—is being fashioned by the most far-reaching trade and financial decisions that European nations have made in the twentieth century. And the consequences of their decisions will extend far into the twenty-first century. The opportunities and challenges arising from the European Union (EU) and the proposed Economic and Monetary Union (EMU) will carry over to the United States, Japan, developing nations, and the transition economies of Eastern Europe, the former Soviet Union, and China.[1]

For private management, both in Europe and outside, the overriding question is how best to position the firm with respect to a unified European market. What will be the effects on costs? on demand? on changes in the competitive structure of industry? on foreign trade? on foreign investment?

For public management, the union raises issues of regionalism versus multilateralism. International policy coordination is also of prime concern. Moreover, a single currency for Europe would have implications for the activities of the International Monetary Fund (IMF). If economic union leads to a tighter political union, the implications for the international public sector will be all the more extensive.

This chapter examines the possible effects of the EU by considering what might be expected from trade and financial decisions already taken and by developments that might occur in the future. We give special attention to the consequences of market integration and the possible effects of monetary integration through the EMU.

FOUNDATIONS OF THE NEW EUROPE

Originally six European nations formed the European Economic Community by signing the Treaty of Rome in 1957. The treaty provided for a customs union (free trade among the member nations but a common external tariff) and envisaged a common market with the four freedoms of free movement of goods, services, people, and capital. Physical, technical, and fiscal barriers among the member states were to be removed. The treaty also looked forward to implementing harmonized policies toward agriculture, energy, transport, competition, and regional development. To that end, a governance structure was established, composed of the commission, council of ministers, court of justice, and assembly. These supranational institutions diminished national sovereignty and became the instruments for decision making and the establishment of community law over national law.

The Economic Community subsequently expanded; in 1985, its twelve member countries adopted the Single European Act that sought a 1992 deadline for the establishment of a Europe without frontiers that would allow free trade in goods and services and the free movement of finance and labor. In 1993, the treaty on European Union (the "Maastricht" Treaty) embraced the objectives of monetary union, a common foreign and security policy, common citizenship, and the development of cooperation on justice and social affairs. The Maastricht Treaty looked forward to a gradual three-stage movement to the EMU that would have a single currency for the EU, a European Central Bank, and a common monetary policy.

Initially, the movement to a European common market was mainly politically motivated—to unite Germany and France in the postwar world. Increasingly, however, the support has been for economic reasons. As Giovanni Agnelli, former chairman of Fiat, observes:

> The current unity of Western Europe is not so much the result of a Utopian dream as it is the political recognition of economic reality: the reality of global markets, the reality of economic interdependence and the reality of competitive pressures—all of which make cooperation essential.
>
> The reason that the project has continued to progress and defy the odds against it is that it does not depend entirely on political good will; [it] was born for sound economic reasons and those forces continue to be its engine. . . . Entrepreneurs and corporations are keeping the pressure on politicians to transcend considerations of local and national interest. We believe that European unity is our best hope for stimulating growth and technological innovation, and for remaining an influential presence in the world.[2]

Decisions being made in the European Union affect a market of more than 340 million customers with a combined GDP in 1995 of over $6 trillion, amounting to 27 percent of world GDP. In comparison, the GDP of the United States in 1995 was $5.2 trillion, and $2.8 trillion in Japan. Table 6.1 indicates the differences in the level of income per head in European countries, and in comparison with Japan, Canada, and the United States.

In a certain number of economic activities the EU's value added is larger than that of the United States: financial services, food products, beverages, tobacco, textiles, leather, clothing, metalliferous ores, and steel products. The European chemical, transport equipment, and industrial machinery industries are comparable to their counterparts in the United States and Japan.[3] The EU lags well behind the United States, but is at a comparable level to Japan, in respect to data processing, office automation, precision instruments, electrical appliances, heavy equipment, industrial and consumer electronics, and telecommunications equipment. These industries have strong demand potentials and high technological content, and are leading in R&D. The present fragmentation of EU industry, however, seriously handicaps these industrial markets. These high-tech sectors require active cooperation or even integration of European firms if the union is to reach the level and effectiveness of R&D expenditure in this area by American and Japanese multinational firms. Economies of scale are also significant in these industries and require production units that are integrated with respect to standards and marketing requirements for a unified market. According to several studies, the EU's industrial base devoted to the production of high-tech goods is still relatively narrow. In the dynamic industries for which world demand is growing sharply, European industrial output is lagging behind that of the United States and Japan.

In much of European industry, labor productivity has also been considerably lower than in American or Japanese industry. The best productivity performances of the major countries are achieved in industries with a large enough national market to compensate for the effect of nontariff barriers: food products, beverages, tobacco, textiles, leather, clothing, nonmetalliferous ores, and building materials. In the high-tech industries, however, European countries have a relatively low level of productivity; this accounts for their weak performance in international trade and a small market share in their own domestic markets in such products as electrical goods and electronics, office machinery, and information technology.

Internal trade among EU members has expanded more rapidly than external trade from the EU. Including trade among member states, the EU accounted for 38 percent of merchandise traded internationally in 1989, up from 23 percent in 1958 when the European Economic Community became effective. Excluding internal trade, one fifth of world trade originated from or was destined for the EU in 1989, slightly less than the EU members as a group had accounted for three decades earlier. External trade has also expanded less than world merchandise trade. Table 6.1 compares foreign trade by country.

As a result of the rapid expansion of internal trade and rising imports from outside the EU, the share of each European country's domestic demand met from its own industrial

TABLE 6.1
Economic Profile of the European Union, North America, and Japan, 1994

	GDP ($ billions)	Population (millions)	GNP per Capita* ($)	Exports of Merchandise ($ billions)	Imports of Merchandise ($ billions)
Austria	196.5	8	24,630	45.2	55.3
Belgium	227.6	10	22,870	137.4	125.8
Denmark	146.1	5	27,970	41.4	34.8
Finland	098.0	5	18,850	29.7	23.2
France	1,330.4	58	23,420	235.9	230.2
Germany	2,046.0	82	25,580	427.2	381.9
Greece	077.7	10	7,700	9.4	21.5
Ireland	052.1	4	13,530	34.4	25.5
Italy	1,024.6	57	19,300	189.8	167.7
Netherlands	329.8	15	22,010	155.6	139.8
Portugal	087.3	10	9,320	17.5	26.7
Spain	482.8	39	13,440	73.3	92.5
Sweden	196.4	9	23,530	61.3	51.8
United Kingdom	1,017.3	58	18,340	205.0	227.0
Canada	543.0	29	19,510	166.0	155.1
Japan	460.0	125	34,630	397.0	275.0
United States	6,648.0	261	25,880	513.0	690.0

*Purchasing power parity.

Source: World Bank, *World Development Report 1996*, Tables.

production steadily declined during the 1980s. Import penetration rates differ widely according to sector. There has been a larger propensity to import high-tech products. Imports from outside the EU have also grown more rapidly than intra-union trade in office machinery and information technology, electrical and electronic equipment, and machinery and transport equipment. Intra-union trade has grown more rapidly than imports for food processing, paper, metal products, and in the chemical and pharmaceutical sectors. Intra-union trade has been especially strong in such capital and skilled labor-intensive industries as steel, chemicals, and paper pulp. The EU's common agricultural policy has also promoted intra-union trade in food products.

Regarding trade in services, the union's balance of trade has been in substantial surplus for banking transactions, air transport, civil engineering, maritime transport, and tourism. Trade in services has been principally outside the EU, with the United States being the union's most important trading partner. The EU has become America's largest market for exports. Table 6.2 indicates the shares of world trade for the United States and the EU. Europe is also the major recipient of U.S. investment overseas (see Table 6.3).

BENEFITS OF MARKET INTEGRATION

The case for European market integration is often expressed in counterfactual terms of what would be the costs of "non-Europe." A year before the Single European Act was signed, the European Commission requested Paolo Cecchini to report on these costs. The

TABLE 6.2
U.S.–E.U. Merchandise Trade, 1980–94

	Value 1994	1980	Share 1990	1994
World Merchandise Exports by Region				
($ billions and percentage)				
United States	513	11.1	11.6	12.5
European Union	1660	37.2	44.6	40.6
World Merchandise Imports by Region				
($ billions and percentage)				
United States	689	12.4	14.8	16.4
European Union	1658	41.0	44.7	39.4

Source: World Trade Organization, *International Trade 1995* (Geneva, 1995), Tables III.1, III.2.

TABLE 6.3
U.S. Direct Investment in the EU, 1995 ($ billions)

Direct investment in the EU	
Petroleum industry	21
Manufacturing	124
Banking, finance, insurance, and real estate	109
Other industries	10
All industries	315
Total U.S. direct investment, all countries	712
Percentage of total invested in the EU(%)	44

Source: U.S. Department of Commerce, *Survey of Current Business* (July 1996), p. 47.

CHALLENGES TO AND FROM EUROPEAN UNION

The European Union is the crucible of reform in the world today. Over the next decade and beyond, Europe will be the first among the major industrial powers to grapple with the challenges of the 21st century:

- How to redefine national sovereignty as individual nations surrender economic autonomy
- How to mesh different cultures with different priorities and different decision-making processes
- How to deregulate separate national economic regimes and to induce competition among national monopolies
- How to establish transnational incentives to promote innovation and technological advance without sacrificing the benefits from, or being captive to, laissez-faire economics

Europe is poised to be the global economy's next great growth engine, pulling along the collapsing economies of Eastern Europe and the moribund economies of Africa, South Asia and parts of Latin America. But a united Europe will also reorder the globe's economic priorities. Europe has suddenly become a focal point for investment and trade. And it poses a threat to U.S. preeminence in the global economy, a challenge that surpasses even that of Japan.

C. Michael Aho (Senior International Economist at Prudential Securities Inc.) *Columbia Journal of World Business*, fall 1994

Cecchini Report has played an important role in the ongoing evolution of the EU. The report established the issues of the continual debate over the benefits and costs proceeding to an integrated market.

Based on studies by twenty-four research teams and questionnaires to some 20,000 industrialists, the Cecchini Report assessed the cost of the barriers that fragmented the European market—the "costs of non-Europe." The ranking of market barriers by businesspeople is summarized in Table 6.4. The barriers assessed fall into three broad types:

- Physical barriers—such as border stoppages, customs control, and associated paperwork
- Technical barriers—for example, meeting divergent national product standards, technical regulations; and conflicting business laws; entering nationally protected procurement markets
- Fiscal barriers—especially differing rates of value-added taxes (VAT) and excise duties.

The survey showed that administrative and customs barriers, coupled with divergent national standards and regulations, were the dominant complaints.

A few examples of the costs considered in the report follow:

- Customs-related costs put a charge on companies equal to a major portion of their profits from intra-European trade; firms in effect pay a penalty dividend—about 25 percent of profits in many sectors—to national border controllers for the privilege of going European

TABLE 6.4
Ranking of Market Barriers by Business

Total Industry	B	DK	D	GR	E	F	IRL	I	L	NL	P	UK	EUR 12
1) National standards and regulations	2	1	1	7	6	1	2	4	2	3	4	1	2
2) Government procurement	6	8	8	8	8	7/8	7	2	8	7	3	4	8
3) Administrative barriers	1	2	2	1	1	2	1	1	1	1	1	2	1
4) Physical frontier delays and costs	3	3	4	3	2	4	3	3	3	2	2	3	3
5) Differences in VAT	8	7	5/6	4/5	7	3	6	7	7	8	8	8	6/7
6) Regulations of freight transport	5	4/5	5/6	4/5	3	5	4	8	5	4	5	5	6/7
7) Restrictions in capital market	4	6	7	2	5	7/8	5	5	4	6	6	7	5
8) Community law	7	4/5	3	6	4	6	8	6	6	5	7	6	4

Ranks are based on the answers to the question: "How important do you consider this barrier to be removed?" Range of ranks:
1 (most important) to 8 (least important).
B = Belgium; DK = Denmark; D = Germany; GR = Greece; E = Spain; F = France; IRL = Ireland; I = Italy; L = Luxemburg;
NL = Netherlands; P = Portugal; UK = United Kingdom.
Source: Paolo Cecchini, *The European Challenge 1992* (Aldershot: Gower, 1988), p. 5.

- Because of inefficiencies imposed by divergent product standards or protectionist procurement, industries in areas like motor manufacturing and telecommunications are losing billions of ECUs (the ECU is the European Currency Unit, a basket composed of the existing currencies in the EU)

- Smaller companies are, to a significant extent, barred from transborder business activity by administrative costs and regulatory hassles

- A bewildering array of national price differences faces customers of essential services and increases the information costs: car insurance may vary by as much as 300 percent between high- and low-price countries; tariffs for telephone services can vary 50 percent from one European country to another; the range of price differences for some key financial services can be even greater

- The public authorities, year in and year out, pay about ECUs $20 billion more than they should in purchasing the goods and services they need because of protective procurement systems over which they themselves preside[4]

The report estimated the size of the costs of non-Europe—and thus a potential for gains—exceeding ECU 200 billion (ECU at 1985 value).[5] These costs would be avoided by completing the internal market of the EU. The Cecchini Report's estimates are probably on the high side, but the types of cost-saving are still significant.

The report regrouped the physical, technical, and fiscal barriers into five categories: tariffs, quantitative restrictions, cost-increasing barriers, market entry restrictions, and market-distorting subsidies and practices.

Of all the types of market barrier, tariffs were the least important when assessing the cost of "non-Europe." Quantitative restrictions had also been considerably reduced within the EU, but some quotas persisted and restricted trade. They were a central feature in the agricultural sector. Effective quotas in the form of licensing and regulatory assistance still applied in air and road transport. Some member states also imposed national quotas on imports—notably of cars and textiles—from non-European countries. These quotas did not raise any revenue for the union's budget but simply allowed the exporter to benefit by way of increased profits.

The report focused on delays at frontiers and technical regulations as "cost-increasing barriers." The overall impact of these barriers was to raise the cost of goods to consumers and to allow a corresponding margin of inefficiency and/or extra profits for domestic producers. The supplier in another member state had to bear the extra costs, and since no tariffs were payable, the unfavorable impact on consumers was not offset.

The other principal type of market barrier related to market entry restrictions. This category included government procurement restrictions, the right of establishment for various service industries and professions, restrictions in some service sectors (insurance, electricity) that prevented or limited direct trading across frontiers, and restrictions on entry into some regulated markets (civil aviation). These types of restrictions excluded competition.

The final type of market barrier comprised market-distorting subsidies and practices. These put foreign suppliers at a competitive disadvantage and sheltered inefficient domestic suppliers. The result for the consumer was higher taxes rather than higher prices.

Although cross-frontier trade between private sectors of the European nations had expanded considerably, this was not true for their public sectors whose purchasing programs usually stopped at national borders. Public procurement, however, was large: In 1986, total purchasing controlled by the public sector was worth ECU 530 billion, amounting to 15 percent of the EU's gross domestic product. By not encouraging intra-European competition, each European country's public sector paid more than it should for the goods it bought and at the same time sheltered suboptimal enterprises that remained less competitive on world markets than they otherwise might be.

The report also noted that technical product regulations and standards forced companies to produce for only a national market and to innovate for a national market, thereby constraining manufacturers to a suboptimal market, or to try and enter new markets via a range of suboptimal plants and excessively narrowly relevant technology. Up to 100,000 regulations affected technical requirements, standards for products and product processes, and testing and certification procedures. Such barriers were an important problem in electrical engineering, mechanical engineering, the chemical industry, the food and tobacco sector, and the precision and medical equipment sectors. Table 6.5 summarizes the costs that resulted from divergent standards and regulations.

Other costs faced by companies that attempt to do business across national borders within the EU involved the extra administrative burden imposed by different auditing and fiscal systems. These were estimated as between 10 percent and 30 percent of the costs of the company departments involved. Most large companies had to produce three sets of figures: those conforming to the national requirements of the parent company; national accounts for each subsidiary; and a standardized system specific to the company used by all of its units for the purposes of internal control. In addition, there were different reporting dates and periods in the various EU countries.

Companies bore considerable administrative costs because of the different fiscal systems among the EU countries. The need to deal with competing national tax authorities raised transaction costs and limited company flexibility. The attempts made by national tax authorities to maximize their share of a European company's tax liability influenced key company decisions, including those on locating group management, production, and R&D. The report estimated that the charge of Europe's regulatory diversity on existing transborder

TABLE 6.5
A Typology of Costs Resulting from Divergent Standards and Regulations

For companies
　Duplication of product development
　Loss of potential economies of manufacturing scale
　Competitive weakness on world markets and vulnerability on European markets as
　　companies operate from a narrow national base

For public authorities
　Duplication of certification and testing costs
　Not getting value for money in public purchasing, whose noncompetitive nature is often
　　reinforced by national standards and certification

For consumers
　Direct costs borne by companies and governments means higher prices
　Direct and larger losses due to industry's competitive weakness and inefficient structure

Source: Cecchini, *The European Challenge 1992*, op cit., p. 26.

operations ran into tens of billions of ECU.[6] The costs were especially high for automobiles, machinery, textiles, telecoms, and pharmaceuticals.

　The costs of non-Europe applied to the service sectors as well as to industrial sectors. Government regulations often constituted a barrier to market entry for many activities in financial services (banking, insurance, and securities). Technical regulations, standards, and procurement also had a sizable impact on the community market, or the absence of it, for telecommunications services. The regulatory situation was more varied for other business services—advertising, engineering, computing, and legal services. The report estimated that the costs of nonintegration in banking and credit, insurance, brokerage, and securities amounted to approximately ECU 22 billion for eight of the EU countries.[7]

　Figures 6.1 and 6.2 summarize the expected benefits from liberalization and the expansion of the internal market in the EU. Figure 6.1 summarizes the microeconomic effects. When these microeconomic gains are aggregated, they will result in macroeconomic gains, as illustrated in Figure 6.2.

　Firms will immediately save costs when barriers and national regulations are reduced. Telecommunications, for example, will benefit by the removal of differing standards and protectionist public purchasing. Most important, the wider market should result in economies of scale. Transaction costs within the EU market will fall. A reduction in barriers to market entry will intensify competition among firms. The wider market will also support greater product diversity, resulting in more intraindustry trade. Restructuring and consolidation within an industry will also occur. There will also be more production by multinational corporations realizing multiplant economies. The increased degree of industrial competition will also reduce price differentials among the member countries and there will be less price discrimination in favor of exports over domestic markets. The need for—and the incentive to realize—dynamic efficiency will also result in more innovations at both the process and product levels.

　The new Europe immediately avoids the costs of non-Europe, but in the future it is the dynamic gains that will be prominent. The dynamic effects on the supply side associated with gains in microefficiency will be more significant than the static once-over trade effects. In the short term, an integrated internal EU market will result in loss of profits to monopolistic firms or those in protected positions. In the longer term, however, the competitive pressures

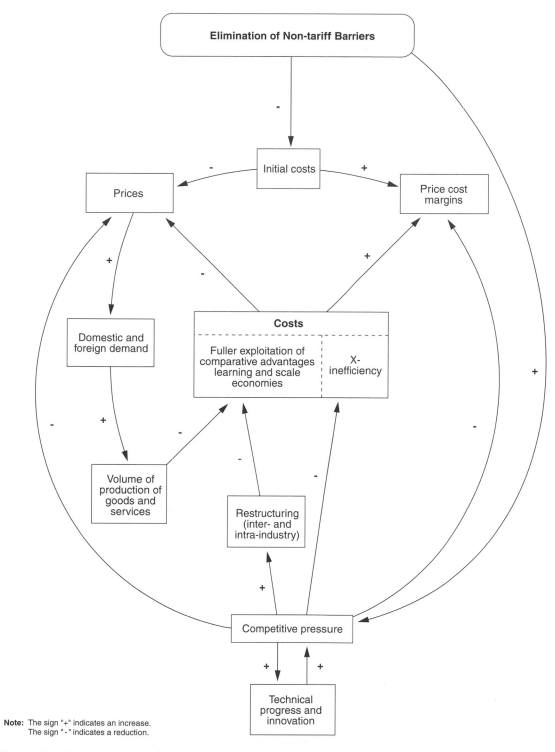

Note: The sign "+" indicates an increase.
The sign "-" indicates a reduction.

Figure 6.1   Microeconomic effects triggered by EU market integration. *Source*: Cecchini Report, *The European Challenge 1992* (Aldershot: Gower, 1988), p. 125.

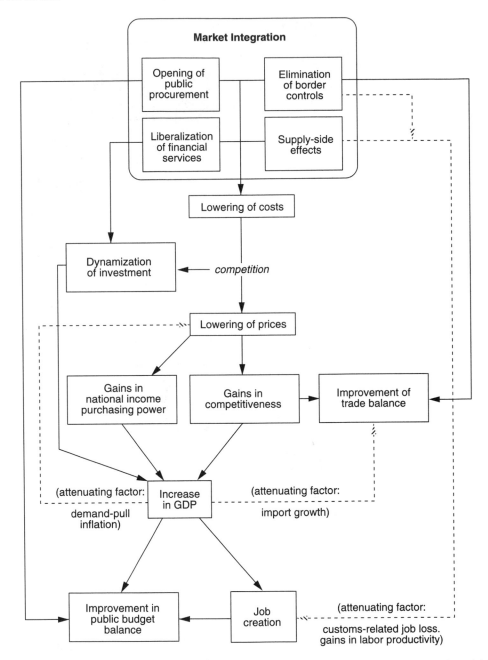

Figure 6.2 Macroeconomic effects triggered by EU market integration. *Source*: Cecchini Report, *The European Challenge 1992* (Aldershot: Gower, 1988), p. 100.

of the integrated EU market should provide dynamic gains to European business. In brief, these gains should come from a scaling up of production (economies of scale of production), gaining experience in how to produce most efficiently (economies of scale of learning or learning curve effect), elimination of management inefficiencies (what the economist calls "X inefficiency"), and by the greater need and improved capacity to innovate. Dynamic supply-side effects will be most significant as a result of higher investment, quicker technological progress, and greater human capital accumulation.[8]

Proponents of the EU maintain that gains in productivity and the lowering of production costs should raise the rate of growth of GDP, reduce inflationary pressures, expand employment prospects, and improve the balance-of-payments position of member countries.

PROGRESS MADE

Under the Single European Act, hundreds of directives have been adopted ranging from such minor matters as common rules for price labels in shops to more complex issues such

---

UNIQUENESS OF THE EUROPEAN UNION

The three aspects of EU uniqueness—the complex institutional structure, the range of policy responsibilities, and the combination of intergovernmental and supranational characteristics—have combined, and are combining, to produce a system which is quite unique in the extent to which it involves states engaging in *joint* action to formulate *common* policies and to make *binding* decisions. As the words "joint," "common," and "binding" imply, the process of working together is resulting in the EU states becoming ever more intermeshed and interdependent.

Clearly a central aspect of the intermeshing and the interdependence, and one of the principal distinguishing characteristics of the EU, is the way in which the member states have voluntarily surrendered some of their national sovereignty and independence to collective institutions. Indeed, in a few policy sectors, such as agriculture and external commercial policy, the requirements of the EU system have resulted in the role of the states being relegated almost to that of intermediaries. However, viewed from a broader perspective, the EU is not only the cause of a decline in national powers, but is also a response to the decline. This is so because much of the rationale of the EU lies in an attempt—an attempt for which there is no international parallel—on the part of the member states to increase their control of, and their strength and influence in, a rapidly changing world. Although all of the states have reservations, and some have fundamental criticisms, about aspects of the EU, each has made the judgment that membership enhances its ability to achieve certain objectives. The precise nature of these objectives varies from state to state but, in virtually all cases, the main priorities are the promotion of economic growth and prosperity, the control of economic and financial forces that are not confined to national boundaries, and the strengthening of political influence. Insofar as these objectives are being attained, it can be argued that the diminution in the role of the state and the loss of sovereignty that arises from supranationalism is counterbalanced by the collective strength of the EU as a whole.

Neill Nugent, *The Government and Politics of the European Union* (London: Macmillan, 3rd edition, 1994), pp. 433–34. Reprinted with permission of Macmillan Press Ltd.

as air transport, vehicle emission, insurance, and the liberalization of capital markets. The European Common Market earlier had eliminated tariffs among the member countries, but nontariff barriers remained. Several of these have been removed by the EU: (1) differences in technical regulations among countries; (2) delays at frontiers for customs purposes, and related administrative burdens for companies and governments; (3) restrictions on competition for public purchases through excluding bids from other community suppliers; and (4) restrictions on freedom to engage in certain service transactions, or to become established in certain service activities in other member countries.

Barriers regarding health, safety, and technical standards are being removed. Product standardization is being achieved. Every member country is now able to participate in government procurement of goods and services. There is also "mutual recognition" for services: For example, an insurance company can operate in all member countries; stock markets are available to all; achieving accreditation in a profession in one country allows accreditation in all countries. No passports are required for travel within the union, and an individual may retire in any country. Financial institutions are liberalized, allowing deposits outside a home country, loans to foreigners, and international credit cards. In 1990, controls on capital flows among the member countries were abolished. A single banking market has come into being.

In 1996, the European Commission issued a report on the progress of the first four years of the single market. Figure 6.3 compares what the early Cecchini Report expected and what has resulted. The optimism of the Cecchini Report has been borne out—but not quite to the extent expected. The single market has had positive effects on growth, employment, trade, and foreign direct investment. The abolition of customs documentation and formalities has led to savings of about ECU 5 billion (£6.3 billion) for businesses trading among EU countries. Telecoms equipment prices, telephone charges, and cross-border freight costs have all been reduced significantly.

Decisions are still to be made on the important issues of harmonization of effective rates of taxation and company law directives. It is hoped that the removal of obstacles to cross-border investment, production, and trade will gradually bring about a community-wide labor market. The Commission's Social Charter would also like to encourage workers' rights and harmonization of working conditions. But progress has not been made on the harmonization of labor rules, and there has been growing opposition to free labor movement. Even more difficult to achieve will be changes in the protectionist Common Agricultural Policy by way of reducing the subsidization of exports and the reliance on price supports. And exceptions, missing links, and long transitional periods still keep Europe from being a wholly integrated market. Continual negotiations are required if market integration is to expand and deepen.

The European Commission lists the following as the main priorities for the next few years:

- The single market for individuals, including full freedom of movement and quick and effective redress for consumers

- A more effective single market for business, including the definitive VAT regime

- Liberalization of energy and telecommunications

What was expected	**Progress made**
• The creation of 1.8m new jobs	• Between 300,000 and 900,000 people who are in work would have been unemployed without the single market
• A significant relaunch of economic activity, adding on average 4.5 per cent to EU GDP over the next five years	• EU GDP in 1994 was 1.1 to 1.5 per cent higher than it would have been without the single market, and investment was 2.7 per cent higher
• Falling inflation, with consumer prices deflating by an average of 6.1 per cent	
• The relaxation of budgetary and external constraints, improving the balance of public finances by an average equivalent to 2.2 per cent of GDP and boosting the EU's external position by around 1 per cent of GDP	• EU trade has risen faster than extra-EU trade, with the share of intra-EU imports in manufactured goods rising from 61.2 per cent in 1985 to 67.9 per cent in 1995
• The structural readjustment of industry in response to new patterns of competition	• The EU absorbed 44.4 per cent of world foreign direct investment flows in the early 1990s, compared to 28.2 per cent between 1982 and 1987
Source: Cecchini Report, (1988)	Source: EU Commission (1996)

Figure 6.3 Progress in the EU. *Source: Financial Times,* October 31, 1996, p. 11.

- Preparing for the information society and the trans-European networks for energy, telecommunications, and transport
- Meshing the single market with EU social and environmental policies
- Helping the countries of central and eastern Europe adapt to the requirements of the single market
- Ensuring that EU law is enforced to equivalent standards in all member states

DPR BY EUROPEAN FIRMS

How will an integrated market in the New Europe affect firms within and outside the EU?

The Cecchini Report concluded, "For firms, the era of the national soft option will be over . . . in short, strengthening European competitiveness leads, so to speak, to the reconquest of the European market. Failure to meet the demands of competitiveness does not mean that the challenges of the European Market will not be mastered. They will. But not by Europeans."[9]

If the potential gains of the European home market are to be realized by European firms, they will have to practice Diagnosis, Prediction, Response (DPR). Business strategies are likely to require restructuring internally or externally. Companies will have to rationalize their activities by specializing in a central line of business and dropping other areas, or they will have to engage in internal restructuring to extend their production and marketing for the enlarged EU market. External restructuring may include takeovers and mergers that enable exploitation of economies of scale, access to new geographical markets, and a greater division of labor among the various parts of the European market. There has already been an increase in the number of takeovers and asset mergers both within the EU and with non-EU partners at the expense of purely national linkups. We may anticipate a rising number of intercompany cooperative arrangements, provided that European company and tax laws facilitate transborder cooperation among firms.

According to a *Business International* study, the industries most affected by integration of the internal market will be[10]:

- Industries that will lose protection and become subject to more competitive pressures
    banking and insurance
    pharmaceuticals
    telecommunication services
- Industries that will shift from local to community-wide markets
    distribution
    food processing
    transport
- Industries gaining economies of scale
    electronics
    packaging
    white goods and other consumer products
- Industries dependent on public procurement
    computer equipment and services
    defense contractors
    telecommunications equipment
- Industries that may substitute EU production for imports
    chemicals
    electrical components and products
    office equipment

The former Chairman of Fiat states:

> As our market opens up more to foreign competition, a greater degree of consolidation and cooperation is almost inevitable. While the U.S. auto industry is divided among three main manufacturers, in Europe there are more than a dozen, with the largest single auto maker, Fiat, holding only 15% of all European sales. Cooperation, joint ventures, research consortia and various kinds of strategic alliances will be necessary for European car manufacturers to compete effectively with our larger American and Japanese rivals. . . . The future growth of Europe's industries lies in their improved access to a continent-wide, even worldwide, economy.[11]

Especially significant for European firms will be the wider range of opportunities for market entry. Their business strategy will also have to reckon with the challenge to European companies occasioned by the rivalry they will face from non-European companies in their enlarged EU market. Intensified competition from Japanese and American competitors can be expected in both the European markets and the global economy. This competition will be especially intense in the high-tech sectors. Unless European firms adopt successful business strategies, the primary beneficiaries of market integration could be non-European firms. Such strategies may involve full exploitation of innovation capacity; the "first mover advantage" for locally established companies; full use of "best practice" production processes to consolidate the first mover market advantage; and close durable and costly-to-replace relations between local suppliers and clients.[12]

Surveys by the European Commission in 1996 of more than 13,500 companies showed widespread satisfaction about the benefits that the EU's barrier-free bloc has yielded. Almost half the companies also recognized that they faced more intense competition as a result of the single market.

EFFECTS OF MARKET INTEGRATION ON NON-EUROPEAN FIRMS

If the single European market becomes as effective as the foregoing discussion indicates, it could produce a new generation of European industrial and banking giants that would put pressure on the top American and Japanese firms.[13] Larger firms in the EU will have an advantage in financing the enormous R&D costs associated with leading-edge technology, sustaining the losses incurred in bringing new products to market, reaping economies of scale, and financing industrial restructuring. The largest banks can also take on greater risks. Japanese firms have already pushed U.S.-based firms down in the rankings of industrial and financial giants. The rise of European giants may be yet another cause of concern to U.S. firms in global competition.

With European multinationals more formidable in foreign markets, many American firms might seek a relaxation in antitrust policy and a revision of banking policy so that they can combine and better compete in world markets. Instead of abandoning procompetitive policies, however, the EU and the United States could conceivably agree to coordinate their antitrust policies and to evaluate jointly the trans-Atlantic corporations engaged in mergers or strategic alliances. Otherwise, the consumer gains from freer trade could easily be lost as giant firms engage in informal market sharing on a global basis.

Of major concern to non-EU firms is the question whether the new Europe will turn into "Fortress Europe." The issue of regionalism versus multilateralism is crucial. (Recall the discussion in Chapter 3, pp. 86–90). Will the European Commission succumb to the demands of its more protectionist members and issue commercial and industrial directives that discriminate against non-European firms? While the EU liberalizes its internal market, it still practices elements of mercantilism without.[14] Far from the tenets of unilateral free trade, EU external trade policy is characterized by discrimination in the form of preferences on imports from some countries and departure from the most favored nation principle, restrictiveness through nontariff barriers, bureaucratic discretion in imposing antidumping and safeguard measures, and pursuit of reciprocity. Although the wider internal market should attract exports from non-EU firms, there is the possibility that external trade barriers will negate these export opportunities for firms in the United States, Japan, and the developing countries. Foreign direct investment might also be adversely affected by EU restrictions. Much will depend on whether the protectionist interests in France, Italy, and Spain will overcome the free trade interests of Germany, the Netherlands, and the United Kingdom. Trade barriers against non-EU firms are more likely where the GATT rules are weak or nonexistent.

Whether Fortress Europe comes about will depend on the outcome of five major issues that are on the U.S.–EU negotiating agenda.[15] They involve:

- Reciprocity
- National quotas
- Technical standards
- Rules of origin and local content
- Government procurement

Reciprocity

EU countries are not likely to extend the benefits of the internal market to outside firms without receiving something in return. Neither GATT nor any other agreement compels the EU to extend unilaterally to outside countries the benefits of the single banking license, open procurement, mutual recognition of technical standards, pan-European TV programming, or any other agreement in support of the single market. The EU countries ask for "reciprocity," which is interpreted by the EU to mean that in a foreign market, an EU firm should enjoy national treatment—that is, the same treatment that a government accords to its domestic firms—plus effective access to that market. A test of meaningful reciprocity is often defined in terms of the market share that EU firms acquire in the foreign country, whether through exports or investment. The EU reciprocity principle will probably be pragmatically adapted to the circumstances of each sector. The principle is likely to be strongly advocated in high-tech sectors, banking and financial markets, and in public procurement. Japan is especially likely to be the target of EU high-tech reciprocity requirements: It will be asked to open private and public procurement of high-tech goods and services, to facilitate European investment in Japan, and to ensure the transfer of Japanese technology to Europe. Regarding banking, the United States and Japan bar banks from entering the securities business, so European bankers could argue they are being denied reciprocal treatment by these countries. Europeans also complain about difficulties in obtaining seats on the Tokyo Stock Exchange and about being able to manage Japanese corporate and government pension funds.

National Quotas

Insofar as in the early 1990s the EU had nearly 700 national quantitative restrictions that limit third country suppliers, it will obviously be significant how these quotas are phased out. Of these quotas, about 70 percent limit textile and apparel imports under the Multi-Fiber Arrangement that restricts imports mainly from developing countries. About 26 percent of the quotas limit other industrial goods. Most of these cover imports from Eastern Europe and the former Soviet Union and are likely to be liberalized. It is unlikely that national quantitative restrictions will be transformed into EU-wide quotas. Nor is there likely to be unilateral abandonment of quantitative restrictions. The future of quotas is likely to be coupled with alternative trade policy measures designed to "safeguard" affected industries and to offset "unfair" foreign practices. The policy choice will depend largely on the sensitivity and the political influence of different industries.

EU-wide "soft" monitoring is probable in the automobile industry. Auto executives from Germany, Italy, and France, together with those of Ford of Europe, demanded transitional EU-wide controls on the sale of Japanese cars through the mid-1990s, and relaxation only in the context of true reciprocity from Japan. Any EU-wide monitoring of Japanese market penetration could also endanger the potential growth of American automobile exports to Europe from Honda firms in Ohio and Nissan firms in Tennessee.

Technical Standards

With the EU's setting of technical standards related to public health, safety, and the environment, American companies will be at a disadvantage if they are excluded from EU standard-setting procedures. The United States and the EU have yet to agree on mutual recognition of testing and certification. Prior to this there will have to be mutual recognition of industry standards.

A prominent concern relates to telecommunications where the EU is establishing common standards. If these standards are not compatible with those used in the United States and Japan, firms from these countries will confront adverse discrimination.

Large U.S. firms, accustomed to operating on a continental scale, stand to gain from the eventual harmonization of European technical standards. If, however, American interests are excluded from EU standard-testing procedures, they could be at a competitive disadvantage, especially in exporting high-tech products to Europe.

A federal advisory group on Europe's mode of testing and certification of goods has urged that the U.S. government help focus industry efforts to harmonize standards. So far, the interests of U.S. industry have been advanced case by case.

Origin and Local Content

Tight rules of origin and stringently applied local content requirements could exclude products from the firms outside the EU. These rules have already had adverse effects on a range of industries as diverse as TV programming and semiconductors. In the case of semiconductors, the EU has insisted that the process of diffusion (laying the circuit on the chip) must take place in Europe to meet the EU rule of origin. The incidence of local content rules will become especially significant as more transplant firms are located in Europe.

Rules of origin and local content will influence plant location and investment decisions insofar as those rules can determine whether a product is exempt from residual national quotas, is eligible for government procurement, is acceptable under EU-EFTA and other preferential tariff schemes, or escapes certain antidumping duties.

Public Procurement

Finally, it will be extremely important for outside suppliers whether the multibillion dollar public procurement market in the EU is also to be open to outside suppliers. The United

States is especially concerned about the further opening of telecommunications markets in Europe. A high rate of growth can be expected in the telecommunications equipment market and in telecommunication services.

The EU still exempts four sectors from open public procurement—energy, telecommunications, transportation, and water supply. The European Commission has directed that public authorities may reject outright any bid that does not meet a 50 percent EU content requirement, and it has imposed a "Buy European" preference margin of 3 percent on bids that do not meet the local content requirement, but, at the option of the public authority, are not rejected. This preference margin will self-destruct on a bilateral basis when another country (e.g., the United States) eliminates its own buy national preference at all levels of government.

OPPORTUNITY EUROPE

Despite uncertainty about how these negotiating issues will ultimately be resolved, most non-European firms regard the internal European market as an opportunity, not a problem. The integrated internal market should lead to greater economic growth within European countries and, hence, higher demand for imports. There is also stronger potential for foreign direct investment in the EU. Already, 45 percent of American capital invested overseas is in European equity ownership. Over the past three decades, the stock of U.S. direct investment in the EU has grown substantially faster than the value of U.S. exports. Moreover, sales of U.S.-owned affiliates within the union amount to several times the value of U.S. exports to the EU. This trend is expected to accelerate in the future. From an investment perspective, the new Europe should be highly attractive to American companies—"Opportunity Europe," not Fortress Europe.[16]

There are daily reports of Japanese and American multinationals investing in EU countries in anticipation of the wider European market. Japanese firms have already been induced to increase their foreign direct investment in Britain, Spain, Greece, and Portugal. Prominent investments in manufacturing plants have been made by Fujitsu, Toyota, Bridgestone, NEC, Nissan, Fuji, and Sony. American acquisitions of companies in the EU have been mainly in automotive concerns, food and food retailing businesses, printing and advertising, oil and gas, electronics, and chemicals and plastics. Financial investment in the EU by American firms would have been even larger in recent years but for the fact that large American manufacturing firms have already become well entrenched in the EU. The U.S. firms, unlike most Japanese companies, already supply almost all their share of the EU market from operations within the EU and depend very little on importing from the United States.[17] Moreover, many American firms already established in the EU are ahead of European firms in treating the EU as a single market. Examples are General Motors, Ford, IBM, Digital Equipment, Unisys, and Hewlett Packard.[18]

The stock of U.S. direct investment in the EU has risen much more than the value of American exports to the EU. Sales of U.S.-owned affiliates within the EU have in recent years amounted to eight to ten times the value of exports from the United States to the EU. Moreover, a third of American exports to Europe already go to U.S.-owned affiliates. There are now, however, more moves toward EU production and joint ventures by nonmanufacturing operations such as distribution and services, by smaller companies,

---

OPPORTUNITIES FOR U.S. FIRMS

Seen from an investment perspective, [the EU] is highly attractive to American firms. It is "Opportunity Europe," not "Fortress Europe." European nations almost unanimously welcome foreign investors; competition policy is favorable to newcomers; and foreign firms established within Europe enjoy numerous opportunities to participate in shaping the internal market. Whatever [the EU] may hold for U.S. exports, it basically holds great promise for General Motors, International Business Machines, Merck, American Telephone and Telegraph, and a long list of other U.S. firms with a strong presence in Europe. Not surprisingly, the principal organizations that speak for U.S. business— the Business Roundtable, the U.S. Council for International Business, the National Association of Manufacturers, and the U.S. Chamber of Commerce—are enthusiastic about the new Europe.

In any event, export concerns do not necessarily conflict with investment opportunities. In some cases, totally new U.S. exports may follow from an expansion of investment ties. In more cases, investment abroad enables the U.S. parent to sell components and earn royalties from its foreign affiliate, in circumstances where the market for the final product would have been lost to a local competitor if the U.S. firm had not established a plant. But, in some cases, U.S. corporations will be faced with a clear choice between locating highly desirable R&D centers in, for example, Grenoble or Rochester, or between expanding semiconductor capacity in Dublin or San Jose.

Gary Clyde Hufbauer, ed., *The New Europe: An American Perspective* (Washington, DC: Brookings Institution, 1990), pp. 24–26

---

by those not previously producing extensively within the EU, and by firms anticipating a share in public procurement.

In the future, the new Europe should become even more extensive with growing connections to the European Free Trade Association (EFTA) countries and Eastern Europe. The growing market should stimulate even more foreign direct investment. And if the EU should impose strict local content rules or other trade barriers, non-European firms will invest directly all the more in Europe to escape these barriers. Numerous mergers and acquisitions by foreign firms and additional joint collaboration on R&D may also be anticipated.

MONETARY INTEGRATION AND THE EMU

The second major force in the evolution of the new Europe is the movement toward the Economic and Monetary Union (EMU). Although the internal market has generally received the approval of public opinion and the support of EU member governments, the provisions of the EMU have been controversial and its implementation still needs to be achieved.

The future of the new Europe depends heavily on international monetary developments. It is desirable—even necessary—that the single market avoid inflation and the uncertainties associated with fluctuating exchange rates. To this end, there have been various proposals, debates, and negotiations toward the formation of an Economic and Monetary Union (EMU). While the "E" embodies the single market integration, the "MU" would feature a common currency, a common monetary policy, and fixed exchange rates among the member countries.

Proponents of an EMU expect it to do much more for monetary integration than does the present European Monetary System (EMS). Under the EMS, each member agrees to fix the value of its currency in terms of the European Currency Unit (ECU) that is defined in terms of a basket of currencies. The ECU has not become a currency of trade although investment in ECU bonds is now an international phenomenon.[19]

The EMS is characterized by a system of pegged exchange rates among the members' currencies, originally with a plus or minus 2.25 percent margin under the Exchange Rate Mechanism (ERM). When there is a speculative attack and the markets try to push a currency outside its band in the ERM, the first line of defense is intervention on the foreign exchange markets: sales or purchases of the currency to hold its level stable. EMS members can also draw on the system's special credit lines. When a currency is threatening to break through its limits, the EMS allows unlimited credit from other central banks in the form of a very short-term financing facility. A second line of defense is a change in interest rates to make the currency more or less attractive to overseas savers. The third line of defense is a change in tax and spending policy: Higher taxes or cuts in public spending curb demand for imports and hence the outflow of the weaker currency. In the last resort, finance ministers of the member countries can agree to change the bands of the ERM either up or down, thereby depreciating or appreciating a currency in relation to the ECU.

A persistent problem with the ERM has been a lack of credibility for the boundaries of the target zones when under speculative attack. Realignments have been necessary for the currencies of countries with higher inflation rates, high rates of money and credit growth and budget deficits, and weak trade balances. For example, during 1992 and 1993, there were mounting pressures on weak currencies in the ERM. Speculative attacks on the pound sterling and lira forced devaluations. EMS currencies were then allowed to float within a 15 percent band around their parity with the German mark.

Many now believe that there cannot be an efficient single internal market with price stability, greater competition, and free movement of capital in the EU without progress from the EMS to the EMU. A strategic report on the EMU was issued in 1989 by a committee of experts chaired by Jacques Delors, president of the Commission of the European Communities. The Delors report recommended a three-stage movement to a definitive EMU, as follows:

> Stage One. The abolition of capital controls and joining of the ERM by all member countries. This has been accomplished.
>
> Stage Two. Creation of a new monetary institution—a Euro-Federal Reserve type of central institution that would exercise full responsibility for monetary policy in the community. This stage also envisages opposition to further parity changes. It started in 1994 with the creation of a new institution, the European Monetary Institute, as a precursor of the European Central Bank (ECB).
>
> Stage Three. Three years from the start of the second phase, it is expected that substantial progress will be made toward an irreversible fixing of exchange rates. The transition to a single monetary policy and a single currency would then be made at the beginning of the third stage. Extending the original date of 1997, EU leaders agreed in

1995 that EMU will begin on January 1, 1999, with the irrevocable locking of exchange rates and the transfer of interest rate and foreign exchange policy to a European central bank.

In 1992, European leaders signed the Maastricht Treaty that designated the criteria for membership in the EMU and the institutions to regulate the new common currency.

To make the conditions for the inauguration of the EMU more favorable, the Maastricht treaty established four criteria for the convergence of prospective members:

- Price stability: an average inflation rate not exceeding by more than 1.5 percent that of the three best performing member states
- Budgetary discipline: a budget deficit of less than 3 percent of GDP and a public debt ratio not exceeding 60 percent of GDP
- Exchange rate stability: a country must have maintained its membership in the EMS for at least two years with no devaluations
- Interest rate convergence: an average nominal long-term interest rate not exceeding by more than 2 percent that of the three best performing member states

The European Council is, however, given some discretion in interpreting these criteria and in selecting member states for Stage III.

The desire for convergence is to ensure monetary stability and credibility for fixed exchange rates.

The treaty asserted that the European Central Bank (ECB) should be independent from national governments, should not finance public-sector deficits, and should seek the overriding object of price stability. The new currency is to be called the "Euro."

The following timetable has been established:

- Early 1998: examination as to which countries, based on 1997 data, meet the criteria for monetary union
- January 1999: irrevocably fixed exchange rates and common monetary policy is set for the EMU countries. National currencies will continue to exist, but with fixed exchange rates. Monetary policy will be conducted by the ECB for the member countries from day one
- January 2002, at the latest: euro notes and coins will be put into circulation and national currencies withdrawn. Within six months national currencies will lose legal tender status

The movement to the EMU has considerable support among many EU members, but its objectives of a single currency union with a grid of permanently fixed exchange rates and a Euro-Fed type of central bank have been subject to considerable negotiation. Although "one market" has been generally approved, "one money and one monetary policy" are subject to much debate over the putative benefits and costs.

Proponents of the EMU expect the benefits to be many. A study by the European Commission lists no fewer than sixteen benefits from the proposed EMU.[20] Among the benefits, the commission argues that EMU would:

EUROPE'S ROAD TO A SINGLE CURRENCY

1994
European Monetary Institute, forerunner of the European Central Bank, is founded in Frankfurt. Europe emerges from recession, but currencies do not stabilize.

1995
Spain devalues peseta. German mark soars. Germany challenges currency's name. Heads of state approve new name, the "Euro." Governments embrace a timetable for transition to new currency.

1996 and 1997
Governments under pressure to cut spending to reduce deficits to fulfill convergence criteria.

Early 1998
Decisions on which countries qualify for Monetary Union. A new European Central Bank will be created.

Jan. 1, 1999
Exchange rates of qualifying countries will be permanently set. European Central Bank takes over monetary policy. Governments issue debt in Euros.

Early 2002
Euro notes will begin to circulate. Stores will price goods in Euros.

June 2002
Old national currencies will no longer be legal tender. Only Euros will be used in member countries.

- Completely eliminate nominal exchange rate variability and exchange rate uncertainty
- Completely eliminate the transaction costs of exchanging currencies
- In combination with internal market integration provide not only once-and-for-all gains, but also dynamic gains in a higher rate of economic growth
- Ensure price stability that would be advantageous for efficient resource allocation
- Foster competitive pressures that should increase the efficiency of public expenditure and taxation
- Still allow changes in real exchange rates and hence international competitiveness provided that wages and prices are flexible
- Result in a saving on transaction costs in international trade, more ECU-dominated financial issues managed by European banks, a saving in the holding of foreign currency reserves, and seignorage gains on foreign holdings of ECU notes

Beyond the microeconomic benefits of the EMU, one might also expect dynamic efficiency gains and a stronger European presence in global financial markets. There may be dynamic gains from greater investment and higher growth rates. Some also expect that the "Euro" can become a strong competitor to the U.S. dollar in the international financial system, with diversification away from the dollar to the Euro and an ECU-denominated portfolio.

European businesspeople recognize substantial benefits from establishment of the EMU. According to a survey of 260 European businesses by Ernst & Young, the prospect of EMU was greeted with enthusiasm. Especially helpful to them would be the savings in the costs of transactions and the avoidance of uncertainty over foreign exchange movements. Seven out of ten companies also thought a common European currency would promote exports and improve their sourcing. More than half believed a single currency would help distribution and marketing strategies. With the exception of banks, the companies surveyed preferred the benefits from a single European currency to the idea of an additional currency operating as a parallel currency alongside the existing national currencies.[21] It is significant that in the Ernst & Young survey, the addition of a single currency to the single integrated market more than doubled the number of enterprises expecting a "very positive" impact on the business climate in the EU.

In contrast, many analysts discount the benefits and focus on the costs of proceeding to the EMU. To MIT's Rudi Dornbusch, "The costs of getting there are large, the economic benefits minimal, and the prospects for disappointment major."[22]

The costs of introducing a common currency begin with the cost of the initial change in accounting units and the cost of converting outstanding financial contracts into the single currency. These are, however, relatively minor once-and-for-all costs. More important is the psychological cost for the public when a nation gives up sovereignty over its currency and introduces the Euro to replace its historical currency.

Most troublesome is the cost of losing the capacity to alter a country's nominal exchange rate as an instrument of balance-of-payments adjustment and to conduct an independent monetary policy for the stabilization of national income and price levels. A member of the EMU would not be able to devalue its currency if it confronts a balance-of-payments deficit or if it wants to be more competitive internationally. When confronting adverse external shocks, a country would have to use fiscal policy—taxes and public spending—as the alternative to monetary policy and exchange rate adjustments. If a country suffers a balance-of-payments deficit because its exports decline, it would have to adopt a deflationary fiscal policy in place of devaluation. If it runs a surplus, inflation would have to occur instead of the remedial policy of appreciation.

There will also have to be considerable reliance on labor mobility instead of an easy monetary policy to alleviate unemployment. And wages and prices would have to be sufficiently flexible to affect competitiveness among the countries by changes in real exchange rates (as distinct from nominal official fixed rates). But European labor markets are not very competitive: Labor tends to be immobile, wages are rigid downward, and social welfare measures prevail.

Moreover, since the new central bank would have sole responsibility for EU monetary policy, European monetary growth by the Euro-Fed would then be instrumental in determining inflation rates. Accordingly, wage bargaining arrangements—instead of exchange rates —would have to affect the unemployment rate that is needed to hold a country's inflation

---

A SINGLE CURRENCY?

The process of European integration is faltering. Indeed, the brakes have been applied so firmly that Europe is at risk of fragmenting once again into separate economic islands.

The blame for this lies in the timid way the debate on economic and monetary union is being conducted. It is getting bogged down in technical detail. No one seems willing or able to restore the momentum that the integration process once had in the late 1980s, when moves to implement the single European market drew investment and envious glances from around the world, and when Euro-sclerosis gave way to single-market euphoria.

Today more than ever, I am convinced that Europe needs a strong, single currency. This would stabilise industry's cost and price structure and make damaging fluctuations between the units of exchange of the main EU member-states a phenomenon of the past. In short, a single currency is essential if stability is to become the trademark of Europe and not just a tantalizing vision.

Helmut Werner, president of Mercedes-Benz, *Financial Times*, May 26, 1995

---

stable. Again, only fiscal policy would be left in a member country's macroeconomic policy tool box. Denied the ability to monetize their public debt, governments would have to convince investors that they were willing to collect enough taxes to remain creditworthy.

Many analysts, however, doubt that the alternative policies to an independent monetary policy and the ability to adjust exchange rates will be sufficient for adjustment to shocks. They claim that wages and relative prices are not sufficiently flexible. And even if markets for goods, services, and capital become more integrated, European labor markets are still so segmented by linguistic, cultural, and educational differences that labor mobility is inadequate for adjustment to asymmetric aggregate supply and demand disturbances across member countries.

Moreover, some economists remain skeptical about the merits of establishing the EMU because it is unlikely in the first place to meet the conditions of an optimum currency area. According to that literature,[23] an optimum currency area should be characterized by similar economic structure in the member countries and substantial intermember trade, real wage flexibility, high mobility of labor, and fiscal integration.

PROSPECTS

The historically unique process of fashioning an economically united Europe has been long, complex, and marked by halting success. Most observers believe that the New Europe should be viewed as an evolutionary process, not to be determined by one fixed operational date. Progress toward the integration of the internal market may be fairly speedy. But the more integrated European markets for goods and services become, and the greater are capital movements, the less acceptable will it be to have exchange rate fluctuations stemming from divergent monetary policies. There is, however, considerable doubt as to when the various stages of the EMU will actually be achieved.

The convergence criteria are severe, and many of the EU countries are unlikely to meet the criteria in time. Figure 6.4 indicates that as of 1996 many countries in the EU had not met the convergence criteria—especially with respect to their public debt and budgetary imbalances. More detailed convergence indicators are given in Table 6.6, including official forecasts for 1997. To reach the Maastricht targets, many members will have to undertake austerity programs. But the price of convergence may be too high for some countries in causing them to sacrifice growth, political stability, or social harmony. If budget deficits and public debts were to be brought down to the required levels, recession might result. Some therefore argue that there has to be either a dilution—or even abandonment—of the convergence criteria, or there will be no EMU except for a minority of countries. Much will depend on how the Maastricht Treaty is interpreted to justify "exceptional and temporary" excesses from the agreed fiscal reference values.

Germany's strong anti-inflation stance, as exemplified by the record of the Bundesbank, will be a factor in controlling the new Central Bank's monetary policy. Germany wants the central bank to be nothing other than a copy of the Bundesbank, and it therefore argues for a slow transitional process with prior economic convergence being a necessary condition for membership.

Officially, thirteen of the EU's fifteen states are dedicated to monetary union, but what is most likely to happen is either a multispeed transition to EMU or no move at all. A multispeed movement would involve an earlier move toward EMU by the "core countries" that have sufficient convergence with low inflation rates and virtually fixed bilateral exchange rates—namely, Germany, Benelux countries, and possibly France. Their currencies would trade at zero-margin fixed exchange rates with par clearing against each other as if they were a single currency. They could also jointly exercise monetary policy. Other countries would follow later when they have attained adequate convergence. After this, the independence of national central banks might be overcome by the establishment of a Euro-Fed. Finally, there may come a single currency.

Given mobile capital, it is technically feasible for European countries to maintain fixed exchange rates via coordinated monetary policy, but they would still pursue independent fiscal policies. To avoid adverse spillovers from one country to another, coordination of fiscal policy would therefore have to be forthcoming. Coordination of fiscal policies, however, is even more difficult politically than coordination of monetary policies. Nigel Lawson, Britain's former Chancellor of the Exchequer, has argued: "Bluntly, I do not see how a single European currency, managed by an independent single European central bank, can make practical sense unless it is matched by a single European Finance Minister and Finance Ministry, and thus a single European government: in other words, the creation of a United States of Europe."[24] And who can say if Europe is politically ready for anything this bold?

The macroeconomic benefits of EMU therefore remain more doubtful than the microbenefits from the integrated internal market. As an IMF study concludes, "Ultimately the debate is about the question of whether, when, and to what extent countries will be ready to surrender sovereignty in the economic and, in the last analysis, the political field to common institutions and to share in a common decision-making process."[25]

As Europe moves through the stages toward EMU, there will, of course, be repercussions on other countries. Anticipating this, the six nations of the European Free Trade Association (Austria, Finland, Iceland, Norway, Sweden, and Switzerland) have negotiated with the EU to establish the European Economic Space (EES). Closer integration between

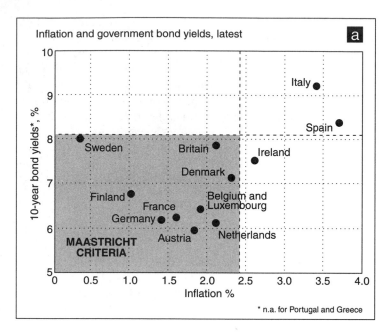

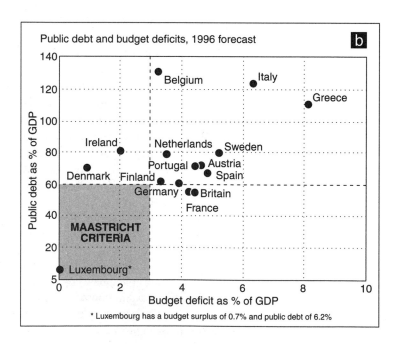

Figure 6.4 Convergence Criteria, 1996. *Sources*: National Statistics, *The Economist*, September 21, 1996, p. 20. © 1995 The Economist Newspaper Group, Inc. Reprinted with permission. Further reproduction prohibited.

the EU and EFTA is likely insofar as about 55 percent of EFTA's exports go to the EU, and 27 percent of the EU's exports go to EFTA nations. Trade between the two groups is more than trade between the EU and the United States.

TABLE 6.6
European Union: Covergence Indicators for 1995, 1996, and 1997 (In percent)

	Consumer Price Inflation			General Government Balance/GDP				Gross Government Debt/GDP[2]			Long-Term Interest Rates[3]
	1995	1996	1997	1995	1996	1997	1997[1]	1995	1996	1997	March 1996
Germany	1.8	1.5	1.5	−3.5	−3.9	−3.4		57.7	60.1	61.1	6.5
France	1.8	1.8	1.8	−5.0	−4.2	−3.6	−3.0	52.3	55.0	56.4	6.7
Italy	5.4	4.4	4.0	−7.2	−6.8	−5.9	−4.4	122.9	121.4	119.5	10.4
United Kingdom[4]	2.8	2.8	2.6	−5.1	−3.8	−2.5		48.8	49.7	49.5	8.1
Spain	4.7	3.6	3.2	−5.9	−4.7	−3.9	−3.0	64.7	65.5	65.4	9.9
Netherlands	2.0	2.3	2.0	−3.8	−3.5	−2.5		79.0	79.5	78.5	6.5
Belgium	1.5	2.0	2.0	−4.5	−3.4	−3.7	−2.5	133.8	132.7	130.6	6.8
Sweden	2.6	2.8	2.9	−6.8	−4.5	−2.5	−2.5	80.3	79.5	78.6	8.8
Austria	2.3	2.2	1.9	−6.1	−5.1	−4.0	−3.0	66.7	69.3	71.3	6.6
Denmark	1.9	2.4	2.6	−1.7	−1.0	−0.6		81.6	81.6	78.3	7.6
Finland	1.0	2.0	2.0	−5.6	−3.0	−0.5	−0.5	60.3	62.5	62.0	7.7
Greece	9.3	7.4	5.6	−9.0	−7.9	−6.5	−4.2	113.2	113.3	113.1	13.3
Portugal	4.1	3.5	3.3	−5.2	−4.5	−4.2	−3.0	72.6	72.6	72.3	9.1
Ireland	2.5	2.3	2.7	−2.1	−2.6	−2.5		85.3	80.0	76.0	8.0
Luxembourg	1.9	1.8	2.0	0.4	—	—		6.3	6.7	6.8	6.8
All EU	3.0	2.6	2.5	−5.1	−4.6	−3.6		72.0	73.0	72.9	7.9
Maastricht convergence criteria reference range/value	2.5–3.3	3.0–3.3	3.0–3.4	−3.0	−3.0	−3.0		60.0	60.0	60.0	8.5–8.8

Note: The table shows the convergence indicators mentioned in the Maastricht Treaty, except for the exchange rate criterion.
[1]Official targets or intentions.
[2]Debt data refer to end of year. They relate to general government but may not be consistent with the definition agreed at Maastricht.
[3]Ten-year government bond yield or nearest maturity.
[4]Retail price index excluding mortgage interest.
Sources: National Sources; and IMF staff projections; IMF, *World Economic Outlook*, May 1996, p. 41.

A more integrated Europe is also an economic and political magnet for Central and Eastern Europe. In the future, what will matter the most for Eastern Europeans is whether the EU will allow greater shipments of agricultural products, steel, and textiles into its markets. In the longer term, the prospect of EU membership is attractive to Eastern Europe. Eastern European countries hope for a series of "association agreements" that will offer free trade into the EU while allowing a transitional period of protection for the East Europeans. Western expertise is also sought through joint projects in banking, R&D, telecommunications, and industrial ventures. Financial aid from the EU to Eastern Europe will also strengthen trade relations.

Despite the halting progress, a new dynamism and spirit of optimism characterize much of Europe. Eurosclerosis has given way to Euphoria. "Before the end of this century there will be a single currency in Europe," Cornelis Van der Klugt, former chairman of N. V. Philips of Holland, has said. "Much of Eastern Europe will be in the European Community, and 20 years from now there will be a Europe of 700 million people able to be equal partners with the U.S., Japan, and the rest of the world."[26] Euro-skeptics may dismiss this as hyperbole, but many businesses inside and outside the EU are optimistic. Accordingly, they are changing their production and marketing strategies to take advantage of more trade and investment in the new dynamic Europe.

NOTES

1. The EU is composed of Austria, Belgium, Denmark, Finland, France, Germany, Greece, Ireland, Italy, Luxembourg, Netherlands, Portugal, Spain, and the United Kingdom.

   The EU has signed association agreements with Bulgaria, Czech Republic, Slovak Republic, Hungary, Poland, and Romania. These agreements aim to establish a free trade area by 2003. Negotiations have also occurred wth the Baltic states and countries in Eastern Europe and the former Soviet Union.
2. Giovanni Agnelli, "The Europe of 1992," *Foreign Affairs* (fall 1989): 62.
3. For details see Michael Emerson, *The Economics of 1992* (London: Oxford University Press, 1988), pp. 11–20.
4. Paollo Cecchini, *The European Challenge 1992* (Aldershot: Gower, 1988), pp. 3–4.
5. The center point of the estimated spread of ECU 174–258 billion is ECU 216 billion.
6. Cecchini, *The European Challenge 1992*, p. 31.
7. Ibid., p. 37. The ECU 22 billion gained from completing the EC internal market is calculated on the basis of estimates of the prices of a standard set of financial products before and after the removal of regulatory barriers.
8. Richard Baldwin, "Measurable Dynamic Gains from Trade," *Journal of Political Economy* (February 1992): 162–174.
9. Cecchini, *The European Challenge 1992*, pp. 74–75.
10. "Gaining a Competitive Edge in the New Europe" (New York: Business International Corp., November 1989), p. 34.
11. Agnelli, "The Europe of 1992," p. 65.
12. A. Jacqemin, *The New Industrial Organization* (Cambridge, Mass.: MIT and Oxford University Press, 1987).
13. Gary Clyde Hufbauer, *Europe 1992: Opportunities and Challenges* (Washington, DC: Brookings Institution, 1990), Ch. 2.
14. Martin Wolf, "Cooperation or Conflict? The European Union in a Liberal Global Economy," *International Affairs* 71, 2 (1995): 333–337.
15. These issues are discussed in detail in Hufbauer, op cit., Ch. 2. The following is a condensation.
16. Gary Clyde Hufbauer, "Europe 1992: Opportunities and Challenges," *Brookings Review* (summer 1990): 13.
17. Robert E. Lipsey, "American Firms Face Europe: 1992," National Bureau of Economic Research, Inc. Working Paper No. 3293 (March 1990), p. 1.
18. Ibid., pp. 12–13.
19. ECU bonds offer a higher yield than the most stable currency in the EU, while, through its basket composition and the political desire for convergence of monetary and fiscal policies, it provides a safe and fairly stable home for funds.
20. Commission of the European Committees, "One Market, One Money," European Economy No. 44 (Luxembourg: European Community Publication Office, October 1990).
21. "Plotting European Union," *Economist*, May 19, 1990, p. 87.
22. Rudi Dornbusch, "Euro Fantasies," *Foreign Affairs* (Sept./Oct. 1996): 113.
23. Robert Mundell, "A Theory of Optimum Currency Areas," *American Economic Review* (September 1961): 657–665; Ronald McKinnon, "Optimum Currency Areas," *American Economic Review* (September 1963): 717–725.
24. Nigel Lawson, "Rules versus Discretion in the Conduct of Economic Policy," Stamp Memorial Lecture, London, November 26, 1990.
25. *The European Monetary System: Developments and Perspectives* (Washington, DC: IMF Occasional Paper #73, 1991).
26. *Wall Street Journal*, July 5, 1990, p. 1.

DISCUSSION QUESTIONS

1. Is the EU a beneficial development for the rest of the world in general and for the United States in particular?

2. Is a multispeed Europe a good idea? Would the innercore ever agree to widen the union? Would there be any problems between the "ins" and the "outs" in a partial monetary union? What would be the implications of a multispeed Europe for financial markets, companies, consumers, and governments?

3. Even if in economic terms the costs of the EMU are considered to be greater than the benefits, might countries still want to adopt a common currency for political reasons? Is it politics rather than economics that will be decisive for establishment of the EMU?

4. Instead of replacing national currencies with the Euro, would it be better to retain national currencies but institute irrevocably fixed exchange rates? What would be the implications of such a monetary regime: for companies that trade and invest in Europe? for governments?

5. In theory there could be a single market among countries each with a separate currency, autonomous monetary policy, and floating exchange rates. But what would you expect to happen in practice under such a monetary regime?

6. Along with the EMU, enlargement is a major goal of the EU in coming years. What strategy for enlargement would you recommend?

7. Do you believe that the Maastricht Treaty that established the convergence criteria should also have provided for more political integration?

8. Do you believe that the creation of a single European market is essential if European firms are to compete successfully with their American and Japanese counterparts?

Chapter

7 WHITHER JAPAN?

Afer making economic history with spectacular advances in its economy since the 1950s, Japan now confronts a number of challenging policy issues. Having caught up to the leading industrial nations, does a "different Japan" now face economic maturity and problems similar to those of the advanced Western economies? Is the sun about to set?[1] Will Japan slip from the top ranks of industrial power? Will it have to reposition itself in the world economy? Answers to these questions will have important implications for managers throughout the global economy.

To seek these answers, we first summarize the outstanding trends and achievements in the Japanese economy, and examine how these achievements relate to Japan's national economic management. After understanding the "whence" of Japan, we can then explore "whither Japan?"

CATCH-UP INDUSTRIALIZATION

Between its prewar peak in 1938 and 1990, Japan's GNP increased from being only 5 percent of the United States's GNP to almost 80 percent (at market exchange rates). Its GDP per head (at market exchange rates) exceeded that of the United States in the 1990s (see Figure 7.1). Although Japan occupies only 0.3 percent of the world's land area and has 2.5 percent of the world's population, it has become the second largest industrial economy in the world, producing 15 percent of the world's output of goods and services. It is also the second largest exporter of manufactured goods. It has enjoyed large balance of trade surpluses with the United States since the early 1980s, and had foreign exchange reserves in mid-1997 of over $207 billion. Of the world's ten largest banks, nine are Japanese, and by the mid-1980s, Japan had become the leading exporter of financial capital.

These achievements reflect a remarkable structural transformation in Japan's postwar economy—a transformation from an agricultural to an advanced industrial economy, with

A. Using Market-Based Exchange Rates

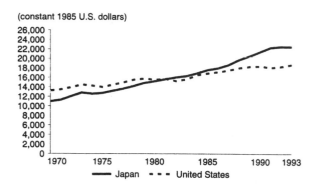

(constant 1985 U.S. dollars)

Japan ▪▪▪ United States

Figure 7.1 Comparing per capita gross domestic product in Japan and the United States. *Source*: World Resources Institute, *World Resources 1996–97* (New York: Oxford University Press, 1996), p. 164.

B. Using Purchasing Power Parity

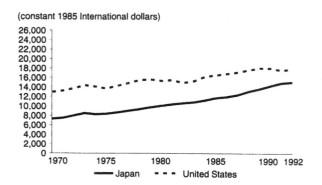

(constant 1985 International dollars)

Japan ▪▪▪ United States

exports of higher–value-added manufactured products becoming ever more significant. Until the oil shocks in the 1970s, Japan experienced superfast growth rates in national income: from 1950–73, the annual real growth of Japan's GNP averaged 10 percent—the highest sustained rate of increase for any country. In the 1960s, Japan's national income grew at the phenomenal average annual real rate of over 12 percent—three times the rate in the United States. The annual growth rate in income per head was an exceptional 9 percent during the 1960s, amounting to a doubling in per capita income in eight years. Table 7.1 compares Japan's growth rates with that of several countries, 1960–90. Between 1960 and 1973, domestic output more than quadrupled. And Japan's international competitiveness improved enormously.

After the first oil crisis in 1973, Japan's growth rate was sharply reduced to 3.8 percent per year from 1973 to 1979. The rate of growth in income per head fell to the 3 percent to 4 percent range during the 1970s. But this fall was true for all countries, and Japan still enjoyed higher growth rates than the OECD average of 2.8 percent per year from 1973–79.[2] Japan's absolute performance has diminished, but its performance relative to other leading industrialist nations is still most impressive. Between 1980 and 1990, national income

TABLE 7.1
Average Annual Real GNP Growth Rates, by Country, 1960–90

Country	1960–69	1970–73	1974–85	1985–90
Japan	12.1	7.5	3.8	4.5
United States	4.1	3.2	2.2	3.4
West Germany	5.7	4.2	1.8	2.7
France	5.8	5.6	2.1	2.8
Great Britain	3.1	3.7	1.3	3.5

Source: International Monetary Fund, *International Financial Statistics Yearbook* (Washington, DC: IMF, various years).

per person rose in real terms nearly 4 percent annually in Japan, compared with less than 2 percent in the United States. Figure 7.2 shows changes in some economic indicators, as does Table 7.2.

We should identify the sources of Japan's growth in order to place Japan's future in perspective. Will the sources of growth that have dominated in the past be as strong in the future? How have government-business relations contributed to the various sources of growth? Will these change in the future? How does Japan's domestic growth rate relate to the international economy? And what are the international implications for the future?

A number of sophisticated statistical and econometric studies have examined the sources of Japan's growth. These studies establish a framework of growth accounting that identifies the causes of Japan's high rate of growth in output in terms of contributions made by increases in factor inputs (labor, capital, land) and by the rate of technical change (increases in total factor productivity). A major study found that five forces contributed more to growth in Japan during 1953–71 than they did in the other industrial countries—namely, increased labor input, increased capital stock, increases in productivity attributed to advances in knowledge (technical change), reallocation of resources away from agriculture, and economies of scale.[3]

Table 7.3 summarizes an intensive study of the sources of economic growth in Japan and the United States. The most important contributor to growth in both countries has been the growth of capital input, accounting for about 5 percentage points of Japan's growth

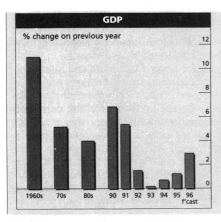
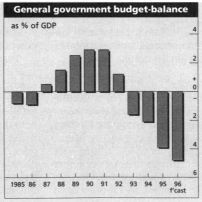
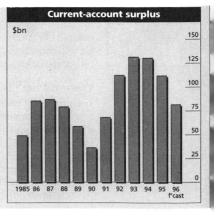

Figure 7.2 Economic indicators, Japan. *Source:* World Bank, *World Tables*, 1995.

TABLE 7.2
Japan: Economic Structure

Economic Indicators	1973	1983	1993	1994	1995
GDP at market prices, ¥ trillions	112.5	281.8	475.4	479.1	480.7[a]
Real GDP growth, %			0.1	0.5	0.9[a]
Exports changes in figures, $ billions	36.9	146.7	351.3	384.2	427.3
Imports changes in figures, $ billions	38.3	126.4	209.8	238.2	292.5
Current-account balance, $ billions	−0.13	20.8	131.5	129.2	110.4
Reserves excludes gold, $ billions			98.5	125.9	183.3
Exchange rate (avg.), ¥:$	271.7	237.5	111.2	102.2	94.1

Principal Exports 1995[a]	$ billion	Principal Imports 1995[a]	$ billion
Motor vehicles	53.1	Mineral fuels	53.3
Office machinery	30.7	Foodstuffs	51.2
Chemicals	30.2	Textiles	24.9
Scientific & optical equipment	18.6	Chemicals	24.7
Iron and steel products	17.5	Wood	10.1

Main Destination of Exports 1995[a]	% of total	Main Origins of Imports 1995[a]	% of Total
USA	27.3	USA	22.4
South Korea	7.1	China	10.7
Taiwan	6.5	Australia	4.3
Hong Kong	6.3	South Korea	5.2
Singapore	5.2	Taiwan	4.3
China	5.0	Indonesia	4.2

[a]Preliminary.
Source: World Bank, *World Tables*, annual.

rate and about 1.54 percentage points of the U.S. growth rate from 1960–79. This amounts to 60 percent of Japanese growth and 40 percent of U.S. growth. Labor input accounted for 1.5 percent of Japan's growth rate and 1.2 percent of the U.S. growth rate. The rate of technical change contributed nearly 2 percent in Japan and 0.7 percent in the United States. After the energy crisis of the 1970s, Japan's slowdown was due to a sharp decline in technical change.

A sizable increase in the capital stock during the period of high absolute growth is related to Japan's overcoming a technology lag and undertaking a catching-up process in industrial development. Japan lagged far behind other industrial countries in technology in the 1950s and 1960s, but it had a large pool of available labor in agriculture, and the social capability to absorb and adapt foreign technology. The Japanese economy was a dynamic market economy, and strong private investment led to high economic growth. Supporting the rise in investment was a steady increase in private savings. In the rapid growth period of the 1960s and early 1970s, gross national saving (by corporate and government bodies and households) was astoundingly high at 35 percent to 40 percent of national income.[4] As indicated in Table 7.4, the national saving ratio was somewhat lower in the late 1970s and 1980s but still relatively high in comparison with other industrial nations (compare in Table 7.5).

As economic growth slowed after the early 1970s, investment also declined, but savings did not fall at a comparable rate, and an excess of savings over investment began to

TABLE 7.3
Sources of Economic Growth, Japan and the United States, 1960–79

	1960–79		1973–79	
	Japan	**United States**	**Japan**	**United States**
Average Annual Growth Rate				
Net output	.083	.035	.038	.028
Capital input	.096	.040	.060	.038
Labor input	.031	.020	.015	.017
Annual Rate of Contribution to Growth				
Capital input	.050	.015	.029	.014
Labor input	.015	.012	.008	.011
Technical change	.020	.007	.001	.003
Quality change of capital input	.018	.004	.005	.003
Quantity change of captial input	.032	.012	.024	.011
Quality change of labor input	.010	.002	.005	.001
Hours worked change	.005	.010	.004	.010
Weighted average of sector technical change	.007	.004	−.012	−.007
Contribution of Allocation Changes				
Net output	.004	.002	.014	.009
Capital input	.009	.001	.005	−.000
Labor input	.001	.000	−.005	.002

Source: Dale W. Jorgenson, *Productivity*, Vol. 2 (Cambridge, Mass.: MIT Press, 1995), p. 378.

TABLE 7.4
Investment and Saving in Japan, 1965–93 (percent of GDP)

Year	Average Gross Domestic Saving	Average Gross Domestic Investment
1965–69	33.8	34.6
1970–74	37.5	38.4
1975–79	31.5	32.1
1980–84	30.9	27.6
1985–89	32.2	29.2
1990–93	33.5	32.7

Source: Annual Report on National Income Statistics (Tokyo: Government Printing Office, various years); World Bank, *World Tables*, 1995.

appear in the private sector. To the extent that the excess private savings were not absorbed by the government's fiscal deficit, the excess savings contributed to a rise in net exports. (Recall the balance-of-payments relationship explained in Chapter 5.)

The rise in excess private savings meant that the private sector was not absorbing through consumption, housing investment, and business investment as much as it was producing. And since the government pursued fiscal austerity especially in the 1980s, the resultant current account surplus in the balance of payments meant that foreign countries were absorbing the goods and services produced but not consumed in Japan. At the same time, the surplus savings flowed abroad as a net capital outflow in Japan's balance of payments.

The demand side of Japan's growth process was driven not only by high investment, but also by high exports. During the 1960s, exports rose at an annual rate of nearly 18 percent.

TABLE 7.5
Industrial Countries: Saving Rates by Sector, 1980–87

Country	Gross Saving Rates[a]			
	Households	Enterprises	General Government	National Total
Japan	16.08	10.85	4.19	31.10
United States	9.71	8.99	−2.10	16.60
Canada	11.88	10.70	−1.87	20.71
France	7.57	13.09	−0.54	20.11
Germany, Fed. Rep. of	8.00	11.92	1.90	21.82
Italy			−6.54	22.36
United Kingdom	7.13	11.08	−0.18	17.53

[a]Gross saving as percentage of GNP.

Source: Organization for Economic Cooperation and Development, *National Accounts* (Paris: OECD, various years).

The fast rate of growth in exports allowed imports to expand at the same rate, and the rising imports supported the high rate of economic growth.

The growth rate of exports fell to 12.7 percent from 1971 to 1974, and to an annual rate of 6.9 percent from 1975–85. But net exports (exports minus imports) increased until 1985. The share of GNP growth based on the expansion of net exports was therefore large, as indicated in Table 7.6.

We should recognize, however, that the leading export industries initially grew out of expanding domestic markets. Textile and garment industries in the prewar period and the 1950s; shipbuilding and electrical appliances in the 1960s; autos, manufacturing machinery, semiconductors, and electronic products in the 1970s and 1980s—the products of all these industries were first tested and widely marketed within Japan.[5] Through learning by doing in the growing domestic markets, these industries improved their productivity and then became internationally competitive.

Government protection in Japan has not been centered on the export industries but rather on low-productivity sectors, such as agriculture and retail. Income has been redistributed from the export industries to the less productive sectors by tax-subsidy schemes and import protection. The redistribution contributed, in turn, to expansion of domestic markets for consumer goods and hence more growth for the high productivity sector.

The structural transformation that occurred during the high-growth period of the 1960s and early 1970s had significant international consequences. Three major changes took place in Japan's international trade. First, Japan's share of world trade rose substantially. Second, Japan moved rapidly up the ladder of comparative advantage. The composition of Japan's exports changed greatly: the share of unskilled labor-intensive products (textiles, light consumer products, sewing machines, and inexpensive cameras) declined, and the share of products of heavy engineering industries (steel, machinery, automobiles) rose markedly (see Table 7.7). Japan's exports of manufactures rose from 8 percent of world exports in 1965 to over 13 percent by 1987. In the same period, U.S. exports of manufactures fell from 19 percent of the world total to 11.7 percent. In this period, Japan was transforming from a latecomer, newly industrializing country having a comparative advantage in labor-intensive products to a highly developed industrial country having a comparative advantage in high–value-added engineering products utilizing sophisticated technologies.

TABLE 7.6
Growth in GNP and Net Exports, Japan, 1975–93

Year	Real GNP (trillions of 1987 yen)	GNP Growth Rate (percent)	Percentage Points of GNP Growth Due to Net Exports[a]	Share of GNP Growth Due to Net Exports[b] (percent)
1975	217.2	2.8	1.0	36.3
1976	226.4	4.2	0.9	20.2
1977	236.7	4.5	1.0	22.8
1978	248.4	5.0	0.6	11.4
1979	262.6	5.7	−2.7	−46.8
1980	271.4	3.4	−0.3	−8.7
1981	280.6	3.4	1.8	52.4
1982	290.2	3.4	−0.1	−2.5
1983	298.1	2.7	1.1	40.8
1984	311.1	4.4	1.1	24.2
1985	327.3	5.2	1.0	18.3
1986	335.6	2.5	0.8	32.7
1987	350.5	4.4	−0.7	−16.2
1988	372.6	6.3	−0.5	−7.3
1989	390.8	4.9	−0.3	−6.7
1990	409.8	4.8	−0.4	−7.7
1991	427.4	4.3	0.6	14.8
1992	433.0	1.3	0.6	46.8
1993	433.3	0.1	0.0	−48.1

[a] Growth of exports and imports is weighted by their shares in GNP. Net exports is exports minus imports. The figures thus show the percentage points of growth due to expansion (or contraction) of net exports.

[b] Percentage points of growth due to net exports divided by GNP growth rate.

Source: *World Tables* (published for World Bank), Johns Hopkins University Press, Baltimore and London, 1995. © 1995 The Johns Hopkins University Press.

Table 7.7
Changing Composition of Japanese Exports, 1965–89 (in percent)

	1965	1970	1980	1985	1989
Capital goods	27.7	31.1	40.1	46.5	54.3
Of which:					
Technology-intensive products[a]				5.7	9.4
Consumer goods	21.3	25.7	28.5	31.0	25.3
Of which:					
Passenger cars	1.4	4.7	12.4	14.5	14.1
Industrial supplies	45.4	38.3	28.5	20.4	18.2
Of which:					
Textiles	12.3	8.4	·3.7	2.7	1.9
Iron and steel	15.3	14.7	11.9	7.7	5.4

[a] Data processing machines, integrated circuits, and telecommunications equipment.

Source: Robert Corker, "The Changing Nature of Japanese Trade," *Finance and Development*, June 1991, p. 7.

The third change was in the balance of payments: Japan's balance on current account turned positive in the 1980s and has been generally in surplus since then. Table 7.8 shows Japan's balance of payments by type of account. The surplus in merchandise trade balance rose rapidly as the pattern of technological progress in Japan, including the introduction of new products and the development of overseas marketing networks, was strongly biased

TABLE 7.8

Japan's Balance of Payments by Type of Account, 1975–95 ($ billions unless specified)

Year	Merchandise Trade Balance	Services Trade Balance	Current Account Balance	Net Long-term Capital	Net Short-term Capital	Yen-Dollar Exchange Rate (¥ per $)
1975	5.0	−5.4	−0.7	−0.3	−1.1	296.8
1976	9.9	−5.9	3.7	−1.0	0.1	296.6
1977	17.3	−6.0	10.9	−3.2	−0.6	268.5
1978	24.6	−7.4	16.5	−12.4	1.5	210.4
1979	1.8	−9.5	−8.8	−13.0	2.7	219.1
1980	2.1	−11.3	−10.7	2.3	3.1	226.7
1981	20.0	−13.6	4.8	−9.7	2.3	220.5
1982	18.1	−9.8	6.9	−15.0	−1.6	249.1
1983	31.5	−9.1	20.8	−17.7	0.0	237.5
1984	44.3	−7.7	35.0	−49.7	−4.3	237.5
1985	56.0	−5.2	49.2	−64.5	−1.0	238.5
1986	92.8	−4.9	85.8	−131.5	−1.6	168.5
1987	96.4	−5.7	87.0	−136.5	23.8	144.6
1988	95.0	−11.3	79.6	−130.9	19.5	128.2
1989	76.9	−15.5	57.2	−89.2	20.8	138.0
1990	63.9	−22.3	35.8	−43.5	21.5	144.8
1991	103.0	−17.7	72.9	37.1	−25.8	134.7
1992	132.3	−10.1	117.6	−28.5	−7.0	126.7
1993	141.2	−3.9	131.4	−78.3	−14.4	111.2
1994	145.9	−9.3	129.1	−82.0	−8.9	102.0
1995	132.1	−13.1	111.25	−84.5	74.9	94.0

Source: Bank of Japan, *Balance of Payments Monthly* (April 1995): 7–8; International Monetary Fund, *International Financial Statistics Yearbook* (September 1996); and *World Tables* (published for World Bank), Johns Hopkins University Press, Baltimore and London, 1995. © 1995 The Johns Hopkins University Press.

toward raising production in exports and import-competing goods.[6] Before 1980, however, there was not much concern in the United States about a trade deficit with Japan because it was offset for the United States by trade surpluses with other countries and for Japan by a large trade deficit with the oil-producing countries. In the aggregate, neither the United States nor Japan had a substantial trade imbalance. But this changed dramatically in the 1980s: The US-Japan trade imbalance grew, and the United States suffered a cumulative trade deficit from 1981 through 1988 of $750 billion, of which 40 percent was in trade with Japan.

"JAPANOMICS"

How are we to account for Japan's remarkable record of growth, structural transformation, and international competitiveness? We have already noted the economic sources of growth. But what policies, by both government and business, contributed to these forces of growth? And what policies accelerated the structural transformation and enhanced international competitiveness?

A leading management consultant based in Tokyo, C. Tait Ratcliffe (president of International Business Information, Inc.), provides some incisive answers:

> Japan has clearly had an industrial strategy, a distinctive "Japanomics," characterized by hard headed pragmatism and minimal attention to economic ideologies.

Some of the principal aspects of the strategy described by Tait include:

- Selective use of protectionism and the threat of market opening to stimulate its infant industries to grow into world giants.
- The existence of clear industrial targets and a sense of mission and direction based on a general consensus established between industry, finance, and government Ministries.
- The adoption of necessary policy measures to assure the maintenance of high saving and investment rates, which reflect the essentially frugal mindset of the Japanese populace.
- Avoiding involvement in geopolitical issues and restraining military expenditures in line with the postwar constitution.

Another important aspect of Japanomics is *jimae shugi*, meaning, "Make, don't buy, whenever possible" and "Retain ownership at all cost."

Under the *jimae shugi* philosophy, Japanese corporations work to be self-sufficient through continued efforts to develop better, lower-cost means of manufacturing goods initially manufactured overseas. Much of the success of Japanese corporations seems to be traceable to this approach. In many respects, *jimae shugi* is the opposite of the principles of comparative advantage and international division of production. Through the introduction of increasingly sophisticated manufacturing techniques and systems, Japan has in fact been able to change its comparative advantage and become competitive in an increasingly broad range of high-value-added manufactured products.

Finally, the determination to retain ownership at all costs is clear from the shareholdings of large Japanese corporations and the low level of mergers and acquisitions activity in Japan. Behind this lies a strong appreciation of the value of markets and market share. In summary, under Japanomics, policies and practices have been formulated to keep control over key industries, over key home markets and over domestic financial resources.[7]

Financial markets have also had unique characteristics through the special relationships, via the *keiretsu*, of Japan's banks with industries. In the early postwar period of growth, controlled interest rates meant that access to credit was crucial, leading to guided capital rationing to favored industry groups clustered around powerful main banks.[8] Relying on indirect financing from banks, Japanese corporations had a high ratio of debt to equity and a low cost of capital. Prominent features of the financial system were its financial product market segmentation, price regulation, and hierarchical organization. By overcoming problems of asymmetric information and monitoring their firms, banks allowed Japanese firms to adopt a long-run view directed to sales growth and market share rather than to focus on short-term share-price maximization.

Moreover, under the traditional financial system, savings were channeled into business investment and were not available to bid up prices of financial assets. After the oil shock in the 1970s, the government sold more securities to cover a growing budget deficit, money and securities markets were subsequently deregulated, and Japan's finance system became more open. These financial changes reinforced the low real interest rates and high expected growth rate that led to the extraordinary rise in asset prices in the 1980s and subsequent collapse of the financial bubble.

Another analyst offers the following perceptive summary of the distinctive characteristics of the Japanese economy.

1. The Japanese work hard.
2. The Japanese are well educated.
3. Japanese work cooperatively in large corporations.
4. There is extensive use of subcontracting in manufacturing.
5. Japan has a managerial, production-oriented capitalism, not a shareholder-dominated form of capitalism.
6. Japan has the most effective form of incomes policy outside Austria and Sweden.
7. Japan has a high saving rate and low rates of interest.
8. Japan is still a relatively "small government" country.
9. Japanese corporations are very good at forming cartels.
10. The Japanese value and honour the public service, and an intelligent industrial policy is one consequence of this.
11. By contrast, the Japanese do not much honour politicians, whose role in running the economy is small.[9]

SPECIAL GOVERNMENT-BUSINESS RELATIONS

Beyond the influence of the Ministry of International Trade and Investment (MITI) in particular industries, many observers attribute the achievements of the Japanese economy more generally to uniquely effective government-business relations, financial-industrial relations, and management-labor relations. The institutional framework provided by the government is especially significant in reinforcing some unique features of the organization of firms in the market.

During the 1950s and 1960s, government and business cooperated most effectively. In that period of high absolute growth, government-business relations facilitated the implementation of an energetic industrial policy that had an effective mix of regulation and competition. Wartime controls of the economy were transformed in more democratic ways that supported the market. Although MITI has tried to diffuse risks and cushion downside costs, its power of administrative guidance can be exaggerated.[10] It is now considerably less influential than in the past—in part because of recent disappointments in sponsored research programs, such as those to develop fifth-generation artificial intelligence, the VT-2500 jet engine, and superspeed, parallel processing computers. More to the point, MITI's influence has diminished because of the very success of Japanese business: In industries composed of large companies, the amount of subsidization MITI can provide is small relative to the research budgets of these companies. Furthermore, the companies normally have better ideas of the likely success of R&D programs than does MITI.

A better interpretation of Japan's political economy since the 1970s is a pluralist interpretation of the distribution of power in economic decision making—an interpretation that takes into account the competition among big business, small business, farmers, labor, the government bureaucracy, the media, consumers, urban residents, and environmentalists.[11]

A multitude of factions and interest groups exists within the government bureaucracy, big business, and political parties. As a major interest group, however, big business retains a close, friendly relationship with a supportive government.

Government-business relations in sectoral economic management of particular sectors have been especially important because growth in and competition among sectors is often regarded as a more important factor than macroeconomic management in explaining Japanese economic performance. The roles played by the bureaucracy, interest groups, and politicians differ from sector to sector. As a student of the politics of economic management in Japan observes, "Bureaucrats, in cooperation with business interests, are entrusted with the task of promoting strategic sectors and nurturing the 'seeds' of growth; politicians mainly exert their influence over distribution of the 'fruits' of economic growth. The allocation of resources can be considered apolitical; income distribution is a political issue over which politicians exert some influence."[12]

Close ties between the financial community and Japanese industry have also supported the nation's economic achievements. Private intermediaries, particularly commercial banks, have been reliable partners of Japanese corporations, financing their endeavors with a view to their long-term success. Further, the marginal role of the stock market allows industry to take a long-term view—not simply a short-term concern with quarterly profits and the position of stockholders. It also insulates management from the threats of outside takeovers. Moreover, government intervention in financial markets during the high-growth period was of a character to provide a relatively stable financial structure. The monetary authorities also acted to promote economic growth and often undertook positive public policies that moved the system in the direction in which market forces would cause it to evolve, but moved it faster.[13]

Further, a highly productive labor force has also been instrumental in promoting Japan's growth. Underlying this, in turn, have been cooperative management-labor relations and a strong emphasis on human resource development. The labor movement has had a local or enterprise base, and unions have been relatively docile. Those who emphasize Japanese culture attribute the harmony of industrial relations to a traditional social system that gives Japanese workers a relatively strong consciousness of enterprise loyalty and a weak consciousness of class. The relationship between employer and employees is even characterized as a relationship of protection and family-like dependence. So too the relationship between employer and enterprise union.

Others point to the favorable effects of the Japanese firm's system of permanent commitment to its employees. Although the system is by no means universal, tenure is offered by many large- and medium-size enterprises. For large Japanese employers, this can be interpreted as a completely rational policy in terms of costs and benefits, the main reason for its survival being economic efficiency.[14] Cooperation between management and labor results in high investment in employee training and development at the enterprise level. Skill development during a long career with one firm contributes strongly to an increase in labor productivity, and employees become valuable assets of the firm.

Another incisive analysis is offered by Masahiko Aoki's characterization of Japanese management and the behavior of the firm.[15] Aoki considers management as a "mediator" that weighs and equilibrates both the implicit and explicit bargaining powers of the firm's constituents. Employees make their interests known to management through the enterprise union, but informal and implicit pressures exercised by subordinates on management may also play an important role. Management, possibly in cooperation with the enterprise union, coordinates wage determination and managerial policy making simultaneously to achieve an efficient mediation outcome. According to Aoki,

> The technology employed by the firm is such that employees' skills are formed and transmitted on the job and in a team context. . . . In order to motivate employers and employees to share the costs of investment in such team-oriented human capital, seniority-related benefits to employees in the form of seniority wages, retirement compensation, and the like have been developed as devices through which both partners can reap returns from their respective investments over time. Without such contrivances, employees might quit in the middle of their careers, causing the value of the human capital accumulated within the firm to be lost. These devices bind employees to the firms in which they are trained, and once they are instituted, the employers are guaranteed returns to shared investment in specific training. On the other hand, the employees are able to substitute expected utilities derivable from job security and better prospects of career advancements within the firm for the immediate satisfaction derivable from current wages. This trade off between current wage levels and managerial policies favorable to the welfare of the employees is the basis for the efficient mediation postulate.[16]

Aoki has also presented a more general analysis of the institutional source of Japan's postwar economic growth. This analysis does not attribute the outstanding growth record to merely an increase in resource inputs. Nor is it because of industrial policy. The institutional framework that had been designed to support centralized control of wartime production survived into the postwar period, however, with some important democratic modifications in its content. And this modified institutional framework became growth inducing as it found a "fit" with private organizational innovations relying on information-processing capacity at the grassroots level.[17] More significant than a simple mobilization of savings to the government and the importation of foreign technology, the sources of Japan's growth involved some homegrown technological progress and a different way of combining inputs in Japan. According to Aoki, technological progress or the rise in total factor productivity can be attributed in large part to what Lau calls the "software" component of investments, broadly defined to include managerial methods and institutional environment, as well as supporting infrastructure.[18] A unique organizational coordination mechanism evolved within and across enterprises, providing the important "software" component of investment that improved the coordination of inputs within the firm. The salient feature of Japan's growth has been the complementarity between this evolving organizational mode and the institutional framework in which the government has been instrumental.

The organizational innovation gave employers a sense of being members of the enterprise as a community, and work organization became strongly team oriented with a broad information-processing capability of workers on the shop floor. The internal organization of the firm facilitated lateral coordination among different task units on the basis of information sharing, joint responsibilities, and help. These cross-functional interactions allowed manufacturing firms in Japan to gain competitive advantage in certain process industries by quickly adapting to continually changing technological and market environments. Aoki characterizes this organizational practice as a "horizontal hierarchy."[19]

At the same time, wartime institutions of governmental control were transformed in the postwar period and supported the development and maintenance of "horizontal hierarchy." The role of governmental controls evolved initially with the declaration that *zaibatsu* holding companies were illegal and the privatization of stocks that were initially transferred to a government committee; the establishment of close relationships between a major enterprise and a single bank; formation of industrial associations to represent common interests of firms in public policy making; and the transformation of a wartime social organization into enterprise unionism. For the evolutionary path, see Table 7.9.

The organizational mode of enterprises and the institutional framework were mutually reinforcing. Stressing that "institutions matter," Aoki states:

> The removal of shareholders' control made it possible for the workers to gain shares in property rights in their firms in terms of job security, accumulation of retirement benefits, [and] opportunities to advance to managerial positions. Their position in the firm as stakeholders provides incentives to invest in team-oriented skills. The potential moral hazard of "insider control" is effectively checked by the prospect of bank intervention contingent on the bad performance of teams. The industrial association puts peer discipline on member firms not to recruit workers from employees of other member firms, which enhanced the effectiveness of the threat of bank discipline on badly-performing firms by reducing outside option values for the workers. On the other hand, the industrial association acted as an intermediary to protect property rights of the stakeholders of member firms *vis-à-vis* outsiders and feed their interests into the bureaucratic process of industrial policy-making and budget allocations.[20]

Finally, Aoki indicates the significance of pluralistic interests being mediated through a bureaucratic process that he terms "bureau-pluralism."[21] Thus, as some industries (machinery, autos) became ever more profitable, the low-productivity sectors (agriculture, retail, services) were protected by the relevant government bureau that introduced policies to redistribute a portion of profits from the high-productivity sectors to the lagging sectors.

TABLE 7.9
Institutional Evolution in Japan

Institutional Transformation	Wartime Design for Centralized Control	Postwar Democratic Reform	Evolution of Complementary Relationships with Horizontal Hierarchy
Stockholder structure	Restriction of *zaibatsu* stockholders' rights	*Zaibatsu* dissolution and stockholding democratization	Management-crafted cross-shareholding as insulation from takeover
Banks and governance structure	Designated banking system	Bank involvement in cleaning up bad debt problem	Main bank system, contingent governance
Industrial association	Industrial controlling association	Industrial association	Bureau-pluralism
Small and medium-sized enterprise	Assigned to a large enterprise for technical assistance	Relationship maintained	*Keiretsu* (relational contracting)
Workers' organization	Industrial Patriotic Society	Factory control movement	Enterprise unionism

Source: Masahiko Aoki, "Unintended Fit: Organizational Evolution and Government Design of Institutions in Japan," in Masahiko Aoki, Hyung-Ki Kim and Masahiro Oknno-Fujinara, *The Role of Government in East Asian Economic Development: Comparative Institutional Analysis*, (New York: Oxford University Press, 1997), p. 245.

This supported a further expansion of domestic markets and also provided a safety net that gave social stability.

TECHNOLOGICAL PROGRESS

Japan's catch-up process of industrialization has depended heavily on technological progress. Japan has been especially adept in commercializing technology and utilizing technological advances to become a global competitor. Until recently, Japan's investment in basic research was not significant. Instead, it has imported foreign technologies, subsequently adapted them, and applied them in creative ways. Although Japan relied on the United States, United Kingdom, West Germany, France, and Switzerland for basic technology, it gained a competitive advantage in such manufacturing activities as production engineering, control of production processes, improvement of production processes and products, quality control, and marketing. Technological applications during the 1950s and 1960s led to decreasing costs of production in steel, automobiles, oil refining, synthetic fibers, petrochemicals, electrical appliances, and other machinery industries. These cost-decreasing industries accounted for a large percentage of value added in manufacturing. In more recent years, Japanese firms have utilized technology to move upscale from low-price and high-volume manufacturing to goods that are less price sensitive and of higher value.

By the early 1980s, Japan had reached state-of-the-art technology in a variety of areas related to iron and steel production, agricultural chemicals, nuclear energy, semiconductors, computer peripherals, office automation, robotics, certain areas of telecommunications, pharmaceuticals, biotechnology, and industrial lasers.

Japanese industry has also developed a unique production system oriented toward rapid product cycles, differentiated markets, continual integration of new product and process technologies, and flexible manufacturing as opposed to rigidly standardized mass production.

The operational components of this system include just-in-time manufacturing, which requires close coordination between suppliers and producers; continual improvement of production processes; flexible, small-lot mass production; a design philosophy emphasizing workability, quality, and frequent, incremental redesign; and a highly skilled, relatively flexible workforce. This has proved an excellent system for highly integrated, computerized production processes and is especially well suited to high-technology industries, where competition takes place in global markets that are volatile and differentiated.[22]

Recognizing Japan's ability for commercial application of technological inventions, Michael Dertouzos, director of the MIT computer science laboratory, says, "We[Americans] value creativity and innovativeness, and we don't value production. But the money is not in invention, it's in production."[23]

From 1965–80 real growth rates in Japan's R&D expenditures rose faster than in any other major industrial state. During the 1980s, Japan's R&D spending as a percentage of GNP continued to increase markedly and has surpassed the American percentage since the early 1980s. The results have been reflected in Japan's share of the world's exports of high-tech products, which has risen from 13 percent in 1980 to approximately 30 percent.

Finally, and most important, the key agent in Japan's growth process has been the business firm. Japanese firms in the leading industries have been characterized by a long-run managerial perspective and a strong motivation for growth. The firm commonly seeks to maximize its market share or achieve higher sales growth rather than endeavoring to maximize profits (share prices). As already noted (p. 274), Aoki's analysis of the Japanese firm provides an explanation of this behavior. Being a mediator among different constituents of the firm, management in the policy-making process strikes a balance between the interests of shareholders and those of employees. If management can organize the activities of the firm in such a way as to realize higher growth at lower costs, it will improve employees' opportunities for promotion within the firm and increase capital gains for shareholders. This will in turn enhance the legitimacy and the reputation of the manager.

When employees can benefit from better opportunities for promotion and job security within the firm, it is better for them to reach some accord with management in regard to a choice of a combination of wage and managerial policy variables. They may agree to trade wage increases for job security or better opportunities for promotion made possible by growth of the firm. Efficient managers in Japanese firms are therefore even more aggressive and growth exploring than managers devoted to a value maximization goal. Management can maximize the share prices for a certain level of employee welfare by coordinating both wage level and managerial policy instruments simultaneously. The firm may be able to maintain and enhance its competitiveness in the market by restraining current wage levels while preserving and accumulating firm-specific human capital. Gains from such efficient mediation by management can be shared between shareholders and employees over time to make both constituents better off.[24]

THE FUTURE

Having identified the central features of the catch-up process and Japanomics, we may now ask what are the implications for the future? If Japan has concluded phase one of heavy industry and phase two of the drive into high technology, what can we expect phase three to be? A very strong position in world finance and the expansion of Japanese industries to truly global standing, as predicted by Ratcliffe? Or, in contrast, as predicted by Emmott, the emergence of grave limitations on Japan's potential as a great power and confirmation that the sun also sets—that Japan's economy, too, moves in cycles?[25] Or, as some analysts suggest, structural changes based on expansionary domestic demand and improvement in the quality of domestic life that will move Japan and the United States in similar directions? Or, as the group of revisionists maintains, no convergence, but instead a basic conflict between Japanese and American interests and the necessity to contain Japan's expansion.

Underlying these predictions, there must be some implicit answers to a number of particular questions. Will Japan's economy become more open? Will Japan's trade surplus disappear? What will happen to savings? investment? capital outflows from Japan? Will there be an international yen? Will the government-business consensus on economic direction continue? labor-management peace? financial-industrial linkages? What will be the nature and scope of industrial policy? technological progress? What will be Japan's relation to Asia? the European Union? the United States?

Within Japan itself, there have been a number of studies that consider the problems and prospects of Japan's future economy. These studies may be characterized as "vision and strategy" exercises that provide a vision of future change and the strategy to shape the future in favorable directions. Focusing on Japan's international status, all the studies recognize that globalization is breaking down Japan's insularity and the "small Japan" psychology. But, as one study states, "It is difficult for the average Japanese citizen to understand the extent of this new influence because this country has not yet reached the level of the West with respect to such factors as commodity prices, working hours, housing, land, social capital, and personal exchanges. In many ways, Japan remains a small country in terms of richness and quality of life. It goes without saying that the gap between Japan's current position as a major economic power and the actual quality of everyday life in the country will have to be eliminated as quickly as possible by increasing investments and reforming various systems relating to individual standards of living. This is one of the most important problems currently facing Japan."[26]

Another study by the Long-Term Outlook Committee of the Economic Council is premised on the fact that "Japan's economic society has now entered a 'post catching-up' maturing stage. As a result, population growth is heading for stability, economic growth is shifting to medium speed, and Japan's international position and responsibility are becoming strongly recognized."[27]

"Thus far, the history of Japan's development has been a history of change to an economic society of the Western type. Nonetheless, now that Japan has economically reached the level of developed nations, and that socially, the troubles of the West European type welfare society are becoming clear, an economic society of the Western type can no longer be a model for Japan.

"From now on, Japan must open up a path of its own both economically and socially."[28]

The report recognizes that Japan cannot depend on the high growth of past decades to achieve its policy goals. Instead, it has entered a maturing stage, and it is now necessary to fashion a new "grand design" looking into the twenty-first century. It is envisioned that, having reached maturity, the Japanese economy will shift from being centered around industrialization and materials to that of knowledge and services. In such a situation there will be more individual and diversified consumption.[29]

The report also argues that Japan can no longer rely on simply receiving technology from industrially advanced countries. Instead, a technical development under the past catch-up formula "will gradually become more difficult. Japan must therefore take on creative and innovative technical development, something it has found hard to deal with."[30] In the field of energy, advances in solar cells, fuel cells, and new type batteries are being put into practical use. The development of technology related to nuclear fusion may not come until after the year 2000. Technological development in the electronics field will progress rapidly, bringing an optical fiber communications system, high performance integrated circuits, and many other sophisticated products to practical use. Among other achievements before the year 2000 will be drugs based on gene restructuring technology, artificial organs, space laboratories, short take-off and landing aircraft, the recovery of uranium from sea water, the recovery of manganese nodules from sea beds, new transport systems, linear motor trains, and a sophisticated information network system.[31]

Further, the report emphasizes that the maturing of the economy will affect the competitive environment. First, it is expected that as the income level increases and values diversify, the people's desire to raise their living standards and social status will wane. Second, if Japan fails to take proper measures in coping with its aging society, there will be a loss of bonds between those who receive welfare benefits and younger workers who must pay for them. There is a fear that this could obstruct vitality at the individual level. Third, with the aging of the labor force, dissemination of higher education, and a shift to medium growth, it is possible that corporations may find it difficult to promote employees and provide other incentives. Fourth, it is possible that as the country's economy shifts to medium growth and the market expansion of enterprises slows down, there will be moves by corporate firms to resort to cooperative actions and monopolies.[32]

For management, the implications of these changes are significant. The report states that looking at the prospects for the twenty-first century, it is expected that firms and their employment practices will be confronted with these changes: (1) a slowdown in the tempo of market expansion and market maturity; (2) progress in technical innovation; (3) a slowdown in the growth of the number of people of productive age, the trend toward an aging labor force, and the trend toward people with higher education; (4) changes in worker consciousness and the diversification of values; (5) internationalization of business development; and (6) a diversified and liberalized money market.[33] The challenge therefore is one of maintaining "vitality in the maturing process." It is especially important that Japan opens up its own creative sources for the maintenance and formation of vitality in its economic society.[34]

Finally, the report proposes that, in the coming era of medium economic growth, the public sector should assume new roles in the midst of internationalization, an aging society, and maturity of the economy. In coping with internationalization, it is expected that government will have to strive for the establishment of a new international economic structure based on free trade as well as international rules, promote measures to open up the domestic market, implement smooth industrial coordination, and expand official assistance to developing countries.

The government also must maintain sound economic management, attaching importance to the prevention of inflation in dealing with the aging society. Moreover, in accommodating the maturing economic society, the government should promote technical development that serves as the foundation for the vitality of economic society; check stagflation with appropriate economic policy; maintain a competitive environment for business; make efforts to preserve a steady supply of energy resources; and promote energy saving in the development of alternative energy sources. Finally, another role the government is likely to assume is the steady accumulation of effective social capital befitting the demands of an era that will have to cope with changes in economic society.[35]

The study group of *Japan's Choices* considers Japan's agenda in the widest context. It maintains that "to switch from a 'catch-up' orientation to a creative-type system that places importance on the selection and responsibility of individuals, Japan must reform the overall framework of such fields as industry, society, daily life, and culture. For this purpose, it is necessary to change the value assessment and source of distribution from the conventional government-led, centralized pattern, to a 'double-track' pattern in which individuals, companies, and public institutions all participate independently. It is also necessary to change drastically various systems with the purpose of forming a free society with a wide degree of selection, and to carry out extensive investment to consolidate the foundation for new styles of industry, daily life, and culture."[36]

Although this report and others are long on vision, they are short on strategy. They also minimize a great deal of disagreement about precisely what Japan's future agenda should be. Various interest groups exercise considerable influence over public policy goals, and among these groups there is still much debate over the extent of the economy's internationalization, its opening to imports, liberalization of capital markets, expansion of government spending, adjustments at the micro level, and environmental issues in a country that has the world's highest GNP per square mile.

It would be a mistake to believe that Japan faces the outside world as a unified entity— as a "Japan, Inc." As an observer of the political process in Japan states, "No one in the United States, whether government official, private business person, or trade association representative, should assume that exerting influence in Japan will involve simply showing how his or her objectives accord with official policy in Japan or are essential to reducing the trade gap, or whatever. Nor should anyone expect that some single switch, in the form of the Prime Minister, the head of Keidanren, an appropriate MITI official, the President of the Bank of Japan, the U.S. Ambassador, or anyone else, can be pulled to effect the desired end. At best, any such effort will be no more than a first step to be followed up by a good deal more convincing, cajoling, and horse-trading."

"At the same time, the potential for foreign influence on specifics is far greater than ever before if and when the appropriate alliances within Japan can be forged. No longer does the foreigner confront "Japan." Instead, it is possible to ferret around in various pockets of power and influence in the search for potential allies in what will inevitably be a political bargaining process, not the exertion of influence by fiat."[37]

Moreover, the visionary goals of 2000, as outlined in these reports, cannot be taken seriously until a number of interim problems are first solved. In particular, how can the necessary rate of growth be attained? How can a more rapid balance-of-payments adjustment be achieved? How can a more open economy be fostered? These questions are inter-related and their resolution will determine, in turn, the future course of the Japanese economy.

IMPORTS AND EXPORTS

In Policy Profile 5.5, we considered the problem of balance-of-payments adjustment between Japan and the United States. The adjustment mechanism appears to be working, albeit slowly. Figure 7.3 shows the continuing current account imbalances. Given the large appreciation in the yen and the depreciation in the dollar since 1985, some disconcerting questions remain: Why doesn't Japan import more from the United States? And why doesn't the United States import less from Japan?

Normally we would expect the appreciation of the yen to raise the price of Japanese exports in terms of the dollar and to lower the price of Japanese imports in terms of the yen. This assumes that the appreciation of the yen will be passed through to the prices of goods and services. For the period 1985–90, however, studies show that the pass through to export prices in terms of dollars was considerably less than the appreciation of the yen. The pass-through has been greater on differentiated products where there is more market power and less on standardized products where Japan faces competition from other countries. The low pass-through can be explained by the fact that initially Japanese firms had a thick cushion of profits accumulated during the period of dollar appreciation, and that they then cut their profit margins to hold on to sales, and finally they have cut costs to remain competitive. Other reasons for the low pass-through on the export side have been the fall in prices of

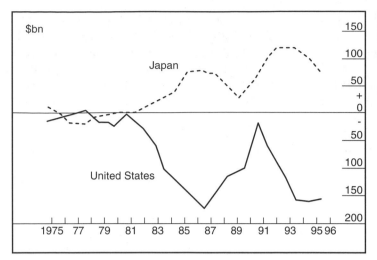

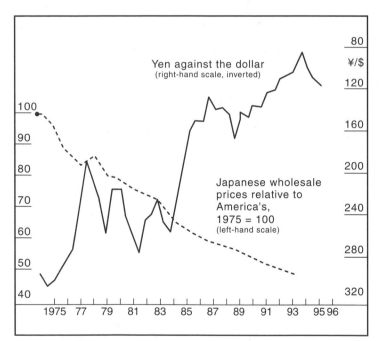

Figure 7.3 Current account balances, prices, and exchange rates, United States and Japan, 1975–96. *Source*: IMF, *International Financial Statistics*, annual.

raw materials (particularly oil), the rapid growth in productivity, and the low inflationary rate in Japan.

The deterioration in the U.S. trade balance with Japan in the 1980s was especially heavy for machinery products. As shown in Table 7.10, the United States had large net surpluses in machinery products in the 1970s. From 1981 to 1985, however, the U.S. trade balance deteriorated in every category of machinery products. And in these industries, Japan experienced the largest increases in net export ratios (surplus of exports over imports expressed as a percentage of domestic sales). Even after the appreciation of the yen, the

U.S. trade balance in machinery products did not improve. Indeed it worsened in some industries (see the period 1985–87 in Table 7.10). Despite the dollar's depreciation, the higher increases in the United States than in Japan in unit labor costs and in unit capital return (profits, interest costs, depreciation) substantially reduced the price competitiveness of U.S. machine manufacturers. And Japanese firms, in contrast with American firms, cut their operating profits, emphasizing increased sales at the cost of some loss in profits per unit.[38]

The volume of Japanese exports has also held up for other reasons. Nonprice dimensions such as style and quality have kept exports high even when their prices have risen. In addition, as U.S. income rises, the United States has a highly elastic demand for imports from Japan. On the other hand, Japan's imports from the United States have a much lower elasticity of demand with respect to changes in Japan's national income.

Another special factor in maintaining a strong demand for Japanese exports is related to the rising amount of direct foreign investment by Japan in the United States. Ron Napier of Salomon Brothers calculates that $1 worth of new Japanese foreign direct investment raises Japan's machinery exports by $436,000. When the investment projects mature, and new offshore production expands, these exports of Japanese machinery should slow down.

Exports from the United States to Japan have had to grow $1\frac{1}{2}$ times faster than imports simply to keep the trade gap from widening. This is because exports are growing from a much smaller base than imports. A need for the United States to run a surplus in merchandise

TABLE 7.10
Comparison of Net Export Ratios (Exports minus imports as a percentage of domestic sales)

Industry	1973	1981	1985	1987
Optical, photographic equipment				
United States	3.1	2.6	−1.8	−2.4
Japan	7.0	16.2	15.3	26.2
General industrial machinery				
United States	17.8	33.2	13.4	5.6
Japan	8.3	14.7	16.0	30.0
Metalworking machinery				
United States	8.1	−3.7	−23.5	−30.8
Japan	5.4	21.6	23.2	29.1
Computing machinery				
United States	26.5	30.0	12.8	7.8
Japan	2.2	20.2	38.5	35.5
Electric industrial machinery				
United States	2.8	5.5	−0.8	−1.5
Japan	8.8	24.2	24.1	30.2
Other electric machinery				
United States	−3.0	−4.6	−11.6	−10.6
Japan	16.8	28.4	25.5	27.0
Motor vehicles				
United States	−2.8	−7.1	−11.4	−17.6
Japan	16.3	36.4	45.2	67.8
Other transportation equipment				
United States	20.1	25.6	16.1	15.5
Japan	75.5	62.1	41.2	34.2

Source: Shinichi Yamamoto, "Japan's Trade Lead," *The Brookings Review* (winter 1989/90): 15.

trade also becomes all the more necessary as growing interest and profits have to be paid to foreigners on their investments in the United States.

Many believe that formal trade barriers prevent an expansion in American exports to Japan. Actually, however, tariffs and quantitative restrictions on nonagricultural products are not high in Japan. Tariff rates are at approximately the same low levels as in the United States, Europe, and Canada. Indeed, trade barriers in Japan were lowered in the 1970s and 1980s—at a time when Japan's trade surplus still improved. But if the formal trade barriers are not especially significant for Japan, the same cannot be said for informal barriers that constitute an "invisible protection." Imports remain limited by standards, testing, labeling, and certification procedures; by biases in government procurement; by lack of intellectual property protection; and by services barriers. Exporters to Japan also charge that multiple tiers in the distribution process make imports too expensive to be competitive, and that the large-scale retail store law, which restricts the expansion of large retailers, deprives imports of their best outlet. Cultural attachment to Japanese products also causes imports to be limited.

Many a would-be exporter has complained about closed Japanese markets. Some of this may simply be personal rationalization in the face of competition, but there are other objective indicators of closed markets to imports. As recently as 1985, when the yen began to appreciate, manufactured imports accounted for only 31 percent of Japan's total import bill. The level of manufactured imports relative to the size of Japan's economy is very low; the low ratio of manufactured imports to GDP and to GDP in manufacturing are evident in Table 7.11. These low ratios contrast markedly with those of West Germany—a country that is also highly dependent on imports of primary products but manages also to import a much higher ratio of manufactured imports to GDP and to GDP in manufacturing.

Moreover, it is striking that intra-industry trade (two-way trade in the same industry), is also low for Japan. On a scale of 0 for no intra-industry trade to 100 for complete intra-industry trade, Japan's intra-industry trade index was only 25 in 1980 compared with 60 for the United States, 66 for Germany, and 82 for France.[39] Not only is the prevalence of intra-industry trade distinctively lower in the case of Japan than for other countries, but the intra-industry trade is especially low in those Japanese industries that export the most—a pattern that is unique among the industrial nations. Moreover, Japan's intra-industry trade is low (and usually because exports are far greater than imports) in those industries that account for most of the U.S. exports to the rest of the world; that is, Japan accepts fewer imports from the United States in precisely those industries of U.S. worldwide competitive strength.[40]

TABLE 7.11
Imports of Manufactured Goods

| | Manufactured Imports as a % of | | | | | |
| | GDP | | | GDP in Manufacturing | | |
	1970	**1980**	**1987**	**1970**	**1980**	**1987**
Japan	2.3	3.0	2.4	6.5	10.3	8.3
United States	2.5	4.8	7.3	10.1	22.1	37.8
West Germany	8.9	12.6	14.4	23.1	38.5	44.7

Source: World Bank, *World Tables* (Washington, DC: World Bank, 1989).

A Smaller Surplus

Japan's trade balance, based on exports and imports that have cleared customs.

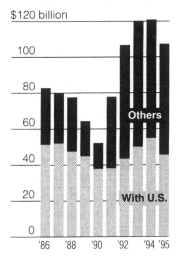

Figure 7.4 Japan's trade surplus. Japan's overall surplus in trade is more than twice what it was in 1990. When measured in yen, however, Japan's trade imbalance has been falling since 1993. But because the yen appreciated in terms of dollars, the surplus reported in dollars continued to grow until 1995. *Source:* Japan's Ministry of Finance; *New York Times*, January 24, 1996, p. C7.

Source: Japan's Ministry of Finance

Some features of industrial organization also suggest collusive insider relationships in Japan that limit imports. A study that correlates industry-structure variables with trade performance concludes[41]:

- Products with high-distribution margins are less likely to be imported than those with low margins, especially when the import-competing Japanese industry is concentrated
- Products purchased by business are less likely to be imported than those purchased by household, especially when the import-competing Japanese industries are concentrated
- Products purchased by government are also less likely to be imported than those purchased by households
- Products with high supplier concentration in Japan are more likely to be both exported and imported than other products

The low import ratios for Japan might also be partially explained by its geographical distance from the United States and Europe, its large domestic GNP, and its need to pay for its raw materials imports by running a trade surplus in manufactures. More to the point, however, is Japanomics—the determination to catch up with the West by building a strong domestic manufacturing base. The combination of institutions, policies, and behavior patterns in industry and government have resulted in informal barriers that exclude or minimize imports. But having caught up, isn't Japan now pushing the process too far and for too long?

In light of the past causes of balance-of-payments problems and trade frictions between America and Japan, what now are the policy options that might best reduce conflict over the balance of payments and also allow Japan to achieve the objectives of Japan 2000?

Balance-of-payments adjustment must come through both macro and micro policies.[42] At the macro level, the United States is spending too much, and Japan, too little. The U.S. fiscal deficit must be reduced and private savings increased. In Japan, it would be desirable if the propensity to save were reduced and consumption increased. Changes in national expenditure will come much more rapidly through the Japanese government than the private sector. On the side of the United States, an easier monetary policy would also be desirable as the fiscal budget tightens. Because a tighter fiscal policy reduces the stimulus to growth in the American economy, a depreciation of the dollar may help offset this by expanding exports and slowing down imports.

The micro remedy for Japan's unequal trade is a continual opening of its markets. The United States must avoid trade protection, managed trade, and aggressive reciprocity, but instead must attempt to harmonize trade barriers downward and not upward. Both the United States and Japan must support the liberalization of trade in goods and services through multilateral efforts of the WTO. Most important in the immediate future, however, will be Japan's efforts to diminish its informal barriers to trade. Such efforts may be expected to be significant for a range of manufactured imports, but not for agriculture or for some high-tech industries.

Since 1985, Japan's imports have indeed risen, but the value of imports of manufactured products from the United States rose only two times between 1985 and 1989, while imports rose nearly fourfold from the European Union, and more than four times from the Asian NICs. Although the ratio of manufactured imports to domestic manufacturing has been historically low, it can be expected to rise to over 10 percent by the late 1990s. Real changes are occurring with respect to imports in Japan. Many observers note a greater inclination on the part of Japanese consumers to import foreign goods, especially as they discover that prices are higher in Japan than abroad. An indication is that in 1988, the average Japanese who traveled abroad brought back through customs $2,200 worth of merchandise. If this is multiplied by the number of Japanese travelers, the total amounts to about 3 percent of all consumer spending by Japanese citizens. The 3 percent figure is a significant commentary on how closed Japan's market has been, but it also indicates growing information about the differential between domestic prices and foreign prices.[43]

"Reverse imports"—finished products of overseas Japanese subsidiaries that are exported back to Japan—are also rising as Toshiba, Hitachi, Mitsubishi Motors, and Honda import from their overseas plants. Transplants are becoming more significant in replacing exports from Japan. For example, Japan's "big three"—Nissan, Honda, and Toyota—have established factories in Britain and are considered as being inside the EU. Government forecasts suggest that by the year 2000, Japanese companies will be producing at least 1.2 million cars in Europe—about 80 percent from plants in Britain—and Japan will account for 20 percent of cars sales in Europe.

Trading companies that were traditionally designed to handle raw material imports and manufactured exports are also discovering that it is profitable to import foreign products. Most significantly, Japanese government officials are now saying that imports are good for Japan. Whereas in earlier government documents the traditional reason for urging an increasing market share was "to fulfill its obligations towards the international community," government documents now urge an increase in manufactured imports to support efficiency and growth in the Japanese economy itself. Recent reports from MITI, the Economic Planning Agency, and the Japan Fair Trade Commission, indicate that the government is now promoting the horizontal division of industry [*Suihei Bungyo*] as a dominant concept, one that encompasses the notion that imported manufactured goods and intra-industry trade are economically beneficial to Japan.[44]

The basis for being optimistic that the balance-of-payments problem and trade frictions will be diminished in the future is the fact that influential Japanese government officials and business leaders are now emphasizing the domestic rationale for higher government expenditures and greater imports. The vision and strategy reports realize that the future path of development for Japan should give much more emphasis to services and the social infrastructure and less to favoring manufactured exports. A higher standard of living and social goals envisaged for Japan 2000 will best be achieved by departure from the Japanomics of the catching-up period and a greater emphasis on more efficient allocation of resources at home, the widening of consumer choice, the opening of markets to imports, and government-funded social infrastructure.

Japan's exports will continue to expand in the late 1990s as a result of the domestic investment of the 1980s that yielded new R&D intensive products and greater productivity through automation. In the longer period, however, Japan's trade surplus is likely to shrink as a result of the decline in household savings as the population ages, rising public expenditures on health care and social services, domestic investment in housing and public infrastructure, and the influence of a new generation who are more consumption oriented and less attracted to a work ethic. Any appreciation of the yen, as a result of interest rate differentials in Japan's favor and reduced outflows of long-term capital, would also contribute to a shrinking of Japan's trade surplus.

Actually Japan's global trade surplus decreased in the mid-1990s. By May 1996, there had been eighteen consecutive months of decline, amounting to a decline of 61 percent globally, and 40 percent with the United States. Much of this was due to the most severe slowdown of the postwar period in the Japanese economy: the result of financial shocks bursting the asset price bubble of the late 1980s and the sharp appreciation of the yen. In mid-1995, the trade-weighted exchange rate for the yen had appreciated by some 63 percent and by 33 percent in mid-1996 over the 1990 rate. In the future, if the yen weakens against the dollar but Japan's economy expands, and there is a continual shift of Japanese manufacturing abroad, the trade surplus will continue to decline, but at a slower rate. More imports on the lower rungs of the comparative advantage ladder will come to Japan from Asian-Pacific countries. The volume of imports into Japan will continue to increase through greater openness. Exports will continue to be upgraded and become more capital intensive and knowledge intensive. Japan will compete more vigorously with advanced products, greater productivity, and through strategic international alliances. Transplants from Japan will also replace some Japanese exports. And the percentage of Japan's manufactured exports to the United States will continue to decline. At the same time as the trade surplus with the United States shrinks, it will increase with the New Europe and Asian countries. Exports from Japanese firms in third-country platforms will increase with more offshore production. "Reverse imports" will also expand with more of the imports being finished products.

REVISIONISTS

If the trade surplus continues to shrink, there will be no case for the revisionists' view of Japan. In several recent writings, a group of revisionists have argued that Japan is different as a political and social system, a player who follows completely different rules, and that the spread of Japanese power must be contained.[45] Revisionists believe in a fundamental conflict between the Japanese and American economies, not only for political and economic reasons, but also because of differences in national character and culture. James Fallows, editor of *U.S. News & World Report*, has stated that, "The conflict arises from Japan's inability or unwillingness to restrain the one-sided and destructive expansion of its economic power. The expansion is one-sided because Japanese business does to other countries what Japan would not permit to be done to itself." Fallows quotes with approval the argument of the Dutch journalist Karel van Wolferen that the ultimate reason why the Japanese deprive themselves of comfort and risk the enmity of the world is because individual Japanese, rather than depriving themselves, are deprived by the country's major power centers—the big corporations, the government regulators—which are always struggling to keep from losing ground to one another or to foreign competitors.[46] Moreover, Fallows maintains that, "On the evidence of what has happened since 1985, normal economic and business pressures are not going to balance Japan's trade accounts. Its surpluses, assets, and industrial strengths will continue to grow in a lop-sided way."[47]

As with other revisionists, Fallows points to differences in national character. "A willingness to overlook cold, pure principle and get down to practicalities can be seen as a virtue by Americans as well as Japanese. But Japanese society's lack of interest in principle has a profound effect that most Americans are slow to recognize. The lack of interest in principle makes sheer power the main test of what is fair. Might makes right anywhere, but in Japan's dealings with the outside world it does so sweepingly. . . . When foreign negotiators ask Japan to embrace the principle of free trade, they run up against not only Japanese special interests that would be hurt by imports but also a broader Japanese discomfort with the very prospect of abiding by abstract principles."[48]

As for recommended policies, the revisionists state that the basic assumptions of convergence through the market working things out must be abandoned. Instead, external pressure must be exerted and Japan must be contained. Washington consultant Clyde Prestowitz also claims that there is no point in discussing common rules. Revisionists generally call for such outside pressure as reciprocity, retaliation, and managed trade. Their emphasis is on micro regulation, not on macro adjustments.

Considering the revisionists' call for managed trade, the *Economist* concludes, "This belief is dangerous nonsense. It would amount to a death sentence on GATT and the multilateral trading system that have so enriched the world since 1945. It would divert America from treating defects of its own that have led to its present economic troubles. And it would slow the radical changes that are, in reality, remaking Japan in a freer market image."[49]

The basic assumption of the revisionists is wrong. Market forces are working. Political leadership and public support are effecting changes. It is a mistake to overlook the positive changes that are coming through the intrinsic strengths of the private sector and the soundness of macroeconomic policies. It would be counterproductive to succumb to revisionist policy that would simply bring about a Japanese backlash, leading to greater power to the bureaucrats, inward-looking policies, a trade war, and the formation of an Asian regional bloc centered on Japan.

CHALLENGING ISSUES

The continued successful performance of the Japanese economy is threatened not by the case of the revisionists, but rather by some other challenging issues relating to Japan's position in the world economy. Foremost is concern over the future rates of productivity and economic growth. The historically high rates of 1960–73 are unlikely to be repeated. The growth of capital input will be considerably less. To achieve moderate rates of growth, Japan will have to give more attention to human resource development for the upgrading of the labor force and for the supply of entrepreneurship. Individual incentives for innovations will also need encouragement. Most important, a moderately high rate of technical change will have to be maintained.

Beyond the maintenance of aggregate growth rates is the challenge of sectoral growth rates. The low productivity sectors of agriculture and services require special attention. So too do the low levels of productivity in some individual industrial sectors. During Japan's high-growth period, productivity was higher in Japan than in the United States for almost all industries. But this is no longer true: The interindustry variation in productivity performance has increased substantially between Japanese and American industries, and is likely to continue to do so with differential rates of sectoral technical change in the two countries.[50]

Changes in government-business relations will also influence growth performance. Greater emphasis on the need for domestic competition should lead to a liberalization of the anticompetitive restrictions in distribution, construction, financial markets, and other domestic service industries. This will, however, create a dilemma for bureau-pluralism—the dilemma between a greater degree of privatization in the high-productivity advanced sectors and the increasing dependence on protective government support of the low-productivity sectors.[51] One possibility, more appealing to an economist than to a bureaucrat, would be to change the role of the bureaucracy from being a pluralistic agent to that of an adversarial regulatory agency.

Instead of undertaking, as in the past, direct interventions and pursuing strategic policies to promote key industries, the government is likely to utilize softer policies and to act in a more complementary way toward the private sector. The ability of Japan's civil service to control the economy will be weaker, the more Japan becomes integrated into the world economy. "Visions" and indicative plans and the sharing of information will help to coordinate activities of private firms, outline goals for the economy, and provide public assistance and incentives so that private firms will act in harmony with the general objectives.

The practice of global management will have to be extended to more Japanese companies. They will have to shift from cost to differentiation strategies and toward higher levels of technological innovation—all within a global strategy.[52] Foreign subsidiaries will have to be coordinated and integrated in a global strategy. Traditionally inward-looking Japanese firms will have to become strong multinationals.

SOME IMPLICATIONS FOR ICA AND DPR

These challenges require policy initiatives by the Japanese government and corporations. Whether or not they will be taken requires close monitoring through international contextual analysis. And, if the analysis of this chapter is valid, there is a wide range of implications to which management—both in and out of Japan—will have to respond. Some of these implications can be briefly summarized:

The high-growth and catch-up phases of Japan's growth being over, the economy will have characteristics of a mature economy—especially that of slower growth and more forces of conservatism.

Japan 2000 will entail rising private domestic demand based relatively more on increasing consumption than in the past. But the saving rate will still remain relatively high through the 1990s. Only later will the aging of the population bring this rate down.

More rapid increases in government expenditure can be expected, especially in housing, public utilities, and social infrastructure.

Government expenditure overseas in the form of foreign economic assistance will also increase. Japan already has the world's largest foreign aid program, and its influence in the developing countries, especially in Asia, will intensify.

Japan will have growing influence in the governance of international financial institutions—the World Bank, the International Monetary Fund, and the multilateral development banks.

Japanese banks and security houses will continue to expand abroad, but less aggressively than before. These firms' main competitive advantage—their low-cost funds—will gradually fade away over the decade.[53]

The yen will be used extensively in Japan's export trade, but this does not mean that it will become an international currency. Its use in commercial transactions between non-Japanese trading partners will remain moderate in comparison with that of the U.S. dollar.

We have already noted (in the previous section) changes in the volume, composition, and direction of Japan's foreign trade. These changes will affect aggregate output and the allocation of resources.

The chief concern of Western firms wanting to export to Japan will no longer be with formal trade barriers preventing market entry but with informal obstacles including restrictions on direct foreign investment in Japan, complexities in the distribution system, and the generally high cost of doing business.

The capital surplus from Japan will also diminish as the excess of capital over home demand declines. And real interest in the United States will no longer be significantly higher than in Japan and European countries. The United States will therefore not be able to finance its budgetary deficit so easily from foreign savings.

Foreign direct investment into the United States will continue but will be far below the high-growth rates of the late 1980s, unless protective trade barriers induce more transplants. Foreign direct investment from Japan is, however, likely to accelerate in Europe and in the Asian countries, especially in the East Asian countries, China, and ASEAN. There will be greater economic integration and more intraregional trade in Asia, based on Japan as the center of the Asia-Pacific region.

CHANGES IN JAPAN'S ECONOMY?

In 1997, the *Wall Street Journal* reported:

TOKYO—Behind the gyrations in Japan's stock market lies a fundamental shift in national economic policy—an apparent decision to let market forces rather than bureaucratic dictates prevail. And behind that change is a highly unlikely reformer, Prime Minister Ryutaro Hashimoto.

Just a year ago, many Japanese feared that the conservative prime minister and his stodgy Liberal Democratic Party were more likely to turn back the economic clock than to push ahead. . . .

But two months ago, he announced one of Japan's biggest reform plans in years. He committed his administration to a far-reaching economic and administrative program by 2001, vowing to push through changes for Japan's long-term good even if, in the effort, he "burst into flame."

Mr. Hashimoto's proposed reforms, though still vague and facing a gantlet of advisory and legislative committees, hold the promise of opening up Japan to a force that it has long sought to deal with only on its own terms: the market. While skeptics abound, Mr. Hashimoto has already made a major down payment: During the stock market plunge here earlier this month, he said the government wouldn't again support the market by buying stocks. His ministers are reiterating that stand despite the market's continuing decline. . . .

Mr. Hashimoto . . . certainly has ambitious plans. He wants to restructure the educational system, which is blamed for producing too many mediocre, uncreative students; bring the deficit, now roughly $175 billion a year, under control with tax increases and spending cuts; revamp the national health-care system; promote deregulation to reduce business costs, and slim down the bureaucracy.

Perhaps most important, he says the government will break down regulatory barriers in financial services, barriers widely criticized for leaving Japan's huge banks and securities companies sheltered and uncompetitive. "If we just ignore these issues, Japan may be left behind by the global tide," he said last November.

If Mr. Hashimoto can keep his promises, he may well go down in history as a great prime minister. His reforms could radically change the economy, overturning decades of business-government cooperation and informal rigging of markets. . . .

Reprinted by permission of the *Wall Street Journal*, January 29, 1997, p. 1. Dow Jones & Company, Inc. All Rights Reserved Worldwide.

As more of their production and marketing occurs overseas, Japanese companies will have to transfer abroad an increasingly wide range of engineering and management functions and rely on local employees to perform them: This process is called "global localization" by Akio Morita, former chairman of Sony. Its effectiveness will determine whether Japanese firms become "insiders" in foreign markets. This move of the *kaisha*—the Japanese corporation—to become multinational in manufacturing and marketing will be the greatest challenge to Japanese management over the coming years.[54]

These implications have been summarized in bald fashion. Their validity must always be subjected to continual international contextual analysis. In practicing ICA, management should analyze the impact on the firm of changes in international market conditions and the indirect impact through changes in national policies. ICA must be continually practiced to modify any prediction. These modifications will, in turn, require revision of strategic responses by the firm as it strives for total efficiency.

There are also implications for international public management. These arise mainly from changes in Japan's pattern of foreign trade, trade policy, capital movements, balance-of-payments adjustment, and activities of Japanese multinationals.

Many of the implications for private management are also related to problems of global competitiveness, as discussed in Chapter 10. And for public management, they relate to problems of global governance, as examined in Chapter 11.

NOTES

1. Instructive are Edward J. Lincoln, *Japan: Facing Economic Maturity* (Washington, DC: Brookings Institution, 1988); Bill Emmott, *The Sun Also Sets: The Limits to Japan's Economic Power* (New York: Times Books, 1989).
2. Dale W. Jorgenson, *Productivity*, Vol. 2: *International Comparisons of Economic Growth* (Cambridge, Mass.: MIT Press, 1995), pp. 376–377.
3. For a detailed discussion, see Edward F. Dennison and William K. Chung, "Economic Growth and Its Sources" in Hugh Patrick and Henry Rosovsky, eds., *Asia's New Giant: How the Japanese Economy Works* (Washington DC: Brookings Institution, 1976), pp. 63–151.
4. In national income accounting, gross private domestic investment is the sum of personal and corporate saving, the government surplus, and the current account deficit in the balance of payments.
5. Masahiko Aoki, et al., *Beyond the East Asian Miracle: Introducing the Market-Enhancing View*, Stanford Center for Economic Policy Research, Publication No. 442, October 1995, p. 33.
6. Ryutaro Komiya and Motoshige Itoh, "Japan's International Trade and Trade Policy 1955–1984," in Takashi Inoguchi and Daniel I. Okimoto, eds., *The Political Economy of Japan, Volume II: The Changing International Context* (Stanford, Calif.: Stanford University Press, 1988), pp. 186–188.
7. C. Tait Ratcliffe, "The Intricacies of 'Japanomics'," *Speaking of Japan* (June 1990): 12–13.
8. David M. Meerschwam, "The Japanese Financial System and the Cost of Capital," in Paul Krugman, ed., *Trade with Japan* (Chicago: University of Chicago Press, 1995), Ch. 7. For a comprehensive description of the main bank system, see M. Aoki and H. Patrick, eds., *Japanese Main Bank System* (Oxford: Oxford University Press, 1994).
9. For elaboration of this list, see Ronald Dore, *Taking Japan Seriously* (Stanford, Calif.: Stanford University Press, 1987), pp. 12–17.
10. For a contrary view that maintains MITI plays a leading role in the "capitalist development state" that characterizes Japan, see Chalmers Johnson, *MITI and the Japanese Miracle* (Stanford, Calif.: Stanford University Press, 1982).
11. Patrick and Rosovsky, *Asia's New Giant*, pp. 49–53.
12. Yutaka Kosai, "The Politics of Economic Management," in Kozo Yamamura and Yasukichi Yasuba, eds., *The Political Economy of Japan*: Volume 1. *The Domestic Transformation* (Stanford, Calif.: Stanford University Press, 1987), p. 576.
13. For details of the financial system, see Koichi Hamada and Akiyoshi Horiuchi, "Political Economy of the Financial Market," in Yamamura and Yasuba, eds., *The Political Economy of Japan*, Vol. 1 (Stanford, Calif.: Stanford University Press, 1987), pp. 223–260 (© 1987 by the Board

of Trustees of the Leland Stanford Junior University); Henry C. Wallich and Mable I. Wallich, "Banking and Finance" in Patrick and Rosovsky, eds., *Asia's New Giant*, Ch. 4.

14. This argument is spelled out by Walter Galenson, in Patrick and Rosovsky, eds., *Asia's New Giant*, pp. 619–626.

15. Masahiko Aoki, *The Cooperative Game Theory of the Firm* (Oxford: Oxford University Press, 1984).

16. Masahiko Aoki, "The Japanese Firm in Transition," in Yamamura and Yasuba, eds., *The Political Economy of Japan*, Vol. 1, pp. 263–268. Reprinted with permission from Stanford University Press.

17. M. Aoki, "Unintended Fit: Organizational Evolution and Government Design of Institutions in Japan," Stanford Center for Economic Policy Research, Publication No. 434, February 1995.

18. Lau 1994, p. 215.

19. Aoki, "Unintended Fit," op cit. pp. 16–18.

20. Masahiko Aoki, "Towards a Comparative Institutional Analysis," *Japanese Economic Review* 47, 1 (March 1996): 11.

21. M. Aoki, *Information, Incentives, and Bargaining in the Japanese Economy* (Cambridge, Cambridge University Press, 1988), Ch. 7.

22. Charles H. Ferguson, "America's High-Tech Decline," *Foreign Policy*, No. 74 (spring 1989): 130.

23. *Wall Street Journal*, June 25, 1990, p. 1, col. 1.

24. For other discussions of the unique qualities of the Japanese firm and Japanese management, see J. C. Abergglen and G. Stalk, *Kaisha, the Japanese Corporation* (Tokyo: Tuttle, 1985); Ronald Dore, *Flexible Rigidities* (Stanford, Calif.: Stanford University Press, 1986).

25. William Emmott, *The Sun Also Sets: The Limits to Japan's Economic Power* (New York: Times Books, 1989).

26. Reproduced from Masataka Kosaka, ed., *Japan's Choices* (London and New York: Pinter, 1989), p. 8. By permission of Pinter Publishers, Wellington House, 125 Strand, London, England.

27. Long Term Outlook Committee Economic Council (Saburo Okita, Chairman), *Japan in the Year 2000* (Tokyo: Japan Times Ltd., 1983), p. 18.

28. Ibid., p. 18.

29. Ibid., p. 148.

30. Ibid., p. 151.

31. Ibid., p. 70.

32. Ibid., p. 152.

33. Ibid., p. 154.

34. Ibid., p. 155.

35. Ibid., p. 176.

36. Kosaka, *Japan's Choices*, op cit., p. 15.

37. T. J. Pempel, "The Unbundling of 'Japan, Inc.': The Changing Dynamics of Japanese Policy Formation," *Journal of Japanese Studies* 13, 2 (summer 1987): 305.

38. Shinichi Yamamoto, "Japan's Trade Lead: Blame Profit-Hungry American Firms," *The Brookings Review* (winter 1989/90): 14–18.

39. Edward J. Lincoln, *Japan's Unequal Trade* (Washington, DC: Brookings Institution, 1990), p. 40.

40. Ibid., pp. 6–7.

41. Peter A. Petri, "Market Structure, Comparative Advantage, and Japanese Trade Under a Strong Yen," in Krugman, ed., op cit., pp. 77–78.

42. Policy Profile 5.5 is again relevant here.

43. Edward J. Lincoln, "Commentary," *Japan Economic Survey* (June 1990): 9.

44. For more details on these government reports and the changing import structure in Japan, see Lincoln, *Japan's Unequal Trade*, Ch. 5.

45. Included in the revisionists are Karel van Wolferen, *The Enigma of Japanese Power* (New York: Alfred A. Knopf, 1989); James Fallows, "Containing Japan," *Atlantic Monthly* (May 1989): 40–54; former U.S. trade official Clyde Prestowitz, *Trading Places* (New York: Basic Books, 1988); and political scientist Chalmers Johnson, *MITI and the Japanese Miracle*. Management guru Peter Drucker also charges in his book, *The New Realities* (New York: Harper & Row, 1989), that Japan practices "adversarial trade" in its resistance to high value imports and its targeting attacks on established foreign industries.

46. Fallows, "Containing Japan," p. 42.

47. Ibid., p. 44.

48. Ibid., pp. 51–52.

49. "The Unhappy Alliance," *Economist*, February 17, 1990, p. 22.

50. On Japan-U.S. industry level productivity comparisons, see Jorgenson, ed., op cit., Ch. 7. For types of technology gap and expected pattern of technology gap, see pp. 372–373.

51. Aoki, *Information, Incentives, and Bargaining in the Japanese Economy*, op cit., pp. 293–297.

52. Cf. Michael E. Porter, *The Comparative Advantage of Nations* (New York: Free Press, 1990), p. 710. For fuller treatment of the Japanese firm, see J. C. Abegglen and G. S. Stalk, Jr., *Kaisha, The Japanese Corporation* (New York: Basic Books, 1985); Keinichi Imai and Ryutaro Komiya, eds., *Business Enterprise in Japan* (Cambridge, Mass.: MIT Press, 1994).

53. See also William Emmott, "The Limits to Japanese Power," in Richard O'Brien and Tapan Datta, eds., *International Economics and Financial Markets, AMEX Bank Review* (1989), p. 16.

54. This problem is emphasized by Abegglen and Stalk, op cit., pp. 282–288.

DISCUSSION QUESTIONS

1. An analyst of the Japanese economy states:

> Japan's success as an economic power is doubtlessly due to many inter-related factors, for example, high saving and investment rates (but why are these so much higher in Japan than in North American or Western Europe?), priority given to building an excellent education system (with the result that Japan easily has the most literate and numerate work force of all the advanced nations), cultural factors (leading to extraordinary ability of organizations to innovate and to adapt to changing circumstance?), effective macromangement of the economy, low priority accorded to the military (but isn't Japan a "free rider" on the United States with respect to national defense?), intense rivalry among the major *keiretsu* groups, lifelong employment practices of major firms (enabling managers to take a "long-run" perspective on their functions?), and, yes, an industrial policy that without question is more activist than anything in the United States (although perhaps today not as activist as that of France).
>
> Which of these factors explain Japan's success? I suspect that they all do to some degree, and I do not claim that my little list is exhaustive by any means. I further suspect that any effort to assign weights to any of these factors is doomed to failure. Any model to calculate such weights will likely be highly overspecified, and the explanatory variables highly collinear.
>
> Edward M. Graham, "Comment on Industrial Policy in Japan,"

in Paul Krugman, ed., *Trade with Japan*, op cit. pp. 302–303.
Reprinted with permission of the University of Chicago Press.

Do you agree with this assessment?

2. Do you think there is any merit to the popular view of "Japan, Inc."? To the view of the revisionists?

3. What are some unique features of various economic institutions in Japan? What are the implications for the management of Japanese firms? For the international competitiveness of Japanese firms?

4. How do fluctuations in the dollar value of the yen affect Japan's exports, imports, and international capital flows?

5. What changes would you expect in Japan's pattern of foreign trade over the next ten years (volume, composition, and direction)?

6. In 1995, Japan generated 60 percent of the world's net capital outflows, while the United States absorbed as much as 45 percent of the inflows. In view of this, is a continual decline in Japan's current account surplus of benefit to the United States? To other countries?

7. Ronald Dore has characterized "Japanese capitalism" as being different from "American capitalism" in five ways: nature of the labor market, social perception of the enterprise, character of interfirm transactions, intercompetitor cooperation/collusion, and role of government as creative umpire. (Dore, "Japanese Capitalism, Anglo-Saxon Capitalism," Ch. 2 in Nigel Campbell and Fred Burton, eds., *Japanese Multinationals*, 1994).

During the 1990s, Japan's "bubble economy" broke, the government's debt grew to nearly 90 percent of GDP (1996), and the profitability of major manufacturing firms fell on sales. In addition, analysts believe that "administrative guidance" is not compatible with the development of new technology, and that liberalization of financial and goods markets will lead to de-industrialization and a shift toward services.

Do you believe that these conditions imply a change in the future character of Japanese capitalism?

Chapter

8 DEVELOPING ECONOMIES

S tating that "development is the most important challenge facing the human race," the World Bank points out that "more than one billion people, one-fifth of the world's population, live on less than one dollar a day—a standard of living that Western Europe and the United States attained two hundred years ago."[1] Two centuries after the Industrial Revolution it is distressing that most of the world is still poor, living in the less-developed countries (LDCs). The future development of the LDCs in the new global economy will, however, affect everyone's future.

DEVELOPMENT PERFORMANCE

The World Bank designates forty-nine of its member countries as "low-income economies" with a GNP per capita of $765 or less in 1995, and fifty-eight other countries as "middle-income economies" with a GNP per capita of more than $765 but less than $9,385 in 1995. The bank's low-income and middle-income countries constitute the LDCs of Africa, Asia, the Middle East, Latin America, and the Caribbean. In contrast, "high-income economies," mainly industrialized members of the Organization for Economic Cooperation and Development (OECD), number twenty-six countries, with an average GNP per capita of over $24,930 in 1995.

The head of the OECD was recently asked what worried him most on the horizon: U.S. budget and trade deficits? Protectionism? Recession? He answered that the serious concern, out about a decade, is "demography." Not the demography of OECD countries, but that of the LDCs. Many of the LDCs are increasing their population at a rate beyond their development effort. Already immigration from the South is a pressing political problem in France and Italy. For the United States the push is also coming from south of the border.

During the next hour, more than 16,000 babies will begin their lives in the world. Of these, nearly 90 percent will be born in the developing countries. The World Bank estimates that by 2050, population in the more-developed countries will increase from the present 1.1 billion to 1.4 billion, while in the LDCs population will increase from 4.1 billion to 8.4 billion, accounting for five sixths of the world's population.

Population growth will make the development process more difficult, but does not make it impossible. Witness the record of development in the densely populated countries of South Korea and Taiwan—the second and third most densely populated countries in the world (after Bangladesh) when they began their development in the 1960s.

When population grows, however, the development process must intensify to provide more jobs for a growing labor force. And if income per head is to rise, it is necessary to achieve a structural transformation of the economy from primary production to industrialization and higher–value-added output.

Three common measures of "economic development" are per capita real income, per capita income corrected for purchasing power parities, and the components of a broader human development index (HDI). The latter measures GNP per capita, life expectancy, adult literacy, and mean years of schooling.

The record of development shows various rates of development performance in different regions, as can be noted in Table 8.1. The outstanding success stories have been in the Asian Newly Industrializing Countries (NICs: Singapore, Hong Kong, South Korea, Taiwan). From 1965–89, the average annual growth rate in GNP per head was 7 percent in South Korea, a doubling of income per head every decade; and 8.2 percent from 1980–93. Many other countries, however, have made little progress. In sub-Saharan Africa, where the total fertility rate is the highest in the world, the growth rate of GNP per head was only 0.6 percent from 1973 to 1980, and a dismal minus 1.2 percent from 1980 to 1994.[2] Per capita incomes actually fell in nearly 70 countries between 1980 and 1995.[3] During the past three decades, the proportion of people enjoying per capita income growth of at least 5 percent a year more than doubled, from 12 percent to 27 percent, but the proportion of those experiencing negative growth more than tripled, from 5 percent to 18 percent.[4] Figure 8.1 shows the regional shares of world population that enjoyed higher or lower incomes in the 1990s than in earlier decades. Even though the Asian NICs are graduating from the less-developed status, the challenge of development remains pressing for most of the LDCs.

Deplorable as the quality of life still is in the poor countries, the challenge of development has not gone unmet. Indeed, in no other period in history has the condition of the world's poor improved as much as during the past four decades when the international community made deliberate efforts to accelerate the economic development of poor countries. GNP per head has risen markedly in the low-income economies—by an annual average of nearly 3 percent from 1965 to 1980 and by 3.4 percent from 1980 to 1994. Average life expectancy increased by over one third between 1960 and 1995, and is now 63 years. Adult literacy rates increased between 1970 and 1995, from 46 percent to 66 percent. Other nonmonetary indicators of food, nutrition, health, and education show marked progress, as can be noted in Table 8.2.

Nonetheless, the challenge of development remains severe, as illustrated by the statistics on deprivation in Table 8.2. Of the world's population, nearly 80 percent are still in the LDCs, earning less than 20 percent of world income.[5]

Compounding the development problem of the future is the fact that the world's labor force is projected to increase by 40 percent over the next two decades, but 95 percent of the

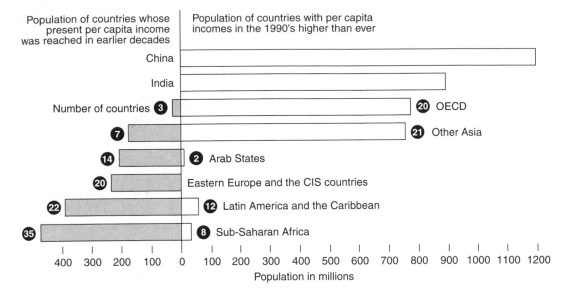

Figure 8.1. Growth has failed for more than a quarter of the world's people. The diagram shows the regional shares of world population. The lighter area to the right of the vertical line represents people in countries with incomes in the 1990s higher than ever before. They number over 3 billion people in about 60 countries, mostly Asia and OECD. The area to the left of the vertical line represents people whose incomes in the 1990s were lower than in earlier decades—about 1.5 billion people in about 100 countries. *Source:* UNDP, *Human Development Report 1996* (New York: Oxford University Press, 1996), p. 3.

TABLE 8.1
Average Annual Growth in Real Per Capita Income by Region, 1960–93 (percent)

Region or Country Group	1960–70	1970–80	1980–90	1990–93
World	2.6	2.8	3.0	2.4
Industrial countries	4.6	2.9	1.9	−3.1
OECD	4.3	2.6	2.0	1.0
Eastern Europe and the CIS	5.2	5.2	1.3	−11.5
Developing countries	2.0	2.8	3.5	4.3
Arab States	2.0	3.6	−0.8	−1.3
East Asia	2.0	4.3	7.2	10.6
Latin America and the Caribbean	2.9	3.7	−0.7	1.0
South Asia	1.8	0.7	3.3	1.2
South-East Asia and the Pacific	2.1	4.1	2.8	4.1
Sub-Saharan Africa	1.4	0.9	−1.0	−1.2
Least developed countries	0.8	−0.1	−0.1	−0.1

Source: World Bank, *World Development Report 1991* (New York: Oxford University Press, 1991), pp. 181–182; *World Development Report 1996.*

increase in the labor force will be in the less-developed countries. And in the next twenty-five years, the working-age population will double in these countries. But these less-developed countries have only 15 percent of the world's capital investment. Surplus labor and capital scarcity constitute their unfortunate factor endowment. Most of the world's people have nothing to sell but their labor. Where are the jobs to come from? How can surplus labor be made more productive so as to earn higher incomes?

TABLE 8.2
Balance Sheet of Human Development—Developing Countries

Progress	Deprivation
Health	
• In 1960–93 average life expectancy increased by more than a third. Life expectancy is now more than 70 years in 30 countries.	• Around 17 million people die each year from curable infectious and parasitic diseases such as diarrhoea, malaria and tuberculosis.
• Over the past three decades the population with access to safer water almost doubled—from 36% to nearly 70%.	• Of the world's 18 million HIV-infected people, more than 90% live in developing countries.
Education	
• Between 1960 and 1992 net enrollment at the primary level increased by nearly two-thirds—from 48% to 77%.	• Millions of children are still out of school—130 million at the primary level and 275 million at the secondary level.
Food and Nutrition	
• Despite rapid population growth, food production per capita increased by about 20% in the past decade.	• Nearly 800 million people do not get enough food, and about 500 million people are chronically malnourished.
Income and Poverty	
• During 1960–93 real per capita income in the developing world increased by an average 3.5% a year.	• Almost a third of the population—1.3 billion people—lives in poverty.
Women	
• During the past two decades the combined primary and secondary enrollment ratio for girls increased from 38% to 78%.	• At 384 per 100,00 live births, maternal mortality is still nearly 12 times as high as in OECD countries.
• During the past two decades fertility rates declined by more than a third.	• Women hold only 10% of parliamentary seats.
Children	
• Between 1960 and 1993 the infant mortality rate fell by more than half—from 150 per thousand live births to 70.	• More than a third of children are malnourished.
• The extension of basic immunization over the past two decades has saved the lives of about three million children a year.	• The under-five mortality rate, at 97 per thousand live births, is still nearly six times as high as in industrial countries.
Environment	
• Developing countries' contribution to global emissions is still less than a fourth that of industrial countries, though their population is four times the industrial world's.	• About 200 million people are severely affected by desertification.
	• Every year some 20 million hectares of tropical forests are grossly degraded or completely cleared.
Politics and Conflicts	
• Between two-thirds and three-quarters of the people in developing countries live under relatively pluralistic and democratic regimes.	• At the end of 1994 there were more than 11 million refugees in the developing world.

Source: UNDP, *Human Development Report 1997* (New York: Oxford University Press, 1997), Chs. 1 and 2.

MONITORING DEVELOPMENT PERFORMANCE

In the global economy of the future, an essential component of long-range strategic management will be the ability to monitor the economic progress of developing countries.

Monitoring the development of the LDCs is necessary to assess their significance as buyers, suppliers, competitors, and users of capital.[6] As potential buyers, they constitute 80 percent to 85 percent of the world's population. Forty percent of U.S. exports already go to

WORLD BANK AND POVERTY ALLEVIATION

The commitment of three World Bank presidents:

There will always be "relative poverty" in the sense of income differentials between richer and poorer, but the World Bank should focus on those in "absolute poverty"—a condition of life so degraded by disease, illiteracy, malnutrition, and squalor as to deny its victims basic human necessities.

Robert S. McNamara, Address to the Board of Governors (Washington, DC: World Bank, September 25, 1972), pp. 8–10

No task should command higher priority for the world's policy makers than that of reducing global poverty.

Lewis Preston, *Implementing the World Bank's Strategy to Reduce Poverty* (Washington, DC: World Bank, 1993), p. 3

I am here, quite honestly, because I have a dream. I really want to make the world a better place. I want to contribute in the best way I can to the improvement of the human condition, to alleviate poverty and to assist in the sustainable development of the world. . . . Above all, I am talking about a bank that has a dream. And I am saying that if you do not have a dream, then why the hell are you working at the Bank? Why not go to Wall Street or some economics department?

James Wolfensohn, *Institutional Investor* (October 1995): 68–69

the developing countries. As suppliers, they account for 20 percent of world exports. A third of American imports come from the developing countries. As competitors, the developing countries account for 25 percent of the more-developed countries' manufactured imports. As capital users, they are host to a fourth of U.S. direct foreign investment, and a third of the assets and liabilities of major international banks are in the developing countries.

What then will determine whether the future development performance of such an important group of countries is one of success or disappointment? Success in meeting the challenge of development depends in large part on improvement in the quality of policy making to accelerate development and reduce poverty. For some insight into the future possibilities, we must first look to development experience. When development efforts began after World War II, economists frequently said that "a poor country is poor because it is poor"—a "vicious circle of poverty" keeps the LDC in a low-level equilibrium trap. Most development economists would now say, however, that "a poor country is poor because of poor policies." The development record shows that some countries have undertaken appropriate policies to relax the constraints on their development while others have not. For the future of development, it is important to recognize how policy reform can overcome the constraints on a country's development.

Some may attribute the success stories of the Asian NICs to favorable sociological and political conditions. The sociologist Peter Burger, for instance, focuses on what he calls "East Asian economic culture. It is characterized by hard work, discipline, and a great capacity for what psychologists call 'delayed gratification' (its economic equivalent is saving); by very pronounced loyalty to one's social group; by respect for authority and learning; and, underlying all of this, by a basic attitude toward the world marked by hardheaded practicality and pragmatism."[7]

Noneconomic attributes certainly do matter. But aside from cultural traits, what are the economic sources of more rapid development? Accelerated development depends on overcoming these four strategic constraints:

- Savings gap
- Foreign exchange gap
- Agricultural lag
- Human resources development

We shall examine the nature of these constraints. Then we shall emphasize the need for policy reform that will have governments undertake a set of appropriate policies, as follows[8]:

- Stabilization of the macroeconomy
- Promotion of the market price system
- Opening the economy to international trade and foreign investment
- Investment in people

ICA and DPR call for an understanding of how the four major constraints affect development and how appropriate policies can relax them to accelerate a country's development.

SAVINGS GAP

Consider the first constraint of the savings gap. When we ask how is development to be financed, we do not mean where are the rupees or pesos coming from. (The country's central bank can answer that, but only with a resultant inflation.) Instead, we mean how can real resources be mobilized to finance development? How can there be a surplus of resources above consumption to be used for investment purposes? How can the "vicious circle of poverty" be overcome? The vicious circle of poverty states that:

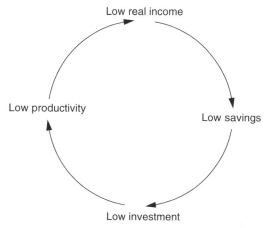

Low real income

Low savings

Low investment

Low productivity

Most of national income goes into consumption, little into savings. There is a real resource gap—a savings gap that does not release sufficient real resources for real investment to increase productivity.

Nonetheless, the vicious circle cannot be so vicious that a country can never break out of it. Over time, in some countries low savings have become moderate, and hence everything else in the circle has become moderate. And eventually moderate savings have become high savings and hence everything else in the circle became high. In South Korea in 1962, for instance, GNP per head was only $100 and domestic savings were negligible. At the same time the annual population growth was a high 3 percent. And yet, Korea succeeded in increasing its savings and its investment. In 1994, gross domestic savings in Korea amounted to 39 percent of national income and gross domestic investment 38 percent. GNP per head in 1994 was over $8,200. This increase in the standard of living is not simply because of the increase in savings and investment. But certainly overcoming the real resource gap—the savings gap—has contributed a great deal to Korea's development.

Table 8.3 indicates savings and investment in various developing countries from 1965–94. In those countries where domestic investment exceeded domestic savings, this was only made possible by an inflow of foreign savings in the form of a capital inflow (recall Chapters 4 and 5).

How have countries overcome the savings gap? Appropriate measures have been taken to provide a high real interest rate, curb inflation, and restrain the rise in wage rates within the increase in productivity. Capital flights have not occurred. Further, over time there has been a more efficient use of an increase in capital, leading to a greater increase in output. Over time, therefore, not so great a fraction of an increase in output has been needed to be saved and invested to produce a subsequent increase in national income. In addition, some governments have succeeded in raising public savings—i.e., taxes—as national income rose. In South Korea, for instance, taxes as a percentage of GDP rose from an annual average of 10 percent in 1963–73 to 18 percent in 1974–80, and up to nearly 20 percent in 1981–87.

For many countries, however, the savings constraint is still severe and is likely to remain so. For purposes of DPR, it is important to recognize how the savings constraint in a country intensifies because of large-scale rural to urban migration. The most rapid rates of urbanization are occurring in poor countries. Twenty-five years ago there were sixteen cities in LDCs with a population of 1 million; now there are seventy, and it is estimated that in twenty-five years there will be 200 with populations of a million or more. High rates of urbanization call for high rates of capital formation in infrastructure and housing. As the structure of industry is transformed to more capital-intensive industries, more savings are also needed. Further, an increase in savings is necessary to combat inflation in these countries, to service external debt, and to help remove deficits in their balance of payments.

FOREIGN EXCHANGE GAP

Most developing countries are small countries and are therefore highly dependent on international trade. If their GNP is to grow, they must import goods and services to support growth. Payments in foreign exchange for these imports can only come from export receipts, inflows of foreign capital, or the use of foreign reserves. The capacity to import from export

TABLE 8.3
Investment and Saving, Selected Developing Countries (Percentage of GDP)

	Gross Domestic Investment			Gross Domestic Saving		
	1965	**1980**	**1995**	**1965**	**1980**	**1995**
Tanzania	15	29	31	16	19	−7
Sierra Leone	12	16	6	8	−1	−9
Malawi	14	25	15	0	11	4
Bangladesh	11	15	17	8	2	8
Kenya	14	29	19	15	18	13
Nigeria	14	22	18	12	32	20
India	17	21	25	15	17	22
Zambia	25	23	12	40	19	3
Ghana	18	6	19	8	5	10
Pakistan	21	18	19	13	7	16
Zimbabwe	15	19	22	23	16	17
China	24	35	40	25	35	42
Côte d'Ivoire	22	27	13	29	20	20
Sri Lanka	12	34	25	13	11	14
Egypt, Arab Rep.	18	28	17	14	15	6
Bolivia	22	15	15	17	19	8
Indonesia	8	24	28	8	37	36
Philippines	21	29	23	21	24	15
Jamaica	27	16	17	23	16	10
Colombia	16	19	20	17	20	16
Peru	34	29	17	31	32	11
Costa Rica	20	27	25	9	16	24
Thailand	20	29	43	9	23	36
Turkey	15	22	25	13	14	20
Venezuela	25	26	16	34	33	21
Botswana	6	38	25	−13	28	23
Brazil	20	23	22	22	21	21
Malaysia	20	30	41	24	33	37
Chile	15	25	27	16	20	29
Mexico	20	27	15	19	25	19
Argentina	19	25	18	22	24	18
Korea, Rep.	15	32	37	8	25	36
Hong Kong	36	35	35	29	34	33
Singapore	22	46	33	10	38	51

Note: Countries are listed in ascending order of per capita income.
Source: World Bank, *World Development Report 1991* and *1997*, Table 13.

receipts (Q_M) depends, in turn, on the quantity of exports (Q_X) times the price of exports (P_X) divided by the price of imports (P_M), or $Q_M = \frac{P_X Q_X}{P_M}$. The inflow of foreign capital depends on government to government aid, cross-border sovereign lending by commercial banks, receipt of private foreign investment, loans from the World Bank, and access to the country's drawing rights in the IMF. If payments for imports exceed the revenue from exports and inflow of foreign capital, the country faces a foreign exchange gap. From balance-of-payments analysis (Chapter 5), we have seen that a domestic resource gap (savings plus taxes less than investment plus government expenditures) will spill over to an external payments imbalance—imports greater than exports. The country must then either give up its target growth rate in national income by reducing investment and government expenditure, or else lose foreign reserves, or try to close the foreign exchange gap by adopting policies to replace imports, or promote exports, or raise its price of exports (P_X) relative to import prices (P_M).

Again, the Asian newly industrializing countries (NICs) serve as models for overcoming the foreign exchange gap. They are small countries or city-states that have chosen to overcome the diseconomies of their small size by a strategy of export-led development. This promotion of exports has served as their engine of growth.[9] They have also sought macrostabilization to reduce pressure on their balance of payments.

What policies allowed the Asian NICs to establish an outward-looking regime that fostered export-led development, thereby overcoming their foreign exchange shortage? Like many other LDCs, South Korea and Taiwan initially adopted an import substitution strategy that relied on tariffs, quotas, and subsidies to bias the allocation of resources toward production of domestic substitutes for imports. But they abandoned this strategy in the early 1960s after the first easy stage of replacing labor intensive, nondurable consumer goods. Instead of trying to proceed on to the more difficult stages of substituting domestic production for imports of durable consumer goods and producer goods, they turned to export promotion—to a strategy of export-led growth that would have as its driving force an expansion of the export of semimanufactures and manufactures. Government and business in Korea and Taiwan realized the high costs of import substitution, recognized instead the principle of comparative advantage, and responded to the rapid expansion of world trade and the opportunities presented for new countries and new firms in the 1960s. They therefore chose to focus on producing what they were good at producing and to exchange these exports for what they wanted to consume. After instituting a set of policy reforms to promote exports, Korea's income per head grew an average of 7 percent a year between 1962 and 1971, compared with only 0.7 percent during the import-substitution period of 1953–61.

To promote exports, Korea and Taiwan corrected policies that were having a negative impact on exports and introduced other positive measures in favor of exports. They liberalized their foreign trade regime by removing quotas and reducing tariffs. They remitted duties on imported inputs for export production and established export processing zones. They also ended the overvaluation of their domestic currency in terms of foreign currency, which had been penalizing exports under the previous import substitution regime. A set of positive measures included cheap bank loans for exporters, the remission of indirect taxes on inputs into exports and on the exports themselves, exemption from corporate income taxes on a part of export earnings, preferential rates for services of public utilities, accelerated depreciation on the assets of exporters, occasional cash subsidies to exporters, and permission for exporters to use all their export earnings on the purchase of imports.

The upshot of these measures was to remove the bias in favor of import substitution and against exports by making it as profitable to export as to replace imports. Technically this is done by making the "effective exchange rate for exports" equivalent to the "effective exchange rate for imports." The effective exchange rate for exports is defined as the number of units of domestic currency that can be obtained for a dollar's worth of exports, taking into account export duties, subsidies, special exchange rates, input subsidies related to exports, and other financial and tax measures that affect the price of exports. The effective exchange rate for imports equals the number of units of domestic currency that would have to be paid for a dollar's worth of imports, taking into account tariffs, surcharges, interest on advance deposits, and other measures that affect the price of imports.

Suppose that initially in Korea the effective exchange rate on imports is 450 won to the dollar and the effective exchange rate on exports is 400 won to the dollar. Resources would then be biased toward the production of import substitutes for which domestic producers could realize up to 450 won compared with a dollar's worth of imports, while producers of exports would gain only 400 won for a dollar's worth of exports. If now through export promoting measures the effective exchange rate for exports comes up to 450 won to the dollar, the trade regime is neutral in its bias or outward oriented. In essence, the foreign trade regime in Korea made the effective exchange rate for exports higher than the nominal official exchange rate throughout the 1970s. (For example, in 1978 the nominal exchange rate was 484 won to the dollar whereas the effective exchange rate for exports was 566.5 won to the dollar.)

In addition, Korean and Taiwanese firms remained competitive on world markets as their governments controlled inflation, restrained wage increases within productivity bounds, and devalued periodically to prevent the real exchange rate for exports from becoming overvalued. Operating with world prices for their inputs and output, the exporting firms became competitive in a virtual free trade regime. Although there was some infant industry protection in Korea, this was done on a carefully selective basis. Moreover, there was continual monitoring of these industries, with pressures to move quickly from being an "infant industry" to becoming an "infant exporter." In general, investment was directed in accord with the pattern of potential comparative advantage. Comparative advantage was created, economies of scale were realized, and the structure of production moved up the ladder of comparative advantage.

An important feature of the export-promoting measures was their credibility for businesspeople. Export incentives will not be effective unless the export-promoting policies can be expected to last for the duration of investments in the export sector. This happened in South Korea as government plans displayed policy consistency and stability, thereby assuring exporters of the permanence of government policies designed to remove the disincentives to exporting and keeping production for export as profitable as that for the domestic market. Moreover, private investment was not crowded out by a large public deficit and by an inflationary tax on savings.

Undertaking a strategy of export-led development, Korea and Taiwan have enjoyed a remarkable rise in exports. From 1965–80, Korea's exports (at constant prices) rose at an average annual rate of 27 percent. By 1981, the proportion of the GNP exported had risen to nearly 34 percent in Korea and 54 percent in Taiwan. Table 8.4 shows changes in exports in Korea and various other developing countries, 1965–94. As their export revenue increased, Korea and Taiwan were able to support rapid growth in national output with imports of capital goods and intermediate goods. As in Korea and Taiwan, it is striking that other countries that adopted outward-oriented trade regimes have experienced the fastest rates of economic growth. World Bank calculations indicate this in Table 8.5.

For several reasons, the foreign exchange constraint has tightened in recent years in many LDCs. The capacity to import based on export receipts fell in the 1980s because of the trough in export prices of primary products and the slow demand for imports in the OECD countries. The real value of the inflow of foreign capital also declined as foreign aid fatigue set in, commercial banks walked away from debtor nations, net lending by the World Bank decreased, and net credit from the IMF was actually negative for 1986–89. Table 8.6 indicates that net financial transfers (international borrowing minus debt service)

TABLE 8.4
Export Volume of Merchandise Average Annual Growth Rate (percent)

	Exports		
	1965–80	**1980–89**	**1990–95**
Tanzania	−4.2	−1.8	10.0
Malawi	5.1	0.1	−1.8
Bangladesh	...	7.5	12.7
Kenya	3.9	2.6	16.6
Nigeria	11.1	−2.4	−1.9
India	3.0	6.3	7.0
Zambia	−0.7	−3.5	26.9
Ghana	−2.6	3.9	9.1
Pakistan	−1.8	9.5	8.8
China	15.6	11.6	14.3
Côte d'Ivoire	5.5	3.3	−7.5
Sri Lanka	0.2	6.3	17.0
Bolivia	2.7	1.7	−5.4
Indonesia	9.6	5.3	21.3
Philippines	4.6	2.9	10.2
Jamaica	−0.4	1.2	1.3
Colombia	1.4	9.7	4.8
Peru	1.6	−1.9	11.0
Thailand	8.6	14.3	21.6
Turkey	5.5	12.0	8.8
Venezuela	−9.5	1.6	−0.1
Brazil	9.3	6.1	6.6
Malaysia	4.6	11.5	17.8
Chile	8.0	5.7	10.5
Mexico	7.7	12.2	14.7
Argentina	4.7	3.1	−1.0
Korea, Rep.	27.2	13.7	7.4
Hong Kong	9.1	15.4	15.3
Singapore	4.7	12.1	16.2

Source: World Bank, *World Development Reports 1991 and 1997*, Table 15.

to all developing countries declined in the 1980s. In the 1990s, capital inflows increased, mainly in the form of private foreign investment. The need for external financing of the foreign exchange gap, however, still remains high. But this now coincides with a worldwide concern over a shortage of capital, as the surplus in Japan's balance of payments diminishes, Germany's surplus vanishes, and the demand for capital intensifies in Central and Eastern Europe at the expense of other developing countries.

AGRICULTURE

The third constraint—that of a country's lack of agricultural development—is a serious bottleneck for its industrial development. Progress in industrialization depends on progress in agriculture to provide an investable surplus and a marketable surplus in support of industrialization. Savings and taxes from the agricultural sector provide an investable surplus that can go into the industrial sector. A marketable surplus of raw materials is

TABLE 8.5

Trade Regimes and Growth (Real GNP per person, average annual % change)

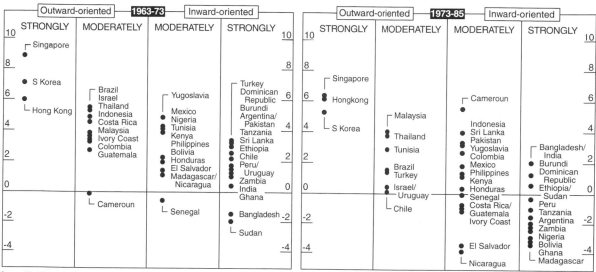

Source: World Bank

Source: World Bank, *World Development Report 1987* (New York: Oxford University Press), p. 86.

important in providing inputs for industrial output. In view of the high rates of rural to urban migration, it is also necessary that the urban workers take their lunch with them from the farm: The agricultural sector must provide sufficient food for the urban industrial sector. Moreover, an expanding marketable surplus from agriculture is essential to raise real income in that sector so that the demand for industrial products will increase. Insofar as most of the population is in agriculture, the extent of the domestic market will depend on rising real income in the agricultural areas. Agricultural development is also vital to reduce pressures on the balance of payments when a country is exporting primary products and must retain its competitive position in world markets. It is also possible to have import substitution in primary products: Where a foodstuff or a primary product is being imported, it may be possible to substitute production at home at competitive costs. Finally, agricultural development is now crucial to reduce the excessively high rural to urban migration. Urban centers simply cannot absorb in productive jobs the large inflow of migrants.

In many developing countries, agricultural development has been neglected in favor of industrialization; but this is premature. It is impossible to have an industrial revolution without having a previous or a parallel agricultural revolution. If its poverty is to be eradicated, a country cannot allow its food production per head to go down (unless the country is in as fortunate a position as is Hong Kong and can export manufactures and import foodstuffs).

The World Bank and other development agencies have recognized that greater effort must be devoted to agricultural development. Although rich countries tend to overpay their

TABLE 8.6
Developing Countries: Capital Flows[1] (*Annual average, in billions of U.S. dollars*)

	1983–88	1989–95	1991	1992	1993	1994	1995	1996
Developing countries								
Net private capital flows[2]	15.1	107.6	136.1	127.4	141.2	118.3	151.2	200.7
Net direct investment	10.4	41.8	26.7	34.3	50.2	69.5	72.5	90.7
Net portfolio investment	3.4	44.0	36.1	53.0	89.3	83.6	16.9	44.6
Other net investments	1.3	22.1	73.2	41.6	2.3	−35.0	61.7	64.9
Net official flows	29.0	21.4	20.8	14.3	23.3	20.4	31.0	−3.8
Change in reserves[3]	8.4	−42.7	−49.7	−45.7	−40.0	−42.2	−60.7	−82.3
Africa								
Net private capital flows[2]	3.5	7.2	5.5	5.7	4.7	12.7	13.6	9.0
Net direct investment	1.1	2.3	2.4	1.9	1.2	3.4	2.3	5.1
Net portfolio investment	−0.9	−0.2	−1.6	−0.7	0.9	0.4	1.9	0.7
Other net investments	3.3	5.1	4.7	4.5	2.5	8.8	9.4	3.2
Net official flows	5.0	6.0	5.9	8.6	6.2	5.5	4.0	6.4
Change in reserves[3]	0.2	−2.3	−3.2	2.4	−1.0	−5.8	−2.2	−4.4
Asia								
Net private capital flows[2]	11.9	43.6	32.4	21.8	52.7	63.2	89.2	94.7
Net direct investment	3.6	25.0	12.1	17.7	34.0	43.6	49.5	54.8
Net portfolio investment	1.2	5.2	0.5	1.8	11.7	10.0	10.2	9.2
Other net investments	7.1	13.6	19.8	3.7	7.6	9.2	29.4	30.1
Net official flows	7.6	8.4	10.6	10.7	10.1	6.2	5.6	7.2
Change in reserves[3]	−2.2	−23.8	−26.7	−15.1	−25.3	−47.4	−28.3	−43.2
Middle East and Europe								
Net private capital flows[2]	1.8	23.9	73.2	44.5	22.0	−2.4	12.6	19.4
Net direct investment	1.1	1.3	1.4	1.9	1.5	0.9	0.8	0.8
Net portfolio investment	4.2	13.5	22.6	21.2	15.6	12.2	12.2	7.6
Other net investments	−3.4	9.0	49.2	21.3	4.9	−15.6	−0.5	10.9
Net official flows	6.7	1.4	1.1	−3.0	5.9	10.3	−1.3	−5.8
Change in reserves[3]	9.9	−4.4	−4.3	−11.7	6.1	−0.1	−6.5	−13.9
Western Hemisphere								
Net private capital flows[2]	−2.0	33.0	24.9	55.5	61.7	44.9	35.7	77.7
Net direct investment	4.7	13.2	10.9	12.9	13.4	21.5	19.9	29.9
Net portfolio investment	−1.1	25.4	14.5	30.6	61.1	60.8	−7.5	27.1
Other net investments	−5.7	−5.6	−0.5	12.0	−12.8	−37.5	23.3	20.7
Net official flows	9.7	5.7	3.2	−2.0	1.1	−1.7	22.7	−11.6
Change in reserves[3]	0.5	−12.2	−15.5	−21.3	−19.9	11.2	−23.6	−20.8

[1]Net capital flows comprise net direct investment, net portfolio investment, and other long- and short-term net investment flows, including official and private borrowing.

[2]Because of data limitations other net investment may include some official flows.

[3]A minus sign indicates an increase.

Source: IMF, *World Economic Outlook*, May 1997, p. 43.

farmers, poor countries should not underpay them. Their governments do so by imposing price controls on their output and charging above world prices for their domestically produced inputs. The green revolution has brought progress to some areas, but it does nothing for rain-fed regions such as in sub-Saharan Africa. There is a need in some countries for land reform, extension of rural infrastructure, improvement in rural credit institutions, and more effective marketing institutions. Moreover, rural development is essential to reduce the excessive differential in real wages between urban and rural areas and help stem the excessive migration. Decentralization of industrial activities to rural sectors is also useful in allowing farm families to increase their income with off-farm jobs. In Taiwan, for instance, it is striking that, by their commuting to nonfarm jobs, the family's income from nonfarm employment amounts to almost three-quarters of the average farm family's income.

HUMAN RESOURCES

The fourth major constraint on a country's pace of development relates to the need for human resource development. Whether in a rich or a poor country, human resources constitute the ultimate wealth of nations. In poor countries, it has become increasingly apparent that an improvement in the quality of human life cannot be simply awaited as an ultimate objective of development, but must be viewed as in itself a necessary instrument of development. Beyond an increase in the quantity of productive factors, it is necessary to improve the quality of people as economic agents. If the development process entails economic growth plus qualitative change, then the qualitative dimensions of development require a greater emphasis on investment in human capital. Human capital is clearly needed to mobilize other resources and to utilize them efficiently. Without a strong human infrastructure, the process of development will not become self-sustaining.

Numerous studies in growth accounting emphasize the value of investment in human capital. Calculations of the historical growth in output in the now developed countries as a function of the increase in their inputs of labor, capital, and natural resources over time indicate that only some 50 percent of the increase in output can be attributed to increases in the quantity of inputs. Another 50 percent represent a rise in "total factor productivity." A rise in total factor productivity means that an increase in the quantity of inputs by x percent will lead to an increase in output of more than x percent. An increase in total factor productivity then implies a decrease in the real unit cost of production. For economic progress, merely increasing the quantity of inputs will not do. A rise in total factor productivity is essential. Much of the rise in total factor productivity can be attributed to investment in human capital that leads to technological progress, improved quality of labor, improved organization, better management, and innovations.

As Table 8.7 indicates, a sizable percentage of the high growth in national output in the more successful countries, such as in East Asia, has come from an increase in total factor productivity. There are, however, a number of econometric studies of the sources of growth in the East Asian NICs that differ in their conclusions as to whether the growth of total factor productivity—rather than factor accumulation—dominated the growth of output per capita. One of the most thorough studies by MIT's Alwyn Young reduced the usually high "naive" estimates of total factor productivity by adjusting for the rise in participation rates of labor, rise in investment to GDP ratios, educational levels, and the intersectoral transfer of labor from agriculture to other sectors with higher value added per worker. These adjustments increase the contributions of labor and capital inputs while reducing that of total factor productivity.

Another study of sources of growth in East Asia from 1960–90 concluded that capital was the most important source, accounting for between 48 percent and 72 percent of the economic growth of the East Asian NICs.[10] There is, however, evidence that technical progress depends directly on the size of a country's capital stock. Of the three factors—capital, labor, and technical progress—capital is the only one that can be readily varied. Insofar as capital and technical progress are complementary, they account for a large percentage of a country's growth.

Beyond the constraints of the savings gap, foreign exchange gap, and agricultural bottleneck, the ultimate constraint on a country's development is the ability of its human resources to increase productivity. Improved labor skills and innovations by an enlarged supply of entrepreneurs are essential.

TABLE 8.7
Contributions to the Growth of Output

Region and Period	Capital	Labor	TFP*
1960–73			
Africa	59	22	17
East Asia	50	16	35
Europe, Middle East, and North Africa	51	10	38
Latin America	55	20	25
South Asia	81	20	0
Total	56	18	26
1973–87			
Africa	92	37	−27
East Asia	62	17	20
Europe, Middle East, and North Africa	68	19	14
Latin America	94	51	−48
South Asia	55	19	24
Total	76	28	−6
1960–87			
Africa	73	28	0
East Asia	57	16	28
Europe, Middle East, and North Africa	58	14	28
Latin America	67	30	0
South Asia	67	50	14
Total	65	23	14

*TFP: Total factor productivity. This measures the growth of national output above and beyond the growth in the use of both labor and capital inputs.
Source: World Bank, *World Development Report 1991* (New York: Oxford University Press, 1991), p. 45.

Economists have long recognized the need for creativity and innovations to bring about technological progress. Long ago, the Cambridge economist Alfred Marshall observed that although nature is subject to diminishing returns, man is subject to increasing returns: " . . . Knowledge is our most powerful engine of production; it enables us to subdue nature and satisfy our wants." So too did Columbia's economist J. M. Clark state, "Knowledge is the only instrument of production not subject to diminishing returns."[11] "Increasing returns" in an economy is related to an increase in total factor productivity stemming from ideas, ingenuity, innovations, and technological progress.

In accepting the Nobel Prize, the noted agricultural economist Theodore Schultz also stated that, while agricultural development is of paramount importance, "The decisive factors of production in improving the welfare of poor people are not space, energy, and crop land; the decisive factor is the improvement in population quality."[12] Schultz emphasized that the returns to various quality components are increasing over time in many low-income countries. Stressing the economic value of human capital, he connected favorable economic prospects with an investment in health and education.

Recognizing the importance of knowledge, the president of the Economic History Association, Richard Easterlin, answered the question "Why isn't the whole world developed?" by stating that development is a function of the rate of technological change—the introduction of new production techniques. The transfer of technological change, according to Easterlin, is an educational process. Thus the spread of development depends on the growth of science and the diffusion of modern education, which, in turn, depends on an incentive structure and new political conditions and ideological forces.[13] Historically, the growth of formal schooling has led to a secular, rationalistic, and materialistic trend in intellectual thought that promoted development. In many less-developed countries, however, this has not yet occurred. Of the infants now being born in the developing world, 10 percent will not reach their first birthdays, and 20 percent will not reach their fifth birthdays. One third of primary school-age children will not be enrolled in primary school and, of those who do enter, 60 percent will not complete more than three years of elementary school. Although literacy has increased markedly in many developing countries, there is still clearly a need for greater investment in human capital.

Education and training play a major role in improving the human infrastructure. Investment in education contributes to growth by increasing productivity and by reducing income inequality.[14] Although each individual commonly views his or her own education as a consumption good, it is more appropriately interpreted as an investment good from the standpoint of the economy's development. To the economist, human beings can be conceptualized as human capital or embodied savings that will yield a future stream of income. It is then an economic problem to determine how much the economy should invest in human capital and, of equal importance, what the composition of that investment should be.

As human resources-rich economies, the East-Asian success stories have been based not on an abundance of natural resources, but on their human resources. All the fast developers have invested heavily in education. The quality of education and extent of schooling and training in East Asian countries have markedly increased in the course of their development. By 1960, just before South Korea's economic "take-off," 90 percent of children were already completing primary school, and over one third were going on to secondary education. Korea's achievement is notable in universalizing primary education at an earlier stage than any other developing country. Secondary and university enrollment have also grown rapidly.

Also striking is the decline in the gender gap (male versus female) in enrollment rates at the primary and secondary levels. By 1987, the East Asian countries had all achieved universal primary education for girls, virtually eliminating the gender gap at that level. In contrast, substantial gender gaps still persist in some forty low-income countries to almost the same degree as in 1965.

The education of girls is extremely important—not only because the private returns to education are similar for women and men, but because the social benefits from educating girls are especially high.

The East-Asian NICs also demonstrate that with education and training a country can progress from inexpensive labor power to relatively inexpensive brain power, with an accompanying structural transformation to higher-value production.

POLICY LESSONS

A number of policy lessons emerge from the contrasting development records of the successful East Asian countries and the disappointments in many other LDCs.

In terms of human resources, it may be said that "the chief personal characteristics that influence development and may be molded by value systems are attitudes to work, to self improvement through the acquisition of knowledge, and thriftiness. Development-minded governments are fortunate if they rule people who, by nature or tradition, work hard, are thrifty, and want to learn."[15] These traits alone, however, are not sufficient for development. Beyond ethnic or cultural causes, we must look to the quality of national economic management.

Disappointments in development can be traced to the super constraint of poor national economic management. Figure 8.2 shows a country's potential rate of development if it relaxes its constraints on saving, foreign exchange, agriculture, and human resources. In reality, however, the actual rate of development in many countries has been below the potential. This is because government has taken inappropriate policies that have handicapped the development effort. National economic management has to implement those appropriate policies that can bring the actual rate of development up closer to the country's potential by improving the allocation of resources, mobilizing more resources, and increasing productivity.

Analysis by the World Bank suggests that there is an interaction between different forms of investment (human, physical, and infrastructure) and the taking of appropriate policies. Among a sample of sixty developing economies during 1965–87, the bank found that those with distorted policies and a low level of education grew, on the average, by only 3.1 percent a year. The economies that had either higher levels of education or fewer policy distortions did better, growing at 3.8 percent a year. But the countries that had both—that is, a higher level of education and fewer policy distortions—grew at an impressive 5.5 percent a year.[16]

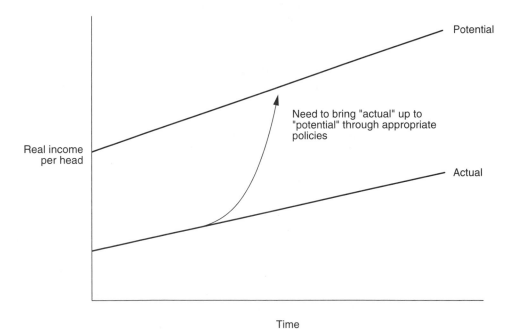

Figure 8.2 Potential and actual development.

The bank's economists also looked at the economic rates of return on 1,200 public and private projects financed by the World Bank group. They calculated the rates of return under different policies and conditions. In particular, the bank examined a variety of economic policy distortions: in trade (tariffs and import quotas), foreign exchange (the premium on black market exchange rates), interest rates (whether positive or negative in real terms), and fiscal policy (the size of budget deficits). On every measure of policy distortion, projects yielded the highest returns where policy distortions were low, and the lowest returns where distortions were high. The substantial improvement in policy is associated with a five- to ten-percentage point increase in the rate of return for projects. This also confirms that market incentives work and that good policies and investments are complementary.[17]

From the perspectives of the firm's ICA and DPR, therefore, what matters the most in monitoring a country's development is an appraisal of the effects of the government's policies.

Appropriate policies have four major objectives:

- To provide stable demand management at the macro level
- To make the market price system more effective at the micro level
- To improve the quality of people as economic agents
- To promote an outward-looking trade regime

Macroeconomic management should be designed to avoid inflation and financial repression. Inflation intensifies the savings gap and the foreign exchange gap, misallocates resources, and worsens the distribution of income. Government intervention on money and capital markets has also resulted in financial repression in the sense of keeping interest rates too low and targeting credit to unproductive sectors. Insofar as governments have combined distorting interest rate regulations with high rates of inflation, interest rates have often been negative in real terms and have perpetuated an excess of demand over supply in the market for credit. The early reforms in South Korea were designed to bring about financial deepening and to raise real interest rates. Experience demonstrates that countries with positive real rates of interest have had better growth records than those with negative rates.[18] In all the attention to policy reform it is now clear that a major component and the necessary first step must be a macrostabilization program. Governments must keep their budgets under adequate control: A poor country cannot afford excessive fiscal deficits that are financed by resorting to the printing press. Programs of monetary stabilization and financial liberalization must be undertaken as complementary strategies.[19]

At the micro level, the quality of national economic management reflects how successful the government is in keeping distortions from entering the market price system. In many developing countries price distortions have been pervasive: Prices have not been honest prices in the sense of reflecting the true scarcity or abundance of what is being valued. In particular, three key prices have commonly been distorted—the interest rate, wage rate, and foreign exchange rate. Given the scarcity of capital, interest rates have been too low. Given the surplus of unskilled labor, the level of wage rates has been too high, and wages have been allowed to outstrip the rise in productivity. The foreign exchange rate has been distorted as the government has kept the value of domestic currency overvalued in terms of foreign currency. When these key prices are distorted, the allocation of resources will be inefficient and the mobilization of additional resources will be limited. It has therefore become common to say, "Get prices right."

Policy reform also looks to an improvement in the performance of state- owned enterprises or to privatization. Many state-owned enterprises in LDCs have accounted for 10 percent to 40 percent of GDP. They have, however, made large and growing claims on the budget and have resorted to external debt for financing. In a number of countries, the public enterprise deficit has been identified as a proximate cause of excessive credit creation, leading to monetary expansion, price inflation, and, ultimately, balance-of-payments pressures. State-owned enterprises also often undertake policies of controlling prices of public services, food grains, and other basic wage goods, which often prevent the public enterprises from covering their costs, with corresponding fiscal and monetary repercussions. Various ways of improving the efficiency in state-owned enterprises are now being emphasized—from the provision of systems for monitoring and evaluating performance to the sale of state-owned enterprises and promotion of privatization programs.[20]

Another major component of a policy reform package is the promotion of an outward-looking trade regime. Trade policy has been heavily researched, and development economists are close to unanimity in emphasizing the benefits of an export-led development over an import-substituting process of industrialization. The costs of import-substituting industrialization have been excessively high. Too many plants have produced too small an output; quality has been inferior; capital has been underutilized; and the industrial structure has become increasingly monopolistic and less competitive. Rare is the firm that has been able to proceed from replacing imports to becoming competitive on export markets. Trade protection has not succeeded in moving firms down their learning curves to lower costs, and hence to the eventual realization of higher profits by establishing a competitive position in export markets. On the contrary, import-substitution policies have simply given the sheltered firms high profits in local currency, but the domestic resource cost to the entire economy has been excessive, and the cost has increased per unit of foreign exchange saved. In some countries, the promotion of import substitutes through tariff rates that escalate with the degree of processing (low on imported intermediate goods and high on final goods) has actually resulted in negative domestic value added. Although high protection of final goods makes production of the import substitute privately profitable in terms of local currency, the value of inputs at world prices exceeds the value of the final product at world prices.

The process of import substitution has generally been socially inefficient. It has resulted not only in inefficient use of resources, but has also often intensified the foreign exchange constraint. For at the same time as policies have subsidized import replacement, they have inhibited expansion of exports. Nor has there been a net saving of imports because the replacement of finished import commodities has required heavy imports of fuels, industrial materials and capital goods, as well as foodstuffs in cases where agricultural development has also suffered. With the tightening of the foreign exchange constraint there has been an increasingly stringent exchange control regime and a growing dependence on foreign capital.

After a period of import-substituting industrialization, the problems of maldistribution of income and unemployment have actually become more serious than they were before the inward-looking policies were taken. Inappropriate policies involving the use of subsidies, maintenance of overvalued exchange rates, rationing of underpriced import licenses, high levels of effective protection, and loans at negative real interest rates have induced the production of import substitutes by capital-intensive, labor-saving methods and have resulted in industrial profits in the sheltered sector and high industrial wages for a labor elite, thereby aggravating inequalities in income distribution. Employment creation in the urban import replacement industrial sector has not kept pace with the rural-urban migration, and the unemployment problem has been aggravated by the transfer of the rural underemployed into open unemployment and underemployment in the urban sector.

Moreover, while the subsidization of the import-replacement industries has implicitly taxed exports and agriculture, it has resulted in additional costs through the practice of "rent-seeking" activities by domestic businessmen. Rents are supernormal profits in a noncompetitive market. When a government intervenes by imposing quantitative controls over imports, or by licensing investment toward import-replacement industries, these restrictions give rise to rents in various forms, and people often compete for these unearned profits. The imposition of a quota on imports, for example, raises the price of imports and gives a rent to the importer who is able to secure a license for the limited quantity of imports. The importable goods can be sold at a premium as the market price becomes higher than the world price. There is a redistribution of income from consumers of the importable to the importer who has acquired the property of the import license.

There is a potential source of profit for somebody if the pattern of protection can be altered in his or her favor. Resources are therefore spent in lobbying governments and

---

DEVELOPMENT THROUGH TRADE

Classical and neoclassical economists did not make the dynamic aspects of trade central to their thought; but to the extent that they did consider the effects of trade on development, they saw no conflict between a country's conformity with its comparative advantage and the acceleration of its development. Indeed, John Stuart Mill stated that trade, according to comparative advantage, results in a "more efficient employment of the productive forces of the world," and that this might be considered the "direct economical advantage of foreign trade. But there are, besides, indirect effects, which must be counted as benefits of a high order." A most important "indirect" dynamic benefit, according to Mill, is

> the tendency of every extension of the market to improve the processes of production. A country that produces for a larger market than its own, can introduce a more extended division of labour, can make greater use of machinery, and is more likely to make inventions and improvements in the processes of production. . . . The opening of a foreign trade . . . sometimes works a sort of industrial revolution in a country whose resources were previously undeveloped.

John Stuart Mill, *Principles of Political Economy*, 2 vols. (1848), Vol. 2, Book 3, Sec. 5, Ch. 17.

in trying to win an increase in the level of protection for one's own business. The rent seekers compete in various ways, some of which are perfectly legal; but other methods involve bribery, corruption, smuggling, and black markets. Rent-seeking activity has no social value although it uses time and resources. In the importer's attempt to capture the restriction-created rents, there is an opportunity cost as real resources are used in lobbying or other rent-seeking activities that produce no greater supply of the restricted quantity. As importers engage in activities to receive the favor of government, resources that go into the rent-seeking activities are diverted from other productive activities. Although the rent-seeking activity may be privately rational in terms of self-interest, it is socially wasteful and represents another cost of import substitution policies.

In contrast to the disappointing performance of those countries that have stayed too long with an import-substitution strategy, the developing countries that adopted an export-promoting strategy have realized the best development records. They have demonstrated superior performance in reducing the savings gap, increasing investment, reducing the foreign exchange gap, raising total factor productivity, increasing employment, enjoying higher real wages, and having a more equitable distribution of income.

Why has export promotion had such a strong favorable impact on development? As for its effect on the balance of payments, one might think that there is little difference between earning a unit of foreign exchange through exports or saving a unit of foreign exchange through import substitution. But the alternative strategies have differed in domestic resource costs: Evidence shows that the cost of earning foreign exchange is less than the domestic resource cost of saving foreign exchange. Moreover, export-promoting countries have become more creditworthy, and their foreign exchange constraint has been relaxed. Export-led development has not only yielded the static gains from trade according to comparative advantage, but also has allowed the country to realize dynamic benefits. While a reallocation

---

SIGNIFICANCE OF EXPORTS

Experience has been that growth performance has been more satisfactory under export promotion strategies . . . than under import-substitution strategies. While it is impossible to specify a particular model of growth process that will simultaneously satisfy all observers, the relationship between export performance and growth is sufficiently strong that it seems to bear up under many different specifications of the relationship. It has been tested over many countries for: (1) rates of growth of real GNP and of exports . . . ; (2) for real GNP net of exports and exports . . . ; and (3) for rates of growth of GNP as a function of rate of capital formation, aid receipts, and export growth. . . . Time-series and cross-section data have been pooled, so that deviations of countries' growth rates from their trends have been estimated as a function of the growth of export earnings. . . . In all of these specifications, rate of growth of exports has turned out to be a highly significant variable.

Anne O. Krueger, "Trade Policy as an Input to Development," *American Economic Review* (May 1980): 288–289.

of resources in conformity with a country's comparative advantage can raise the country's level of national income, the dynamic gains have been most important in increasing the rate of growth in income. There has been increased capacity utilization of plants, realization of economies of scale, the creation of employment through export of labor-intensive products, and an increase in total factor productivity. There is evidence that the faster export output grows, the faster is the growth in productivity. This is because of economies of scale, higher investment embodying capital of a more productive later vintage, and a faster pace of innovation in processes and products.[21]

After reviewing the high quality of national economic management in the Asian NICs in their support of a market price system, stable demand management, and export-led development, Australia's Helen Hughes concluded that "Many aspects of policy effectiveness remain unsolved, but enough is known to accelerate growth in slowly growing countries. There is now no excuse for the governments of developing countries that do not approach the high, long-run GNP growth of the East Asian countries."[22]

It is not, however, simply a matter of economists knowing what should be done and advising governments what to do, for governments must also have the capacity and the political willingness to undertake policy reforms. Political rationality determines what governments do. When political rationality conflicts with economic rationality, the task of policy reform becomes extremely difficult. UCLA's Arnold Harberger, a long-time adviser to developing countries, may contend that "economics is good for you," but political objectives may make governments ignore economic rationality.[23]

Nonetheless, economic rationality may eventually win out. When the state becomes overextended in an underdeveloped economy, government may ironically lose control of the economy. Inflation, the rise of parallel markets, the breakdown of a price system, rent seeking, and corruption may then eventually force policy reform for the government to regain a grip on the economy. Actual experience with the adverse consequences of inappropriate policies may be more influential in bringing about policy reform than any prescriptions by economists. As Bhagwati observes, "Many developing countries learned [the policy lessons] the hard way. . . . Perhaps learning by other's doing and one's own undoing is the most common form of education!"[24]

STATE OR MARKET?

In considering what the World Bank characterizes as *The East Asian Miracle*,[25] the bank's analysts identified many of the policy lessons that we outlined in the preceding section. Emphasis was given to macroeconomic stability, outward orientation, low price distortions, and heavy investments. To the extent that the East Asian governments undertook appropriate policies, their development performance has not been a "miracle." True, in the 1950s, the "initial conditions" of these economies were inauspicious and their subsequent rapid rate of development not expected. But analysis of the public policies selected and implemented dispels the quality of being a "miracle." They simply attest to the force of economic logic and the competence of national economic management.

Analysts of the East Asian countries differ, however, regarding the respective roles of the state and the market. The bank study concludes that for the most part government interventions were market friendly and that industrial policies were not so influential except to the extent that they were market conforming. (By industrial policies is meant specific government interventions to alter industrial structure to promote productivity-based growth.) Mainstream neoclassical economists also emphasize the market-friendly policies. A more recent group of revisionists, however, sees in the success of the East Asian countries evidence that highly targeted industrial policy was effective. Instead of the "invisible hand," the revisionists see the visible hand of government in selecting certain industries as "winners," protecting infant industries, and promoting exports. It is contended that not "market supremacy" but "government leadership" matters.[26]

The bank's balanced conclusion is that selected interventions were neither as important as their advocates suggest, nor as irrelevant as their neoclassical critics contend. The bank observes that "One of the main characteristics of interventions in the East Asian countries is that in general they have been carried out within well-defined bounds limiting the implicit or explicit costs. Whether these interventions contributed to the rapid growth made possible by good fundamentals or detracted from it is the most difficult question we have tried to answer. It is much easier to show that the East Asian countries limited the costs and duration of inappropriately chosen interventions—itself an impressive achievement—than to demonstrate conclusively that those interventions that were maintained over a long period accelerated growth. We conclude that promotion of specific industries generally did not work and therefore holds little promise for other developing economies. Directed credit has worked in certain situations but carries high risk. The export push strategy has been by far the most successful of the three sets of policy intervention and holds the most promise for other developing economies."[27]

In contrast to the bank's equivocal conclusion, the University of Sussex's Robert Wade has maintained that instead of having the state follow the market, there has been a "governed market" or "developmental state" in Korea and Taiwan that has undertaken industrial policies that lead the market. The policies assisted the firms to do what they would not do otherwise. Government was the rule maker and first player in a multistage game, with the moves by the government influencing the credible options of the other players. Intervention was at the sectoral, product, and even firm levels and aided industries by affecting investment and production decisions. Thus, Wade rejects the claims of those who interpret the East Asian story as a vindication of either free-market principles or the confinement of government intervention to only promoting exports and correcting market failures.[28]

Oxford's Sanjaya Lall also contends that industrial policy was significant in raising the technological competence and technological deepening in the East Asian countries. He argues that the bank's conclusion that industrial policy had little structural effect "flies in the face of overwhelming micro-level evidence that most promoted activities would not otherwise have been undertaken. . . . The most successful industrializers have been dynamic precisely because their governments intervened heavily in the process of building up technological capabilities."[29]

So too does Harvard's Dani Rodrik contend that Korea and Taiwan could not have experienced their economic take-off under decentralized market conditions. "Chief among these reasons are the imperfect tradability of key inputs (and technologies) associated with modern-sector production, and some increasing returns to scale in these activities. These conditions created a situation of coordination failure. In other words, while the rate of return to coordinated investments was extremely high, the rate of return to individual investments remained low.

"Governments in [Taiwan and South Korea] undertook a set of measures starting in the late 1950s that not only removed some policy-induced distortions, but also served to coordinate and subsidize private investment. These measures included: credit subsidies, tax incentives, administrative guidance and public investment.

"This active government role helped remove the coordination failure that had blocked industrial growth. As private entrepreneurs responded to these measures, the resulting investments turned out to be profitable not only in financial terms, but in social terms as well."[30]

Regardless of where one comes out regarding the efficacy of industrial policy in the East Asian countries, the controversy does point up more generally the conditions for successful industrial policy. A distinction should be made between industrial policy in a functional sense and an industry-specific sense. In a functional sense, government policies operate across many industries, and are related to such functions as labor training or R&D. One of the world's most extensive programs of government support for R&D has been in Israel and has certainly brought the country to leading-edge technology. Selective industrial policies are, however, industry specific and are intended to affect investment and production decisions in particular industries or even firms. The conditions for their efficacy are much more rigorous.

The economic justification for government intervention is the presence of market failures. Among the several sources of market failures are information problems, imperfections of competition, increasing returns, learning by doing, externalities, and rents. The real issue, however, is whether government intervention is better than private efforts in view of market failures. Government failure may replace market failure. Policies directed at reshaping the structure of output may be costly in attempting to promote premature production of high-tech differentiated products that divert the nation's scarcest resources—in particular its skilled people, its research capability, and its investment capital—away from their most productive uses and toward industries in which the nation is presently uncompetitive.[31]

A case for industrial policy is arguably strongest for new export-oriented industries that create externalities. Criteria for selecting industries should of course be economic, not political. Industry expertise is also essential. Another student of industrial policy in South Korea presents these guidelines:

> First, the overriding objective of the intervention must be the achievement of dynamic efficiency in the sense of obtaining international competitiveness within an explicit medium-term time horizon.

> Second, information relevant to judging potential comparative advantage must be sought continually from every possible source.

> Third, detailed industry-specific strategy should be reformulated as needed to reflect the accumulation of pertinent information and experience acquired during the course of implementation.

> Fourth, only a small number of industries should be targeted at any one time, so as not to spread scarce and specialized technical and entrepreneurial talent too thinly.

Fifth, the government's intervention should not overly constrain the exploitation of comparative advantage in well-established industries.[32]

Finally, it is essential not to confuse the competitive advantage of a firm with the comparative advantage of a nation.[33] The confusion between appropriate strategies for the firm and the nation results in the misconception that industrial policies aimed at directly influencing the composition of output can accelerate a country's development. The sequence should be the other way around, from the development of dynamic comparative advantage on the supply side to the eventual transformation of the structure of output as a consequence of the development process, not its cause. If industrial policy focuses on reshaping the structure of output itself, it does not necessarily produce development of the economy's resource base and may in fact retard it. Attention may be diverted from the central policy issues of efficient resource allocation, macroeconomic stability and appropriate development of the nation's resource base. When deliberate transformation of the structure of output is viewed as a cause of the development process—rather than as a consequence of the process—the result is likely to be protectionist policies that retard rather than promote economic growth.[34]

Reviewing the East-Asian experience, Masahiko Aoki rejects the view that markets and governments are rival institutions. Instead, he propounds an intermediate position that he terms the "market-enhancing view" because it emphasizes the role of government action in promoting private sector coordination and providing incentives for private market advancements.[35] Instead of introducing a substitute mechanism for resolving market failures, government can increase the capabilities of private sector institutions to do so. For instance, when coordination problems involve increasing returns to scale and asymmetric information in the private sector, the government by facilitating information exchange and strengthening private sector intermediaries can promote private sector coordination better than the market or comprehensive government intervention can. In such a case, the government does not substitute for private coordination, but plays a complementary role in shaping an institutional environment conducive to a type of organizational coordination.

Government can also increase the capabilities of private sector institutions by creating "rent opportunities" in the private sector. For instance, by restricting entry into the banking system, the government can bestow a "franchise value" for banks that induces them to become more stable institutions with better incentives to monitor the firms they finance and manage the risk of the loan portfolio. The government can also sometimes target rents for specific bank activities to compensate for market deficiencies, such as the lack of long-term lending.[36] The rents are not resource-wasteful rent transfers as in ordinary rent-seeking activity through government controls, but rather rent opportunities that are contingent on an agent's productive activity. Korea's use of export subsidies, for example, was tied to the objective criterion of an export target to be fulfilled by the private sector. By creating an opportunity for profits, the government can perform a complementary role in inducing coordination and cooperation in private sector institutions. Even when confronting market failure, government may do better by pursuing market-enhancing policies than by intervening with direct specific controls.

On the issue of state or market, we can conclude that the most important questions about the role of the state are not how large should be the public sector or how much government intervention there should be, but rather what kind of intervention. What can government do best? Can public policy work through markets? As Dwight Perkins of the Harvard Institute for International Development observes, "Making markets work is a much more complex process than slogans such as 'getting the prices right,' 'privatization,' or 'getting rid of controls' would imply. Making markets work involves fundamental changes in enterprise behavior in most cases and substantial changes in the way government itself carries out its functions. Finally, most developing nations are never going to be willing to turn as much over to the market as, say, Hong Kong. Nonmarket controls or hierarchical commands will continue to play a major role in many sectors of most economies. Reform, therefore, is not just a matter of getting rid of such commands. A high growth economy must learn to make both the market and the bureaucracy perform efficiently."[37]

FUTURE NICS?

The experience with export-led development in the Asian NICs has yielded strong policy lessons, but we are left with the question whether other countries can follow their success stories. Can the East Asian model of development be generalized? For the practice of DPR, it is important to ask whether another tier of NICs can in the future follow the Asian NICs up the ladder of comparative advantage and succeed in exporting manufactures. As in the 1950s and 1960s, some observers are now pessimistic about the prospects for exports from additional NICs. The old export pessimism focused on dim prospects for primary product exports and led to the import-substituting industrialization strategy. The new export pessimism is now skeptical about the potential for exports of manufactures from additional NICs. Export pessimists believe that the countries that have been able to follow export-led industrialization have done so only because of favorable conditions that cannot be replicated elsewhere. They also assert that future demand will not support exports from additional developing countries.

Such pessimism, however, is not justified for the following reasons. First, it is not true that the East Asian NICs developed because of favorable conditions not to be found in other countries. On the contrary, their initial conditions were actually very unfavorable—lacking natural resources, severe population pressure, and political instability. Their development success cannot be attributed to especially favorable conditions, but rather, as we have seen, to the choice of appropriate policies by the government and a dynamic response on the part of the private sector to these policies. The lesson of the Asian NICs is that effective demand management and efficient supply-oriented policies have been the strategic forces accounting for successful development performance. As Yale's Gustav Ranis notes, we must differentiate between those elements of "non-transferability" that relate to obstacles "in nature" and those that relate to obstacles "in man." The latter obstacles can be overcome by institutional choices and the political process. Appropriate measures need not be confined to any one country. The lessons of the Asian NICs can be transferred to other countries by the creation and extension of social, economic, and political institutions and mechanisms that promote the mobilization and efficient allocation of resources and an increase in total factor productivity.

It is true, however, that the Asian NICs initially took advantage of world market opportunities from 1945–70, which was an historically unique period of high growth in

TABLE 8.8
Market Failure and State Intervention

Reasons for Market Failure

(i)   Markets may be monopolised or oligopolistic.
(ii) There may be extermalities.
(iii) There may be increasing returns to scale.
(iv) Some markets, particularly insurance and futures markets, cannot be perfect and, indeed, may not exist.
(v)   Markets may adjust slowly or imprecisely because information may move slowly or marketing institutions may be inflexible.
(vi) Individuals or enterprises may adjust slowly.
(vii) Individuals or enterprises may be badly informed about products, prices, their production possibilities, and so on.
(viii) Individuals may not act so as to maximise anything, either implicitly or explicitly.
(ix) Government taxation is unavoidable and will not, or cannot, take a form which allows efficiency.

Some Problems of State Intervention

(i)   Individuals may know more about their own preferences and circumstances than the government.
(ii) Government planning may increase risk by pointing everyone in the same direction— governments may make bigger mistakes than markets.
(iii) Government planning may be more rigid and inflexible than private decision-making since complex decision-making machinery may be involved in government.
(iv) Governments may be incapable of administering detailed plans.
(v)   Government controls may prevent private sector individual initiative if there are many bureaucratic obstacles.
(vi) Organisations and individuals require incentives to work, innovate, control costs, and allocate efficiently and the discipline and rewards of the market cannot easily be replicated within public enterprises and organisations.
(vii) Different levels and parts of government may be poorly coordinated in the absence of the equilibrating signals provided by the market, particularly where groups or regions with different interests are involved.
(viii) Markets place constraints on what can be achieved by government, for example, resale of commodities on black markets and activities in the informal sector can disrupt rationing or other non-linear pricing or taxation schemes. This is the general problem of "incentive compatibility."
(ix) Controls create resource-using activities to influence those controls through lobbying and corruption—often called rent-seeking or directly unproductive activities in the literature.
(x)   Planning may be manipulated by privileged and powerful groups which act in their own interests and further, planning creates groups with a vested interest in planning, for example, bureaucrats or industrialists who obtain protected positions.
(xi) Governments may be dominated by narrow interest groups interested in their own welfare and sometimes actively hostile to large sections of the population. Planning may intensify their power.

Source: Nicholas Stern, "The Economics of Development," *Economic Journal* (September 1989): 616.

world trade. But the growth of manufactured exports from developing countries was as high in the 1970s as it had been in the 1960s, even though the industrial economies grew only half as fast on average.[38] And when we look at the 1980s—a period of world recession in trade and slower growth in the more-developed countries—the export of manufactures still increased during those years at an annual rate of 14 percent from Korea, 15 percent from Hong Kong, and 12 percent from Singapore. What has proved so important is the supply side of the equation—that is, the ability of these countries to remain competitive in supply and thereby maintain high rates of growth in exports of manufactures despite a slowdown in the rate of growth of world trade.

Even if growth in the more-developed countries slows, exports to those markets need not then slow by as much, or even at all, because the NICs can increase their market share in the more-developed countries by underpricing producers in those countries. This is exactly what has happened. The share of manufactured goods in the developing countries' nonfuel exports increased from 10 percent in 1955 to 65 percent in 1986. The trend is not confined to the Asian NICs. Even excluding the Asian NICs, the proportion of manufactures in the developing countries' exports went up from 10 percent to 45 percent between 1955 and 1986. These goods are in competition with domestically produced manufactures. The demand for them is therefore sensitive to price. To that extent, the exporters' success depends less on the growth of demand in the more-developed countries and more on their own supply side efficiency.

Despite past experience, one might think, "Well, if many other countries follow the Asian NICs and export manufactures, won't the market be saturated?" The answer is that not all countries are going to export the same types of export products at the same time and at the same rate. It is not to be expected that additional NICs will reach the exceptionally high rates of growth in exports that the Asian NICs experienced in the earlier period. But they will still be able to export, and the market will not be saturated because we are considering manufactures and semimanufactures, not primary products. For manufactures, the products are differentiated and there is scope for horizontal specialization and greater intra-industry specialization. A niche in dynamic world markets can be found. Empirical studies show that intra-industry trade through horizontal specialization has increased and that the extent of intra-industry trade conducted by industrialized countries has grown much more rapidly with the developing countries than with other industrialized countries.

Most important, the ever-changing structure of comparative costs (as discussed in Chapter 2), allows a country to proceed up the ladder of comparative advantage—specializing in turn on resource-intensive exports, unskilled labor-intensive exports, skilled labor-intensive exports, capital-intensive exports, and finally knowledge-intensive exports. And as a given country moves up the ladder, another country in the queue is able to follow it up another rung on the ladder. Thus we have seen that as Japan rose on the ladder, the East Asian NICs became major suppliers of Japan's former exports. Now, as the East Asian NICs proceed through the higher stages of comparative advantage, there is room for other Asian nations—Thailand, Malaysia, Sri Lanka, Indonesia, and the Philippines—to take over the markets vacated by the earlier exporting countries.

Export pessimists fear, however, a protectionist backlash. But the penetration into import markets in the more-developed countries is still very low. The share of developing countries in world trade and manufactures is still only about 15 percent. About 55 percent of the manufactured exports from LDCs are from the Asian NICs; many countries, such as Mexico, Brazil, Argentina, and India, still have very low export proportions and can increase their supply. The consumption of imports of manufactured goods from LDCs in the more-developed countries is still only a little over 3 percent of their total consumption of manufactured goods. Furthermore, protectionist sentiment tends to be based more on the size of a country's trade deficit than its volume of imports. In the United States, for example, during the 1980s when protectionist sentiment became stronger, the share of imports in America's GDP remained about the same while the share of exports in America's GDP fell. It was the trade deficit—not the scale of imports in relation to the overall economy—that made protection a political issue. We should also recognize that if additional NICs are able to expand their exports to the more-developed countries they, in turn, will import more from the industrial countries.

Finally we must realize that there is considerable potential for expanding trade among the developing countries themselves. Inter-LDC trade is now under 20 percent of the exports of non-OPEC LDCs. The East Asian NICs now export only about 3 percent of their total exports to South Asia, while Asian countries export only some 4 percent to other Asian countries. There is considerable scope for more trade among the LDCs for food, fertilizers, cement, steel, and light manufactures. These exports from LDCs to other LDCs could replace imports from the more advanced countries.

As the *Economist* concludes, "The adding up problem echoes the popular prejudice that there are only so many goods to be produced in the world: if one group of countries produces them, there is nothing left for the others to do. It is the lump of production fallacy. Global production and consumption are not somehow fixed. Trade increases the output that can be squeezed from any given collection of resources, and the consumption that can be obtained from any given set of production possibilities. The parties at both ends of the transaction profit. Trade is, in short, a positive sum game."[39]

PRIVATE FOREIGN INVESTMENT IN DEVELOPING COUNTRIES

Along with export-led development, a greater potential for private foreign investment in the developing countries is now of increasing importance. This is because many developing countries desire to extend the market price system and support the private sector, to encourage privatization programs, and to mitigate the external debt crisis by attracting more private foreign investment. In Chapter 4, we discussed the determinants of foreign direct investment and saw how it has increased rapidly in recent years. FDI flows to the developing world rose from an annual average of approximately $13 billion in 1980–85 to $110 billion in 1996, accounting for nearly 40 percent of all FDI flows compared with only 12 percent in 1990. Table 8.9 indicates net FDI in recent years. As Table 8.10 summarizes, there has also been a surge in portfolio equity and debt investment since the early 1990s. As a total, private capital flows to developing countries rose by $60 billion in 1996, to $244 billion—up from $44 billion in 1990.

The ultimate decision to invest in a developing country will depend on the result of negotiations with the host government. It is common to negotiate over the terms of entry, conditions of performance, and duration of the investment. More investment projects are now the outcome of a cost-benefit analysis in negotiations between the foreign investors and host governments but as yet, a comprehensive economic analysis is only approximated to various degrees in actual negotiations. Nonetheless, it is still desirable to have an ideal model in mind when negotiating. This type of model attempts to rationalize the mixture of incentives and restrictions that host governments place on foreign investment. It also may suggest arrangements that will give a higher payoff for both investor and host country.

Typical restrictions on FDI cover: sectors of the economy from which a foreign investor is excluded; maximum percentage of foreign ownership; withholding and other taxes on profit and capital remittances; performance obligations, including minimum investment periods and/or required reinvestment of earnings; restricted access to local capital markets;

TABLE 8.9
Net Foreign Direct Investment in Developing Countries, 1990–96 (*billions of U.S. dollars*)

Country or country group	1990	1991	1992	1993	1994	1995	1996[a]
All developing countries	24.5	33.5	43.6	67.2	83.7	95.5	109.5
Sub-Saharan Africa	0.9	1.6	0.8	1.6	3.1	2.2	2.6
East Asia and the Pacific	10.2	12.7	20.9	38.1	44.1	51.8	61.1
South Asia	0.5	0.5	0.6	0.8	1.2	1.8	2.6
Europe and Central Asia	2.1	4.4	6.3	8.4	8.1	17.2	15.0
Latin America and the Caribbean	8.1	12.5	12.7	14.1	24.2	22.9	25.9
Middle East and North Africa	2.8	1.8	2.2	4.2	3.0	−0.3	2.2
Income group							
Low-income countries	4.5	7.1	13.9	32.0	39.1	41.6	49.5
Middle-income countries	20.0	26.3	29.8	35.2	44.6	53.9	60.0
Major recipient countries							
China	3.5	4.4	11.2	27.5	33.8	35.8	42.3
Mexico	2.5	4.7	4.4	4.4	11.0	7.0	6.4
Malaysia	2.3	4.0	5.2	5.0	4.3	5.8	6.2
Brazil	1.0	1.1	2.1	1.3	3.1	4.9	5.5
Indonesia	1.1	1.5	1.8	2.0	2.1	4.3	5.8
Thailand	2.4	2.0	2.1	1.8	1.4	2.1	2.9
Argentina	1.8	2.4	2.6	3.5	0.6	1.3	2.0
Hungary	0.0	1.5	1.5	2.4	1.1	4.5	1.7
Poland	0.1	0.3	0.7	1.7	1.9	3.7	4.2
Chile	0.6	0.5	0.7	0.8	1.8	1.7	2.2
Memo item							
Low-income countries excluding China	1.0	2.7	2.7	4.5	5.3	5.8	7.2

[a]Preliminary.
Source: World Bank Debtor Reporting System. World Bank, *Global Development Finance 1997*, (Washington, DC, 1997), p. 29.

discriminatory income taxes; foreign exchange restrictions; and restrictions on percentage of expatriate staff, and local content requirements.

On the other hand, there are investment incentives that can include: direct financial inducements such as tax holidays, investment allowances, locating in free export zones, labor training subsidies; and indirect economic benefits such as sheltering through protective tariffs and quotas, price floors and ceilings, and granting of foreign exchange guarantees or privileges.

The central problem now for a developing country is to devise policies that will succeed in both encouraging a greater inflow of private foreign capital and ensuring that it makes the maximum contribution feasible toward the achievement of the country's development objectives. Private investors must be aware, therefore, of the developmental objectives and the priorities of the host country and understand how their investments may contribute to the country's development strategy. The foreign investor has to be prepared to demonstrate the contribution of private foreign capital in terms beyond private profit. At the same time, the government must recognize that if risks are too high, or the return on investment is too low, FDI will be inhibited from making any contribution at all. The negotiation process should establish policies that will meet the mutual interests of private investor and host country.

Government as negotiator must go beyond political rhetoric. And foreign investor as negotiator must go beyond simply asking for the platitude of a "favorable climate." It is necessary to examine the role of private foreign capital more systematically by appraising

TABLE 8.10
Portfolio Equity and Debt Flows to Developing Countries by Region, 1989–95

Region	1989	1990	1991	1992	1993	1994	1995[a]
Equity Flows ($ millions)							
Sub-Saharan Africa	0	0	0	144	144	860	465
East Asia and the Pacific	2,623	2,268	1,049	5,102	18,107	12,613	12,230
South Asia	168	105	23	380	2,025	6,228	1,430
Europe and Central Asia	71	235	0	65	191	1,934	1,590
Latin America and the Caribbean	434	1,099	6,228	8,229	25,149	13,159	6,200
Middle East and North Africa	0	0	0	0	0	106	85
Memo							
Global[b]	76	36	253	137	2,900	1,477	—
All developing countries	3,372	3,743	7,552	14,057	45,615	34,895	22,000
Debt Flows (gross) ($ millions)							
Sub-Saharan Africa	0	0	0	724	0	1,417	1,340
East Asia and the Pacific	260	872	2,993	5,749	13,358	22,424	23,691
South Asia	530	274	200	0	556	1,078	800
Europe and Central Asia	2,116	1,646	800	7,483	13,605	7,518	8,360
Latin America and the Caribbean	960	2,673	8,730	12,587	26,536	19,465	24,409
Middle East and North Africa	164	90	0	0	0	678	1,000
All developing countries	4,030	5,555	12,723	26,543	54,054	52,580	59,600

— = not available.

[a]Preliminary

[b]Global funds that invest across emerging markets.

Source: World Bank, *World Debt Tables 1996*, pp. 101–102.

the prospective benefits and costs of private foreign direct investment. Such an appraisal may then provide a more rational basis for determining the type of policy that is most appropriate for securing the maximum contribution from FDI.

In essence, the foreign investor must convince the host government that the increase in real income resulting from the investment project is greater than the resultant increase in the income of the investor. If the value added to output by FDI is greater than the amount appropriated by the foreign investor, social returns exceed private returns. The negotiating objective of the foreign investor is to convince the host country that the benefit-cost ratio of the FDI is greater than unity and to secure the most favorable conditions for entry and operation.

To this end, the foreign investor may point to a considerable list of benefits from the investment, including the following: local value added, inflow of foreign exchange, creation of employment, infusion of skills, contribution of taxes and royalties, and the creation of external economies elsewhere in the economy beyond the investment project itself.

As long as foreign investment raises productivity, and this increase is not wholly appropriated by the investor, the greater product must be shared with others, and there must be some direct benefits to other income groups in the host country. These benefits can accrue to domestic labor in the form of higher real wages, consumers by way of lower prices, the government through higher tax revenue or royalties, and the indirect gains elsewhere in the economy through the realization of external economies.

For a developing country, the inflow of foreign capital may be significant not only in raising the productivity and real wages of a given amount of labor, but may also allow employment of a larger labor force. The international flow of capital can thus be viewed as an alternative to labor migration from the poor country: When surplus labor cannot emigrate to rich countries, the substitution of domestic migration of labor to the investment project becomes the most feasible alternative.

In order that labor and consumers might benefit from the higher productivity in foreign enterprises, the overseas withdrawal by the investors must be less than the increase in the output. But even if the entire increase in productivity accrues as foreign profits, this requirement may still be fulfilled when the government taxes foreign profits. Taxes on foreign profits or royalties from concession agreements can amount to a large proportion of total government revenue.

External economies can be especially important. Foreign direct investment brings to the developing country not only capital and foreign exchange—which help to fill both the savings gap and the foreign exchange gap—but also managerial ability, technical personnel, technological knowledge, administrative organization, and innovations in products and production techniques—all of which are in short supply in the host country. One of the greatest benefits to the recipient country is the access to foreign knowledge that private foreign investment may provide—knowledge that helps fill the managerial gap and the technological gap. This is a form of private technical assistance, and its "demonstration effects" may spread and have beneficial results in other sectors of the economy. The rate of technological advance in a poor country is highly dependent on the rate of capital inflow. New techniques accompany the inflow of private capital, and, by the example they set, foreign firms promote the diffusion of technological advance in the host country. In addition, foreign investment may lead to the training of labor in new skills, and the knowledge gained by these workers can be transmitted to other members of the labor force, or these workers might be employed later by local firms. FDI might also be beneficial in stimulating additional domestic investment. If the foreign capital is used to develop the country's infrastructure, it may directly facilitate more investment. Even if the foreign investment is in one industry, it may still encourage domestic investment by reducing costs or creating demand in other industries. Profits may then rise and lead to expansion in these other industries. A whole series of domestic investments may thus be linked to the foreign investment.

Offsetting these benefits, however, are various costs. The investor as negotiator must be aware of these costs to meet the objections of the government negotiators. Governments are likely to point to such costs as concessions that they have to offer to attract the foreign investment, adverse effects on domestic saving, discouragement of domestic entrepreneurship, problems of balance-of-payments servicing, loss of domestic economic autonomy, inappropriate technology, and negative externalities.

To encourage foreign investment, the host government may have to provide special facilities, undertake additional public services, extend financial assistance after tax concessions, or subsidize imports. These have a cost in absorbing governmental resources that could be used elsewhere.

Once foreign investment has been attracted, it should be expected to have an income effect that will lead to a higher level of domestic saving. But this effect might be offset by a redistribution of income away from domestic capital if the foreign investment competes with domestic enterprises and reduces profits in domestic industries. Foreign enterprise may also inhibit local entrepreneurship in a competitive field.

More serious than the foregoing costs are those arising from balance-of-payments adjustments. If the outflow of interest, dividends, and profits on foreign investment causes the developing country to experience a net capital outflow, the indirect costs of debt servicing then come into play. The country has to create a surplus on current account equal to the debit items on account of the payment of interest, dividends, profits, and repatriation of the foreign investment. The country then has to incur the costs of the adjustment mechanism in its balance of payments by undertaking policies such as deflation, devaluation, or direct controls on imports (recall Chapter 5).

Less visible may be the cost in loss of domestic autonomy and policy making whenever a government retreats from some policy objective or sacrifices a particular policy instrument in deference to the interests of the foreign investor. If the government would have acted differently in the absence of the foreign investment, the presence of the foreign enterprise is then of some cost to the government.

Governments may also complain that the transfer of technology is too capital intensive and does not provide sufficient employment. The advanced labor-saving technology that the foreign investor uses in his home country may be considered inappropriate in the developing country. The foreign investment may also create negative externalities such as pollution or environmental damage.

The foregoing discussion indicates in a broad way the various benefits and costs of FDI. A more rigorous analysis, however, would require application of the techniques of project appraisal. This type of analysis values the time profile of the benefits and costs and uses shadow prices (accounting prices) that correct for market price distortions by revaluing the output or input according to a measure of its social worth in terms of social objectives. The calculation of shadow prices provides more "honest prices" for wages, inputs, foreign exchange, and interest rates to reflect their true value. The analysis also allows for the nonmarket effects of externalities that are not included in the calculation of a private rate of return. Social analysis may also give welfare weights to the benefits of employment creation or a more equitable distribution of income. These corrections make social benefit-cost analysis different from the private business discounted cash flow methods of investment appraisal. "National economic profitability" differs from private financial profitability; it is the former that matters to the host country. The foreign investor should therefore be aware of how such a calculation can be made.

The following equation summarizes the calculation of net social benefit or national economic profitability from an investment project:

$$NSB = [(P_s) \cdot (O)] - [P_s \cdot \text{inputs}] + [\text{net externalities}$$
$$+ \text{ capital inflow } + \text{ return to domestic investors}$$
$$+ \text{ taxes and royalties}] - [D \text{ and } K \text{ repatriated in foreign exchange}]$$

where NSB = net social benefit
  P_s = the shadow (or accounting) price
  O = output
  D = dividends, interest, and profits
  K = capital

Considering the streams of social benefits and social costs and discounting to the present, it would be in the best interest of the host government to allow entry if the present value of the (NSB) is greater than 0 at a social discount rate. The social discount rate reflects the time preference of society: that is, the community may be willing to wait for a longer payoff period on the investment than would a private investor. Mindful of future generations, society may value saving more than current consumption. Under these conditions, the social discount rate is less than the private market rate of interest.

Regarding the issue of termination of the investment, the government would be rational to insist on fade-out or divestment when the present value of NSB becomes less than 0, or when the NSB of a substitute domestic investment becomes greater than the NSB of the foreign investment.

In short, the present value of NSB criterion says that a project should be undertaken as long as the sum of the future social returns minus social costs, discounted back to the present, is positive. The foreign investor should realize that this type of analysis may actually make the case for FDI even stronger than one based on simply private profit. When shadow prices are used and social benefits are included, the social net benefit may in some cases turn out higher than the private net benefit.

The negotiating process is also likely to focus on an entire spectrum of arrangements for securing foreign capital and scarce managerial and technical knowledge. The foreign investor may initially desire a wholly-owned subsidiary for an unlimited time duration. The host government, however, may insist that after a certain period of time any expansion be with local equity, or it may insist on a joint venture initially, or it may stipulate that the foreign investor should divest after a certain period of time.

At the other end of the spectrum, the government may attempt to unbundle the package of inputs and secure each input separately at a lower cost in the form of technical collaboration agreements, licensing, and management contracts—instead of through one foreign equity investment. The benefit: cost ratio of these contractual arrangements has to be compared with the benefits and costs of a foreign direct investment. Quasi-equity arrangements might also be considered in the form of production sharing, revenue sharing, or profit sharing.

Each of these alternative possibilities amounts to an alternative foreign investment proposal with a different production structure and concession terms. If the proposals are alternative, only the best alternative in the set will have a positive present value of NSB. In the negotiation process, the upper limit of concessions offered by the host government will lie just below the scarcity value to the host government of the services of the FDI. The lower limit to concessions will be just what is necessary to induce the FDI (net of rent, leaving only a normal return on investment).

Although countries may have nominal restrictions on the extent of foreign ownership, there is still the important issue of whether control can be exercised by the foreign investor even without majority ownership. Even with minority equity, the foreign investor may retain control, especially when the host country is short of technical and managerial expertise. Conceding management rights on paper may still mean that foreign management remains in control because it has the resources and abilities to make effective decisions. There may also be minority ownership by foreigners, but the local ownership can be so widely dispersed that the foreign owners retain managerial control. In some cases, control without majority ownership can be exercised through such devices as technical agreements and management contracts or by requiring more than a simple majority vote for decisions in certain key management areas. For the export of manufactures by multinationals from developing countries, the existence of minority ownership with technology contracts, management contracts, and marketing contracts may be just as effective indicators of the presence of close relationships between buying and selling firms and of the potentiality for foreign control as is majority ownership.[40] It is also possible that, as has happened in Indonesia, foreign firms may respond to the pressure for greater localization by increasing their debt equity ratios and by maintaining control through long-term licensing and management contracts. Moreover, if majority ownership is not possible, a foreign enterprise may issue two classes of shares (i.e., voting and no-voting) so that the parent company can maintain management control even though it holds a minority equity position.

In sum, it is necessary to distinguish between de jure and de facto control. As Edith Penrose states, "Ownership wholly or in part is not a sufficient condition to assure control of a foreign enterprise. Stated in this bald form, there will probably be few who would not agree that the mere acquisition of shares is of little economic consequence without the ability and willingness to take advantage of the powers that ownership confers. If we assume that governments acquiring ownership interests in foreign companies want to exercise some effective control (as distinct from merely receiving their share of the distributive profits), we have then to inquire into their capacity to do so. . . .

"One of the greatest sources of the power of multinational corporations lies in their knowledge, which includes technological knowledge, and knowledge of markets and finance, as well as of managerial skills. It follows that the only really effective way of reducing this power lies in the development of similar knowledge in the host country. The question then arises of whether the acquisition of equity control of foreign enterprises accelerates the acquisition of the relevant knowledge or makes possible a more effective use of the knowledge already in hand."[41]

Recognizing that control may be exercised without majority ownership, the foreign investor may find it advantageous in a negotiation to trade off reduced equity participation for increased effective control, a trade-off that may be preferable if increased equity participation (because it is highly visible) carries a greater perceived cost to the host government, but effective control does not because it is more difficult to discern, monitor, and regulate.[42] The foreign investor may find it advantageous to bargain, not for increased equity ownership, but for control over the variables critical to the success of its foreign subsidiary.

Appreciating the positive role that FDI can have in supporting development, a host government should not pursue policies of aggressive economic nationalism against foreign investment. Indeed, the ideal would be to treat domestic investment and foreign investment alike. As in nondiscriminatory trade policy, so too are gains to be realized from nondiscriminatory treatment of foreign investment.

Why then should there be any government intervention—either in screening the entry of foreign investors, specifying performance requirements, or monitoring their activities? From the perspective of economic theory, the answer is simply that intervention results because of departure from standard neo-classical competitive assumptions: The government attempts to correct the market imperfection or the market power of the foreign investor or to correct the market imperfection of externalities in production. From this standpoint one might explain the desire to establish minimum labor requirements, minimum export requirements, or minimum local content inputs.

Although our emphasis on securing net social benefit from FDI might be interpreted as implying screening institutions and monitoring procedures, we must realize that in practice these institutions and procedures are likely to be complex and time-consuming. The majority of foreign investments should be subject to national treatment without any special screening. When, however, incentives are offered to attract FDI, the investment should be subject to screening to ensure a high net social benefit and there should be monitoring to ensure performance as expected. Similarly, if FDI is being attracted into production of import substitutes because of high effective rates of protection on the import substitutes, it is necessary to screen such investments to ensure that domestic value added is not negative when valued at world prices. The existence of domestic price distortions creates the same problem and calls for shadow pricing with efficiency (economic) prices.

From the perspective of the "new political economy" that departs from the economist's usual notion of a benevolent state acting in the public interest, government intervention may, however, be influenced by the interest of local entrepreneurs, workers and unions, political parties, or government bureaucrats. For instance, insofar as manufacturing activities may provide more linkages to local interest groups, the government may direct foreign investment to manufacturing and exclude it from raw materials. Joint ventures instead of 100 percent foreign equity may also allow some interest groups to capture natural resource rents or the monopoly rents from import substitution.

The task now is to improve the quality of policy making with respect to foreign investment. National objectives should be clearly identified. Then it is necessary to ensure their consistency.

General economic conditions are most important in determining a country's attractiveness for FDI. Established property rights, transparent regulatory and legal regimes, economic stability, and political stability are of first consideration to a prospective investor. Freedom to import inputs and freedom to remit dividends and profits are also crucial. The effects of special incentives and restrictions on foreign investment are more questionable.

As liberalization in a developing country continues, so that internal prices conform more closely to world prices, there will be less need for screening: The foreign investor's calculation of financial internal rate of return will then be closer to the nation's economic rate of return that social benefit-cost analysis would yield. The removal of domestic price distortions and the reduction of trade barriers will promote not only freer trade, but also the freer movement of international capital. A continued process of liberalization is thus necessary to realize the full potential of foreign investment and allow foreign investment to complement foreign trade in accelerating a country's development.

IMPLICATIONS FOR MORE-DEVELOPED ECONOMIES

In the early development days of the 1950s and 1960s some argued against the neo-classical view of mutual gains from trade. They alleged that asymmetrical power relationships allowed the center (Western Europe, Britain, and the United States) to dominate the periphery (the newly emerging countries). The developing economies were alleged to be dependent economies that should reverse their dependency by "delinking" from the international system and adopting inward-looking policies of import substitution and restrictions on foreign investment. As we have noted, such policies actually inhibited the development process while superior development performance has been achieved by the outward-looking countries that became ever more integrated in the world economy.

Given the rapid development of the NICs, however, many now ask the opposite question: Is growth in developing countries detrimental or beneficial to developed countries?[43]

The concern is not new. Since the first industrial revolution, there has been a continual succession of NICs. In the period when continental European countries were industrializing as the late-comers after Britain, there was a commonly expressed belief that the industrialization of the late-comers would diminish Britain's trade prospects. But in fact industrialized nations have become each other's best trading customers.

Nor did the nineteenth century outflow of British capital to the regions of recent settlement diminish British home investment. The expansionary effect of the capital inflow overseas led to a greater demand for imports from Britain and stimulated the British economy. Over time, the borrowing countries became mature debtors and repaid their debts.

As in the earlier historical period, fears are now expressed that the flow of capital and transfer of technology to the developing economies will allow them to "outcompete" the more-developed countries. True, a rising share of imports in the advanced economies is coming from the LDCs. But this, in turn, must mean that a rising share of exports from the advanced economies is going to the LDCs. As production expands in the LDCs, income rises, and this implies higher expenditure—some of which is for the exports of more-developed economies. Indeed, the rapid growth in output in the East Asian NICs has been associated with a more-than-proportionate growth in imports. Developing countries purchase a quarter of industrial country exports and, on present trends, that could rise to more than a third within a decade. For the United States, more than 40 percent of its exports went to developing countries in 1995.

Moreover, lower-priced imports must raise the real income of consumers in the developed countries. As Krugman emphasizes, "When world productivity rises (as it does when Third World countries converge on First World productivity), *average* world living standards must rise: after all, the extra output must go somewhere. This by itself presumes that higher Third World productivity will be reflected in higher Third World wages, not lower First World incomes. Another way to look at it is to notice that in a national economy, producers and consumers are the same people; foreign competitors who cut prices may lower the wage I receive, but they also raise the purchasing power of whatever I earn. There is no reason to expect the adverse effect to predominate."[44]

As we discussed in Chapter 3 (pp. 71–74), the decline in the wages of unskilled workers in the United States (and the unemployment rates in Europe) can not be attributed in any large degree to imports from the LDCs. The evidence points to other causes—particularly, technical progress. At a symposium held by the Federal Reserve Bank of New York, the consensus among both labor and trade economists was that for the United States only about 10 percent of the relative reduction in wages of low-skilled workers could be attributed to foreign trade; the remainder was due to technical change (60 percent) and other factors (30 percent), such as immigration and wage-setting practices.[45]

In general, technical change within a country causes much more dislocation than do imports. In Schumpeter's words, innovations and technical progress lead to "creative destruction." The new industry outcompetes the old. Similarly, senile or lower-productivity industries in the more developed countries lose their markets to imports. Just as technical change in the domestic economy should not be inhibited, neither should the workings of dynamic comparative advantage in the world economy. In neither case should the benefits of economic change be sacrificed for the sake of avoiding the cost of dislocation.

Further, the cost of dislocation in job displacement as a result of imports is often exaggerated. Not only is the number of those directly displaced lower, but in a general equilibrium analysis that allows for indirect consequences there may actually be an increase in employment. This may happen when the importation of lower-priced intermediate inputs allows an expansion of the final output with greater employment in the final stages of production. An increase in consumers' real income as a result of lower-priced imports may also increase demand for other products and expand employment in the other industries.

The flow of capital from the more-developed to the less-developed countries should also be of benefit to the investors from the advanced countries. Foreign direct investment is based on higher expected returns. Much of direct investment is also associated with intracompany trade. Any discouragement to domestic investment in the source country is likely to be small, given the low ratio of foreign direct investment to domestic investment in the more-developed countries. Portfolio investment in the emerging markets is also of benefit by allowing diversification of risk for the investors.

IMPLICATIONS FOR DIAGNOSIS, PREDICTION, AND RESPONSE (DPR)

In practicing DPR in the changing global economy, management must be aware of the growing importance of the developing economies and the continually new international division of labor. The process of national economic development in the context of the global economy has major implications for companies. Companies in all countries will be affected by the future of the developing countries in Asia, Africa, Middle East, the Caribbean, and Latin America. It is therefore important to monitor the rate and pattern of development in these countries. In monitoring their development, management should focus on the key performance indicators as related to the relaxation of the four major constraints of the savings gap, foreign exchange gap, agriculture, and human resources. To anticipate movement in these key performance indicators, it is essential to monitor whether national economic management is based on appropriate policies. For this will determine whether the government undertakes stable demand management, strengthens the market price system, promotes an export-led strategy of development, and invests in human capital—the priority policy objectives.

The rate and pattern of development will clearly be important for the operation of any business within a developing country. Promotion of private enterprise in a developing economy is intimately related to the operation of a private market price system and market-oriented policies. The private market price system has the merit of contributing to efficient resource allocation and providing incentives for economic growth. The market mechanism is also an effective administrative instrument that can be used to achieve policy objectives while avoiding the inefficiency, rent-seeking, illegal parallel markets, bureaucratic exploitation, and corruption that result from direct quantitative controls such as quotas and licensing. When participants in the market are private enterprises, undistorted prices play the important roles of providing information, allocating resources, rationing scarce resources, mobilizing additional resources, and distributing income. All these are important in allowing private enterprise to contribute to a country's development by responding with total efficiency to the market signals of a price system. In many developing countries, a greater role for private enterprise will depend on the government undertaking market-friendly policy reforms: introducing and extending market institutions, privatizing state-owned enterprises, providing physical infrastructure, protecting property rights and the legal rules of contract, and investing in people. Such supportive market institutions and the extensions of the private market price system can provide incentives to private enterprise while reducing those types of government intervention that in themselves create nonmarket failure.

The central issue thus becomes how to achieve these liberalizing measures of policy reform that will support private enterprise—both domestic and foreign—in the interests of accelerated development. Business should not opt for laissez faire but for the government undertaking appropriate policies in conformity with market opportunities. The need is for mechanisms to overcome political obstacles to policy reform and to avoid nonmarket failure in the future.

The pace and pattern of development in the LDCs will also have significant external effects. The volume and composition of their exports will change. Their markets for the importation of goods and services from the more-developed countries will grow and evolve in composition. The developing countries will also become ever more important users of capital. In the immediate future the debt overhang in several poor countries will remain a major problem. The capacity to deal with the debt problem will depend on the government's capacity to reduce the internal fiscal deficit. Moreover, any shortage of capital on a global basis will remain a handicap for accelerated development. The long-run potential for private foreign investment in the developing world is, however, high. And much of this investment will be associated with the international transfer of technology.

As they reach economic maturity, the four dragons among the Asian NICs cannot be expected to maintain the remarkably high rates of growth that they enjoyed previously. Problems typical of a more mature economy—such as those of troublesome industrial relations, rising real wages, and rising consumption—are already being experienced.

The next tier of NICs, however, will emerge as more countries switch from import substitution to export promotion and adopt more appropriate policies of stabilization and liberalization. We may expect that the next tier of NICs in Asia will comprise Thailand, Malaysia, Sri Lanka, the Philippines, China, and Indonesia. To these countries will also come a greater inflow of private foreign investment from Japan, Korea, and Taiwan. In Africa, the next tier of NICs may comprise Kenya, Maritius, Botswana, and Senegal; in Latin America, Chile, Colombia, Costa Rica, Venezuela, Brazil, and Mexico.

As more of the developing countries look outward and forward to meet the challenge of development, the challenge to management will, in turn, intensify—within the LDCs and in the more-developed countries alike. The challenge to management will be to diagnose, anticipate, and respond to how the LDCs are overcoming their four major constraints (savings, foreign exchange, agriculture, human resources) with appropriate policies in the four priority policy areas of macro stabilization, marketization, human resource development, and integration into the global economy.

NOTES

1. World Bank, *World Development Report 1991* (New York: Oxford University Press, 1991), p. 1. Per capita real income is taken as the index of economic development, but it is also highly

correlated with life expectancy, infant mortality, nutrition, literacy, and other nonmonetary indicators that represent a physical quality of life index.

2. World Bank, *World Development Report 1996* (New York: Oxford University Press, 1996), Table 1.

3. United Nations Development Programme, *Human Development Report 1996* (New York: Oxford University Press, 1996), p. 11.

4. Ibid., p. 2.

5. Ibid., p. 13.

6. James E. Austin, *Strategic Management in Developing Countries* (New York: Free Press, 1990), Ch. 1.

7. Peter L. Berger, "Asian Capitalism and the Future," *Speaking of Japan* (February 1989), p. 10.

8. These policies are emphasized in the World Bank, *World Development Report 1991*, especially Ch. 8.

9. Contrary to the standard story of export-led growth, Dani Rodrik maintains that the economic take-off in South Korea and Taiwan was due more to an increase in private investment than to exports. Also, there were distinctively favorable initial conditions—the relative abundance of human capital and equitable income and wealth distribution—that made the return to capital accumulation high. For Rodrik's full argument, see "Getting Interventions Right: How South Korea and Taiwan Grew Rich," *Economic Policy* (April 1995): 55–107.

10. Alwyn Young, "The Tyranny of Numbers: Confronting the Statistical Realities of the East Asian Growth Experience," *Quarterly Journal of Economics* (August 1995): 641–680, with bibliography of other studies; Jong-Il Kim and Lawrence J. Lau, "The Sources of Economic Growth of the East Asian Newly Industrialized Countries," *Journal of the Japanese and International Economies* 8 (1994): 235–271.

11. J. M. Clark, *Economics of Overhead Costs* (Chicago: University of Chicago Press, 1923), p. 120.

12. Theodore W. Schultz, "Nobel Lecture: The Economics of Being Poor," *Journal of Political Economy* (August 1980): 640.

13. Richard Easterlin, "Why Isn't the Whole World Developed?" *Journal of Economic History* (March 1981): 1–17.

14. Nancy Birdsall, et al., "Inequality and Growth Reconsidered: Lessons from East Asia," *World Bank Economic Review* (September 1995).

15. Ian M. D. Little, "An Economic Reconnaissance," in Walter Galenson, ed., *Economic Growth and Structural Change in Taiwan* (Ithaca, NY: Cornell University Press, 1979).

16. World Bank, *World Development Report 1991*, p. 5.

17. Ibid., pp. 7–8.

18. For a good review of financial experience, see World Bank, *World Development Report 1989* (New York: Oxford University Press, 1989).

19. Recent experience with stabilization programs and financial liberalization have been reviewed by Rudiger Dornbusch, "Stabilization Policies in Developing Countries: What Have We Learned?" *World Development* (September 1982); Vittorio Corbo and Jaime de Melo, eds., "Liberalization with Stabilization in the Southern Cone of Latin America," *World Development Special Issue* (August 1985).

20. On problems of management and control, see World Bank, *World Development Report 1983*, (New York: Oxford University Press, 1983), Ch. 8. Also Steve H. Hanke, *Privatization and Development* (San Francisco: ICS Press, 1987).

21. Alice H. Amsden, "The Division of Labor Is Limited by the Rate of Growth of the Market: The Taiwan Machine Tool Industry in the 1970s," *Cambridge Journal of Economics* 9 (1985): 271–284.

22. Gustav Ranis and T. Paul Schultz, eds., *The State of Development Economics* (Oxford: Basil Blackwell, 1988), p. 142.

23. For an elaboration of why governments do what they do, see Gerald M. Meier, ed., *The Politics of Development Policymaking: Perspectives from the New Political Economy* (San Francisco: ICS Press, 1991).

24. Jagdish N. Bhagwati, "Export Promoting Trade Strategy: Issues and Evidence," *World Bank Research Observer* 3, 1, p. 41.

25. World Bank, *The East Asian Miracle: Economic Growth and Public Policy* (New York: Oxford University Press, 1993).

26. Robert H. Wade, *Governing the Market: Economic Theory and the Role of Government in East Asian Industrialization* (Princeton, NJ: Princeton University Press, 1990).

27. World Bank, *East Asian Miracle*, p. 354.

28. Robert Wade, "Industrial Policy in East Asia: Does It Lead or Follow the Market?" in Gary Gereffi and Donald L. Wyman, eds., *Manufacturing Miracles* (Princeton, NJ: Princeton University Press, 1990), Ch. 9.

29. Sanjaya Lall, "The East Asian Miracle: Does the Bell Toll for Industrial Strategy?" *World Development* 22, 4 (1994): 651.

30. Dani Rodrik, "Getting Interventions Right," *Economic Policy* (April 1995), p. 78.

31. Peter G. Warr, "Comparative and Competitive Advantage," *Asian-Pacific Economic Literature* 8, 2 (November 1994): 10.

32. Larry E. Westphal, "Industrial Policy in an Export-Propelled Economy: Lessons from South Korea's Experience," *Journal of Economic Perspectives* 4, 3 (summer 1990): 57.

33. This is done by Michael Porter, *The Competitive Advantage of Nations* (New York: Free Press, 1990).

34. Warr, "Comparative and Competitive Advantage," op cit., p. 11. For a formal analysis of the rigorous conditions under which the promotion of specific industries is justified, see Gene M. Grossman, "Promoting New Industrial Activities," *OECD Economic Studies*, No. 14 (spring 1990): 89–119.

35. Masahiko Aoki, "Toward a Comparative Institutional Analysis," *Japanese Economic Review* (1996).

36. Thomas Hellman, et al., "Financial Restraint," Stanford Graduate School of Business, Research Paper Series, April 30, 1995, pp. 2–3.

37. Dwight H. Perkins, *Reforming Economic Systems in Developing Countries* (1), p. 45.

38. Clive Crook, "The Third World," *Economist* (September 23, 1989): 33.

39. Ibid., p. 34.

40. Gerald K. Helleiner, "Direct Foreign Investment and Manufacturing for Export in Developing Countries: A Review of the Issues," in *Policies for Development: Essays in Honor of Gamini Corea,* ed. (Cambridge, MA, Harvard Institute of International Development, 1991).

41. Edith Penrose, "Ownership and Control: Multinational Firms in Less Developed Countries," in G. K. Helleiner, ed., *A World Divided* (Cambridge: Cambridge University Press, 1976), p. 154.

42. Donald J. Lecraw, "Bargaining Power, Ownership, and Profitability of Transnational Corporations in Developing Countries," *Journal of International Business Studies* (spring–summer 1984): 41.

43. Richard Cooper, "Is Growth in Developing Countries Beneficial to Developed Countries?" in World Bank, *Annual Conference on Development Economics*, 1995; Paul Krugman, "Does Third World Growth Hurt First World Prosperity?" *Harvard Business Review* (July–August, 1994): 113–121.

44. Krugman, op cit., p. 114.

45. Federal Reserve Bank of New York, "Colloquium on U.S. Wage Trends," *Economic Policy Review* (January 1995).

DISCUSSION QUESTIONS

1. Why are poor countries poor?

2. What determines an increase in total factor productivity?

3. What type of trade strategy would you advocate for a country that wants to accelerate its development?

4. What type of industrial policy, if any, would you advocate to accelerate a country's development?

5. What policies would you advocate to absorb surplus labor in productive employment?

6. Do you think that foreign direct investment in a developing country should be subjected to a screening process? If so, what kind?

7. How would you determine whether a developing country is able to service its external debt?

8. How could economic growth in the less-developed countries be detrimental to the more-developed countries? Do you believe that it has been?

9. Of what benefit, if any, is it to the more-developed countries to invest in less-developed countries and transfer technology to them?

10. Do you think there is a trade-off between faster economic growth and a more equitable distribution of income?

11. The "reform of the state" in a developing economy means different things to different policy makers. What do you think it should mean?

Chapter

9 TRANSITION ECONOMIES

O f all the countries in the world, those in Central and Eastern Europe (CEE), the Commonwealth of Independent States of the former Soviet Union (CIS), and China are likely to experience the greatest changes in the near future. With the breakdown of centralized economic planning, these countries are in a widespread process of restructuring as they attempt to marketize their economies. The repercussions of their transforming efforts will extend far beyond their borders as their measures of reform affect international trade and international capital movements.

These efforts, however, are still subject to great uncertainty. For politics still dominate economics. More than in the other countries we have considered, economic reform remains dependent on political reform. Market institutions and the market price system are still so rudimentary and fragile that they can be readily politicized. The process of economic reform must cover years and decades. Applied to these economies in transition, the practice of ICA and DPR must therefore be heavily grounded in country risk analysis.

Although political and economic conditions are extremely fluid, we may ask what are the prospects for solving the problems involved in transforming a socialist or communist planned economy into a market price system. Problems of transformation extend beyond those of devising market-friendly policies (as in the policy reform experience of the developing countries). At a more fundamental level, they entail the creation or reform of institutions—economic, social, and political—and organizational change. How successful has the transformation process been in different economies? What major problems remain to be solved if controls are to be replaced by individual incentives and the private sector is to perform efficiently? And what are the implications for a DPR strategy by domestic and foreign firms? This chapter tackles these complex questions.

THE BREAK FROM PLANNING

Despite its ideology and visionary theory, central planning has failed in practice. The adverse effects have been pervasive and are widely recognized. At the macro level, the government deficit in Eastern European countries became an extraordinarily high percentage of GNP, resulting in inflation or suppressed hyperinflation. A breakdown of distribution and transportation characterized what might be termed a "shortageflation." Grey and black markets abounded. A large ruble overhang confronted empty shop shelves in the republics of the former Soviet Union. In Poland and Hungary, the external debt became excessive.

National economic management was impotent. In allocating resources, micro management by the government proved highly inefficient. Decisions were overly centralized, subject to bureaucratic politics, and characterized by excessive quantitative controls. Most enterprises were state owned and subject to continual financial crises that have been covered over by a "soft budget" that bails out the inefficient firms. Technological progress has been extremely limited, and much of the productive technology is internationally noncompetitive. So too has the quality of output suffered. The performance of the industrial sector has been woefully inadequate; production of consumer goods has been neglected in quantity and quality; and agricultural output has lagged badly. Many industrial sectors were protected through trade restrictions and subsidized by very low energy prices. At world prices, however, the value of their output was negative. Moreover, the export sector has been noncompetitive: The benefits of international trade have been missed, and hard currency is sorely needed.

The inefficiencies of planning, low and declining rates of economic growth, a falling return on investment, worsening of living standards—all these weaknesses made countries in CEE and NIS turn to reforms in the 1990s. China introduced some initial rural reforms as early as 1978.

POLICY LESSONS OF THE SOUTH FOR THE EAST AND CHINA

The situation in countries that now seek some market solutions to their problems is analogous to the crisis in planning faced by less-developed countries in the 1970s and 1980s. In the South, many of these countries also suffered from an overdeveloped state in an underdeveloped economy, as they now do in the East. Recognizing the weaknesses in planning, a number of developing countries turned to policy reform. What is the relevance of their policy lessons for the emerging market economies of Central and Eastern Europe and China?

If the transition economies are to realize a self-sustaining increase in real income per head, they must be reorganized to achieve a relaxation of the four basic constraints on a country's development: inadequate savings, shortage of foreign exchange, agricultural bottlenecks, and the inadequacy of human resources as economic agents. (For an elaboration of these constraints, see Chapter 8.)

The experience of government failure in many developing countries should also serve as a warning to those now offering economic advice to governments in the transition economies. Only too often such advice is predicated on the assumption that governments want to promote the "public interest" or at least to approximate it by achieving efficiency in the allocation of resources through a well-functioning market price system. But experience shows that normally government policy makers are more concerned with the distribution of income—who gets what—rather than efficiency in resource allocation; or are concerned with meeting the demands of lobbying constituencies whose support is necessary for the government's staying in power, or are concerned with the wishes of bureaucrats, or with state interests such as maximizing revenue or power. In following these political objectives, policy makers frequently violate economic rationality. An adviser must recognize these political economy problems and seek to avoid government failure.

Guided primarily by international leverage through the IMF and World Bank, a number of developing countries have undertaken policy reforms. The transition economies now need similar policy reforms. Their transformation is, however, more difficult. Obstacles and handicaps abound because of the reaction from hard-liners, entrenched ministries, and the bureaucracy. Economic policy is politicized. Market institutions are not developed, and a socialist or communist ideology of the past still mistrusts capitalism, private property, and a market price system. There is also fear of the political-social costs of fast liberalization: unemployment, inflation, and inequality. Whether people will tolerate the hardships remains to be seen.

REPLACING STATE WITH MARKET

Nonetheless, despite these obstacles, many within and outside the transition economies are seeking ways to introduce market institutions and strengthen the market price system for directing and coordinating economic activities.

A natural first step is to try and add some elements of capitalism to the pre-existing socialist system. Yugoslavia, Poland, and Hungary have gone through such a phase of market socialism. The USSR also made the attempt with perestroika, but stalled until the aborted coup of 1991. The rationale of market socialism is that while state firms should remain in state ownership, appropriate conditions should be created to make these firms act *as if* they were part of a market. In this sense, market socialism equals state property plus market coordination.[1] This idea has failed, however, in Yugoslavia, Hungary, China, Poland, and now in Russia.

As the Hungarian economist Janos Kornai observes, market socialism has simply been classical socialism falling apart. It has not resulted in a coherent and robust system to replace classical socialism. It is a political monopoly with overcentralization in decision making and state-owned enterprises. It has been impossible to establish a contract between the state and firms. Business has been politicized. And the government does not act in terms of the public interest but instead seeks to maintain political power or military power or economic growth. Property rights are insufficient for decentralized decision making. Bureaucratic interventions prevent market coordination.

Moreover, the mixture does not allow true discipline to be exercised by market forces. Instead, a soft budget supports the bailout of state-owned enterprises whenever they make losses. "Tiny isles of the private sector are surrounded by an ocean of state-owned firms,"[2] subject to bureaucratic regulation rather than market coordination. The holding of wages in line with productivity is also lost, and cost discipline is not established. Further, without truly free markets, the experiments with market socialism have not allowed free entry and exit of firms: monopolization—not competition—has characterized industrial structure.

Against the background of these failures of classical state socialism and market socialism, the attempt now is to introduce a more robust and more extensive market price system. How to make the transition is the subject of numerous studies. Recognizing that market socialism will inevitably fail in practice, Kornai advocates nothing less than a nonviolent revolutionary transformation of the whole political and economic system away from the socialist system to a decentralized free-market system. On the need for private ownership, Kornai states, "It is my firm conviction that history is not like a film reel that can be stopped at any moment, or run on fast forward, or backward at will. Socialist state ownership means the complete, 100%, impersonalization of property. We cannot simply reverse this process in an attempt to reduce the percentage gradually to 95%, 90%, 85% and so on. The reel must be fully rewound and played from the beginning. . . . The first engines of capitalist development in all countries are individual entrepreneurs . . . I consider it desirable to increase the proportion of the private sector as fast as possible to a point where this sector counts for the larger part of the country's gross domestic product."[3]

Beyond the shift in property relations toward privatization, Kornai also advocates a package of measures needed for stabilization, liberalization, macroadjustment, and the strengthening of political support for these changes. All these reform measures are intertwined; none can be accomplished without implementing the others. The need for a comprehensive set of measures to be undertaken together makes the desired transformation process extremely difficult to implement.

Numerous proposals have been made for the reform of the former Soviet Union. Like Kornai, a committee of American economists, including five former presidential advisers, issued a report on the Soviet economy that excluded the possibility of a "third way" between socialism and capitalism. Price decontrol and fiscal restraint are advocated. Beyond that, new institutions and attitudes are required for effective competition. State-owned enterprises must give way to private enterprise. A banking system needs to be established to ration credit according to economic criteria, not political favoritism. Convertibility of the ruble is recommended to open the economy to foreign competition. During a difficult transition period, a safety net must be provided for the very poor and unemployed that meets standards of fairness without discouraging productive work or enterprise.

Another joint study by the IMF, World Bank, Organization for Economic Cooperation and Development, and the European Bank for Reconstruction and Development also advocates a "radical" reform strategy for the former Soviet Union. The study points out that early and comprehensive price decontrol is "essential to ending both the shortages and the macroeconomic imbalances that increasingly afflict the economy."[4] It argues that market clearing prices are necessary to eliminate the economic disruption resulting from hoarding, barter, the black market, dollarization, and restrictions on the free internal movement of goods. A robust private sector also requires an equally robust financial sector. Private commercial banks are essential, and specialized state banks need to be converted into universal joint stock enterprises. Increasing competitiveness among enterprises is necessary to stop the diminishing return from large-scale investment, the excessive use of raw materials and energy, low-labor productivity, and overstaffing. The study also advocates shifting from a system of centrally administered foreign trade to one in which exports and imports are market determined. It urges a shift to world market prices for future transactions.

Recognizing that the transformation of a formerly planned economy is bound to be extraordinarily complex and will take many years to complete, the major thrust of the report is to advocate action in three closely related areas at the outset of the process: (i) macro-economic stabilization, including fiscal, monetary, trade and payments, and incomes policy; (ii) price reform in an environment of increased domestic and external competition; and (iii) ownership reform, involving the rapid privatization of retail trade and small enterprises, along with the commercialization of large, state-owned enterprises. Rejecting the conservative, or gradualist, approach to economic reform as being insufficiently comprehensive and without staying power, the report advocates a more radical approach that would begin with a strong macroeconomic stabilization program, designed to reduce the budget deficit rapidly to or below the level of 2 percent to 3 percent of GDP, accompanied by immediate decontrol of most prices and the start of privatization of small-scale enterprises.

As in the reports of many policy advisers, this chapter concentrates on liberalization, stabilization, privatization, financial systems, and integration into the world economy.

LIBERALIZATION

The central focus of the transformation process is on liberalization. This involves a series of measures. Price distortions have to be removed. Prices have to be freed to move toward market levels. Competition has to determine prices for both domestic and external transactions. To bring foreign trade prices closer to world market prices, export controls and taxes must be eliminated, and import quotas and high tariffs have to be replaced by low to moderate import duties.

Beyond the freeing of prices, liberalization also means that market transactions should replace state orders and procurement, state production and trading monopolies, and the centralized allocation of foreign exchange. Freedom of entry for new firms is essential.

The advantages of a decentralized market price system are well-known. Especially important are the provision of individual incentives, information, and depoliticized prices that can guide the allocation of resources more efficiently, raise productivity, and stimulate a higher rate of growth. Prices that are market determined, instead of controlled, reflect the true value of inputs and output, and determine the pattern of production according to the true scarcity or abundance of what is being priced. The liberalization of prices leads not only to a more efficient use of resources: It can also help mobilize resources if inflation is avoided, especially saving and investment because of the greater capacity to save out of a higher income and the inducement to save by a higher real rate of interest. Price and trade liberalization also stimulates industrial restructuring—changes in output and employment at the firm level, entry of new firms, innovations, and shifts of output among industrial subsectors.

At the start of the transition period, government must decide whether the liberalization process should be rapid—a "big bang"—or gradual. The case for undertaking as many reforms as possible as rapidly as possible is that this will minimize the costs of the transition period, achieve the benefits sooner, and prevent backsliding. In contrast, the gradual approach is meant to be more cautious, building on the success of partial reforms, acquiring credibility, and establishing the basis for the more difficult institutional changes.

Poland adopted the "big bang" approach. Within six months in 1990, the government eliminated most subsidies and price controls, both to cut the state budget deficit and to set prices at scarcity values linked to world market levels. State trading monopolies were abolished, and most trade barriers eliminated. The currency rate was sharply devalued, unified, and made convertible for current transactions.

Growth has been rapid—as much as 7 percent in 1995. But the "shock therapy" has also brought insecurity to farmers, pensioners, bureaucrats, and other state employees.

Despite the rapid reforms in Poland, Jeffrey Sachs cautioned that "While a 'big jump' may indeed be possible in initiating reform, the results will necessarily be gradual."[5] Sachs recognizes that the ultimate test of the government and its economic policies will hinge on institutional change—mainly the privatization of much of state industry and the reallocation of the workforce and capital within the economy. "The long run promise of Poland will certainly remain unfulfilled . . . if political barriers impede the transformation process. The most immediate risk is that economists and policymakers, misled by faulty data or spurred by populous politics, might attempt to arrest the recession through a renewal of inflationary policies. . . . The second risk is a paralyzing debate over privatization.

"The third risk is a descent into protectionism, if coalitions of workers, managers, and bureaucrats tied to declining sectors wage a successful lobbying battle to preserve their jobs in the face of adverse market forces. . . . Poland and the rest of Eastern Europe, with their legacy of powerful state enterprises, bureaucratic entrenchment, and monopolistic industrial organization, may be especially prone to this tragic denouement unless political leaders act bravely and decisively to fend off protectionist pressures."[6]

Figure 9.1 indicates the progress of liberalization by country. Figure 9.2 shows the growth in the private sector.

In contrast to a "big bang," China has adopted a gradual approach. Initial reforms in 1978 were in the rural economy where the household responsibility system decollectivized agriculture: Traditional agricultural communes were broken up into small farm leases. Agricultural producer prices were raised, and rural communities were permitted to keep the bulk of their income as savings and invest them in nonagricultural activities. Beginning in 1984, the government relaxed restrictions on "nonstate" industrial firms—those owned by local governments and collectives—and allowed new entry into a variety of businesses. New small size township and village enterprises (TVEs) were permitted to operate on market principles outside official price and output controls that still controlled the heavy industry state sector.

TVEs became the main engine of Chinese growth. A TVE is a communal industrial enterprise located in a township or a village and is owned by the local residents. These producer cooperatives have grown rapidly (from fewer than 800 in 1980 to over 7,000 in 1990) and have proved to be more efficient than the state sector. Compared with state-owned enterprises, TVEs do not rely on government for any financing and have to face a hard budget constraint. Nonetheless, the state sector has shrunk, particularly in those industries where they faced competition from the TVEs. By 1994, the percentage of industrial output produced by state enterprises was down to 34 percent while the share from TVEs was over 40 percent (up from only 10 percent in 1980).[7]

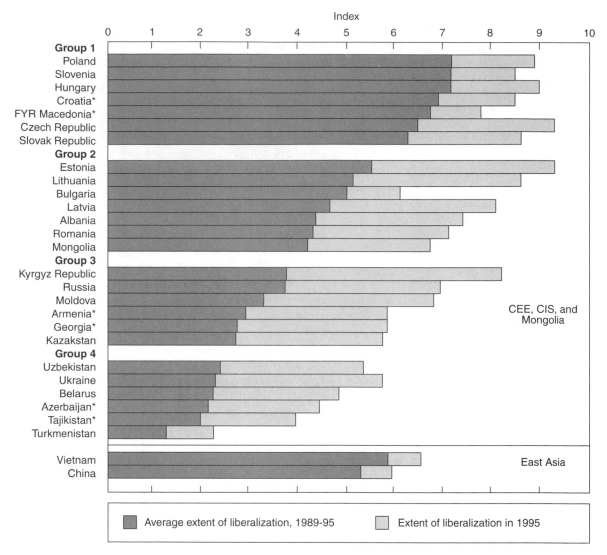

Figure 9.1   Economic Liberalization by Country. Note: Bars indicate the extent to which policies supporting liberalized markets and entry of new firms prevailed in 1995 and on average over 1989–95. Asterisks indicate economies severely affected by regional tensions between 1989 and 1995. The index is a weighted average of estimates of liberalization of domestic transactions (price liberalization and abolition of state trading monopolies), external transactions (elimination of export controls and taxes, substitution of low to moderate import duties for import quotas and high tariffs, current account convertibility), and entry of new firms (privatization and private sector, or nonstate, development). The weights on these components are 0.3, 0.3, and 0.4, respectively. *Source*: World Bank, *World Development Report 1996*, p. 14.

Foreign trade was also gradually liberalized with the establishment of special economic zones outside the control of state trading monopolies. Subsequently reforms have spread slowly to the urban economy, and institutional reforms have begun while the role of the central plan has been reduced. Political power and control have been diffused toward

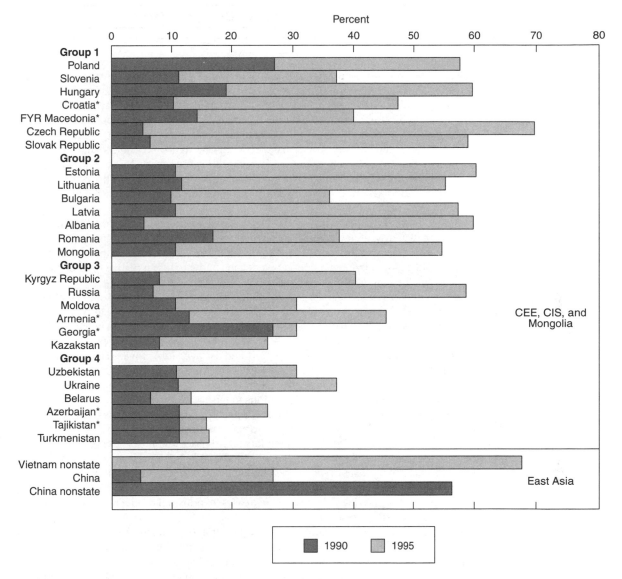

Figure 9.2 Private Sector Output as a Share of GDP. Note: Firms are considered private if less than 50 percent state owned. For China, the nonstate sector includes collectives and TVEs as well as private firms; agriculture is considered private in 1995, although land is held through long-term leases. Asterisks indicate economies severely affected by regional tensions between 1989 and 1995. *Source*: World Bank, *World Development Report 1996*, p. 15.

a regionally based system with local planning. By the early 1990s, the distinction between the special economic zones and the rest of the economy had diminished, all enterprises had more equal access to foreign trade, and the economy was more open to world markets.

China's gradualism has involved a dual-track approach: One track has been the "plan track" that maintained traditional institutions and practices of a command economy; and a

MARKET-ORIENTED REFORMS IN CHINA

Five elements are needed to make a market work well, and these five categories also describe the concrete steps that a Soviet-type command economy must take if it is to evolve into a functioning market economy. The five steps are: (1) achieve macro stability, meaning an acceptable level of inflation and a balance of payments not in serious disequilibrium; (2) make inputs and outputs available for purchase and sale on the market, rather than allocated administratively through a state bureaucracy; (3) free up prices to reflect relative scarcities in the economy; (4) remove barriers to market entry so that competition between firms in different localities becomes possible; (5) change key elements of the institutional framework so that decision-makers in the production unit (farms and industrial or service enterprises) have an incentive to maximize profits by cutting their costs or raising sales.

For Chinese agriculture, achieving the first four elements of a market economy was not particularly difficult. Macro instability was not a problem and there were no effective barriers to entry in farm production. Making goods available on the market was accomplished gradually over a period of a decade and a half, but many goods become available on the market almost immediately. . . .

The "household responsibility system" that resulted from decollectivization embodied some elements of the property rights required to generate market-oriented incentives for farm households, and went a long way toward meeting the fifth profit maximization criterion of a functioning market economy. Households are natural profit maximizers (subject to the usual caveats about uncertainly and risk aversion) provided that they have the right to keep the income that is earned. This objective was achieved by dividing up the commune land and allocating it to individual households who kept all income from that land after meeting certain tax obligations to the government. . . .

The task of reforming state-owned and private industrial enterprises is not fully analogous to creating market conditions from farm households and small shops. Not only do industrial enterprises have much larger and more complex internal structures, these enterprises are embedded in external institutions, a banking system, a tax system and much else, that are a product of the old command economy. Reforming all of these institutions together is a complex task, but failure to do so carries with it the danger that partial reforms may not lead to sustained increases in industrial productivity, the central goal of the industrial reform effort.

China began a systematic effort to reform industrial enterprises in 1984. In terms of the five components needed for a functioning market system, the first, macroeconomic stability, was not a problem in 1984. As for components 2 and 3, China made large quantities of industrial inputs available on the market rather than through the administrative allocation system of the government. Inputs (and outputs) allocated by the state were sold at fixed state-set prices, but inputs distributed through the market were sold at much higher market-determined prices. This dual price system soon provided many with the opportunity to earn easy profits and the resulting corruption contributed to urban discontent in 1989. But the dual price system did mean that market-determined prices governed a large share of enterprise allocation decisions. Component 4, opening up the system to competition, was achieved by abolishing the regional monopolies that until then had determined where almost all industrial enterprises, including small ones, could sell their products. . . .

As for component 5, the enterprise's objective function was changed to emphasize profits rather than gross value output and a myriad of other plan targets. Selling off large state enterprises to private investors was ruled out in both the 1980s and early 1990s, largely on the ideological and political ground that such a move would not be consistent with socialism. The 1988 constitution did include a formal statement allowing private property, and foreign joint ventures and small-scale firms can be private. There was much discussion and numerous experiments with a responsibility system for enterprises which, among other things, was supposed to increase enterprise autonomy vis-à-vis the government ministries. In November 1993, the Central Committee of the Party issued a directive that spelled out terms for moving state enterprises even further toward complete autonomy from the central government, at least on paper.

Dwight Perkins, "Completing China's Move to the Market," *Journal of Economic Perspectives* (spring 1994): 27–28, 35–36

second "market track" with progressive liberalization at the margin outside state controls. The case for the "dual-track" approach over the "big bang" approach was mainly the avoidance of large and sudden distributional changes and the minimization of political opposition to reforms. A "two-tier" price system for urban consumer goods maintained pre-reform prices within the limits of pre-reform rationed quantities while allowing purchases beyond these quantities at free market prices. The role of official prices declined after the dual price system was introduced in the early 1980s. Now official prices for most products have been merged with market prices and dual prices have disappeared.

Unlike reformers in Eastern Europe and Russia, however, the Chinese government had no deliberate intention of creating a full market system. As a leading analyst of China observes, "It was as much by luck as by design, therefore, that China stumbled on a strategy that has proved remarkably successful in moving the economy from a Soviet-style command system to what by the early 1990s was an economy governed in large part by market forces, however distorted some of those market forces may have been. That the economic reforms initiated in December 1978 and continuing thereafter have been successful cannot be seriously doubted."[8]

Many economists attribute the success of China's economic reforms to the practice of gradualism, the instituting of competition across regions, the growth of the nonstate sector, and to the experimental and bottom-up approach. Especially significant are the new forms of corporate entities—cooperatives and particularly TVEs—alongside state-owned firms that have become more regionally (locally) controlled.[9]

Compared with the Former Soviet Union, the initial conditions in China made reform less costly. This was because there was a lower share of negative–value-added industry and military output to start with, and the agricultural sector was originally taxed and had a clear surplus of labor. Price liberalization and the opening to foreign trade in China then shifted resources out of agriculture into light industry, industrial exports, and services without involving a sharp decline of an important share of output—namely, the negative value sector of industry—that occurred in Russia.

According to differences in their history, initial economic and social conditions, and politics, countries are following different paths of liberalization. Figure 9.1 summarizes their

---

CHINA AND OTHER TRANSITION ECONOMIES

The Chinese example refutes some of the more simplistic versions of the now familiar argument that the best transition is always the fastest. There are, however, important ways in which China's experience and circumstances differ from those in other transition economies. We highlight five.

1. China has been politically and economically stable. Notwithstanding changes in leadership since 1978, the basic approach to reforms has been remarkably consistent.

2. China's prereform economy differed from the command economies of the Soviet Union and Eastern Europe in some major respects. The economy was already highly decentralized in the sense that local governments had a great deal of discretion. This decentralization has made it possible to introduce piecemeal reforms and allow experimentation without disrupting the whole economy. Moreover, since much of industrial output was distributed outside the centralized supply system, the barriers to setting up new enterprises were comparatively low. Inputs for new activities could be obtained relatively easily.

3. An overwhelming percentage of the labor force was, and still is, located in rural areas and organized largely at the household level. Market-oriented reforms are easier to introduce in such an environment than in an economy dominated by large-scale industry and economic organizations. This rural-community-household structure means that market incentives can be introduced without building entirely new institutions. Much activity can be generated merely by lifting the restraints on economic activities. The flexibility of the rural labor market has been crucial in facilitating the growth of TVEs.

4. China began its reform process with none of the major macroeconomic handicaps that afflicted many other postcommunist transition economies. The inflation rate was low, and government finances were in balance. China had no international debt. Notwithstanding the acceleration in inflation since the mid-1980s, the savings propensity of Chinese households continues to be very high, making it much easier to sustain a high growth rate without runaway inflation.

5. Hong Kong has played a crucial role in the rapid expansion of exports and the large inflow of foreign direct investment. It has been the largest source of foreign capital, a major conduit for Chinese exports, and an invaluable source of commercial know-how for exporting to industrial market economies.

In sum, these differences tell us that while China's example debunks some simple slogans masquerading as rigorous analysis, it does not necessarily provide a model for all transition economies.

Athar Hussain and Nicholas H. Stern, "Comment," Proceedings of the World Bank Annual Conference on Development Economics 1994, pp. 161–162

---

experience, 1989–95. By 1995, many countries in CEE and CIS were essentially market economies with open trade, current account convertibility, and liberal policies toward new entry and private business. Some, however, had retreated from earlier reform programs. And Russia's extent of liberalization has been only about one half of that of the leaders in group 1 in Figure 9.1.

STABILIZATION

Regardless of which path of liberalization the transition economies follow, they must achieve macroeconomic stabilization if the transformation process is to succeed. Inflation has to be brought down from the triple-digit levels prevailing in the early phases of transformation in many of the transition economies. Without macroeconomic stabilization, distortions in relative prices within markets will persist, and reform of the micro structure cannot be achieved.

Stabilization requires disinflationary measures of tight money and tight fiscal policies, control of credit, reduction of the government deficit as a percentage of GNP, and hard budget constraints on firms. Disinflation down to at least moderate two-digit levels is essential to stimulate more productive investment, improve the allocation of resources, raise efficiency in firms, build confidence in the domestic currency, avoid distributional hardships, stop the redistribution of wealth from savers to borrowers, and make credible the policies of reform.

Experience with disinflationary measures has been mixed. Table 9.1 shows recent rates of inflation in groups of transition economies corresponding to the groups in Figure 9.1. Lower rates have been difficult to achieve because of incomplete price reform, rapid monetary expansion, failure to reduce government budgets, inadequate tax policy, and large capital inflows that add to the money supply and put pressure on prices in some countries.

China has experienced moderate inflation, but with stop-and-go cycles in prices and output (see Figure 9.3). The inflationary periods have come with rapid credit expansion, followed by a strengthening of financial policies through administrative controls. Inflationary forces persist when reforms are incomplete, especially in the enterprise and financial sectors.[10]

Contributing to China's inflation have been soft budget constraints, the maintenance of low real rates of interest, government subsidies to enterprises whose prices remain fixed at artificially low levels, and large declines in government revenue. In most countries, these conditions would have led to much higher inflation, but in China this has been avoided because of the exceptionally high demand for cash and bank deposits to hold by enterprises and households. This fall in velocity contrasts with the rise in CEE and CIS where a flight from money has intensified inflationary problems. In mid-1996, the governor of the People's Bank of China (central bank) claimed that after three years of tight monetary policy, China had sharply cut its inflation without slowing its robust growth rate. But a shortage of tax revenue is a persistent problem.

There is, moreover, the danger that in the half-reformed banking system the state banks will continue to ease state-authorized loans to state-owned enterprises, many of which still operate at a loss. The demand for money to hold is likely to grow more slowly in the future because money balances are already exceptionally high, alternatives to bank deposits—equities, enterprise bonds, foreign currency, and real assets—are becoming increasingly available, and capital movements are being liberalized. Further, Chinese leaders have been—and may continue to be—reluctant to use fully anti-inflationary measures because they fear the political consequences of a major slowdown in economic activity. At the same time, enterprises have high investment ratios and a strong demand for bank credit. As Dwight Perkins concludes, "Until the financial system is fully reformed, even real GNP

TABLE 9.1
Annual Inflation in Europe and Central Asia (Percent change in average Consumer Price Index)

	1990	1991	1992	1993	1994	1995	1996
Central Europe and the Baltics	16.1	117.7	211.2	85.0	35.9	25.0	18.8
Albania	0.0	35.5	226.0	85.0	22.6	7.9	10.2
Bulgaria	64.0	238.9	82.6	72.8	96.0	62.6	117.0
Croatia		122.6	663.6	1517.1	98.0	4.1	3.0
Czech Republic	9.6	56.6	11.1	20.8	10.0	10.0	8.0
Estonia	23.1	210.6	1069.0	89.0	47.7	28.8	21.0
Hungary	28.9	35.0	23.0	22.5	18.8	28.2	23.5
Latvia	10.5	172.2	958.7	109.2	35.9	25.0	18.8
Lithuania	16.1	224.0	1162.7	291.4	51.4	27.5	30.2
FYR Macedonia		114.9	1092.0	229.5	121.8	16.0	12.0
Poland	585.8	70.3	43.0	35.3	32.2	27.8	20.0
Romania	4.7	161.1	211.2	255.2	136.8	30.8	50.0
Slovak Republic	10.4	61.2	10.0	23.2	13.4	9.9	5.2
Slovenia	549.7	117.7	201.3	32.3	19.8	12.6	11.0
Eastern Europe and the Caucasus	5.6	91.2	1210.0	1188.0	1427.7	188.7	40.2
Armenia	10.1	80.1	677.9	3731.9	5273.4	176.7	22.1
Azerbaijan	7.5	82.8	1350.9	980.9	1427.7	411.7	20.6
Belarus	4.5	94.1	970.0	1188.0	2222.0	709.0	71.3
Georgia	3.3	78.7	637.3	19257.9	17271.5	162.7	40.2
Moldova	14.8	136.1	1276.0	788.5	330.0	30.6	24.5
Russia	5.6	92.6	1354.0	895.3	303.2	188.7	47.4
Ukraine	4.2	91.2	1210.0	4735.0	891.1	376.0	79.0
Central Asia	4.8	90.7	1007.0	1075.0	1281.0	176.0	35.3
Kazakstan	18.9	87.4	1622.6	1255.5	1880.0	176.0	38.5
Kyrgyz Republic	4.8	113.7	1007.0	782.1	278.1	43.0	29.4
Tajikistan	—	—	—	—	350.4	635.0	729.0
Turkmenistan	—	—	—	—	1748.0	1005.0	N/A
Uzbekistan	3.5	90.7	717.6	1075.0	1281.0	117.0	32.0

Source: World Bank data.

growth of 9% or 10% is likely to trigger accelerating inflation followed by retrenchment. Stop-and-go growth in output and prices appears to be a characteristic of an economy in the twilight zone between command and the market."[11]

CEE and CIS began their transformation process with repressed inflation—controlled prices but a monetary overhang. Given limited output, queues and black markets were pervasive. When prices were freed, they soared as inflation became high and open. But after further liberalization and tight financial policies, inflation was brought down. The experience with inflation is shown in Figure 9.4. Price reform is, however, incomplete: The prices of energy and some services are still far below world market levels, and will have to increase in the future. To avoid inflation, public expenditure will have to decrease, tax revenue increase, credit allocation be depoliticized, deeper financial markets established, savings increased, and structural reform measures completed to expand productive capacities. For Russia and the Ukraine, the amount of international financial assistance, especially from the IMF, and the effectiveness of its monitoring will also determine future rates of inflation. For all the transition economies, the future of inflation and the success of democratic economic reforms are interrelated.

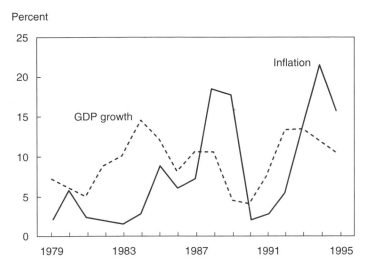

Percent

Figure 9.3   GDP growth and inflation in China. *Source*: World Bank, *World Development Report 1996*, p. 34.

PROSPECTS FOR PRIVATE ENTERPRISE

Besides efforts at liberalization and stabilization, the transition economies are pursuing policies of privatization (majority private ownership of an enterprise) and encouragement of new private enterprises. The objective of creating and expanding the private sector is to overcome the deficiencies in the legacy of central planning by transferring power from bureaucrats and state-owned enterprises to markets and private enterprise. Liberalization and stabilization must be complemented by establishment of private property rights, privatizing of existing state-owned enterprises, and the encouragement of freedom of entry for new business enterprises. Without private ownership, markets cannot function properly. Nor can the benefits of decentralized investment be achieved. Further, an increase in total factor productivity is to be attained not only by technological innovation, but also by the improved organizational mode and managerial methods of private enterprises.

Privatization is, however, a difficult process. The scale of the task is enormous—in Hungary and Poland, for example, 90 percent of all enterprises were state owned. Obviously the first problem is to decide which state-owned enterprises are to be privatized. According to the principles of public economics there may be justification for state ownership of some enterprises—for example, public utilities or enterprises in which the social benefits exceed private profit. But even in these exceptional cases, public regulation instead of public ownership may be the first best policy. Moreover, if prices are distorted—that is, they do not reflect the true scarcity or abundance of the outputs or inputs that are being valued—it is difficult to undertake any benefit-cost analysis to determine whether state ownership of an enterprise is economically justified. Ideology and politics are only too likely to maintain too many enterprises in state ownership. Government ministries that have acted as the "owners" of the state enterprises will naturally be reluctant to lose their power and are likely to oppose privatization of their enterprises. If privatization is to proceed, it may first be necessary to institute political changes that promote decentralization of decision making and minimize

Percent per year

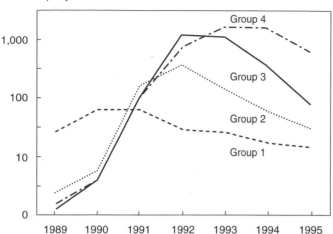

Figure 9.4 Time Profiles of Inflation by Country Group. Note: Countries in CEE and the CIS are grouped by their average liberalization index scores for 1989–95 (see Figure 9.1). Countries severely affected by regional tensions are excluded. Annual inflation rates are simple averages for each group. Inflation is plotted on a logarithmic scale. *Source*: IMF and World Bank data, World Bank, *World Development Report 1996*, p. 39.

the power of ministries and the economic bureaucracy in order to subordinate them to market forces (no subsidies or tax breaks).

If state owned enterprises are to be converted into joint stock companies and sold to private investors, the next question becomes at what price? How to value the assets and liabilities of these enterprises? How can the value be determined when there are not market prices for the output and inputs of the enterprise?

Assuming that the valuation problem is solved, the next question is: Who will buy the enterprises? Most proposals for privatization envisage the sale of stock to individuals, workers, state pension funds, and foreign investors. But can individuals and workers afford the purchase of shares in these enterprises, especially if there is also a squeeze on household liquidity and wealth as a result of a stabilization program? To avoid this problem, some advocate simply giving the enterprises away. Poland and Hungary, however, rejected giveaway schemes, believing that only real owners, confronting financial risks, will want the enterprises managed according to the discipline of the market. To provide proper incentives, property rights must be clearly established. Moreover, lack of capital markets, security markets, and a modern banking system enormously complicate the task of selling to individuals. (We discuss the financial system on pp. 358–60.)

It has been difficult to privatize large and medium-sized enterprises. Essentially three types of privatization approaches are being attempted. Sales of state enterprises to outsiders—"real" owners with capital and managerial skills—may be preferred, but have been few in number. Management-employee buyouts have been more frequent, especially in Russia. Given the autonomy of managers of state enterprises and the political power of workers (as in Poland), "insider control" can be gained rapidly and easily through preferential treatment in voucher-based programs. But corporate governance may be weak: Inefficient use of the enterprise's assets has been common when there is no external discipline exercised by outside stockholders in efficient securities markets or commercial banks that monitor managerial performance.[12] Privatization through the distribution of vouchers in an equal-access manner across the population has also been followed, especially in the Czech Republic, where the mass privatization program has been the most successful to date.

Table 9.2 shows the various methods of privatization of large enterprises in some transition economies. Table 9.3 indicates some criteria by which to evaluate the various approaches.

Privatization of small firms has been much easier and more extensive than for the larger enterprises. They are easier to value, are attractive to more owners, less subject to political opposition, and can quickly display progress—especially in services. In the Czech Republic, locally administered auctions have been open and competitive, with good results. In Hungary, the small private business sector has grown mainly through the entry of new private competitors. Although Russia has divested most of its small units, ownership has been acquired mainly by insiders with questionable results.

A great deal of privatization must depend on attracting foreign investors, not only because capital is limited, but even more significantly because the new companies will need Western management and technology. The sale to foreign investors, however, is difficult. Ideology and beliefs of the previous communist era may still carry over and oppose foreign ownership or control of a domestic enterprise. Foreign investors in turn are reluctant to invest in an economy that lacks domestic economic stability, is still heavily controlled by

TABLE 9.2
Methods of Privatization for Medium-size and Large Enterprise in Seven Transition Economies (percentage of total)

Country	Sale to Outside Owners	Management-employee Buyout	Equal-access Voucher Privatization	Restitution	Other[a]	Still in State Hands
Czech Republic						
By number[b]	32	0	22[c]	9	28	10
By value[d]	5	0	50	2	3	40
Estonia[e]						
By number	64	30	0	0	2	4
By value	60	12	3	10	0	15
Hungary						
By number	38	7	0	0	33	22
By value	40	2	0	4	12	42
Lithuania						
By number	<1	5	70	0	0	25
By value	<1	5	60	0	0	35
Mongolia						
By number	0	0	70	0	0	30
By value	0	0	55	0	0	45
Poland						
By number	3	14	6	0	23	54
Russia[c]						
By number	0	55	11	0	0	34

Note: Boxed numbers show the dominant method in each country. Data are as of the end of 1995.

[a]Includes transfers to municipalities or social insurance organizations, debt-equity swaps, and sales through insolvency proceedings.
[b]Number of privatized firms as a share of all formerly state-owned firms. Includes parts of firms restructured prior to privatization.
[c]Includes assets sold for cash as part of the voucher privatization program through June 1994.
[d]Value of firms privatized as a share of the value of all formerly state-owned firms. Data for Poland and Russia are unavailable.
[e]Does not include some infrastructure firms. All management buyouts were part of competitive, open tenders. In thirteen cases citizens could exchange vouchers for minority shares in firms sold to a core investor.
Source: World Bank data, *World Development Report 1996*, p. 53.

TABLE 9.3
Trade-offs among Privatization Routes for Large Firms

Method	Objective				
	Better corporate governance	Speed and feasibility	Better access to capital and skills	More government revenue	Greater fairness
Sale to outside owners	+	−	+	+	−
Management-employee buyout	−	+	−	−	−
Equal-access voucher privatization	?	+	?	−	+
Spontaneous privatization	?	?	−	−	−

Source: World Bank data, *World Development Report 1996*, p. 52.

the state, and in which enterprises operate with obsolete technology and low-productivity techniques of production.

Although privatization has proceeded slowly in Eastern Europe, a number of financial firms have established offices to advise on privatizations. Budapest has become the most internationalized financial center in Eastern Europe. Among the Western financial institutions selected by the Hungarian government to advise on privatizations are Barclays de Zoete Wedd, Coopers & Lybrand, N. M. Rothschild, and Nomura International. Bankers Trust Co. has also established a joint investment bank with Commercial and Credit Bank Ltd. of Hungary to form the new Budapest-based bank, Magyar Trust Ltd., which will undertake fee-related business.

Despite the financial advice that governments are receiving, policies still need to be clearly established on who should be given access to shares on favorable conditions, the role to be allowed foreign investors, procedure for listing denationalized companies on exchanges, and what proportion of state assets should be sold.

QUEUES IN TRANSITION

The transformation of the Russian economy is well illustrated by three front-page photos from *Izvestiya* in July 1994. They picture Russians in 1985, queuing for vodka, and in summer 1992, queuing for bread—but in 1994, they are shown queuing to buy shares. In the winter of 1991 and 1992, people feared famine in Russia. By the summer of 1994, the major concern was financial scandals with the potential of hurting millions of private speculators who had large savings and a high acceptance of risk. It is difficult to imagine a faster transition in popular concerns, and this in turn reflects the successful transformation of the Russian economy. Before 1988, most Russians seemed convinced that the Russian nation was fundamentally unsuitable for entrepreneurship. In 1994, a standard Russian saying ran: "Those who do not take risks will not drink champagne." An entire culture had been transformed.

Anders Aslund, *How Russia Became a Market Economy* (Washington, DC: Brookings Institution, 1995), p. 312

CREATING PRIVATE ENTERPRISES

Starting from less than zero in November 1991, a small, determined, and often beleaguered group of Russian reformers—with some important external support—has been able to:

- Devise and implement, in the face of strong resistance, a "corporatization" program that turned about half of Russian state-owned enterprises into joint stock companies.
- Persuade the most important "insider" stakeholders who might have opposed privatization—workers and managers—to take part in the process by offering them shares in the firms in which they work for free or at a low price.
- Conceive and implement a voucher program, giving 144 million participating Russians a chance to become, along with insiders, owners of enterprises.
- Create a national voucher auction system in more than eighty-five regions, with 750 bid reception centers.
- Facilitate the creation of some 650 private investment funds that compete for vouchers and convert them to diversified shareholdings in newly privatized enterprises.

The result is that by the end of June 1994, between 12,000 and 14,000 medium-size and large enterprises had been transferred to private ownership. These firms employed more than 14 million people, or about half of those employed in Russia's industrial sector. About 40 million Russian citizens had become owners of shares in privatized firms.

These achievements border on the miraculous, having taken place in the absence of consensus on the desirability, scope, and pace of liberalizing reform in general, and privatization in particular, and in the absence of what normally would be considered the requisite administrative and financial resources to implement, monitor, and enforce a privatization program of this magnitude. Yet it was done. The only potentially comparable privatization experiences are those of the former East Germany and the former Czechoslovakia. . . .

WHAT NEXT?

The Russian privatization team thus opted for the method that they judged would yield results—and they got them. But as a consequence, the results were tentative and partial. Transfer of ownership to insiders was a striking step, but only a first step. It must now be followed by equally essential second steps opening ownership of privatized firms to external investors and owners. These, in turn, will bring needed capital, market access, managerial know-how, and a bottom-line mentality to privatized companies. External investors will complete the restructuring of firms begun by the transfer of ownership. A significant percentage of restructured firms will become profitable as well as nationally and internationally competitive, and Russia will be well launched on the process of growth and integration into the global economy. Such is the hope.

ISSUES TO BE RESOLVED

To put it mildly, much stands in the way of the achievement of this grand aspiration. Ignoring the evident macroeconomic and macropolitical deficiencies of present-day Russia, and concentrating solely on the privatization process, one encounters a number of critical issues:

- Insiders fear that the restructuring brought about by external investors will cost them their jobs, thus they do their best to prevent or minimize sales of large blocks of shares to external investors.

- The voucher scheme expired on June 30, 1994. The current political configuration apparently will not tolerate a second voucher issue. But 12,000–14,000 enterprises remain uncorporatized, unprivatized, and lacking the voucher mechanism to spur their divestiture.

- Small-scale privatization in Russia is impressive in absolute terms (with some 85,000 small business units divested), but lags relative to similar programs in the Czech Republic, Estonia, Hungary, and Poland, where a much larger percentage of the entire small-scale base has been divested. Small-scale privatization schools both new owners and consumers in market economics and has proved critical in job creation, essential to the absorption of surplus labor flowing out of the large-enterprise sector.

- Twelve to fourteen thousand medium-size and large firms are now in private hands. But there are few who believe that their future operations will be left entirely to determination by pure market forces, since the current Russian variant of the market deviates so sharply from the textbook model. Privatized firms urgently require technical assistance (to help in the preparation of business plans and in restructuring), credit to finance working capital, trade, and investments, and equity injections to provide both long-term money and active governance.

- Important as privatization is, it is only a part of the transition process, alongside new entrants and greenfield investments.

World Bank, *Development Brief,* January 1995

Recognizing the unreality of expecting widespread and rapid privatization, Kornai has proposed a number of more positive measures[13]:

1. Although it may be comparatively simple to transfer smaller units from state ownership into the hands of an individual or group of individuals, it is unrealistic to count on private entrepreneurs to purchase huge state-owned firms. This, however, might be facilitated by breaking up enormous state-owned enterprises that artificially unite a number of smaller units. These units could then be sold to private entrepreneurs.

2. Irrespective of its size, state property to be sold to a private owner should change hands at a real market price. Property should generally be auctioned, utilizing independent bodies to quote the asking price. Evaluation of an enterprise could begin with the initial question of how much the private entrepreneur would have to invest from his own money to establish a producing unit similar to the one offered.

3. A credit institution related to the sale of state property to private owners must be established. This is necessary so that the upper limit on sales to private parties is not determined by the current total of private wealth. A mortgage, however, should be tough, and once the investor fails in his payment, he should face the complete loss, even of his initial capital.

4. The practice of leasing out state assets to private individuals may be followed provided that the rentals are rational and realistic. The rental system can also serve the transition to sales utilizing well-known formulas for converting rents into nonrecurrent capital value.

5. Foreign investment should be welcomed but in accordance with a benefit-cost calculation so that the recipient country does not have a bargain basement sale of national wealth. Although it may be desirable to place an upper limit on the proportion of state-owned property that foreigners may buy, there should be no limit placed on direct foreign investment involving setting up a new installation, largely with foreign resources. Up-to-date equipment and managerial business and technical expertise are sorely needed.

6. A state-owned firm may have to be converted into a joint stock company, but it is essential that the conversion ultimately achieves its purpose of leading to a *real* privatization of the firm. One cannot therefore simply allow the current managers to appropriate the firm and convert themselves from employees paid by the state into owners, or more precisely into owner-managers combining the roles of ownership and management. The new owners should have a free hand in appointing the management. They should be able to keep the old management if they like, or appoint new executives if they prefer. It should also be up to the new owners to decide how to fix executive salaries and financial incentives. It would be inadmissible for the previous managers themselves to choose who the new owners should be or promote themselves to the top of the list of new owners. Moreover, it would be undesirable for the firm's workforce as a whole to receive the entire equity so that state property becomes the state collective property of the firm's employees. Wealth embodied by the firm at the moment of ownership transfer has not been created exclusively by that firm's workers, and it would be unjustifiable for this small, select group of citizens to acquire the wealth as a gift. Moreover, some labor collectives could do very well, while others would become owners of a heavily indebted, loss-making, negative wealth enterprise.

Of most importance, however, is not the legal entitlement to acquire the property, but rather the prime consideration of being able to run it well. Kornai reiterates that only private property can supply enough incentive to guarantee permanently an effective use of the resources. Instead of disbursing the ownership too widely among shareholders, Kornai believes that it would be desirable for a dominant individual shareholder or small group of shareholders (national or foreign holding at least 20 percent or 30 percent of the shares) to have a decisive say in the appointment and supervision of the firm's executives. A sizable shareholding is necessary to give the owners a strong interest in the firm's success.

Finally, the marketing of state wealth should be a fully public process. The legal framework and organizational framework should be clearly established. Extensive information should be readily available to potential buyers and sellers.

Even if Kornai's proposals were followed, the success of privatization would depend only in part on instituting an economically rational process of privatization. That is only a preliminary step to establishing a thriving market economy. Most important is the establishment of a genuinely competitive environment. There is no merit in transforming state monopolies into private monopolies. The creation of private monopolies has to be avoided; if they do exist, they have to be regulated. There should be no barriers to entry for new firms. Moreover, market pricing for inputs and outputs are necessary to promote competition. If market prices are to prevail, it is necessary to liberalize foreign trade and to calculate with free trade prices. A new independent central bank is also essential to pursue monetary policy in accord with appropriate demand management. To have economic agents act rationally in accord with market-determined prices, it is also necessary to have a commercial banking system and a financial structure that allow intermediation between savers and investors. This is especially important for capital accumulation to promote technological progress.

The experience with privatization is still very limited, and it will be a long-term process to achieve privatization in any substantial way. For the next decade or two, it can still be expected that state-owned enterprises will have a significant role in Eastern European economies. At best, small-scale private enterprises, especially in the service sector, may grow quickly. Larger state-owned enterprises, however, will be "destate-ized" only slowly. As Kornai suggests, once the state-owned enterprises become small islands in a sea of the private economy, they too will be compelled to behave almost as if they were privately owned. However, for a long while to come, the reverse situation will prevail: The tiny isles of the private sector will be surrounded by an ocean of state-owned firms. In Kornai's opinion, for the next two decades, Hungary will have a dual economy with its two constituent parts: the state and the private sectors.[14]

FINANCIAL SECTOR REFORM

Liberalization, stabilization, privatization—all these objectives will be more effectively implemented if there are well-functioning capital markets. Although measures of liberalization and stabilization might be introduced fairly rapidly, privatization and development of a financial system involve longer-term institutional development. They are also interdependent: The restructuring of enterprises and restructuring of the financial system are parallel requirements.

If properly developed, capital markets can fulfill important functions. These can be summarized as:

1. Transferring resources from savers to borrowers or investors.

2. Agglomerating capital in projects that require more capital than any one saver or small group of savers can accumulate.

3. Selecting projects that are most productive.

4. Monitoring to ensure that funds are used as promised.

5. Enforcing contracts.

6. Transferring, sharing, and pooling risks. The rules that specify the conditions of repayment effectively determine who bears what risks.

7. Diversifying risk by pooling a large number of investment projects together.[15]

To achieve these objectives there needs to be reform of banks and other financial institutions. A legacy of planning is a weak banking system that is undercapitalized, beset with nonperforming loans, low profitability, or insolvency covered over by a soft budget. Rather than being capable of performing the functions of a vigorous banking sector, the banks have been simply accounting agencies that passively accept household deposits and account for financial transactions according to the allocations of the central plan. Moreover, other components of an effective financial system were not established under planning. The rudimentary character of the financial sector must be overcome if there is to be stabilization and enterprise restructuring.

Early on in the period of transition it is most important to harden the budget restraint. In the past, state-owned banks had only soft budget constraints as deficits were made up by the government. If the banks face only soft budget constraints, they will not discipline their borrowers—state-owned enterprises—who, in turn, may not care about losses as long as they too enjoy soft budget constraints. Privatization of the financial sector is the most direct way to remove any reliance on government credit and to make the budget constraint bite for financial institutions and for enterprises more generally throughout the economy.

Banking reform calls for the liquidation of over-indebted state banks, commercialization of state banks, and the encouragement of entry of new banks. Russia has taken this approach. Hungary and Poland, however, have chosen to recapitalize existing banks, undertake programs to improve them institutionally, and to privatize as soon as possible.[16]

In privatizing and encouraging the entry of new banks, a transition economy faces the issue of how much competition is desirable. Excessive competition among banks would tend to limit the economic return to a bank and hence diminish the bank's efforts to maintain its reputation. In contrast, excessive limitation of the number of banks would result in insufficient competition. It is difficult for a government to establish the "right" level of entry.[17]

Another decision has to be made regarding whether reform of the banking system should follow the universal banking model of having banks own shares in enterprises and engage in a variety of financial activities or have separate commercial and investment banks. Either way, regulation and supervision must be instituted to monitor transactions. Capital requirements need to be set at a sufficiently high level, uniform accounting guidelines established, large exposures limited, and substantial enforcement powers given to the central bank. The central bank, in turn, must be politically independent.

As with the general problem of creating legal frameworks and a rule of law for private sector development, it is necessary to develop the legal system so that banks can be clear on procedures for collateral recovery, bankruptcy, and enforcement of their claims. Capital markets also must rely on company laws to define the rights of shareholders and their influence on management.

Nonbank financial institutions also have an important role. Mutual funds, venture capital funds, and leasing companies are especially significant for small and medium-sized firms. Capital markets rely, however, on well-functioning banks and on money markets to provide a basis for pricing securities. Although they are growing rapidly in transition economies, equity markets are not of prime importance. They do increase liquidity, but relatively little capital is raised in equity markets. Long-term investments—sorely needed in the transition economies—are unlikely to be determined by stock market prices. Some argue that equity markets provide a basis for the exercise of corporate governance; but to the extent that managers do pay attention to stock market prices, they are likely to focus excessively on short-term profits.

What is most important in the establishment of the roles of banks, capital markets, and other financial intermediaries is recognition of their important functions, listed at the beginning of this section (p. 358). From initial programs of privatization, the financial system should evolve and deepen over the longer term to fulfill these functions more effectively.

BECOMING OUTWARD ORIENTED

The future of private enterprise in the transition economies is also highly dependent on the extent to which these economies can become outward oriented and link their domestic markets to world markets. Competition within the domestic economy will be promoted the more the economy removes restrictions on its foreign trade and encourages private investment from overseas. Benefits from greater integration into the world economy will be realized not only from the gains from trade based on comparative advantage, but also from the dynamic gains from exports and capital inflow.

The potential for trade growth is high. Already from 1978 to 1992, China rose from being the world's thirty-second largest exporter to its tenth largest. China's imports and exports doubled between 1990 and 1995.

Exports from China have not only grown rapidly—about 20 percent annually—from 1986 to 1996, but have also shifted from primary products to manufactures. Tables 9.4–9.6 show trends in China's trade. China has a large trade surplus with the United States, amounting in 1996 to nearly 20 percent of the total U.S. trade deficit. Since 1994, foreign exchange has been traded at a unified rate. This has promoted exports and an increase in capital inflows. Foreign exchange reserves also increased more than 2 times from 1994 to 1997, and China's foreign reserves are second largest in the world after Japan. This has allowed China to undertake more liberalization of trade and investment—cutting tariffs, eliminating many import quotas, moving toward currency convertibility, and easing restrictions on operations by joint ventures with foreign shareholders.

Other transition economies are also trying to be more outward oriented. Between 1990 and 1995, the CEE countries' imports from OECD countries increased 216 percent and its

TABLE 9.4
China: Exports and Imports, Destination (1994) ($ billions)

	Import (from)	Export (to)	Total
Japan	26.32	21.57	47.89
Hong Kong	9.46	32.36	41.82
Taiwan	14.08	2.24	14.39
Republic of Korea	7.32	4.40	11.72
Singapore	2.48	2.56	5.04
Germany	7.16	4.76	11.92
U.K.	1.77	2.41	4.18
France	1.94	1.42	3.36
Italy	3.07	1.59	4.66
Netherlands	0.71	2.27	2.98
Switzerland	0.99	0.36	1.35
Russia	3.50	1.58	5.08
Canada	1.83	1.40	3.23
USA	13.97	21.46	35.45
Australia	2.45	1.49	3.94

Source: China Publishing House, *Statistical Yearbook of China, 1995*; Goodhart and Xu, op cit., p. 72. Note that Hong Kong acts as an entrepot, or gateway, for trade flows with unspecified third parties.

TABLE 9.5
Foreign Trade of China Since 1976 ($ billions)

	1976	1980	1985	1990	1992	1993	1994
Exports	6.5	19.4	20.6	62.1	85.0	91.3	124.0
Imports	6.2	21.5	31.8	53.4	80.7	103.4	118.6
Balance of foreign trade	0.3	−2.1	−11.2	8.7	4.3	−12.1	5.4

Note: Data are in US$ 1990 year prices.
Source: China Publishing House, *Statistical Yearbook of China, 1995*; Goodhart and Xu, op cit., p. 2.

TABLE 9.6
Balance of Payments of China ($ billions) (current value)

	1991	1992	1993	1994
Exports (fob)	58.92	69.57	75.66	102.56
Imports (fob)	50.18	64.39	86.31	95.27
Trade balance	8.74	5.18	−10.66	7.29
Current account	13.27	6.40	11.90	7.66
Capital account	8.0	−0.25	23.47	32.64
Reserves	21.72	19.44	21.20	51.60

Source: Chicago Publishing House, *Statistical Yearbook of China, 1995, 1995;* Goodhart and Xu, op cit., p. 73.

exports to them 159 percent. Growth in trade between the EU and CEE is becoming ever more significant, especially in intra-industry trade and processing and assembly activity by CEE firms.[18] Only Russia, Slovakia, and Bulgaria had a current account surplus in 1995. Other CEE countries were in deficit, with Hungary having a current account deficit as large as 5.7 percent of GDP.

For the near future, the composition of export trade from Central and Eastern Europe will resemble that from a labor-intensive developing country. The low quality of consumer goods and the lack of upscale exports will limit the expansion of exports to Western Europe. New export markets are more likely to be in Southern Europe and Asia. The upgrading of exports may come, however, with the transfer of technology and know-how from the more-developed countries. Joint ventures may bring Western technology to the resources and labor of the transition economies, with a subsequent movement up the ladder of comparative advantage as has occurred in other developing economies. As exports eventually grow to the West, so too will the transition economies become larger markets for imports.

In the past, the Soviet-led bloc of countries was inward looking, with state monopoly of a limited amount of foreign trade. Much of the foreign trade involved bilateral trade agreements within the framework of the Council for Mutual Economic Assistance (Comecon). In 1991, the Comecon trade bloc was dissolved, and a new Organization for International Economic Cooperation instituted. The difficult task now is to move away from the heavy dependence on reciprocal relations and trade based on a transferable ruble that existed in Comecon and turn outward to the West on a convertible currency basis. The restructuring of trade toward the West will have a high cost—requiring new investment, upgrading of technology, retraining of labor, and changes in the transportation infrastructure. Beyond the physical restructuring to support a reorientation of trade to the West, it will also be necessary to dismantle the state monopoly of foreign trade and transform domestic enterprises into competitive enterprises that can calculate the profitability of exports and imports at world

---

JOINT VENTURES IN EASTERN EUROPE

DRT International's survey, comprising all of its big manufacturing, retail, and trading clients in addition to major financial institutions, found that most Western corporations currently in Eastern Europe are active in import/export. But the results indicate that joint ventures will be the favored form of the future. Early entries in the joint-venture field include these major multinationals:

- The United Kingdom's BREL, one of Europe's largest producers of rail vehicles, signed a cooperation agreement with the Czech firm CKD Tatra, the world's largest manufacturer of trams and light-rail vehicles.

- General Electric paid an initial $150 million to begin a joint light bulb-manufacturing venture with Hungary's Tungsram.

- General Motors signed a preliminary agreement with RABA (the Hungarian Railway Carriage and Machine Factory) to assemble automobile engines and Opel Kadett cars. GM estimates that the venture will produce more than 100,000 engines a year and assemble up to 25,000 cars. GM has entered joint ventures to make cars and transmissions in the Czech Republic. GM is also preparing to invest as much as $400 million by 1996 to revive Poland's automotive industry.

- Honeywell and the Soviet Ministry of Mineral Fertilizer Production formed a joint venture company, Sterch, that provides digital process-control systems for chemical fertilizer manufacturing plants. Honeywell is contributing products and management expertise to the venture.

- VW created a joint venture with Skoda of the Czech Republic to produce 400,000 automobiles annually in 1997.

- Unilever has bought 80 percent of a Polish detergent maker with the government retaining 20 percent of the privatized firm.

- Procter and Gamble Co. has formed joint ventures in Hungary and Poland.

- Firms such as Apple Computer, CSX, Dutch Shell, Fiat, Hoechst, Sony, Microsoft, Phillip Morris, and Siemens also plan to invest.

---

market prices. To facilitate these micro decisions, the government must practice rational macro management that will ensure competitive real exchange rates and suitable policy measures for balance-of-payments adjustment.

The most critical foreign trade problem facing East European countries is their chronic shortage of foreign exchange and the problem of supporting convertible currency trade. If currency convertibility is to be meaningful, there must also be commodity convertibility—i.e., foreign exporters should be able to convert their currency receipts to imports that are not predetermined by state control of exports. To allow full convertibility, effective reforms are needed to "demonopolize" foreign trade, restructure the economy toward exports to hard currency countries, remove trade restrictions, allow a flexible market-clearing exchange rate, and exercise sufficient discipline in monetary and fiscal policy to avoid balance-of-payments imbalances.

CURRENCY CONVERTIBILITY

By early 1991, all Eastern European countries, with the exception of the former U.S.S.R., had established the essential elements of currency convertibility. There are, however, significant differences in the practical implementation of external sector reforms, which are largely related to the specific economic situation and, in particular, the availability of foreign exchange. The differences include the degree of the unification of exchange rates, the restrictions on convertibility for the nonenterprise sector, the determination of exchange rates, and the scope of restrictions on profit remittances and capital account transactions.

Most countries have established a unified official exchange rate for commercial transactions, although some restrictions on payments for current transactions remain in place.

There are considerable differences across countries in the way exchange rates are determined on the basis of a peg, degree of flexibility, number of rates, and payments restrictions.

For features of exchange arrangements, see I. M. F. *Exchange Arrangements and Exchange Restrictions*, Annual Report.

If the Eastern European countries are to become more outward oriented, they will also have to become more hospitable to private and foreign investment. As already noted, foreign direct investment could have a more significant role in the privatization programs. Beyond that, the receipt of direct investment from overseas could confer significant benefits to economies that wish to undergo a transformation to more open markets. We have already listed (in Chapter 8) the benefits that direct foreign investment brings to a developing country—a contribution to the filling of the savings gap and the foreign exchange gap, technological advancement, know-how, employment, increase in domestic value added, and government revenue. These benefits are equally important for CEE, CIS, and China.

After being without a market economy for a half century, the postwar centrally planned economies now especially need to benefit from the "educative effect" of foreign private investment—that is, the international transfer of knowledge, the demonstration of more efficient management, innovations in products and processes of production, and marketing outlets. To attract private foreign investment, however, there must be political stability and credibility to a government's reform program. The Asian NICs offer a lesson in the preconditions that need to be established to attract direct foreign investment. The CEE countries, however, have not been as encouraging to private foreign investors as are the Asian NICs. Moreover, because of the government's reluctance to allow majority equity and the paucity of attractive local partners, private foreign investment has so far been limited.

Foreign investors in Russia are especially concerned about confiscatory taxes, the difficulty of legally enforcing commercial contracts and property rights, crime and corruption, and the hostility of some local bureaucrats. The Russian government recognizes these problems and has been attempting to improve the environment for foreign investment.

In 1996, net foreign direct investment in the CEE and CIS was $11 billion, a five-fold increase from 1991. Capital flow to China has been much greater, although more than half of the inflow has been from Hong Kong. Table 9.7 shows the sources of foreign direct investment into China in 1994. By 1996, annual net private capital flows to China were over $50 billion. Between 1979–97, China received about a quarter of all foreign direct investment to developing countries. Some 200 of the world's 500 largest multinationals have entered China since 1990, investing in joint ventures and increasingly in wholly foreign-owned ventures. Foreign investment is growing in large infrastructure projects and in industries such as petrochemicals and motor vehicles. Table 9.8 indicates foreign direct investment in some CEE countries and CIS from 1990–95 and a forecast of a sizable increase in 1996–2000. The Economist Intelligence Unit bases this forecast on "optimistic expectations" of strong economic growth rates, an improving business environment, and less political risk. Although Hungary, Poland, and the Czech Republic were the main recipients of FDI in the years 1990–95, Poland and Russia are forecast to be the main destinations for the rest of the decade.[19] Portfolio investment has also increased, especially in association with privatization. In the Czech Republic, it amounted to 3.5 percent of GDP in 1994—considerably more than FDI.

Official development finance to CEE and CIS averaged nearly $9 billion in 1990–95. China is becoming the World Bank's largest recipient of loans, coming close in the mid-1990s to the bank's ceiling to any one country of a tenth of the bank's total lending. The major share of official financing is for balance-of-payments and budgetary support and debt relief. Insofar as conditionality is attached to the official financing, it can be significant in ensuring liberalization, stabilization, and institution building. The policy dialog is an important complement to the receipt of financial resources from the IMF, World Bank, and European Bank for Reconstruction and Development (EBRD).

New institutional arrangements may be introduced to speed up the inflow of private sector foreign investment. The EBRD can channel funds from international capital markets to the transition economies. The bank is especially directed "to promote private and entrepreneurial initiative in the Central and Eastern European countries committed to and applying the principles of multiparty democracy, pluralism and market economics." With an initial capital base of $12 billion, the majority of the bank's exposure will be in the private sector, through loans and equity investments. At least 60 percent of the bank's exposure over the first five years must be in the private sector or in state-owned enterprises that are shifting to private ownership and control.

TABLE 9.7
Foreign Direct Investment in China, 1994
(gross inflows: $ billions)

Hong Kong/Macao	20.2
Taiwan	3.29
USA	2.49
Japan	2.48
Singapore	1.18
South Korea	0.72
UK	0.69
Germany	0.26
Thailand	0.23
Total	31.54

Source: China Statistical Publishing House, *China Statistical Yearbook 1996*, p. 600.

TABLE 9.8
Foreign Direct Investment in Eastern Europe ($ millions)

	1994	1995	1990–95	1996–2000
Hungary	1,146	4,400	11,200	12,968
Poland	1,875	2,500	7,148	21,969
Czech Republic	878	2,500	5,666	15,466
Slovakia	187	200	775	2,150
Slovenia	87	150	501	3,052
Albania	53	75	205	583
Bulgaria	105	150	412	1,428
Romania	340	400	933	4,017
Other Balkans	120	100	300	2,210
Baltics	430	400	1,280	1,890
Russia	1,000	2,000	4,400	26,960
Ukraine	91	113	574	1,400
Other CIS	640	800	2,300	5,085
Eastern Europe	4,791	10,475	27,140	63,847
E. Europe & former USSR	6,952	13,788	35,694	99,186

Source: Economist Intelligence Unit; *Financial Times*, March 25, 1996.

The World Bank has also offered to create an international fund to promote industrial restructuring in Poland. The fund, which could amount to well over $1 billion, would be provided not only by the bank itself, but also by other official institutions, such as the European Investment Bank, the European Bank for Reconstruction and Development, and possibly the European Union. The fund would help finance Polish enterprises seeking to establish joint ventures with foreign companies in priority sectors.

The future inflow of public capital from the World Bank and access to the facilities of the IMF will be influential in determining the progress in marketizing and becoming more outward oriented. Both the World Bank and IMF can engage in policy dialogues with the governments of transition economies and can exercise considerable international leverage toward policy reform. The IMF, for instance, granted in 1991 a $1.8 billion standby agreement to Czechoslovakia, less than four months after it rejoined the fund. At the time it was the largest loan to an East European country and was expected to induce additional financial aid from the European Union and the World Bank. The reform program worked out with the IMF included removal of price controls on 85 percent of goods sold, closing inefficient state-owned enterprises, establishing commercial banks, and making the Czechoslovakian crown convertible.

Poland has also received balance-of-payment support from the IMF, but the government has been even more keen to have Western creditors forgive a large part of Poland's external debt. In his first major speech to a Western audience in 1991, the new prime minister of Poland, Jan Krzysztof Bielecki, called on creditors to forgive 80 percent of Poland's $46 billion foreign debt (of which approximately three-quarters is to official creditors and the remainder to commercial banks). "This debt is a major destabilizing influence," he said. "It badly affects the climate for investment, particularly for foreign investment."[20] In 1991, Western governments did agree to forgive about half the $33 billion that Poland owed them.

The total gross foreign debt of the six Eastern-bloc countries (Poland, Bulgaria, Hungary, former Soviet Union, Czechoslovakia, Romania) rose from $88 billion in 1985 to $143 billion in 1990. Since 1985, the debt-service burden has risen in all the countries except

Poland and Romania. In 1995, Hungary had the highest debt-export ratio of 250 percent of annual exports. In the absence of adequate finance from commercial banks, international development agencies, and foreign aid, the debt overhang will remain an obstacle to price liberalization, currency convertibility, and an inflow of private foreign investment. Whether there will be sufficient underwriting of economic reform remains a major question.

IMPLICATIONS FOR INTERNATIONAL MANAGEMENT

Management's greatest uncertainty with respect to the practice of DPR for CEE, CIS, and China centers on the process of prediction. There is wide agreement on analysis—what needs to be done. An analysis of the economic environment in the transition economies would stress the policy reforms outlined in this chapter—the need to remove price distortions and promote competitive market pricing, monetary and fiscal discipline, foreign trade liberalization, "destate-ization," establishment of property rights, and the institutionalizing of legal, regulatory, accounting, and banking frameworks for competitive markets.

A transition economy must reduce the activities of its overextended state. The state must transfer many of its previous activities to the private sector, substitute markets for state commands, and limit government interventions to the correction of market failure. Yet, while state involvement is to be diminished, government still has the formidable tasks of ensuring macroeconomic stability, supporting the market economy with public goods and an appropriate legal and institutional environment, and providing a safety net for vulnerable groups. In micro terms, government must deal with externalities in production, natural monopolies, and cases of imperfect information.

The daunting challenge for management is to predict whether the proper functions of state and market will occur and how rapidly. The outcome is very much a function of political stability and whether it is in the government's interest to institute radical economic reforms. Although Poland benefits from a degree of political unity, this is still unknown elsewhere in East Europe. In CEE and CIS the "new" political leadership in some countries consists of a handful of former opposition politicians who straddle layer upon layer of politicians and bureaucrats, who may have changed their party affiliation, but not necessarily their Marxist mentality. Political reformation may run only skin deep.[21]

Generally in CEE and CIS there remains a high degree of uncertainty with respect to the successful implementation of policy reforms. This is because the reforms are vulnerable to conservative reaction. The extension of the private sector may be only marginal while the state sector remains subsidized and overextended. The old controlling institutions may be maintained while new institutions supporting the market price system are neglected. Economic reforms depend on political and institutional reforms.

Response by firms outside of the transition economies to developments in these economies will depend heavily on diagnosis and prediction with respect to the growth of the private sector and the movement toward an outward-oriented economy. The death of Comecon should open opportunities for Western firms and investors—especially in the form of export markets for the West, possibilities for direct foreign investment, new activities in investment banking, project finance, and dealing with the emerging private sector. The significance of these opportunities, however, will be determined by the extent to which foreign trade becomes based on world market prices, more favorable conditions for private foreign investment are implemented, currency convertibility and commodity convertibility occur, and creditworthiness is established. So far the opportunities have been greatest in former East Germany, but it may be expected that Poland, Hungary, and the Czech Republic will follow.

Indicators of future growth in CEE, CIS, and China can be best diagnosed and predicted by monitoring the country's progress in market liberalization, price stabilization, property rights, and open trade policies.

Considering how these policy reforms affect a country's growth in GDP, the European Bank for Reconstruction and Development has ranked countries according to their intensity of reform (on a scale of 1 to 4, with a higher number indicating greater intensity as in Table 9.9). Table 9.10 shows that all of the strong reformers had achieved positive growth by 1994, but that none of the other countries had done so.

Whereas negative growth rates were experienced in CEE and CIS during the early years of reform, China has achieved an extremely fast rate of growth since the late 1970s (see Table 9.11). This table also shows the differential growth rates between China and other transition economies.

TABLE 9.9
Progress in the Transition to a Market Economy

	Private Sector Share of GDP, 1994 (percent)	Privatization		Restructuring of Companies	Prices, Competition	Trade, Foreign Exchange	Banks
		Large Firms	Small Firms				
Albania	50	1	3	2	3	4	2
Armenia	40	1	3	1	3	2	1
Azerbaijan	20	1	1	1	3	1	1
Belarus	15	2	2	2	2	1	1
Bulgaria	40	2	2	2	3	4	2
Croatia	40	3	4	2	3	4	3
Czech Republic	65	4	4	3	3	4	3
Estonia	55	3	4	3	3	4	3
Georgia	20	1	2	1	2	1	1
Hungary	55	3	4	3	3	4	3
Kazakhstan	20	2	2	1	2	2	1
Kyrigyz Republic	30	3	4	2	3	3	2
Latvia	55	2	3	2	3	4	3
Lithuania	50	3	4	2	3	4	2
Macedonia, former Yugoslav Republic of	35	2	4	2	3	4	2
Moldova	20	2	2	2	3	2	2
Poland	55	3	4	3	3	4	3
Romania	35	2	3	2	3	4	2
Russia	50	3	3	2	3	3	2
Slovak Republic	55	3	4	3	3	4	3
Slovenia	30	2	4	3	3	4	3
Tajikistan	15	2	2	1	3	1	1
Turkmenistan	15	1	1	1	2	1	1
Ukraine	30	1	2	1	2	1	1
Uzbekistan	20	2	3	1	3	2	1

Score: 4 = market economy; 1 = little progress.
Source: European Bank for Reconstruction and Development. This table appeared in Masahiko Aoki and Hyung-Ki Kim, "Corporate Governance in Transition Economies," *Finance & Development* (September 1995), p. 21.

TABLE 9.10
Reform and Growth Rates of Transition Economies (percent)

Country	Strength of Trade Reform	Year of Trade Reform	Cumulative Growth 1989–94	Growth 1994
Strong Reforms				
Hungary	4	1990	−17.94	2.00
Poland	4	1990	−9.23	5.00
Bulgaria	4	1991	−26.41	1.40
Czech Republic	4	1991	−15.49	3.00
Slovak Republic	4	1991	−19.53	5.00
Slovenia	4	1991	−13.26	5.00
Albania	4	1992	−22.89	7.00
Estonia	4	1992	−29.15	5.00
Romania	4	1992	−30.79	3.00
Croatia	4	1993	−31.04	1.00
Latvia	4	1993	−39.52	3.00
Lithuania	4	1993	−55.44	2.00
Average			−25.89	3.53
Moderate Reforms				
Kyrgyzstan	3	1994	−42.30	−10.00
Russia	3	closed	−47.29	−15.00
Average			−42.61	−12.50
Weak Reforms				
FYR Macedonia	2	1994	−51.30	−7.00
Moldova	2	1994	−54.30	−25.00
Armenia	2	closed	−61.60	0.00
Kazakhstan	2	closed	−51.01	−25.00
Uzbekistan	2	closed	−11.75	−3.00
Average			−45.99	−12.00
Weakest Reforms				
Belarus	1	1994	−35.93	−22.00
Azerbaijan	1	closed	−54.32	−22.00
Georgia	1	closed	−85.35	−35.00
Tajikistan	1	closed	−70.37	−25.00
Turkmenistan	1	closed	−38.29	−20.00
Ukraine	1	closed	−51.36	−23.00
Average			−55.94	−24.50
Overall average			−38.63	−7.58

Source: European Bank for Reconstruction and Development, "Transition Report, 1994," Table 2.1, p. 10. Growth rates from Jeffrey D. Sachs and Andrew Warner, "Economic Reform and the Process of Global Integration," *Brookings Papers on Economic Activity* I (1995).

Growth performance in some CEE countries and Russia has improved since 1995. So too have indicators of inflation (see Table 9.12). Higher productivity, rising investment, and growing integration into the world economy have been favorable results of policy reforms. Unemployment, however, remains high.

China's growth potential is especially high, based on its abundance of natural resources, large domestic market, and unlimited supply of labor. As long as China follows "open door" and reform policies, the forces of growth will be strong. Imported capital and technology should play an increasingly important role. So too should the huge internal market make up for any possible future decline in exports. The recent transfer of power to the next generation of Chinese leaders raises some question of political stability, but it can be expected that the current growth-oriented policies of reform will be continued.

TABLE 9.11
Economies in Transition: Annual Growth of GDP (%) (annual averages)

	1980–85	1985–90	1991	1992	1993
China	10.2	7.8	8.4	13.8	13.9
Russia	3.2	1.3	−13.1	−19.7	−12.0
Bulgaria	4.3	2.6	−13.5	−6.1	−5.4
Czech	n.a.	1.8	−14.2	−7.1	−0.3
Slovak	n.a.	1.5	−16.2	−6.3	n.a.
Hungary	1.8	0.6	−12.0	−4.8	−2.0
Poland	0.7	0.3	−7.6	1.8	4.0
Romania	3.8	−2.1	−13.4	−14.9	−4.4

Source: Charles Goodhart and Chenggang Xu, *op cit.*, Table 1.6.

An elaborate econometric model of the Chinese economy estimates future rates of growth of selected economic indicators in a projection period to 2020, as indicated in Table 9.13. The model assumes peace and political stability and the continuation of economic reform policies. Although the rates of growth of exports and imports are lower than in past periods, the projections show that China will continue to grow at approximately 8 percent per annum between 1995 and 2020. Interestingly, China's real GDP will approach $4.5 trillion (in 1990 prices) in 2020, or somewhat less than the current U.S. real GNP, but it will have made the Chinese economy the third largest in the world.[22]

Some analysts are also optimistic about the prospects for CEE. A review of progress in the CEE countries concludes:

> There is no doubt that the CEEs have achieved a stupendous breakthrough in allocative efficiency since the start of market reforms. The introduction of market forces, underpinned by administrative, political, and legal changes, has allowed these economies to become full-fledged market economies in a relative short period of time, approximately one-half decade. As the 1995 Transition Report of the European Bank for Reconstruction and Development makes clear, the leading reformers (Czech Republic, Estonia, Hungary, Poland, Slovakia, and Slovenia) have completed the basic tasks of legal and institutional reform, and have even reached Western European best practices in several key areas, such as the openness of the economy to international trade. Within another few years, the CEEs should rival the Western European economies in other areas of legal and administrative reform.
>
> There is also little doubt that the rise in allocative efficiency is already paying off, in export-led GDP growth. All of the leading reforms have restored positive growth in 1995, after several years in which the introduction of market reforms forced the downsizing or liquidation of the old, heavy industrial enterprises. Much of the new growth is coming in small, export-oriented enterprises, as well as in services. Foreign direct investment is also starting to increase, with foreign-owned enterprises in the CEEs increasingly helping to integrate the region into European-wide, or even global, production networks.
>
> By 1995, the CEEs had made considerable progress in all of the major areas of reform. In the crucial area of trade and exchange rate liberalization, the EBRD judges that six of the countries (Czech Republic, Hungary, Poland, Romania, Slovakia, and Slovenia) have reached the standards of the advanced industrial economies. Nonetheless, there is still considerable work to complete on the basic industrial re-ordering, even

TABLE 9.12
European Economies in Transition and the Russian Federation: Key Economic Indicators[a]

	1994	1995	1996	1997
Bulgaria				
Output	1.4	2.5	2.5	3.0
Inflation	125.0	33.0	40.0	30.0
Unemployment	12.8	11.1	13.0	12.0
Fiscal balance	−5.6	−6.8	−6.5	−6.0
Current account	0.1	0.3	0.0	0.0
Poland				
Output	5.2	7.0	5.5	5.0
Inflation	29.0	22.0	19.0	15.0
Unemployment	16.0	14.9	14.0	13.0
Fiscal balance	−2.7	−2.9	−2.8	−2.5
Current account	−0.9	−2.1	−2.9	−3.5
Romania				
Output	3.5	6.9	4.0	4.0
Inflation	62.0	28.0	25.0	20.0
Unemployment	10.9	8.9	10.0	10.0
Fiscal balance	−1.0	−3.6	−2.5	−2.5
Current account	−0.4	−1.5	−1.5	−1.0
Russia				
Output	−15.0	−4.0	1.0	3.0
Output/revised series	−12.6			
Inflation	226.0	131.0	50.0	30.0
Unemployment	6.0	8.0	9.0	10.0
Fiscal balance	−10.1	−4.0	−4.0	−3.5
Current account	0.0	7.0	2.5	−0.6
Slovak Republic				
Output	4.9	7.4	5.0	5.0
Inflation	11.7	7.2	7.0	7.0
Unemployment	14.8	13.1	12.5	12.0
Fiscal balance	−1.2	0.7	−1.5	−1.0
Current account	0.7	0.5	0.0	0.0
Slovenia				
Output	5.5	4.5	5.0	5.0
Inflation	19.0	9.0	10.0	10.0
Unemployment	14.2	13.5	13.0	12.0
Fiscal balance	−0.2	−0.9	−0.5	−0.5
Current account	−0.5	0.0	0.3	0.1

[a]Output data are average annual percentage changes of real GDP. Inflation refers to the year-end percent change in consumer prices. The fiscal balance is expressed as a percentage of GDP while the current account balance is in $ billion.
Source: OECD, *Economic Outlook*, June 1996, p. 134. © OECD, 1996, Economic Outlook. Reproduced with permission of the OECD.

for the three leading CEEs (Czech Republic, Hungary, and Poland). These countries still have a state sector of 30% or more of GDP, according to the EBRD estimates. They also lag behind the advanced industrial countries in several areas of legal and administrative development, including: banking reform, securities market development, and competition policy.[23]

A study published by the London-based Center for Economic Policy Research shows both the potential for and the limitations to opportunities in Eastern Europe. The report states that in a period of ten years, the countries of Eastern Europe could double their GDP. This implies an annual growth rate in income per head of about 7 percent, but because

TABLE 9.13
China: Comparisons of the Average Annual Rates of Growth of Selected Economic Indicators

	1979–92 Reform	1992–2020 Projected
Real GDP	8.9	8.6
Real GDP/capita	7.4	7.5
Real gross value of:		
Agricultural production	5.9	5.2
Light industry	14.8	10.2
Heavy industry	11.9	12.3
Real personal consumption	8.7	7.4
Real consumption/capita	7.2	6.3
Gross fixed investment	10.2	11.7
Capital stock	8.7	9.2
Employment	2.9	2.3
GDP deflator	5.2	7.3
Retail price index	6.0	7.1
Exports (in current U.S. dollars)	16.7	11.3
Imports (in current U.S. dollars)	15.4	11.7
Telephones/thousand persons	12.0	NA

Source: Lawrence J. Lau, "The Chinese Economy in the Twenty-First Century" (Stanford, CA: Asia/Pacific Research Center, 1994), p. 19.

the existing capital stock of Eastern Europe is, as the report suggests, worthless, any substantial and sustained growth in GDP would require an investment inflow averaging more than $100 billion per year. The report sees no indication that capital inflows on this scale will be forthcoming. Western investors remain cautious, waiting for the governments of Eastern Europe to set up the legal instruments necessary to attract foreign capital. They seek assurances that profits can be repatriated and that the countries are stable. Even if these conditions are met, there is still always the fear that the population will rebel against the liberalization of prices, a cutback in consumer spending, and unemployment. As the report says, "The issue is how both investment and consumption needs can be financed."

A similarly cautious summary is taken by Morgan Guaranty Trust Company: "Foreign investors require credible and predictable legal, regulatory, and fiscal arrangements to define property rights and allow profit repatriation at will or within an acceptable time horizon. These arrangements are needed in any event for markets to function. But they will not come into place overnight, least of all while political systems remain in flux.

"An ideal investment environment from the standpoint of resource allocation, would forswear arbitrary export performance requirements of foreign investors, ownership limits, or other discrimination against them. This will not be easy for economies subject to ethnic or nationalist sensitivities, of which foreign investors in turn must be mindful. Still, nondiscrimination is important in investment matters. Not least so that the Eastern economies may develop constituencies in the West to improve their trade access to Western markets, in particularly to those of the European Community. All told, the Eastern countries will need many years to transform themselves into dynamic, market economies."[24]

Surveying the prospects for transition from plan to market, a World Bank report also cautions that even where policy change is rapid, institutional change is slow, and transition will not be complete until institutions effectively underpin markets. There are severe bottlenecks:

- All countries have taken steps to reform the legal framework, but the extent and coherence of reform vary. The reform of judicial institutions and enforcement mechanisms lags far behind, and corruption has become an acute concern in some countries. These are areas of high priority for the future.

- More advanced reformers now have some banks capable of delivering services at least comparable to those available in middle-income countries, but they also have a substantial share of financial assets in poorly functioning banks. Serious conflicts of interest plague many financial systems, and in most countries the scope of market-based finance is limited by poor debt recovery mechanisms. Virtually all countries have many nonperforming loans, which pose a major policy dilemma.

- Most governments have substantially reoriented their roles to meet the needs of a market economy, but in such critical areas as tax administration, public administration, and fiscal decentralization, reforms are still at an early stage in many countries. This has hurt the economy and in some cases has adversely affected regional equity. The power and administrative authority of central governments have diminished in some countries with the considerable, and sometimes chaotic, decentralization of revenues and functions to subnational governments. There is frequent confusion over the roles of the executive, the legislature, and the constitutional courts.[25]

The study also concludes:

The next stage of reforms in the [transition economies] will be more complex and difficult than their past efforts, as they tackle reform of the core of their state sectors and the institutional underpinnings of their economies. Maintaining growth and improving the distribution of its rewards are central goals, because these are still poor countries, and it is also necessary to sustain support for reform. This requires improving the efficiency with which savings are allocated and, in parallel, developing better indirect tools of macroeconomic management. Continuing fiscal reform, including recentralization of the budget in China, is one priority. So are raising capacity in the banking and legal systems and anticipating the need to deal with the many problem clients that will emerge as banks become more commercial and policies shift away from subsidizing credit. A clear definition of the role and scope of the state sector is called for, and this will almost certainly involve reducing its size. Also important are mechanisms to encourage effective corporate governance and accountability in state, nonstate, and private firms and to avoid an ownership vacuum. Social policy reforms should focus on sustaining broad access to key social services and improving their quality, both for increasing mobile populations and in poor areas. Disentangling of social benefits from state enterprises is needed to unlock the door to further reforms.

    With sustained reforms, transition countries have the potential to achieve strong growth. CEE can exploit the catch-up effect from its favorable location close to large, high-income markets. The CIS can look to major gains from far more efficient use of its natural resource and human capital endowments, and [China] combines abundant labor, a tradition of high rates of saving, and large opportunities to increase the efficiency with which these resources are allocated. A successful transition therefore promises long-term growth rates considerably above world averages.[26]

A cautionary outlook is indeed justified. Close monitoring of economic policies will be essential to determine if reform measures are actually being implemented. As with LDCs, country risk analysis will be extremely important in determining a firm's response to developments in the transition economies.

NOTES

1. From *The Road to a Free Economy* by János Kornai. Copyright © 1960 by János Kornai. Reprinted by permission of W. W. Norton & Company, Inc.
2. Ibid., p. 59.
3. Ibid., pp. 73, 80.
4. International Monetary Fund, et al., *The Economy of the USSR: Summary and Recommendations* (Washington, DC: IMF, 1991).
5. Jeffrey Sachs, "My Plan for Poland," *International Economy* (Dec. 1989/Jan. 1990): 28.
6. Jeffrey Sachs and David Lipton, "Poland's Economic Reform," *Foreign Affairs* (summer 1990): 63–64.
7. Goodhart and Xu, *op cit.*, Table 1.8.
8. Dwight Perkins, "Completing China's Move to the Market," *Journal of Economic Perspectives* (spring 1994): 24.
9. Gary Jefferson and Thomas Rawski, "Enterprise Reform in Chinese Industry," *Journal of Economic Perspectives* 8, 2 (1994); Charles Goodhart and Chenggang Xu, "The Rise of China as an Economic Power," *National Institute Economic Review* (February 1996).
10. This section summarizes World Bank, *World Development Report 1996*, op cit., pp. 34–40. But cf. Ronald I. McKinnon, *Gradual versus Rapid Liberalization in Socialist Economies* (San Francisco: ICS Press, 1994).
11. Dwight Perkins, "Completing China's Move to the Market," *Journal of Economic Literature* 8, 2 (spring 1994): 43.
12. Masahiko Aoki, "Towards a Comparative Institutional Analysis: Motivations and Some Tentative Theorizing," *Japanese Economic Review* 47, 1 (March 1996): 7. For the relation of privatization and post-privatization reforms to corporate governance, see Maxim Boycko, Andrei Shleifer, Robert Vishny, *Privatizing Russia* (Cambridge, MA: MIT Press, 1995), Chs. 1, 4, 5.
13. Kornai, *The Road to a Free Economy*, op cit., pp. 82–93. Copyright © 1990 by János Kornai. Reprinted by permission of W. W. Norton & Company, Inc.
14. Ibid., pp. 59, 101.
15. Joseph E. Stiglitz, *Financial Systems for Eastern Europe's Emerging Democracies* (San Francisco: ICS Press, 1993), pp. 9–10.
16. For details in various countries, see World Bank, *World Development Report 1996*, op cit., Ch. 6.
17. Stiglitz, op cit., pp. 25–26.
18. World Bank, *World Development Report 1996*, p. 133.
19. *Financial Times*, March 25, 1996.
20. *New York Times*, February 3, 1991, p. C-1.
21. Karen Elliott House, "In East Europe, Only Poland Makes Hard Decisions," *Wall Street Journal*, June 5, 1990, p. A22. See also Andrei Shleifer, "Government in Transition," Harvard Institute for International Development, Discussion Paper No. 573, March 1997.

22. Lawrence J. Lau, "The Chinese Economy in the Twenty-First Century," processed, January 1994, pp. 15–18. This model has been constructed jointly by the Chinese Academy of Social Sciences, the State Statistical Bureau of China, and Stanford University.

23. Sachs and Warner, op cit., pp. 42–43, 45.

24. Morgan Guaranty Trust Company, "World Financial Markets," 1990, Issue 1, pp. 15–16.

25. World Bank, *World Development Report 1996*, op cit., p. 13.

DISCUSSION QUESTIONS

1. What measures do you believe a government should adopt to transform its economy from a centralized command economy to a decentralized market economy?

2. In what order should these measures be taken?

3. What are the implications of these measures for business?

4. How would increased trade between CEE countries and China with the EU affect the EU? Developing countries?

5. Would the transition economies benefit from membership in the WTO? In the EU?

6. What are the disadvantages, if any, of having the privatization process result in insider control by managers and workers of former state enterprises? If you were a management consulting firm advising the government of a CEE country on how to privatize, what would you recommend?

7. What should be the role of the financial sector in supporting privatization and enterprise restructuring?

8. If you were undertaking country risk analysis for a foreign direct investment in a transition economy, to what would you give special attention?

9. How do you account for the fact that there has been more rapid economic growth and relatively low inflation in China than in CEE and CIS?

10. What do you believe will be the major problems confronting China over the next five to ten years?

PART **IV**

 SYNTHESIS

For private management, the major implications of global economic change relate to global competitiveness. Many of the topics in our preceding discussion of the analytics of the international economy and the relative roles of state and market are relevant to the international competitive advantage of a firm. Chapter 10 synthesizes these topics in a consolidated analysis of the determinants of international competitiveness. The chapter focuses not only on competitive advantage of the firm, but also on the relative economic performance of nations, especially in terms of productivity and domestic public management for the objective of economic growth.

For the practice of international public management, Chapter 11 synthesizes some problems and prospects of global governance. In view of the international economic tensions and competition among national policy makers that we have noted in preceding chapters, Chapter 11 evaluates various international governance structures for establishing international economic order. We shall emphasize in particular the functioning of the international public sector.

Chapter

10 GLOBAL COMPETITION

In the changing global economy, the exhortation to be competitive is frequently heard. But "competition" needs clarification. Firms compete: Kodak versus Fuji. Internationally, firms compete for markets between two countries or in third countries. For a firm producing a tradable product, being internationally competitive comes down to having your product outsell a competitor's product at satisfactory returns to the firm. The competitive game is zero sum: What one firm gains, the other loses.

To speak of competition between countries, however, is misleading.[1] Countries are not companies and they do not compete in the way that firms compete. What one nation might do, however, is outperform another in the sense of increasing its standard of living or some measure such as GDP per head. National performance, or what the British term "league tables," might then indicate some form of international competition. But what one country gains is not a loss to another country. From a welfare standpoint, it is the absolute increase in a country's standard of living that matters—not the change relative to another country. It is possible for all countries to improve their economic welfare, even if none becomes more competitive relative to the others.

Similarly, it is a mercantilistic fallacy to think of competition among countries as a rivalry to acquire the largest export surplus. What is the competitive advantage of an export surplus? Recall what is meant by the mutual gains from trade (Chapter 2). As we will discuss, exports or inward investment are, of course, essential to pay for imports, but it is only in this sense that we can say that a country must be sufficiently competitive to pay for those imports that are induced by the country's desired rate of economic growth.

We have seen how developments in Europe, Japan, the NICs, and the transitional economies are intensifying competition in world markets. This has important implications for the firm's practice of ICA and DPR. In practicing ICA, management should be concerned with what determines a nation's economic performance, different trends in national performance, and what policies should now be recommended to enhance the economic standing of a country. In practicing DPR, management should diagnose what are the future strategies that are essential to allow a firm to be globally competitive, and the diagnosis and prediction should quickly establish competitive response advantages.

WHAT IS THE COMPETITIVENESS PROBLEM?

Profitability in an industry depends on the prices of the products it sells, input prices, wages, and productivity. Given a stock of capital in the industry and the production function, the rate of return on capital (profitability) depends on the product prices and the nominal wages to labor in the industry. A rise in productivity will raise profitability for given prices and wages. If, however, wages rise faster than the prices of the products that are sold, profitability will fall, and the industry's output and employment are also likely to fall. A rise in input prices also reduces profitability, given the final goods' prices, wages, and productivity.

Consider a model with exportables (X), importables (M), and nontradables (N), with no produced inputs. Utilizing this model to clarify the competitiveness problem, we may distinguish among three cases, as follows[2]:

- Case I represents a sectoral competitiveness problem: Profitability of X (or alternatively, of M) declines, and this is offset by increased profitability of M (or, alternatively, of X). Profitability has declined within the tradables sector, but the average profitability of tradables has not necessarily declined. There are gainers and losers. The loss of competitiveness is only sectoral, with a redistribution of competitiveness among export and import-competing industries, not an overall national decline. The remedial policy is devaluation of the country's currency to stimulate the export- or import-competing industries.

- Case II represents a real appreciation problem: Here the average profitability of tradables has declined, but not the average for the entire economy. A current account deficit appears, or a previous deficit increases. This can be associated with a real appreciation, the domestic prices of tradables falling relative to those of nontradables. Profitability in tradables (in both X and M) then falls and in nontradables (in N) rises. Again, there are gainers and losers, and although overall profitability may not necessarily have declined, it can be said that the country has become internationally less competitive. There has been a general loss of competitiveness of the country's tradables sector.

- Case III represents a decline in national profitability. Here the profitability of tradables (X and M) and nontradables (N) all decline, and the output of all industries falls. This denotes an economy-wide problem of low or declining productivity growth. Appropriate depreciation of the exchange rate can offset the low or declining productivity growth and thereby maintain the competitiveness of the tradables sector. As we saw in Chapter 5, there is some exchange rate together with appropriate absorption policy that can maintain internal and external balance. With the proper exchange rate adjustment, an increase in foreign productivity growth would not reduce the home industries' competitiveness. Moreover, it should be noted that the rate of growth of real income in the home country does not depend on relative productivity growth between the countries but on the rate of growth of productivity at home.

WHAT DOES INTERNATIONAL COMPETITION MEAN?

First, it can refer to the performance of countries in terms of their relative overall productivity growth. While countries with very different levels of productivity can gain from trading with one another, the living standards of each will be determined largely by their own productivity level. This is determined by the whole gamut of domestic economic policies—for savings, for investment and for the introduction of competitive pressure, including from trade.

Second, it refers to the overall cost level of a country, given its productivity. If domestic costs are out of line with domestic productivity, the real exchange rate is overvalued and all industries producing tradable goods and services will suffer. Then either the country will have a large external deficit in its trade, or it will suffer from a recession as the price of putting its external account in order. The solution to this form of uncompetitiveness is a real depreciation of the exchange rate, again something that depends on a country's domestic policies.

Third, it can refer to the fate of particular firms or enterprises. They must compete with other domestic firms for the services of factors of production as well as with foreign firms that produce competing outputs. But the failure of particular firms does not mean that the economy as a whole is uncompetitive. Japan, for example, suffered from a progressive loss of competitiveness in the production of clothing after the 1950s. This was not, of course, an indication of economic failure, but rather one of success. Its comparative advantage was shifting to other, more sophisticated industries.

Martin Wolf, "The EU in a Liberal Global Economy," *International Affairs* (April 1995): 329

MACRO DETERMINANTS OF COMPETITIVENESS

A country's real income depends on a high and rapidly rising level of productivity, but this increase in productivity must be realized through the operation of private firms. If businesses are to increase productivity, both macroeconomic and microeconomic factors must be conducive. Practicing ICA, management must first understand the macroeconomic environment in order to begin achieving total efficiency.

Macroeconomic factors that are most important in determining a nation's productivity are:

- The rate of national saving and investment
- Interest rates and the cost of capital
- Foreign exchange rates
- Investment in education and training of labor
- The country's physical infrastructure
- A noninflationary economy

Tomorrow's productivity will depend very much on the investment made today. By "investment" we mean any use of current resources for the purpose of achieving a future return. Investment therefore includes not only business spending for plant and equipment, but also the use of public resources to improve the nation's physical infrastructure (transportation and communication networks). Capital formation can also be broadened to include investment in human capital through education and training. Funding for R&D is also investment.

To achieve a high rate of national investment, however, there must also be a high rate of national saving. A firm must acquire investable funds, either by borrowing, by selling equity, or by accumulating its own retained earnings. If a country has a high rate of national consumption, it can generate only a low rate of national saving. Resources for investment will then be limited and the cost of capital will be high. The higher the required rate of return on investments by firms, the fewer investments will qualify when the cost of capital is high.

A high cost of capital will also cause firms to substitute labor for capital, and with a declining capital:labor ratio in the production process, labor productivity may fall. Many

---

A COMPETITIVENESS INDEX?

It is tempting to seek a measurement of global competitiveness. The World Economic Forum's *Global Competitiveness Report 1997* attempts this by focusing on "eight factors of competitiveness" that it believes "gauges the ability of a national economy to achieve high rates of growth in GDP per person" over the next five to ten years. The factor indexes are:

- Openness of the economy to international trade and finance
- Role of the government budget and regulation
- Development of financial markets
- Quality of infrastructure
- Quality of technology
- Quality of business management
- Labor market flexibility
- Quality of judicial and political institutions

These factors are measured on a cross-country basis, and the results are summarized in a simple Competitiveness Index. The 1997 report ranks Singapore the highest in potential growth, followed in order by Hong Kong, United States, Canada, New Zealand, Switzerland, United Kingdom, Taiwan, and Malaysia.

The index can be criticized for its problematic selection of factors of competitiveness and for the arbitrary weights given to the individual factors. The real value of the exercise is not the index but the procedure of trying to assess what national policies influence a country's potential standard of living.

have argued that the main reason for slow productivity growth in the United States is the low rate of capital formation attributable mostly to the high cost of capital to American firms, which they blame on the low national saving rate.

Another important macroeconomic variable is the country's foreign exchange rate. If it is to be competitive in foreign markets, the nation must have a real exchange rate that takes account of differential rates of inflation between the home country and foreign countries. If inflation in the home country is at a higher rate than abroad, the home country's currency must be depreciated in terms of foreign currency for exporting firms to remain competitive in price.

A general macro environment of noninflationary prosperity is also conducive to rising productivity. The government's monetary policy and fiscal policy must be directed toward maintaining high and stable levels of full employment of labor and capital in the economy. An excessively large deficit in the government's budget must be avoided so as not to crowd out private investment. Tax policy will also play an important role in determining the relative advantages of saving and consumption, and hence the level of national investment.

MICRO DETERMINANTS OF COMPETITIVENESS

Although macroeconomic factors exercise significant influence on a nation's productivity, they are only part of the story and probably the lesser part. For even though all the national firms are operating in the same macroeconomic environment, it is obvious that some firms do much better than others, both from a productivity perspective and in international competition. Microeconomic factors at the level of the firm must therefore also play a strategic role in determining productivity and competitiveness. To sell abroad or compete against imports, a firm must maintain its cost competitiveness and its product competitiveness. Cost competitiveness will depend on the prices of inputs and their productivity (output per unit of input), and the firm's internal efficiency in achieving the least cost combination of inputs to produce a given output.

On the side of inputs, the cost of labor and its productivity are especially important in determining the firm's international competitiveness. To a considerable extent, international competitiveness is a function of relative labor cost in a common currency per unit of output. Given the exchange rate, competitiveness will be determined by a four factor analysis: the wage rate times the reciprocal of labor productivity times profit margin times exchange rate. The cost of labor (its earnings) comprises wages plus taxes, fringe benefits, and social insurance costs borne by the employer. Earnings multiplied by the inverse of labor productivity will give the firm's labor cost. If earnings are high and labor productivity low, the only way the firm can remain competitive is through a reduction in profit margins or through a depreciation of the country's foreign exchange rate. To be competitive, it is therefore essential to keep wage rates within the bounds of productivity and not allow labor costs to rise relative to other countries.

Beyond cost competitiveness, a firm's product competitiveness is important in achieving the nonprice dimensions of a competitive advantage. These nonprice dimensions involve design of product, quality of product, punctuality in delivery, and service facilities. Especially significant are innovations that differentiate the firm's product and hence give some monopoly element for the firm's product. Innovations are also important in bringing

A FOUR-FACTOR ANALYSIS OF COMPETITIVENESS

Nobel laureate Lawrence Klein offers the following analysis of the components of competitiveness:

"In the final analysis, competitiveness is determined by relative prices, for given products, between country pairs. If the U.S. price is lower than those of [other countries], when measured in common currency units, then we are competitive. Relative price for a product or service of given quality fixes 'the bottom line.' That is straightforward enough. But in order to understand the price relatives and in order to recommend appropriate policies for reaching or maintaining competitiveness, it is useful to show how the price relatives are determined. For the U.S. price, a four-factor decomposition is useful: Unit cost (wage rate) × reciprocal of (labor) productivity × profit margin × exchange rate (L/$) = price in local foreign currency, where L stands for 'local' currency unit, to be compared with the U.S. dollar unit ($).

"Unit cost refers here to cost per unit of productive factor input. A productive factor is a composite of labor, capital, materials, and fuel. The most important productive factor in making up cost of U.S. goods production is labor. . . .

"The second term is the reciprocal of labor productivity. If the wage rate is quoted as wage per hour, then the corresponding productivity measure should be output per hour. . . . The product of wage rate and reciprocal of labor productivity provides a measure of unit labor cost, an important efficiency measure. As labor productivity rises we have an offset to wage cost; the reciprocal falls, and unit labor cost falls. To become competitive, a country should try to hold down its unit labor cost and may do so on two fronts, either through wage restraint or through productivity enhancement, or through a combination of both.

"The profit margin is in the form of a percentage mark-up over cost, in this case unit labor cost. The more profit restraint that we find, the lower will be price; conversely, high profit margins can contribute to lack of competitiveness.

"Finally, the exchange rate converts costs (with mark-up) from a domestic price quotation in dollars ($) to a foreign price quotation in local currency (L). As the dollar depreciates, this factor falls and contributes to a lower price to foreign buyers. Many countries have tried to cover up lack of cost effectiveness by depreciating their currency in order to become more competitive. In a sense, the exchange rate, where it can be controlled or manipulated, becomes a 'crutch' whereby a country tries to gain in competitiveness."

Reprinted with permission from Lawrence R. Klein, "Components of Competition," *Science* 241, 15 (July 1988): 309 Copyright 1988 American Association for the Advancement of Science.

technological progress to the processes of production. Unlike the situation two or three decades ago when differences in labor and capital costs were more significant in determining industrial competitiveness than they are today, technological innovations have become increasingly crucial. Clearly, companies are now continually, and with increasing speed, bringing onto the market new product lines that possess advantages in technical quality rather than in cost and price. And the leader gains market share.

In the 1980s came a shift to managing time rather than cost. In that decade many Japanese corporations, led by Toyota, shifted to a new flexible production strategy. Their success was attributed to operation/manufacturing that significantly reduced costs, increased their productivity rate three to four times the American rate, improved quality, and reduced time to markets (less than one-half the time for some products).

The focus on operation/manufacturing time-based competition has become a competitive weapon. In their book *Competing Against Time*, the authors from the Boston Consulting Group state: "Today's innovation is time-based competition. Demanding executives at aggressive companies are altering their measures of performance from competitive costs and quality to competitive costs, quality, and *responsiveness*. Give customers what they want when they want it. This refocusing attention is enabling early innovators to become time-based competitors. Time-based competitors are offering greater varieties of products and services, at lower costs and in less time than their more pedestrian competitors. In so doing, they are literally running circles around their slower competition."[3]

When they compress time, time-based competitors acquire a competitive advantage for these reasons:

- Costs decrease
- Prices can be increased (because of the premiums paid for rapid delivery)
- Risks are reduced (risks of incorrect forecasting as well as costs of errors)
- Market share increases

In an attempt to determine what factors are most important in determining international competitiveness, a recent empirical study estimated the quantitative significance of many of the factors that we have discussed. The study concluded that international competitiveness as given by the share of market is mainly a function of relative unit labor cost, technology competitiveness (indicated by differentiated products), and time competition in delivery.[4]

INTERNATIONAL PRODUCTIVITY

A number of empirical studies compare differences in economic performance on the basis of national trends in productivity growth rates. For the advanced industrialized countries of the OECD, these studies show substantial rates of growth in productivity during the 1950s and 1960s, but considerably lower rates after the early 1970s. Most strikingly, they reveal that in comparison with other industrialized countries, the United States has sadly lagged. Figure 10.1 charts the course of labor productivity in the United States 1960–95: An average annual rate of growth in productivity of 1.9 percent from 1960 to 1973 fell to only 1.0 percent from 1973 to 1995.

In 1996, the U.S. Labor Department recalculated productivity numbers and found that labor productivity had risen only 1.2 percent annually since mid-1990.[5] The recalculated rate from 1979 to mid-1990 was only 1 percent. The slow rates were despite the corporate downsizing and re-engineering of the 1980s and 1990s.

Productivity in manufacturing—although accounting for less than 25 percent of national output—improved more rapidly: at a rate of 3.2 percent from mid-1990 to 1995 and at a rate of 2.6 percent in the 1979–90 period.

TIME AND WORLD-CLASS AUTOMOBILE COMPANIES

The responsiveness gap some Japanese companies have opened over their Western competitors is simply astounding. [Consider] basic response times for the fundamental value delivery systems of world class automobile competitors in the West and in Japan. Japanese companies require between six and eight days to get an order from the field to line set, the point at which managers know the exact time the order will be manufactured. This compares to 16 to 26 days for the better Western automobile companies. Manufacturing itself takes the best Western companies 14 to 30 days per order compared to two to four days for the fastest Japanese manufacturers. Most important of all is the time required to develop and introduce new automobile designs to the market. The fastest Japanese automobile companies can accomplish this in two and one-half to three years. Western automobile companies require four to over six years to introduce new designs—two to three times longer than the fastest Japanese companies.

The implications of being two to three times faster than the best Western companies are fresher product offerings that have a higher degree of technological sophistication. . . .

Time compression is the fundamental change enabling the Japanese to increase the variety and technological sophistication of the products and services they offer. Time is the secret weapon of business because advantages in response time lever up all other differences that are basic to overall competitive advantage. Some Western managements know this, others are learning, and the rest will be victims.

George Stalk, Jr. and Thomas M. Hout, *Competing Against Time* (New York: Free Press, 1990), pp. 29–31 Reprinted with the permission of The Free Press, a Division of Simon & Schuster. Copyright © 1990 by The Free Press.

Another measure of productivity as we have seen is that of total factor productivity (TFP), which represents the difference between the growth of output and the growth of a composite of all inputs. It therefore shows the extent to which output may grow beyond the increased use of inputs (the residual in a production function relating output to inputs). If, for example, doubling inputs will more than double output, then there is an increase in TFP.

Table 10.1 shows growth trends in TFP for American manufacturing industries in selected periods. Comparing 1949–73 with 1973–92, most industries exhibit a slowdown: In total manufacturing, the growth rate dropped from 1.8 percent to 0.8 percent per year. Table 10.2 shows growth in output as the result of increase in all inputs and TFP.

The implications for competitiveness are these: An increase in productivity growth allows a competitive position to be enhanced without requiring price reductions in inputs; or an input price increase may be offset by the increase in productivity; or input prices may be raised without necessitating a rise in output price.

With such slow rates of growth in U.S. labor productivity, labor's real compensation per hour has also been able to increase at only a very slow rate (see Figure 10.2).

Although productivity growth has generally slowed for major industrial countries since the early 1970s, America's growth rate is the lowest (see Figure 10.3 and Table 10.1).

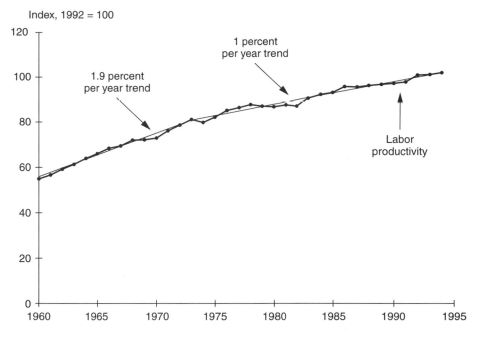

Figure 10.1   Actual and trend labor productivity, United States, 1960–95. *Source*: Department of Labor, Bureau of Labor Statistics, *Economic Report of the President 1996*, 332.

TABLE 10.1

Input, Output, and Total Factor Productivity Growth, United States, 1949–92 (compound average annual growth rates)

Industry	Capital	Labor	Intermediate Inputs	All Inputs	Total Factor Productivity	Output
Total manufacturing						
1949–73	4.1	1.4	2.6	2.3	1.8	4.1
1973–79	4.6	.3	4.1	2.5	−.1	2.4
1979–92	3.6	−.9	.7	.6	1.2	1.7

Source: *Monthly Labor Review*, July 1995, p. 23.

TABLE 10.2

Relative Levels of GDP per Worker, Selected Countries, 1950–87 (percent of U.S. = 100)

Country	1950	1960	1970	1980	1987
United States	100.0	100.0	100.0	100.0	100.0
Canada	77.1	80.1	84.2	92.8	95.5
Japan	15.2	23.2	45.7	62.6	70.7
France	36.8	46.0	61.7	80.1	85.3
West Germany	32.4	49.1	61.8	77.4	81.1
Italy	30.8	43.9	66.4	80.9	85.5
United Kingdom	53.9	54.3	58.0	65.9	71.9

Source: Barry P. Bosworth and Robert Z. Lawrence, "America in the World Economy," *Brookings Review* (winter 1988/89): 44.

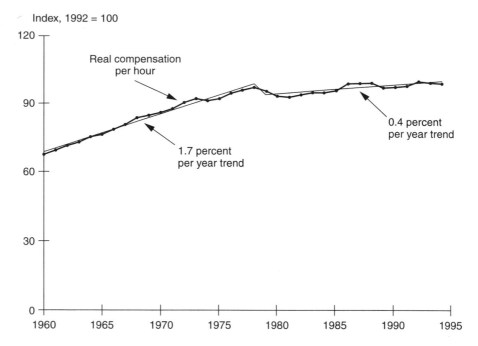

Index, 1992 = 100

Figure 10.2. Real compensation per hour, United States, 1960–95. Note: Hourly compensation in nonfarm business sector divided by the consumer price index. *Source*: Department of Labor, Bureau of Labor Statistics, *Economic Report of the President 1996*, 332.

A revealing comparison of relative levels of productivity is also presented in Table 10.2 that indicates how other countries have improved their levels of GDP per worker relative to that of the United States. For instance, in 1950, Japan's level of GDP per worker was only some 15 percent of the United States's level, but by 1987 it was nearly 71 percent of the U.S. level.

The differences in levels of output per worker between the United States and other countries, as calculated in Table 10.2, are based on purchasing power parity exchange rates (equivalent cost of the same basket of goods in different countries). In 1987, the average French, German, and Japanese worker produced approximately 15 percent, 19 percent, and 29 percent, respectively, less than the average American worker. If in a country there is faster growth of productivity in the traded than in the nontraded goods sectors relative to its trading partners, then there is a real appreciation of its currency. Accordingly, if comparisons are based on 1987 market exchange rates, instead of purchasing power parity exchange rates, then the GDP per employed worker was 11 percent, 5 percent, and 4 percent higher in Germany, France, and Japan, respectively.[6]

These comparisons highlight an important difference between the United States and its international trading partners: Other major industrial countries have matched or exceeded American performance in tradable goods industries that export or compete with imports, but they lag far behind the United States in their ability to produce nontradables, primarily in the distribution, food, and service sectors. Their standard of living would be much higher

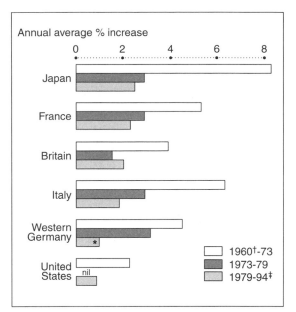

Figure 10.3. Labor productivity, selected countries. *Sources*: OECD; *Economic Report of the President.*

*All Germany after 1991   †Or earliest   †Or latest

if they could buy nontradable goods from the United States, rather than at home. Because of the high cost of domestic nontradables, these nations, particularly Japan, have much lower overall living standards than their efficiency in producing tradable goods would suggest.[7]

For competitiveness, especially significant are unit labor costs. Changes in output per hour together with hourly compensation determine changes in unit labor costs (L). Unit labor costs in terms of national currency are then altered to dollar currency units by the exchange rate in dollars: per national currency unit times unit labor costs (L). Table 10.3 shows how unit labor costs for several countries were determined from 1960–89 by the connections between labor productivity, compensation, and exchange rates. Over the entire period, the United States had the lowest and Japan the highest growth rate of labor productivity. But hourly compensation increased the least in the United States over the same period, so that unit labor costs in the United States show the smallest average annual increase on a national currency basis over the entire period, although running ahead of Japan and Germany in the post-1973 period. When unit labor costs are measured on a U.S. dollar basis, however, American labor costs rose less than in Japan and European countries in 1973–79, continued to rise as dollar appreciation actually increased unit costs elsewhere from 1979–85, and then fell slightly as unit labor costs rose rapidly outside the United States with dollar depreciation during 1985–89.[8]

Since the mid-1980s, hourly compensation for manufacturing production workers in Japan, many European economies, and the Asian NICs have risen considerably (see Table 10.4). From 1992–95, output per head in manufacturing rose more rapidly in the U.S. than Japan, and compensation per hour rose less in the U.S. than in Japan. Consequently, unit labor costs in the U.S. fell by 3.4 percent while they rose by 3.4 percent in Japan on a national currency basis.[8a]

TABLE 10.3
Manufacturing Productivity and Related Measures, Twelve Countries

Item and Country	1960	1970	1982	1989
Output Per Hour[a]				
United States	56.9	75.2	100.0	130.1
Canada	51.6	76.9	100.0	123.8
Japan	17.2	48.0	100.0	144.8
Belgium	24.2	44.2	100.0	—
Denmark	32.4	57.2	100.0	106.8
France	30.7	58.5	100.0	125.1
Germany	36.9	65.2	100.0	119.6
Italy	28.9	54.3	100.0	133.8
Netherlands	27.3	54.1	100.0	134.7
Norway	47.8	74.5	100.0	131.7
Sweden	36.5	69.6	100.0	119.3
United Kingdom	49.4	70.8	100.0	144.1
Compensation Per Hour[b]				
United States	22.5	35.9	100.0	128.8
Canada	16.4	28.7	100.0	143.8
Japan	6.5	24.8	100.0	129.9
Belgium	9.1	23.1	100.0	—
Denmark	7.7	22.3	100.0	147.8
France	7.4	17.8	100.0	155.5
Germany	13.7	35.1	100.0	136.0
Italy	3.9	11.6	100.0	194.4
Netherlands	9.1	28.5	100.0	125.7
Norway	9.9	24.6	100.0	183.3
Sweden	9.3	24.4	100.0	180.7
United Kingdom	7.2	14.9	100.0	164.3
Unit Labor Costs: National Currency Basis (L)[c]				
United States	39.5	47.7	100.0	99.0
Canada	31.9	37.3	100.0	116.1
Japan	37.9	51.6	100.0	89.7
Belgium	37.8	52.3	100.0	—
Denmark	23.8	39.0	100.0	138.3
France	24.0	30.4	100.0	124.3
Germany	37.2	53.8	100.0	113.7
Italy	13.6	21.4	100.0	145.4
Netherlands	33.4	52.7	100.0	93.3
Norway	20.6	33.0	100.0	139.1
Sweden	25.5	35.0	100.0	151.4
United Kingdom	14.6	21.0	100.0	114.0
Unit Labor Costs: U.S. Dollar Basis ($)[d]				
United States	39.5	47.7	100.0	99.0
Canada	40.6	44.1	100.0	121.0
Japan	26.2	35.9	100.0	161.8
Belgium	34.7	48.2	100.0	—
Denmark	28.8	43.4	100.0	157.7
France	32.2	36.2	100.0	128.2
Germany	21.7	35.8	100.0	146.8
Italy	29.6	46.2	100.0	143.4
Netherlands	23.7	38.9	100.0	117.5
Norway	18.7	29.8	100.0	130.0
Sweden	31.0	42.5	100.0	147.4
United Kingdom	23.4	28.7	100.0	106.9

— = Data not available.

[a] Value of goods and services in constant prices produced per hour of labor input.

[b] Wages and salaries of employees plus employer's contribution for social insurance and private benefit plans, and the wages, salaries, and supplementary payments for the self-employed—the sum divided by hours at work.

[c] Labor compensation costs expended in the production of a unit of output and are derived by dividing compensation by output.

[d] Exchange rate in $ per national currency unit × unit labor costs (L). Calculated at the market exchange rates.

Source: Monthly Labor Review, January 1991.

TABLE 10.4
Competitive Positions: Relative Unit Labour Costs (Indices, 1991 = 100)

| | 1991 | 1992 | 1993 | 1994 | 1995 | Projections | |
						1996	1997
United States	100	96	95	92	90	92	91
Japan	100	106	129	138	144	125	123
Germany	100	107	114	114	121	118	116
France	100	99	102	100	103	104	103
Italy	100	95	79	76	67	73	74
United Kingdom	100	98	89	91	90	90	92
Canada	100	91	84	80	79	82	83
Australia	100	90	83	87	87	97	100
Austria	100	100	100	97	98	96	94
Belgium-Luxembourg	100	100	99	102	106	103	103
Denmark	100	101	105	105	109	110	111
Finland	100	77	62	67	76	71	69
Mexico	100	113	124	125	82	83	94
Netherlands	100	104	106	103	106	103	103
New Zealand	100	89	92	99	105	112	113
Norway	100	97	96	97	102	102	103
Portugal	100	110	108	110	116	117	120
Spain	100	101	89	82	83	85	86
Sweden	100	98	72	72	72	80	82
Switzerland	100	98	100	109	117	116	116
Korea	100	94	91	96	96	100	102
Chinese Taipei	100	107	104	106	103	106	108
Hong Kong	100	102	116	127	125	133	137
Singapore	100	107	106	107	109	113	115

Note: Indices are expressed in a common currency and concern the manufacturing sector. The relative unit labour cost indices take into account both export and import competitiveness.
Source: OECD, Economic Indicators, June 1996. © OECD, 1996, *Main Economic Indicators*. Reproduced with permission of the OECD.

Data from the less-developed countries indicate that a low-wage country may actually have high unit labor costs. What matters is the link between wages and productivity. If low wages are accompanied by low productivity, then labor costs will be high. As Figure 10.4 shows, labor costs may actually be higher in the Philippines or India than in the United States, and the differences among countries in labor costs are much smaller than we would expect from differences in wages alone.

If, however, we disaggregate, productivity will vary in different industries. A competitive advantage will then exist for those industries that can combine high productivity with low wages (as determined by the average productivity in manufacturing). Recall Ricardo's analysis, Chapter 2.

CATCHING UP?

Is the gap in productivity between a leader country and a group of follower countries being reduced?

Historical trends in productivity growth do indicate that productivity levels in other countries have converged toward the level of productivity in the United States. This has been

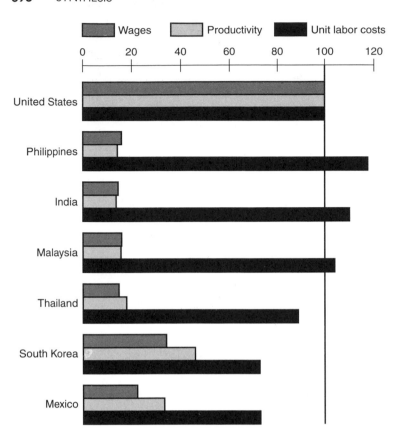

Figure 10.4. Manufacturing productivity and labor costs, developing countries, 1990 (U.S. = 100). *Source*: Stephen Golub, "Comparative and Absolute Advantage in the Asia-Pacific Region," Federal Reserve Bank of San Francisco, Working Paper, 1995.

most noticeable for the convergence of Japan's productivity level to that of the United States. Figure 10.5 shows that while the United States's productivity level rose from an initial index base of 2,500 in 1960 to approximately 4,300 in 1981, Japan's productivity level rose from an index of only 700 in 1960 to the same index level of 4,300 in 1981. The convergence of productivity levels and the slower rate of productivity growth in the United States means that the international competitiveness of many American industries is threatened.

A comparison of the differences in the growth of "total factor productivity" in Japan and the United States is also revealing. In manufacturing, the growth in total factor productivity can be thought of as an average of the productivity growth rates of inputs of labor, capital, energy, and materials. Although labor productivity is usually considered the better measure of economic welfare because it bears an approximate correspondence to income per head, total factor productivity is considered a better measure of an economy's efficiency and its rate of technical progress because it measures the ratio of output to the sum of all basic inputs. Changes in the measurement of total factor productivity reflect changes in technology, shifts in the composition of the labor force, changes in utilization of plant capacity, R&D, skill and effort of the labor force, and more efficient management.

Table 10.5 compares the growth in total factor productivity in the United States and Japan from 1966–78. Although the growth in labor productivity was much higher in Japan than in the United States, the growth in total factor productivity—while still higher in Japan

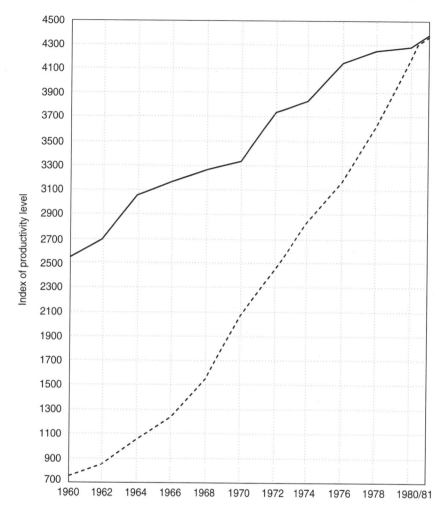

Figure 10.5. U.S. and Japanese manufacturing levels. *Source*: William J. Baumol and Kenneth McLennan, eds., *Productivity, Growth, and U.S. Competitiveness* (New York: Oxford University Press, 1985), p. 15.

than in the United States—was considerably lower than the growth rate of labor productivity. It is also evident from Table 10.5 that although capital productivity was falling in Japan, the tremendous gains in labor productivity allowed total factor productivity to increase. As the price of labor rose, producers raised labor productivity by increasing the input of capital, energy, and materials and decreasing labor input. It is also striking that the rate of energy productivity growth more than doubled in Japan after 1973 as Japan developed energy-saving technology.

It is clear that the more rapid growth in Japan of other inputs—capital, energy, and materials—accounts for most of the difference between American and Japanese rates of labor productivity growth, compared with the rates for total factor productivity. For instance, the difference in total factor productivity growth contributed only about 1 percent

TABLE 10.5
Average Annual Rates of Growth of Productivity Factors in U.S. and Japanese Manufacturing, Gross Output Basis (percent)

	Capital Productivity		Labor Productivity		Energy Productivity		Materials Productivity		Total Factor Productivity	
	United States	Japan	United States	Japan	United States	Japan	United States	Japan	United States	Japan
1965–73	−.011	−4.09	2.50	11.08	0.05	1.50	−0.14	1.03	0.59	0.91
1973–78	−0.87	−0.78	1.83	5.42	−0.73	3.27	0.00	1.15	0.38	1.64

Source: J. R. Norsworthy and David H. Malmquist, "Input Measurement and Productivity Growth in Japanese and U.S. Manufacturing," *American Economic Review* 73 (December 1983), Table 3, p. 954.

a year in the post-1973 period, compared with a difference of 3.6 percent a year in labor productivity. Although total factor productivity in Japanese manufacturing has not shown such remarkable progress relative to that of American manufacturing, the rapid growth in capital and material inputs in Japan has been a major source of Japanese growth. The Japanese worker has had more capital services to work with than has American labor, and the rapid growth in the capital stock has raised the workers' capacity to process a greater volume of materials. It is to be expected that when, as in Japan, the capital labor ratio is generally increasing over time, labor productivity will rise more rapidly than capital productivity, and total factor productivity will be in an intermediate position.

The relative economic performance of nations can be assessed in terms of "convergence" analysis. Figure 10.6 shows the gap in labor productivity between the United States and fifteen other industrialized countries (their mean) between 1870 and 1987. Since the 1950s, the gap has been shrinking—considerably during the period 1950–73 (in spite of rapid American productivity growth) and then somewhat less rapidly in the 1980s and 1990s.

What is the explanation of the "catch-up" of followers to leaders? A prominent interpretation of catch-up and convergence emphasizes the forces of "technological congruence" and "social capability" between the productivity leader (the United States) and followers.[9] Stanford's Moses Abramovitz and Paul David analyze how these forces relate to a country's growth potential and its actual ability "to make the technological and organizational leaps" that the convergence hypothesis envisages.[10] The constraints on the potentials of countries are divided into two categories. First, there are limitations of "technological congruence"— limitations that arise because the frontiers of technology do not advance evenly in all dimensions among nations—that is, with the same proportional impact on the productivities of labor, capital, and natural resource endowments, and on the demands for the different factors of production and on the effectiveness of different scales of output. The lagging countries have difficulty in adopting and adapting the current technological practices of the leader.

The second class of constraints relates to "social capability" (or perhaps more aptly, the "learning rate" of an economy). This comprises levels of education and technical competence; commercial, industrial, and financial institutions; and political and sociocultural characteristics that influence risk-taking, incentives, and rewards of economic activity.

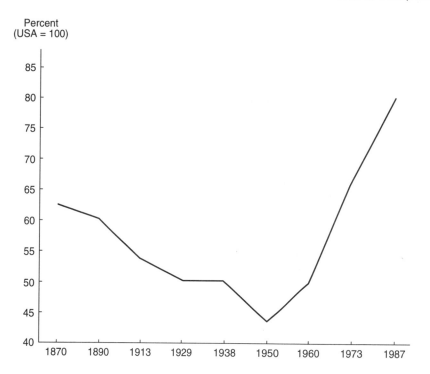

Figure 10.6 Catching up or falling behind? GDP per man hour in fifteen industrialized countries relative to the United States. *Source*: Jan Fagerberg, "Technology and International Differences in Growth Rates," *Journal of Economic Literature* (September 1994): 1157.

Over time, a lagging country's ability to achieve its potential changes. As Abramovitz and David state, "In the short run, a country's ability to exploit the opportunities afforded by currently prevailing best practice techniques will remain limited by its current social capabilities. Over the longer term, however, social capabilities tend to undergo transformations that render them more complementary to the more salient among the emerging technological trajectories. Levels of general and technical education are raised. Curricula and training facilities change. New concepts of business management, including methods of managing personnel and organizing work, supplant traditional approaches. Corporate and financial institutions are established, and people learn their modes of action. Legal codes and even the very concepts of property can be modified. Moreover, experience gained in the practical implementation of a production technique enhances the technical and managerial competencies that serve it, and thus supports further advances along the same path. Such mutually reinforcing interactions impart "positive feedback" to the dynamics of technological evolution. They may for a time solidify a leader's position or, in the case of followers, serve to counter the tendency for their relative growth rates to decline as catch-up proceeds. . . .

"To summarize our general proposition: countries' effective potentials for rapid productivity growth by catch-up are not determined solely by the gaps in levels of technology, capital intensity, and efficient allocation that separate them from the productivity leaders. They are restricted also by their access to primary materials and more generally because their market scales, relative factor supplies, and income-constrained patterns of demand make their technical capabilities and their product structures incongruent in some degree with those that characterize countries that operate at or near the technological frontiers. And they are limited, finally, by those institutional characteristics that restrict their abilities to finance, organize, and operate the kinds of enterprises that are required to exploit the technologies on the frontiers of science and engineering.

"Taken together, the foregoing elements determine a country's effective potential for productivity growth."[11]

Applying their analytical schema to the United States and followers, Abramovitz and David see the strong catch-up in investment and the convergence of productivity during the postwar years in the gradual elimination of weakening of the obstacles to "technological congruence" and "social capability" in the followers of the United States.

Especially significant in the "catch-up" of Europe and Japan was their emphasis on growth as the premier goal of public policy. "Throughout Europe and in Japan, programs of public investment were undertaken to modernize and expand the infrastructure of roads, harbors, railroads, electric power, and communications. The demand for output and employment was supported by monetary and fiscal policy. The supply of labor was enlarged by opening borders to immigrants and guest workers. Productivity growth was pursued by expanding mass and technical education, by encouraging R&D, and by providing state support for large-scale firms in newer lines of industry. The expansion of international trade was promoted by successive GATT rounds and by the organization of the Common Market and the European Free Trade Area."[12]

Moreover, other conditions also promoted the realization of the strong potential of Japanese and European catch-up. New conditions favored the diffusion of technology. Industry was able to satisfy a growing demand for labor without encountering tight labor markets that might otherwise have driven up wages. Governmental policies at both the national and international levels favored investment, trade, and the spread of technology.

In the 1990s, however, there was weakening of many of the elements forming the previous conjuncture of strong potential for catch-up and the social capability to realize the potential. The rate of catch-up and convergence slowed down between the United States and other advanced industrialized countries. Abramovitz and David conclude that "The post-World War II conjuncture of forces supporting catch-up has now largely done its work. It has brought the labor productivity levels of the advanced, capitalist countries within sight of substantial equality. The significant lags that remain among the advanced economies in the course of catching up are no longer to be found in a marked persistence of backward technology embodied in obsolescent equipment and organizations. Rather, they lie in the remaining differences between American, European, and Japanese capital-labor ratios, and in the sphere of politics and social sentiments that protect unduly low-productivity agricultural sectors and traditional forms of organization in both farming and retail trade. The great opportunities for rapid growth by modernization now belong to the nations of eastern Europe, South and Southeast Asia, and Latin America. . . .

"Among the presently advanced capitalist nations, the question is whether substantial equality in productivity levels will long persist. Will a new bend in the path of technical advance again create a condition of superior technological congruence and social capability for one country? Or will conditions that support the diffusion and application of technical knowledge become even more favorable? Will technology continue to pose demands for "readjustment and rehabilitation" that many countries can meet? For the foreseeable future, convergent tendencies appear to be dominant. But the full potential of the still-emergent Age of Information and Communication is yet to be revealed. The industrialization of the huge populations of South and Southeast Asia may change the worlds of industry and commerce in ways that are now still hidden."[13]

An empirical study of growth rates in some 100 countries from 1960 to 1990 is also instructive.[14] The conditional convergence property is posed as an empirical hypothesis: The lower the starting level of real per capita GDP, the higher is the predicted growth rate. The growth rate is considered to be a function of not only the propensity to save, the growth rate of population, and the position of the production function, but also of government policies with respect to levels of consumption spending, protection of property rights, and distortions of domestic and international markets. The study finds a strong empirical regularity for predicted conditional convergence: For a given starting level of real per capita GDP, the growth rate is enhanced by higher initial schooling and life expectancy, lower fertility, lower government consumption, better maintenance of the rule of law, lower inflation, and improvements in the country's terms of trade. For given values of these variables, growth is negatively related to the initial level of real per capita GDP. As predicted by convergence theory, the poorer country catches up in technology, capital, and management faster than the richer country is able to make new advances.

EXPLAINING PRODUCTIVITY PERFORMANCE

How to explain the differences in productivity performance?

From convergence analysis we may conclude that the country that comes from behind has the advantage of advancing more rapidly through imitation of the leading economy. But as the performance gap narrows, this advantage becomes self-terminating.

Other differences among economies are more fundamental in determining productivity performance. We can identify as especially important the rates of saving and investment, expenditures on R&D and technology, and provision of education and training of labor.

As repeatedly stressed: If a country is to enjoy high rates of growth in productivity, it must have rates of investment supported by high rates of saving. Investment in manufacturing (modern plant and equipment and capital-deepening) and in infrastructure (transportation and communications) are especially needed. But net national saving rates (i.e., after depreciation) declined in virtually all OECD countries, from an average of 15 percent of GDP in the 1960s to only 9 percent in the 1980s. Table 10.6 shows net national saving ratios.

National savings come from three sectors: government, household, and business, as can be noted in Figure 10.7. In most countries, the largest part of the decline in national saving since the 1960s has been the drop in government savings; several governments changed from being net savers in the 1960s to dis-savers in the 1980s. Moreover, almost everywhere household savings fell in the 1980s. Household savings in the United States, Britain, and France are much lower than in Japan; they are also lower than they were in these countries in the 1960s. Because low rates of national saving keep the level of productive

TABLE 10.6
Net National Savings Ratios, % of Net National Product (averages)

	1960–70	**1971–80**	**1981–87**
United States	20.6	8.9	3.9
Japan	25.6	24.6	20.2
West Germany	19.9	14.3	10.7
Britain	11.2	8.2	6.2
Italy	15.0	12.1	12.8
Canada	11.3	13.3	9.4

Source: OECD statistics, annual national income accounts.

investment in plant and equipment low, the growth in productivity remains low as capital equipment per worker remains low and the level of technology does not rise. As differences are compounded year after year, a country with low rates of saving and investment is bound to have a lower rate of growth relative to other countries. Table 10.7 shows saving and investment rates for OECD countries from 1960 to 1994. (Note that the saving rate in this table is for gross saving including depreciation.)

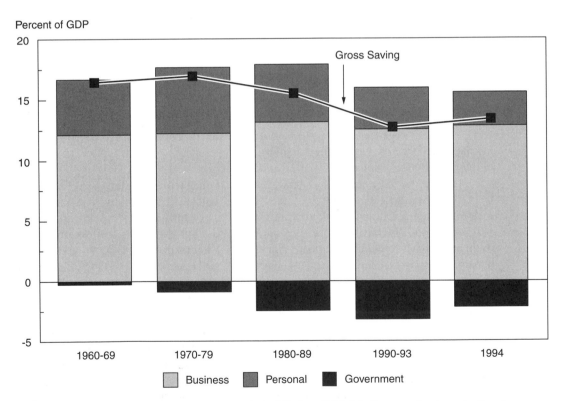

Figure 10.7. Components of Gross Saving, United States, 1910–94. Gross saving has declined since the 1970s, partly because the personal saving rate has declined and partly because the public sector has run much larger deficits. Net saving has fallen even more rapidly than gross saving, partly because of a shift in investment to more rapidly depreciating equipment. *Source*: Council of Economic Advisors, *Economic Report by the President 1995*, p. 118.

TABLE 10.7
Saving and Investment Rates

	Saving Rate[1]				Investment Rate[2]			
	1960–69	1970–79	1980–89	1990–94[3]	1960–69	1970–79	1980–89	1990–94[3]
United States	20.0	19.8	17.8	15.4	18.3	19.1	19.0	16.3
Japan	34.4	35.3	31.8	33.5	31.6	33.1	29.1	30.6
Germany	27.3	24.4	22.4	22.2	24.8	22.6	20.3	20.1
France	26.3	25.9	20.4	19.9	23.4	24.1	20.6	19.9
Italy	28.2	26.0	21.8	18.4	24.7	24.0	21.3	18.5
United Kingdom	18.5	18.0	16.6	13.3	18.0	19.2	17.5	16.5
Canada	21.5	22.4	20.1	14.7	22.5	23.0	21.5	19.4
Australia	24.4	23.7	20.2	16.3	25.6	24.3	24.3	20.7
Austria	27.6	27.8	24.1	25.4	26.2	27.1	23.5	24.8
Belgium	22.6	23.2	16.6	21.3	21.5	21.9	17.3	18.8
Denmark	23.3	20.8	14.8	17.5	23.5	23.1	17.9	15.8
Finland	25.2	26.3	23.7	15.9	25.9	27.4	25.0	19.4
Greece	19.6	26.5	17.8	14.9	20.9	24.2	19.6	18.4
Iceland	26.3	25.3	17.6	15.4	28.1	28.3	21.7	17.3
Ireland	17.1	19.2	15.3	19.6	18.8	24.3	21.1	16.2
Luxembourg	31.7	42.3	57.8	60.7	25.8	25.7	23.8	27.9
Mexico	18.7	18.6	21.4	16.8	18.0	20.8	20.4	20.0
Netherlands	27.7	25.0	23.1	24.4	25.8	22.9	20.1	20.0
New Zealand	21.1	21.9	19.2	17.3	21.7	24.4	22.8	17.9
Norway	27.1	26.3	26.9	22.7	28.3	31.1	26.5	19.6
Portugal	24.5	27.4	24.7	25.2	25.9	28.7	28.9	26.3
Spain	24.6	25.4	20.9	19.9	23.6	24.8	21.1	22.0
Sweden	24.0	21.1	17.3	14.6	23.8	21.1	19.4	17.2
Switzerland	30.1	29.7	29.9	30.6	27.5	25.2	24.5	24.3
Turkey	14.9	18.1	20.6	21.0	15.7	19.2	21.3	23.9
OECD Average[4]	24.3	24.8	22.5	21.5	23.6	24.4	21.9	20.5

[1]Gross national saving as a percent of gross domestic output. Presented averages are average of yearly rate.
[2]Gross fixed capital formation as a percent of gross domestic product. Presented averages are average of yearly rates.
[3]The latest available year is 1993 for Greece and Norway and 1992 for Luxembourg.
[4]Unweighted average.
Source: OECD, *National Accounts*.

Industrial R&D is also a major source of productivity: It leads to innovations in the production process that economize on inputs, raise the level of technology, and introduce innovations at the product level. All these changes improve the firm's international competitiveness. Moreover, industrial R&D normally yields dynamic scale economies that are not limited by national borders. This is especially significant for global competition. Although the United States still spends more on total R&D than the next four largest industrialized countries combined, some international competitors—especially Japan and Germany—have surpassed the United States in R&D expenditures as a percentage of GNP. It is significant that if only nondefense R&D is considered, Japan and Germany have been ahead of the United States for nearly two decades. Moreover, their rate of civilian R&D investment as a percentage of GNP has been rising faster than that of the United States since 1981.

By 1986, Japan had a higher proportion of scientists and engineers per 10,000 workers than America did. And it is wrong to believe that Japan is simply an imitator of technological change in other industrial countries. One indication of this is the growth in Japanese-invented

U.S. patents. In 1975, 65 percent of the new patents in the United States were for inventions by Americans, 9 percent were for Japanese inventors, 8.5 percent Germans, and 7.5 percent British and French inventors combined. In the following decade, America's share fell by ten percentage points, to less than 55 percent. West Germany's share rose slightly, Britain's dropped a bit, and the French stayed much the same. But Japan's slice more than doubled to almost 19 percent. Japanese inventors now own more new patents in the United States than those from Britain, Germany, and France.[15]

Japanese patenting in the United States emphasizes certain specific technology fields that are commercially important such as photocopying, information storage and retrieval, photography, motor vehicles, and typewriting machines.[16] The level of utilization of advanced manufacturing technologies in the United States has also lagged behind other countries. Robotics technologies, for instance, have been adopted more rapidly in Sweden, West Germany, and Japan and are utilized in greater numbers (on a per capita basis) in the manufacturing sectors of these nations than is true of the United States.

Evidence that the United States lags in adoption suggests that the gap between "best practice" and "current practice" in the United States may be greater than is true of other industrial economies. The Council on Competitiveness recently reviewed ninety-four technologies and concluded that American companies were far behind and no longer a factor in world markets in a third of the technologies.[17]

From 1977–88, employment of scientists and engineers in private business in the United States expanded at more than twice the rate of total employment. American university students, however, show a downward trend in their choice of undergraduate majors in some natural science and engineering fields. The shift away from these majors portends reduced science and engineering degrees in the coming years. The increases in graduate science and engineering enrollments also slowed from an average annual of 2 percent from 1980 to 1987, to an annual 1 percent increase in the late 1980s. Foreign students continued to increase their share of the graduate enrollments and the share of American citizens decreased.[18]

High investment in human capital through education and training also results in higher productivity. As we noted for the Asian NICs (p. 311), such investment in human capital has resulted in an upgrading of labor skills and in innovations from an enlarged supply of entrepreneurs. An improvement in the quality of people as economic agents is key to realizing increasing returns in an economy.

This is closely associated with a rise in total factor productivity. The "residual" difference between the rate of increase in output and the rate of increase in physical capital and labor inputs encompasses many "unidentified factors," but a prominent element is the improvement in the quality of inputs. Although some of this progress may be incorporated in physical capital, the improvements in intangible human qualities are often more significant. Knowledge, creativity, innovations, technical progress—the results of investment in human capital—contribute to the better quality of labor, technical progress, improved organization, and more efficient management that underlie an increase in TFP. These inferences from human-capital theory have been given a strong empirical base through analysis of rates of return to investment in human capital, the production function approach to the sources of growth, and comparative cross-country studies of investments in human resources.

Other causes of an increase in TFP may be related to macro determinants of competitiveness (p. 379–81) and to broader factors such as those considered in the World Economic Forum's Competitiveness Index (p. 380).

Especially important are government policies that enhance or contravene the market price system through government expenditures, tax and subsidy programs, and regulatory policies. National differences in relations between labor and management also affect comparative productivity performance.

A particular feature of the slowdown in U.S. productivity is the poor performance in services. Unlike causes in other industries, the weak bargaining position of labor is a better explanation of the slow productivity growth in services. A structural shift in the labor market has increased the supply of labor in services. A large amount of labor input per unit output results from weak unions, a decline in the real minimum wage, and substantial immigration.[19] To the extent that more education and training for less-skilled workers would reduce the supply of the less skilled in low-productivity activities, there would be an improvement in productivity.

TRADE PERFORMANCE

If an increase in productivity is to support a rising standard of living without the country encountering balance-of-payments problems, the country must be able to export (or receive an inflow of capital). For when national income rises, the demand for imports also rises. If imports become greater than exports, and there is not a sufficient inflow of capital, the country must then deflate or devalue its currency relative to foreign currencies, or impose direct controls on imports (recall Chapter 5). To avoid these adjustment costs, the country needs to increase its exports and improve its trade balance while simultaneously enjoying a rising standard of living through higher productivity.

Productivity growth will be a major determinant of a firm's ability to compete in world markets. For the ability of a firm to compete in price is highly dependent on its relative unit labor costs. A rise in such costs will make exports uncompetitive. As we have seen, labor unit cost in a country may rise relative to other competitive countries because labor earnings in national currency rise faster than in other countries, or the foreign exchange rate is improving relative to other countries, or productivity growth is lower than in other countries. Firms in that country then lose their competitive price advantage. In contrast, high productivity growth that is not offset by higher labor earnings will translate into falling relative labor costs and allow the country's exports to be more price competitive. The home country's industries that compete with imports will also be more competitive.

Exports also depend, however, on nonprice considerations. Especially vital is the firm's capacity to innovate—to compete with new technology, new products, new methods of production, and the opening up of new markets. As the Austrian economist Joseph Schumpeter observed:

> Economists are at long last emerging from the stage in which price competition was all they saw. . . . In capitalist reality, as distinguished from its textbook picture, it is not that kind of competition which counts, but the competition from the new commodity, the new technology, the new source of supply, the new type of organization . . . —competition which commands a decisive cost or quality advantage and which strikes not at the margins of the profits and the outputs of the existing firms but at their foundations and their very lives.[20]

TABLE 10.8
Average Annual Growth Rate of Merchandise Exports (percent)

	1980–90	1990–94
Argentina	3.1	−1.0
Australia	5.8	8.1
Brazil	6.1	6.6
Canada	5.7	8.4
Chile	5.7	10.5
China	11.4	14.3
Germany	4.6	2.2
Indonesia	5.3	5.7
Israel	5.9	10.0
Italy	4.4	6.0
Jamaica	1.2	1.3
Japan	5.0	0.4
Korea, Republic	13.7	7.4
Mexico	14.7	5.7
Peru	−1.9	11.0
Philippines	2.9	10.2
Poland	4.8	3.9
Taiwan	11.6	5.9
United Kingdom	4.4	1.8
United States	3.6	5.6
Venezuela	1.6	−0.1
World	4.8	5.7

Source: World Bank, *World Development Report 1996*, Table 15.

Table 10.8 allows a comparison of growth rates in exports for various countries.

If a country has a trade deficit, many view this as a symptom of the country's inability to compete. But as we have emphasized, the external imbalance of a trade deficit is a reflection of the domestic imbalance between savings plus taxes and investment plus government expenditures (recall Chapter 5). Neither a country's surplus nor deficit is, however, the issue for national performance—rather it is productivity and the standard of living.

What is relevant is that trade does affect a country's living standards in three significant ways: through the country's capacity to import, dynamic gains from exports, and the terms of trade. Our discussion of comparative costs recognized the efficiency gains from trade and the gains from trade in terms of imports (Chapter 2). Dynamic gains from exports are realized by allowing the exporting country to overcome the diseconomies of the small size of its domestic market, stimulate investment, realize dynamic learning scale economies, and quicken the pace of innovations in various industries.

A country's terms of trade (price of exports relative to price of imports) also matter insofar as the higher are the terms of trade associated with a given trade balance, the higher is the country's real income because the purchasing power of a unit of its exports rises. In contrast, if a significant proportion of a country's income is spent on imports, and its terms of trade worsen, then the standard of living would be significantly reduced.

A change in the terms of trade, however, is merely a summary index of underlying forces such as changes in productivity, factor prices, and demand conditions. For the effect on a country's standard of living, we must go behind the nominal change in the terms of trade to an analysis of the causes of the change. If, for instance, the terms deteriorate because productivity in export production increases and export prices fall, this would not necessarily have any adverse effects. For in this case the deterioration in the terms of trade reflects only the increased productivity. As long as productivity in the export sector is rising faster than the price of its exports are falling, the country's real income rises despite the deterioration in its terms of trade. If the prices of exports relative to imports fall by a smaller percentage than the percentage increase in productivity, the country actually benefits by being able to obtain a greater quantity of imports per unit of factors embodied in the production of its exports.

OVERCOMING THE U.S. SLOWDOWN

Compounded over more than two decades, America's lower rate of productivity growth relative to other countries in the 1970s and 1980s has had a costly impact on the standard of living and the international competitiveness of American business. The severity of the productivity crisis in the United States can be summarized by realizing that if productivity growth had only continued since 1965 at the pre-1965 rate, U.S. output would have been at least 50 percent higher in 1990 than it actually was, with no additional labor used in production.

What can now be done to reverse America's slowdown? From an analysis of the reasons for America's lagging performance, our policy proposals must focus on both the macro environment within which business firms operate and on the firm's managerial quality.

Public policy is necessary to improve the macro environment. Most important are measures to:

- Encourage a higher rate of private investment
- Improve the nation's physical and social infrastructure
- Expand R&D outlays
- Improve the quantity and quality of education

An increase in the national rate of saving is the central priority. Private investment should not be crowded out by a high federal budget deficit and high cost of capital. A reduction in the budget deficit and an easier monetary policy would help translate an increase in savings into a higher rate of domestic investment in new plants and equipment that could promote productivity growth. Tax policy should also stimulate saving and investment—for example, by the taxation of real rather than nominal capital gains, by reducing the effect of the tax rate on income from capital relative to consumption, and by tax simplification through broadening of the tax base and reduction in marginal rates. Closer attention should also be given to the effects that the regulations on safety, health, environment, and product liability have on productivity.

We have repeatedly seen that the slow pace of innovation is an especially strong cause of low productivity growth. Although innovation is intimately related to individual qualities of entrepreneurship, it is also affected by R&D activities. R&D expenditures in the United States have slowed down in real terms. Federal financing of basic research has also declined, and as a result total spending on research in the United States (basic or applied, whether federally or privately financed) has stagnated in the 1990s.

Stanford's Paul Romer, whose model of growth explains how knowledge in the shape of technology and human capital can be created and spread through the economy to give increasing returns to capital, has said: "We are eating our seed corn"—by still squeezing products from the aging cornucopia of breakthrough technologies that came during and after World War II. "If this continues, [the U.S.] will no longer be the nation that is on the cutting edge of new technologies, new products and new markets."[21] An improvement in the results from R&D, however, depends on more than raising expenditures: Redirection of R&D to activities that yield greater value added is needed. This would involve more basic R&D at universities, increased attention to the development components of R&D, and greater emphasis on improving manufacturing processes.

To advise a government to stimulate "advances in knowledge" is an elusive objective. Greater public encouragement of R&D is justified, however, because of the high social returns that frequently come from R&D expenditures. University of Pennsylvania's Edwin Mansfield found that a great deal of the knowledge that R&D generates provides benefits not only to the company performing the R&D, but also to other companies and consumers. Competitors may benefit by copying or "reverse engineering" new products and by hiring away key personnel. Or key personnel become competitors by setting up their own companies. Consumers benefit when information about new technologies spreads to several companies and generates competition. Only a part of this social return to R&D becomes a private return to the company that has paid the bill. Spillovers from R&D can be significant. In his study of a group of specific innovations, Mansfield actually found a social rate of return of 56 percent while the private rate was 25 percent. From other studies, it would be conservative to maintain that the social rate return to R&D is 35 percent to 60 percent above the return to ordinary capital.[22]

It would be desirable for the government to support small company R&D activities instead of simply concentrating government subsidies for R&D spending on the largest companies. Studies undertaken in the early 1980s by America's Small Business Administration found that small firms produced more than twice as many innovations per employee as large ones. Although one might question the value of General Motors's R&D expenditures, computer software and biotechnology have been dominated by innovative, small firms. A greater percentage of government support on R&D should also be earmarked for basic research in universities while business concentrates more on market commercialization of innovations. Tax credit for R&D may also be stimulating. And if projects promise social returns, some public funding would be in order. It is, however, questionable whether government support for commercial R&D consortia is beneficial. Many argue that government support of consortia would not encourage more effective R&D but simply increase interest rate charges in the federal budget deficit and refill the troughs of big company lobbyists.[23]

The promotion of "advances in knowledge" through R&D involves not only pushing out the technological frontier to develop leading-edge industries, but also the diffusion into existing industries of technological advances that have been made at the leading edge. More support needs to be given to the diffusion of technology and to projects of applied research that have commercial applications with results that are too general to make them attractive to private companies on their own. The challenge for technology policy is to maintain the advantages of private market incentives while supplementing the incentives to obtain greater diffusion of existing technology so that technological opportunities will not be missed.

Human Resources

To improve a nation's standard of living, it is essential to realize that human resources ultimately constitute the wealth of nations. The role of capital and natural resources in production may be subject to the law of diminishing returns, but the role of human resources can be one of increasing returns. It is therefore crucial to upgrade the most

---

MISSED OPPORTUNITIES

Studies of a number of U.S. industries indicate that slow growth in the United States has reflected missed opportunities. One study concludes:

"The United States was the pioneer in computer technology and continues to hold a substantial lead there. This edge created a built-in opportunity for the U.S. machine tool industry to become the world leader in computer-controlled machinery, which, in turn, could have helped many other manufacturing industries boost their own productivity. These opportunities were missed.

"As the pioneer in computers, the United States also had the opportunity to reduce labor in white-collar activities by seeking ways to take advantage of the new technology. Although economists lack, as yet, a full understanding of the behavior of white-collar productivity, it is clear enough that streamlining labor needs in service activities has failed to provide the source of growth that it might have.

"The United States was the pioneer in nuclear energy and made important developments in supercritical turbine technology. These developments in applied science provided opportunities for innovation, but the new technologies were not implemented successfully and did not result in productivity improvement.

"The U.S. chemical industry found that its sources of growth had been exhausted, but there were advances in materials science, in biotechnology, and in the manipulation of molecular structures that could have opened up new opportunities. . . .

"To summarize: for productivity to keep growing, there have to be new ideas and the economy has to take advantage of them. Japan and Europe increased productivity not only because advanced technology was available to be borrowed, but also because they became adept at the activity of borrowing and even at improving on what they borrowed. As they approached the frontier, Japan and Europe faced an inevitable slowdown.

"The slowdown in the United States was not inevitable in the same way. It occurred more because the U.S. economy failed to incorporate new technology effectively into production than because the scientific frontier stopped expanding."

Martin Neil Baily and Aloh K. Chakrabarti, *Innovation and the Productivity Crisis* (Washington, DC: Brookings Institution, 1988), p. 105

competitive asset—human resources—through investment in human capital. Critics of American education can rightly say that a Japanese eighth grader typically knows more mathematics than an American MBA.[24] Only 1 percent of American 18-year-olds take advanced physics examinations compared with 11 percent of Japanese. On science and mathematics achievement tests, American school children continue to perform below the levels reached by their age groups in other countries. In a 1988 international mathematics and science assessment of 13-year-olds in six countries, American children scored lowest of all the populations in mathematics and below the mean in science.[25] It is clearly necessary to upgrade the teaching of science and mathematics in American schools, and measures should be undertaken to reverse the decline in the proportion of U.S. undergraduates majoring in science and engineering and in the number of Americans receiving advanced degrees in these fields. It is also essential to decrease the number of school dropouts.

Moreover, not only is it distressing that one out of five American 18-year-olds is illiterate, but it is unfortunate that many high school graduates with enough qualifications to go to college cannot afford it. For those who cannot or do not wish to attend college there is a need to have training for jobs that are becoming ever more complex. Older workers also need to be able to enjoy lifelong learning through university courses televised for industry or through community college classes to upgrade manufacturing supervisers' skills. Unless their productivity is raised through education and training, the lesser-skilled workers will confront increasing competition from workers in the newly industrializing countries and their wages will stagnate because of technical change.

Expenditures on public elementary and secondary education have shown little increase in real terms. At the same time, the demands on public education have significantly increased. The President's Commission on Industrial Competitiveness, Business Roundtable, White House Conference on Productivity, and Business-Higher Education Forum have all focused on the urgent need for improving the quality of the nation's educational system. They generally recognize that as important as is government expenditure on education, better results also depend on higher standards, rigorous assessments, and greater accountability.[26] Federal resources, state and local activities, and intensified concern by industry must be combined to upgrade skills and provide the human resources base for technological change.

Deficiencies in educational and training practices will become even more evident as the composition of the labor force changes in future decades. The majority of new entrants to the labor force will be drawn from groups that have been disadvantaged, and minority and immigrant workers will constitute larger proportions of the labor force. The MIT Commission on Industrial Productivity therefore advocates that the federal government adopt programs for K-12 education that will lead to greater technological literacy. It maintains that the task of upgrading the primary and secondary schools is probably the single most important challenge facing the country. The commission recommends adopting more rigorous educational standards, establishing national examinations, increasing the focus on science and mathematics in early grades, and lengthening the school year. The government should also encourage continual education and training for the U.S. workforce, with special attention on the increased participation of women, African Americans, and Spanish-speaking Americans. Further, the commission would encourage public-private partnership for job training, retraining of the unemployed, and perhaps giving tax benefits to corporations for investments in education and training.[27]

Anti-Trust Policy

The foregoing emphasis on measures to raise saving and investment, support R&D, and improve education are generally approved in the policy-making community. Other proposals, however, such as liberalizing anti-trust policy and a national industrial policy are subject to considerable disagreement.

Some, including the MIT Commission on Industrial Productivity, have advocated that anti-trust restrictions be relaxed to allow more cooperative relationships among firms in the same industry. The MIT study points to several instances in which the absence of horizontal cooperation led to the underprovision of such collective goods as joint R&D, standardization, and education and training, which were instrumental in promoting technological innovation and productivity growth in those same industries in Europe and Japan. Congress did pass in 1984 the National Cooperative Research Act, which gave industry an anti-trust exemption for joint R&D projects. Joint manufacturing and marketing consortia are not exempted, however, and some claim that further legislation may be needed to overcome the fear of litigation of companies contemplating such consortia.[28]

Nonetheless, the MIT commission finds other causes for declining U.S. industrial performance—including outdated strategies, short-term horizons, technological weaknesses, neglect of human resources, and government and industry tension. The responsibility of U.S. anti-trust law for this catalogue of failures is actually minimal. Others also conclude that over-zealous anti-trust enforcement is scarcely an explanatory cause of lack of competitiveness. The courts and enforcement authorities already include foreign competition in their analysis. Sweeping modifications of anti-trust law are unnecessary. If enacted, they will invite anti-trust risk, needlessly complicating legal standards and distracting public attention from the more fundamental issues that impede U.S. competitiveness.[29] Instead, further enforcement of established anti-trust policies is likely to promote business efficiency through the beneficial pressures of domestic competition and thereby also enhance competitiveness in global markets.

A National Industrial Policy?

The advocacy of a national industrial policy is especially controversial. In part, this is because of its vague meaning. If it comprises only the government's intention to promote economic stability through monetary and fiscal policies and to correct instances of market failure, there is little criticism.[30] Or if a national industrial policy simply means support of exports through a more active government role in promoting adequate export financing and removing disincentives to U.S. exports, there is again little criticism.[31] Such policies would include maintenance of a competitive real exchange rate in the United States; an increase in the size and scope of the Export/Import Bank; relaxation of national security, foreign policy, and short supply controls that prevent sales abroad; and trade negotiations to improve increased market access overseas.

If, however, the scope of a national industrial policy is extended to mean that the government should select certain industries as "champions" and give them special support, then there is much more controversy. This approach involves selective industrial policies, but proponents of such policies are divided on the issue of which sectors should receive help.

INDUSTRIAL POLICY OR MARKET ALLOCATION?

Proponents of a national industrial policy divide on which industries should receive government support. Advocates of a defensive approach seek to aid "sunset" industries. Others advocate an offensive approach to support "sunrise" industries.

Of both approaches, Robert Z. Lawrence states:

"As even their proponents acknowledge, these selective industrial policies require considerable time to take effect; design, implementation, operation, and evaluation impose long lags. Selective policies are also costly to consumers and to taxpayers. Because they confer benefits on powerful domestic interests, they are probably irreversible. Also, nations abroad might emulate selective policies of the United States, with the accompanying risk of a rise in global levels of protection. It is crucial, therefore, that proponents provide a plan that (1) focuses on permanent trends and not transitory shifts due to business-cycle or exchange-rate fluctuations for which monetary and fiscal policies are more appropriate tools, (2) in principle has the potential to improve resource allocation, and (3) in practice improves resource allocation if implemented in the U.S. political and institutional context. . . .

"Efficiency requires decision making at the margin and a continuous reevaluation of the areas in which resources are most needed. There is no such thing as an absolute need. Instead there is need for continuous trade-offs. The market system can accomplish this through millions of independent consumers guiding marginal resource allocation decisions with their dollar votes. No central committee is likely to do better. Rather than assuming that some simple rules could select the truly deserving industries, a superior approach is to leave resource allocation to market forces unless there is a clear case of market failure.

"The search for criteria to define a basic or essential industry usually reflects a desire to find a reason of supporting an industry that is no longer required. If an industry producing commercial goods needs government support in order to function, in fact, that signals it is no longer basic."

Robert Z. Lawrence, *Can America Compete?* (Washington, DC: Brookings Institution, 1984), pp. 89, 105–106

Should it be a defensive approach to a troubled "sunset" industry such as steel, automobiles, glass, rubber, and other basic industries? Or is it to focus on "sunrise" industries—those with the greatest potential for growth and international competitiveness?

Regardless of which industries are selected, the major criticism of selective industrial policies is that they allocate resources to various industries in ways different from those of the market. Some industries will be favored and others will not. The issue then is whether the criteria used for the selective industrial policies are superior to the criteria of the market place. Many would say "no."

Examining the popular support for an industrial policy that would encourage the entry of national firms into new industrial activities—primarily technology-based and skilled-labor intensive—Princeton's Gene Grossman has also been skeptical:

Few of the valid arguments for intervention rely explicitly on the existence of international competition. Where growth of some new activity is too slow, it often is so for the world as a whole. Rarely does the national identity of the new firms matter for the argument. The exceptions to this rule are arguments in favour of strategic promotion of domestic interests in their competition with foreign rivals. These arguments have been shown to be especially sensitive to the details of market structure and conduct and to rely on information that the government is not likely to have at its disposal. Moreover, strategic interventions seek gain at the expense of trade partners, and so invite retaliation. When countries head down this road, mutually harmful subsidies or protection can easily be the outcome. Countries may need on occasion to invoke strategic trade policies to safeguard their interests, but the ultimate goal in all cases ought to be a co-operative outcome in which all parties desist from pursuit of strategic gains.

Finally, from the limited empirical evidence available to date, it appears that the strongest case for government intervention may arise in the early stages of development of a new, technologically innovative product. When the introduction and improvement of a new product involve substantial research outlays and costly learning-by-doing, private firms often are unable to capture more than a fraction of the benefits they create for consumers and for other firms in the industry. . . . A strong case can be made for government support for research and development, and for favourable tax treatment of operating losses, during initial stages of a new product's history. It will, of course, be difficult for the policy analyst to identify the deserving innovations and to delimit the period of government support to the time when substantial externalities are being generated. But the magnitude of the foregone gains that have been estimated for several industries suggest the existence of a margin for error.

One last caveat is in order. In any public policy program the parties that stand to benefit from government support have more than ample incentive to plead the merits of their own cases. The success of an industrial policy program hinges as much on the protection that it builds into the process to prevent it from being co-opted by interested parties as it does on the ability of economists and policy makers to identify market failures and to propose appropriate remedies under idealised analytical conditions. The potential societal gains from an activist policy can easily be sacrificed if opportunities for wasteful rent seeking are created or if the criteria for selection become the political clout of the applicant rather than the economic merits of the case.[32]

Further, when a national industrial policy involves "targeting industries" it is only too likely also to embrace "managed trade." This may have political appeal, but the economic costs are high. In Chapter 3, we already saw the costs of protectionism and the misconceptions involved in advocating a "level playing field." Many, however, believe that industrial policy "remains an important and neglected tool for reducing the country's balance of trade deficit in manufacturing," and is applicable not only to "old fashioned products," but to preventing the virtual disappearance of such key twenty-first century industries as robotics and semiconductors.[33] To go on and advocate "orderly marketing agreements," such as for steel and textiles, is to misjudge, however, the causes of the balance of trade deficit and to use the wrong remedial measures. An industrial policy should not be a bailing-out policy. An industrial policy should not inhibit competition, for through competition comes the efficiency that makes an industry internationally competitive. Only too often an industrial policy would divert international energies from innovation-producing and productivity-enhancing activities in competitive markets to rent-seeking from government regulations.

CHALLENGE TO INTERNATIONAL MANAGEMENT

There are many causes for the United States's anemic record in productivity and for a decline in the international competitiveness of some American firms. Among the multiple causes, deficiencies in the management of firms should be of as much concern as the macro causes that we identified in the previous sections. Too many managers have unduly narrowed their horizons both geographically and temporally. Their outdated strategies are deficient in a number of functions:

- Too narrow a focus on short-term financial objectives
- Neglect of manufacturing performance
- Deficient management of the innovation process
- Failure to commercialize applications from R&D expenditures
- Undervaluation of human resources
- Lack of understanding of changes in the global economy
- Insufficient attention to time-based strategies

The concentration by business on short-term financial objectives has led to decision making geared to short-term cost reduction and short-term profits, rather than to long-term development of technological competitiveness.[34] Concentration on the short term may be a rational response to high interest rates in the macroeconomic environment, but it is also frequently simply a manifestation of uncertainty about the future of inflation, interest rates, and foreign exchange rates. This uncertainty deters long-term risk taking. A better understanding of how these economic variables operate in the international environment would reduce the perceived risk to longer-term investment. In practicing DPR, an improvement in diagnosis and prediction of these variables would bring a more efficient response.

An extension of management's time horizon would help prevent American firms from giving ground to overseas competitors despite their holding an early lead in technology or sales. They would be more willing to live through a period of heavy investment and forgo short-term profits, in order to secure a foothold in a growing market.[35] Although American firms were the first to introduce video recording technology, Japanese firms were the ones willing to invest heavily in both product development and process development for more than two decades, while cash returns were low and growing only slowly. Over the same period, many U.S. firms were retreating from consumer electronics markets, progressively ceding products and functions to foreign competitors and diversifying into less risky and more profitable businesses, completely unrelated to their original line of work.

In several of the industry studies by the MIT commission, the following pattern was observed. Japanese firms enter a new market at the low-cost end of the product range. American firms choose not to contest these market segments, often in spite of

REGAINING THE PRODUCTIVE EDGE

An MIT Commission on Industrial Productivity took a bottom-up approach to America's industrial performance and focused on the organizational patterns, the plant, the equipment, and the people—from factory workers to senior executives, who combine to conceive, design, develop, produce, market, and deliver goods and services to the consumer.

The study observed recurring patterns of weakness in productivity performance across the eight industrial sectors examined. The following interrelated patterns of behavior were found to best characterize the evidence:

- Outdated strategies
- Short time horizons
- Technological weaknesses in development and production
- Neglect of human resources
- Failures of cooperation
- Government and industry at cross-purposes

The MIT Commission summarized its recommendations to industry as follows:

- Focus on the production process, with the objective of improving long-term productive performance.
- Adopt as an exclusive objective of the production process the delivery of high quality products to market in a timely fashion at competitive prices.
- Develop techniques to measure and improve the efficiency and quality of the production process, and identify opportunities for progressive improvement in its performance.
- Emphasize product variety and manufacturing flexibility in the development of production systems.
- Cultivate a more involved, less specialized, continually learning work force.
- Flatten organizational hierarchies to give employees greater responsibility and broader experience.
- Integrate and (where feasible) perform concurrently the functions of research and development, product design, and process design to achieve greater efficiency and a shorter time to market.
- Cooperate with suppliers, rather than treating them as adversaries.
- Insist that key employees have an adequate understanding of foreign cultures.
- Adopt the best practices of world industry to improve productivity and quality in the manufacturing process.
- In the area of labor-management relations, support diffusion of cooperative industrial relations by accepting labor representatives as legitimate and valued partners in the innovation process.

MIT Commission on Industrial Productivity, *Made in America* (Cambridge, MA: MIT Press, 1989), pp. 44, 148–150

their high growth potential, because the immediate or near-term profit margins are lower. The Japanese then exploit their growing market presence, reputation, and the effects of the learning curve to move up-market and challenge directly the American producers. This pattern has repeated itself in a broad range of markets, including machine tools, copiers, consumer electronics, semiconductors, sophisticated broadcast video equipment, and medical-imaging equipment.[36]

An illuminating survey of 500 major American and Japanese companies compares the differences in corporate objectives in the United States and Japan. Table 10.9 shows that for American executives, return on investment was clearly the highest priority, followed by share-price increases and market share. New product introductions ranked only seventh out of nine objectives. In contrast, for the Japanese firms, market share was the most important objective; return on investment ranked second; new product introductions were third; and share price ranked last.

Commenting on the contrast in this study, two Boston Consulting Group consultants state that:

> Judging from the realities of competition, the elevation by U.S. management of the return on investment goal over the goals of market share and refreshment of the product portfolio would seem to be illogical. In the West, as in Japan, high profits and hence high return on investment come with superior competitive position. Superior competitive position is achieved with good products and maintained with new products, and the measure of superior competitive position is market share. . . . If in the pursuit of market share Japanese companies find that they must make certain capital or expense investments to hold or gain share, the investments are made with little regard for the short term returns of the project. Not making the investments risks a loss of competitive position; the business may well never earn much money.[37]

A survey of Fortune 500 executives also reveals the underemphasis on manufacturing. When asked what functional area offered the greater opportunities for advancement, one third said marketing, one fourth finance, and one fourth general management; but, in contrast, fewer than 5 percent considered production or manufacturing a logical choice.

TABLE 10.9
Ranking of Corporate Objectives: United States and Japan*

	United States	Japan
Return on investment	8.1	4.1 (2)
Share price increase	3.8	0.1
Market share	2.4	4.8 (1)
Improve product portfolio	1.7	2.3
Rationalization of production and distribution	1.5	2.4
Increase equity ratio	1.3	2.0
Ratio of new products	0.7	3.5 (3)
Improve company's image	0.2	0.7
Improve working conditions	0.1	0.3

*291 Japanese companies and 227 U.S. companies ranked factors weighted 10, for first importance, to 1, for least importance.
Source: James C. Abegglen and George Stalk, Jr., *Kaisha, the Japanese Corporation*, (New York: Basic Books, 1985), p. 177. Copyright © 1985 by Basic Books, Inc. Reprinted by permission of Basic Books, a division of Harper Collins Publishers, Inc.

Management should realize, however, that the innovative process depends on manufacturing to capitalize on the commercialization of an innovation and to achieve continual improvements in products and in processes.

We have repeatedly emphasized the need for innovations to increase productivity and promote competitiveness. Innovations, however, depend on entrepreneurship, but too many managers merely follow routine and traditional procedures. Joseph Schumpeter is noted for drawing a sharp contrast between the "entrepreneur" and the "manager." The entrepreneur undertakes the special process of carrying out new combinations of the means of production. Through innovations, the entrepreneur introduces new processes of production, new products, discovers new markets, and implements new ways of doing business to attain competitive advantage. The manager, in contrast, runs his or her business as other people run their businesses. While the manager follows routine, the entrepreneur carries out a new plan. The entrepreneur is a special type, with qualities of creativity and leadership. Clearly, more managers need to become entrepreneurial. They must avoid the inefficiencies in the current practices of other managers and instead practice ICA and DPR to respond effectively to the potentialities of profitable innovation.

To the extent that R&D underlies innovations, would-be entrepreneurs should now give more attention to application and development for the actual utilization of inventions. The commercialization of new technologies is needed, especially for the development of advanced manufacturing process technologies and for strengthening downstream technical performance. Much innovation, however, need not involve big science solving big problems. Instead, most innovations may be incremental. In this vein, Ralph Gomory, president of the Sloan Foundation and former IBM senior vice president for science and technology, emphasizes that management's mastering of "cyclic development process" is critical. He emphasizes attention to the product improvement end of the cycle. Cyclical process is dominated by manufacturing engineers, making incremental improvements to existing products. While a current product is in the manufacturing stage, a development team should be working on the next generation of the product. One generation of a project needs to succeed another. Frequently, the repeated incremental improvement of a product determines who will be dominant in an industry. A company with the shorter cycle will obviously develop an advantage over its competitors. Again, attention to the successful execution of cycle strategies requires close ties between manufacturing and development.[38]

In sum, management must become more entrepreneurial, not only in responding to change, but also in actually creating change by using information, experience, creativity, and leadership to introduce continually new products and processes.

Human resource development within the firm is also of prime importance. To meet the challenge of improving manufacturing productivity, firms must have a technologically knowledgeable and competent labor force at all levels. In a survey of American employers, however, Cornell economist John H. Bishop found that most never even requested a job seeker's high school transcript. "In Europe, a diploma establishes that someone is above a certain level," he said. "Here, it doesn't even provide an assurance of literacy."[39]

Firms must identify training needs relevant to current and anticipated industry practices. As the president of the National Association of Manufacturers urges, "We have to incorporate employer training as a standard part of work if we are going to compete in the global economy. Investment in people will become as critical as investment in new technology." Similarly, Levi Strauss's chief executive Robert Haas observes: "The potential for human technology is at least as potent as the investment we would make in robot serving heads. With the world changing as rapidly as it is, we need to invest heavily in skills-building."[40]

Indeed, management must change its view from "controlling labor inputs" or viewing workers as having only limited skills and being interchangeable to "employing human capital" and upgrading multiskilled workers. Employers now spend more than 10 percent of the initial cost of their machinery to maintain it, but less than two percent to maintain the skills of their employees. The American Society for Training and Development estimates that more than 40 percent of all U.S. workers required, but did not receive, training in 1989. It is also predicted that within the next ten years, 75 percent of Americans on the job today will need retraining for new skills. Currently, only one in ten employees ever gets formal training, and most of these are upper-level managers. Too few American firms have programs of comparable relative size to those of the corporate leaders in job training—IBM, General Electric, Xerox, Texas Instruments, Motorola, Honeywell. Even in these corporate leaders, total training expenditure for job training amounts to only 2 percent to 5 percent of the payroll. More extensive job training is needed to develop general transferable skills, as well as specialized capabilities. American employers need to realize that skill acquisition through company training is a way of developing human capabilities over the long term. So widespread is the neglect of human resources, that the MIT Commission on Industrial Productivity concluded that "without major changes in the way schools and firms train workers over the course of a lifetime, no amount of microeconomic fine-tuning or technological innovation will be able to produce significantly improved economic performance and a rising standard of living."[41]

Further, in practicing DPR, executives must focus on being a time-based competitor in the firm's entire value-delivery system. In the use of all the firm's assets—whether for achieving the competitive advantage of flexible manufacturing, innovating, or raising labor productivity—management must choose time consumption as the critical strategic parameter within the organization.

Stalk and Hout suggest that to become a time-based competitor, a corporation must accomplish three tasks:

1. Make the value-delivery systems of the company two to three times more flexible and faster than the value-delivery systems of competitors.

2. Determine how its customers value variety and responsiveness, focus on those customers with the greatest sensitivity, and price accordingly.

3. Have a strategy for surprising its competitors with the company's time-based advantage. . . .

    The journey to becoming a time-based competitor is demanding. It begins with a vision of what could be. The vision needs to be sufficiently clear and attractive to motivate the organization to rethink the structure and activities of its entire value-delivery system so as to maximize its performance.

    Initiating and executing a program that improves the responsiveness of an organization is not easy. Such a program must compete with other programs for attention. . . . Senior management must shift its focus from cost to time, and its objectives from control and functional optimization to providing resources to compress time throughout the organization. Senior management, as keeper of the vision, must believe that time is the organization's number-one competitor.[42]

This vision is congruent with our emphasis on total corporate efficiency. Management must shift from focusing on only internal efficiency (cost) to external efficiency and dynamic efficiency (time).

To acquire the greatest competitive advantage for its firm, management must analyze the international environment and diagnose, predict, and respond appropriately to changes in the new global economy. Management has to make continually a number of global choices.

Where to locate? A firm's activities should be located in a country according to the comparative advantage of the country (recall Chapter 2). Competitive advantage for the firm will disappear, however, if the nation loses its comparative advantage in the firm's product. If a country in which a firm is located subsequently loses its comparative advantage in the firm's product, the firm may find it profitable to produce overseas where another country has the comparative advantage. This has happened extensively with the international migration of textile and apparel firms and consumer electronics.

Where to source inputs? Again, management must be aware of the comparative cost structure among nations to secure inputs at the lowest factor cost. World-class competitors disaggregate their production functions and locate different activities around the globe according to national comparative advantage in the respective activities. Instead of exporting, should the firm license its technology, or engage in foreign direct investment to produce the product overseas? Management must consider the benefits and costs of these alternatives and be aware of the shifts in their relative profitability over time.

Should the firm enter into international alliances? The potential for joint R&D has increased with the more rapid pace at which industrial technologies can now be transferred across national borders. The international diffusion of process and product technology will make it increasingly difficult to place a national label on a product that incorporates numerous components or subassemblies.[43] The potential for high temperature superconductivity was first demonstrated in a Swiss industrial research laboratory operated by IBM. Texas Instruments maintains a software engineering laboratory in India. Boeing has formed a five-year alliance with the Paris-based Thompson-CSF S.A. and with Deutsche Airbus/Deutsche Aerospace of Germany to cooperate in identifying and pursuing new business opportunities and to capitalize on each other's technology and product lines.

To diagnose, predict, and respond to this ever-changing international division of labor is one of management's major challenges. In so doing, management must evaluate the net benefits that might come from learning from an overseas partner, gaining access to new markets overseas, sourcing inputs on a global basis, undertaking product development, manufacturing, and marketing. Collaborative ventures with foreign firms may be especially significant for "young" industries (biotechnology, robotics). Management has also to consider whether the financial and political risks of innovation and foreign marketing are reduced through a collaborative venture, instead of engaging in direct foreign investment, licensing, or exporting. Although the potential difficulties of collaborative ventures should not be minimized, American management needs now to recognize that changes in the technical capabilities of foreign firms and in the nature of product demand have increased the potential contributions that foreign firms can make to collaborative ventures.

In sum, to be internationally competitive a company must institute a global approach to its strategy. The understanding of international contextual analysis (ICA) and the practice of diagnosis, prediction, and response (DPR) in individual firms will ultimately determine total corporate efficiency, and hence the firm's international competitiveness. Internal efficiency must be combined with external efficiency and dynamic efficiency. To this end, rapid changes in the world beyond the firm compel less management of the routine, but more entrepreneurship based on the practice of ICA and DPR.

This entire book has immersed the reader in various elements of ICA. How successfully the reader will practice DPR as the international environment changes will depend on his or her entrepreneurial skills.

NOTES

1. Samuel Brittan, *Capitalism with a Human Face* (Edward Elgar, 1995), Ch. 10; Paul Krugman, "Competitiveness: Does It Matter?" *Fortune* (March 7, 1994).
2. Max Corden, *Economic Policy, Exchange Rates, and the International System* (Oxford University Press, 1994), Ch. 15.
3. George Stalk, Jr. and Thomas M. Hout, *Competing Against Time: How Time-Based Competition Is Reshaping Global Markets* (New York: Free Press, 1990), p. 1. Reprinted with permission of The Free Press, a Division of Simon & Schuster. Copyright © 1990 by the Free Press.
4. J. Fagerberg, "International Competitiveness," *Economic Journal* (June 1988): 371.
5. The new system uses price rather than income measures to calculate the value of output, has new groupings of companies, and uses chain-weighted measures of output.
6. Barry P. Bosworth and Robert Z. Lawrence, "America in the World Economy," *Brookings Review* (winter 1988–89): 45.
7. Ibid., p. 45.
8. For a more detailed analysis, see Arthur Neef, "An International Comparison of Manufacturing Productivity and Unit Labor Cost Trends" in Bert G. Hickman, ed., *International Productivity and Competitiveness* (New York: Oxford University Press, 1991), Ch. 6.
8a. *Monthly Labor Review*, February 1997, p. 88.
9. For summary expositions, see Jan Fagerberg, "Technology and International Differences in Growth Rates," *Journal of Economic Literature* (September 1994): 1156–1166; Moses Abramovitz and Paul A. David, "Convergence and Deferred Catch-up: Productivity Leadership and the Waning of American Exceptionalism," in Ralph Landau, et al., eds., *The Mosaic of Economic Growth* (Stanford: Stanford University Press, 1996), pp. 21–62. Quoted with the permission of the publishers. Additional references and a mathematical exposition are given in Robert J. Barro and Xavier Sala-l-Martin, *Economic Growth* (New York: McGraw-Hill, 1995), Ch. 1 and References.
10. Abramovitz and David, op cit., pp. 32–35.
11. Ibid., pp. 33–34.
12. Ibid., p. 57.
13. Ibid., pp. 60–61.
14. Robert J. Barro, "Determinants of Economic Growth: A Cross-Country Empirical Study," National Bureau of Economic Research, Working Paper 5698 (August 1996). For the theoretical framework of modern growth theory, see Robert J. Barro and Xavier Sala-l-Martin, *Economic Growth* (New York, McGraw Hill, 1995).
15. *Economist*, May 20, 1989, p. 91.

16. National Science Board, *Science and Engineering Indicators, 1989* (Washington, DC: U.S. Government Printing Office, 1989), p. 128.

17. Council on Competitiveness, "Gaining New Ground: Technology Priorities for America's Future," reported in *New York Times*, March 21, 1991, p. C2.

18. National Science Board, *Science and Engineering Indicators, 1989* (Washington, DC: U.S. Government Printing Office, 1989), pp. 2, 6.

19. Robert J. Gordon, "Problems in the Measurement and Performance of Service–Sector Productivity in the United States," National Bureau of Economic Research, Working Paper 5519, March 1996.

20. Joseph Schumpeter, *Capitalism, Socialism and Democracy* (London: Unwin, 1943), p. 84.

21. *New York Times*, October 8, 1996, p. C8.

22. Martin Neil Baily and Alok K. Chakrabarti, *Innovation and the Productivity Crisis* (Washington, DC: Brookings Institution, 1988), p. 39.

23. "Out of the Ivory Tower," *Economist* (February 3, 1990), p. 66.

24. Richard Rosecrance, "Too Many Bosses, Too Few Workers," *New York Times Forum*, July 15, 1990, p. 11.

25. National Science Board, *Science and Engineering Indicators, 1989* (Washington, DC: U.S. Government Printing Office, 1989), p. 7.

26. John F. Akers, "Let's Get to Work on Education," *Wall Street Journal*, March 20, 1991, p. A20.

27. MIT Commission on Industrial Productivity, *Made in America: Regaining the Productive Edge* (Cambridge, MA: MIT Press, 1989), pp. 152–153.

28. Ibid., pp. 105–106.

29. Joseph F. Brodley, "Antitrust Law and Innovation Cooperation," *Journal of Economic Perspectives* (summer 1990): 111.

30. For the advocacy of a national industrial policy that would go entirely beyond these limited policy measures, see Don E. Kash, *Perpetual Innovation* (New York: Basic Books, 1989); George C. Lodge, *Perestroika for America* (Boston: Harvard Business School Press, 1990).

31. Bergsten, "R_x for America: Export-led Growth," pp. 2–6.

32. Gene M. Grossman, "Promoting New Industrial Activities," in OECD, *Economic Studies* No. 14 (spring 1990), p. 119. © OECD, 1990, *Economic Studies*. Reproduced with permission of the OECD.

33. John B. Judis, "Time for an American Industrial Policy," *Wall Street Journal*, February 14, 1991, p. A13.

34. For an emphasis on this management failure, see Robert H. Hayes and William J. Abernathy, "Managing Our Way to Economic Decline," *Harvard Business Review* 58 (July–Aug. 1980): 67–77.

35. For an analysis of how this has affected several industries, see MIT Commission on Industrial Productivity, *Made in America*, Ch. 4.

36. Ibid., pp. 54–56.

37. James C. Abegglen and George Stalk, Jr., *Kaisha, The Japanese Corporation* (New York: Basic Books, 1985), pp. 176–177.

38. Ralph Gomory, "Of Ladders, Cycles, and Economic Growth," *Scientific American* (June 1990): 140.

39. *New York Times*, March 14, 1991, sec. 6, p. 1.

40. "Levis' New Strategy," *San Francisco Chronicle*, March 28, 1991, p. C4.

41. MIT Commission on Industrial Productivity, *Made in America*, p. 81. For a detailed proposal see Ch. 6 and pp. 309–314.

42. Stalk and Hout, *Competing Against Time*, op cit., pp. 36–37. Reprinted with permission of The Free Press, a Division of Simon & Schuster. Copyright © 1990 by The Free Press.

43. For a more extensive analysis, see David C. Mowery and Nathan Rosenberg, *Technology and the Pursuit of Economic Growth* (Cambridge: Cambridge University Press, 1989), Ch. 8.

DISCUSSION QUESTIONS

1. What determines the international competitiveness of a firm that exports on international markets?

2. What meaning, if any, can be given to "national competitiveness?" Do you believe "national competitiveness" is a major economic problem?

3. Can the state use industrial policy to improve on the market? If so, with what kind of industrial policy? For what type of country?

4. What determines a firm's capacity to take advantage of new technological developments?

5. What is the methodology of growth accounting?

6. How would you explain the slow growth in productivity in the United States after 1973?

7. What would you advocate to increase productivity in the United States?

8. How are ICA and DPR related to a firm's international competitiveness?

11 | GLOBAL GOVERNANCE

W e have concentrated in previous chapters on issues of international trade and welfare, trade and stability, and trade and development (interpreting "trade" broadly in terms of goods, services, capital, technology, and ideas). And we have sought an understanding of such trade at three levels of discourse: theory, application, and policy making. The normative discussion of policy making, however, has been limited primarily to national public policies. Now we want to consider international public management more fully by synthesizing some of the issues of trade, welfare, stability, and development in the context of global governance.

The problems of international resource allocation, the determinants of the pattern of world trade, the gains from trade, the relative merits of free trade and protection—all these problems relate to trade and welfare. The central issues involve economic efficiency and dynamic change in the international economy, and this becomes, in large part, an application of international welfare economics.

Some of the more prominent manifestations of the trade and welfare problem appear in the operation of GATT and the WTO, the new regional arrangements, the United States's Trade Acts, and the proliferation of nontariff distortions of trade. Policy problems in this area have become more complex as an earlier generation's concern with "freer trade" has had to accommodate to recent demands for "fair trade" and "managed trade" (Chapters 2 and 3).

The second problem area—trade and stability—involves the interrelationship between international trade and national income. The focus is on balance-of-payments problems. In the interwar period (1919–39), international currency disorder aroused widespread concern as the relative international economic harmony of the pre-1914 era disappeared with the sufferance of mass unemployment, abandonment of the gold bullion standard, spread of trade controls, exchange controls, and competitive currency devaluations. Since World War II, this problem area has appeared most prominently in the context of the operations of the IMF, a series of international monetary crises, and the efforts at international monetary reform since 1971. Policy issues in this area have become more complex—and national policy making has become more competitive—as nations strive to achieve both internal and external balance (Chapters 4 and 5).

The third problem area—trade and development—poses many vital policy issues. Particular examples of the problems of trade and development are to be seen in national development plans of the poor countries, foreign aid programs, policies with respect to multinational enterprises, the operation of the World Bank, and the problem of external debt (Chapter 8).

Despite—and in some cases because of—the globalization of economic transactions, we have frequently encountered international economic conflicts that arise because each nation strives to acquire a larger share of the gains from trade or foreign investment, or a country tries to avoid being damaged by external forces, or a national government seeks to maintain its domestic autonomy in policy making when confronting an international shock. (These conflicts were discussed in more detail in Chapter 1).

Now, recognizing the stresses that are inherent in the internationalization process, we must ask by what means are the conflicts resolved or at least mitigated? There is no well-defined international normative process to keep pace with other features of the internationalization process. We therefore must search for a normative order that will accommodate conflicts, make better policy choices, and control change. Is it possible to establish more effective international public management, so that there will be an economic order with less discord? Can nations improve the quality of their own policy making, without injuring other nations? What rules, norms, or standards can be invoked to control the behavior of nations in the world economy?

Answers to these questions cannot come from a set of institutions that are already in place for economic management with a transitional reach. The world economy is a decentralized system that involves decisions by households and firms within each nation, national governments, regional organizations, multinational corporations, and international agencies. There is no central decision mechanism, and in a literal sense there can be no "management" of the international economy. The relevant issue is whether global governance can be improved. Can there be more effective mechanisms or structures of governance to shape the international economic conduct of private business and national governments? We cannot yet appeal to an international public sector that might engage in international economic management as extensively as does national economic management. There is no international central bank. There is no international fiscal policy. There is no international anti-trust legislation. There is no international industrial policy. There is no international regulation of the natural environment. What then are the institutions and procedures for making decisions that might govern international order?

MECHANISMS OF INTERNATIONAL GOVERNANCE

Although there is no fully developed international public sector, there are elements of such a sector—for instance, the IMF, World Bank group, GATT and WTO, and the specialized agencies of the United Nations. In combination with the operation of international market forces, these institutions establish a variety of international governance mechanisms. As private management attempts to analyze the international context of its activities, it confronts the complex task of anticipating not only what national governments will do in reaction to international conflicts, but also what types of international governmental mechanisms will be operating and what their effects will be on the business enterprise.

The various international governance mechanisms are as follows:

Market Price System

- In a pure market, supply and demand operate freely to determine changes in price and quantity. Market forces are pervasive and micro driven.

- In a modified market, demand and supply may be affected by public policies such as tariffs and subsidies. Governments intervene in international markets, especially for protectionist and balance-of-payments purposes.

Extra-Market

- Direct quantitative controls are imposed by the government, such as quotas on imports, voluntary export restraints, and orderly marketing arrangements.

- There is an international code of conduct subscribed to by member nations. The International Monetary Fund, for example, establishes a code of conduct regarding exchange rates and balance-of-payments restrictions. The World Trade Organization (WTO) establishes some agreements on conduct in trade policy.

- There is an international treaty, such as for double taxation, or a Treaty of Rome establishing the European Economic Community, or a North American Free Trade Agreement.

- Negotiation or bargaining occurs. For example, there is the Organization for Petroleum Exporting Countries (OPEC), or there is the Paris Club of governments that lends to governments of developing countries and negotiates debt reschedulings with the debtor countries.

- There may be arbitration—for instance, by the World Bank's Center for Investment Dispute Settlement that may arbitrate a dispute between Alcan and the government of Jamaica. There may also be private arbitration such as between IBM and Fujitsu over intellectual property issues.

- Adjudication may be another means of resolving conflict. The US International Trade Commission, for example, hears complaints about unfair trade policies and domestic injury and adjudicates these cases. WTO committees may also engage in dispute settlements over trade policy issues.

- Finally, policy coordination among countries may be sought to resolve conflict. Countries may reach a collective decision such as when they established the Special Drawing Rights (SDRs) in the International Monetary Fund through an agreement among members of the IMF. There may also be attempts to harmonize fiscal and monetary policies among countries. A noncompetitive type of agreement may be reached such as in the 1985 Plaza agreement or the 1987 Louvre agreement that attempted to maintain foreign exchange rates within a certain target zone for the dollar, deutschmark, and yen.

A particular policy problem may involve the operation of several of these decision mechanisms. For instance, the role of the dollar in the international monetary system depends on the market price system (with flexible exchange rates), intervention in foreign exchange markets by national central banks, the operation of the IMF, and such policy coordination as the Plaza or the Louvre agreements.

In reality, pure market forces do not rule. The world economy is certainly not characterized by free trade and by freely flexible rates without any government intervention. Nor do international codes of economic conduct prevail. National governments, therefore, frequently act unilaterally and undertake policies in an ad hoc and competitive manner. Outcomes frequently depend on national bargaining power. As a result, firms must be aware of the consequences of different governmental policies and the possible impact on their activities of the different decision mechanisms that operate internationally.

EVALUATION OF GOVERNANCE MECHANISMS

Given an international policy problem, what mechanism of governance is most appropriate? Most of these problems do not lend themselves to mathematics-intensive policy analysis or to "optimization science." The problems normally involve multiple principals and agents, an ill-defined objective function, variables that are not amenable to subjective probability analysis, and outcomes that cannot be converted to a single utility index. Especially significant is the distinction between "instrumental rationality" and "constitutive rationality." The former is the basis of a rational choice model in which an objective is predetermined, dominant weight is given to the attainment of efficiency relative to other values, and one seeks the most effective policy instrument to achieve the objective. In contrast, constitutive rationality requires a "constitution"—that is, decisions about how decisions are to be made. Many issues of global governance need to determine the way in which decisions will be made and the boundary of the decisions. Most of the tensions and conflicts that arise from changes in the world economy require for their resolution a governance mechanism that will ameliorate the conflict, provide some social control of the allocation of benefits and costs, and exercise some means of monitoring orderly change.

Although at the level of global governance, policy analysis cannot be as rigorous as at the national level, we may at least establish some criteria by which to evaluate the different mechanisms of international governance:

When evaluating a particular policy, a benefit-cost analysis would consider the fulfillment of the objective of the policy, its external benefits, economic costs to the governing agency and the affected parties, detrimental externalities, and the transition or adjustment costs to the final state.

There are also other objectives to be evaluated beyond the fulfillment of the policy's immediate objective—namely, efficiency, equity, and the appropriateness of the process or procedure for reaching the policy decision.

Finally, there are criteria of "policy technology": the information needed, speed of implementation, specificity in results, simplicity in operation, reversibility or corrective mechanisms, and the jurisdictional domain (correspondence between the reach of the policy and the operational area of the activity being controlled).

Various governance mechanisms will meet these criteria to different degrees. The market, for instance, would receive high marks for such criteria as efficiency, process, information, implementation, and simplicity. But the state might devise governance mechanisms that would merit higher marks for equity, specificity, reversibility, and jurisdictional domain.

Among the various governance mechanisms, centralized decision making and codes of conduct are the most difficult to establish. Although commonly advocated, a code of behavior has its drawbacks. To reach agreement among the diversity of countries, any code will have to contain loopholes and escape clauses that will render the code ineffective, or it will have to be written to satisfy the demands of the lowest common denominator. Otherwise, the code is likely to impose undesirable rigidity, provoke unnecessary controversy, and overstress control or the negative aspects instead of facilitating the creation of opportunities, providing incentives, and promoting desired behavior. Even the GATT and WTO are not really legalistic, but a form of what has more aptly been called "diplomats' jurisprudence."

Nor did the Articles of Agreement of the IMF attempt to specify the meaning of the key condition of "fundamental disequilibrium," but left it to future consultation. The ambiguity in the operations of these international organizations demonstrates that their effectiveness depends on consensus, and that nations must agree on the constitutive rationality of rules. Insofar as the global economy is a decentralized system, the relationships among the decentralized units of decision making within the system are often uncertain and cannot be readily controlled. Absent global government or adherence to a definitive international code of conduct, the international economic conduct of firms and states needs to be shaped by other forms of global governance.

The need for an international reach in policy making is simply a corollary of the principle that the level at which a decision is taken should be high enough to cover the area in which the impact is nonnegligible. In order that the decisions regarding necessary policy instruments be optimal, there must not be "external" effects—i.e., the influences exerted on the well-being of groups outside the jurisdiction of those who make the decision should be weak. The area in which the impact of the instrument will be felt determines what decision level will be optimal. For many issues that we have discussed, the nation–state is an inappropriate decision-making unit. Decisions taken at the national level are often far too low to be optimal.[1] Governance must reach beyond national jurisdiction.

BRETTON WOODS SYSTEM

The main structure of the international public sector was formed in 1944 at the Bretton Woods Conference that established the IMF and International Bank for Reconstruction and Development (World Bank). The fund was designed to mitigate balance-of-payments problems, avoid the competitive devaluations of the interwar experience, and provide stability in international monetary affairs. The bank was to support investment in productive projects in countries recovering from the war and in need of development support. A third international institution was anticipated to complement the fund and bank—an International Trade Organization that was proposed in the Havana Charter. This was to govern not only trade barriers, but also private foreign investment, intergovernmental commodity agreements, and restrictive international business practices. The Havana Charter, however, met opposition in the American Congress, and only the trade policy chapter was adopted in the form of the GATT, a provisional arrangement that lasted until the WTO was established.

Some issues of governance raised at Bretton Woods and Havana—but not settled— still remain unsettled. And with intensified globalization, new issues have come to the fore. True, the Bretton Woods institutions have evolved with added functions and powers.

But now the central question is whether these institutions have evolved sufficiently to be effective in meeting the present—and future—problems of the world economy.

The IMF, World Bank, and WTO do exercise some functions of global governance. Initially, the IMF established the then-radical principle that countries were to give up national sovereignty over exchange rates, which were to become a matter of international management. Exchange rates were to remain fixed in the short run, but would have some flexibility in the long run insofar as the fund could approve an alteration of exchange rates when the country experienced "fundamental disequilibrium." With, however, the United States's unilateral action in 1971 of removing two foundations of the IMF—namely, the par value system of exchange rates and the gold convertibility of the dollar—the fund's management of exchange rates has been weakened by the establishment of floating exchange rates, albeit with interventions by central banks and monetary authorities. The IMF has also been marginalized through actions of the G-7 and regionalism.

The IMF was also to be a source of official international liquidity. Drawing rights at the fund were to be in sufficient amount to allow a deficit country time for the adjustment mechanism to operate on its balance of payments without having to resort to deflationary measures or trade restrictions. When utilizing the upper tranches of credit, however, the deficit country would be subject to "conditionality." This has become important in shaping the policies of deficit countries. Much of the success from adopting appropriate policies within developing countries and transition economies now depends on the conditionality exercised by the fund, together with the policy advice offered by the World Bank.

Despite the increase in international liquidity provided by the IMF and the loans from the World Bank, the international public sector has not yet solved the international saving-investment problem. Bretton Woods was unwilling to follow Keynes and create more international official liquidity and also to put pressure on chronic surplus countries. Instead, the international financial intermediation task of transferring savings from rich countries to investment in the poor countries and transition economies was met first through the United States balance of payments until 1971, and then through the World Bank group, IMF, and Eurocurrency loans from commercial banks. Not only do problems of debt servicing and conditionality remain, but so too does the severe fundamental problem of providing a greater net resource transfer to the LDCs and the transition economies. These challenges mean that if the domestic public sector in the LDC or transition economy is to be diminished through policies of stabilization, liberalization, and privatization, the international public sector will actually have to be strengthened. The IMF, World Bank, and WTO will have to support the economy's structural transformation through demand management and supply management based on project and program loans, budgetary support, and balance-of-payments support.

Prospects for debt flows are limited. The worldwide competition for private capital combined with a decline in official development assistance intensifies the demand for increased flows from the World Bank group. At the same time, resources of the World Bank are not increasing sufficiently in real terms. Replenishments of the International Development Association (IDA), the soft loan window of the bank, are still insufficient to meet the growing needs of eligible countries. A capital increase for the International Finance Corporation (equity lending agency of the bank) is also required.

In the changing world economy, it is most important that the World Bank, IMF, and WTO recognize the interdependence of trade, investment, and finance and coordinate their operational activities accordingly. The WTO should complement the programs of the bank and fund more than did GATT. Joint consultations among the three institutions are needed to consider how trade policy affects the balance of payments or other monetary issues, and, in turn, how monetary affairs, including exchange rates, can affect trade policy. An integrated approach is especially relevant for governing the developing countries. Although the time has not yet come for a merger of the IMF and World Bank, they too will have to collaborate more closely on common problems of governance.

This is not the time, however, for a second Bretton Woods Conference. Not only would such a conference with over 180 delegations be infeasible; it is not necessary insofar as the Bretton Woods institutions already possess the procedural powers to continue to evolve in a substantive manner. But what would be desirable is the addition of a fourth pillar to the Bretton Woods system that would govern "social relations" among countries. The managing director of the IMF has proposed such an institution for social issues, education, and technology.

It may be asked why not simply leave the "rules of the game" with respect to international trade and an international monetary regime to the operation of international market forces? Governments have answered that this will not be allowed. Governments intervene to affect the direction, composition, and terms of trade. And they intervene to affect the foreign exchange rate. An international public sector is therefore necessary—not only to remedy international market failure, but also to mitigate competitive policy making by national governments. If the IMF was initially concerned with the avoidance of competitive devaluations, international economic agencies now have to be concerned with international competitive monetary policies, competitive subsidization policies, competitive trade policies, and competitive foreign investment policies. The forces of globalization and liberalization create conflicts in international monetary and trade affairs that call for surveillance over international economic conduct and efforts at international economic peace-keeping. Improvement in global governance is as important as improvement in domestic governance.

Of prime importance is governance with respect to trade policy, international monetary affairs, international development, and multinational enterprises.

CASE OF TRADE POLICY

As we have seen in Policy Profile 3.3, at the same time that GATT promoted multilateral negotiations, nations chose to bypass GATT. In recent years, the U.S. government has given more extensive relief from import competition through escape clause cases (Trade Act "section 201" cases), antidumping, antisubsidy or countervailing duties, unfair trade practices actions ("301 cases" and Super 301 action), unfair import practices ("337 cases"), and market disruption ("406 cases"). Both the United States and the European Union have imposed more voluntary export restraints (VERs) and quotas on imports. The new protectionism has hence intensified since the mid-1970s in the form of nontariff barriers such as quotas, VERs, import targets, and domestic trade-diverting subsidies.

We also analyzed in Chapter 3 trade policy from the perspective of welfare economics. Welfare economics asks whether a situation, after a policy is adopted, is Pareto-superior to the pre-policy situation. But even if the final result of a policy of trade liberalization is Pareto-superior to restricted trade, there are still adjustment costs that must be borne by some groups in some countries. The costs of the path to the new position must be appraised, and compensatory policies devised for the injured. This problem requires more analysis, and then the adoption of more appropriate policies in the context of international economic law.

The present practice of imposing market safeguards and involving escape clauses under GATT, national legislation, and by executive discretion lacks any rationale in welfare economics. How can the deficiencies in the present mixture of policies be overcome and a first-best remedial policy be established to monitor problems of trade adjustment?

First, the conditions of "market disruption" and "domestic injury" in the importing country must be more clearly established. If there are to be safeguards for the importing country, what are the different effects of protecting via the suspension of a tariff concession, introduction of a tariff on the imports that are found to cause "injury," the imposition of quantitative restrictions, or the institution of "voluntary export restraints?" What relevance does the principle of "nondiscrimination" have? In turn, as the exporting country loses exports, should it receive compensation? In what form—another tariff concession or financial compensation? If the latter, to the government or the exporting industry? From the importing country's government or a multinational fund? In this connection, do the legislative terms of "orderly marketing," "fair share," and "equitable share" have any economic meaning?

If, on the other hand, safeguards are disallowed, and the importing country instead chooses to undertake adjustment policies to ease the transformation costs, who should receive compensation in the importing country and in what amount? Should only workers? Or also owners of capital? In which industries, and under what conditions?

Finally, because the market safeguards of one importing country will have an effect on another importing country (as exports are redirected to the other country), should there be some form of multilateral surveillance of these safeguards? Similarly, would not multinational coordination of domestic adjustment policies be welfare superior to only national policies taken independently?

These several questions indicate that the welfare states of all these various schemes need to be compared before the welfare superiority of a new set of policies can be established for trade adjustment. Although policies have been instituted in a piecemeal and ad hoc fashion, mainly designed for so-called "emergency" situations, new policy initiatives to meet the problem of trade adjustment require that policies be founded on systematic welfare analysis and be directed to the consequences of an ever-changing international division of labor. If this is not done, there will continue to be distortions in the patterns of comparative advantage, and the liberalization of trade will not be facilitated.

Welfare economics is also usually cast in terms of only national policies. But the first-best national policy may be second best or n[th] best compared with a number of other multinational policies. This limitation is apparent in the questions we have raised about trade adjustment policies. Safeguards against market disruption need to be considered as complementary policies for adjustment assistance. If adjustment assistance is designed to increase the speed with which change can be absorbed, the safeguards against market disruption must be designed to slow down the speed of the change that has to be absorbed. Optimum policy with respect to change associated with shifting comparative advantage requires joint optimization of safeguards and adjustment, not prior choice of one line or other of policy and subsequent optimization with respect to it alone.[2]

Although there is now no international agreement on measures that will permit short-term market safeguards while adjustment policies are undertaken, it has been suggested that new rules for these safeguards should be established in conformity with the following three principles. First, emergency protection should have a finite time limit and be progressively reduced over the period. Second, market safeguards must be accompanied by a definite effort by the importing-country's government and industry to adjust, modernize, or diversify into competitive lines of production. Third, some multilateral organization, such as the WTO, should establish multilateral surveillance over both safeguard and adjustment measures.

Aside from their growing incidence, the changing nature of nontariff barriers should be of concern: Increasingly, nondiscriminatory trading policies are being replaced by unilateral or bilateral discriminatory arrangements. Nations have bypassed GATT, and GATT's fundamental principle of nondiscriminatory, most favored nation treatment has been severely impaired. Also weakened has been GATT's principle of reciprocity based on a broad balancing of multilateral concessions instead of only concessions in specific industries of one country.

In the 1980s and 1990s, through bilateral negotiations, the United States either renegotiated existing barriers or negotiated new ones on textiles, automobiles, sugar, steel, machine tools, and semiconductors. Bhagwati has labeled this "aggressive unilateralism"—that is, the practice of the United States imposing on others its unilaterally defined views of unfair trade practices.[3] Bhagwati condemns especially the use of section 301 and Super 301 provisions of American trade legislation, as updated in the 1988 Trade Act. Super 301 demands negotiations from specific countries on "priority" practices that the United States finds unacceptable, regardless of whether they are proscribed by the GATT or another treaty, and seeks their abolition on a tight time schedule set by the United States, using tariff retaliation by the United States if necessary. In contrast to the principles of GATT and the WTO, the practice of imposing unilateral or bilateral discriminatory arrangements is a threat to an open trading system. Only too readily can the misguided view of international competitiveness turn into international economic warfare. Economic peacekeeping and the maintenance of an open trading system require continual multilateral surveillance. International economic diplomacy is required to sustain economic peacekeeping. America's leadership was responsible for previous rounds of GATT negotiations. Its leadership should not now be diverted to aggressive unilateralism against an individual country. Indeed, to strengthen the WTO, the U.S. government should again exercise leadership in establishing hard rules in an international code for trade conduct instead of lending its voice to such ambiguous slogans as "managed trade," "fair trade," or "results-oriented trade."

The rise of regional trading blocs may also be a threat to economic peacekeeping. We discussed such a possibility in Chapter 3 (pp. 86–90). From the standpoint of governance, we should recognize that deeper forms of regional arrangements that involve common policies among the member countries and common systems of governance are an alternative to national governance rather than simply a means of liberalizing trade among members. As Lawrence observes,[4] there is no reason to maintain that public goods and regulatory regimes should all be implemented by the nation–state. Some goods and rules are better provided through plurilateral international arrangements. It may be welfare enhancing to change or harmonize domestic policies through deep integration, as proposed for competition policy, standards, regulatory practices, and technology policies in the European Union (recall Chapter 6). In response to globalization, a curtailment of national sovereignty through

---

THE MARKET VERSUS SOVEREIGNTY

Markets are global and individualistic. Politics are collective and, particularly in democracies, redistributive. Politicians and those who seek favors from them often justify the interventions they propose by reference to the view that trade is war.

The main purpose of the international trade regime is to protect the market from the free play of politics. Given its origin in the 1930s, this should be perfectly obvious. Nor should it be objectionable. Domestic constitutions, with their entrenched rights and divisions of power, serve the same purpose. Even the notion of representation is a restriction on democracy, which could instead be implemented through referenda. Moreover, in the case of international trade, by restricting one's own country's freedom of maneuver, one simultaneously restricts that of other countries. How else can a degree of predictability be introduced into the law and regulations that govern the global economy?

John Jackson, in Peter B. Kenen, ed., *Managing the World Economy* (Washington, DC: Institute for International Economics, September 1994), p. 170

---

deep regional integration may be in order to harmonize national differences and integrate institutions and laws. The form of integration, however, should be "open," so that other countries are not excluded, and multilateral benefits might accrue.

CASE OF INTERNATIONAL MONETARY REFORM

Although the Bretton Woods Conference wanted to establish international monetary order, some of the same fundamental issues of monetary reform still demand attention. There is still concern about what should be the exchange rate mechanism, the amount of official international liquidity, and the respective responsibilities of deficit and surplus countries. If the world's monetary regime is to cease being characterized as a "nonsystem" or merely an "evolving status quo," these persistent issues will have to be revisited.

As long ago as 1972, the executive directors of the IMF published a study on *Reform of the International Monetary System*. This report identified five main problem areas of the international monetary system that call for new arrangements through international discussion and negotiation:

1. The exchange-rate mechanism, including both the indications of when changes in par values are necessary and the respective responsibilities of the deficit and surplus countries for making par value changes

2. The reestablishment of convertibility and the arrangements for the settlement of imbalances among countries

3. The position in the system of the various reserve assets and in particular the status and function to be given to foreign exchange reserves, gold, and SDRs

4. The problem of disequilibrating capital movements and what might be done to lessen the intense market pressures that accompany them

5. The possibility of new provisions in the fund arrangements for the special needs of developing countries.

A quarter-century later, this is still a succinct summary of the agenda for international monetary reform.

The dimensions of an international monetary system involve foreign exchange rates, nature of official reserves, and degree of convertibility. The functions involve provision of liquidity, adjustment mechanisms, and confidence. The dimensions and functions may be established by any of a number of organizing principles: automaticity (as in the pure gold standard with spontaneous governance by the market and complete domestic autonomy), supranationality (as with the IMF and its extra-market code of conduct), hegemony (as when the United States was the hegemonic power and the dollar ruled), or negotiation (as in the Plaza and Louvre agreements or establishment of the SDR based on international agreement). Application of these principles affect national sovereignty, the degree of domestic autonomy in policy making, and especially the burden of the adjustment mechanism.

Exchange Rates: We have recognized (in Chapter 5, pp. 179–86) some strong reasons for believing that freely floating exchange rates is the best exchange rate regime. The impersonal and nonpoliticized market price system may be favored by economists. But the exchange rate is a special type of price affecting all tradables, and governments reveal their preference for intervention to manage their exchange rates. Policies that go against the market, competitive depreciations, and the use of the exchange rate as an instrument of trade policy may then occur. To counter these actions, a clear and predictable code of conduct with some sanctions would be desirable.

Since the beginning of managed floating in the early 1970s, the IMF has been marginalized, and the best it can do is attempt some surveillance of exchange rates. "The importance of effective Fund surveillance," according to the managing director of the IMF, "has increased with globalization. The world really does need effective Fund surveillance to help prevent crises by pinpointing policy weaknesses and emerging tensions at an early stage. Surveillance needs to be strengthened, particularly in terms of its continuity, its monitoring of data, and its attention to capital account developments and financial flows."[5]

Although the IMF may profess surveillance as an absolute priority, the present monetary regime still makes the practice difficult. The fund is limited in its ability to control volatile exchange rates, disequilibrating capital movements, and governmental interventions. The provision of data to the fund and consultations help, but—absent a strong code of conduct—the fund's governance of member actions remains weak.

For those seeking a stronger system of governance, the concepts of "objective indicators" and "target zones" have recurrent appeal. In the early 1970s when managed floating began, the Secretary of the Treasury George Shultz proposed that a country's balance-of-payments policies be judged according to some "objective standard" of its reserve holdings. A "base" level of reserves would be established for each country. A "low point" below the base level and an "outer point" above the base level would also be set to ensure the undertaking of adjustment policies, including exchange rate depreciation or appreciation. If reserves moved to the low point (or outer point) the country would be obligated to depreciate (or appreciate) its currency or else face international sanctions imposed by the IMF.[6]

Two governing features would be the requirement that the bands be shifted before their edges are reached so as to prevent a buildup of competitiveness problems, and a "soft

AVOIDING MONETARY CONFLICT

Monetary relations are a necessary means for facilitating trade and the gains that it provides, but they can also be a mechanism for transmitting shocks. The most persistent problem facing monetary policy-makers has been the spillover of potentially damaging effects from the outside world through the international system. The most enduring debate has been over the extent to which human ingenuity can invent an abstract procedure or rule, or a way of looking at the world, that makes the instrument of exchange less controversial, avoids the need for consultation or negotiation, and eliminates the possibility of arguments, clashes, and mutually destructive behavior.

Harold James, *International Monetary Cooperation Since Bretton Woods*, 1996, p. 1

band" provision allowing the band to be temporarily disregarded if there is a speculative attack (thereby allowing depreciation rather than an increase in interest rates).

The proposal was, however, a nonstarter insofar as countries were unable to agree on the magnitudes of the "objective indicators" and were unwilling to submit to any sanctions by the IMF. And politically the scheme was objectionable, as Japan's minister of finance retorted, "No computer has been appointed Minister of Finance."

Similarly, countries appear unwilling to undertake the degree of international policy coordination required to maintain exchange rates within target zones. The leading proposal of target zones, advocated by John Williamson of the Institute for International Economics, would commit the G-7 countries to using monetary and fiscal policy, as well as intervention, to keep their exchange rates within bands of plus or minus 10 percent around an "internationally agreed" estimate of the "fundamental equilibrium exchange rate," which would be automatically adjusted to allow for differential rates of inflation (in effect, a system of crawling pegs surrounded by bands). Monetary policy would be designed in part to avoid real exchange rate disequilibrium while fiscal policy would be assigned to stabilizing domestic demand. The IMF would be responsible for servicing the international policy coordination process.[7]

Of this proposal, however, the *Economist* states:

"As Benjamin Cohen, of the University of California at Santa Barbara puts it, 'International monetary cooperation, like passionate love, is a good thing, but difficult to sustain.' Experience shows that policy coordination between the three big economies, America, Japan and Germany, is politically impractical, because governments are not willing to subordinate national economic policy to an international target. It is hard enough to get agreement on interest-rate changes; on fiscal policy it is near impossible. And yet it was fiscal policy that was largely to blame for the two greatest exchange-rate upsets in recent years—in America in the 1980s and Germany after unification.

"Another snag is that nobody is sure what might be the 'right' level for the dollar, or any other currency. There is no reason why governments should be better judges than the markets. Moreover, even if the governments of the big three economies could agree on policies to keep currencies within their bands, target zones would still be vulnerable to speculative attack as rates approached their limits. In a world of highly mobile capital, there may be no comfortable middle ground between floating exchange rates and permanently fixed rates. Pegged but adjustable exchange rates tend to be unstable."[8]

Far short of the ideal of macroeconomic governance of the exchange rate regime, the feasible arrangements that nations will tolerate in the near future are probably limited to more intensive surveillance by the IMF and the imposition of the fund's conditionality over a country's exchange rate and macro policies when it draws on its upper credit tranches in the fund.

Liquidity. The amount of liquidity created by the IMF also affects the governance of balance-of-payments policy. The greater the amount of official international liquidity and the more accommodating is the lender of last resort, the less is the discipline exercised by the balance-of-payments. As we saw in the Cooper-triangle, p. 185, the more readily a country can move toward the Liquidity vertex, the less does it have to submit to internal measures or external measures to correct its balance-of-payments deficit.

Just as there is a question of what is the "right" exchange rate, so too is there a question of what is the "right" amount of liquidity—and how should it be created and for whom?

With the internationalization of financial markets and the large flows of private capital, one may argue that there is no shortage of liquidity. If creditworthy, countries can engage in sovereign borrowing from international capital markets. The issue, however, is the adequacy of a country's "owned reserves," without recourse to debt.

The IMF still believes that official reserves should be provided by an international institution. An international decision to increase quotas in the IMF and possibly a new allocation of SDRs could be more efficient and equitable than resorting to independent accumulation of "borrowed reserves" from private capital markets. And, of course, if the IMF were ever to evolve into a World Central Bank, it would have to influence or control international liquidity creation.

Those who favor the provision of increased liquidity by the IMF point to the long-term need for international reserves as world output and trade grow. "Owned reserves," unlike "borrowed reserves," do not need to be periodically financed; they avoid the higher cost of acquiring reserves through borrowing; and they are not subject to abrupt withdrawal.

The management of the IMF estimated that the global demand for reserves would expand by several hundred billion SDRs during the sixth allocation period of quotas (1992–96). Moreover, at the end of 1992, 20 percent of the developing countries, and nearly 40 percent of the transition countries held nongold international reserves equivalent to less than eight weeks of imports. An allocation of owned reserves is deemed especially necessary for the growth of the LDCs and transition economies.

Even though in the last two decades the share of SDRs in world reserves has averaged only some 5.3 percent, the share has actually diminished in recent years. If the SDR is ever to become "the principal reserve asset" of the international monetary system as specified in the IMF's Articles of Agreement, an increase in SDRs will be necessary. Although some would favor a special SDR allocation to the developing countries, such special and differential treatment has been denied previously, and it remains unlikely to happen as the IMF reasserts its principle of uniformity in governance. Opposition to an increase in SDRs is also likely to come from industrial countries that enjoy low costs of holding other reserves and see little benefit from SDR allocations that do not give a rate of return above that of other reserve assets.

Adjustment. The issue of international governance over balance-of-payments adjustment policies is subsumed under the feasible degree of governance over exchange rates, macro policy coordination, and provision of official liquidity. Underlying this issue, however, is the stumbling block of imposing symmetric adjustment responsibilities on the deficit country and surplus countries. And how can the burden of adjustment be minimized?

While deregulation of national capital markets and the liberalization of international banking and capital markets have been beneficial, they have also imposed costs of greater financial instability and fragility. Systemic risk across markets has become more internationalized. Policy issues related to exchange rates, liquidity, and adjustment are being increasingly shaped by the rapid expansion of global financial markets.

This expansion raises policy questions of global supervision and regulation. Together with the Bank of International Settlements (BIS), the IMF must become more involved with harmonizing different national regulatory authorities and avoiding financial crises that create major international adjustment problems. The Mexican peso crisis in 1994 (pp. 208–24) illustrates the need for the IMF to help countries deal with temporary balance-of-payments difficulties that stem from capital flows. To help governments cope with speculative attacks on their foreign exchange markets, the IMF may have to establish an intervention fund.

In the future, the degree and quality of global governance of the international monetary regime will be determined mainly by activities of the IMF. Although the IMF has been the prime agent in governing adjustment policies, greater collaboration with the World Bank and the WTO is desirable. A study of the fund's historical evolution and the key issues in the future concludes as follows: "The world faces an institutional choice between an order in which these aspects of surveillance (over management of global liquidity, adjustment policies, confidence, and trade policy) are fragmented and treated in separation, with a smaller IMF (as in Figure 11.1) or, preferably, one in which the elements of surveillance are more effectively coordinated, with a stronger IMF (Figure 11.2). The case for greater coordination between international institutions rests on the substantial extent of the linkages that exist between different global economic problems. Issues such as interest rate levels, macro-economic orientation, debtor problems, and capital flows cannot be treated adequately in isolation from each other."[9]

CASE OF INTERNATIONAL DEVELOPMENT

All the elements of governance, discussed above, apply generally to the LDCs as well as to the more-developed countries. In addition, there is the particular issue of whether there should be special and differential treatment for the LDCs. We have seen that in their evolution the Bretton Woods institutions have responded somewhat to the special needs of developing countries. Initially, the GATT held to the principles of nondiscrimination and most favored nation treatment, but later incorporated Part IV of GATT to allow some special treatment for LDCs: preferences on imports from LDCs and the waiver of reciprocity. Initially, the IMF adhered to the principle of uniform treatment for all member countries, but later the fund instituted some special financing facilities that are used by LDCs.

In the interest of rules-oriented trade policy, few economists now argue for more special treatment for LDCs. Many, however, recommend that the IMF should help integrate the poorest countries into the globalized economy. The managing director of the fund

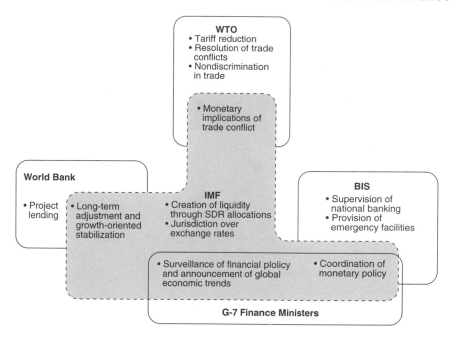

Figure 11.1 Small IMF.

agrees: "In our increasingly unified world, the persistence of zones of extreme poverty is a scandal—a scandal that is potentially more disruptive to the world than ever before. . . . Globalization increases the danger that poor performers will be further marginalized from the mainstream of global growth. If this danger is to be averted, as it must, we need to give decisive support to the poorest countries.

"The Fund's key instrument for this purpose is the enhanced structural adjustment facility (ESAF). It has enabled us to provide concessional assistance for growth-oriented adjustment programs in 38 low-income countries over the past eight years. . . . But ESAF alone cannot suffice. The replenishment of the International Development Association (IDA) is essential, as is an adequate level of concessional support from bilateral donors and other multilateral development banks. Debt reduction is (also) an important contribution to easing the burden of bilateral office debt."[10]

As well as the IMF, the World Bank recognizes that its mission is to diminish poverty in the developing world. More than a half century ago at Bretton Woods, one could not have imagined the success stories of East Asia. But the developing nations now confront the challenge that in the next twenty years the world's labor force will increase by 40 percent, and 95 percent of this increase will be in developing countries that will account for less than 15 percent of the world's capital investment.[11] This leads to the critical question: How can the Bretton Woods institutions be more effective in promoting the appropriate policies that an effective antipoverty strategy requires?

To improve the pattern of growth—and hence reduce poverty—the World Bank and IMF have to direct their analytical and operational support to four crucial sectors of the client economy: the rural sector, urban informal sector, export sector, and social sector. The policies that they support should be designed to provide the incentives and means for

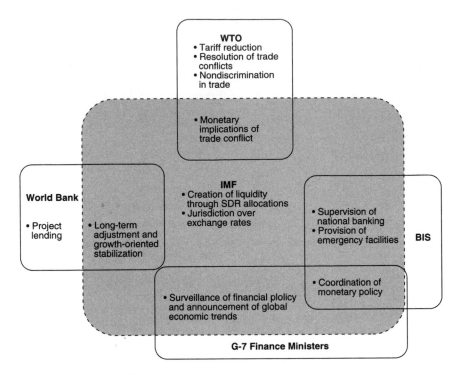

Figure 11.2 Large IMF.

the poor to rise above the poverty line. They are not the short-term palliatives of transfer payments or a redistribution of existing assets from nonpoor to poor. Instead they call for "shared growth": All must share in the benefits of growth.

To this end, the World Bank must give more attention to the beneficiaries of its loans. Country assistance strategies need to concentrate on promoting employment of labor in all sectors of the economy—agricultural, organized, informal, and export sectors. This is not a matter of only macroeconomic policies that would raise the demand for labor through a higher rate of growth in national output. It also requires removing distortions in labor markets and structural changes in the economy. More attention should be given to the question of who benefits from public expenditures and to possible programs that target the poor. Greater understanding on how policy reform—stabilization, liberalization, and privatization—affect the incidence of poverty is also necessary. When the effects are favorable, the bank and fund must provide more resources to validate these market-oriented reform programs.

A major responsibility of the IMF is to aid developing countries in implementing sound budgetary, monetary, and exchange rate policies. To the extent that the IMF can influence and help developing countries control their inflation, the poor will benefit. For the transition years of an orderly program of policy reform, the fund may also have to provide adequate balance-of-payments assistance. In structural adjustment programs and in support of policy reform, the fund must go beyond attention to macroeconomic aggregates and also recognize structural changes and the effect on the condition of vulnerable groups. The

FINANCIAL REGULATION

A significant problem in the regulatory arena is the openness of borders and the threat to the territorial sway of regulators. The borders that are falling are not just between nations but also between different financial sectors—between insurance and banking, between commercial banking and investment banking, and so on. Defining the territory is difficult when markets exist primarily on computer networks and when the turf can no longer be described by physical location.

In such a world, governments could respond by getting together to establish global regulations. To date, this has meant setting global standards, such as common minimum capital standards for international banking, which then have to be enforced by individual governments. However, no sooner has one long process been completed than the market has moved on to cause other problems. In this fast-paced environment, regulators are entrusted not only with preserving a system they no longer thoroughly control but also with controlling a system that neither they nor the players thoroughly understand.

Reprinted by permission of Harvard Business School Press. From Richard O'Brien, "Who Rules the World's Financial Markets?" *Harvard Business Review,* Boston, MA (March–April 1995): 151 Copyright © 1995 by the President and Fellows of Harvard College; all rights reserved.

fund's exercise of conditionality should be extended to "social conditionality" in the sense of improving the quality of life for those in poverty. The fund's activities, as well as the bank's, should be of increasing value in laying the groundwork for attracting more private foreign investment to developing countries.

Because of the importance of their export sectors and their efforts at liberalization, developing countries are justifiably exercised by the nontariff barriers that have multiplied since the 1970s as countries bypassed GATT. It is estimated that industrial country protection reduces developing country national income by roughly twice the amount provided by official development assistance.[12] Developing countries have been harmed not only by "aggressive unilateralism,"[13] but also by the multiplication of regional arrangements at the expense of multilateralism. Ideally, the establishment of the World Trade Organization (WTO) and future negotiations may counter this trend. Indeed, the WTO may usefully revisit some issues of the abortive ITO. To that end, Sir Leon Brittan (EU commissioner for competition) has advocated that the WTO incorporate policies dealing with world competition policy—cartels, mergers, and public monopolies. The WTO will also have to consider new issues such as the links between trade and the environment, trade and investment, and trade and labor standards.

Moreover, the G-7 must meet their problem of slow growth and the new challenge of a rapidly changing international division of labor by ways other than protection. Invocation of the pauper labor argument against imports of labor-intensive manufactures from the LDCs will not solve the problem of real wages of unskilled labor in the industrialized countries. As we have seen, available evidence does not indicate that less-skilled workers in the more-developed countries have been disadvantaged because of imports from developing countries. But import quotas, voluntary export restraints, the extensive use of countervailing duties and antidumping measures, and the threat of "social dumping" measures do exacerbate the problem of poverty in LDCs that would like to enjoy the dynamic gains of export-led development.

Although the Bretton Woods institutions have country-specific challenges, it is essential that they extend and coordinate more comprehensive policies at the international level. National development occurs within the context of the world economy. Support therefore must come from the three main agents in the international public sector—the IMF, World Bank, and WTO—even as liberalization reduces the extent of the domestic public sector within developing countries and transition economies.

Not only do problems of debt servicing and conditionality remain, but so too does the severe fundamental problem of providing a greater net resource transfer to the LDCs and the transition economies. The latter have some characteristics of developing countries, and some policy lessons of the South can now be applied to the East. The establishment of one market depends on the establishment of another market (for example, the labor market depends also on the housing market). Export-led development is desired. Stabilization is essential before liberalization and convertibility can occur. All these challenges mean that if the domestic public sector in an LDC or transition economy is to be diminished, the international public sector will actually have to be strengthened. The IMF, World Bank, and WTO will have to support the economy's structural transformation through demand management and supply management based on project and program loans, budgetary support, balance-of-payments support, and an outward-looking development strategy.

Prospects for debt flows are limited. The worldwide competition for private capital, combined with a decline in official development assistance, intensifies the demand for increased flows from the World Bank Group to the poorer countries. At the same time, resources of the World Bank are not increasing sufficiently in real terms. The bank's concessional affiliate—IDA—is underfunded to meet the growing needs of the poorest countries. A capital increase for the IFC is also required for additional equity lending. Without additional resources, the bank's role in global governance will be severely weakened.

In many respects, the power of the IMF has been diminished through actions of the G-7, floating exchange rates, and regionalism. Nonetheless, although the fund is now less significant for G-7 countries, its functions are of extreme importance to developing countries. In the future, the fund may become even more influential if it devises mechanisms to meet the serious international problem of incomplete risk markets. At the same time, as international financial markets have been liberalized and exchange rates have floated, the risks from volatile price changes have increased. Added to the volatility in international commodity prices, the repercussions of wide movements in exchange rates and interest rates have increased the risks for many developing countries. Although the solution is not to fix prices, some institutional changes—led by the IMF—should be devised that would allow world capital markets to spread risk and permit it to be borne more efficiently.

MULTINATIONALS, STATE, AND MARKET

Other questions of global governance arise from the influence of multinational corporations. In a letter to the editor of the *Independent* (Oct. 24, 1995), Lord Desai (director of the London School of Economics Center for the Study of Global Governance) stated:

If we agree that it is economic power we are discussing and we define it as the power of a state (any state) to shape its macro-economic policy autonomously, then there has been a diminution of the power of the state. The key difference has been the mobility of capital—both portfolio capital and direct investment—since the late 1970s. Keynes knew perfectly well that capital mobility would wreck his scheme. This is why the Bretton Woods arrangements restricted capital movements.

Once capital can be mobile, governments can no longer pursue policies that alarm the markets. It is no good arguing with the markets that some sort of cooperative game will benefit everyone rather better than selfish behavior. Keynes relied on that, but bound the hands of capitalists and bondholders so that they were willing to accept the class compromise whereby full employment and high wages coexisted with a high and stable level of profits.

What broke this equilibrium was the erosion of profit rate when real wages started rising faster than productivity, and neither inflation nor incomes policies could act as a solvent. At the same time, technological progress in transport and communication had made it possible for factories to be relocated from the center to the periphery.

The state remains powerful but not autonomous in macro-economic affairs. Rivaling the state in power is the global corporation. We have been used, for too long, to think of the world as being constituted by nation states; after all the economic statistics are arranged by countries. But it will be more useful, in my view, to think of the world as constituted by the 200 or so global corporations. Their internal trade becomes international trade; their treasurers' decisions to shift the petty cash—an odd billion dollars or so—can cause an exchange rate crisis. Their production decisions bind countries together in an international division of labor.

A Brave New World is being created out there. Not, as one hoped, by one-world idealists or UN diplomacy, but by the global corporations for the simplest of all reasons—profits. The state can either play along with them or have delusions of grandeur. The cost of delusions will be severe and will be paid not by politicians but by the citizens.

The multinational enterprise's strategy is bound to be a function of different governmental regulations. The very differences in national governmental policies determine the multinational's strategy in the presence of national policy divergences in taxation, foreign exchange controls, tariffs, etc. Multinational regulation through harmonization and coordination of national policies is therefore needed for a first-best policy in the sense of achieving the greatest possible present value of social net benefit for the host countries. Without multinational policy coordination, the multinational corporation will continue to operate on the national policy differentials. And sovereignty will remain at bay,[14] as the multinational escapes complete regulation by a national government. Any first-best policy of regulating the multinational must entail multinational policy making because the multinational can evade national regulation in one jurisdiction by shifting assets, production, markets, etc. Multinational regulation is necessary to limit tax avoidance, harmonize any concessions offered by host governments to attract foreign investment, control the terms of technology transfer, and acquire jurisdiction over restrictive business practices. If the multinational's activities can span several nations, it is impossible for a single nation, without the cooperation of other nations, to impose a first-best policy in the sense of the greatest possible increase in net benefit. The individual nation may be overregulating the multinational corporation at the same time as the corporation is underregulated internationally. As long as the jurisdiction of national policy does not correspond with the operational domain of the multinational, the optimal terms of foreign investment cannot be achieved.[15]

Concern with the activities of the multinational corporation (MNC), such as that expressed by Lord Desai, has led some to advocate an international code of conduct that would be binding on multinationals.[16] Instead of imposing obligations on firms, many would seek the governance of international investment through an instrument that is binding on governments. Possible investment agreements can be bilateral, or regional (EU or NAFTA), or truly multilateral. Bilateral treaties have the disadvantage of having to be large in number and hence subject to inconsistencies and nonuniform behavior. A truly multilateral agreement would be best negotiated at the WTO level.[17] But because of their different perceptions of what substantive standards the agreement should contain, nations are not yet ready to proceed through the WTO. There is still too much disagreement on a host of provisions such as national treatment, minimum criteria for transparency, dispute settlement procedures, global MFN treatment, screening of inward investment, performance requirements, and investment incentives. On policy issues related to the governance of multinationals, there remains a fundamental divergence among global welfare, source-country welfare, and host-country welfare.[18] In the near future, the most that can be expected are regional agreements and possibly some agreement within the OECD that might subsequently be extended to incorporate other countries.

INTERNATIONAL COOPERATION

Another form of governance operates at the level of policy cooperation among nations, especially for the design and implementation of their macroeconomic policies. The degree

---

ECONOMIC AND POLITICAL JURISDICTIONS

In the past two decades, a substantial amount of literature has been concerned with the response of governments to the growing significance of the cross-border activities of firms, and the acknowledgment that the key assets to wealth creation—viz. technology, entrepreneurship, and organizational skills—are often highly mobile across national boundaries. But, while the quicksilver nature of these assets has widened the arena of market based organizational modalities, including private hierarchies, the domain of national governments has remained mainly unchanged. It is this growing dichotomy between the boundaries of economic and political jurisdiction that is necessitating a reappraisal of the role of national governments. Sometimes, this means a reorientation of their overseeing roles, and sometimes, of their regulatory participatory or advisory roles. But, sometimes, it also suggests that governments—like firms—should engage in cross-border alliances to exchange information and ideas, and, where appropriate, coordinate policies.

John H. Dunning, "Governments and the Macro-Organization of Economic Activity," Carnegie Bosch Institute Conference on Governments, Globalization and Business, June 15, 1995

of cooperation, however, can vary from the exchange of information and consultation to the coordination of policy decisions among nations. Or they might even agree on presumptive rules that limit national discretion and constrain the use of international policy instruments.[19]

Periodically "top level" negotiations among nation–states may reach understandings or formal agreements that establish the "rules of the game" for a given area of international economic conduct. An international regime environment is thus created. Such a regime has at least two dimensions or attributes. One dimension refers to the incidence of agreements among national governments and the principles, norms, rules, and decision-making procedures around which their expectations converge. Another dimension indicates the numbers and strengths of international or supranational institutions and the forums, processes, and decision-making procedures that may be associated with them. International regimes may vary from complete decentralization of authority among nation–states to regimes in which there is more centralization of authority through international or supranational institutions. For any given degree of decentralization, there can be cooperative activity through the establishment of agreed principles and norms, or, in contrast, national sovereignty with little or no international cooperation. A special region might entail "mutual governance" facilitated by strong federal supranational institutions.[20]

Some types of international regimes also have another dimension denoting the extent of rule versus discretion. Strong governance in an international monetary regime, for example, would emphasize rules of conduct over the discretionary action by national governments. The collapse of the Bretton Woods regime in the early 1970s with a move to flexible exchange rates diminished international cooperation and allowed more national discretion with respect to exchange rates. Through economic summits with the G-7, consultations within the OECD, meetings of the Bank for International Settlements, and greater surveillance by the IMF, in the future there could be a weak movement toward more international cooperation and governance of the international monetary regime.

FUTURE IN PERSPECTIVE

Few would deny the desirability of greater global or transnational governance. But feasibility is another matter.

A summary case for more governance over international economic transactions can be made as follows. "Spontaneous" governance through international markets is not sufficient because some markets are missing, incomplete, or subject to market failure.[21] Especially significant are externalities that spill over from one country to another. Not valued by any market, these externalities have to be internalized by mechanisms of governance. When the cross-border spillovers are detrimental, other nations need to be protected from damage. When the externalities are beneficial, a greater supply needs to be encouraged. The forces of globalization are now increasing cross-border spillovers that call for more international management.

The market also underestimates international public goods (the environment, monetary stability). Moreover, competitive policy making by nations needs to be avoided. Instead of allowing "beggar-my-neighbor" policies, mechanisms of governance should seek policy optimization in the sense of making all countries better off (avoidance of trade wars,

---

A COMMUNITY OF NATIONS

The world is organized into nation-states, and it is generally presumed that the nation is the appropriate jurisdictional level of governance. Under some circumstances, however, international governance may produce better results than would emerge from independent and uncoordinated national action.

The argument that shallow integration would produce internationally the best results depends on two assumptions: that markets operate efficiently—in other words that there are no international market failures—and that political systems are legitimate—that national governments reflect the interests of their citizens and thus no constraints need be imposed on their actions, an assumption analogous to consumer sovereignty. If markets or political systems fail, the case for international cooperation or discipline would strengthen.

The decision on when the case for international cooperation is strong enough for nations to cede some part of their autonomy or to force other nations to cede some autonomy is sensitive and subtle. International cooperation permits nations to internalize and deal with market failures, such as those arising when one nation's production generates pollution in another. It permits nations to cooperate to provide international public goods, such as basic scientific research, to police opportunistic national actions, and to take advantage of international economies of scale. But decentralized national decisionmaking accommodates diversity in national preferences and conditions, the need for accountable government, uncertainty about appropriate policies, the importance of common historical and cultural experiences in developing communal solidarity, and the ability to realize economies of scope in governance.

The insights from these possibilities and analytical considerations point to the desirability of a global community of nations that balances openness, diversity, and cohesion. Openness improves competition and discourages trade and industrial policies that exploit monopoly power. Diversity accommodates varying national conditions and preferences and allows for innovation and experimentation. Cohesion and trust in one another's institutions and practices and in international institutions is essential if increased openness is to be viable.

Robert Z. Lawrence, Albert Bressand, Takatoshi Ito, *A Vision for the World Economy* (Washington, DC: Brookings Institution, 1996), pp. 105–106

---

avoidance of competitive depreciation). Intergovernmental cooperation and coordination are required.

Governance beyond the nation is also necessary to give jurisdictional reach over economic conduct that is international in scope. For example, as we have noted, the activities of MNCs cannot be covered by simply national regulations. Nor can the allocation of the world's resources that are shared among nations (ocean mining, space) be solved by only national legislation.

The feasibility of transnational governance, however, is limited for a number of reasons. National governments are unwilling to give up sovereignty or their domestic autonomy in policy making. Prisoners' dilemma type of situations also apply. Each country has an incentive to act rationally at the other's expense, but the result is collective irrationality

BUILDING A NEW INTERNATIONAL ECONOMIC ORDER

Because of the political setting and the nature of the task, the process of international economic reform will be piecemeal and evolutionary. Reform will result, in part, from international negotiations such as multilateral trade negotiations. It will arise from the evolution by negotiation of international institutions such as the IMF, IBRD, and GATT. Reform will also grow out of common law, the establishment of rules and procedures through trial and error and through *ad hoc* responses to problems. International monetary management through consultations among central bankers and finance ministers of the group of seven will most likely evolve through such a process. Reform will come not only from such international agreement and managed change but also from sporadic crises. It was the currency crises of the 1960s and 1970s, not international agreement, that led to the floating exchange rate system. And the near crises in Venezuela and Mexico led to a new approach to the debt problem. In the absence of agreed-upon rules, structures, and processes, such disturbances may multiply.

The outcome of these reform processes will not be a comprehensive international economic order. The political bases are too weak and the problems too complex to lead to anything approaching world economic management. In some areas, management will be effective and relatively comprehensive. Issues of interdependence will most likely be managed because they are of greatest concern to the developed market economies. As we have seen, work has progressed on guidelines for exchange rate management, rules on nontariff barriers, and codes for the behavior of multinationals. Because interaction will continue to be limited, progress on regulating East-West interaction is possible. The reduction of U.S. tariff barriers and guidelines for state trading behavior in international markets, for example, are likely.

But progress on international equity is much less likely. In most cases, the efforts of the less-developed countries to challenge the power and authority of the developed countries has failed. Evidence suggests that political weakness will continue to plague the South in the future. Some changes—aid for the least developed and greater market access in the North—will be offered by the developed market states. The Third World may also benefit indirectly from the management systems devised by the North for money, trade, and multinationals. No major redistribution, however, will occur. As a result, the confrontation between the haves and the have-nots will persist as an element of international economic relations.

Copyright © 2/90. From Joan Edelman Spero, *The Politics of International Economic Relations*, 4th ed. (New York: St. Martin's Press, 1990), pp. 334–335. Reprinted with permission of St. Marin's Press, Inc.

as both lose if both act according to only self-interest. In their self-interest, countries pursue a protectionist trade policy, although it would be in their collective interest to follow free trade. But free trade is not a natural order; it must be enforced by governance mechanisms that lead each country to act in its self-interest and collective interest.

Governance that promotes a common goal or common interest among nations can be viewed as an international public good.[22] All countries benefit, irrespective of whether they have contributed to its costs or not. But the free rider problem then results in an undersupply of international public goods. Each country, knowing that others may not contribute, lacks the incentive to contribute to something that benefits others, including itself. If countries want to be free riders and not contribute, or if they fear that, even if they do contribute, no other country does, then the outcome will be that no country contributes.

In game-theoretic analysis of strategic interactions among individual decision-makers, the "supply of cooperation" often falls short of what would be mutually beneficial because collective action is a public good. Individual agents making decentralized and rational decisions, may fail to achieve their mutual interest. These general results for individuals are all the more likely to occur when national governments are the individual decision-making agents.[23]

A corollary is that "public bads" are oversupplied. A single country tends to have no incentive to remove or reduce them, without assurance that others will also share the costs (situations of competitive depreciation, protection, monetary instability, global pollution, overexploitation of exhaustible resources to which no property rights are attached). Again, nationally rational actions will result in a suboptimal collectively irrational outcome.

It might be thought that if there are well-established property rights and low transactions costs, then there can be efficient negotiations among decision makers, as postulated in the Coase theorem.[24] But negotiations among national governments over the issues we have been considering are limited because property rights may not be well defined, the nation–state does not act as a unitary agent (different bureaucratic interests and various domestic constituencies), information may be asymmetric, and outcomes are unpredictable.[25]

Finally, the intellectual underpinning for mechanisms of global governance is ambiguous and subject to differing interpretations. Competing models of international economic behavior have different implications for the degrees and kinds of governance.[26] When no professional consensus exists about the single best model, international cooperation becomes all the more remote.

The problem of rival models is especially severe for matters of global governance when the type of rationality involved is what we have termed "constitutive" rationality— that is, decisions have to be made about how decisions are to be made.[27] This contrasts with the normal type of rationality considered in economic analysis—namely, instrumental rationality: what policy instruments to use to satisfy an objective function. Insofar as the task of designing a structure of governance is akin to writing a constitution, it is more difficult than simply selecting policy instruments.

In addition to "model uncertainty," the feasibility of international cooperation is also limited by other types of uncertainty—about the objectives and intentions of national governments, their ability to perform on agreements, and about their ability to monitor the compliance of other governments.[28]

Given the barriers to global governance, how can they be overcome? In the future, as in the past, agreement on some form of governance is most likely to emerge under conditions of crisis management. Governments may then share a common aversion and cooperate to avoid a particular outcome.[29] Aside from the need to take action in a crisis, nations may also submit to more governance, the more often are the attempts to institute such governance (as in repeated games). Progress is also more likely, the fewer the number of nations involved, such as in regional arrangements.[30] As Olson emphasized,[31] cooperative solutions are easier to attain in smaller than larger groups for three reasons: the fraction of a collective benefit enjoyed by any individual agent tends to decline as the size of the groups increases; larger groups are less likely to exhibit the small-group strategic interactions that

COOPERATIVE DECISION MAKING

Applications of game theory in economics make more precise the insight, recognized in political and economic theory for centuries, that decentralized, noncooperative decision-making can produce outcomes that are decidedly inferior to a set of efficient, Pareto-optimal outcomes attainable through collective action. Numerous studies of market failures, externalities, public goods, and strategic interactions within national economies identify instances in which unconstrained maximization by individual decision-making agents, though rational for each agent, can produce suboptimal outcomes for all agents together. The possible suboptimality of decentralized decisions extends naturally to many types of interactions between national governments and to international collective goods. In principle, therefore, when transnational externalities are important and if coordination among governments is feasible, it may be possible to "internalize the externalities" and reach mutually preferable outcomes through cooperative decision-making. This fundamental insight is the starting point for most of the literature adopting the policy-optimization perspective.

A closely related insight is the appreciation that neither international cooperation nor explicit coordination is a synonym for altruism or benevolence. On the contrary, cooperation and coordination can result from completely selfish bargaining. Coordination does not require that national governments have common or even compatible goals, or that some governments must sacrifice their own goals in deference to the goals of others. Cooperation and coordination merely imply the self-interested mutual adjustment of behavior. The potential for large gains from cooperation in all its forms may well be greatest when goals are inconsistent and discord is high.

Bryant, op cit., pp. 407–408

facilitate the supply of collective goods; and organization costs tend to increase with an increase in group size.

Clearly, global governance is still rudimentary. There is a long way to go before legal and political institutions catch up with the potential of economic globalization. There must be wider understanding of the potential benefits from global governance. Ultimately, political leadership must promote this understanding and provide the incentives for commitment to global cooperation. Meanwhile, if globalization continues in the de facto sense, there will be less need for mechanisms of global governance in the de jure sense when global markets deepen, become more complete, and more perfect. For the future, however, as in the past, the central issue for both private and public management will be how states and markets confront the challenge of increasing the "size of the pie" (through efficiency and growth) and distributing it (with equity or fairness). In helping to meet this challenge, mechanisms of global governance need to remedy failures in international markets and avoid failures of the international public sector.

When moving the acceptance of the Final Act at Bretton Woods, Keynes concluded: "Mr. President, we have reached this evening a decisive point. But it is only a beginning. We have to go from here as missionaries, inspired by zeal and faith. We have sold all this to ourselves. But the world at large still needs to be persuaded." That is still true. But instead of simply zeal and faith, we now need deeper understanding of how to reduce the conflict between cross-border economic integration and national political sovereignty, avoid international policy competition, and promote international cooperation in the changing world economy. This book has attempted a modest contribution in that direction.

NOTES

1. Jan Tinbergen, "Building a World Order," in J. N. Bhagwati, ed., *Economics and World Order from the 1970s to the 1990s* (New York, 1972), pp. 145–157.

2. H. G. Johnson, "Technological Change and Comparative Advantage: An Advanced Country's Viewpoint," *Journal of World Trade Law* (Jan./Feb. 1975): 13.

3. Jagdish Bhagwati, "Multilateralism at Risk," *World Economy* 13, (June 1990): 158. See also Bhagwati, *The World Trading System at Risk* (Princeton: Princeton University Press, 1991), Ch. 4.

4. Robert Z. Lawrence, "Regionalism: An Overview," *Journal of the Japanese and International Economies* 8 (1994): 365–387; "Futures for the World Trading System and Their Implications for Developing Countries," in Manuel R. Agosin and Diana Tussie, eds., *Trade and Growth* (New York: St. Martin's Press, 1993), Ch. 2.

5. Michel Camdessus, "Presentation of the Fiftieth Annual Report," IMF Summary Proceedings, Annual Meeting, 1995, p. 33.

6. Memorandum on "The U.S. Proposals for Using Reserves as an Indicator of the Need for Balance-of-Payments Adjustment," reprinted in *Economic Report of the President* (January 1973), pp. 162–171.

7. For details, see J. Williamson and M. Miller, "Targets and Indicators: A Blueprint for International Coordination of Economic Policy," Institute for International Economics, September 1987; Williamson and C. Randall Henning, "Managing the Monetary System" in Peter B. Kenen, ed., *Managing the World Economy* (Washington, DC: Institute for International Economics, September 1994), Ch. 2.

8. *Economist*, October 7, 1995, p. 30.

9. Harold James, *International Monetary Cooperation since Bretton Woods* (New York: Oxford University Press, 1996), pp. 617–620.

10. Address by the managing director of the International Monetary Fund, Summary Proceedings, Annual Meeting 1995 (Washington, DC: International Monetary Fund, 1995), pp. 35–36.

11. Lawrence Summers, "Research Challenges for Development Economists," *Finance & Development* (September 1991): 5.

12. J. Michael Finger and Patrick A. Messerlin, "The Effects of Industrial Countries' Policies on Developing Countries" (Washington, DC.: World Bank, 1989), p. 29.

13. Jagdish Bhagwati, *Protectionism* (1988), pp. 123–127.

14. See Raymond Vernon, *Sovereignty at Bay* (New York, Basic Books, 1971); *Storm Over the Multinationals* (Cambridge, MA: Harvard University Press, 1977).

15. For further discussion of the relationship between globalism of firms and nationalism of governments, see Sylvia Ostry and Richard R. Nelson, *Techno-Nationalism and Techno-Globalism* (Washington, DC: Brookings Institution, 1993).

16. For a compromise in the interests of source countries and host countries, see Organization for Economic Cooperation and Development, *The OECD Guidelines of Multinational Enterprises* (Paris: OECD, 1979).

17. C. Fred Bergsten and Edward K. Graham, *Global Corporations and National Governments* (Washington, DC: Institute for International Economics, 1995).

18. For an incisive analysis of the divergence, see Richard E. Caves, *Multinational Enterprise and Economic Analysis*, 2nd ed. (Cambridge: Cambridge University Press, 1996), Ch. 10.

19. This section follows the analysis of Ralph C. Bryant, "International Cooperation in the Making of National Macroeconomic Policies: Where Do We Stand?" in Peter B. Kenen, ed., *Understanding Interdependence* (Princeton: Princeton University Press, 1995), Ch. 11.

20. For a more detailed discussion, see Bryant, op cit., pp. 394–395.

21. For the distinction between "spontaneous" governance and "intentional" governance structures, see Oliver E. Williamson, "Economic Institutions: Spontaneous and Intentional Governance," *Journal of Law Economics and Organization* (1991): 159–187.

22. Paul P. Streeten, *Thinking About Development* (Cambridge: Cambridge University Press, 1995), pp. 90–95; C. P. Kindleberger, "International Public Goods Without International Government," *American Economic Review* (March 1986).

23. Bryant, op cit., p. 408.

24. For elaboration, see Richard N. Cooper, "The Coase Theorem and International Economic Relations," *Japan and the World Economy* 7 (1995): 29–44.

25. Another recent approach to international organization stems from the new institutional economics that focuses on contracting. See Beth V. Yarbrough and Robert M. Yarbrough, "International Contracting and Territorial Control: The Boundary Question," *Journal of Institutional and Theoretical Economics* 150, 1 (1994): 239–264.

26. Bryant, op cit., pp. 427–434.

27. See also above, p. 420.

28. Bryant, op cit., pp. 427–430. For a critique of international cooperation—and the belief that it should not even be attempted—see Martin Feldstein, "Distinguished Lecture on Economics in Government: Thinking about International Economic Coordination," *Journal of Economic Perspectives* 2, 2 (spring 1988): 3–13.

29. Arthur A. Stein, *Why Nations Cooperate* (Ithaca: Cornell University Press, 1990), Ch. 2.

30. Beth V. Yarbrough and Robert M. Yarbrough, "Regionalism and Layered Governance: The Choice of Trade Institutions," *Journal of International Affairs* 48, 1 (spring 1994): 95–117.

31. Mancur Olson, "The Logic of Collective Action: Public Goods and the Theory of Groups," 2nd ed. (Cambridge, MA: Harvard University Press, 1971).

DISCUSSION QUESTIONS

1. What problems of governance are associated with international trade and welfare? With trade and stability? With trade and development?

2. Bretton Woods depended on the concepts of universality, equality, and progressive liberalization. To what extent have these been achieved in reality?

3. Were the Bretton Woods institutions weakened by being the product of an Anglo-American wartime alliance? By establishing fewer rules and more discretion?

4. Does the increasing freedom of capital movements complicate global (or transnational) governance?

5. Is game theory useful in illuminating problems of global governance?

6. Short of the establishment of supranational institutions, what other forms of global governance are possible?

7. What are the barriers to global governance?

8. How might these barriers be overcome?

9. "More international cooperation is not necessarily better than less." Do you agree?

10. "Cross-border economic integration and national political sovereignty have increasingly come into conflict, leading to a growing mismatch between the economic and political structures of the world. The effective domains of economic markets have come to coincide less and less with national governmental jurisdictions." —Preface to the Brookings Institution's *Studies on Integrating National Economies*.

What are the implications of this statement for public management of the globalized economy? For private management in the globalized economy?

INDEX

UNIVERSITY OF WOLVERHAMPTON
LEARNING RESOURCES